Water-Related Death Investigation

Water-Related Death Investigation

Practical Methods and Forensic Applications

Second Edition

Kevin L. Erskine and Erica J. Armstrong

CRC Press
Taylor & Francis Group
Boca Raton London New York

CRC Press is an imprint of the
Taylor & Francis Group, an **informa** business

Second edition published
by CRC Press
6000 Broken Sound Parkway NW, Suite 300, Boca Raton, FL 33487-2742

and by CRC Press
2 Park Square, Milton Park, Abingdon, Oxon, OX14 4RN

First edition published by Routledge 2010

CRC Press is an imprint of Taylor & Francis Group, LLC

ISBN: 978-0-367-25154-3 (hbk)
ISBN: 978-0-367-76456-2 (pbk)
ISBN: 978-0-367-33229-7 (ebk)

Typeset in Minion
by Deanta Global Publishing Services, Chennai, India

To all souls who seek to know the truth.

Erica J. Armstrong, MD

Contents

Preface

> To the living we owe respect. To the dead we owe the truth.
>
> **—Voltaire (1694–1778)**

On June 6, 1996, our department was requested to respond to one of our park areas for the report of a female found floating in the lake approximately 100 yards offshore. A jet skier had been motoring along when he found himself adjacent to her body floating face down in the water. A police boat responded to the scene, retrieved the body, and transported it to the public boat ramp facility in the area. No on-scene body assessment was conducted by any responding agencies. At that time, no responding officers had the necessary training or experience in conducting a water-related death investigation, so the officers did what they were trained to do, which included securing the scene for body recovery, obtaining any witness statements, and attempting to identify the victim in question. The divers on the scene had no other obligation than to pull the victim's lifeless body onto the rescue boat for transport to shore.

I happened to be off that day and was informed of the incident by other officers during casual conversation. This case caught my attention because it was believed to be a homicide. Several people involved in the body recovery would later tell me that they recalled seeing distinctive marks around the victim's neck, and she was found floating in the lake the very same day she went missing. These were signs of foul play not commonly found in a water-related death.

In the months following the recovery, I would soon begin to learn valuable information regarding the specialized field of water-related deaths as I began our department's own investigation into the incident. It was fascinating to me to interview the pathologist who conducted the autopsy on the victim. This fascination was enough to prompt me to begin seeking formal training in the field as well as seeking information through personal research. Many indicators of foul play were evident in the case, which I would later term "red flag indicators" of foul play. The case was ultimately ruled as a suicide by a neighboring agency, and I was ordered to cease my investigation.

The intent is not to find fault in those who participated in this recovery and investigation but rather to learn from our mistakes and move on in the hope of not making those same mistakes again. Responding personnel who possess even the basic knowledge of what to look for at the scene can boost the investigation drastically by assisting the pathologist in determining time, cause, and manner of death.

What is a water-related death? Those cases of two people swimming together at the beach and one frantically runs up to a lifeguard claiming the other was overcome by waves and his or her head was submerged. A group of fishermen in a boat in the middle of a lake suddenly returns one man short, and the others claim he fell in trying to untangle his line from the boat propeller, or an elderly lady sight-seeing along a scenic trail "accidentally" slips in and was overcome by the current. These are all cases of water-related deaths. But are they truly accidents? Is a body found near a body of water still regarded as a water-related death? Without knowing what to look for on the scene, this is difficult to determine.

All too often, police called to the scene of a drowning may consider it an accident before they even arrive. Their sense of pity for the family is overwhelming, and they may even have siblings or children the same age as those involved. Our culture almost always perceives drowning as an accident. Responding officers often feel helpless due to the lack of a specially trained dive team, responsibilities of controlling on-lookers, family members' presence, and obtaining witness statements. Complicating matters further, the officer may be required to give a death notification on the scene to any family members.

An added problem is that drowning is one of the most difficult causes of death to determine. Drowning as a cause of death is determined only after a meticulous examination with a complete autopsy and after all other causes of death are ruled out. Furthermore, to rule a drowning a homicidal act is extremely difficult, mainly because it is difficult to overcome that preconceived belief that all drowning incidents are an accident. At the scene of a homicide, foul play is usually obvious, but a drowning incident is regarded as an accident because the majority of road officers do not possess the specialized training needed to process the scene properly. Larger departments have a heavy caseload, and "accidents" allow them to move forward with higher-profile cases. Likewise, smaller departments do not have the extra manpower necessary to conduct a proper follow-up. More investigative work is typically done at the scene of a motor vehicle accident than is done for a pool, tub, or open water death. To rule out foul play, it must first be considered.

During the Susan Smith case, Sheriff Howard Wells stated that there was such an outpouring of sympathy from the public that no one wanted to believe a mother could have murdered her own children by strapping them into their car seats and driving her vehicle into the lake. This statement reinforces the belief that the death must have happened another way.

A new form of recreational sex has hit society in the form of erotic drowning. Individuals, both men and women, gain sexual gratification and excitement from submersion in water. Subjects hold their partner's head under water during various sexual acts to heighten orgasm. How easy would it be to pass this off as an accident? A thorough investigation is warranted.

In ancient history, dunking was used frequently as a form of punishment. This form of water torture was common in many cultures and even used as a form of execution. Even in the Bible, Book of Genesis, God created the Great Flood to cleanse the earth and serve as the ultimate punishment for all mankind.

Sudden deaths in infants initially suspected upon scene visitation as sudden infant death syndrome (SIDS) or sudden unexpected infant death (SUID) have later been found at autopsy to have resulted from shaking with impact (nonaccidental head injury) or blunt force trauma to the trunk. In these cases, homicidal violence initially may not have been considered due to the lack of visible injury. Does this also hold true with drowning incidents? Historically, many water-related cases have been ruled accidental only to have additional information or evidence obtained months or even years later. In retrospect, investigators cannot go back and collect evidence and conduct interviews with witnesses or potential suspects. All evidence is lost, requiring investigators to learn from their mistakes, which may ultimately affect the credibility of the agency involved.

This book will cover, in part, red flag indicators of foul play. Such indicators may more accurately lead the investigator to believe that this tragic incident was in fact not an accident, but possibly an intentional act, whether by suicidal or homicidal means. These indicators will help steer the course of the investigation. Moreover, water-related death investigation does not end with the scene. The coroner or medical examiner is charged with the determination of not only why the person died but by what means and under what circumstances. This book will additionally cover the processes involved in the medicolegal death investigation of water-related deaths and stress the importance of correlation of the investigative and scene findings with findings generated by complete autopsy performance, including laboratory testing.

Kevin L. Erskine
Master Water-Related Death Investigator, Retired

Acknowledgments

I wish to extend a huge amount of gratitude to the following:

My coauthor, Dr. Erica Armstrong, for her patience with me through this strenuous and tiresome process of authoring a book of this magnitude. Although I have authored several books, I severely lacked in the documentation of my sources and references. She had to patiently and constantly correct many of my oversights and offered many enhancements to my work. I quickly realized she was bringing out my best and making me not only a better investigator but a more efficient writer as well. I am thankful that she was receptive to my request to have her as a coauthor in this huge undertaking, and I learned a lot from her over the course of our writing.My sons, Kameron and Kollin Erskine, for their patience in assisting me with photo shoots.

Fireman Charles (Chuck) Cali, for his help with drone information and photos.

James Wentzel of the Cuyahoga County Coroner's Office, for his generosity both through the camera lens and on the computer in creating high-quality photographs and drawings for this project. Jim's talents as the coroner's head of photography have helped me in many endeavors, but none have compared to this huge "work of art," and his expertise and enthusiasm are greatly appreciated. He is a credit to his profession.

Bernadette Jusczak, former coroner's employee, for her dedication and talents in drawing the body figures for cold water immersion. She was able to take my rough sketches and bring them to life, immensely improving the quality of this work.

Gene Ralston, for assistance in providing information and insight into his specialty of side-scan sonar. His cooperation and support regarding underwater search and recovery incidents and sonar images are greatly appreciated. He is deeply dedicated to assisting families in need of underwater searches and has travelled thousands of miles to do so.

Roger and Joanne Pierce, for support and permission to feature the sonar search and recovery operation of their son from Lake Cumberland. I am truly sorry for your loss.

Mark Atherton, author of *Echoes and Images*, for his support and assistance in providing images and information regarding the Kongsberg Meso Tech 1000 sonar unit.

Walt "Butch" Hendrick and Andrea Zafares of Lifeguard Systems, Inc., for their continuing dedication to educating and assisting search and rescue units in the specialized field of public safety diving. Many water and ice accident victims are alive today due to their training programs, publications, equipment designs, public speaking engagements, and actual rescue efforts. They are the leaders in the water rescue industry.

Deep Trekker, for insight and photos for underwater drones.

Parabon Snapshot, for their cooperation with this unique technology, photos, and case study.

Former Sheriff Howard Wells of Union County, South Carolina, for taking the time to allow me to interview him regarding the investigation of the Susan Smith murder case.

Public safety diver Richard Burdette, for taking the time to work out all those formulas and figures to create the body drop rate chart.

Euclid Police Department Detectives Susan Schmid and Michael Grida, for conducting an excellent pool drowning investigation, which I was able to feature as a model case in this project.

Cuyahoga County Coroner Frank Miller, for opening up his staff and facility to assist both authors in this project.

Mike Carlson and Lab Director Edward Golla of TRI, Inc., for their assistance in providing photos and information regarding scuba fatality investigations.

ODNR Watercraft Officers Jim Gorman and Maggie Brown, for providing insight into the complicated task of watercraft accident investigation.

Kevin L. Erskine (Retired)

The completion of this book would not have been possible but for the diligent efforts of many influential, talented, and dedicated professionals. First, accolades to Officer Kevin L. Erskine, coauthor, dedicated investigator, and originator of this textbook, who has long recognized the need for a better and more thorough water-related death investigation. Sincere thanks go to Mr. James Wentzel, Ms. Kate M. Snyder, Ms. Bernadette Jusczak, Ms. Amy Koons, and Mr. Brendan Curtin for their tireless efforts with the creation of illustrations, compilation of images, and photographic expertise. Gratitude is for Mr. Eric Lavins and Mr. Szabolcs Sofalvi for their dedication to the important work of postmortem forensic toxicology, in addition to helpful recommendations and retrieval of toxicology articles. Finally, I am forever grateful to Drs. Elizabeth Balraj and Frank Miller, who since the beginning of my career have remained a source of encouragement and mentorship within the realm of forensic pathology.

Erica J. Armstrong, MD

About the Authors

Kevin L. Erskine graduated from Hocking College in 1982 with an associate's degree in natural resources law enforcement. He also obtained mountain rescue, search and rescue, and EMT certifications. He began his career with the Ohio State Park Police in 1986 and developed the only State of Ohio dive team in 1998. In 2000, he codeveloped the Children's Ice Drowning Prevention Workshop, which teaches children self-rescue techniques in the event of an ice accident. He designed a multiagency training scenario for an airplane crash in Lake Erie. Within months of the training scenario, an actual plane crash occurred within a quarter-mile of the training site. In 2005, he developed the Master Water Death Investigator curriculum for the Ohio Peace Officer's Training Academy (OPOTA). He is an OPOTA-certified Master Criminal Investigator who has earned numerous life-saving awards for rescues of drowning victims in the waters of Lake Erie. He was recognized as "Citizen of the Year" by the Cleveland Fire Department in 2006 for the rescue of an active drowning victim within his jurisdictional waters. He has attended police diver symposiums in Hamilton, Ontario, Canada; West Point; and Indianapolis. In 2011, he retired after 25 years of service to the State of Ohio. He currently serves as the training coordinator for Hope Christian Church First Responder Team in Avon, Ohio, where he lives with his wife and two sons.

Erica J. Armstrong, MD is a forensic pathologist and deputy medical examiner at the Cuyahoga County Medical Examiner's Office (CCMEO) in Cleveland, Ohio. She is a graduate of Case Western Reserve University School of Medicine. She completed her training in anatomic and clinical pathology at the University Hospitals Cleveland Medical Center-Institute of Pathology. She completed her training in forensic pathology at CCMEO from 2000 to 2002 under the mentorship of former Cuyahoga County Coroner Dr. Elizabeth K. Balraj and the late Deputy Chief Coroner Dr. Robert C. Challener. She is the Director of Medical Education at CCMEO and utilizes the position to provide a comprehensive educational experience to visiting medical students, medical residents, allied health students, and other students and professionals with a connection to medicolegal death investigation. She holds academic appointments at medical and osteopathic schools. She is author and coauthor of several journal articles on the topics of forensic pathology, forensic toxicology, anatomic and clinical pathology, and the biological sciences. She has authored a textbook on the topic of death reporting and death certification and maintains an educational blogsite on this subject matter.

Introduction

1

ERICA J. ARMSTRONG

Drowning: A Diagnosis of Exclusion

Deaths due to drowning and other water-related deaths remain both a local and worldwide problem with far-reaching human and economic consequences, prompting ongoing data collection, analysis, and research. A number of task forces made up of experts involved in water safety from around the world were established in 1997 in order to define recommendations and reduce the number of drowning victims and improve the outcome of casualties. These recommendations were discussed during a number of meetings held at the World Congress on Drowning in Amsterdam in 2002. A definition of drowning has been adopted and recommended for widespread use by the World Congress on Drowning, which defines drowning as "the process of experiencing respiratory impairment from submersion/immersion in liquid."[1] *Merriam Webster's Collegiate Dictionary* describes "to drown" in part as "to suffocate by submersion, esp. in water."[2] *Dorland's Illustrated Medical Dictionary* defines "drowning" as "suffocation and death resulting from filling of the lungs with water or other substance or fluid, so that gas exchange becomes impossible."[3] Drowning does not always end in fatality and can be non-fatal whereby the victim is resuscitated and recovers but may suffer medical complications as a result of lung damage, also known as secondary drowning.[3] Forensic pathologists, who are involved in the determination of cause and manner of death, generally define drowning as an asphyxial death in which the body is deprived of oxygen as a result of impairment of oxygen exchange ultimately within the lungs after partial or complete submersion in a liquid, usually water, with subsequent inhalation of some quantity of the liquid deep into the airways of the lungs. Partial or complete *submersion* specifically involves partial or complete coverage of the external airways (nose and mouth). All of the above definitions have in common that drowning involves a compromise of respiratory function that if prolonged, can result in irreversible neurological and organ injury or death. Death may occur acutely within minutes and upward of 24 hours after submersion, or may be delayed beyond 24 hours, in which the victim can develop a number of medical complications arising from direct lung injury by the inhaled fluid or water or oxygen deprivation. This delayed death is also referred to as **near drowning** by forensic pathologists while the World Congress on Drowning uses the terminology to refer to victims who survive the drowning event. Forensic pathologists consider the determination of death due to drowning as a diagnosis made by the exclusion of other potential causes of death by the performance of a complete autopsy with a review of medical records, test results, and all investigative and scene information. While there are a number of autopsy findings *supportive* of drowning, there is no one definitive test or autopsy finding that can absolutely unequivocally define drowning, and not all individuals recovered from a body of water can be presumed to have drowned.

Bodies recovered from water are often prematurely labeled as accidental drownings; however, a significant number of drownings and other water-related deaths occur as a result of natural disease or by homicidal, suicidal, or undetermined means. For those who are involved in the investigation of drowning deaths, this is important to recognize in order to maintain an open mind and not overlook clues that may indicate circumstances other than accidental. The cause of death of an individual recovered from a body of water may actually be as a result of natural diseases, such as heart disease that causes collapse and death prior to, upon, or during submersion (i.e., while swimming). While the scene investigation suggests that the individual has accidentally drowned, the autopsy findings may show complete blockage of a coronary artery with damage to the heart muscle supplied by that blocked artery, with very little or lack of supportive findings of drowning. More importantly, while the scene where an individual recovered from a body of water may appear accidental in nature, the individual may have expired prior to submersion or upon submersion from injury or intoxication by illicit drugs or prescription medications. Accidental injury prior to or upon submersion (i.e., impact on rocks or impact with the bottom of a pool) may alone result in death or contribute to drowning. In other words, the individual is made more susceptible to drowning with the addition of an incapacitating injury.

Fatal drowning may occur passively after an attempted revival by immersion in cold bathwater of an individual who is suspected to have taken an overdose of illicit drugs or prescription medications. Death may also result from the overdose or intoxication alone, just prior to passive submersion from slumping over or collapsing into the body of water. In this case, the performance of comprehensive toxicological testing in addition to a complete autopsy and review of all investigative information is essential for the proper determination of the cause of death and the manner in which the death came to be (i.e., accidental manner of death solely by an acute overdose/intoxication *or* by drowning during or as result of an overdose/intoxication). Because the autopsy findings of drowning and overdose are often similar, it may be difficult to clearly identify which was actually the cause of death.

In some cases, the determination of drowning as the cause of death is certain; however, the manner in which the death came to be is uncertain or cannot be determined. Take, for example, an individual with a debilitating neurological disorder such as multiple sclerosis who had prior to her untimely death voiced to an acquaintance her frustration and sadness with coping with her worsening condition. She was found submerged in 3 feet of debris-filled water near the shoreline of a lake in the late spring. She was accompanied by her acquaintance, who did not witness the event, reportedly due to being turned away from her during the moments leading up to submersion. There are no other witnesses. Her walking cane, which she always used by necessity, is not recovered and is otherwise not found. Autopsy findings are supportive of drowning and specific for multiple sclerosis. There are no other significant injuries, including injuries consistent with homicidal violence. Results of toxicological testing are noncontributory. The **cause of death**, defined as the injury or disease leading to death, most probably is drowning. The difficulty for the forensic pathologist, in this case, is in determining how the death came to be—the **manner of death**. Did the acquaintance push her in, leaving no marks of injury? Did she bid "farewell" and simply just walk over the edge of the pier into the lake as the acquaintance tried to restrain her from taking her life? Did she venture too close to the edge and, because of the unsteadiness caused by her illness, slip and fall in? When there is insufficient information to allow for the categorization into one of the four main categories for the manner of death (**natural**, **accident**, **suicide**, or **homicide**), the death is ruled as "undetermined" and the cause and manner of death are entered onto the death certificate. Should additional information or evidence arise at a later time (i.e., a confession from the acquaintance that after a heated argument he took her cane from her and pushed her in), the death certificate may be amended with a change in the categorization for the manner of death (i.e., from "undetermined" to "homicide").

Identification of any body recovered from a body of water such as a lake, river, or ocean is of primary importance. The determination as to whether badly decomposed remains, whole or partial, are even human may be the first task to complete, and the condition of those remains could potentially preclude subsequent identification. Nevertheless, knowledge of the decedent's identity may not only assist the investigator in uncovering the circumstances surrounding the death, but also bring to light information about the decedent's medical and psychiatric history, lifestyle, and swimming ability. Knowledge of medical and psychiatric history may be the key to deciding whether natural disease or death by suicide precipitated by a psychiatric condition played a part. Without this information, and with a lack of definitive autopsy findings supportive of drowning or another cause of death, the determination as to the cause and manner of death may both be designated as undetermined. In one previous study, it was found that among the unidentified individuals in a series of 123 drowning deaths, 97% were certified as undetermined manner of death, compared to 25% in the identified group. Of the unidentified deaths without mechanical trauma, 30% were certified with an undetermined *cause* of death compared to only 5% in the identified group.[4]

Individuals recovered from water cannot automatically be presumed to have drowned accidentally. Individuals killed by other means, such as strangulation, sharp force injury, or blunt force injury, may be disposed of in water in the hopes that the body may not be recovered or recovered only after the onset of extensive decomposition, rendering identification and the determination of the cause of death difficult or impossible. In the case of an individual who cannot be readily identified, the most important task for both the investigator and the forensic pathologist obviously is to establish the identity. Identification can not only facilitate the investigation into the circumstances surrounding the death, but can also serve the purposes of providing notification to the family and the proper certification of death for the correct individual. Collection and preservation of evidence with the performance of a complete autopsy should quickly commence and are essential pieces of the puzzle within the whole realm of investigation of water-related deaths, particularly those of suspicious nature. Moreover, an individual may have been killed and then placed into a body of water to make it appear as if he or she drowned, with the addition of an elaborate or inconsistent story told by the perpetrator(s) or accomplice(s) as to how the decedent "accidentally" drowned: the so-called *staged drowning*. The autopsy may disclose recent injury in a pattern consistent with suffocation, strangulation, and other homicidal blunt and sharp force injuries inflicted prior to submersion. Homicidal violence must also be considered, particularly in suspicious drownings involving not only adults, but the more vulnerable members of our society, namely infants, children, the physically disabled, and the elderly.

The investigation of bodies found in water requires the coordinated efforts of law enforcement, medicolegal death investigators, forensic pathologists, forensic scientists, and other ancillary scientific experts. The most accurate determination of the cause and manner of death will follow the review and correlation of all available investigative and autopsy information. As previously stated, not all bodies recovered from water can be presumed to have drowned, for a variety of important reasons, which need to be considered by all involved in this type of death investigation. The forensic pathologist knows that an autopsy alone may not provide all of the answers, including the cause of death. Furthermore, when death due to *accidental* drowning is strongly favored, one must consider whether or not certain human and environmental factors could have predisposed an individual to drowning. The late Dr. Joseph H. Davis, a well-known forensic pathologist and former Chief Medical Examiner of Miami-Dade County, referred to this as the "drowning equation," in which drowning is the constant (and end result) and certain human and environmental factors are the variables.[5] Consideration of the equation can help answer questions regarding how and why the individual became submerged and why the individual was unable to self-extricate. The investigation may uncover aspects of the medical or social history or certain hazards of the environment. The autopsy can confirm known aspects of the medical history or uncover a totally unexpected finding that either predisposed the individual to drowning or in and of itself caused the death of the individual, who happened to have been in the water at the time of death. The findings from toxicological testing on body fluids recovered at autopsy may confirm that an individual was in fact overdosing prior to and during submersion which then led to the drowning. Finally, consideration of the components of the drowning equation may help in the differentiation between unintentional/accidental and intentional (suicidal or homicidal) drownings. Lack of predisposing human factors and problems with the environment should bring to mind other possible causes and prompt additional inquiry and investigation.

Drowning Statistics and Epidemiology

Globally, unintentional (accidental) drowning remains a significant public health concern prompting ongoing research regarding where, how, and why these deaths occur in order to prevent future deaths. The World Health Organization (WHO) collects, compares, and reports injury and mortality data provided by participating countries. Specifically, the Violence and Injury Prevention and Disability Department of WHO is charged with raising awareness regarding the degree and consequences of injuries, violence, and disability through the collection, analysis, and dissemination of injury- and disability-related data in order to improve health services, foster research, prevent injuries and death.

As of 2015, an estimated 360,000 deaths were due to drowning, making it the third leading cause of unintentional injury death globally, after road traffic accidents and falls, and represents 7% of all injury-related deaths.[6] The more current figure excludes deaths due to cataclysmic events such as floods and transportation accidents, thereby underestimating the true number of drowning deaths. Moreover, distinctions between unintentional and intentional drowning deaths (i.e., suicides and assaults) are unclear, since some may not be reported or may be misclassified. The majority of drowning deaths occur in low- and middle-income countries within the Western Pacific, Southeast Asian, and African regions.[6] Among age groups, children five years of age and younger have the highest drowning mortality rates globally.[6] Within the United States and Australia, drowning mortality rates were higher among the indigenous populations than the white population.[6] The fact sheet also cites an extensive list of major risk factors for drowning. Those factors notably include male sex, young age, water-related occupation, weather extremes, unsafe boats, lack of boating safety equipment, alcohol impairment, low socioeconomic status, and access to unsafe/unsecured water environments.

In the United States, the magnitude and distribution of drowning deaths parallel those noted globally, including age- and sex-related risk factors and socioeconomic status. Between 1999 and 2017, a total of 66,805 unintentional (accidental) drowning deaths (excluding transportation-associated incidents) were recorded. In 2017 alone, there were a total of 4,508 deaths due to drowning by unintentional (accidental), homicidal, suicidal, and undetermined intents, for all ages and races, and for both sexes: 3,709 deaths were accidental, 35 homicidal, 479 suicidal, and 285 undetermined.[7] Death by drowning ranks fifth among the leading causes of unintentional deaths. [7]

According to the CDC "Water-Related Injuries Fact Sheet," in 2005, for unintentional drownings occurring within the United States, men, children, and minorities were most at risk.[8] Drowning in infancy and childhood remains the second-most common cause of accidental death in recreational settings.[9] Analysis of these deaths has revealed a number of risk factors. Lack of barriers around sites containing water (bathtubs, buckets, toilets, and swimming pools) and lack of supervision of young children who have access to these sites are noted. Recreational and natural water settings such as lakes, rivers, and oceans are the common locations for drowning in individuals greater than 15 years of age. The lack of adherence to safety measures, including the use of approved flotation safety devices while boating or proper use and operation of personal watercraft, constitutes another risk factor for not only direct drowning deaths but also water-associated deaths due to trauma, hypothermia, and carbon monoxide poisoning. Alcohol intoxication, which is known to affect motor skills and judgment, was found to be yet another significant risk factor associated with water recreation and boating. Underlying medical conditions such as seizure disorders also confer risk. Individuals with seizure disorders are at an even higher risk of drowning, with the bathtub as the site with the highest drowning risk.[8]

Preventative measures have been proposed by various national, international, and global study groups in order to reduce the number of risk factors and thus the risk for injury or death. These include providing barriers and fencing to pools and small natural bodies of water, discouraging alcohol consumption during water recreation, promoting swimming and cardiopulmonary resuscitation education, and promoting the use of approved flotation devices.

The Drowning Process

Respiratory (Pulmonary) Physiology

The human respiratory system conveys oxygen-containing air into the body via inhalation and is comprised of the nasal and oral passages, larynx, trachea, bronchial tubes, and lungs (Figures 1.1 and 1.2A and B). The flexible and tubular larynx, trachea, and bronchial tubes are kept open or patent by rings of cartilage allowing unobstructed movement of oxygen-containing air into the lungs with inhalation and carbon dioxide waste products out of the lungs and body upon exhalation. The cells lining the airways have microscopic hairs and produce mucous which along with the cough reflex help trap particulate matter and bacteria and keep the airways free and clear of obstruction. The nerves of the larynx also sense pressure caused by the inhalation of foreign objects including fluids and can trigger brief closure or spasm, known as **laryngospasm**, as an additional protective mechanism to prevent obstruction of the airway and further interference with oxygenation. The skeletal muscles between the ribs (intercostal muscles), and the skeletal muscles attached

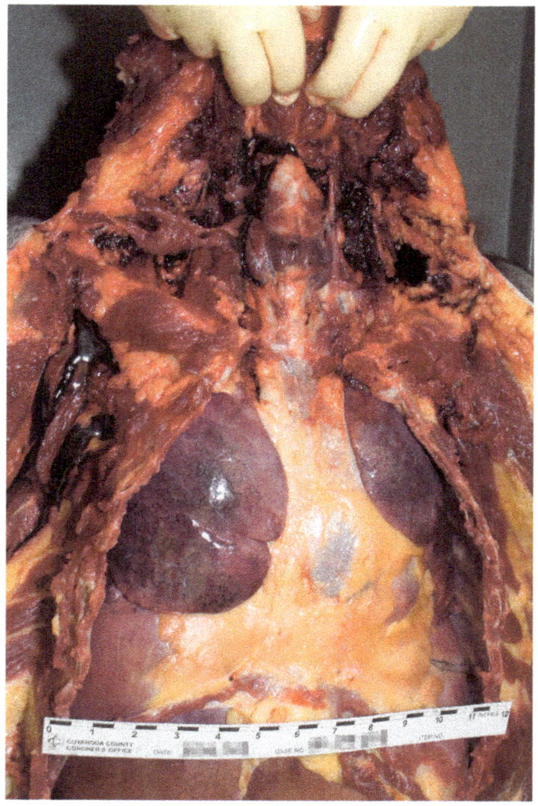

Figure 1.1 Gross anatomic photograph of the trachea, larynx, and lungs *in situ*.

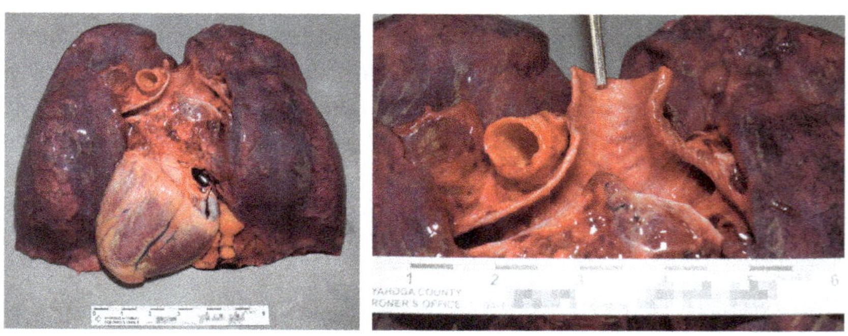

(a) (b)

Figure 1.2 A and B (A) Gross anatomic photograph of lungs with attached trachea and right and left bronchial tubes and heart (posterior view) and (B) Gross anatomic photograph of lungs with attached trachea and right and left bronchial tubes, featuring rings of cartilage supporting trachea and bronchial tubes (posterior view).

to the sternum, the diaphragm, and the abdominal muscles are all important structures in respiration, as they work to expand and contract the rib cage during inspiration and expiration of air (Figure 1.3).

Respiration, or the process of gas exchange that occurs during **inhalation** and **exhalation**, is an involuntary process that is under the control of the central nervous system (CNS). The terms **inspiration** and **expiration** are used synonymously also to refer

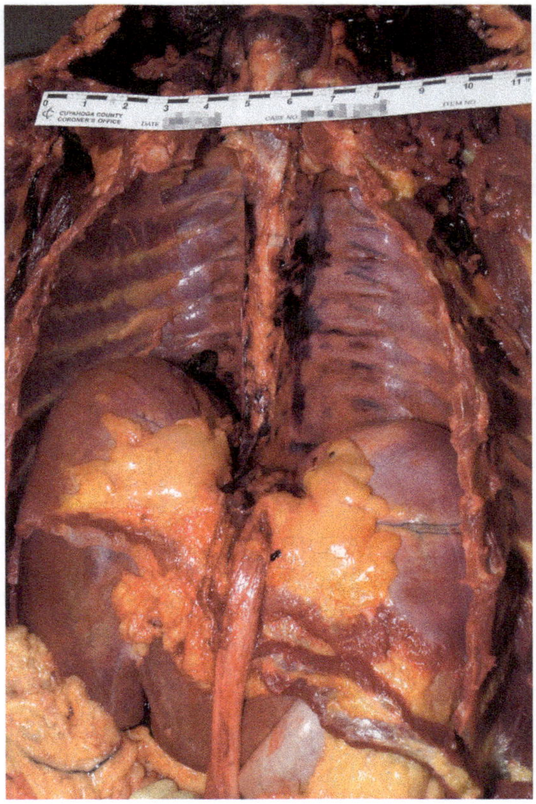

Figure 1.3 Gross anatomic photograph of the thoracic cavity after removal of the heart and lungs, featuring intercostal muscles and diaphragm.

to inhalation and exhalation, respectively. The CNS senses and monitors both the body's oxygen and carbon dioxide (CO_2) levels and can moderate those levels as needed in part by controlling the rate and depth of breathing. CO_2 is a waste product of cellular metabolism and is expelled during exhalation.

The lungs are spongy elastic organs, usually pink-red in color, with each adult lung weighing normally between 325 and 570 grams, with the right lung normally slightly heavier than the left. The right lung normally has three lobes and the left lung two (Figure 1.4A and B). The blood supply to the lungs originates from the heart, which gives rise to the right and left pulmonary arteries, and from the aorta, a large vessel arising from the heart that gives rise to the bronchial arteries (Figure 1.4C). Lungs inherently have a great capacity for expansion upon the inspiration of air. They contain innumerable tiny air sacs called **alveoli**, the deepest and terminal-most parts of the airways, that arise after innumerable branching of the larger airways (bronchi and bronchioles) (Figure 1.4D). The alveoli lack the cartilaginous rings of the upper airways and would be prone to collapse, due to the forces of surface water tension, but for the presence of **surfactant.**[10] Surfactant is a natural chemical comprised of proteins, phospholipids, and ions secreted by specialized epithelial cells (**type II pneumocytes**) that line the alveoli. Surfactant reduces the surface water tension and prevents collapse of the alveoli, which if collapsed would become unavailable for O_2–CO_2 exchange. The alveoli are adjacent to tiny blood vessels or **pulmonary capillaries**. Capillaries

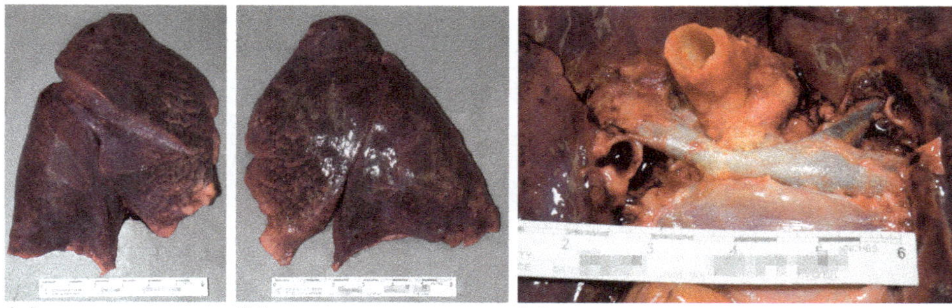

Figure 1.4 A–D (A) Gross anatomic photograph of right lung with three lobes, (B) Gross anatomic photograph of left lung with two lobes, (C) Gross anatomic photograph of posterior view of lungs with heart, and (D) Gross anatomic photograph, close-up view of cut surface of lung, featuring numerous tiny air sacs (alveoli) in lung with mild emphysema.

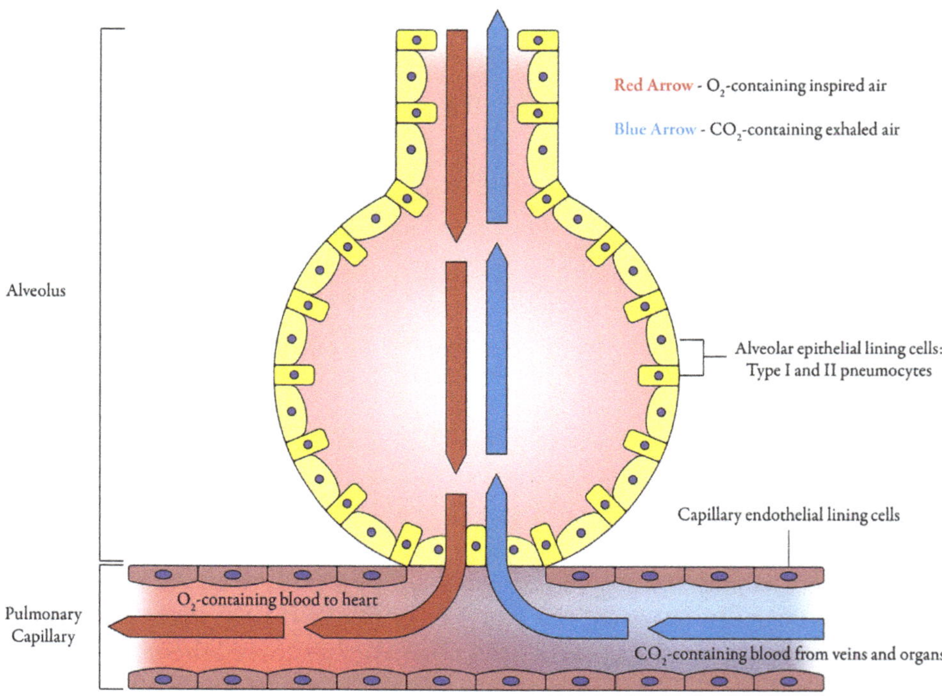

Figure 1.5 Illustration of the alveolar-capillary interface and movement of O_2 and CO_2 in alveolar ventilation.

are low-pressure conduits that connect blood flow from the veins to the arteries. The alveolar-capillary interface is the site of O_2 and CO_2 exchange, also known as **alveolar ventilation**[10] (Figure 1.5). With inspiration, O_2-containing air is brought in and down into the alveoli with the diffusion of O_2 into the pulmonary capillaries, where it circulates attached to red blood cells back to the heart, which pumps the oxygen-rich blood to the rest of the organs via the arteries. CO_2, collected and circulated by the veins from all of the organs to the heart and subsequently the lungs, diffuses from the blood within the pulmonary capillaries into the alveoli and is conveyed out of the airways during exhalation (Figure 1.5).

Pathophysiological Effects of Drowning

Our current knowledge of the effects of drowning in watery environments is a result of prior clinical observation of hospitalized human victims, experiments performed on human volunteers, animal experiments, and findings of postmortem (autopsy) examinations. Drowning occurs as a result of prolonged submersion in a liquid such as water with the gradual reduction in the blood and tissue/organ oxygen levels, leading to abnormal physiological states (also known as pathophysiological). These importantly include **hypoxemia** and **hypoxia**, respectively, which can lead to cardiopulmonary arrest and eventually death if not treated. Oxygen (O_2) is an odorless gas produced from water by certain bacteria, algae, and plants by the process of photosynthesis and released into the atmosphere. The normal percentage of oxygen in the atmosphere is approximately 21%. It is essential for the life of countless organisms, both seen and unseen. Within the human body, O_2 binds with the red blood cell protein **hemoglobin** and is carried by the red blood cells within the blood circulation and delivered to the tissues and organs. Within the cells that comprise the organs, oxygen is used to produce energy for the maintenance of normal cellular functions, and thus tissue and organ function. **Neurons** are cells found in the brain that control many functions of the body. Certain regions of the brain contain neurons that are especially sensitive to reduced or absent oxygen states **(hypoxia** or **anoxia)** and can become irreversibly damaged or die, thus compromising brain functions including those that control cardiac and respiratory functions. Irreversible neuronal cell damage may begin approximately four to six minutes after sustained O_2 deprivation, and the degree of functional recovery is dependent on the extent of the irreversible brain damage and the promptness of resuscitation efforts. In drowning, the exchange of inspired oxygen is impaired deep within the lungs by the presence of inhaled fluid and sometimes debris, preventing the gas from entering the bloodstream and being circulated to the organs, including the brain (Figure 1.6). Cells deprived of oxygen switch to an alternative pathway

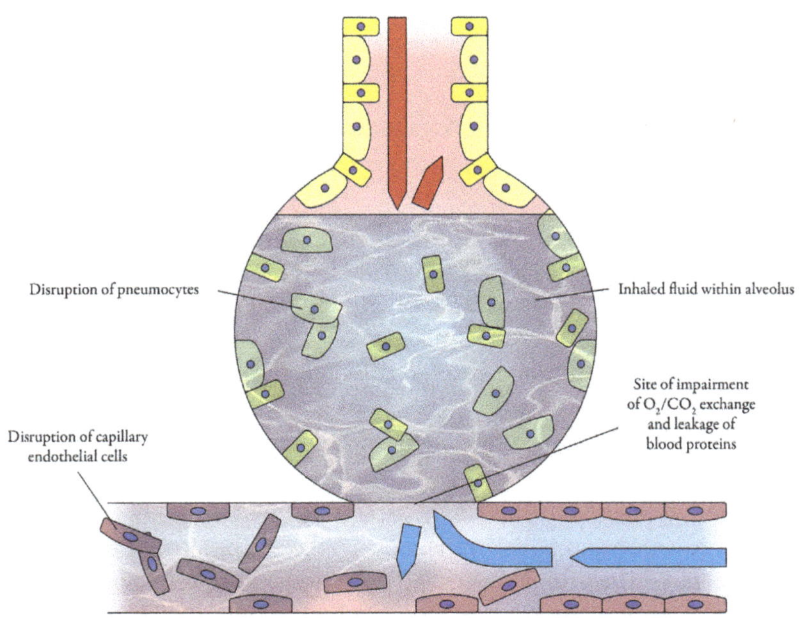

Figure 1.6 Illustration of the alveolar-capillary interface featuring disruption of the alveolar and capillary lining cells with impairment of O_2–CO_2 exchange and inhalation of fluid during drowning.

of energy production with the generation of acid, which enters and circulates within the bloodstream. In addition, CO_2 builds up in the blood. The combination of increased acid and CO_2 leads to a pathophysiologic change called **metabolic acidosis**, which is measured clinically in near-drowning patients by the analysis of arterial blood for levels of certain metabolic products and pH. The volumes of inhaled fluid causing these pathophysiologic effects may be relatively small, and the lungs do not necessarily need to be completely filled with inhaled fluid.

Individuals who are resuscitated and hospitalized following a submersion event may fully recover, expire, or develop a number of complications triggered by the inhalation of water. In forensic pathology practice the phrase **near-drowning** has been used on death certificates to refer to an individual who expires after the development of certain complications despite the administration of therapy, within a day but as long as days or even weeks of survival. Clinical complications, ones that may be lethal, include anoxic-ischemic encephalopathy (brain dysfunction resulting from low or absent O_2, respiratory failure), cerebral edema (brain swelling), pulmonary edema (lung fluid), pneumonia (lung inflammation and infection), **acute respiratory distress syndrome** (**ARDS**), sepsis (widespread bacterial infection and/or multiorgan dysfunction), and multiple system organ failure. Particularly, ARDS can arise as a result of direct lung injury by inhaled fluid or aspiration of gastric contents with subsequent development of aspiration pneumonia. Other also potentially lethal complications include a rapid breakdown of the muscles (rhabdomyolysis) and metabolic acidosis which can have adverse effects on multiple organ systems leading to multiple system organ failures and abnormal blood clotting **(disseminated intravascular coagulation** (**DIC**) if not reversed.

Post-immersion syndrome, also referred to as **secondary drowning**, is another potentially lethal complication in which the lasting damaging effects of water inhalation and the insufficient production of surfactant causes deterioration of respiratory function and the need to be re-hospitalized. [13]

The Process of Drowning

Prior experiments on submerged awake dogs (ethically inappropriate by today's standards) have reported five phases of drowning, lasting a total of 3½–4 minutes:[11–13]

- Nonpurposeful then purposeful movements, first five to six seconds
- Mouth closure, no respiratory movements, lasting one minute
- Profound respiratory movements, foam on water surface, gradual cessation of movements, lasting one minute
- Arrest of circulation, immobile thorax, dilated pupils, and lack of corneal reflex, lasting one minute
- Three or four respiratory movements and no further evidence of life

In humans, drowning can take place in as little as a few inches of water, which may be encountered in puddles, streams, bathtubs, and buckets. Thus the submersion of the face with the involvement of the entry points to the airway (nose and/or mouth) rather than the entire body is the main focus. Children, intoxicated individuals, individuals with seizure disorders, injured individuals, and those with physical and mental disabilities are particularly at risk for drowning at any depth, but especially in shallower bodies of water.

The process of drowning encompasses two general phases: **immersion** and **submersion**. Immersion involves the initial contact of the body with the watery environment that occurs before the head along with the nose and/or mouth becomes submerged. During the immersion phase, one or more factors that ultimately precipitate the drowning process may be at play.[14] These include environmental factors inherent to the watery environment such as temperature extremes (particularly cold water) and strong currents. Additionally, human factors, such as panic, fear, swim inability, drug and alcohol impairment, physical disability, physical injury, and whether the face is the first point of contact with the water versus the rest of the body, may each or in combination be at play. The wrong combination of certain human and environmental factors may put even the experienced swimmer at an increased risk of drowning.

The sequence in the process of drowning in humans, particularly in deeper bodies of water, has some similarities to that described in animal experiments.[11–14] Following the immersion phase and upon initial submersion of the head into the water, there is a period of voluntary breath-holding (apnea) as the victim struggles to maintain the position of the nose and mouth above the surface of the water. Psychological factors such as panic and fear may also be at play at this point. The length of the apnea period is variable and based on many factors such as physiological tolerance, swim and diving experience, psychological factors, and environmental factors (particularly water temperature extremes). As breath-holding continues, the CO_2 will continue to rise along with the fall of O_2 to critical levels referred to as the **break-point**. All organs are vulnerable to lowering O_2 and CO_2 levels but the brain is especially sensitive. Upon reaching the break-point, the urge to breathe causes involuntary gasping. At this point, if the swimmer has become fatigued and is no longer able to maintain the face above water, gasping with inhalation of water (along with any debris) instead of air will result. The amount of water inhaled varies between individuals and need not be great. [11] During this time, a brief spasm of the upper airway (laryngospasm and bronchospasm) may occur triggered by the inhaled water but whether or not this prevents water from getting into the lungs has been a subject of debate. Eventually, with the worsening hypoxia, the spasming will cease allowing entry of water. Also during the period of inhalation, large quantities of water may be swallowed, and vomiting with the aspiration of acidic gastric contents into the lungs can occur simultaneously, which can lead to further lung damage. The asphyxial nature of drowning and the resultant brain hypoxia causes loss of consciousness simultaneously or shortly after inhalation of water. Lowered brain oxygen as a result of continued submersion will lead to the development of seizures, respiratory failure, and arrest, and after a period of several more minutes of continued heart activity, cardiac arrest. The development of an abnormal heart rhythm (arrhythmia) leading to cardiac arrest can occur at any time during the drowning process. Involuntary loss of urine, feces, and seminal fluid may also occur during the drowning process. In the terminal, near-death period (also referred to as agonal), spontaneous respiratory efforts occur and may permit further penetration of the fluid into the lungs in addition to the fluids that have already been inhaled or have formed as a result of the physiological responses to the drowning, mainly pulmonary edema. [14] It is currently not possible to determine the proportion of fluid that was inhaled versus the fluid that was produced as a result of the physiological response to the drowning. [14]

The development of hypoxemia with hypoxia can develop within minutes. The time to death as a result of low oxygen states has been said to range from 3 to 10 minutes in water greater than 15–20°C (58–68°F).[12–14] Survivability of individuals, especially children, submerged for prolonged periods in colder water with subsequent rescue and resuscitation has been reported. [15] Even with resuscitation following prolonged submersion, irreversible damage and cell death of the most vulnerable neurons may result leading to permanent brain damage and disability. [14]

The sequence of events may be altered with deliberate hyperventilation prior to submersion, as may be practiced by individuals in order to increase endurance during diving activities. The process of hyperventilation, with the taking of several deep breaths prior to submersion and descent, can cause a significant *decrease* in CO_2 levels (bypassing the involuntary trigger that initiates breathing), with subsequent rapid drops in O_2 alveolar and blood levels upon ascent to the surface. The individual may lose consciousness due to cerebral hypoxia and spontaneously resume breathing with the inhalation of water and drowning, before reaching the surface. This phenomenon is also known as **shallow water blackout**.[16,17]

With the entry of water/fluid into the lungs, other physiological changes occur.[13] Inhalation of fluid causes laryngospasm, resistance to airflow to the terminal airways, constriction of the small pulmonary vessels, decreased lung compliance, and alteration of alveolar/pulmonary capillary gas exchange and capillary blood flow. Moreover, the presence of water (saltwater or freshwater) within the alveoli diminishes or cancels the effect of surfactant, leading to alveolar collapse. Water within the alveoli moves across the pneumocytes into the adjacent capillaries, causing disruption and damage to both the alveolar lining cells and capillary lining cells (**endothelium**). This disruption and damage allow for leakage of red blood cells and blood proteins into the alveoli (**pulmonary edema**), and with the mixture of water, surfactant, and air already within the lungs, the production of a white or blood-tinged foam will occur. This foam or froth moves into the upper airways, including the trachea and larynx, and may make its way out of the nose and mouth, forming a **foam column** or **foam cone** (Figure 1.7). The presence of the foam is nonspecific for drowning and may be seen in other types of deaths, including drug overdoses, stroke deaths, and deaths caused by certain heart and lung diseases. The presence and the degree of the foam may be reduced or made absent by resuscitative attempts, which cause the foamy fluid to flow out more rapidly. In addition, a drowned individual dead for an extended period of time (with or without obvious signs of decomposition) may present with little or no foam.

Freshwater vs. Saltwater Drowning

Whether freshwater or saltwater is inhaled, the end result of prolonged submersion in either media leads to the disruption of the alveolar-capillary membrane along with O_2/CO_2 exchange, accumulation of edema fluid within the alveoli, formation of ARDS, and lowered blood and brain O_2 levels, the effects of which have already been discussed.[14] Freshwater, which is generally hypotonic, directly alters, damages, or dilutes surfactant at its source, thereby increasing the alveolar surface tension allowing the collapse of the alveoli and impairing gas exchange, unless pulmonary edema has already developed and the alveoli are already filled up. Saltwater, which is hypertonic, rapidly draws proteinaceous fluids from the capillaries into the adjacent alveoli also damaging surfactant, impairing gas exchange, and causing pulmonary edema.[17,18] Depending on the amount and type of water inhaled, changes in blood volume and blood electrolyte levels have been reported in hospitalized drowning victims with greater changes seen when large amounts of either

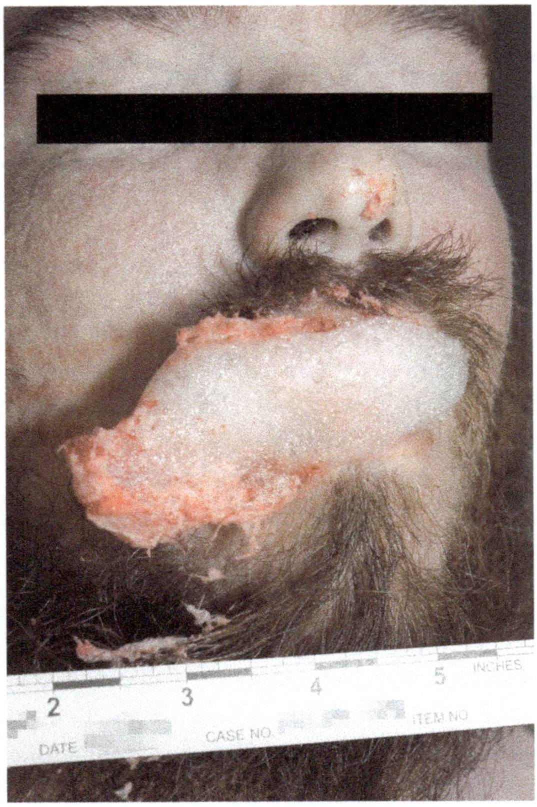

Figure 1.7 Gross anatomic photograph of the foam column in an individual dead from a drug overdose.

freshwater or saltwater have been inhaled, the effects of which are not always fatal. The influx of relatively hypotonic freshwater into the alveoli, especially in large quantities, allows rapid entry of water into the blood circulation, with some increase in blood volume and decrease in the electrolyte levels as a result of dilution.[18] This increase in blood volume can strain the heart and contribute to the development of pulmonary edema or lead to the development of abnormal cardiac rhythms and death. The influx of large amounts of relatively hypertonic saltwater into the alveoli causes a rapid inflow of fluid from the blood circulation into the alveoli leading to elevated blood electrolyte levels but life-threatening changes have infrequently been reported.[18]

"Dry Drowning"

Most drownings involve some degree of water or fluid penetration into the lungs resulting in lungs of increased but variable weights, with the production foamy fluid and edema evident (to variable degrees) at autopsy and microscopically, thus representing the so-called **wet drowning**. Previous animal and clinical research studies have reported the apparent lack of inhalation of water occurring in approximately 5–15% of drownings.[11] In deaths where drowning was suspected, the lungs and upper airways lacked foam and edema suggesting the occurrence of so-called **dry drowning**. Dry drowning was thought to have occurred as a result of involuntary spasm and closure of the larynx or **laryngospasm**, with subsequent formation of a plug of mucus, foam, and froth, preventing the entry of appreciable amounts of fluid into the lungs.[11,13,19] More recent critical appraisal of the past literature alongside the examination of a large number of adult drowning victims indicate that the actual incidence of true dry drownings likely represents a very small segment of 2% or less and other causes of death including natural and other non-natural causes must be actively sought. [11,20] Whether or not the so-called dry drowning actually occurs still remains unclear and unproven prompting the World Congress on Drowning to recommend abandoning the use of the term. [1,11,14,20] Therefore the so-called dry drowning remains a controversial topic among forensic pathologists who will exercise caution before designating a death due to drowning in the absence of supportive lung findings. The absence of these supportive findings necessitates consideration and the search for other causes of death, including natural disease, intoxication/poisoning, injury, or other types of asphyxial deaths.

Drowning Tests

Since it is known that inhaled fluid can cause changes in the lungs, the blood circulation, and other organs, various tests have been developed to detect these changes as ways to diagnose drowning or determine the location of the drowning event. Despite these efforts, both past and present, there currently remains no scientifically valid, reliable tests that provide consistent and easily interpretable results in all cases. Efforts to develop such tests that are also widely available, cost-efficient, and timely are ongoing. This is particularly the case in bodies that have been submerged for prolonged periods and are badly decomposed or injured bodies where water can enter passively through wounds. Therefore currently the diagnosis of drowning as a cause of death remains one made in the context of all available historical and investigative information and supportive autopsy findings with the exclusion of other potential causes of death. More recent efforts continue in the pursuit of better diagnostic tests, however.

Historically, tests for ocular (vitreous humor) fluid electrolytes and magnesium ions and the Gettler serum chloride test on ventricular heart blood were devised in attempts to diagnose drowning or differentiate freshwater from saltwater drowning.[19,20] Other tests attempted to measure the specific gravity differences in blood taken from the cardiac chambers in order to diagnose and differentiate freshwater from saltwater drowning with inconsistent and unreliable results. More recently, the analysis of ocular fluid has been shown to be potentially useful in distinguishing freshwater and saltwater drowning by measuring the sodium level. [21]

Diatoms are the microscopic skeletons of single-celled algae-type organisms that are widespread and found in air, soil, and natural bodies of water, including freshwater, saltwater, and brackish water. They have been used to assist in aquatic crime scene investigation by the method known as **forensic limnology**.[22] During the drowning process, diatoms gain entry into the circulatory system, tissues, and organs through the disrupted alveolar-capillary membrane, and thus their identification in human tissues has been used as a supportive or definitive evidence of drowning. Diatoms may also gain entry into the body in non-drowning instances such as through breathing in air or dust or aspirating drinking water. Postmortem passive entry into the internal organs during prolonged submersion with the onset of decomposition, during resuscitation efforts, and during the preparation of the tissue sample for testing are potential sources of contamination that have been identified as giving rise to false-positive test results that were interpreted as drowning when no such drowning had occurred. [23]

The unique species-specific structures and size characteristics of diatoms have been used to differentiate freshwater drowning from domestic water drowning.[23] Extraction and analysis for the presence, characteristics, and density of the diatoms have been performed on a variety of tissue samples, although bone marrow and lung tissue are the preferred specimens. Results of tissue analysis have been compared to the results of the analysis on the water from which the individual was recovered to aid in the diagnosis of drowning and the determination of the location of drowning. [23] Due to the widespread occurrence of diatoms, however, their presence in non-drowned individuals, and the propensity to be retained within the body indefinitely, the controversy remains regarding the interpretation of results and usefulness in the diagnosis of drowning and the location of drowning.[19,21,23]

The perfect test remains elusive and efforts through research and development of better, faster, more reliable, and more accurate diatom tests that can be applied to a variety of tissues and bodily fluids (i.e., lung, liver, kidney, bone marrow, and cavity fluid) in conjunction with drowning media are ongoing. [24, 25, 26]

Scientists continue their efforts through research to identify other methods to assist in the diagnosis of drowning or drowning location. The detection of certain bacteria common in certain natural aquatic environments from drowned bodies may aid in the determination of drowning as a cause of death.[27] The detection of elevated levels of the trace element strontium in the blood of drowning victims has been shown to be highly sensitive for freshwater and seawater drowning.[19,28] A fairly recent study has shown differences in the production of surfactant proteins in drowning deaths as compared to other types of deaths using human lung tissue. [29] Differences in the electrolyte concentration in pleural effusion fluid as well as the detection of the presence or absence of marine bacteria have been used to differentiate between freshwater and seawater drownings.[30–32] The suppression in the genetic expression of aquaporin-5 (AQP5) by Type I alveolar epithelial cells (Type I pneumocytes) has been demonstrated in the lungs from the victims of freshwater drowning.[33] The application of imaging techniques such as the whole body computed tomography (WBCT) has shown usefulness in the non-invasive workup of drowning deaths with the finding of excess fluids and sedimentary debris in the sinuses and cavities of the head and chest, mouth, lungs, and the gastrointestinal tract. [34] WBCT has also demonstrated changes in the spleen of freshwater drowning victims indicative of dilution of the blood as a result of the drowning process. [34]

Even without the performance of such specialized tests, which may be further limited by availability, budget, and technical feasibility, a general microscopic comparison of the overall characteristics of various debris that may be identified within the lung tissue and stomach contents of a drowning victim to a sample of the water or fluid from which the victim was recovered (the medium) can still be done. This comparison may be helpful in confirming or refuting the location from which the victim was recovered. It is perhaps conceivable that chromatographic-mass spectrophotometric and scanning electron microscopic technologies utilized in toxicology and trace evidence labs, respectively, could also be applied to water or fluid samples that may contain chemicals and unknown substances for the purpose of identifying them and determining or confirming their origins.

Cold-Water-Related Deaths

The physiological responses to cold water immersion put one at particular risk of drowning. [14] Prolonged contact with water at a temperature between approximately 25°C (77 °F) and 15°C (59 °F) is sufficient to trigger these responses that are divided into four stages: skin cooling or **cold shock**, cooling of superficial nerves and muscle, cooling of deep tissues, and post-immersion collapse. [35] With prolonged submersion in cool or cold water, cooling of the deep tissues leading to **hypothermia** results. Even with rescue and resuscitation, the physiological effects of hypothermia alone (with or without the effects of drowning) may persist leading to the decreased function of multiple organ systems and ultimately cardiovascular collapse and death and is known as **post-immersion collapse**. Death may result from drowning at any of the stages, from cardiac arrest, or as a result of the effects of hypothermia.

After a fall into cool or cold water with the cold shock response (the first stage), the initial breath-holding response is rapidly overcome by involuntary gasping and hyperventilation which, if the head is underwater, will lead to water inhalation triggering the drowning process. With face-first cool or cold water immersion, not only will the gasp reflex be triggered but also the dive reflex simultaneously. The **diving reflex** (also known as the **diving response** or **mammalian diving reflex**) is an involuntary reflex triggered by face-first immersion that causes activation of the autonomic part of the nervous system. It is prominent in diving mammals, reptiles, and human infants and children. The ultimate effect of this reflex is the conservation of O_2 by slowing its consumption via reducing the heart rate (bradycardia), constricting the blood vessels and raising the blood pressure (hypertension), and causing the O_2-containing blood flow to shift from the skin, extremities, and other organs to the brain which needs it the most. While the dive reflex activates the autonomic part of the nervous system, the effects of the cold shock response activate the sympathetic part of the nervous system. This causes an increase in heart rate (tachycardia). The activation of these two opposing parts of the nervous system creates what is known as the **autonomic conflict** and represents a perilous time in which the spontaneous development of abnormal and potentially lethal heart rhythms (arrhythmias or dysrhythmias) can occur.[14] Individuals who have an underlying genetic predisposition to arrhythmias or heart disease may especially be at risk for the development of arrhythmias. These abnormal heart rhythms may also occur even before the point of autonomic conflict, in the first few seconds following submersion and after the breath-holding period is overcome by cold shock. Arrhythmias that follow cold water submersion can result in absence of water inhalation (drowning) and would not be detectable by autopsy examination of the heart. Moreover, the spontaneous gasping movements in the last moments of the drowning process may allow water to enter into the lungs, adding to the appearance of drowning at the time of autopsy examination of the lungs.

With continued cool or cold water submersion, the biochemical processes and electrical impulses of the nerves to the skin and importantly the muscles slow leading to muscle fatigue and loss of strength resulting in impaired ability to maintain head above water or to self-rescue. Therefore, the risk of drowning is heightened. [14] This encompasses the second stage.

With continued contact with cold water, deep tissue cooling (the third stage) signifies the onset of hypothermia. Immersion of bodies in cold water for prolonged periods puts one at particular risk for drowning due to the physiologic effects of hypothermia, and death can result from hypothermia alone.[14,17,18] Hypothermia causes suppression of the body's metabolism, blood flow, and brain function which translates to reduced O_2 requirements and virtually all organ systems are ultimately affected. The normal core body temperature is approximately 37°C (98.6°F). Hypothermia occurs when the core body temperature falls below 35°C (95°F). Cold water has a conductivity 25 times that of air causing the body to cool four to five times faster in water than in air. This is in addition to body heat lost through respiration, urination, and sweating.[14,17,18] Previous studies have found that prolonged immersion (upward of six hours or more) and cold water temperatures ranging from below 0°C to just below 20°C (or 32–68°F) are important risk factors for death due to hypothermia. Other studies have illuminated additional risk factors, including lower body fat, lack of clothing, exertional activity, intoxication, and the use of certain prescription medications that can accelerate the onset of hypothermia.[14,17,18]

The body experiences a number of symptoms alongside a series of physiologic changes with the development of hypothermia.[14,17,18] Initially, there is diffuse body pain followed by shivering, which is the body's attempt to generate heat and is accompanied by increased respiratory rate, heart rate, and blood pressure. With falling body temperature, pain and shivering abate and vital signs change, with a decrease in respiration, heart rate, and blood pressure. Decreased muscle strength is also noted. With continued cooling to around 33.9°C (93°F), disorientation and confusion ensue. Reduced and eventual loss of consciousness appears with core body temperatures ranging from 30°C to 32°C (86°F to 90°F). With the loss of consciousness, submersion occurs more readily with subsequent drowning. When the core body temperature reaches 30°C (86°F) or lower, death becomes more likely and even more so at a core body temperature of approximately 24–28 °C (75–82°F). The time to death after cold water immersion is dependent on the temperature of the water and the length of exposure and the colder the water the faster the time to death. For example, incapacitation and death will likely occur within 30 minutes to an hour, respectively, in water at a temperature of 6°C (43°F).[14,17,18] The rate of body cooling and the temperature at which certain signs and symptoms occur or when death occurs will be dependent on the temperature of the water and on a number of human factors including the degree of fitness, the amount of body fat, sex, and the type of clothing or protective gear worn. Full neurological recovery following cold water immersion has been reported in children, and rarely in adults, and is believed to be due to a more rapid deep body cooling of a smaller body in combination with the decreased metabolism and oxygen demand of the brain and heart.[15,36,37] Rarely, sudden cardiac death occurs upon immediate immersion into freezing water secondary to rapid changes in heart rate and blood pressure as a result of the secretion of hormones called catecholamines.[14,17,18]

Warm-Water-Related Deaths

Recreational warm and hot water immersion or bathing gives rise to subjective feelings of euphoria, relaxation, and a sense of well-being, making this an attractive social activity. Hot water immersion may be part of cultural tradition such as Ofuro tub bathing in Japan in which immersion in deep hot water (38–43 ° C or 100–109.4°F) as high as the neck for up to 15 minutes is done.[14] The water within older recreational hot tubs can reach temperatures as high as 43°C (109.4°F).[36] Prolonged immersion in very warm and hot water can be problematic in the body's ability to regulate the core temperature as normal cooling via sweating and evaporation from the skin is impaired and limited to the head and neck only leading to elevated body temperature or hyperthermia. Other effects include elevated heart rate, abnormal heart rhythms, dehydration, thickening of the blood, and fainting. and produce physiological changes that may result in hyperthermia. These effects also put a particular strain upon the cardiovascular system, which could be deleterious in those with preexisting heart disease, such as hypertensive heart disease and coronary artery disease. Individuals with diabetes and seizure disorder may also be at greater risk for complications of these conditions precipitated by prolonged warm water immersion. The physiological effects with or without preexisting medical conditions put one at risk for submersion and drowning or death due to hyperthermia. The very young and the elderly are particularly at risk for hyperthermia due to the body's lessened ability to regulate body temperature changes at those age extremes. Other activities such as competitive swimming and deep diving in warm tropical waters pose an increased risk of hyperthermia and drowning.[14]

Individuals who have consumed alcohol or taken drugs and medications that cause central nervous system and respiratory depression or have side effects of drowsiness or light-headedness are at risk of drowning and hyperthermia during prolonged warm water immersion.[38,39] These risks are magnified in individuals with preexisting medical conditions, such as heart disease and seizure disorders.

Position of Body in Water after Drowning

With drowning in large, deep, natural bodies of water, the body will assume different positions within the water column, dependent upon a multitude of factors both human and environmental.[40,41] Human factors affecting buoyancy and density include the types of clothing worn, body fat composition, presence of air or exogenous fluid in the lungs and gastrointestinal organs, whether the individual was alive or dead upon submersion, and the degree of body decomposition. Factors relative to the water include water depth, water temperature, water salinity, and entrapment by underwater debris. Characteristics of waves and currents are additional factors that relate to the degree of body displacement from the original location of the drowning. Many of these factors will be of interest to or will be encountered by water death investigators and technical recovery personnel and their recognition will aid in providing direction for search and recovery efforts. A more detailed discussion on this topic also follows in subsequent chapters.

Generally, in calmer freshwater, as the fluid displaces air in the lungs and gastrointestinal tract and with increased density, the increase in specific gravity will cause the unencumbered body to sink to the bottom, assuming a prone position with face down, buttocks up, and arms and legs dangling down. This has been referred to as the **drowner's pose**. In saltwater, the body will assume this position but may not sink to the bottom, as a result of increased buoyancy. Exposed body regions, such as the forehead, back of arms, and knees, may come in contact with and scrape against the bottom surface (being propelled by the wave and current action) causing injury in the form of abrasions and lacerations. Injury to the more accessible parts of the body, such as the face, may also result from predation by marine life. Deep currents and snags may keep the body submerged, and currents alone may move the body great distances. Bodies may also be intentionally weighted down and may be kept from resurfacing for a time, but eventually, internal gas production due to decomposition will allow the body to rise to some level remaining submerged or rise to the surface. The time to resurfacing will be dependent upon water temperature, whereby bodies in warmer waters resurface within days and those in cold and deeper waters, weeks or longer.[17] A body submerged in cold water with delay in resurfacing will also delay its visual location and recovery, (absent the use of other types of underwater location methods) until such time that decomposition with gas production is sufficient enough to bring the body to the surface.

Waterborne Illness

Although not directly related to drowning, exposure to various water sources may lead to illness and death as a result of contact with various microorganisms and chemicals. The Waterborne Disease and Outbreak Surveillance System (WBDOSS) collects data on waterborne disease and outbreaks associated with treated and untreated recreational water, drinking water, and environmental and undetermined exposures to water. WBDOSS is a national surveillance system started in 1971 as a partnership between the Centers for Disease Control and Prevention (CDC), the Council of State and Territorial Epidemiologists (CSTE), and the U.S. Environmental Protection Agency (EPA). Surveillance summary reports regarding sources of outbreaks, circumstances, and numbers of individuals involved, over specified time periods, are available from the Centers for Disease Control and Prevention website and provide important public health recommendations such as maintaining and improving pool water quality by adherence to the Model Acquatic Health Code (MAHC) (www.cdc.gov/mahc/pdf/2018-MAHC-Code-Clean-508.pdf). Recent reports cover the time periods 2000–2014 and 2011–2012. [42,43]

Surveillance of outbreaks associated with treated recreational water covering 2000–2014 time period identified 27,219 cases and 8 deaths.[42] Certain chemicals along with a variety of pathogens causing gastrointestinal and respiratory illness were identified and included Cryptosporidium, Giardia, Legionella, Pseudomonas were identified. Cryptosporidium continues to be the most common pathogen due to its resistance to even the recommended level of chlorine. Hotels were the most frequent setting associated with outbreaks. Pools, hot tubs/spas, water parks were the typical sources of the pathogen or chemical exposure.

During the 2011–2012 time period, 21 outbreaks were reported with the Escherichia coli O157:H7 pathogen, which can cause severe gastrointestinal illness, identified in a third or 7 of those cases.[43]

Recreational water activities in predominantly saltwater environments can also result in toxic exposures from pathogenic bacteria and other microorganisms and their toxins. Surfers are particularly prone to lacerations caused by contact with the surfboard. These injuries may become infected with a number of types of pathogens, including *Streptococcus* spp., *Escherichia coli*, *Pseudomonas aeruginosa*, *Mycobacterium marinarum*, *Staphylococcus aureus*, and *Vibrio* spp., which must be diagnosed and treated with the appropriate antibiotics.[44] Surfers and swimmers alike are at risk of exposure and envenomation by stinging organisms called coelenterates (jellyfish, Portuguese man-o'-war, and box jellyfish). These organisms cause painful skin lesions and potentially systemic anaphylactic reactions, which can become life-threatening. Deaths are specifically caused by a hypersensitivity reaction or the direct effects of toxins on the heart, brain, and kidneys.[45,46] The so-called sea bather's eruption results from exposure to larval coelenterates, causing an itchy skin rash and a hypersensitivity reaction.[46] Dinoflagellates are a diverse group of microalgae and the major cause of harmful algal blooms (HABs) and liberate harmful neurotoxins and hepatotoxins that cause poisoning upon consumption of contaminated shellfish or respiratory illness through water or aerosol exposure.[47]

Additional discussion regarding water-related environmental hazards appears in Chapter 2.

Importance of a Good Scene Investigation

It cannot be emphasized enough that the determination of cause and manner of death does not occur in a vacuum in which the autopsy alone provides all of the answers, especially as it pertains to water-related deaths. Certain key questions surrounding any death must be answered and correlated with the autopsy and toxicological findings within the context of all available historical data:

- Who is the decedent?
- How, where, and when was the decedent discovered?
- How did the decedent get to the location in which he or she was discovered?
- What is the cause of death and how did the death come to be?

For bodies recovered from the water, Dr. Davis stresses questions of investigative importance that should be considered:[5]

- Was the victim alive or dead before entry into the water?
- Did the victim drown?
- Why did the victim get into the water in the first place?
- Why was the victim unable to survive the water?

The body and the death scene can possess a wealth of information and evidence which must be identified, documented, and carefully preserved. This may be difficult in certain natural watery environments with moving or swift water. Identification of a decedent and proper collection with preservation of evidence are critical factors in any investigation, especially those in which the death may be suspicious for foul play. The recognition of these critical factors not only builds toward the accurate determination of cause and manner of death but also helps to eliminate questions regarding contamination and improper handling of evidence, which could potentially compromise or prolong future court proceedings.

The medicolegal death investigator (MDI) is the "first responder" of the coroner or medical examiner's office. MDIs are trained individuals and may be certified by the American Board of Medicolegal Death Investigators (ABMDI) upon successful completion of a training course and an examination. They may otherwise have previous medical, legal, mortuary, and law enforcement training and experience and serve as the coroner's or medical examiner's death investigator. As representatives of the coroner's or medical examiner's office, medicolegal death investigators serve as an initial point of contact for law enforcement and technical recovery personnel and the conduit of information between these personnel and the forensic pathologist. The MDI is instrumental in obtaining relevant death scene information through scene visitation with photographic documentation followed by completion of a report, which will be reviewed by the forensic pathologist. Generally, the investigator will document bodily findings relative to a submerged body in addition to the environmental and water conditions whether in a natural setting or indoors. Documenting the position of the body *as found* prior to their arrival becomes vitally important in determining if the victim was submerged at all and if so to what degree as in the case of bystander resuscitation in which the body has been removed from its original submerged position or otherwise repositioned. Noting the presence, condition, and state of dryness or wetness of the body and the presence or absence of clothing is important for any death scene, especially for water-related deaths. Certain scenes will require a focus on documenting or uncovering additional pertinent findings. Signs of bathing, such as the presence of nearby wet towels, the position of the bathtub drain, the proximity of electrical devices, and any evidence that the Ground Fault Circuit Interrupter (GFCI) was tripped, the height soap scum level in the bathtub, or signs that the body was moved, are some important factors for bathtub drownings. In pool drownings, the presence of a lifeguard, video surveillance, witnesses to a person in distress, unsecured access points, and victim swim ability are relevant investigative information. In drownings occurring in natural environments, underwater and land topography, weather conditions, water temperature and conditions, use of safety gear if any, signs of intoxication, state and type of dress, and signs of bodily injury are important to note. Other important information includes any medical and psychosocial history or history of remote or recent trauma that can indicate a physical disability. Deaths occurring under homicidal or unknown circumstances or in which unusual bodily findings are reported may warrant consultation with and scene visitation by the forensic pathologist.

The investigation of sudden deaths in toddlers and older children necessitates answering of similar key questions of investigative importance. Furthermore, the investigation of sudden deaths in infants, particularly ones from 1 to 12 months of age, requires a systematic and consistent approach to documentation. The **Sudden Unexplained Infant Death Investigative Reporting Form** (SUIDI-RF) is a guide for death investigators that allows for the standardized collection of demographic, social, and medical history and information regarding the terminal events preceding the infant's death. This form provides essential information to the pathologist prior to the performance of the autopsy to assist in the identification of certain environmental hazards that may pertain to the cause of death or aspects of the medical history that necessitate further investigation via laboratory testing. MDIs will utilize this form to guide their investigation. The downloadable form, including instructions on how to use it, is available on the Centers for Disease Control and Prevention website.[48]

The Role of the Coroner/Medical Examiner in Medicolegal Death Investigation

Forensic medicolegal death investigation involves the application of the scientific disciplines of forensic pathology and the forensic sciences for the resolution of medicolegal issues and in order to inform the public and the broader scientific community of the outcome of an investigation into any death. It is through completion of the death certificate, provision of an annual death statistical report, provision of expert court testimony, and community education that the lay, legal, and scientific communities become informed about deaths resulting from disease, infection, or injury. The reporting of death trends has far-reaching benefits for both local and global health through the fostering of epidemiological and medical research, allocation of health care dollars, and the creation of strategies to reduce morbidity and mortality.

In the United States, there are two types of death investigation systems: the coroner (C) and the medical examiner (ME) systems. Both systems coordinate the systematic investigation of sudden, unexplained, unnatural, and suspicious deaths and have jurisdictional authority derived from federal, state, and local laws, with jurisdictions covering a single county, counties, or whole states. Some states have purely coroner's systems or purely ME systems. Others may have a mixture of coroner and ME systems. Still others may have state ME systems that may provide autopsy services to the coroners within their states. The C/ME takes jurisdiction over deaths after the time of pronouncement of the death by the physician in the hospital or hospice/nursing facility, or at the scene by the emergency medical response team under the direction of a medical control physician. The pronouncement of death is made after evidence of cessation of pulse, respirations, reaction of the pupils to light, and response to tactile stimuli or brain death as determined in the hospital. The official pronouncement of the date and time of death may instead be made by the physician C/ME at the scene or shortly after arrival at the C/ME's office.

Approximately 20–40% of all deaths within the United States will be reported to the C/ME. Up to two-thirds of those reported deaths will be accepted as C/ME cases and have a death certificate completed by the C/ME, with the majority of those deaths resulting from natural causes.[46] The remainder of the deaths will be certified by the primary physician who cared for the decedent or has knowledge of the decedent's medical history.

The coroner, an elected official, who may or may not be a physician, depending on state requirements, functions as the chief death investigator and certifier of death for a particular jurisdiction. This function is supported largely by trained pathologists, pathologist assistants, death investigators, forensic photographers, forensic scientists, and forensic chemists and toxicologists who apply their expertise to assist the forensic pathologist in the determination of cause and manner of death or other investigators in the reconstruction of events leading up to and surrounding a death. A coroner may also hold an inquest, in which the facts and circumstances surrounding a death are reviewed, calling upon jurors to assist in the determination of how the death came to be. Occasionally, professionals working in additional specialized fields, including entomology, anthropology, radiology, odontology, and engineering, are needed in the death investigation. The death investigator specifically refers to an individual, who under the direction of the coroner or medical examiner assists the investigation by gathering and documenting the scene information, including interviewing police, family, and witnesses, with completion of a report. Optimally, the death investigator is a board-certified medicolegal death investigator (MDI).

The ME system has similar goals and modes of operation. A significant proportion of the U.S. population (50%) is served by an ME system.[49] In contrast to the coroner, the ME is appointed by a local body of government and is almost always a physician and often a forensic pathologist. Some variability in the definition of the duties of the ME exists. Depending on the jurisdiction, the ME may send bodies to a pathologist for autopsy or the ME is actually the coroner's pathologist. Like the coroner, the ME has access to scientists whose expertise is applied to the death investigation and also utilizes death investigators. As far as investigative systems go, the national trend has been a slow but continued shift toward the ME system headed by a physician pathologist, preferably with specialized training in forensic pathology.

The **pathologist** is a specially trained physician (doctor of medicine—MD or doctor of osteopathic medicine—DO) who makes medical diagnoses via the scientific examination of tissues and body fluids. Abnormalities found in the tissues or body fluids constitute forms of pathology. Specifically, **pathology** is the study of disease and a branch of medicine. Completion of a four-year undergraduate degree, medical school, and a medical residency in either anatomic or anatomic and clinical pathology is required to become a pathologist. This arduous but rewarding process currently takes 11 or 12 years. The pathologist is a licensed physician and is usually board certified in either anatomic or anatomic and clinical pathology after successful completion of an examination.

After the coroner or medical examiner, the **forensic pathologist** is the primary individual responsible for the collation and interpretation of all information, including autopsy and toxicological test results, for the purpose of determination of cause and manner of death. A forensic pathologist is a specially trained pathologist who has completed an additional one to two years of training in forensic pathology and has specific knowledge in the identification and interpretation of recent and remote injury and acute and chronic diseases and their sequelae. The autopsy is one of the forensic pathologist's tools for uncovering signs of injury and disease. The interpretation of autopsy findings, along with toxicology test results, medical history, and all available investigative information, allows for the most accurate determination of cause and manner of death. The forensic pathologist and other forensic scientists routinely communicate their findings to law enforcement to assist or guide them during their investigation surrounding the circumstances of a death. Communication may also take the form of pretrial meetings with attorneys and court testimony in civil or criminal proceedings. Finally, communication with members of the family provides them with the anxiously anticipated answers as to why and how their loved one died in order to at least provide understanding, if not some degree of closure.

Reporting a Death to the Coroner or Medical Examiner: General Information and Requirements

The National Association of Medical Examiners (NAME) is a professional organization whose membership includes physician medical examiners and coroners, medical death investigators, and medicolegal system administrators working throughout the United States and other countries. It was founded in 1966 with the dual purpose of "fostering professional growth of physician death investigators and disseminating the professional and technical information vital to the improvement of medical investigation of violent, suspicious, and unusual deaths." As of 1993, NAME has recommended that authority be given to C/MEs to investigate certain deaths that fall under the following categories, which are expansions of or additive to categories previously listed under the 1954 Model Postmortem Examinations Act:[50]

- Criminal violence
- Suicide
- Accident
- Sudden death when the decedent was in apparent good health
- Death unattended by a practicing physician
- Death under suspicious circumstances
- Abortion

- Poisoning
- Diseases constituting a threat to public health
- Disease, injury, or toxic agent resulting from employment
- Death associated with diagnostic or therapeutic procedures
- Death in a prison or penal institution
- Death when in legal custody
- Death in which a body is to be cremated, dissected, or buried at sea
- Unclaimed bodies
- A body brought into a new medicolegal jurisdiction without proper medical certification

State statutes have incorporated the above categories to varying degrees, including the provision of specific examples of types of reportable deaths (i.e., sudden unexpected deaths of infants and children). There is no uniformity or standard among the states, however. If there is any question as to whether a death should be reported to the C/ME, it is wiser to contact the office serving that jurisdiction for guidance. Many C/ME offices have websites containing information on which deaths are reportable and how to report a death. Not surprisingly, a water-related death is an automatic C/ME case.

Anyone can report a death to the C/ME, but this duty ultimately falls to medical personnel within a hospital, nursing, or hospice facility or law enforcement personnel. On occasion, a funeral director may report the death of an individual who has sustained some kind of injury that was not initially reported by the medical facility to the C/ME. The C/ME death investigator will need to obtain medical information, including information about the injury from the medical facility, to determine if the circumstances meet the criteria for a C/ME case and, if so, accept the case so that the determination of the cause and manner of death and completion of the death certificate can be performed ultimately by the C/ME. Deaths reported by medical personnel require the conveyance of decedent identifying information, medical history, a summary of events during hospitalization, and the date and time of pronouncement of the death. Deaths reported by law enforcement personnel require the exchange of key pieces of information in addition to the historical information. Police investigators initially need to provide their name, badge number, city of jurisdiction, and a phone number where they can be reached for additional information or questions. The decedent's name, address, birth date/age, race, sex, marital status, and social security number are also needed. If the identity of the decedent is unknown, the decedent can be reported as "unidentified" and will remain so until identification is made visually or scientifically using one or more methods, such as fingerprint matching, dental or body x-ray film comparison, or DNA comparison. Identification of badly decomposed or skeletonized remains will require the application of scientific methods. The C/ME may request the assistance of law enforcement or other investigators (including their own medicolegal death investigators) in obtaining fingerprints from the decedent or otherwise utilize automated fingerprint identification technology. Law enforcement and medicolegal death investigators also assist in obtaining x-ray films and locating close relatives to assist in the confirmation of identification. The name and telephone number of the next of kin should also be reported, if known. The C/ME routinely requests reports, including any supplemental reports and death scene photographs, from law enforcement and other agencies. Hospital and paramedic reports are also routinely requested.

Regarding death scenes, the C/ME needs answers to specific questions. The medicolegal death investigator, who acts as a delegate of the C/ME, is often the first point of contact for law enforcement when taking the report of death over the telephone or when physically responding to the death scene and will seek out information to answer the following:

- Who found the decedent?
- Where was the decedent found?
- What time was the decedent discovered?
- When was the decedent last seen alive and by whom?
- In what position was the decedent found?
- What was the condition of the body (frozen, burned, decomposed, soiled, wet)?
- Any evidence of foul play or trauma?

If the death is believed to be suspicious, this should be specifically stated or pointed out to the medicolegal death investigator along with the reason for that belief. This would include observations of evidence of a break-in, missing personal effects or valuable items, signs of a struggle, the presence of drug paraphernalia, the presence of empty or near-empty pill bottles, and the presence of weapons or objects that could be used as weapons. Weapons or objects with apparent biological tissue or fluids on them are also important to document. The notation of the presence of a suicide note, whether on paper or in electronic form (i.e., audio recording, computer entry, or cell phone text), is especially informative in suspected suicide deaths. If the body is decomposed, important scene markers or clues as to how long the individual may have been dead include piles of mail or newspapers, calendars with successive dates marked off, last date on a tear-off style calendar, type of clothing worn by the decedent, or type of meal that was being prepared. The medicolegal death investigator has formal training and/or practical experience in seeking out and documenting pertinent death scene information as well as communicating with law enforcement.

For decedents found at home and otherwise not within the confines of a medical facility, obtaining the medical information is of particular importance. This can be done by interviewing the family, coworkers, acquaintances, or a neighbor, or by examination of medical documentation found at the scene. Information regarding the treating physician's name and telephone number and the last doctor's visit may be found on medical documents. Importantly, an inventory of all accessible medications, whether prescribed to the decedent or not, along with the prescribing physician's name and telephone number, is needed.

Finally, notation of the presence of the emergency medical response team, including names, squad number of the crew, and time dispatched, is important. If, via the emergency medical response team, the medical control physician has pronounced the patient dead, obtain and convey the time pronounced.

Ultimately, the medicolegal death investigator responsible for obtaining all of the above information from either the law enforcement agency or the medical facility where the death took place and determining whether the death is indeed a C/ME case. As stated, the death investigator may also physically respond to the scene to continue and complete documentation of the circumstances surrounding the death, working with and alongside law enforcement.

For deaths occurring in medical facilities, if the death does not meet the criteria required for a medicolegal death investigation, then it is released from the jurisdiction of the C/ME.

In this case, the decedent's primary care physician will be responsible for certifying the death and the next of kin can commence making the funeral arrangements. Otherwise, the death is accepted as a C/ME case, custody of personal property and medications are taken, and the decedent is conveyed to the C/ME's office by a courier service. After the assumption of jurisdiction over the death, the medicolegal death investigation process will begin, with or without the performance of an autopsy, as dictated by the circumstances of the death and at the discretion of the C/ME.

References

1. vanBeeck, E., and Branche, C. 2014. Definitions of drowning: A progress report. Ch. 9. In *Drowning: Prevention, Rescue, Treatment*, ed., Bierens, J. L. M. Heidelberg: Springer.
2. *Merriam-Webster's Collegiate Dictionary.* 10th ed. 1997. Springfield, MA: Merriam-Webster, Inc.
3. *Dorland's Illustrated Medical Dictionary.* 27th ed. 1988. Philadelphia, PA: WB Saunders Co.
4. Lucas, J., Goldfeder, L., and Gill, J. 2002. Bodies found in waterways in New York City. *J Forensic Sci* 47(1):137–41.
5. Davis, J. H. 1986. Bodies found in water—An investigative approach. *Am J Forensic Med Pathol* 7(4):291–97.
6. World Health Organization. 2017. Drowning fact sheet. 2017 May. Geneva: World Health Organization. [cited July 29, 2019]. http://www.who.int/mediacentre/factsheets/fs347/en/. (accessed August 18, 2019)
7. Centers for Disease Control and Prevention, Injury and Prevention and Control. Web-based Inquiry Statistics Query Reporting System (WISQARS) fatal injury data, fatal injury reports 1981–2017. https://webappa.cdc.gov/sasweb/ncipc/mortrate.html (accessed August 18, 2019).
8. Centers for Disease Control and Prevention–National Centers for Injury Prevention and Control. 2005. Water-related injuries fact sheet. http://www.cdc.gov/ncipc/factsheets/drown.html (accessed September 2, 2019).
9. Gilchrist, J., Gotsch, K., and Ryan, G. 2004. Nonfatal and fatal drownings in recreational water settings: United States, 2001–2002. *MMWR Morb Mortal Wkly Rep* 447–52.
10. Guyton, A. C., and Hall, J. E. 1996. *Textbook of Medical Physiology.* 9th ed. Philadelphia, PA: W.B. Saunders Company.
11. Modell, J. H., Bellefluer, M., and Davis, J. H. 1999. Drowning without aspiration: Is this an appropriate diagnosis? *J Forensic Sci* 44(6):1119–23.
12. Orlowski, J. P., and Szpilman, D. 2001. Drowning. Rescue, resuscitation, and reanimation. *Pediatr Clin North Am* 48(3):627–46.
13. Pearn, J. 1985. Pathophysiology of drowning. *Med J Aust* 142:586–88.
14. Bierens, J. J. L. M., Lunetta, P., Tipton, M., and Warner, D. S. 2016. Physiology of drowning: A review. *Physiology (Bethesda)* 31(2):147–66.
15. Bolte, R. G., Black, P. G., Bowers, R. S., et al. 1988. The use of extracorporeal rewarming in a child submerged for 66 minutes. *JAMA* 260(3):377–79.
16. Caruso, J. L. 2003. Bodies found in water. In *Handbook of Forensic Pathology*, ed. R. C. Froede, 203–12. 2nd ed. Northfield, IL: College of American Pathologists.
17. Spitz, D. J. 2006. Investigation of bodies in water. In *Medicolegal Investigation of Death—Guidelines for the Application of Pathology to Crime Investigation*, ed. W. U. Spitz, 846–81. 4th ed. Springfield, IL: Charles C Thomas Publisher Ltd.
18. Layon, A. J., and Modell, J. H. 2009. Drowning: Update 2009. *Anesthesiology* 110(6):1390–401.
19. Piette, M. H. A., and de Letter, E. A. D. 2006. Drowning: Still a difficult autopsy diagnosis. *Forensic Sci I* 163:1–9.
20. Lunetta, P., Modell, J. H., and Sajantilla, A. 2004. What is the incidence and significance of "dry-lungs" in bodies found in water? *Am J Forensic Med Pathol* 25:291–301.

21. Stephenson, L., van den Heuvel, C., and Byard, R. W. 2019. The persistent problem of drowning: A difficult diagnosis with inconclusive tests. *J Forensic Leg Med* 66:79–85.
22. Siver, P. A., Lord, W. D., and McCarthy, D. J. 1994. Forensic limnology: The use of freshwater algal community ecology to link suspects to an aquatic crime scene in southern New England. *J Forensic Sci* 39(3):847–53.
23. Levkov, Z., Williams, D. M., Nikolovska, D., et al. 2017. The use of diatoms in forensic science: Advantages and limitations of the diatom test in cases of drowning. Bath (UK): Geological Society. p.261–77. https://www.researchgate.net/publication/318108836_The_use_of_diatoms_in_forensic_science_advantages_and_limitations_of_the_diatom_test_in_cases_of_drowning (accessed September 27, 2019).
24. Zhou, J., Liu, C., Bardeesi, A. S. A., et al. 2017. The diagnositic value of quantitative assessment of diatom test for drowning: An analysis of 128 water-related death cases using microwave digestion-vacuum filtration-automated scanning electron microscopy. *J Forensic Sci* 62(6):1638:42.
25. Diaz-Palma, P. A., Alucema, A., Hayashida, G., et al. 2009. Development and standardization of a microalgae test for determining deaths by drowning. *Forensic Sci Int* 184(1–3):37–41.
26. Lin, C. Y., Yen, W. C., Hirsch, H. M., et al. 2014. Diatomological investigation in sphenoid sinus fluid and lung tissue from cases of suspected drowning. *Forensic Sci Int* 244:111–5.
27. Huys, G., Coopman, V., Varenbergh, D., and Cordonnier, J. 2012. Selective culturing and genus specific PCR detection for identification of Aeromonas in tissue samples to assist the medico-legal diagnosis of death by drowning. *Forensic Sci Int* 221(1–3):11–15.
28. Perez-Carceles, M. D., Sibon, A., Gil Del Castillo, M. L., et al. 2008. Strontium levels in different causes of death: Diagnostic efficacy in drowning. *Biol Trace Elem Res* 126(1–3):27–37.
29. Miyazato, T., Ishikawa, T., Michiue, T., and Maeda, H. 2012. Molecular pathology of pulmonary surfactants and cytokines in drowning compared with other asphyxiation and fatal hypothermia. *Int J Legal Med* 126(4):581–7.
30. Kakizaki, E., Takahama, K., Seo, Y., et al. 2008. Marine bacteria comprise a possible indicator of drowning in seawater. *Forensic Sci Int* 176(2–3):236–47.
31. Kakizaki, E., Kozawa, S., Sakai, M., et al. 2009. Bioluminescent bacteria have potential as a marker of drowning in seawater: Two immersed cadavers retrieved near estuaries. *Leg Med (Tokyo)* 11(2):91–96.
32. Usumoto, Y., Sameshima, N., Hikiji, W., et al. 2009. Electrolyte analysis of pleural effusion as an indicator of drowning in seawater and freshwater. *J Forensic Leg Med* 16(6):321–24.
33. Hayashi, T., Ishida, Y., Mizunuma, S., et al. 2009. Differential diagnosis between freshwater drowning and saltwater drowning based on intrapulmonary aquaporin-5 expression. *Int J Legal Med* 123(1):7–13.
34. Vander Plaetsen, S., De Letter, E., Piette, M., et al. 2015. Post-mortem evaluation of drowning with whole body CT. *Forensic Sci Int* 249:35–41.
35. Golden, F. C., and Harvey, G. R. 1981. The "afterdrop" and death after rescue from immersion in cold water. In *Hypothermia Ashore and Afloat*, ed. Adam, J. A. Aberdeen University Press, Aberdeen.
36. Orlowski, J. P. 1987. Drowning, near-drowning, and ice-water submersions. *Pediatr Clin North Am* 34(1):75–92.
37. Edwards, N. D., Timmins, A. C., Randalls, B., et al. 1990. Survival in adults after cardiac arrest due to drowning. *Intensive Care Med* 16(5):336–37.
38. Press, E. 1991. The health hazards of saunas and spas and how to minimize them. *Am J Public Health* 81(8):1034–37.
39. Yang, K. M., Lee, B. W., Oh, J., Yoo, S. H. 2018. Characteristics of sauna deaths in Korea in relation to different blood alcohol concentrations. *Forensic Sci Med Pathol.* 14:307–313).
40. Mateus, M., de Pablo, H., and Vaz, N. 2013. An investigation on body displacement after two drowning accidents. *Forensic Sci Int* 229:e6–e12.

41. Ellingham, S. T. D., Perich, P., and Tidball-Binz, M. 2017. The fate of human remains in a maritime context and feasibility for forensic humanitarian action to assist in their recovery and identification. *Forensic Sci Int* 279:229–34.
42. Hlavsa, M. C., Cikesh, B. L., Roberts, V. A., et al. 2018. Outbreaks associated with treated recreational water-United States, 2000–2014. *MMWR Morb Mortal Wkly Rep.* https://www.cdc.gov/mmwr/volumes/67/wr/mm6719a3.htm (accessed October 1, 2019).
43. Hlavsa, M. C., Roberts, V. A., Kahler, A. M., et al. 2015. Outbreaks of illness associated with recreational water-United States, 2011–2012. *MMWR Morb Mortal Wkly Rep.* https://www.cdc.gov/healthywater/surveillance/pdf/mm6424.pdf (accessed October 1, 2019).
44. Zoltan, T. B., Taylor, K. S., and Achar, S. A. 2005. Health issues for surfers. *American Family Physician* 71(12):2313–17.
45. Burnett, J. W., Calton, G. J., and Burnett, H. W. 1986. Jellyfish envenomation syndromes. *J Am Acad Dermatol* 14(1):100–6.
46. Wang, D. 2008. Neurotoxins from marine dinoflagellates: A brief review. *Mar Drugs* 6:349–71.
47. Steensma, D. P. 2007. Exacerbation of asthma by Florida "red tide" during an ocean sailing trip. *Mayo Clin Proc* 82(9):1128–30.
48. Centers for Disease Control and Prevention. Sudden infant death syndrome (SIDS) and sudden unexpected infant death (SUID): How to use the sudden, unexplained infant death investigation reporting form. 2020. https://www.cdc.gov/sids/pdf/SUIDI_instruct_508.pdf (accessed January 28, 2021).
49. Hanzlick, R. 2006. Death investigation systems. In *Basic competencies in forensic pathology*, ed. J. A. Prahlow, 15–22. Northfield, IL: College of American Pathologists (CAP).
50. Hanzlick, R., Parrish, R. G., and Combs, D. 1994. Standard language in death investigation laws. *J Forensic Sci* 39(3):637–43.

Investigative Duties on Scene

2

KEVIN L. ERSKINE

The investigation starts at the location where the body is found. The scene may include more than one location, such as where the body entered the water, where the decedent's personal effects were located, or where the means of transportation was found. There may also be an additional crime scene location in the case of a body dumped after a homicide.

Any item within the immediate area of the recovery must be considered to have evidentiary value until proven otherwise. Nothing should be touched or moved. If the body is removed from the scene due to resuscitation efforts, immediate documentation of the location and position originally found is mandatory. It is very important to protect and preserve the scene immediately to preserve any possible evidence. Documentation of the recovery location may prove to yield an abundance of physical evidence as well as potential witnesses. The scene boundaries are established with "Police Line—Do Not Cross" tape, and access is limited to only those required to be there, including potentially pathologists and coroner or medical examiner death investigators. Any location of the decedent's personal effects or vehicle must also be secured for processing.

Each individual scene will have specific characteristics that will need to be documented. Individual environmental conditions will dictate specific duties to be completed by the investigator.

Securing the Scene

It is not uncommon for an agency to receive a report of a body found in or near a body of water and to have that responding agency arrive, recover the body, and leave without conducting even the most basic investigation. Oftentimes, the area is not roped off, photographed, or searched for evidence. Furthermore, investigators are not conducting an on-scene body assessment to collect data that will begin to change immediately upon removing the body from the water. A properly trained investigator can conduct an on-scene body assessment in approximately three minutes. This allows the investigator to obtain valuable information that is often missing for use by the pathologist conducting the autopsy.

The practice of accepting witness and complainant accounts at face value prohibits any further inquiry. More documentation is usually done at the scene of a motor vehicle accident than that of a water-related death scene. Because the environment is constantly changing, it is imperative the investigator collect all available data while initially on the scene. Even a delay of one to two hours will allow so many factors to change about the scene that any attempt to return for omitted data will render inaccurate results. Environmental changes such as water and air temperature, water depth, and clarity may have already occurred. Witnesses have left the area, and the immediate recovery site has been trampled by curious onlookers.

It is imperative that all water-related death scenes be processed as a crime scene until enough evidence is obtained to determine otherwise. The immediate scene must be taped off, limiting access from unauthorized persons. Detailed crime scene sketches and photographs should follow, depicting accurate details regarding body positioning and location. A search of the area should then be conducted to locate and retrieve any evidence of a crime. Finally, witness information and statements are obtained.[1]

Determining Scene Boundaries

Generally speaking, it is the first responding officer's judgment to determine the external boundaries of the area to be secured. If the scene is a private residence, the answer is simple: secure the entire home. Valuable evidence of a crime may be located in other rooms of the house. For example, the laundry room may provide evidence that an attempt was made to clean up the scene. The garage might contain possible weapons used in the commission of a crime. If a commercial location, such as a hotel or pool area is involved, secure the immediate area and any additional areas that may contain evidence.

The first responding officer might locate wet footprints or a blood trail leaving the scene. These areas would need to be contained within the secured area.

Outdoor scenes present a more difficult challenge. The first officer on the scene must make a quick assessment of the area based on:

- Location of the body
- Presence of any physical evidence
- Eyewitness accounts or statements
- Presence of natural boundaries, such as buildings, riverbanks, fence rows, hillsides, etc.

The largest area possible should initially be considered. The area can always be narrowed later.

Factors the officer may consider include:

- Type of location
- Foot traffic
- Recreational activities, such as boat traffic or swimming areas
- Crowds and onlookers
- Paths of exit and entry
- Weather or tidal conditions

The most important issue to keep in mind is isolating the body and any potential evidence of a crime to keep them from being altered in any way.[2]

Documenting the Scene

During an active drowning scenario, it will be virtually impossible for the investigator to document the scene accurately. Responding rescue personnel and dive team members will inevitably alter the scene in their attempts to save a life. In this instance, the investigator can only do his or her best to document the scene after the decedent has been removed from the area. But, they will employ much the same techniques as those utilized during the recovery of a body known to be deceased.

After scene boundaries have been established, it is important to take a series of photographs documenting where the decedent was located within that area. Distant photos, as well as close-ups, may prove invaluable during the course of the investigation. A scene sketch should also be done to document the entire layout of the scene. This will help establish the location of certain items that may become an issue later in the investigation. A simple bird's-eye view is sufficient. This type of sketch is similar in nature to a floor plan for a home-related incident. It should include all relevant items, such as a bathtub, shower, swimming pool, or hot tub, as well as any barriers, such as walls that occur within those parameters. Possible noise sources or distractions, such as a television, telephone, or stereo, should also be documented. For outdoor scenes, draw the area the best you can, including any unmovable objects present for reference points (Figures 2.1 and 2.2). Care must be taken to document the exact positioning of the body upon the initial response.

This can be done by using a simple triangulation method in which measurements are taken in a straight line from two distant, unmovable reference points. This is especially useful in outdoor scenes. To document the positioning of a submerged body, the dive team should use color-coded floats affixed to different body parts. For example, the head can be marked using a red float, the hands are marked using yellow floats, and the feet are marked using blue floats[3] (Figure 2.3). A special weighting system is used on the floats to eliminate slack in the line, providing a more accurate positioning of the floats directly above the body. A line is attached to the target (in this case, a body) and then passed through a ring

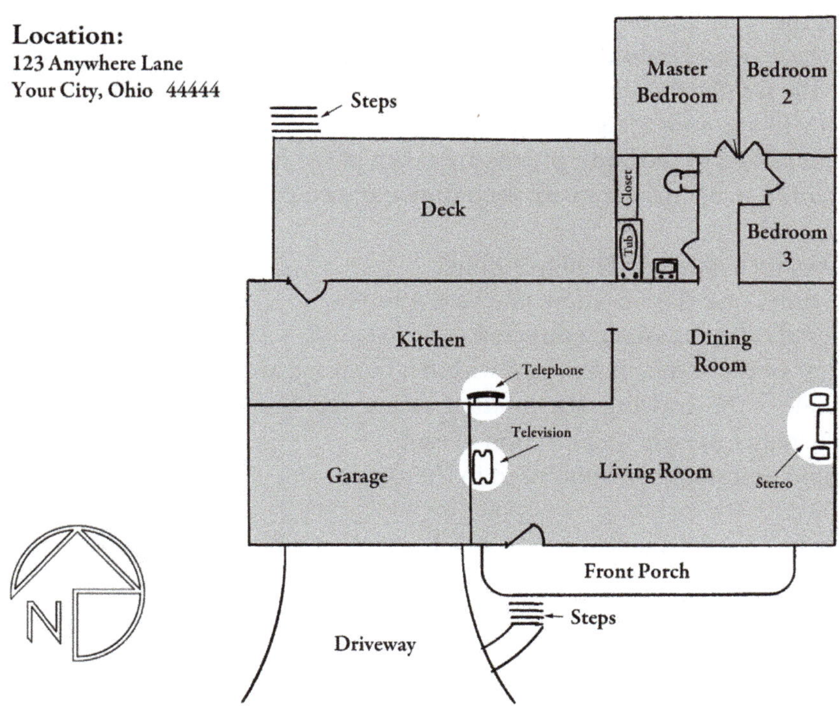

Figure 2.1 A floor plan drawing should be done for in-home water deaths to establish the location of the incident. This may assist the investigator in determining discrepancies in the witness's account of the incident.

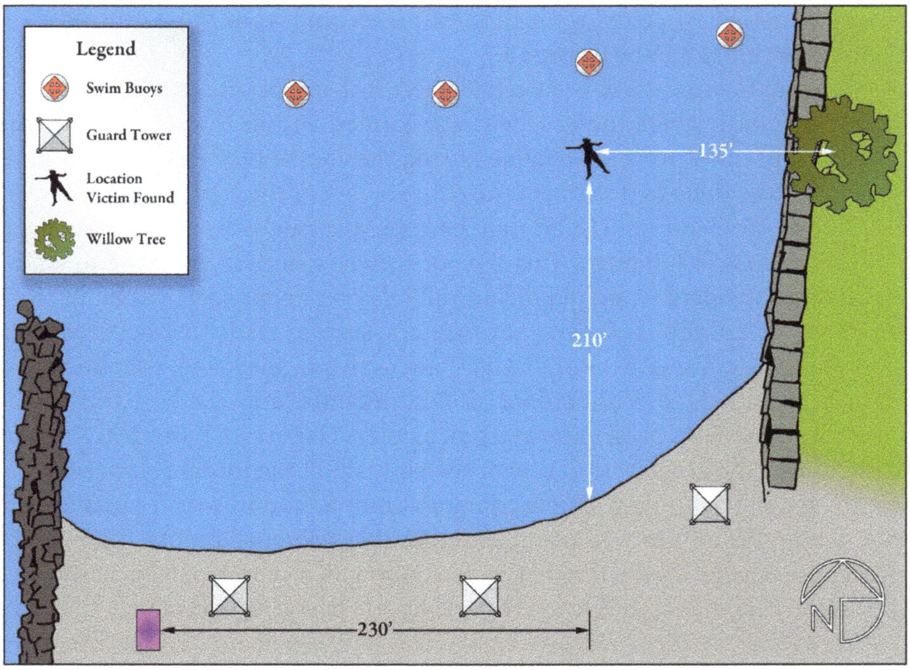

Figure 2.2 A sketch of an outdoor scene will assist investigators in a re-creation of the incident to verify or discredit statements of witnesses.

underneath the float. The free end of the line has a weight attached to it. This weight hangs free below the float and pulls the slack out of the line, which positions the float directly over the target. The weight should be as heavy as possible without exceeding the weight of the target. This will accommodate any ripple or wave action that may move the weight. After the floats are affixed to the body, photos are taken of the floats on the surface (Figure 2.4).

Information to be included with each drawing includes:

- Investigator's name and badge number
- Date, time, case classification, and case number
- Names of officers assisting on scene
- Address of the scene, its location within a building, and compass direction
- The scale of the drawing or a notation indicating "Not to scale"
- Any evidence present and location of each
- A legend describing symbols used in the sketch

A sketch can be used to enhance areas in which a photograph cannot, as well as assisting in the clarification of information obtained on the scene and at a later date. It is often utilized during questioning of witnesses as well as possible suspects and clarifies the scene for court purposes.

Search for Evidence

Special care must be taken during the body recovery process to preserve any evidence that may be present on or near the body. The best way to minimize evidence loss is to bag the body

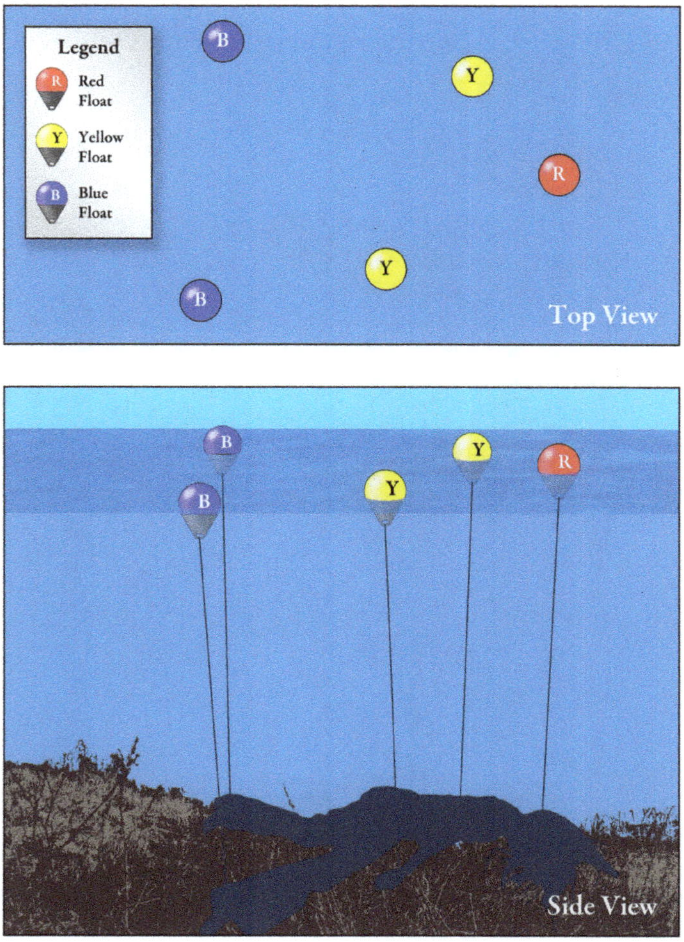

Figure 2.3 Floats attached to the body mark a submerged body for documentation of position and location.

where it is found. Even in a submerged environment, bagging the body prior to moving is the preferred method. When bagging the body, move the bag underneath the body. Do not lift and move the body to the bag. This may disturb crucial evidence clinging to the underside of the body or in the immediate area. Ideally, the dive team will have an underwater body recovery system, which consists of a body bag that has a mesh bottom to allow water to escape during recovery, yet retains any evidence left behind. This system may also have an integrated lift bag, which assists in lifting the body from extreme depths. If a body bag is not used during the recovery, at the very least ensure that the head, hands, and feet are bagged. These are the areas most likely to harbor evidence of foul play, and they need to be preserved. Before the dive team clears the water, have them take water and soil samples from the immediate area of the recovery. They should also be able to provide the following information:

- Depth at which the body is recovered
- Water clarity and temperature
- Photographs of the body and surrounding area, if visibility is conducive during recovery
- Diagrams of body positioning before moving

Figure 2.4 A weighted float system allows for more accurate marking of a submerged object, such as a body, by eliminating slack in the line.

Unmanned Aerial Vehicles (UAVs or drones)

The use of UAVs for a multitude of applications has exploded in recent years, and law enforcement is no exception. Many departments have instituted drone use for a variety of assignments such as surveillance, traffic collision reconstruction, investigation of active shooter incidents, search and rescue, and crowd monitoring. Many agencies are unaware that drone use can also be applied to searches for bodies in and near the water environment and the discovery of potential obstacles which may have caused injury to the recovered body. For instance, a body recovered from a river may have broken bones, cuts, or lacerations that need to be explained. A cursory search of the river may reveal waterfalls, rocky areas, and/or strainers that may have caused these injuries.

The introduction of drones for the purpose of a water-related body search has the potential to reduce the risk to ground crew personnel. A drone operator using a camera can determine the type of terrain involved prior to placing search personnel in a potentially hazardous environment. Once the type of terrain is identified, ground crews can prepare

Figure 2.5 Simulated picture of the body on shore taken from a drone at 100 feet. (Photo courtesy of Charles Cali, Pilot in Command, Medina County All Hazards UAV Team.)

for that type of terrain with proper clothing and equipment. In areas where the terrain is too dangerous or not accessible to ground search teams, a drone can be used to search those areas with virtually no risk to searchers. Drones can cover larger areas in a short amount of time with the potential to minimize the ground areas needing to be searched, literally "turning a mountain into a molehill."

Lakes, ponds, and riverbanks often have tall seagrass, debris, and brush along the water's edge. A body hung up in these areas may be camouflaged from ground searchers, making it virtually impossible to find the body. A drone overhead can see into these areas with a bird's eye view (see Figure 2.5). Lower elevations for photos will yield a more clear vision of target images compared to higher elevations, which will have less clarity but cover a larger search area (see Figure 2.6).

CASE STUDY

April 1, 2012, in Liberty County, Texas, a two-year-old boy wandered away from his home while his mother was taking a nap. A nearby pond was searched by searchers in kayaks, and he was not located. The same pond area was later searched using a drone. His red shirt was spotted in a drone photo in tall grass that was not visible to the kayakers. Because of the presence of alligators in the area, had the body not been found by the drone, the family likely would never have had closure as to what had happened to the toddler. His death was ruled accidental. [4]

Complicating matters further, light reflecting off the water will not allow a searcher to see below the water's surface. A view from the air is not adversely affected by this glare of light, so with ideal water visibility conditions, subsurface searches are possible in shallower depths (see Figure 2.7).

Figure 2.6 Same simulated picture of the body on shore taken from a drone at 200 feet for comparison. (Photo courtesy of Charles Cali, Pilot in Command, Medina County All Hazards UAV Team.)

Figure 2.7 Location of a missing vehicle using a drone. Searchers could not see the vehicle from shore due to light reflection from the water's surface. (Photo courtesy of Charles Cali, Pilot in Command, Medina County All-Hazards UAV Team.)

A properly trained and equipped drone operator can be deployed in under ten minutes, whereas a ground search crew, under ideal conditions, could take four to six hours or even days to organize. In many of these cases, time is of the essence as evidence of potential foul play can change or be lost altogether in a matter of hours (see Figure 2.8).

A drone utilizing a camera and/or thermal imaging equipment may be able to locate a body as well as documentation of the location the victim is located. Aerial photographs may

Figure 2.8 Drones can be deployed at a moment's notice with very little preparation. (Photo courtesy of Charles Cali, Medina County All-Hazards UAV Team.)

also inadvertently reveal potential and unexpected evidence of a crime, such as tire tracks or a weapon. Once the grid search for the drone is determined and set, documentation of the entire search area is possible as well as providing court-ready 3D maps and photos.

While drones provide many positive capabilities, there are some disadvantages. Drones have a limited flight time, usually between 20 and 30 minutes. Depending on the size of the search area, some of that flight time is required for the drone to return to home (RTH). The effectiveness of the drone is limited to the ability and experience of the pilot and the person interpreting the information gathered. Extensive training and knowledge with interviewing skills can drastically reduce the search area if the investigator can determine a last seen point for the victim. Therefore, a disorganized incident command structure can limit success. All too often, drones are deployed in haste due to peer pressure from loved ones and the public before all the necessary information is gathered, which is a recipe for disaster.

Body Search Missions

Equipped with an on-board camera, drones can stream live video and data to the operator using real-time technology. Terrain-following technology allows the drone to fly at a constant and precise distance from the ground using automatic search pattern tools which achieve faster results.

By displaying video streams from the drone in real time, the operator can take manual control of the camera. This way, if the operator sees a point of interest, they can hold the drone's position to

focus and zoom in on the object. The operator can mark specific locations to allow for further investigation by ground personnel.

Body Search Operations Checklist

- Set up the drone
- Set up the centralized drone operations center
- Connect the drone and upload pre-determined flight paths Stream video feed from the drone to the operations center Monitor the flight and video feed
- Drone pilot place-marks locations for detailed investigation by ground crew
- Place-marks provide body coordinates to the operations center
- Ground crew converges on coordinates to investigate and potentially recover the body
- stream video feed from the drone to the operations center
- monitor the flight and video feed

Challenges of Drone Use for Body Searches

- Federal Aviation Administration (FAA) regulations prevent flying the drone beyond visual line of sight. This means the operator must be able to see the drone from the ground at all times. Trained team members placed along the flight plan may act as observers to extend the potential search distance from the operator.
- Most multirotor drones are limited to a 20-minute flight time at 20 mph flight speed.
- The operator cannot see the ground through treetop canopies and dense vegetation.
- Seeing a human at an altitude is very difficult even to the highly trained eye.
- Terrain and vegetation interfere with drone control and data links.
- It is difficult for field personnel to see clues due to screen size, glare, and motion (Figure 2.9).

Aviation compliance, disaster coordination, and future planning require accurate data about flights. For each flight, record the following:

- Drone type, weight, dimensions, payload, control method, and planned route. Date, time, and duration of flight
- Mission details
- Team members present
- Wind and weather conditions (temperature, precipitation, cloud cover, average altitude, base elevation, furthest distance from home)
- Satellite image of the area (Google Earth) with landing zone, planned path, pattern of flight, sensor coverage, and quadrants of imagery
- Aerial image of the area (possibly multiple images "stitched" together or a panoramic view) [5]

Figure 2.9 Photo of drone pilot taken from 400 feet. In this example, the operator can be seen relatively easily because he is standing on an open snowy ground. Imagine if your target subject was white in color. (Photo courtesy of Charles Cali, Pilot in Command, Median County All-Hazards UAV Team.)

Search area planning must include:

- An established probability of the area which determines the likelihood of the subject being in that particular area.
- A probability of detection which is the condition that the search of an area using drones would locate the subject.
- Sweep width characterizing the average ability of a given sensor to detect the body under a specific set of environmental conditions.
- Average maximum detection range (the average distance beyond which a searcher cannot see a typical search object set out for the purpose of measurement).
- Critical separation or the spacing in a grid search where, if the body is halfway between two searchers, it will be at the limit of the visible range of both searchers.

Coordinating with Ground Teams

The success in using a drone, regardless of the application, such as search and rescue, searching for a deceased victim or evidence searches, relies more heavily on the preparation and planning applied before the aerial search even begins. Thus, the success or failure of a mission is governed not by the type of drone being flown but in the quality of the information gathered ahead of time. For example, considering the limited flight time of all drones, there is not enough time and battery life available to search large areas by air. Effective interviewing skills are needed to help narrow the search area. Search and rescue type missions rely on the last known location and personal habits and skill levels. Added to this information are a well-trained team and strong incident command system, knowledge of the terrain, environment, and weather conditions. For example, using thermal imaging equipment to find someone on an extremely hot day will not be effective. Thermal imaging relies on temperature differences, and on a hot day, everything is giving off heat. Likewise, heavily wooded areas make the best drones in the world ineffective by blocking both visual and thermal images. The key to a successful mission involves specialized pilot training and experience coupled with the best combination of aircraft, payload, technology, and tactics.

Keys to a successful mission include:

- Essential planning and development of a search strategy
- Inter-agency cooperation and cross-training to assure all responding agencies complement efforts rather than hinder them.
- Victim familiarization—Gathering of known facts about the missing person such as physical description, comfort level in this environment, outdoor experience, and interests.
- Using the gathered information about the victim to guide the flight operation and strategy.

Loc 8 Image Scanning Software

When the call comes in, incidents have many unanswered questions. Drones armed with high-resolution cameras or thermal imaging equipment can help find the answers.

Loc8 revolutionary image scanning software is capable of independently searching still images taken by drones which ease the process of finding missing persons, subjects, and items/evidence. Large aerial searches using drones may be disrupted and end poorly due to the impossibility of humans physically scanning hundreds of aerial images while looking for small pieces of information. Compounded by fatigue and expending lots of time and resources, many such operations end without a positive result. Drone pilots do not possess the systematic approach to searching for small objects, aside from combing through thousands of photos in search of 1 or 2 pixels to find a person.

Loc8 searches color palettes within the images to identify possible "hits." Searchers can then be navigated to those coordinates to get an "in-person view" of the object in question. Let's say for instances that a missing person was last seen wearing a purple hoodie. All images taken from within the search area would be scanned, and any areas containing a purple pixel would be flagged as a possible point of interest. This technology will improve the process of drone searches tremendously not only in the United States but worldwide. Loc8 software has already been successful in locating stolen vehicles, evidence, and missing persons. [6]

CASE STUDY

July 2005, a retired special education teacher went missing near Wimberley, Texas. Her abandoned vehicle was located by a Texas Trooper along a roadside. She was a certified herbalist and had been known to stop and collect plants along her drives. More than 100 searchers on land were not able to find her, so the assistance of a drone operator, working for the local fire department was requested to fly over the area and take aerial photographs in an attempt to locate her. More than 200 aerial photos were taken and turned over to the Hays County Sheriff's Office, who found nothing noteworthy in the photos. Her body was located a few days later by cadaver dogs, dead from an apparent snake bite. Later examination of the photos revealed the victim was visible in 14 of the 200 photos. This was the first time the agency had used a drone for an operation, and the personnel were not trained to observe aerial photos for clues.[7]

Thermal Imaging

Thermal imaging makes pictures by using heat, not visible light. Heat or infra-red thermal radiation and light are both parts of an electromagnetic spectrum. Cameras that detect light cannot see thermal images and vice versa. Thermal cameras detect differences in heat as small as 0.01°C. This information is then displayed on a screen using various colors in thermal software and computer apps.

Everything on the earth gives off thermal energy, even ice. The hotter something is the more thermal energy it emits. Temperature also affects wavelength and frequency. Objects at room temperature radiate energy as infrared waves. Energy radiating from objects is a range of wavelengths. As an object temperature increases, the wavelength decreases. Hot objects emit shorter wavelengths and higher frequency radiation. Thermal camera specifications list technical details as Noise Equivalent Temperature Differences (NETD), which is a measure for how well a thermal camera can detect thermal differences. NETD are typically expressed in milli-Kelvin or mk. The scientific details of thermal imaging can be very complex, yet the equipment is very easy to use with little training, and the color-coded images are easy to understand and interpret.

Thermal Imaging Limitations

Since thermal imaging is based on differences in thermal radiation that objects emit, fog and rain severely limit these differences by scattering light off droplets of water. The higher the density of water droplets, the more the thermal radiation is diminished.

Thermal Imaging for Drones

Thermal imaging is a heat signature-emitted thermal image. Thermal imaging equipment is capable of detecting heat coming from almost any object and turns them into images and videos. One might ask if it is possible to detect a dead body using equipment to detect a thermal image and to the surprise of many the answer would be yes. But how can a dead body emit heat? There are two ways.

1. Heat signature from the decomposition of the body.
2. Heat signature of decomposition of the surrounding vegetation.

Body Decomposition Heat Signatures

After death, the body begins the decomposition stage, which is actually the self-digestion of the body tissue. Decomposition causes body temperatures to rise as bacteria build in the body, generating heat. A body is considered "fresh" within 24–48 hours after death. Then it moves into the decomposing stage, where significant color changes and skin slippage occur. Finally, the body reaches the "dry" stage when there are dry skin, cartilage, and bones. The bones may become bleached white if exposed to sunlight for an extended period of time. During the fresh and decomposing stages, the heat signature is produced by the rise in temperature of the body due to decomposition. From a 5- to 30-day period, the body may have a rise significantly above ambient temperature.

Decomposing Vegetation Heat Signatures

Once the body reaches the dry stage, the body will no longer be producing a heat signature as there is no remaining flesh to digest. However, during the decomposition stage, the body begins to bloat and rupture due to the buildup of internal gases caused by the decomposition. The rupturing allows digestive fluids to be expelled from the body onto the surrounding vegetation. Released lactic acid during decomposition can poison surrounding vegetation, which is detectable with thermal imaging. This lactic acid causes the surrounding vegetation to die, which begins the decomposition of the vegetation (see Figure 2.10).

In both these instances, the heat signature can be detected using thermal imaging equipment on a drone. Setting the thermal imaging equipment to detect slightly higher than ambient temperature may hasten the search drastically. Vegetation poisoning can also aid in locating skeletal remains and may also occur with bodies buried in shallow graves. Using the drone, scan large areas for heat signatures. Target individuals can be alive or recently deceased, sometimes deceased 4–5 months depending on external influences. Early morning searches with the drone yield the best results due to colder ambient temperatures, which offer a greater contrast in temperature differences.

Aside from climate influences such as wind, temperature, and humidity, anthropophagy can hasten the process of decomposition by exposing the body tissue to the elements more rapidly than if left untouched. Mammals feeding on body flesh excel decomposition, often leaving nothing but bone. UAVs in this manner can search large areas of land with short notice, minimizing exposure of land searchers to harsh environmental and geographical conditions.

Detailed aerial photos can be taken to preserve any trace evidence prior to land personnel entering an area and possibly destroying items of evidentiary value. Larger areas

Figure 2.10 Decaying animal with poisoned vegetation dying around the animal. (Photo courtesy of Charles Cali, Pilot in Command, Medina County All-Hazards UAV Team.)

Figure 2.11 Photo of a missing person located by drone in 10 feet of water. (Photo courtesy of Charles Cali, Pilot in Command, Medina County All-Hazards UAV Team.)

can be searched using the same equipment, which is adaptable to fixed-wing aircraft or helicopters.

Some limitations for drone searches include:

- Not within 5.5 km of an airport no higher than 400 ft.
- Must stay 120 meters from other aircraft searching the same location.
- Take off/landing zone must be clear of personnel, buildings, and obstacles.
- Only those involved in the drone operation should be located within a 30-meter radius of the take-off/landing zone.
- Flight time may be limited to 15–20 minutes based on wind and payload of the drone. Operator needs both UAV training and thermography [8].

Drones used to document outdoor crime scenes are able to hover to take aerial photos and zoom in or out to show the position of witnesses, suspects, and victims or location of evidence. They provide a 3D map of the area to be used in the courtroom. They also allow searchers to survey and evaluate terrain before arriving on the scene to conduct a search for bodies or missing persons (Figure 2.11).

Mapping Missions for SAR

Lower altitude requires more photographs and takes longer, but you have better resolution of photos.

Thermal Vision Cameras for Drones

Detect heat coming from almost any object and turns them into images and video.

Some of the best heat vision cameras for drones on the market include the following:

- FLIR Vue Pro—affordable heat vision package with on-board recording and flight controller integration.

- FLIR Vue Pro R—captures accurate temperature measurements and saves images with calibrated temperature data embedded in every pixel.
- FLIR Duo Pro R—single integrated package coupling a thermal and a high definition 4K color video, which allows the operator to capture actionable thermal and visible data in a single flight.
- DJI Zenmuse XT Premium—compatible with the DJI Inspire 1, Matrice 100, 200, and 600 series and is available in a 640 × 512 or 336 × 256 resolution. It integrates a high-resolution FLIR thermal sensor and 4K visual camera with DJI stabilization and machine intelligence technology, which transforms aerial data into powerful insights. Dual sensor Heat Track locks onto the highest temperature objects. Quick Track locks onto any desired object (such as a body floating in moving water), and Temperature Lock alerts on any objects exceeding a set limit (e.g., set at 95°F, the temperature alarm alerts on any living person with a normal body temperature of 98.6°F).

Drone Models

DJI Inspire Quadcopter

Specs include:

- 3-axis gimbal
- Capture 4K video and 12 mega pixels (MP) photographs
- WUp to 1.5-mile radio range
- Live 720p HD monitoring with light bridge
- Retractable carbon fiber arms
- Comes ready to fly (RTF) meaning no major assembly required
- Radio controller included (Figure 2.12)

DJI Matrice 200 Quadcopter

Specs include:

- Foldable body, removable landing gear
- Obstacle avoidance sensors
- Foul weather resistant, operable down to −4°F
- DJI Go Flight program
- Precise GPS positioning
- Subject tracking
- Built-in FPV camera
- 51.4 mph maximum speed
- 4.3-mile range
- 20–27 minutes maximum flight with varying payloads
- Remote controller compatible with smartphones and tablets
- One downward-facing gimbal mount
- 16 GB micro SD card; compatibility with card up to 128 GB
- Automatic/manual camera control
- Compatibility with a range of thermal imaging and video/still cameras
- Adaptability to dual controls

Figure 2.12 DJI Inspire drone. (Photo courtesy of Charles Cali, Pilot in Command, Medina County All-Hazards UAV Team.)

Parrot Bebop Pro Thermal Quadcopter

Specs include:

- Compact and easy to fly
- FLIR ONE Pro camera
- Parrot Skycontroller 2
- Free Flight thermal app (allows live broadcast of visible and thermal images on mobile device or tablet)
- 2 integrated camera capability (ideal for stills and video)
- Backpack

DJI Mavic Air

Specs include:

- 4K ultra HD camera
- Folding controller
- Intelligent flight batteries & charging hub
- Folding drone arms for easy transport
- 21 minute flight time

Figure 2.13 Authors DJI Mavic in its carrying case.

- 42 mph max. speed
- Flight autonomy 2.0 offers three-directional environment sensing for precise piloting
- Dual band WiFi allows HD video transmission from up to 2.4 miles away
- SmartCapture lets you launch and control the drone with hand gestures
- Active Track modes follow you anywhere (Trace, Profile, and Spotlight)
- Easy QuickShots selfie modes: Rocket, Dronie, Circle, Helix, Asteroid, and Boomerang)
- Dock your smart phone and use its touch screen navigation
- USB 3.0 type C port for data transfer
- 3 1/4″ W × 1 15/16″ H × 6 5/8″ D
- Weight: 15.16 oz
- Handy carrying case for easy transport (Figure 2.13)

Grid Searches

The use of the latest computer apps available on the market will assist your search team in providing a safer, more complete automated flight. The DJI Drone Deploy app allows the user to pre-plan flights on a desktop and then have pilots in the field automatically synchronize the plan. It organizes pre-planned flights from take-off through the entire search, then lands the drone. This app also allows the user to create accurate, high-resolution maps, reports, and 3D models, as well as real-time live maps for immediate analysis. The operations are safer as multiple drones can fly in close proximity to others while avoiding each other and obstacles in the area. Drone deploy takes the guesswork out of securing a systematic and thorough grid search while capturing images that can be uploaded for further review. Just select the area you want to map, upload geotagged images, and then launch a completely automated flight. The DJI Go App synchronized with Drone Deploy assures the drone is Ready To Fly (RTF) by checking all systems prior to flight. A quick Internet connection can be accomplished by using a cellphone hotspot or other remote Internet connection. The Drone Deploy App has a preexisting grid on a formatted SD card. The only equipment needed is a backpack containing a drone, spare fully charged batteries, cables, transmitter, and memory cards. Drone Deploy is simple to use (Figure 2.14):

1. Click and drag the grid boundaries to cover the search area needed and change the shape of the grid as needed. The app will give the duration of flight time to complete the mission, flight speed, and altitude. (Higher altitude will complete the mission quicker but will have lower resolution photos.)
2. After the grid is set, hit the green checkmark on the screen. This will display the mission search pattern.
3. Make sure the duration of the flight is within the parameters of available battery life.

Figure 2.14 Example of a set grid search pattern for a drone. (Photo courtesy of Charles Cali, Pilot in Command, Median County All-Hazards UAV Team.)

4. After all clear, the screen will display the drone camera image which faces forward. The camera will tilt downward once the drone reaches the pre-set altitude for flight.
5. Hit the green start button to launch the mission.
6. The drone starts the grid search at the furthest waypoint and works its way back so as battery power is depleted, the drone is closer to home.
7. The drone follows the pre-set flight path and takes photos along its route. These photos allow personnel to view the search area after the flight to look for the target that may have been missed while viewing the live image of the search.
8. After the mission is complete, the RTH feature allows the drone to return to its starting point. Some drones will land automatically, while others may require the operator to land them.
9. Manual review of the data captured is done by inserting the SD card into a computer and reviewing the photos. A map processing program will "stitch" the photos together to form one image. This app allows you to view the area in 3D which reveals elevation differences and rough terrain. [9]

Drone Laws

Drone laws are constantly changing and improving and differ from state to stage. Therefore, they will not be printed in this reference book. To learn about your state laws and requirements, please visit: www.uavcoach.com. Search for your state listed alphabetically.

Underwater Drones

Much like the UAVs, underwater drones are becoming more popular for underwater searches. They are often used in tandem with rescue and/or recovery divers. But, underwater drones are the newest innovative technology used with or without diver assistance. Divers have time restrictions, such as equipment setup, restricted downtimes, depth restrictions between 130 and 300 feet, and multilevel dives. They also require a minimum of three personnel: a diver, tender, and a backup diver.

The Deep Trekker (DTG2 & DTX2) can be deployed in 30 seconds with one operator and allows for better visibility and 1,000-feet depth (see Figure 2.15a, b, and c). The batteries last up to eight hours, which allows for longer search times than your average search and rescue diver's downtime of an hour. Underwater drones can also keep divers out of dangerous underwater obstacles and unpredictable conditions.

They can be interpreted with sonar platforms such as TriTech Multibeam sonar and MicroNav positioning systems. Sonar allows the operator to navigate through zero visibility waters and quickly identify targets of interest. The Deep Trekkers patented pitching system allows the operator to tilt the sonar angles. It is easy to transport and deploy to allow for alternative views around an object. Once a target of interest is located, divers can follow the tether down to the object and affect a recovery.

Underwater drones are extremely portable. Being housed in a single carrying case makes it easy to transport and deploy. No generators or bulky equipment needed, which allows operations in rugged areas where divers cannot access. The handheld controller is located on a gaming pad, which allows for quick learning to master the piloting controls. An internal rotating high definition camera allows for wide-sweeping of large areas in 4K resolution. [10]

(a) (b) (c)

Figure 2.15 **a, b, c**. Photos of the Deep Trekker DTG2 and DTX2 underwater drones with mechanical arm. (Photos courtesy of Deep Trekker. For more information, visit www. Deeptrekker.com.)

Underwater drones were used to locate bodies and motorcycles which were aboard an overloaded vessel that sank in June 2018 in Indonesia, with an average water depth of 1,500 feet (450 m). Underwater drones armed with navigational sonar systems have proven to be ideal for black water search and recovery operations. Navigational sonar gives the underwater drone operator the gift of sight even in the darkest waters, with visibility often only a few inches. These conditions would hinder a diver from even seeing a hand placed upon his/her face mask. Low/no visibility for divers is a major safety concern as potential hazards are virtually undetectable. Underwater drones, coupled with sonar, have produced greater success rates in safer and more effective recovery operations. For evidence recovery, the underwater drone can be equipped with an attached grabber arm, which can pick up items of interest and bring them to the surface.

Underwater exploration, surveys, and searches can be critical across many industries. As these industries find new and improved ways to use underwater drones, the market will continue to grow. Improved technology is making the underwater world accessible to everyone. Manufacturers are creating rugged, easy-to-use underwater drones that can be deployed at a moment's notice to reveal the underwater realm in a unique way as well as enhancing any dive missions.

CASE STUDY

DRONE USED TO IDENTIFY FLOATING REMAINS IN WATERWAY (VISUAL EVIDENCE RECOVERY)

The body of a female was observed in the waters of the Ohio River by a tug boat operator and reported to authorities. At the time, there was no safe access point to respond to the scene. The body had been seen near the Dashields Locks and Dam. The body was trapped for more than a day in the rushing water of the low head dam. Authorities were monitoring the location of the body and then eventually lost sight of it. Compounding recovery efforts was a large amount of floating debris, logs, sticks, and even animal carcasses, which get torn up by the powerful force of the dam. Recent rainfall had raised the level of water, making recovery impossible. Allegheny County police responded with a drone to get a closer look at the body. While hovering over the body, the drone operator was able to zoom the camera in on a large tattoo on the woman's left shoulder. The tattoo was very distinctive, containing wording identified by police. While observing the body, the force of the water was constantly pushing the body below the surface, churning the remains over and over again. Eventually, authorities lost sight of the body. They have high hopes that the images captured of the tattoo will help identify the body and give closure to loved ones. Identification will also aid investigators in determining where her body entered the water and what circumstances led to her death. [11]

Underwater Search Techniques

Search Patterns for Divers

There are a number of different types of search patterns used by public safety divers while attempting to locate a missing person or evidence of a crime. The individual search pattern is designated by the type of target to be located. Here are some of the most frequently used basic patterns and a brief description of the advantages and disadvantages of each. These drawings do not depict safe diving practices but are included as a general reference for search teams. A more comprehensive description of patterns and search techniques can be found in *Public Safety Diving* by Hendrick and Zafares.

1. **Sweep pattern.** The sweep pattern is used frequently by dive teams because it is simple to set up and allows the tender to remain stationary throughout the entire search. The diver fins out to the farthest distance of the search area and begins the sweeps back and forth. With each completed sweep, the tender pulls the diver in a maximum of

2 feet and then instructs the diver to sweep back in the opposite direction. The 2-foot maximum pull from the tender allows the diver to overlap the search area for a more thorough search. This pattern is helpful in situations where debris or obstructions onshore make it difficult for the tender to traverse the search area. It is also efficient for boat-based operations. The sweep allows for a systematic search of an area and works the diver closer to shore with each pass, which increases the safety of the diver by working the diver closer to shore as the search progresses. In the event the diver would need assistance, the reduced distance allows for a quicker response from a backup diver. This procedure also allows the diver to finish the search while closer to shore when he or she is fatigued. If the target sought is large in size, such as a boat or car, this pattern may allow the diver to snag the tether line on the object during the first sweep, which results in the immediate location of the target.

The obvious disadvantage to this pattern is the wedge-shaped search area, which requires overlapping searches to cover the dead zones of the search area. Another disadvantage is search areas that contain many obstacles, such as rocks, pier pilings, or vegetation, which constantly cause the tether line to become snagged (Figure 2.16).

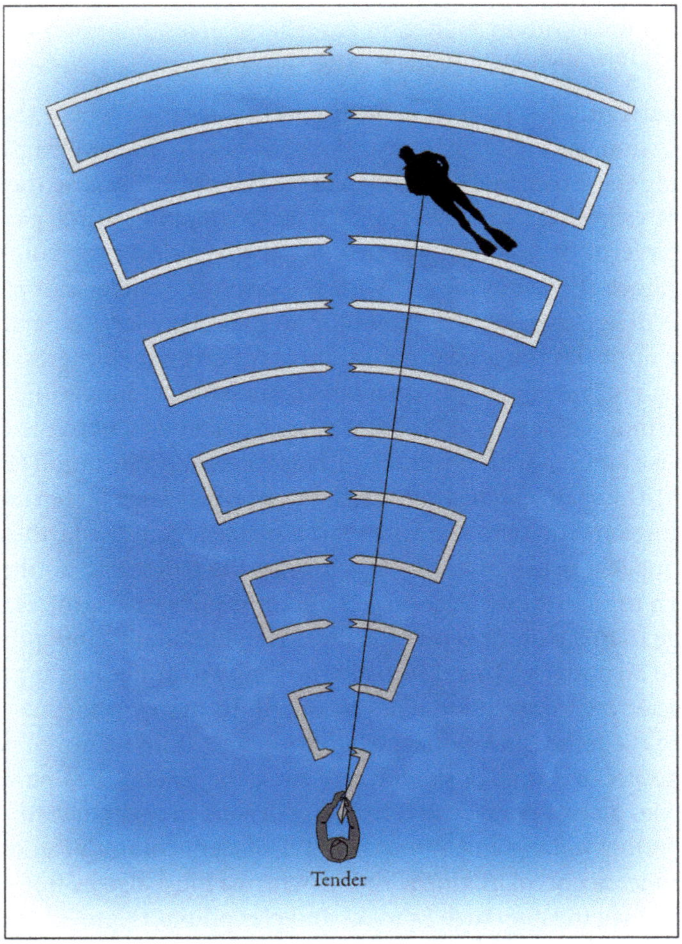

Figure 2.16 Sweep pattern used by divers to cover large areas in a short amount of time.

Figure 2.17 A pier-walk pattern is used to cover large areas, but requires an unobstructed shoreline or pier to allow the tender to move with the diver.

2. **Pier-walk pattern.** This pattern is most effective in areas where the shore is free from obstruction, such as a pier, boat dock, or beach. The tender moves with the diver, keeping the tether line perpendicular to the shore. Because the search area is rectangular in shape, it eliminates the need for overlapping search patterns. As with the sweep pattern, this pattern also works the diver closer to shore as the search progresses. Since the tender moves with the diver, the tender can pace the search speed of the diver. This pattern allows for an extremely large search area, limited only by any obstacles the tender may approach during the progress of the search. Disadvantages include the requirement of an unobstructed shoreline. It is not effective around moored vessels or other obstructions and is not efficient where the search area is cluttered with obstacles such as rocks and vegetation (Figure 2.17).
3. **Snag search.** The snag search is only used for extremely large targets, such as a car or boat. It requires the diver to start the search pattern from the farthest point of the search and make a sweep in an attempt to snag the tether line on the target. It is a quick pattern used to locate large targets and minimizes a lengthy search time. The disadvantage to this pattern is that the diver is intentionally attempting to snag the tether line on an obstacle. This eliminates the ability to utilize line tug signals should the underwater communication equipment fail. In many instances, the diver may not be aware the tether line is snagged on the object until he or she passes over his or her own tether line as he or she starts to circle the object. The line snagged on the object becomes a pivot point, and the diver will start to wrap the tether line around the object. Serious entanglement may result if efficient communication between the diver and tender is not maintained. The search area must also be free of other obstacles that may snag the line, such as rocks and pier pilings (Figure 2.18).
4. **Grid search.** This pattern utilizes a 2-foot-square grid, made of ¾-inch PVC pipe and 90- degree elbows. The square grid is assembled underwater to allow the pipes

Figure 2.18 Snag search is used when searching for large objects, such as a car.

to fill with water, which eliminates the buoyancy of the grid. The grid is then placed on the bottom of the waterway, and the diver sweeps his or her hands only within the confines of the 2-foot-square grid. After this small area is searched, the forward edge of the grid acts as a pivot point and the grid is flipped forward. The new grid area is searched, and then the grid is flipped again. When the search requires a turn to the right or left, that side edge becomes the new pivot point and the search continues. This search pattern is effective when looking for very small objects but requires a relatively flat search area, free from objects that do not allow the grid to lie flat. This search is an extremely slow yet thorough process (Figure 2.19).

5. **Overhead search.** This pattern is slow and meticulous around obstacles such as pier pilings and large rocks. It requires the diver to descend and search a small area and then the tender pulls the diver up to allow for lateral movement. Then the diver descends again, searching another area. This pattern minimizes snags on obstacles and vegetation that do not allow for other types of search patterns. The disadvantages include the risk of sinus and barotraumas or lung overexpansion injury from the constant ascending and descending of the diver. It may also require the diver to constantly adjust his or her buoyancy, which may result in too

Figure 2.19 Grid search utilizes a 2-feet-square grid, which allows a diver to conduct a systematic and thorough search for small objects.

fast an ascent. The tender may also pull the diver up too fast, which can result in decompression illness. It is a very slow process, but the team may have no other efficient alternative if obstacles hinder other search patterns (Figure 2.20).

Diver-Held Sonar

A diver-held sonar unit is typically housed in an underwater flashlight case (Figure 2.21). The unit projects acoustic energy in a narrow cone underwater and receives returned energy that has bounced off a reflective target. It is held by a submerged diver and is aimed in the last-known direction of a target. The diver submerges at the point closest to the determined last seen point of the target. Then the diver begins to sweep the unit back and forth in that direction in an attempt to acquire a reflected signal from the target. Since most targets will be on or near the bottom, it is most effective to hold the unit close to the bottom, allowing the beam to be projected parallel to the bottom. The sweeping motion must be slow so as not to pass by smaller targets. For targets that are likely to stand up from the bottom, it is most effective to skim the bottom with the sonar beam (Figure 2.22). Objects that may not

Figure 2.20 Overhead search allows divers to search areas with submerged obstructions such as boulders or tree stumps.

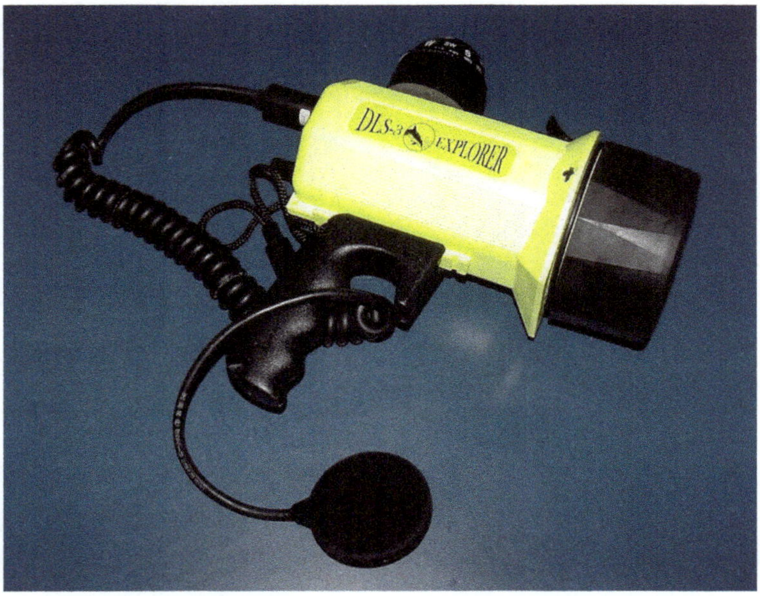

Figure 2.21 The DLS-3 Explorer is a diver handheld sonar unit that is used for underwater searches.

stand up from the bottom may require the unit to be held from a position of some elevation (Figure 2.23). Large targets, such as a car or boat, would best be searched from a distance close to the bottom with the beam running parallel to the bottom (Figure 2.24).

This procedure will minimize the acquisition of unwanted targets such as rocks and other debris. The returned energy is processed by the sonar unit, and an audio signal is sent to an earphone. If the target in question is in close proximity to the unit, the signal will

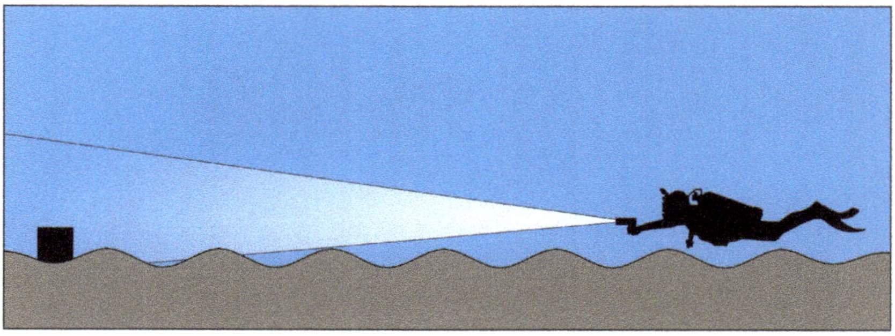

Figure 2.22 Positioning of the handheld sonar unit when searching for objects that are likely to stand up from the bottom. A reflective coefficient defines how much acoustic energy is reflected back to the sonar unit. The fact that different submerged targets have different reflective coefficients allows the diver to distinguish between different targets. Reflective coefficients range from –1 to +1 and define how much energy is reflected vs. how much is passed through the target. A low reflective coefficient (close to zero) allows almost all the acoustic energy to pass into the material. The recognition of the different audible tones is only mastered with extensive practice with the unit. Some typical examples of reflective coefficients are given below. (Table 2.1 shows reflective coefficients of various substances that may be detected using the diver-held sonar unit.)

Figure 2.23 Positioning of the handheld sonar unit when searching for objects that are not likely to stand off the bottom.

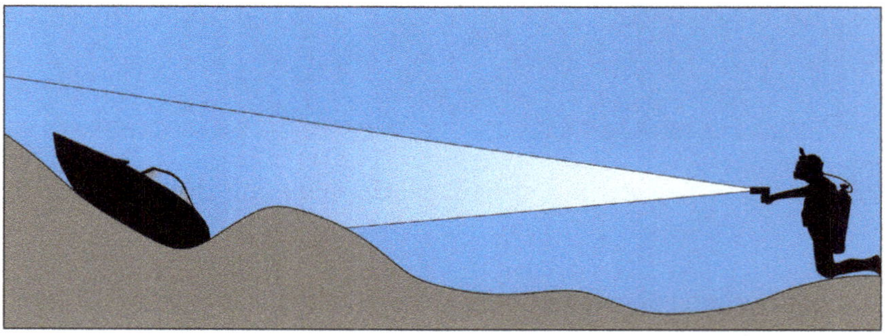

Figure 2.24 Positioning of the handheld sonar unit when searching for large objects such as a car or boat.

Table 2.1 Reflective Coefficients of Various Substances

Material	Reflective Coefficient
Wet fish flesh	0.02
Wet fishbone	0.24
Rubber	0.08
Granite	0.82
Quartz/sand	0.81
Clay	0.67
Sandstone	0.66
Concrete	0.68
Steel	0.94
Air	-1.0
Aluminum	0.83
Human flesh	0.02
Human bone	0.66

Data from Harris Acoustic DLS-3 Owner's Manual.

be low in pitch. If the target is far away, the tone will be high pitched. Some units have an external compass attached that allows the diver to take a compass bearing once the sonar has acquired a target. Provided there is adequate underwater visibility, the diver can follow the compass bearing to the target, aided by the audible tone from the unit. If visibility does not allow the use of the compass, the diver must follow the audible tone only. As the diver gets closer to the target, the tone pitch will progressively get lower. If the diver swims off course, the signal will be dropped, requiring the diver to reacquire it. Our dive team has used the DLS-3 Explorer, manufactured by Harris Acoustic Products, for several years now with outstanding success. Divers literally bump into the acquired target while following the audible signal. Purchasing this piece of equipment is only half the battle in locating a missing person or evidence of a crime. Much practice is required to be able to utilize this unit effectively. Like any piece of equipment, experience in its use is mandatory.

By reviewing the reflective coefficients listed, it is easy to see why military submarines coat the exterior of the hull with rubber to avoid detection (compare the coefficients of steel and rubber). It is important to remember that air (or any gas) has a stronger reflection of acoustic energy than any of the metals. Considering the extremely low reflective coefficient of fishbone and flesh, it is easy to understand that a sonar unit such as a fish finder picks up reflective energy from fish swim bladders. If it were not for these swim bladders in fish, which they use for buoyancy, fish would be invisible to sonar.

CASE STUDY

At Edgewater Park in Cleveland, Ohio, we had a woman report her boyfriend missing, last seen in the water near the end of a stone jetty on the west end of the main swimming beach. The waves were 2–4 feet, and he was a poor swimmer. A dive team member was in the immediate area and responded within minutes of the report. He retrieved the diver-held sonar unit from the dive vehicle and placed the unit under water. The diver was not in dive gear but rather held the unit under water while standing in the rough surf. Within minutes, he acquired a target and was able to direct other swimmers to the location of the missing swimmer in only 6 feet of water. Unfortunately, resuscitation efforts failed and the man was pronounced dead with the cause of death ruled a drowning.

Side-Scan Sonar

High-resolution sonar systems are essentially an improvement upon oceanography exploration equipment designed to map features and topography of the seafloor. With recent emphasis on counterterrorism, higher frequency and resolution equipment have been manufactured. This improvement of sonar devices has increased the resolution for low-reflection coefficient targets such as submerged bodies. Efficiency, not only in the operation of the equipment but also in the interpretation of images obtained, is limited due to the lack of training and the minimal amount of time most agencies have to practice with the unit.Table 2.1.

Side-scan sonars are comprised of a towfish, tow cable, and electronic recording device such as a laptop computer. As the towfish is towed through the water, acoustic pulses are sent out and reflected by the seafloor and objects that lie upon it. These pulses are processed by the unit into an image similar in nature to an aerial photograph and stored by the computer. This is a highly efficient instrument that is effective for searching large areas of a waterway in a relatively short period of time. Generally, one sonar unit on a vessel can search a football-field-sized area in a much shorter time frame than it would take an experienced dive team to cover in weeks. Emphasis on proficiency in interpreting the results cannot be overstressed, as apparent in the following case studies.

CASE STUDIES

EAST FORK STATE PARK, OHIO

April 2, 2007, in Clermont County, Ohio, a 38-year-old man and his 75-year-old father disappeared during a fishing trip on East Fork Lake. The southern Ohio lake had kept its secret for 2 months until a sonar image was sent 1,700 miles away to shed light on the mystery. Gene Ralston and his wife, Sandy, were requested to assist the Columbus Division of Police dive team in locating the missing men. Ralston and his wife viewed the images from their Idaho home and centered their attention on two irregularities in an otherwise unremarkable stretch of the bottom of East Fork Lake. The untrained eye might have overlooked the shapes or perhaps written them off as rocks or debris. But when it comes to finding victims using side-scan sonar, the Ralstons are as skilled as they come. Based on the images before them, they were fairly certain the objects in 78 feet of water were the bodies of the missing men. Their empty boat was found circling this area soon after they launched. Those involved with the operation said the recovery hinged on the ability of side-scan sonar to open a previously closed window into the depths. A Columbus police diver believed that without side-scan sonar, the bodies would never have been located. "Equipment is one thing, but knowing how to use it and interpret images is really the key," Ralston said. "The trick is to use it enough so that you become familiar with what a body is going to look like under all kinds of conditions." A friend of the victims had no kind words for the agency that initially began the search, saying they bungled the search from the start. He maintained the workers didn't run their side-scan sonar properly by running too fast and not knowing what the images are that they locate. The workers said they only began using side-scan sonar two years prior to this incident and admitted they needed time to become proficient in its use. "It's an art, and you have to practice that art. And we are getting better." The worker also envisions homeland security uses for side-scan sonar that goes beyond recovering bodies or locating wreckage. "It is an awesome system and the possibilities are unlimited."[12]

LAKE CUMBERLAND, KENTUCKY

After driving more than 2,000 miles, Gene and Sandy Ralston got up the next day, loaded and set up their special equipment, and within six minutes had located the body of a missing man. Dozens of searchers had unsuccessfully searched for his body on numerous occasions since he fell out of his boat at high speed just weeks before. The victim's father had found the couple on the Internet and had requested their assistance in locating the body of their missing son. The Ralstons, members of Idaho Mountain Search and Rescue, came at the family's request to assist in the search for their son. A Kentucky Fish and Wildlife officer lead the Ralstons to the locations where he had found the boat and where witnesses said they saw the man fall overboard. The officer had recorded the GPS coordinates during his first attempt to find the missing man. The Ralstons entered the information into their GPS, established a grid search pattern, and lowered the towfish into the water. Six minutes into their first line of the pattern, they had a clear image of a body on the mud approximately 90 feet deep (Figure 2.25). The team returned to the dock to retrieve their remotely operated submersible. It was decided that the submersible would be used to retrieve the body rather than delaying the recovery by deploying a dive team. Once the search vessel was back on the scene, Ralston piloted the submersible to where the body was located. The onboard camera allowed him to grasp the wrist of the man with a robotic grappling arm on the device

Figure 2.25 Side-scan sonar image of a body in 90 feet of water. (Photo courtesy of Gene L. Ralston, Ralston and Associates.)

and bring the body to the surface. The county services director praised the skill of the Ralstons and their generosity for traveling the long distance to assist in the search and recovery of the missing man.[13]

Kongsberg Sonar

The reality of working in the field of public safety diving is that rarely is the diver able to see more than a few feet under ideal conditions. More often than not, a diver will be in zero visibility, where sensory input is limited to only touch. It seems impossible, but there are times when a diver can shine an underwater light directly into his or her face mask and hardly see the glow of the bulb. The key to a safe operation is being capable of monitoring the diver's search area. Real-time data from a scanning sonar give surface support personnel the perspective of what is happening on the bottom. The sonar can see beyond the eyes and touch of the diver. The Kongsberg Mesotech 1000 scanning sonar is ideally suited to the following search and recovery operations:

- Search assignments
- Recovery/salvage operations
- Guiding a submerged diver
- Monitoring the dive site

For monitoring search areas, the diver should be tethered via an umbilical to the surface for air/gas supply and hardwire communications. The sonar head should be in a fixed position and mounted to the tripod mount (Figure 2.26) to allow maximum acoustic coverage of the search area (Figure 2.27). If the head is maintained in one location, an extremely

Figure 2.26 Kongsberg sonar tripod mount.

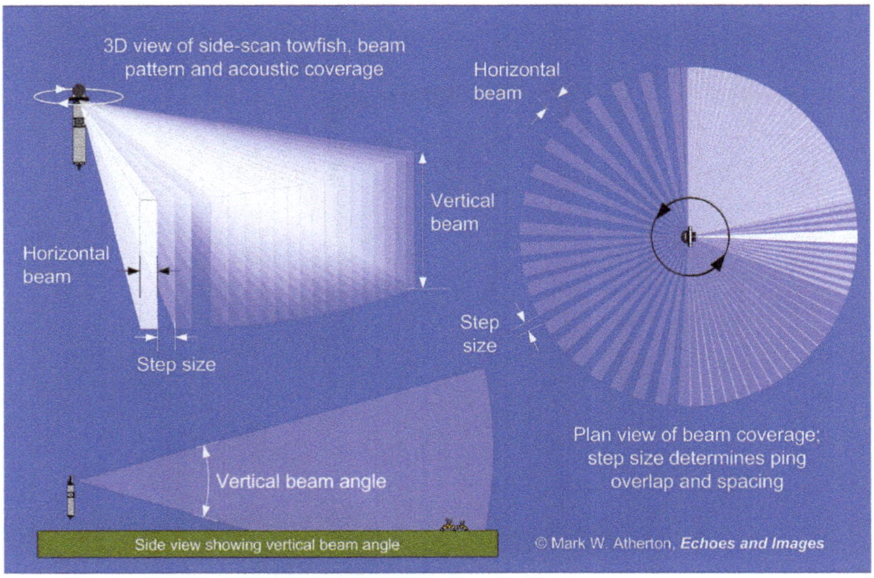

Figure 2.27 View of the side-scan sonar beam pattern and acoustic coverage. (Courtesy of Mark W. Atherton, Echoes and Images.)

accurate search can be conducted without having to utilize an expensive integrated positioning system.

It is important to maintain communication with the diver. The communication system is positioned next to the MS 1000 processor (Figure 2.28). Diver's tanks and bubbles make excellent acoustic targets. If, however, the diver is lost among other bottom targets, instruct the diver to maintain position and exhaust some air. The bubbles will be very visible on the sonar screen. With the sonar head in a fixed position, there is a simple method to determine that the area has been thoroughly searched. With the track plotter program, the geographic position of the diver can be updated and marked on display. When the search area is filled with diver position marks, the area has been covered.

The sonar can be used to direct the diver to a specific target. Instructions can be given to the diver to move in a specific direction and use the reverse scan and cursor functions to continually update the diver's position. The use of the scanning sonar head will greatly assist many diver- related tasks. Information regarding the search area can be obtained before the diver is deployed, eliminating the uncertainty of where things are under water to maximize diver efficiency and safety. Diver safety is of paramount importance. Kongsberg offers a two-day introductory course covering the theory and operation of the unit, but proficiency is only mastered after much practice and experience with the unit.

In the summer of 2007, our jurisdiction had a double drowning in progress at our main swimming beach area. Our divers were able to determine a good last seen point from witnesses on the scene, but due to the extremely high waves, in excess of 12 feet, we were unable to deploy into the rough surf to search for the bodies. Brecksville Fire Department had loaned the MS 1000 to Cleveland Fire Department, and they responded to the scene. Our dive team assisted in setting up the unit by placing the mounting tripod close to the last seen point. A hardwire cable was extended from the tripod to a laptop onshore. Within minutes, the bodies were located and divers were directed underwater to the bodies. The bodies were located directly at the point described by the witnesses. The

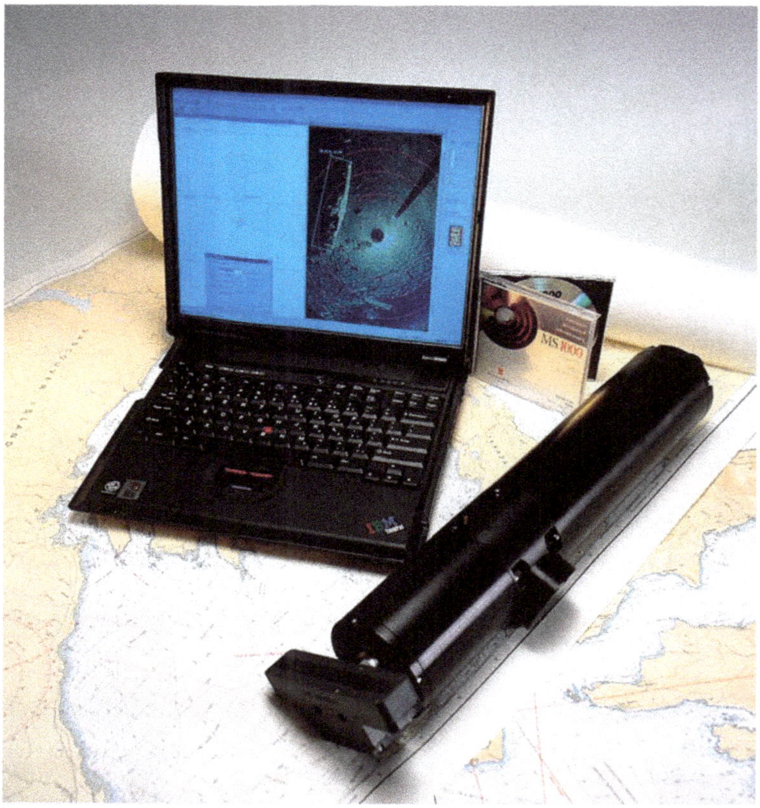

Figure 2.28 Kongsberg MesoTech 1000 sonar system.

high waves prevented divers from reaching this point on the surface, but having the capability of submerging the divers first, and then directing them to the location of the bodies, proved to be paramount to the recovery effort and safety of all rescue personnel on scene.

CASE STUDY

December 2008 in Minnesota, a 39-year-old woman appeared to have fallen through some ice while attempting to rescue a dog. Dive teams spent most of the night trying to locate her body in the frigid waters of the Mississippi River. The divers swam through dangerous icy water full of debris for hours, feeling their way around. Communication equipment and air lines failed due to icy conditions. They were placing air masks in hot water to thaw them out. Local sheriff's deputies responded with a Kongsberg MS 1000. Now they were able to direct divers to specific target areas, and one of their volunteer deputies located the victim. A deputy stated that they get many calls of people going out onto poor ice conditions to assist animals that are stranded on the ice, and there are times when the animal makes it back and the would-be rescuer does not.[14]

K-9-Aided Searches

Recent improvements have been made incorporating search dogs into water-related cases where the last known location of the victim is unknown, either on land or in waterways. Before a lengthy search commences in any waterway, it is first recommended that the area be searched using dogs to make sure the victim didn't simply walk away from the area or perhaps leave the area by other means, such as abduction. In cases involving eyewitness accounts, this may not be necessary. But it is always advisable to establish that the missing person is, without a doubt, located somewhere in the waterway before putting the lives of search divers in harm's way.

There are two basic types of search dogs. Some dogs are tracking dogs, and others are air scent dogs. Both types are similar in nature, but the training is different for each, as well as how they will be used for any specific operation. Tracking dogs search with their nose to the ground, or on nearby vegetation, over many types of terrain. These dogs are not really searching but following a specific scent. They required a last seen point and an uncontaminated trail. This means that the area must not be trampled upon by a multitude of searchers, which contaminate the scent for the dog. If a child has wandered from a play area and is believed to have possibly drowned in a local pond, the tracking dog would be used to follow the child's scent immediately after the disappearance, before law enforcement or other searchers have contaminated the trail.

Air scent dogs work with their nose in the air. They pick up human scent anywhere in the area, but they don't need a last seen point and time is not an issue. Air scent dogs pick up a human scent and seek its origin, which is the area with the greatest concentration of the scent. They may be used to locate a missing hiker in a park area and are often used as specialty dogs, such as cadaver dogs or water search dogs.

CASE STUDY

A girl had wandered off near a reservoir near Baltimore. A search was conducted by the state police. A dog search team was contacted late on day 7 of the search. Five and a half search hours later, a dog in a canoe on the reservoir air scented the girl and led the handler to shore 200 yards into the woods, where she was found alive.

Cadaver dogs are trained to seek out the scent of human remains. They pick up on the smell of decomposing flesh and can detect an object as small as a single drop of blood. Water dogs are used to locate drowning victims by picking up on the human scent rising in the water column. They are usually deployed on a boat but can also search from the shoreline. When a body is under water, gases and skin particles rise to the surface, allowing dogs to pick up on the scent. The dogs are trained to alert on the scent by biting at the water surface, digging at the bottom of the boat, or they may whine, bark, or even attempt to jump into the water at the point of the highest concentration of the scent. Because wind and current are often present, dogs cannot pinpoint the location of a submerged victim. Searchers will usually use multiple search dogs or make several passes with one dog, coupled with wind and current patterns, to estimate a possible location of the body. Cadaver and water search dogs are the only dogs specifically trained to alert on human remains. Many wonder how long a body can give off sufficient scent for a dog to detect. Research is limited in this area, but cases have been documented for remains missing close to a year.

CASE STUDY

A water search dog detected a body under water in the Kern River, in California, after 192 days. A recovery diver stated that the body was wedged up into some rocks so tightly that it had to be pried free. The diver noted that since the body was not located on the bottom, he quite possibly would have missed it had the dog not alerted to the area. During the same search, the dog alerted on human bones that, according to the pathologist, had been in the river for not more than one year.

The National Water Search Report was developed in 1984 to collect data as they relate to water searches using dogs. Its purpose was to document the fact that dogs have been responsible for detecting drowning victims in waterways and to document certain techniques used to aid in the location of these victims. In 1988, a report was published with these findings:

A study was based on 122 water search reports to the National Association of Search and Rescue (NASAR) from search and rescue (SAR) dog units around the country. Twenty-six different SAR dog units were involved, sometimes operating in multiple dog unit searches. Of 130 drowning victims involved, 84 were found by dogs, 24 were recovered out of the search area, and 22 have never been recovered. Of the 22 never recovered or found, the dog alerts in nine incidents could not be followed up on by divers or draggers due to the hazardous locations involved. These locations included depths in excess of 150 feet and flooded valleys with trees, buildings, and bridges under water, making diving or dragging impossible. The bottom line is that water searches with dogs are possible. The dogs will alert to human scent. The intensity of the scent is affected by multiple factors, such as water depth, air and water temperature, length of submersion, the experience of the handler, the presence of current and thermoclines, and the weather. It is up to the handler to read and interpret that alert, which may be subtle or require more than one pass of the area.

Evidence Recovery

Police officers by nature are curious creatures. Human curiosity can be an extremely damaging factor at the scene of a crime. Even after months of tedious crime scene management training, they must consciously remember not to pick up or disturb evidence at a crime scene. The same holds true for the water environment. It is a waste of everyone's time to spend hours, maybe days, looking for submerged evidence, only to have a careless diver place a spent bullet casing, or other evidence of a crime, into his pocket without any regard for its evidentiary value. Once evidence is treated carelessly, it is rendered useless. Attorneys (defense or plaintiff) may be present during subsequent evidence collection, upon revisit to a scene, or after the arrest of the suspect. If a defense attorney can put any doubt at all about **evidence** continuity into the minds of jurors and judges, the evidence will not be admissible. Care must also be taken to include the recovery diver in the chain of custody. It would be very easy for a diver to hand off a piece of evidence and have his or her name omitted from the chain of custody. An effective practice is to have the officer accepting the evidence from the diver print the diver's name on the evidence tag and then have the diver sign it after clearing the water. This will maintain the proper chain of evidence. Your local dive team should have some rigid type of container they can submerge for evidence retrieval. It is preferable to retrieve evidence in the medium in which it is found. Opening an evidence cylinder under water and placing the item inside will preserve the item until it can be analyzed at the lab. Resist the urge to open the evidence container on the surface to look at the item. This is particularly important with metal types of evidence. Once air hits metal objects that have been submerged, rapid rusting or oxidation begins, which could render these items worthless for lab and ballistic tests.[3] It is also advisable to mark the evidence cylinder with wording indicating that it contains a large amount of water. Any time evidence can be photographed prior to removal, do so. In the underwater environment, this is a rare occasion due to suspended silt from the search process. In these instances, mark the location of the evidence with a float and photograph the float from the surface. This shows distances from shore, a boat ramp, or any other location pertinent to the case. Diagrams depicting evidence positioning or direction may also be helpful. The direction a car was facing may help support testimony as well as deteriorate statements of the accused.

Types of Evidence

Some examples of evidence that may be located at the scene of a water-related death include the following:

1. **Objects** such as towels, discarded clothing, weapons, tools, sexual aids, bondage paraphernalia, notes, letters, photographs of loved ones, cigarette butts, purse, wallet, and car keys
2. **Body substances** such as semen, urine, vomit, blood, feces, skin tissue, and saliva
3. **Impressions** such as footprints, tire marks, skid marks, fingerprints, damaged guardrails, damaged vegetation, evidence of a collision, or any other damaged areas

Extreme care must also be taken in the preservation of evidence. Since the majority of the evidence will be wet or damp, it must be carefully sealed in paper bags or other breathable containers. If plastic is used, the moisture will create mold and mildew and the evidence is destroyed. When the evidence is dropped off at the lab, make sure the receiving personnel are aware the evidence is wet. Steps can then be taken to dry the evidence in a safe, controlled environment.

Latent Prints from Submerged Evidence

Since the beginning of time, man has viewed waterways as the perfect means to dispose of anything he no longer wanted, or more importantly, didn't want others to find. The attempt to hide evidence of a crime was simple. Just toss the item into a nearby waterway, and the evidence was hidden and lost forever. But modern science has put an end to this common misconception.

More agencies than ever before are forming highly trained dive teams to recover evidence that once was thought to be gone forever.

How do fingerprints survive the harsh environment of an underwater environment? Sebaceous prints are formed when a subject touches oily substances such as hair, skin, and other oil-coated surfaces. Sebaceous prints are less soluble in water, making it possible to detect and develop latent prints on objects after being submerged in water. These prints, under ideal conditions, may be detectable after 70 days of submersion in cold, freshwater. Warmer water and saltwater drastically reduce the opportunity to detect prints.

Handgun Evidence

Dive team protocols must be adopted to assure that recovery of handguns within the 70-day window dictates that every precaution will be taken during the recovery process to prevent the destruction of the latent fingerprint evidence. This includes limited handling of the weapon by divers and a rigid recovery container capable of containing water from which the weapon was recovered. Weapons that will be processed for fingerprints should be recovered in a rigid container while still underwater. Thus, the container will be full of the water in which it was submerged and no air will be present inside the container. An 8- to 10-inch diameter PVC pipe with a threaded cap is ideal for this application. This container should be clearly marked that it contains water so as to avoid problems in the lab upon opening the container.

The handgun must be processed immediately upon recovery to prevent rust from deteriorating the prints. Polymer handguns do not produce viable prints as the surface is too porous. Stainless steel handguns produce the best results as the surface is not compromised by rust. The case investigator must determine upon submerged weapon recovery if it will be processed for ballistics comparison or fingerprints. The method of preservation of the weapon will vary drastically depending on which is desired. Ballistic comparison will normally yield a higher rate of success as compared to the viability of useful fingerprints.

These facts must be taken into consideration by recovery divers as to how the weapon should be handled and preserved upon recovery from water. Weapons being tested for ballistic comparison can be preserved using any water-displacing liquid such as WD-40, Blaster, Liquid Wrench, or Acetone. The use of these products to preserve a weapon to be processed for fingerprints will render fingerprint analysis useless.

Lifting prints from these weapons produce more challenges for the investigator or lab technician. A very good product to use for lifting prints is AccuTrans Transparent. The chemical name is Polyvinylsiloxane. The benefits of this product are as follows:

- Dries clear like blue gel glue and cures quickly
- Sets in six minutes at 72°F
- Low viscosity and is self-pooling on horizontal surfaces giving it an excellent flow rate and coverage benefits
- On sloped or vertical surfaces, additional workability is easily accomplished.
- Can be spread across the print surface before it is cured using standard lift tape or any flat object such as a tongue depressor.
- After curing, the material is easy to remove from the surface.
- Lifted prints are durable and will not smudge.
- Lift can be secured to a standard fingerprint card or secured to clear acetate.
- Conforms much more effectively to curved surfaces where standard lift tape would cause wrinkles, resulting in a broken print.

- Has been used successfully on difficult surfaces such as keys, coins, computer housings, and drink bottles.

This product was used to successfully recover AFIS-quality prints involved in a homicide case in Akron, Ohio. This is a state-of-the-art technology to aid in quality print recovery from challenging surfaces.

Tape

It has become commonplace to use duct tape for a variety of applications outside the realm of its intended use. In many instances, duct tape remains attached to items even after becoming wet and it is readily available in most department and home improvement stores. The fact that it is found in many people's homes makes it ideal to use for criminal activity. Some types of these activities may include:

- Hands and feet of homicide victims being bound using this tape
- Submerged IEDs (Improvised Explosive Devices)
- Packaging for submerged drugs
- Attaching weights to bodies or evidence to aid in submersion

Submerged duct tape must be handled carefully as it often contains very good latent print evidence. It must be separated manually to produce the best results. Adhesive separating agents, such as Goo Gone, are not recommended as it destroys latent prints. Generally, submerged fingerprint evidence on tape is still viable for up to seven days in both fresh and saltwater (on the sticky side of the tape). Recovery protocol shall mandate that the tape be packaged while still underwater, and immediate transportation to the lab is imperative. Allowing the tape to dry will cause it to crack, rendering prints useless.

Weapon Recovery

Metal evidence should be immediately immersed in acetone or pure (anhydrous) alcohol. These liquids will immediately displace the water molecules, and the metal will be prevented from any further rusting.

CASE STUDY

SUBMERGED EVIDENCE RECOVERY

Submerged fingerprint resilience was evidenced during the recovery of the S. S. Brother Jonathan, a paddle steamer that was loaded with 244 passengers and crew, along with a large shipment of gold coins. It struck an uncharted rock along the coast of California on July 30, 1865. Only 19 passengers survived, making it the deadliest maritime disaster of its time. In 2006, divers began the recovery of the Pacific Coast wreck and documented recovery of $20 Double Eagle coins, which were heavily corroded and unrecognizable. Team members were able to remove the corrosion chemically, which revealed the coin characteristics. The coins being restored to perfect condition revealed a human fingerprint, fully intact and discernible.

Dive Team Equipment

There is a whole multitude of equipment available on the market for public safety divers, yet due to budget restrictions, most teams must start with the most basic and then acquire other specialized equipment when funding is available. The following is a general list of basic equipment that allows teams to work a variety of scenes in a safe manner.

Hardwire Communication Equipment When a diver submerges to conduct an underwater search of an area, he or she has no reference point as to which direction he or she is facing. Often, during the diver's descent, the diver is spinning around and is not even aware of it, especially in low or no visibility water. This is because the diver cannot see any reference point to make him or her aware of this spinning. For this reason, it is imperative that all searches be conducted using a tether line. This allows the diver to use the tether as an underwater reference as to what direction he or she is facing. Even in zero visibility, the diver can feel the direction the tether line is coming from, which tells him or her which direction is the shore, or at least in which direction the tender is located. Underwater communication equipment increases the safety margin of the diver considerably. This equipment allows for direct verbal communication between the diver and tender, or between the diver, tender, and backup diver. This eliminates the guesswork as to when a diver is experiencing difficulty or requires assistance. The hardwire communication wire runs through the middle of the tether rope and allows for knots to be tied in the rope as well. A well-prepared dive team would be wise to practice communication failure procedures should this equipment fail. Universal line tug signals have been established to allow dive teams to utilize the same signals, which could prove to be a valuable procedure, especially in instances of multijurisdictional searches.

Exposure Protection *Dry Suits.* Depending on the specific environment in which the team will be diving, some form of exposure protection is necessary. Dry suits, while expensive, afford the best overall protection from both the colder water at depth and contaminated environments. Many dive teams perform a variety of vehicle recoveries within their jurisdictions, which causes the diver to be exposed to many different petroleum products. With a dry suit, the diver is completely enclosed, except for the head, within a layer of air while wearing warm insulated undergarments. Many newer suits also provide attached gloves and boots to keep the extremities warm as well. This type of suit keeps the diver warm and dry, minimizing the potential for contamination from impurities in the water.

Hoods. Even with the use of a dry suit, a separate hood is often required to provide warmth to the diver's head and prevent heat loss. Most dry suits have a thin rubber outer shell designed to slip over an insulated hood. If the diver will be using a full face mask, special hoods lined with rubber can be used to provide a better seal around the face.

Harness Public safety divers will always be searching for an object underwater, whether it is a body, evidence, or weapons. To allow for a better search, the diver should wear a harness that he or she can connect to a tether line. This tether line connects the diver to a surface tender and allows the diver to use both hands to search. Many of today's teams have the diver hold the tether line, which limits the diver's searching ability, since he or she can only search with the free arm. A harness is also the safer choice since it is less likely the harness will become detached during a search. If a diver is in trouble and drops the tether line, the backup diver will not be able to locate the diver in trouble in a reasonable amount of time.

Contingency Line A backup diver descending to assist a primary diver in trouble should utilize a contingency line. This is a short line, usually only a foot in length, which connects the backup diver's harness to the primary diver's tether line. This attachment allows the backup diver's hands to be free, allowing for other tasks, such as equalizing and cutting the primary diver free from entanglement. This allows the backup to maintain continuous contact with the primary's tether line. If the backup were to lose contact with the primary's tether, the only sure way to locate it in black water would be to the surface, causing a severe delay in rescue of the primary diver.

Cutting Tools Many recreational divers carry knives, but the use of a knife for a public safety diver is limited and dangerous. While working in low- or no-visibility water, it would be very easy to accidentally jab oneself or another with the sharp tip of a dive knife. Knives also have limited cutting ability. They usually require two hands to cut and will not cut many submerged debris, such as wire or fish hooks. Paramedic shears are a much safer, far superior choice of a cutting tool. They have a blunt end, which prevents accidental stabbing, they cut a wide variety of materials, and they can be used with only one hand. They should be worn somewhere within easy reach by either hand, near the chest area of the diver. Avoid strapping tools to the diver's legs, as this only causes a potential entanglement if snagged on something. Paramedic shears are also much cheaper to purchase, which allows the diver to wear multiple pairs. As a backup, the diver should wear a pair of wire cutters, which would be able to cut heavier-gauge wire such as fencing.

Weight Belts or Harnesses Weights are required to be worn by divers so they can descend under water. Many weight belts today are comprised of soft weights, similar to beanbags but filled with lead shot. This allows the diver to wear the weight belt with greater comfort than the old hard lead weights. Some departments using dry suits may choose to use the separate weight harnesses, which have a quick-release mechanism built into them so the weights can be dropped quickly in case of an emergency. Many buoyancy control devices (BCDs) also have weight pouches incorporated into them. The drawback to these incorporated weights is that they make the BCD extremely heavy and cumbersome to handle onshore. Regardless of which weight system your team chooses to use, it is strongly recommended to practice ditching the weights on a regular basis. Ditching should be second nature in the event of an emergency. Many dead divers are found still wearing their weight belts when something as simple as ditching them would have saved their lives.

Buoyancy Control Device (BCD) A BCD is an inflatable vest worn by the diver to allow the diver to adjust buoyancy within the water column. By adding air to the device with a power inflator, which is connected to the air supply, the diver can surface and float. By dumping air from the device, the diver can descend to the bottom. For public safety diving use, the BCD should have a minimum lift capacity of 35 pounds. This allows the diver to support a potential adult victim on the surface. The BCD should have many pockets to hold tools. Avoid BCDs with many clips and D-rings, which may pose an entanglement hazard.

Cylinders and Pony Bottles The air tank should have a minimum capacity of 80 cubic feet. Ideally, it should be made of aluminum, which is easier to maintain in good condition and cheaper than steel. The tank should be free of a tank boot, which may prevent a dropped weight belt from falling free of the diver. Tanks also require a visual inspection once per year as well as a hydrostatic test every three years. Evidence of these current inspections can be found on the side of the tank. The visual inspection sticker (VIP) will appear on the side of the tank, and the hydrostatic test will be stamped into the metal near the neck of the tank.

A contingency tank should be kept at the dive site as well. This is a full tank that has an attached regulator to be used in the event of an entanglement. It is taken to the entangled diver by the backup diver to supply air to the diver during rescue procedures.

Pony bottles should be worn by all divers entering the water. This is a much smaller tank with an independent regulator attached, having a minimum capacity of 18 cubic feet. It is attached to each diver's primary tank by a quick-release mechanism, which allows a diver to pass it off to another in an out-of-air situation.

Full Face Mask Public safety diving almost always requires divers to enter contaminated water. There is also the occasion they may be called to the scene of an ice rescue. For these reasons, a full face mask is a necessity. For cold water and ice diving, it provides extra protection from cold water to the face. In contaminated water, it allows the diver to protect the majority of the face from contaminants. It is recommended that the full face mask be a positive-pressure style so that in case of a leak, air escapes but does not allow contaminated water to enter the mask. Positive pressure masks may also help keep an unconscious diver's airway dry, increasing chances of survival.

Analog Gauges vs. Computers Dive computers should be avoided since they are harder to read in low-visibility water. Computers are excellent for recreational divers because they allow multiple dives in longer duration, yet most public safety diving is limited in both depth and length of submersion (usually not more than 30 minutes), so dive computers are not recommended. An analog pressure gauge and depth gauge should be equipped with a phosphorescent backing, which allows for easier reading in murky water or darkness.

Fins Fins should be constructed of a durable material and be free of hanging straps and buckles. The free end of the fin strap can be taped down with duct tape to reduce the risk of entanglement. Keeping the inside strap free of tape allows the diver to adjust the fins and remove them easily.

Tether Line The preferred method of searching the underwater environment is the solo diver method, in which one diver is deployed on a tether line to conduct a search pattern. This allows for a thorough, methodical search of an area with minimal risks. The diver is merely an extension of the line tender on the surface, who directs the diver to search a specific area. This is done by a hardwire communication line between the diver and the tender. The communication line allows the tender and diver to talk freely to one another, much the same as if talking on a telephone. The communication unit held by the tender also allows another diver, such as the backup diver, to join the conversation. Both divers can talk to each other as well as communicate with the tender on the surface. This dramatically increases safety in the event of an emergency by clarifying specific needs, rather than having the tender trying to guess what the problem is. The hardwire line runs through the middle of a nylon kernmantle rope, which increases its strength and durability. The rope can be tied in knots without affecting the hardwire contained within.

Having a diver attached to a tether line also gives him or her a reference point under water. Otherwise, the submerged diver would have no way of knowing which direction he or she is facing. Finally, a tether line allows for the most methodical search of an area. The diver keeps the line taut and sweeps an area, and then the tender pulls them in a specified distance and the diver sweeps back. Without a tether, divers would submerge and swim off in every direction, making it impossible to record what areas have or have not been searched.

Equipment Familiarization One of the most important things to remember about team equipment is that it needs to be uniform, meaning each piece of equipment should be the same as the next piece of the same type. It is much easier for one diver to render assistance to another if all of their equipment is the same. In instances where wildcat teams or other volunteer teams are formed, and each member is using personal gear, have the divers take the time to become familiar with everyone else's equipment. It would be disastrous to have a backup diver respond to assist the primary, only to find out that he or she can't find the power inflator, or doesn't know how to drop the primary's weights, and so on.

The planning and logistics involved in the public safety diving field are much too extensive and complex to describe in detail in this forum. This information has been provided as a general overview of dive team needs. An excellent in-depth resource for public safety dive teams is *Public Safety Diving* by Walt "Butch" Hendrick and Andrea Zafares.

Significance of the Absence or Presence of Clothing or Other Coverings on the Body

Occasionally, recovered bodies from the water will have a portion or all of their clothing removed, which may erroneously lead the investigator to believe the incident is possibly sexually motivated. It is not uncommon for bodies found in water to have the clothing partially or completely removed. There are several factors that may play a role in this phenomenon, such as body composition, water temperature, current or tidal action, type of clothing, or the manner in which the body came to be located in the water itself. The presence of other wrappings may serve to retard the progression of decomposition, preserve evidence, and help rescuers locate and identify victims.

Body Composition

Individuals who have a higher body fat ratio will generally decompose more rapidly than an individual with less body fat. Fat is a good insulator and slows the rate of fall of the body's core temperature, thus keeping the body warmer for a longer period of time, allowing for continued steady decomposition—a warmer body will decompose at a faster rate. A body that swells more quickly due to rapid decomposition will tend to retain its clothing better than a body that is not bloated. Also, heavier individuals tend to have tighter-fitting clothing prior to water entry, thus making it more difficult for the water action to remove the clothing.

Water Temperature

Clothing is more likely to be removed in cold water drowning incidents due to the slower onset of decay and bloating. Slower bloating of the body results in the clothing fitting loosely, whereas bloating is more rapid in warmer water, causing the clothing to be held intact by the swelling of the body.[15]

Current or Tidal Action

The action of the current or tide may cause the removal of the clothing. Immediately upon drowning and sinking to the bottom, the body will be exposed to very little movement from tides or current. But during the refloat process, the body is moving horizontally higher in the water column, where it is exposed to the movement and force of the water. If the body becomes trapped on submerged debris, this will increase the water pressure on the body and possibly rip away every piece of clothing.

CASE STUDY

After drowning in a kayaking accident, a victim's body was located several miles downstream. It had been totally stripped of clothing and jewelry by the strong current. The clothing can often be located downstream from where the body is located.[16]

Type of Clothing

Clothing made of nylon, lycra, or other stretchy fabric, or those containing elastic waistbands, tend to wash off the body easier. If clothing is secured using belts, ties, suspenders, and the like, they tend to remain secure. Also, clothing with a loose-fitting design, such as halter tops, t-shirts, or baggy pants, also remove easier. The clothing or other covering that remains on recovered bodies can be beneficial for several reasons, including the retardation of decomposition and predation, the preservation of evidence, the facilitation of infants to float on the surface, and the aiding in the recovery or identification of the decedent.

Manner of Water Entry

Individuals who enter water from great heights, such as cliff jumpers or suicidal individuals jumping from a bridge, tend to have their clothing stripped free upon impact with the water. There have been documented cases of individuals recovered from water after being ejected from submerged vehicles who hit the water at such a great force that their clothing is partially or totally removed.

Retardation of Decomposition

A body covered with clothing or other covering, such as those found rolled up inside carpets or rugs, will be separated from the elements, aiding in slower decomposition. The body will be sheltered from fish and animal feeding as well as postmortem wounding.

Preservation of Evidence

When a person is murdered and immediately rolled up in a rug or carpet to dispose of the body or is left clothed, this may preserve evidence that would normally be washed away by the current or during the body recovery phase. Clothing has also been beneficial in holding a badly decomposed body together. If death was induced by a weapon assault, the clothing may help determine entry wounds or other evidence of the crime.

Infant Deaths

Babies less than six months old that are involved in water incidents, even after being ejected from a submerged motor vehicle, will tend to float. This in part is attributed to the higher body fat layer as well as air being trapped in clothing, diapers, and blankets. Disposable diapers with plastic liners contribute greatly to the buoyancy of infants.

Aid in Recovery or Identification

Fast-moving currents often remove clothing and jewelry from victims, which makes it very difficult to locate the decedent. Search teams may attempt to locate the body using a highly visible clothing description, such as a red parka. A body stripped of clothing is difficult to observe because the flesh tones tend to camouflage the body in white water. If the incident is likely to be an accident, chances are great that the decedent will have some form of identification in his or her pockets. Engraved jewelry/watches, unusual and unique jewelry, tattoos, unusual scars, deformities of the limbs, and limb/finger/toe or other amputations can help in the presumptive identification process.

Investigative Characteristics of Selected Scenes

Bodies in Submerged Vehicles

Submerged vehicles can be present in any jurisdiction possessing waterways for a multitude of reasons. On occasion, vehicles are submerged to conceal the vehicle itself or the evidence inside. Suicidal individuals drive vehicles into lakes and rivers as a means to end their lives. In this instance, the vehicle upon recovery may have the driver contained inside (Figure 2.29). An occasional homicide may be concealed as an accident by submerging a vehicle in a waterway with the victim inside the vehicle. This was true in the highly publicized Susan Smith case in Union, South Carolina. On October 25, 1994, in an effort to murder her two young sons, Susan Smith placed them in their car seats and rolled her car into John D. Long Lake, drowning both of them. She would claim to police that a black man had stolen her car at gunpoint with her sons still inside, but she was later charged with their murder after confessing to the act. During testimony at her trial, a recovery

Figure 2.29 Driver found inside recovered submerged vehicle after 21 years of submersion.

diver would explain the limited underwater visibility of about 12 inches at a depth of 18 feet where her car was located. The diver explained how he pressed a light up against the window and could see a small hand against the glass. The car was standing with its grill in the mud, and the boys were hanging heads downward still strapped into their car seats.[17]

For these reasons, it is imperative that the recovering agency process the vehicle for evidence. Upon locating a submerged vehicle, the position of the vehicle underwater should be documented. If possible, have divers determine the position and location of any occupants prior to recovery. During victim removal, care should be taken not to disturb any possible evidence. Once victims are removed, a cursory search inside the vehicle should be made, if safety permits, to locate and seize any possible evidence. In some jurisdictions, it is possible to recover the vehicle with the occupants inside and transport the vehicle to the coroner or medical examiner's office for processing (Figure 2.30). It is highly advisable to have divers close any doors or windows to minimize the loss of any possible evidence. Also prior to recovery, have divers document any exterior damage to the vehicle since it is likely the vehicle will be damaged during the recovery process. Damage will be an important factor in determining the cause of any impact-related injuries found on the occupants.

After the vehicle is safely on land, extensive notes should document the following:

- What gear the transmission is in (Figure 2.31).
- Radio on or off? What station is it tuned to? Newer vehicles have buttons/toggles instead of on/off knobs, and they have digital/LCD displays, and if the accident rendered the car nonoperational, one may not be able the hear the radio or see a display. In this instance, it would be necessary to obtain information from the powertrain control module (PCM).
- Anything present that could have been used to depress the accelerator, such as an axe handle or inflatable toy
- Any cigarettes, liquor, or beer

Figure 2.30 Processing recovered vehicle at the coroner's office with the body still inside.

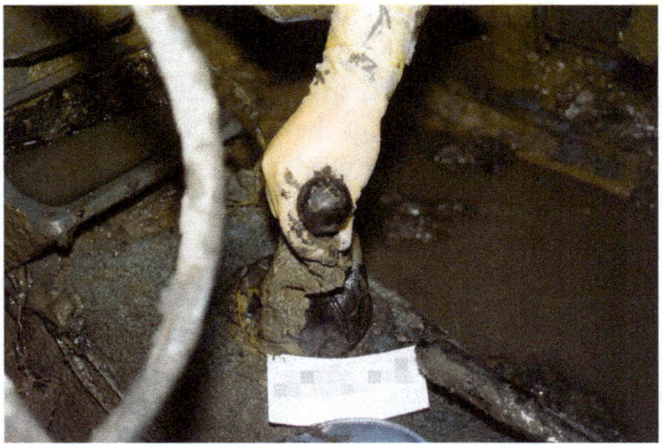

Figure 2.31 Photo documentation of what gear the vehicle was in.

Figure 2.32 Photo documentation of exterior damage and marine growth.

- Emotional valuables, such as photos, ornaments, etc.
- Headlights on or off? Is this consistent with time missing?
- Windows up or down?
- Heat or air conditioning on or off, and is this consistent with season missing?
- Position of driver's seat and mirrors? Seat position can be documented by measuring from accelerator to front edge of the seat
- Ignition on or off? Keys in ignition?
- Marine growth and body damage (Figure 2.32)
- Wipers on or off? Consistent with the weather when missing? The position of the blades (if in the up position, this would suggest they were on at the time of submersion)?
- Document speed on impact with the water, if possible

For newer model vehicles (starting with the year 2000), the powertrain control module (PCM), which is often referred to as the "black box," can be retrieved and analyzed by a certified technician to determine many factors, including whether lights and accessories were in operation and speed on impact. For assistance, contact Vertronics at 1-800-321-4889. For older vehicles, the impact speed may be determined by one of two ways. First, the impact may have bent the needle, freezing it at that speed. Second, the impact may have caused the speedometer needle to dent the soft metal backing at the speed of impact (Figure 2.33). All these observations can be used to assist the investigator in determining if foul play is involved, who was driving, time of day or time of year the vehicle was submerged, and length of submersion. It is imperative that the investigator maintain close contact with the dive team on the scene to ensure that all these observations are documented before and after recovery.

In the fall of 1992, the Michigan State Police conducted a study called the Submerged Transportation Accident Research Project, or simply Project STAR. The study was conducted to determine various characteristics of submerged vehicles, including the length of float time to allow for a means of escape, length of time the power will remain functional, and damage sustained upon impact with the water, and to discount the belief that a pocket of trapped air remains in the rear of the vehicle, allowing occupants to plan for their escape. During the study, vehicles of various makes and models were driven off a floating dock to observe float characteristics. The results were surprising. The study revealed that ample time was available with all passenger vehicles to allow the driver to unfasten his or her safety belt, roll down the window, and escape the vehicle in less than ten seconds. Also, the power remained functional for over ten minutes, but there is no trapped air pocket anywhere inside the vehicle. If the vehicle entered water deeper than the length of the car, the car would flip over on its roof, but if it was submerged in water shallower than its length, it would land under water on its wheels. This study will aid investigators in understanding submerged vehicle dynamics to determine if the damage sustained to a submerged vehicle can be the cause of injuries found on its occupants.

A few years later, a second part of the STAR Project was conducted, which tested float characteristics of school buses. This study was prompted due to a fatal accident in Alton, Texas. At 7:30 a.m. on September 21, 1989, a truck hit a school bus and knocked it into a gravel pit filled with water. Twenty-one children drowned and six were injured. This was the

Figure 2.33 Documentation of speedometer needle indicating the speed of vehicle upon impact with the water.

worst school bus accident in Texas history.[18] The study concluded that the average school bus sank in less than 20 seconds, largely due to the implosion of the front windshield upon impact with the water. This implosion of the windshield most likely killed the driver or rendered him or her unconscious, preventing the only adult on the bus from assisting the children in their escape. Also, the quick influx of water and floating seat cushions blocked any chance for escape. The smaller 25 passenger buses sank in just 9 seconds. This was due largely to the failure of the engine cowling covering the engine, allowing water to rush in at an alarming rate.

CASE STUDY

In Amsterdam, Holland, in 1971, a 27-year-old male was in a vehicle that entered the water off a small bridge at approximately 25 miles per hour. Impact with the steering wheel caused several broken ribs and minor internal damage. His right leg was broken just below the knee by striking the dashboard. He sustained blunt force trauma to the back of his head. At first, the investigating agency believed this case to be an auto accident resulting in his death by drowning, but there was no damage to the roof of the vehicle or any heavy objects inside that could have caused the head injury. This case was ruled a homicide at the conclusion of the investigation.[1]

Bucket Drowning

A bucket drowning involves 5-gallon buckets or often janitor-style mop buckets on wheels. Infants and toddlers who have reached the cruising and walking stages of motor development may push the bucket around the room until the wheels get caught on something. Or infants or toddlers may pull themselves up onto their feet and attempt to play with the liquid inside. Their forward momentum causes them to lose balance, and they fall headfirst into the bucket, submerging their head in liquid. The lack of upper body strength prohibits them from getting out, and they drown. In these instances, the investigator should seize the entire bucket and its contents as evidence. The water contained in the bucket should be placed in a sterile container and transferred to the coroner or medical examiner's office with the decedent for chemical testing. These drowning incidents have prompted the Consumer Product Safety Commission to mandate warning labels on large mop buckets[19] (Figure 2.34).

When considering that foul play may have taken place, a bucket drowning investigation should include a search in the media for other previously reported incidents of bucket drowning. It is believed that reports of prior incidents in the media serve as "instructional videos" for caretakers of small children. In Pennsylvania, there had been no bucket drownings reported for 4 years, yet after a bucket safety broadcast, there were three reported drowning incidents within 30 days.[1] It is believed the caretakers were intentionally drowning the children in buckets based on what they heard and saw in the media. The U.S. Consumer Product Safety Commission has received reports of 275 bucket drownings since 1984. The 5-gallon bucket presents the greatest hazard since the sides are 14 inches high, roughly half the height of the average child. Combined with the stability of the bucket, it is nearly impossible for children to free themselves when they fall in headfirst.[19]

Figure 2.34 Bucket drowning warning label found on all 5-gallon buckets.

CASE STUDY

October 28, 2007, in Quincy, Massachusetts, a nine-month-old girl drowned after she fell into a bucket filled with bleach. The mother was reportedly watching three children in her home when her daughter crawled out of sight and fell into the bucket. She was rushed to a nearby hospital, where she was pronounced dead. A preliminary autopsy report revealed no signs of trauma, and drowning was ruled as the cause of death.

Scuba Fatalities

Scuba fatality investigation presents a unique set of circumstances to the investigator. If the investigator possesses a general understanding of scuba diving, he or she can start to compile the facts in the case, interview witnesses, and conduct a thorough investigation. Investigators who do not have knowledge regarding scuba diving should seek professional assistance from one of the following agencies:

1. Lifeguard Systems, Inc. at LGS@teamlgs.com or by phone at 1-914-331-3383
2. Divers Alert Network (D.A.N.) at 1-800-446-2671

Steps to a scuba fatality investigation should include the following:

1. Interviews of dive buddy and recovery diver
2. Location and recovery of the diver
3. Equipment preservation and evaluation
4. Autopsy
5. Formulating conclusions
6. Scuba fatality report

Dive Buddy Interview

Since the majority of scuba-related fatalities are attributed to panic (aside from natural causes, such as a heart attack), it is important to gain as much information about the decedent as possible from witnesses, the dive buddy, and anyone else who can inform the investigator as to the extent of experience, training, and mental and physical condition of the decedent.

All interviews should be done in a semiprivate setting, one on one. The interviewer should be someone familiar with scuba diving to understand the terms used. Rarely are incidents absent of any witnesses since scuba diving requires the buddy system. The interview of the buddy helps determine the last seen point to aid in locating the body. For instance, if the diver states he last saw his buddy while diving on a specific wreck, the wreck site will be the last seen point, and the search for the missing diver will begin at that location. The dive buddy may also be able to clarify specifics as to what may have happened to the missing diver. The buddy should know if the diver was entangled, entrapped, experiencing problems equalizing, or having equipment problems. This interview will also determine what the diver was doing just prior to death. Be cognizant of discrepancies in the buddy's account of what occurred. Although intentional deception is never ruled out as a possibility, it is common for the diver to feel a sense of guilt for having "let his buddy die," and he may change or enhance the facts that actually occurred. If the pair are frequent dive buddies, they should know basic information about the general health of one another. The buddy will be able to provide predive information, such as the overall health of the diver, preexisting diseases, medications, alcohol or drug use, and mental status before the dive. The dive buddy may indicate the diver was complaining about physical ailments such as chest pain or muscle cramping, as well as mental issues such as problems at home or work, financial worries, or other stressors, which may all be contributing factors in the death.

CASE STUDY

May 30, 2003, a diver was found dead at the bottom of an undersea cave in 162 feet of water, with a knife protruding from his chest. The autopsy confirmed death due to both drowning and the penetrating knife wound. The incident was first considered a homicide, and two suspects were arrested. Careful forensic analysis of the diver's profile, stored on his dive computer, dimensions of the undersea cave, as well as other forensic findings showed that the incident was a suicide, which the diver most likely committed while running out of air in an attempt to avoid the agony of drowning.[20]

Recovery Diver Interview

The recovery diver must be interviewed prior to leaving the scene. It must be determined if the diver's equipment was altered in any way during the recovery. For instance, it is a common practice during a recovery to make the victim buoyant by removing his or her weight belt or adding air to his or her buoyancy compensator device (BCD). If the weights were dropped during the recovery, they must be retrieved as evidence since overweighting may be a contributing factor in the diver's death. Also, the recovery diver can advise what problems were encountered by the victim, such as entrapment, entanglement, noticeable surges, strong currents, animal life, cold temperatures, and bottom topography. If the bottom topography changed frequently, this would cause varying depth changes for the diver, which may contribute to diving illnesses such as air embolism, lung overexpansion injury, or decompression sickness. The recovery diver can also provide information regarding water clarity or visibility. It must be remembered that issues that may seem minor at the time should be well documented and not passed off as being unimportant. For example, small fish are known to nibble on living diver's ears, mask strap, and fingers. The presence of these fish during the dive may be a contributing factor to the diver's death, especially with a new or inexperienced diver. Also, unexpected visitors may have been a source of panic. While many divers relish the opportunity to encounter a shark or dolphin during a dive, others may not be so accepting of the idea. Likewise, friendly and playful seals have been known to pull at masks and fins, which cause this equipment to become dislodged or pulled off.

General information that should be obtained during the interviews includes the following:

Who: Victim's name, age, diving history, and experience; predive assessment of victim's mental and physical condition; use of alcohol, prescription, or illicit drugs; complaints of problems or discomfort.

What: What happened (sharing air, entanglement/entrapment, attempts to rescue buddy); dive objective obstructions.

Where: On bottom, during ascent, on surface; determine accurate last seen point and time (having the buddy drop a marker buoy may aid in this process); weather and water conditions; temperature; surge; and current pollution and topography.

When: Time last seen will determine rescue or recovery mode for the dive team. Generally speaking, dive rescue teams will operate in rescue mode for up to one hour after the last seen time (referred to as the golden hour), then regroup and operate in recovery mode. May also determine how much air the diver has remaining in the tank. The "when" may also aid in locating the victim. For instance, if the "when" was during the end of the dive, the victim will most likely be found near the predetermined exit point.

Location and Recovery of the Diver

There are many training agencies and publications offering excellent information on diving operations and training. Two excellent books regarding dive operations are:

Public Safety Diving by Walt "Butch" Hendrick and Andrea Zafares, Fire Engineering, 2000.
Devil's Triangle: A Guide to Drownproofing Divers by Kevin Erskine, Infinity Publishing, 2003.

The buddy interview should reveal the last seen point, which is where the search will begin, although the body may be a considerable distance away. A tethered search pattern is mandatory unless the search area is very small or the underwater visibility is excellent. A sonar device may decrease the size of the search area considerably, as well as increasing the overall safety of the operation.

Equipment Preservation and Evaluation

Care must be taken to ensure that all the diver's equipment is recovered and preserved in the state in which it is found. Any alteration of the equipment must be avoided until a qualified person can examine it for defects or malfunctions. This will allow the investigator to determine if the equipment played a role in the death of the diver. Even items of seeming unimportance must be seized. This includes cameras, spear gun, flashlights, collection bag, etc. It is possible that some of these items may have contributed to the diver's death by overloading him or her or requiring the diver to carry on multiple tasks. Immediate testing of the equipment should be done so that leaks, malfunctions, or mishandling does not prejudice the conclusions. A bulky item such as a large camera may have required multitasking the diver was not prepared for or may have caused overweighting of the diver, making it difficult to surface.

Basic Equipment Examination (Not All-Inclusive)

1. The gear should not be disassembled.
2. Make notes regarding the tank pressure on the pressure gauge (the face of the gauge can be marked using a permanent marker showing the position of the needle).
3. Record and photograph the tank VIP (visual inspection date) and hydrostatic date stamped on the tank (Figures 2.35 and 2.36).
4. Make a note of any scratches or breaks on the victim's face mask where the diver may have been subjected to trauma to the face.
5. Record the amount of weight on the weight belt and note if any additional weights are found in the BCD pockets.
6. Ensure the quick-release buckle is working properly on the weight belt.
7. Have the remaining air in the tank tested for impurities.

Air Quality Standards for Scuba Tanks

Breathing air for scuba cylinders must meet the following air standards as specified by the Compressed Gas Association (CGA Pamphlet G-7.1) and referenced in OSHA 29, Code of Federal Regulations (CFR 1910.134):

CGA grade E Component maximums:

- Oxygen—20–22%/volume
- Carbon monoxide—10 ppm/volume (.001%)
- Carbon dioxide—1,000 ppm/volume (.1%)
- Condensed hydrocarbons—5 mg/cubic meter
- Water vapor—Not specified
- Objectionable odors—None (any bad odor must be noted on the datasheet)[21]

Sampling Scuba Cylinder Air

In order for the investigator to determine the air quality within the scuba cylinder, it will be necessary to obtain a sample of the air and have it tested by an independent lab, such as TRI Air Testing, Inc. TRI is a highly reputable company that is used by the U.S. military for its air testing needs. TRI offers fast 24-hour analysis and online report access with accurate

Figure 2.35 Visual inspection (VIP) sticker on the scuba tank.

Figure 2.36 Hydrostatic test date stamped into a scuba tank.

third-party lab results. The sampling process will require TRI to send your agency a mini-sampler to obtain the cylinder sample.

Sampling instructions are:

1. The sample will be drawn directly from the scuba tank.
2. Attach TRI's double sampling yoke to the cylinder and attach the mini-sampler to the other side of the sample yoke (see Figure 2.37).
3. Unscrew the black shipping cap from one of the bottles and screw on the white sampling cap.
4. Record the bottle number on the datasheet (Appendix A).
5. You are ready to take a sample. Open the valve on the air supply. There is no need to adjust the airflow; the mini-sampler contains a limiting orifice that regulates the flow of air.
6. Note that most of the air escapes through the large hole in the fitting, while only a small fraction passes through the center needle in the air transfer fitting.
7. Insert the bottle with the white sampling cap onto the needles of the air transfer fitting. (Do not twist the bottle when inserting or removing because it may result in damage to the needles.)
8. Observe the white float inside the bottle. The float will rise with a positive airflow. If it does not occur, cautiously place your finger close to the vent hole, partially restricting the flow. *Do not completely block this hole.* If the float does not rise, please contact TRI. To acquire an accurate sample, the bottle must stay in place, with the white float remaining at the top for one minute. *Remove the bottle before the white float is allowed to fall and then shut the tank flow off.*
9. Remove the white sampling cap and replace it with the black shipping cap. *Tighten the black cap securely to prevent loss of the gas sample.* Make sure your air supply valve is shut off, and remove the mini-sampler from your sample site.
10. Return the bottle and mini-sampler to the foam container and return the package to TRI (return shipping label enclosed).

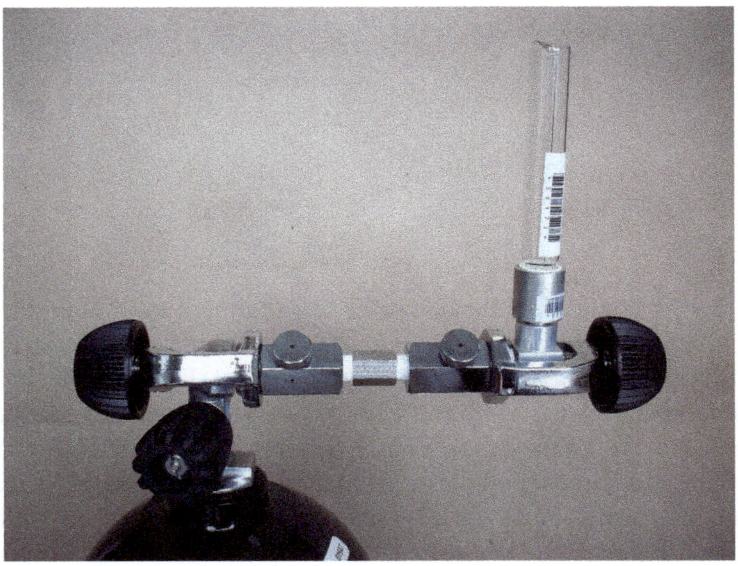

Figure 2.37 TRI mini-sampler attached to a scuba tank to obtain an air sample.

Equipment inspections must be conducted by an individual knowledgeable about diving. Some regulators are designed to leak at the first stage to prevent freezing. To an unknowing investigator, this may appear as a defect or malfunction.

Rarely is a scuba fatality caused by an equipment failure. Regulators are designed to malfunction in a free-flow manner, which delivers a constant flow of air to the diver. But poorly maintained equipment may be a contributing factor. Careful examination may also indicate deliberate tampering or mistreatment of equipment, such as plier marks on a fitting that is designed to be adjusted with a wrench.

Poorly maintained equipment displays a poor attitude toward diving safety by the victim. In most diving accidents, diver error is the cause, not equipment failure. In other words, equipment failure equals diver error in maintenance, fitting, and use of the equipment.

Autopsy

Performance of a complete autopsy, with toxicological testing on the blood and other body fluids, is necessary to reveal any preexisting natural disease, remote or recent injury, and evidence of impairment by drugs, including alcohol or medications, which may have contributed to or caused the death. Additionally, the autopsy may reveal findings supportive of drowning or pressure-related trauma (**barotrauma**). All autopsy-related information is reviewed within the context of the entire case, with the inclusion of investigative information, prior to the determination of the cause and manner of death. Information regarding methods of general autopsy performance and findings in drownings and scuba-related deaths appear in subsequent chapters.

Formulating Conclusions

Any contributing factors must be considered and well documented when drawing conclusions in an investigation. Seemingly unimportant facts must be included. Some common contributing factors include:

- Exposure to cold temperatures
- Entrapment or entanglement
- Equipment failure
- Fatigue
- Panic
- Intoxication by drugs or alcohol
- Environmental hazards
- Multitasking

Rarely does a diving fatality involve one piece of equipment malfunctioning or one element of diver error or misjudgment.[14] It is usually a combination of several factors, each one complicating the next task, causing a snowball effect. For example, let's say a newly certified diver submerges with his brand new underwater camera excited to photograph sea life. He descends and encounters a small amount of seaweed. He struggles to free himself from the entanglement and dislodges his mask. His stress level increases dramatically as he searches for his mask when he snags his regulator hose on a branch, ripping his regulator from his mouth. He panics, holds his breath, and surfaces, causing a lung overexpansion injury that ultimately leads to his death. None of the factors leading up to the breath holding are life threatening. But, when combined, each one complicating the next, scuba accidents result.

Common Factors of Scuba Fatalities

- There is sufficient air left in the tank, usually exceeding 700 psi.
- When found at depth, there is very little air in the BCD.
- The weight belt is still worn with no obvious attempts to ditch it.
- Inspection of the regulator fails to reveal any major problems.
- Air analysis from the scuba tank is well within accepted limits.
- Equipment was worn correctly by the victim and in good condition.
- Diving conditions were seemingly acceptable.
- Buddy contact was good until the fatal incident.
- No major safety violations were identified.
- The victim was found with the regulator out of the mouth.

Many of these common factors are the result of panic. Basic skills such as dropping weights or adding air to the BCD to ascend are not done. Sufficient air left in the tank suggests that either the diver lost the regulator and couldn't retrieve it or simply panicked. Many of these basic skills are forgotten by divers who simply do not practice them on a regular basis. A diver can be certified and not do any of these skills for years and years. Then when an emergency situation arises, tunnel vision sets in and fine motor skills are lost.

CASE STUDY

A man and woman had been diving together when they lost track of time in Hood Canal east of Seattle in northwest Washington. They both began an ascent with an insufficient air supply. The male checked his air and stated to investigators that he had an insufficient amount of air to make a safe ascent. As the pair ascended, the woman signaled she was out of air. Once they reached the surface, she panicked and was not able to release her weight belt or inflate her buoyancy compensator, according to the report. The male called for help while he attempted to hold on to her but lost his grip in the rough water. Other divers found the woman on the bottom in about 20 feet of water a short time later. Medics treated her onshore and rushed her to a nearby hospital. She was later transferred to a medical center, where she died the following day.

Scuba Fatality Reports

The final report should be written so that even a nondiving person can read and understand it. It should be accompanied by many photographs of equipment, which will aid the layperson in understanding the points to be made. Even if a particular piece of equipment played no role in the accident, photographs will simplify understanding. Should the report be needed for litigation or criminal proceedings, these will aid the judicial authorities and pending jurors in understanding what happened.

Suicidal Drowning

In some cases, a suicidal drowning will be made obvious by the decedent because it is important to them to give the surviving family immediate closure. Unlike homicidal acts of drowning, evidence in the case, as well as the location of the body, will be apparent. The subjects will usually go out of their way to assist investigators by leaving a note in a conspicuous location and neatly stack their clothes and belongings on the shoreline near the point of entry. This location of their property is often referred to as a "suicidal headstone." No attempt to hide their belongings or delay the recovery of their body will be evident.

CASE STUDY

The winter of 1990, our jurisdiction had a middle-aged white male park his vehicle in an adjacent neighborhood. It was an extremely cold winter day, and he aroused the attention of a local resident because he was severely underdressed for the weather conditions and left the windows rolled down in his car. He walked over a hillside leading to one of our beach areas. When he did not return after several hours, she reported the incident to our department. Upon our arrival, we could see his wallet and car keys neatly placed on the front seat of his car, which still had the windows rolled down. A check of the vehicle registration revealed the owner had several prior attempts at suicide. Our officers searched the adjoining shoreline for the man but did not locate him. Lake Erie was frozen at the time, and it was believed he had jumped through the ice. After searching the area for the next couple of weeks, the lake began to thaw. During a foot patrol of the shoreline, I noticed an object pressed up underneath the breaking ice that resembled a basketball. Upon further inspection, it was determined to be the face of a human body. It took me and one other officer nearly an hour to chop the body free of the ice. The individual was identified as our missing man.[22]

In this case, there was no suicide note, but his suicidal headstone was located in the front seat of his vehicle, directly next to the location in which his body was located. By placing his belongings in such a conspicuous location, he had made it clear he had no intentions of returning to his car.

Suicides may also present themselves as a homicide. In cases where individuals have had several prior attempts without success, they will go to the extreme to make sure their next attempt is successful. It is not uncommon to find a suicidal individual who has secured himself or herself into the front seat of a car with rope or chains and a padlock (Figure 2.38). In other cases, such individuals may combine several means of death into one attempt, such as drinking a poison like a radiator fluid and then jumping into a lake completely naked in the middle of winter.[14] They may even weigh themselves down with rocks or concrete blocks before jumping into the water. All these extremes may be misleading to the investigator by giving the appearance of a dumped victim of a homicide. The investigator needs to search for suicide notes of multiple forms (on paper, diary, electronic-computer, cell phones), evidence of preparation-wills, etc., life stressors, caretaking responsibility for elderly parents or sick or disabled children, and hardships. There may be

Figure 2.38 Suicidal persons may tie themselves to the driver seat with a rope before driving into a waterway.

no signs other than possibly a foam cone, or there may be signs of prior or recent attempts, such as cutting injuries or scars of the wrist, weights, or tethers.

Pool Drowning

According to the National Safe Kids campaign, a swimming pool is 14 times more likely than a motor vehicle to be involved in the death of a child four years old and under. Many of these incidents can be attributed to accidents in which the child was left unattended, or the appropriate measures to restrict child access were not in place. But a pool drowning incident, like other drowning incidents, must not automatically be viewed as an accident. Each individual case must be investigated as a possible homicide until all other manners of death have been ruled out. The emphasis should be to keep an open mind that a water-related death may not be an accident but may be a suicide, accident, homicide, or natural death. Care must be taken to not assume it can only be a homicide, as one may overcall certain findings, leading to an erroneous conclusion/ruling by the investigator and potentially the coroner or medical examiner, who makes the ultimate ruling on the case.

Upon initial response to the scene, the investigator must take the necessary precautions to ensure the scene is secured to allow for the collection of evidence and to interview any possible witnesses. The investigator's first actions should entail documenting the location and position of the body if it is still on scene. If the body has already been removed from the scene, the location found needs to be determined through extensive witness interviewing. The location of the body alone may assist the investigator in determining if foul play is involved. For instance, a body descending in water with no current will not move more than 1 foot horizontally for every 1 foot of depth (i.e. if the water is 6 feet deep, the body will not move more than 6 feet horizontally during the drowning process).[1] If the complainant states a child fell off a pool deck into a depth of 6 feet, yet the body is found 10 feet from the deck of the pool, this body location would indicate the child was pushed in, not falling accidentally as stated by the complainant.

Other important observations will include determining if there is any indication of a delayed call for rescue personnel. If the complainant states he or she pulled the child out of the water and began CPR, the pool sides or pool deck would most likely be wet. Likewise, the would-be rescuer's clothes would also be wet. An investigator can ascertain dampness on clothing by touching the complainant in a kind and supportive gesture of sympathy. As in any drowning incident, it is imperative the investigator determine the accuracy of information obtained on the scene. Does the evidence on the scene support or contradict witness statements? Evidence collection on the scene should include:

- Recording ambient temperature. This can be used to determine how long the pool deck would have stayed wet after pulling the victim out of the water.
- Water samples from the pool.
- Seizure of clothing worn by the would-be rescuer.
- Photographs of any barriers in place to restrict access to the pool (Figure 2.39).
- Inspection of the house to determine:
    - Any evidence of a cleanup, such as mop buckets, wet towels, or fresh load of clean and dry towels in laundry.
    - Bathroom in disarray or other evidence that may indicate the drowning took place in the home, and the body was moved to the pool.
- Photographs of any toys or flotation devices present. These may be determined to have grabbed the curiosity of the child, luring him or her to the water's edge.
- Clothing worn by the decedent, if not worn on the body.
- Canvass of the neighborhood for witness statements.
- Sketch of location.
- Audio and video documentation of the scene and conveyance to the medical examiner.

Before clearing the scene, the investigator must determine if evidence found at the scene coincides with witness accounts and statements. If something doesn't make sense, second interviews should be done to expose and clarify discrepancies.

Figure 2.39 Barriers present that restrict access to a pool.

CASE STUDY

August 21, 1990, a two-year-old boy from Long Island drowned in his backyard swimming pool after leaving the comfort of his house. His mother and babysitter were home at the time the incident occurred. The 42-year-old mother stated she last saw her son behind a secure gate on the second floor of the house when she went downstairs for a few minutes.[1]

Hotel, School, and Recreation Center Pools

These larger and most often indoor pools present additional circumstances the investigator needs to be aware of when conducting an investigation in this type of environment. Unlike outdoor backyard pools, these often larger pools have a variety of different circumstances that may hinder visibility, safety, and judgment of those who are using them. All these circumstances must be considered when drawing conclusions regarding a drowning incident.

Lighting

In a large pool setting, the pool is often located within an enclosure consisting of a high ceiling that is illuminated with many fluorescent lights. These very bright lights can cast shadows in certain areas while producing a glare on the surface of the water in others. The angles in which witnesses were located during an alleged incident become very critical in determining how much the witness could have seen. This positioning would be determined during the "show me" phase of the interviewing process. It is imperative that the exact conditions are re-created during this process to allow for the most accurate scene assessment. The absence of just one light can have drastic results in changing the visibility of the scene. The investigator must also check or have the appropriate expert (electrician) check the integrity of the pool lighting and its power source for any defects that can pose an electrical hazard and explain a direct cause of death (electrocution) or contributing factor in a pool drowning (paralysis of the respiratory muscles). The interview should also include specific questioning as to whether anyone in the pool, including the victim, complained of tingling, pinprick, or other similar sensation while in the pool or near the pool lights.

Noise

These larger pool locations provide much-needed space to accommodate large groups of swimmers and spectators alike, yet the size is a disadvantage when attempting to communicate within the confines of the structure. A person standing on one side of the pool, yelling instructions to another on the opposite side of the pool will not be able to distinguish the communication clearly. This is because these structures are not acoustic friendly. Anyone speaking loudly will hear an echo inside the building, and this echo distorts what the person is trying to convey. Other distractions often present are a loud radio playing music in the background. Normal communication is extremely difficult. The mere cry of a swimmer in trouble can go unnoticed completely.

Surface Ripple

When attempting to view an object at the bottom of a pool, it is extremely difficult to see distinct shapes because of the surface ripple. Movement in the water causes a small wavelike action on the surface of the water that hinders vision. This ripple has much the same effect as the rippled glass placed in many restroom facilities. The ripple acts like a prism and distorts a clear view of objects beyond it. The movement of one swimmer alone is enough to cause this ripple effect. Determining the positioning of other occupants of the pool is critical. A swimmer 30–40 feet away will not cause the same ripple effect as that of a swimmer within an arm's reach of the victim. Once swimmers exit the water, the ripple effect is calmed almost instantly.

False Sense of Security

Water clarity can be very deceiving to an observer in the area. When people can see the bottom of the pool, they may not consider obstacles that may hinder their view. Even lifeguards in a high chair by the water's edge may not be able to see a victim on the bottom if the victim is positioned near an obstacle such as black racing stripes painted on the bottom of many pools, which are used during swim meets to designate swim lanes. A swimmer wearing dark swimwear, or a dark-skinned swimmer, will be extremely difficult to see from the surface if he or she is positioned over one of these areas. Also, pool drains will have the same camouflage effect. Entanglement is also a possibility if swim lane lines become disconnected. Swimmers can get their legs and arms tangled enough to prevent freedom of movement, which may be enough for them to slip their head below the surface and aspirate water.

Unusual Hours of Operation

Many hotel pools have a "swim at your own risk" policy since they do not employ lifeguards. The need to accommodate travelers requires a wide range of hours to access the pool. Many people also travel alone and may go for an evening swim alone. This action limits potential witnesses to an accident. Many travelers may also have a few alcoholic beverages to help them relax prior to going for a swim, which may hinder their judgment and ability to swim. Many of these facilities locate the pool in a less conspicuous location, which limits passersby. A potential victim could be submerged for hours and go virtually unnoticed.

High Concentration of Swimmers

Many of these pools are accessed by numerous swimmers participating in some form of a formal swim program. High schools have swim teams and swim meets as well as physical education classes. Recreation centers provide water aerobics classes, swimming lessons, and open swim. All of these activities severely hinder visibility since there is a high concentration of swimmers in a relatively small area. It is extremely difficult to see everyone in the pool when the swimmers are so close together. One swimmer slipping below the surface can easily go unnoticed.

Interview of Lifeguard (If One Was on Duty)

Ask questions pertaining to formal training, how long on the job, and whether a lifeguard was on duty at the time or scheduled to be so, in addition to accounts from other witnesses in or out of the water.

Investigative Techniques

During the interview process, it is important to utilize the "show me" technique by leading any potential witnesses through their actions, starting with what they were doing just before the incident through to what they did during the incident. This will establish the positioning of the witnesses, which may expose potential problems in determining what they could or could not see. A sketch should be done of the scene with particular attention to the position and location in which the victim is found. This may prove invaluable later if a reenactment is warranted. Body positioning must be well documented in the sketch because the original witness who found the decedent may not be available at a later time to establish positioning in the event of a reenactment.

Establishing the location found may also reveal discrepancies in information discovered during the course of the investigation.

In some instances, a reenactment may be warranted to clarify information or resolve questions that remain unanswered, such as "Why didn't anyone see the victim at the bottom of the pool?" In this instance, the investigator should obtain a rescue manikin or other object that can be used to show the victim's position and location. The manikin or other object should resemble the victim's description as closely as possible to allow for the most accurate assessment. Place the manikin in the position in which the decedent was located and have each potential witness stand where he or she was at the time the incident occurred. Many will be surprised at how difficult it can be to see a body at the bottom of a swimming pool, even in the best of conditions.

CASE STUDY

The body of a teenage boy was found at the bottom of a high school swimming pool by the school security guard after regular school hours. Several occupants of the school were present after hours and pulled the boy from the water and began CPR in an attempt to revive him and continued until relieved by fire rescue personnel. The school security director stated that after all students are cleared from the pool area, all access doors are locked to prevent anyone from reentering the pool area. The victim's belongings were found in an open locker in the boy's locker room, which included his school ID card. The parents of the boy were contacted, and they stated they were in the process of looking for him since he was not at his normal pickup location at the end of the school day. The mother made a positive identification of her son at the hospital mortuary. It was unclear how the boy came to be in the pool after regular school hours.

An investigation revealed that the boy's last class of the day was physical education and that class was held at the school pool. There were 33 students in the class, yet only 12 were in the water that day. The rest of the students sat along the wall during their class but didn't swim. Security cameras near the pool entrances were checked, and no one was observed entering the pool area after hours. The activity for the physical education class was water basketball, and the decedent reportedly took part. All the students in the class were interviewed, and the decedent had been seen in the water by most of the students in the class, as well as the instructor. Upon exiting the water, many of the students recalled seeing the decedent in the shallow end of the pool, near the rope that divides the shallow end from the deep end of the pool. Students were not permitted in the deep end of the pool during class. Many also would recall they did not see the decedent exit the pool, although one student thought he saw him enter the locker room after class. At the end of the class, the instructor inquired as to the whereabouts of the decedent and, thinking he left early, docked him some points. The instructor was adamant that he checked the pool before leaving the pool deck after class.

The decedent was a black male, wearing only light blue shorts, and was located in the deep end of the pool in the vicinity of one of the black swim lines painted on the bottom of the pool. He was face down, with his head toward the shallow end and his feet toward the deep end of the pool. There was no significant trauma to the body. The victim was not a very good swimmer (did not like to submerge his face) and in fact preferred the shallow parts of the water but would occasionally be observed to inch toward the divider between the shallow and deep ends, as he was observed doing prior to the drowning incident. It was unclear how 32 students and a class instructor could have been in the pool area and not noticed the decedent. Detectives decided to conduct an experiment. They obtained a rescue manikin and placed it at the bottom of the pool in the exact location and position where the decedent was found. Witnesses were asked to look to the bottom of the pool from where they were located during the incident. No one could see the rescue manikin. Even one detective, having prior knowledge where to look for the manikin, could not see it. Although the circumstances in this case remain unclear, in all likelihood and based on all of the recorded investigative information, the victim went too far into the deep end, and because there was no additional investigative information that something other than an accidental death occurred, the coroner in this case ruled the death an accidental drowning.[23]

Bathtub and Hot Tub Drowning

Like the swimming pool drowning, every effort should be made to gather any possible evidence at the scene of a bathtub or hot tub drowning incident. Since dunking is still a widely practiced form of punishment, it would be very easy for a dunking incident to inadvertently become a homicide. As with pool incidents, a timeline must be established to determine if there was any delay in a call for rescue personnel. Evidence to be obtained will include:

1. Determine if floor or sides of tub are wet.
2. Any cleanup attempts, such as numerous wet towels, a fresh load of towels in the dryer, a mop bucket present.
3. Water samples from the tub. If the tub has already been drained, use a bulb syringe to extract a sample from the drain trap.
4. Water temperature. High temperature may indicate punishment by dunking in scalding water. Low temperature may indicate a delay in call for help.
5. Document presence or absence of toys or bath accessories. (Figure 2.40). Also make a note of nearby or submerged electrical devices that may have resulted in

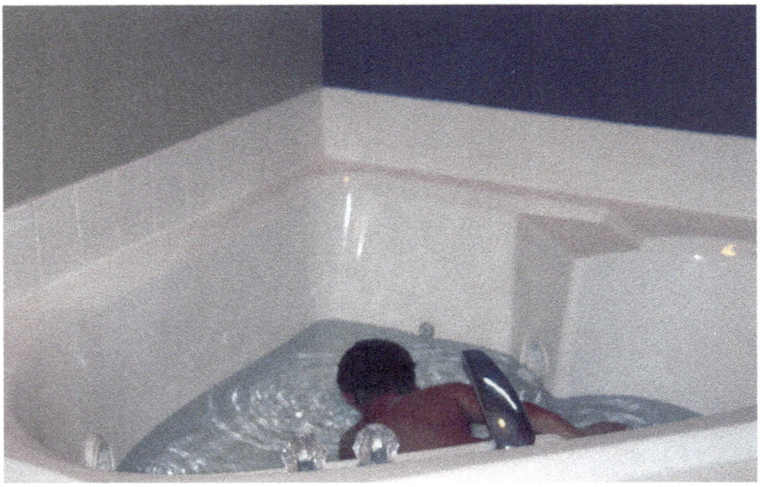

Figure 2.40 Documentation of the presence or absence of toys for tub drowning incidents.

an electrical shock. These should be examined by an electrician for defects, such as wiring, grounding, ground fault circuit interrupter (GFCI) operation, etc.

6. Sketch of location in reference to the rest of the house.
7. Presence of soap scum line on side of tub. A measurement from the tub bottom will assist in determining the depth of water (Figure 2.41).
8. Residency for the past five years. This may reveal any prior incidents in the child's history.
9. Age of the hot tub, when purchased, where purchased (reputable store or representative, garage sale, etc.), and temperature of hot tub water.

While processing the scene of a bathtub drowning, it is imperative the investigator inspects the stopper to the drain for continuity. Many stoppers are made of rubber, which over time, may become damaged or dry rotted, making them ineffective for stopping water from draining the tub. The finding of a damaged stopper may indicate that a bath could not have actually taken place since it would not have been possible for the tub to hold any water.

In addition to taking water samples from the trap in the drain, the investigator must make sure that the drain is not clogged. In the event of foul play, the tub may have been drained hastily by the perpetrator, possibly washing evidence down the drain that may have inadvertently clogged it. In addition, if the drain was clogged prior to the incident, this may indicate that a bathing of the victim never occurred since it would have been impossible to drain the water from the filled tub.

It is not uncommon to have an accidental drowning of a child in a tub and have the caregiver drain the tub upon finding the child submerged. But a water sample should indicate the presence of soap, mucus, urine, and possibly vomit. If the sample reveals clear tap water, this is a discrepancy indicating possible foul play. Care must be taken to conduct a thorough on-scene body assessment, paying particular attention to the child's head, neck, and behind the ears (Figure 2.42). The head is the portion of the body the child is fighting to keep out of the water to breathe, so this is where the majority of external injuries will be located.[1] It would be relatively easy, though, for an adult to forcibly submerge a small child or infant without leaving any injuries due to the difference in strength.

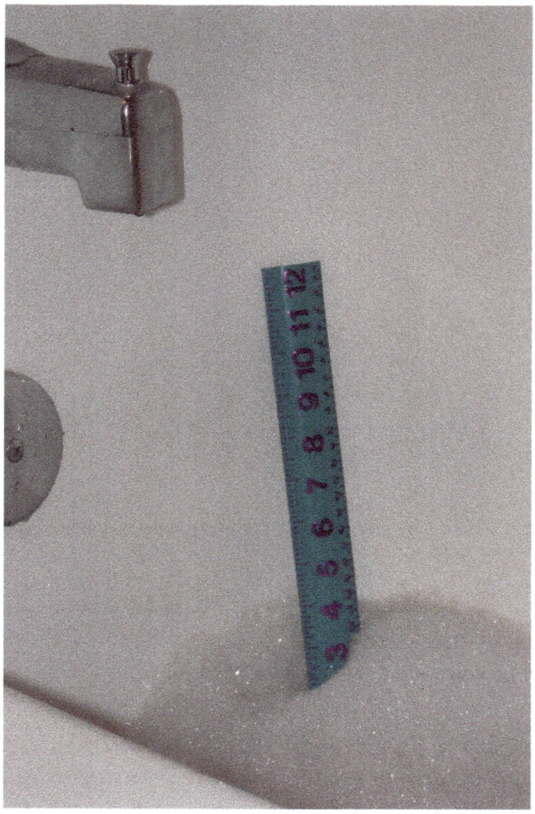

Figure 2.41 Documentation of water depth in a tub drowning.

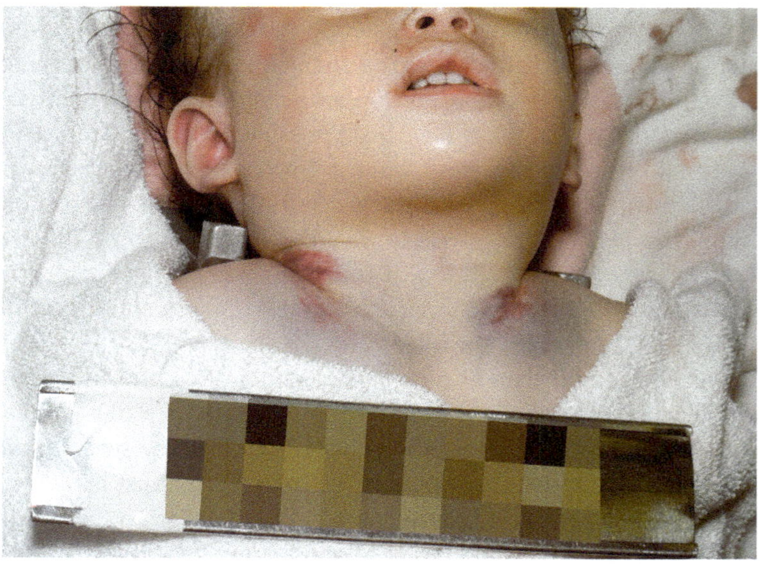

Figure 2.42 Bruising around the child's neck in a tub drowning incident.

Look for bruising around the neck, fingernail scratches behind the ears, or possibly a footprint on the head. Also, look for abrasions on the face around the mouth and nose—caused by the perpetrator, and bruising on the arms and legs—suggestive of restraint by the perpetrator.

Interviews with the parent or caregiver should include the "show me" technique to expose any possible inaccuracies or deception in their account of what occurred. For instance, if a mother states she was giving her son a bath and only left for a minute to answer the phone, reenact the exact circumstances as the incident. Was the television on? Windows open with exterior noise? Stereo playing music? Other children playing or screaming in the house? Can she hear the phone ring or hear a splash from where she states she was located? Is it possible for her to see into the bathroom from where she states she was? An accurate sketch of the home, similar to a floor plan, that shows barriers such as walls is mandatory. Again, do not clear the scene until all discrepancies are exposed and clarified.

CASE STUDY

In Chicago, November 1997, a woman held her three-year-old son's head under water to teach him not to be afraid of it. She said that she then left the room to get a towel and came back to find her son completely limp. Autopsy results revealed death due to drowning as well as fresh bruises on his body and a broken leg. The child had been removed from the home two years earlier by the Department of Child and Family Services because of abuse. The mother was charged with first-degree murder.

Information to look for in a child's history includes:

- Extreme fear of water
- Repeated incidents of pneumonia
- Unexplained apnea incidents (apnea is a pause in breathing for more than 20 seconds) or multiple hospitalizations for apnea incidents without a clear cause
- Previous reports of child abuse
- Other unexplained deaths of siblings

Pneumonia and other respiratory problems are a common result of near-drowning incidents. A medical history of pneumonia may indicate a history of water-related torture or punishment. Consider a parent holding a child's head under water in a tub or sink to stop him or her from crying. For infants and toddlers, ask the pathologist to place a lighted flashlight in the decedent's mouth and close it. This will illuminate the mouth cavity and reveal subsurface bruising that may not be visible otherwise.

CASE STUDY

On December 25, 1997, in South Lyons, Michigan, a mother reported she had left her four-year-old son in the bathtub for a few minutes and returned to find him unconscious, lying face down in the water. She changed her story when she was reinterviewed, and the autopsy showed no signs that he had fallen or suffered a seizure. Finally, during a follow-up interview, she confessed to drowning her son. She stated the boy was splashing the water in the tub and acting unruly, and although she told him to stop, he continued and got her wet. She became angry, grabbed him, and held his head underwater until he stopped struggling. She was charged with first-degree murder.[1]

Hot tubs pose yet another hazard in that, unlike bathtubs, they have a cover. The hot tub cover is usually several inches thick to provide adequate insulation to the hot water below. These covers can be helpful in the prevention of an accidental drowning by restricting access to the water by a small child. They can also pose an entrapment threat to small children who crawl underneath them and become trapped in the water under the heavy weight of the cover.

Hot tubs also have much hotter water than an ordinary bathtub. Hot water is a necessary part of a hot tub to help relieve stress and sore muscles. Various methods to heat the water include electric, natural gas, and sometimes even firewood. If the water temperature is not monitored properly and is allowed to exceed 110°F, the heat can cause sleepiness, which in turn may contribute to drowning. Raising the body temperature to higher levels can also cause heat stroke, heart attack, skin burns, and in extreme cases, brain damage. The hot temperature can have adverse effects on people with preexisting high blood pressure or heart conditions.

Hot tub drownings often involve adults. The investigation should note any evidence of intoxication by drugs, including alcohol or medications.

CASE STUDY

A two-year-old girl drowned in her family's aboveground hot tub at the family home near Tucson Mountain Park. The girl was playing in the backyard when she somehow fell into the uncovered spa. The child's grandfather was in the backyard with her but was inside a work shed when the girl fell in. Other family members were inside the house at the time. It was unclear how long the girl was under water before her grandfather found her. The girl was taken to a local hospital where she was pronounced dead. The grandfather was also treated at the hospital for chest pains.[24]

Moving Water Drowning

Any factors involving moving water incidents that change from moment to moment must be documented as soon as possible to obtain the most accurate data possible. One of the most important factors to obtain is the current speed. A simple test must be done upon arrival at the scene since the current speed can change at a moment's notice, due largely to environmental and weather conditions. Here are some basic formulas regarding body drop rates that can be used to assist in locating the body as well as determining the accuracy of witness statements and other information provided to the investigator on the scene.

Current Speed

$$1 \text{ knot} = 100 \text{ feet per minute}$$

To calculate current speed, drop a float in the water and measure how far it travels in one minute. If it travels 100 feet in one minute, the current speed is 1 knot. Two hundred feet in one minute, and the speed is 2 knots, etc.

Body Drop Rates

Freshwater = approximately 2 feet per second Saltwater = approximately 1.5 feet per second

For this example, let's say the freshwater depth is 20 feet and the speed is 2 knots.

1. Convert the current speed to a fraction: 200 feet ÷ 60 seconds (200 ÷ 60 = 3.33) seconds.
2. Locate the last seen point and determine water depth (20 feet, in this example).
3. Calculate drop time in seconds (20 feet divided by 2 feet rate = 10 seconds).
4. Multiply drop time by the current (3.3 × 10 = 33 feet).

In this example, a body leaving the surface in a 2-knot current in 20 feet of water would be located 33 feet from the last seen point.

Now, let's say a mother states her son fell from a dock and submerged immediately in a water depth of 20 feet. You determine the current speed to be 2 knots or 200 feet per minute. Using the above formula indicates his body should be located within 33 feet of the dock. If the actual distance is much greater than 33 feet, you know that either her statement regarding the last seen point is inaccurate or her account of what occurred is incorrect. It is the duty of the investigator to determine which statement is inconsistent with the evidence. Variables that may affect drop rates include surface or submerged debris, algae growth, and any possibility of trapped air in clothing or other buoyancy possessed by the victim.

A simplified version is provided in Appendix B. All the mathematics has been done. All you need to know is current speed and water depth to cross-reference the information, determining the location of the body. Once on the bottom, a body will not move until the process of refloat begins. Other factors involved in moving water incidents will include possible postmortem wounding from the movement of the body with the current. Signs of travel abrasions will be apparent in cases where the body has gone through the refloat process. Also, other postmortem wounding may be present due to the body striking the surface or submerged objects. If it is suspected the body may have traveled a great distance during refloat, it is advisable to obtain a soil sample from the decedent's clothing, if present. Soil samples, and in some cases maggots, can be used to determine the geographical origin of the body. A survey of the area in which the body has traveled should be conducted to determine possible causes of wounding and other observations on the body. Strainers, rapids, low-head dams, and waterfalls should all be documented on a sketch of the area and photographed (Figure 2.43).

Figure 2.43 Photograph strainers, rapids, or other obstacles that may cause postmortem wounding.

Homicidal Drowning

An investigator may not want to believe that a parent or loved one could have intentionally drowned a child. But, just as parents might shake, beat, strangle, stab, burn, and suffocate a child, they are also capable of drowning a child. Such was the case when Andrea Yates intentionally drowned all five of her children in her bathtub. In this case, immediately following their murders, she called the authorities and admitted to the act.

In cases where there is great disparity (age, intoxication/impairment, gender, other injuries, underlying medical conditions) between the perpetrator and the victim where resistance to the attack will be little to none, little in the way of injury will be found unless there is antemortem torturing or postmortem mutilation of the victim. Otherwise, the victim will put up a good fight to the extent and force that his or her strength allows, and there will be numerous injuries, including defensive types. A perpetrator may attempt to disguise a homicidal drowning or other lethal injury inflicted prior to submersion, as an accidental drowning. Investigators need to recognize that while an autopsy may reveal findings supportive of drowning, the classification of drowning is best made after a review of all of the information, including scene findings, witness information, and information about the victim. The autopsy of a homicidal drowning may appear identical to that of an accidental or suicidal drowning unless there are patterns of injury on the body or results of toxicological tests consistent with a homicidal manner.

There are many other causes of death that one can attempt to conceal as an accidental drowning, so the investigator needs to be familiar with pathological aspects of many manners of death to be able to differentiate between each case.

Erotic Drowning

There is a new sexual experience being practiced in the form of erotic drowning. Individuals, both men and women, gain sexual excitement and gratification from submersion in water.

Subjects hold their partner's head underwater during various sexual acts to heighten orgasm. This is the same theory practiced in an autoerotic death in which some form of ligature device is used to cut off the oxygen supply to the brain. But, in erotic drowning, the "ligature device" is water. Many websites featuring erotic drowning can be found on the Internet. One such site is called Men Underwater. This site offers several services for the water enthusiast, including instructions on erotic drowning, warnings about shallow water blackout and autoerotic immersion asphyxia, tips on how to avoid these dangers, a chat room where participants can write blogs about their experiences, and a message board that allows participants to post ads in search of others interested in the sport.

Shallow water blackout causes a sudden loss of consciousness due to oxygen deprivation to the brain. It occurs suddenly and without warning. Different individuals have different tolerance levels, which complicates matters considerably. One person may be able to sustain several minutes of submersion with no ill effects, while others may experience a blackout in a much shorter time frame. There is no predisposed knowledge of these tolerance levels. A participant who has a regular partner may be accustomed to holding his or her head under water for several minutes, yet if he or she attempts this with another person, that person could have a much lower tolerance, black out, and ultimately drown.

One tip to avoid these dangers instructs participants to "watch for the bubbles." This requires players to watch for the bubbles expelled from their partner's mouth and nose when they exhale air because they can no longer hold their breath. Bubbles are the signal to allow the partner to surface. During a brief pause in attention, this signal can be easily missed, causing an unintentional drowning.

The "buddy page" offers a message board for participants to post profiles, looking for other players to meet. The following is a warning that appears on this page:

> Warning! Underwater breath holding to the point of passing out is *dangerous* and can cause permanent brain damage. It is most likely that anyone without medical training will not be able to resuscitate/revive you if you pass out underwater. Inhaling water is likely to cause death. The webmaster takes no responsibility for the actions or consequences of those who choose to engage in underwater edge play. Don't play alone and please play responsibly!—Thank you!

Some examples of postings may include:

> GWM, 45, 5′11″, 175 lb, brown hair, brown eyes. Love being and seeing guys underwater. I can hold my breath for 2 minutes and 13 seconds. This is my personal best when totally relaxed, which is rare.
>
> WM, 5′8″ free diver, bodybuilder, and ex-swimming champion. Live in London. Like guys between 25 and 40 who love to have sex underwater. Travel a lot to Italy and Greece and hoping to move to Florida soon.
>
> 30-year-old male, 6′1″, 170 lb, I love neoprene, rubber, latex, gas masks, full face masks. I love breath control. I love to be in full rubber suits for several hours. Looking for guys who love it too. Click here for photos of me.

On the underwater games page, several "rules" are posted and explained. Here is a brief list:

1. Never ever jump into a pool on top of another guy. You could knock him out or cause him damage.

2. When dunking another guy, allow him to take a deep breath, which will allow you to hold him underwater longer.
3. Watch for escaping bubbles, which means he is running out of air. He must be allowed to surface within 10 seconds.
4. Wear a nose clip, which restricts water from entering your nostrils. Also, provided you keep your mouth tightly closed, you cannot swallow any water.[25]

These postings and rules are included to provide the investigator with a better understanding of this activity, which may aid in the identification and collection of evidence on scene as well as prompt possible questions to be asked during interviews. Evidence to look for on scene may include:

1. Bondage paraphernalia
2. Restraints, chains, handcuffs, and weights
3. Sexually related reading material, magazines, or videos
4. Condoms or the presence of semen on the floor or in the water
5. Inadvertent admissions or statements of deviant sexual behavior
6. Computer websites visited on the Internet
7. Video cameras or other recording devices

It is important to remember that most jurisdictions require a search warrant to view any electronic files contained on a computer, video recorder, cell phone, or camera.

An autoerotic death by using submersion as an asphyxia method is called autoeroticum. The victim will most likely be found nude and have restraints and complex bondage devices present.

CASE STUDY

Montreal, Quebec, posted that on April 17, 2005, a 25-year-old man was found nude under a homemade plastic body suit and restrained by complex bondage. He was submerged, tied under water to a boat, and was using a homemade diving apparatus for air supply. Death was ruled as accidental autoerotic asphyxia from rebreathing, caused by the faulty air supply device.[26]

Imagine the potential for problems as you read the following descriptions of underwater games posted on this site.

"DUCK ROUND THE HOUSE"

This is a game for two or preferably three or more naked guys who are into bondage and dunking. One guy is chosen to be the "victim" by drawing straws. The victim has his hands strapped behind his back, is picked up and carried by the others throughout the house, dunking his head into various receptacles. The guys make sure that the victim is struggling and sending up plenty of bubbles before they bring him up for air. While dunking him they masturbate him. A 5-gallon bucket and the bath or hot tub are very good places to dunk the victim, and if the guys wish to be extra wicked, they can hold him down till he is desperate for air, bring him up for a frantic gasp, then send him straight down again for a second helping. The toilet for the royal flush is another good one, as the victim is lowered headfirst into the bowl, and then held down for the duration of the flush before being pulled up.

"KEEP HIM DOWN"

This is a game played by three guys and they choose one to be the "victim." The victim has his hands strapped behind his back and is pushed into the deep end of a pool, while the other two don scuba gear. To play the game properly, a bench should have been lowered into the pool and the victim is then strapped to it by the other two. The scuba guys wait till the victim's lungs empty before giving him a breath from a regulator. Afterward, one guy positions himself between his legs and performs oral sex on him. The other guy straddles the bench and gives the victim air every time his lungs have completely emptied.

Perhaps the most interesting and puzzling aspect of the site includes the underwater reference guide in which everyday TV commercials and movies are listed as forms of sexual excitement that participants can view. Some of these include:

1. The Nestea plunge, in which a woman dives into a pool, swims underwater to the other side, exits the water, and sips from a glass of iced tea.
2. Air Force commercial (1999), where a guy is underwater in a pool with goggles on.
3. *The Abyss*—An R-rated movie where a man and his estranged wife are trapped in a mini-sub filling with water. The husband dons scuba gear while his estranged wife drowns. He then tows her underwater to a submerged lab where he performs CPR on her and she is revived.
4. American Dairy Association cheese commercial (2000), where Mr. Giggles throws a man barefaced underwater into a kiddy pool.

It is important to remember, as in these examples, that not all incidents will necessarily include a sex act. These TV commercials and movies have no sexual connotation at all. Just the fantasy or thought of immersion or submersion is enough for the gratification to occur.

Drowning of the Elderly

With current advances in medical technology, our senior citizens are living longer lives. Many younger people are shouldering the burden of caring for their elderly parents, causing both mental and physical burdens. Furthermore, the deteriorating mental capabilities of the elderly are causing frustration and stress on the relationships of their caretakers. All these factors create a sense of helplessness, which fuels the thought of death by drowning as a feasible solution. The fact that many children are also named as beneficiaries in health insurance policies adds to the temptation of putting them out of their misery.

Surprisingly, some life insurance policies actually have a higher payoff amount if death is caused by an accident rather than natural causes. For this reason, it may be possible in questionable scenes that the elderly person died of natural causes, yet caregivers staged the scene to look like an accident.

A tub drowning involving an elderly person may or may not involve trauma to the body. A tub drowning involving an elderly person where trauma is absent could be a red flag indicator of possible foul play, but not necessarily so. It is possible for the elderly person to succumb to natural disease such as seizures or heart disease while bathing, causing him or her to gently slip underwater without sustaining any bodily injury and without striking the head to cause unconsciousness. Elderly persons may sustain injury, however, if they collapse while getting into, standing in, or getting out of the tub, or if they slip due to unsteadiness doing any one of these things. The extent of the resulting injury may or may not be lethal and can include abrasions, bruises, fractures of the arms, hips, and legs, and internal bleeding over the surface of the brain. There may be underlying natural disease that precipitated the fall or collapse. Bruises and abrasions at various stages of healing that cannot be explained by normal daily activity or by a known history of unsteadiness with frequent falls, in an elderly person who has drowned in a bathtub need to be explained with a complete investigation and autopsy.

The investigator should inquire about any history of heart disease, high blood pressure/hypertension, and seizures/epilepsy, as these conditions may predispose one to drowning while bathing or preparing to bathe. The investigator should also inquire about medications and actively look for prescription bottles or medical papers that may list medications.

Other red flag indicators of nonaccidental or homicidal deaths may include:

1. A disability that may have caused a burden to the caregiver
2. Alzheimer's disease
3. Increased or recently purchased life insurance policy, unusual transactions from the victim's accounts, missing valuables' or the sale of valuables
4. Severe or terminal illness
5. Recent injury, illness, or disability of the caregiver that would indicate that the caregiver was not physically capable of providing care to the victim
6. Adult protective service reports or claims made by others (whether substantiated or unsubstantiated)
7. History or witness accounts of seclusion of the elderly victim from family, friends, or functions and outings
8. Prior domestic violence reports (whether substantiated or unsubstantiated)

Evidence during the on-scene body assessment that may indicate possible foul play would include:

1. Lividity inconsistent with body positioning found at scene.
2. Rigor mortis inconsistent with body positioning.
3. Patterned lividity that may suggest the decedent died elsewhere, such as bed sheet impressions.
4. The presence or lack of clothing on the body. For instance, is it feasible an elderly person could get to water in which he or she is found naked, or dressed in a nightgown, etc.? Aspects of the body of water in which the victim was recovered, such as current and waves that may have removed clothing, as previously discussed.
5. Ambient temperature. Could the person have traveled great distances in extremely hot or cold temperatures?

6. Did the person have the physical capability to get to the location found? Are there trees or obstacles restricting access to the location found?
7. Did the decedent have the physical strength to get to the body of water over hills or rough terrain?

The footwear worn should be seized and examined for evidence that the decedent trekked to the location on his or her own. Lack of footwear would be a red flag indicator of foul play.

Boating and Personal Watercraft (PWC) Accidents

Generally, powerboats such as runabouts, cabin cruisers, and personal watercrafts are the most common watercraft involved in boating accidents. Most injuries are caused by either propeller accidents or collisions. Because personal watercrafts such as jet skis cannot be steered when the throttle is released, inexperienced operators often cannot avoid a collision in an emergency. Serious injuries and death can occur from collisions or a person falling overboard and drowning. Many of these drowning incidents could be avoided if the persons on board were wearing a personal flotation device (PFD).

Statistics show that almost all boating accident victims are male (91%), and take place during recreational activities (National Boating Fatalities Report 2003)[27] The most common contributing factors are not wearing a PFD, alcohol use, inexperienced operators, and risk-taking behavior. While boating deaths overall are down, not wearing a PFD is still a contributing factor to the drowning problem, and alcohol consumption is involved in 38% of boating fatalities. Many deadly factors can be prevented if boaters learn to operate their vessel more safely, including wearing the proper gear.

While conducting a boating fatality investigation, it is important for the investigator to thoroughly document any contributing factors involved in the accident and subsequent fatality, including the following:

- Was the vessel being operated at a safe speed for the conditions?
- Is there evidence of alcohol or drug use, such as empty containers throughout the vessel?
- Does the condition of equipment on board indicate the boater has a poor attitude toward boating, such as poorly maintained equipment, insufficient amount of PFDs onboard, overloaded vessel?
- Was the boater following the "rules of the road" for safe boating?
- Has the boater completed a safe boating course?
- Did the boater file a float plan?
- Was the boater taking unnecessary risks, such as boating during poor weather, rough seas, in a hazardous area, etc.?
- What were the weather conditions, for example, rain, wind, fog?
- Was there a full moon that could have caused glare on the water surface that may have hindered visibility?
- Did the boat have properly working lights on after dark?

Table 2.2 will assist the investigator in determining water conditions based on wind speed in knots. This table is provided because, as a whole, there is a general tendency to underestimate small wave heights and to overestimate large wave heights.

Table 2.2 Chart Showing Water Conditions Based on Wind Speed

Knots	Water Conditions	Probable Wave Height in Feet
0–1	Calm—Water smooth and mirror-like	0
1–3	Ripples without foam crests	¼
4–6	Small, short waves; crests do not break	½
7–10	Some crests begin to break with the appearance of foam	2
11–16	Small waves, becoming longer with frequent foam crests	4
17–21	Moderate waves with a more pronounced long form; many white foam crests with some spray	6
22–27	Large waves begin to form; white foam crests are more extensive everywhere; spray	10
28–33	Near gale—Sea heaps up and white foam from breaking waves begins to blow in streaks along the direction of the wind; spindrift begins	14
34–40	Gale winds—Higher waves with greater length; edges of crests break into spindrift	18
41–47	Strong gale; high waves; wave crests begin to topple and roll over; spray may reduce visibility	23
48–55	Storm; very high waves; water surface is white in appearance; wave tumbling becomes shock-like	29
56–63	Violent storm; exceptionally high waves that may obscure small and medium ships; visibility reduced	37
64–71	Hurricane; air is filled with foam and spray; no visibility	45

Each and every fatality has a human element as a contributing factor, and the investigator must thoroughly investigate each incident to determine this factor, whether accidental, intentional, or negligent.

Determining the Location of the Crash

It is important for the investigator to determine the location of the crash to allow the recovery and collection of evidence. Search and rescue personnel that may have responded to the scene may be able to provide Global Positioning System (GPS) coordinates. The vessels involved may also have information stored on their own GPS that may indicate the location. If a general location is known, divers may be able to locate items from the vessel that would sink to the bottom without any chance of drifting, such as fishing rods, flashlights, and toolboxes. Divers may also be able to locate drag marks on the water bottom, which may determine the direction the vessel drifted. After determining the location of the accident, a sketch should be completed that indicates the following:

- All the vessels involved and their relative course
- Relation to aids of navigation, such as marker buoys, channel markers, etc.
- Location of any fixed objects, including lighthouses, land, water intakes, etc. (Figure 2.44)

Photographs of any pertinent damage to a vessel should be taken. In cases of a watercraft striking a person on the water surface, damage to the vessel will be absent. The investigation should include the recovery of any items thrown overboard as a result of a collision. This includes an entire sunken vessel.

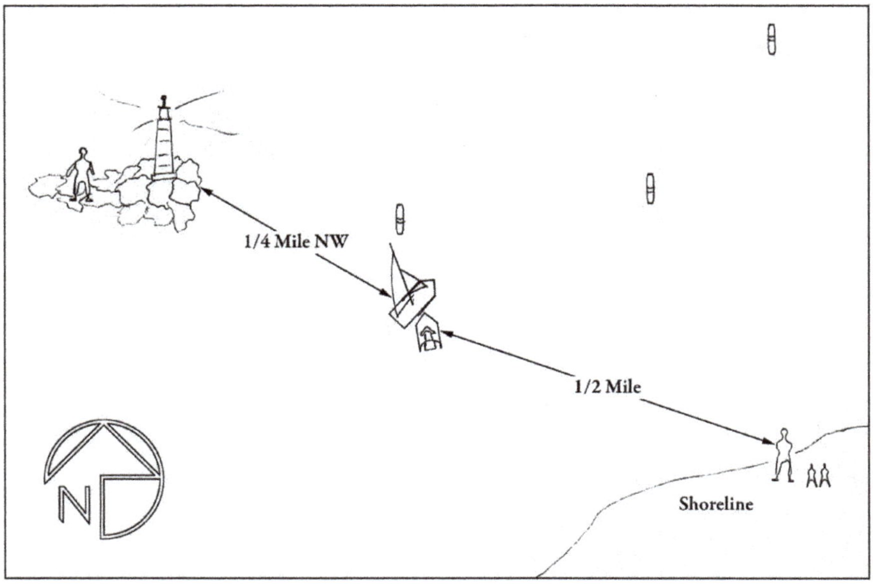

Figure 2.44 Sketch documenting boating accident location and positioning of witnesses.

Light and Lamp Examination

Lights may play an important role in the investigation process. Statements made by witnesses claiming a vessel was running without lighted lights can be difficult to prove if proper procedures in the recovery of evidence are not followed. The fact that a light switch is on or off is not always a good indicator to determine if the lights were functional at the time of the incident. Light bulbs from the lights themselves can be analyzed to determine if they were on at the time of a collision. Therefore, retrieval of all light bulbs is imperative for accidents that occurred in darkness. Burning light filaments break in a certain fashion upon impact, which is different from an unlighted filament. Ideal conditions require removal of the entire light assembly prior to vessel recovery, since the lights can be damaged during the recovery process. The investigator must ensure that proper documentation is done to record the location in the vessel in which the light has been recovered. Lamps that are located closer to the point of impact will have different fracture patterns than those found a greater distance away. The direction of impact can be determined by the direction in which the filament has been broken. Carefully package all light assemblies and transport them to the crime lab for analysis. At best, bulb analysis is not as clear-cut as one might anticipate. The examination of bulb breakage is often a case of drawing on extensive experience and weighing in all the factors involved in the accident in order to form an accurate conclusion. Bulb examination terms (Figure 2.45a) include the following:

- **Incandescent (4,000–6,000°)**: An electrical current was in the filament, causing it to heat to the point where it produces light.
- **Hot (2,000°)**: No current or light being generated. The filament may be hot from just being turned off, or it is hot from close proximity to another incandescent filament.
- **Cold (filaments cool very quickly)**: A cold filament with no electrical current or light being generated.

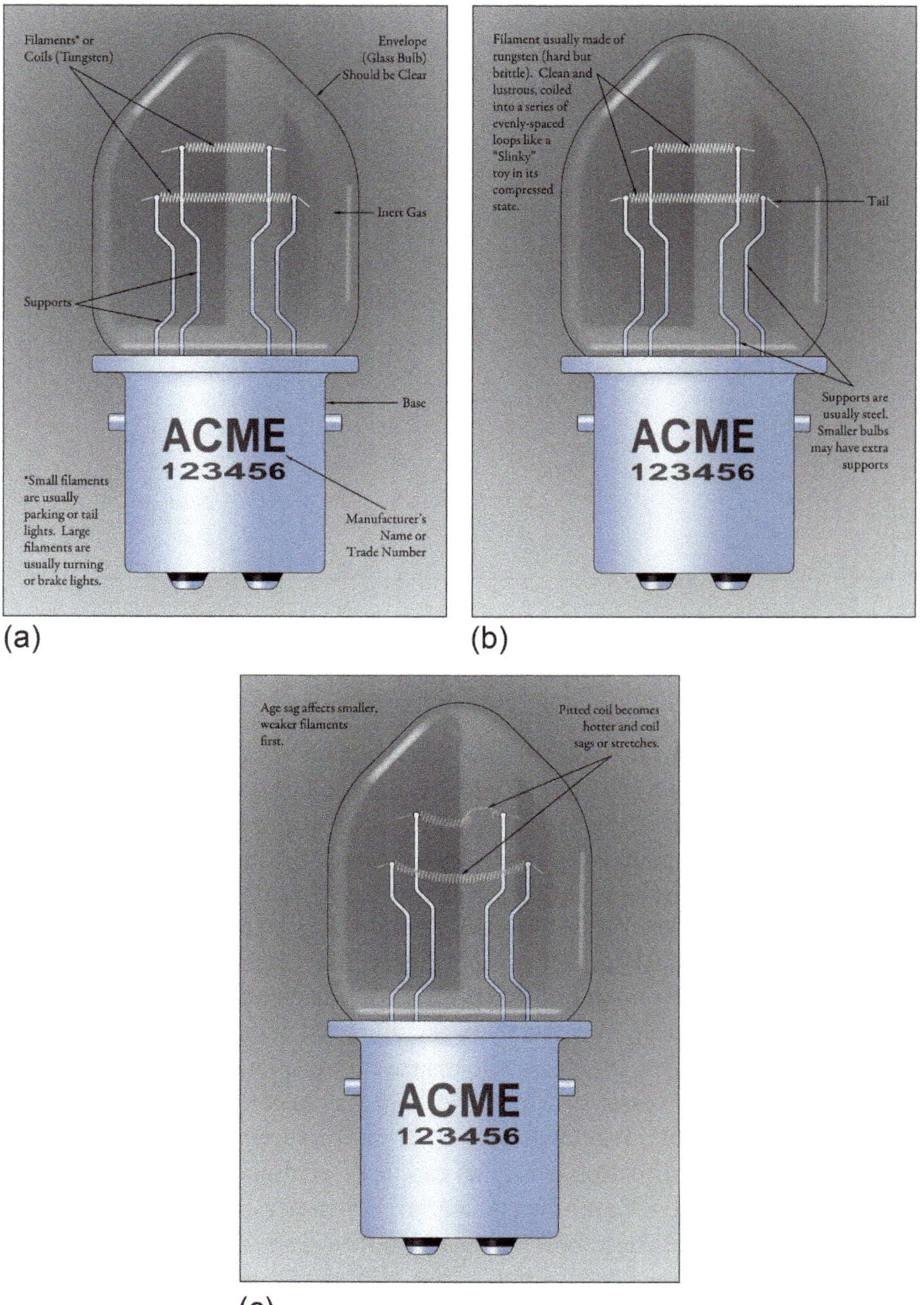

Figure 2.45 (a) Bulb nomenclature. (b) Normal lamp. (c) Age sag.

Light bulb or lamp analysis would be done by a qualified technician at the crime lab, but a general overview, considering a normal lamp or bulb, follows to help the investigator understand the evidence at hand:

1. Bulb is new and off (Figure 2.45b):
    a. The filament or coil is made of tungsten, has evenly spaced coils, and is clean and lustrous.

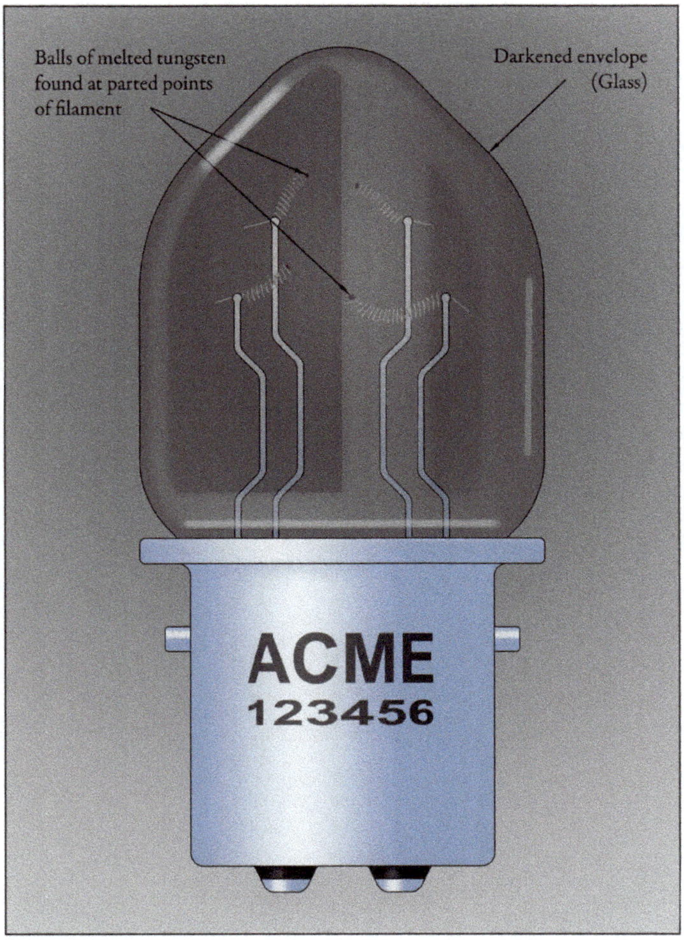

Figure 2.46 Burned out light bulb.

   b. The filament has a tail.
   c. The filament has supports.
   d. The glass bulb (envelope) should be clear.
   e. Inert gas that will not support a flame, such as argon or nitrogen, is present inside the envelope. This inert gas will not permit oxidation inside the bulb.
   f. **Age sag** is found in an older, nondamaged bulb. Over time, the filament becomes pitted, causing a weak spot, which in turn causes the filament to sag or stretch (Figure 2.45c).
2. Bulb is burned out (Figure 2.46):
   a. Evaporated tungsten darkens the bulb glass.
   b. The coil breaks at the weakest point.
   c. An electrical arc is caused when the coil separates.
   d. The filament ends are tapered and balls of melted tungsten may develop.
3. Cold shock (broken while off) (Figure 2.47):
   a. The filament is cold and brittle upon impact.
   b. Heavy impact near bulb causes ends of the filament to break, appearing jagged and sharp.

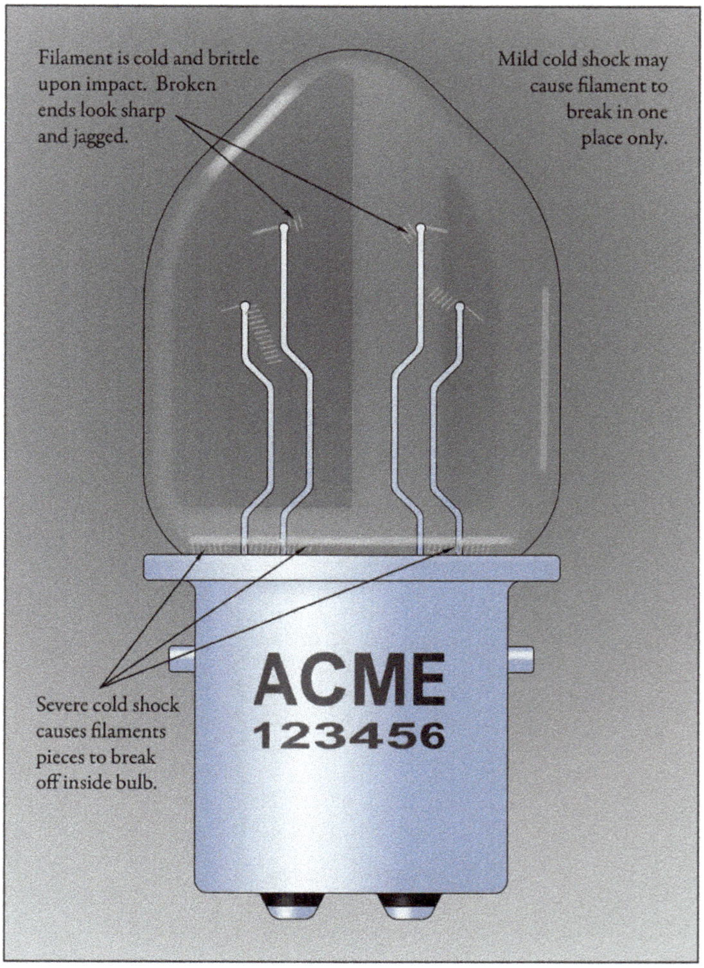

Figure 2.47 Cold shock (bulb is broken while off).

   c. In severe shock, filament pieces may break off inside the bulb.
   d. In mild cold shock, the filament breaks in one place only.
   e. Cold stretch may happen in heavy impact.
4. Hot shock (bulb is broken while on) (Figure 2.48):
   a. The filament is hot and pliable upon impact.
   b. The filament rarely separates because it is pliable when hot.
   c. The filament stretches or arcs from the force of the impact.
   d. The filament remains deformed after a crash.
   e. The filament may etch the inside of the glass.
5. Hot bulb break (Figure 2.49):
   a. The envelope is broken.
   b. Glass pieces may be fused to the filament, indicating the filament was incandescent when the glass was broken. (Glass fragments can be seen under magnification as glass droplets or a fine dust that resembles whiskers.)

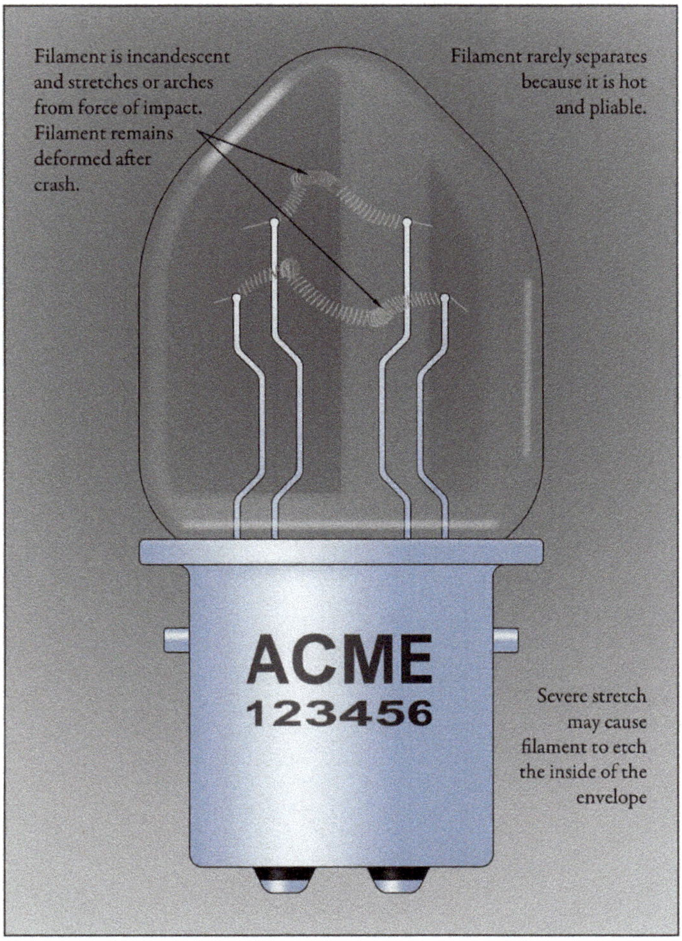

Figure 2.48 Hot shock (bulb is broken while on).

c. Oxidation on the filament indicates that either the filament was hot (on) when the glass was broken or the filament was cold when the glass was broken but the circuit was turned on after the crash.*

Any flotsam (floating debris) must also be recovered. Any floating debris may prove to be valuable evidence, which may include biological evidence such as skin or pieces from damaged organs. Special attention to the boat propeller is warranted. This is the most common external area of a vessel that may trap human remains. The surface search may require the use of a search boat. Recovery divers may also be deployed from this vessel to search for sunken evidence. Special care must be exercised in the recovery of sunken evidence since

* For this reason, it is very important for the investigator to remember not to activate any light switches after the crash. Moving a light switch to the on position can destroy valuable light bulb evidence, which may lead to a determination that the lights were off at the time of the crash.

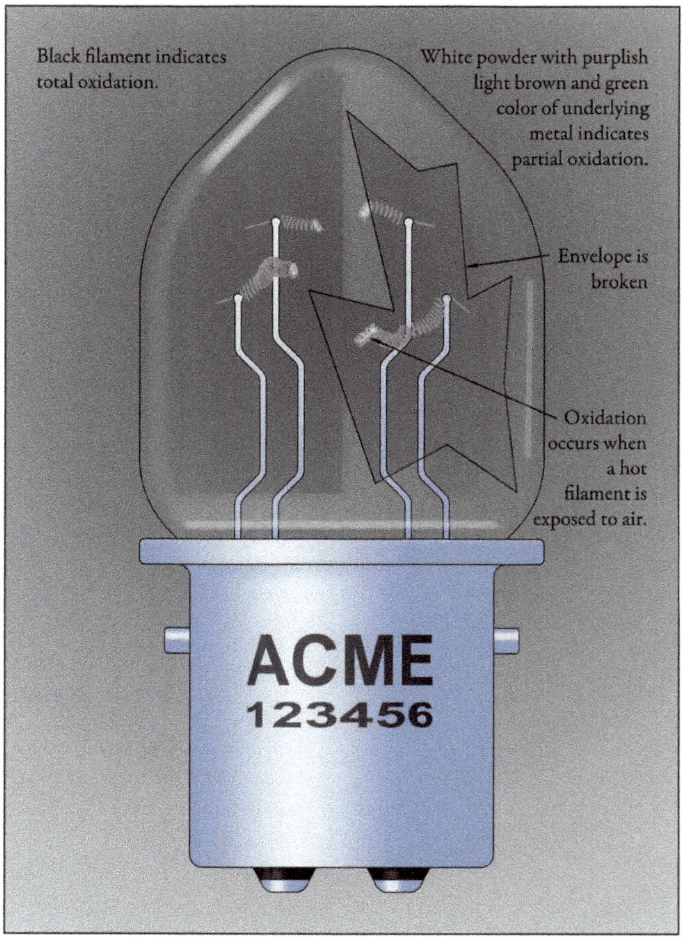

Figure 2.49 Hot bulb break.

in most cases the diver will need to locate the items by means of touch. Most underwater search conditions have less than 1 foot of visibility, making a search by site impossible.

A critical portion of the investigation is acquiring information regarding the weather conditions around the time of the incident. The value of this evidence was clearly established in the investigation of the 1975 sinking of the *Edmund Fitzgerald* in Lake Superior, a tragedy that claimed the lives of 29 mariners. A review of the ship's course and wind patterns allowed investigators to determine that the shift of the wind took the vessel away from the protection of the shore and placed it in the path of huge waves. That investigation also stressed the importance of examining any and all communications made from the victim's vessel to other vessels nearby. In the case of the *Edmund Fitzgerald*, it was determined that the captain was not aware of the severity of their situation until the ship became swamped with water and sank.

Computer simulations can be utilized to reconstruct an accident scene. A simulation may prove to be an important tool in determining what happened to the vessel and persons on board by using a vessel model in a specially designed pool that can create waves. The National Center for Inland Waterways in Burlington, Ontario, Canada, has a pool where these simulations can be conducted. The center can be reached at 1-819-997-2800 or by e-mail at enviroinfo@ec.gc.ca. Accident reconstruction can be a complex matter at best. It must incorporate many aspects of information from a variety of sources. Regardless of how well the reconstruction is conducted, it will always be scrutinized by experts acting on behalf of their clients.

Inspection of PFDs

The investigator can determine the quality and effectiveness of the PFDs onboard by conducting an inspection. Factors to evaluate include the following:

- PFD must be U.S. Coast Guard approved (in the United States) and will be marked as such (Figure 2.50).
- Type of device and size was appropriate for the wearer.
- PFD is in good condition. Check for rips, tears, and holes in the material. Make sure the buckles and straps are functional.
- PFDs must be readily accessible. They must not be stored in plastic bags or under heavy equipment. They lose buoyancy when crushed.
- There must not be any nonfactory alterations.
- Buoyant material must not be crushed, water or oil soaked, rotted, or deteriorated.
- Any other structural component that fails when tugged.

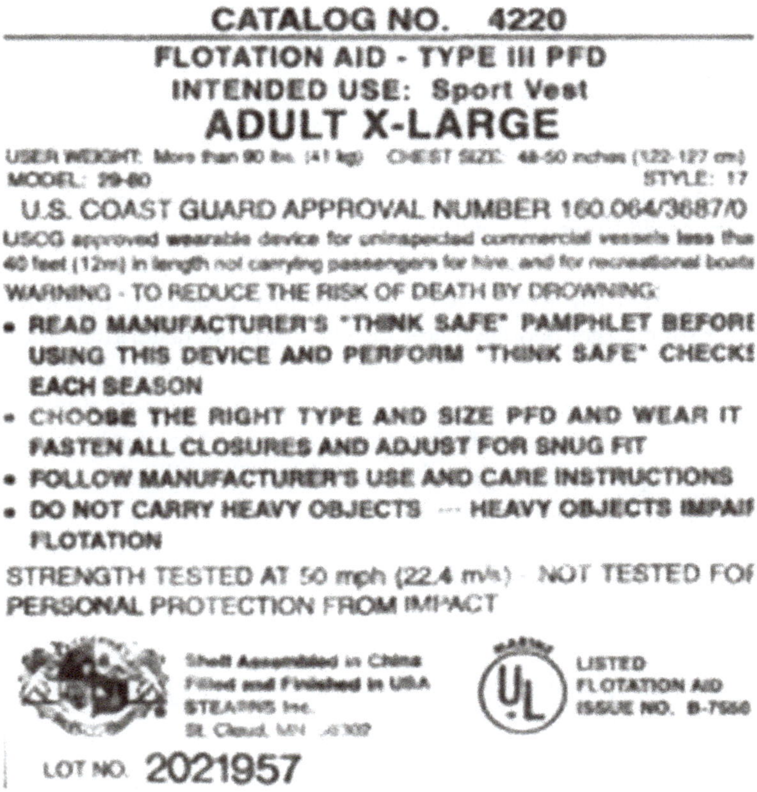

Figure 2.50 U.S. Coast Guard label found on approved PFDs.

Table 2.3 PFD Buoyancy

Type of PFD	Buoyancy in Pounds
Type I—Offshore lifejackets	22
Type II—Near-shore vests	15.5
Type III—Inflatable	22.0
Type III—Buoyant foam	15.5
Type IV—Ring buoys	16.5
Type IV—Boat cushions	18.0
Type V—Hybrid inflatable	22.0

Source: ODNR Boating Safety Course, Ohio Department of Natural Resources, Division of Watercraft, Columbus, Ohio.

Buoyancy is based on Archimedes' principle, which states that any body partially or completely submerged in fluid is buoyed up by a force equal to the weight of the fluid displaced by the body. Most people will naturally float in water because they have residual air in their lungs. The average-sized adult weighs approximately 8–10 pounds in water, so he or she only needs an additional 8–10 pounds of buoyancy to keep his or her head above water. This is why a PFD with 15 pounds of buoyancy can provide adequate lift for an adult. Table 2.3 indicates PFD buoyancy, and Figure 2.51 shows different types of PFDs.

There are factors that may overcome the wearing of a PFD, which may result in drowning:

- Being trapped in an overturned boat
- Being held under by a boulder or log in a strong current
- Removing the PFD for any reason, such as a swim to shore
- Suffering other injuries that lead to drowning
- Becoming hypothermic due to the duration of exposure to cold
- PFD not approved for specific activity

Be aware that cold water can lower the body temperature, causing hypothermia. Smaller people cool faster than larger people; therefore, children cool faster than adults. Even good swimmers drown in cold water because swimming lowers their body temperature due to exertion. Even if a person is wearing a PFD, his or her body will cool down 25 times faster than in the air. Children panic when they fall into water. They flail their arms and legs, making it hard to keep their head out of the water. A PFD will keep a child afloat, but it may not keep his or her face out of the water.

Interviews with witnesses and friends of the decedent may reveal evidence that the decedent was suffering from hypothermia. Signs and symptoms are listed in order of severity:

1. Shivering, slurred speech, blurred vision
2. Bluish lips and fingernails
3. Loss of feeling in extremities
4. Cold, bluish skin
5. Confusion
6. Dizziness

Figure 2.51 Types of PFDs.

7. Rigidity in extremities
8. Unconsciousness
9. Coma
10. Death

Cold Water Immersion

Cold water immersion (Figure 2.52) kills in several ways. The colder the water, the greater the chance of death.

Stage 1—Cold shock: Occurs in the first three to five minutes in cold water. Sudden immersion causes an involuntary gasp reflex, which can result in the inhalation of water. This aspiration of water will cause panic, hyperventilation, and vertigo. Sudden immersion can also cause a rapid change in heart rate and blood pressure, which in itself may lead to death.

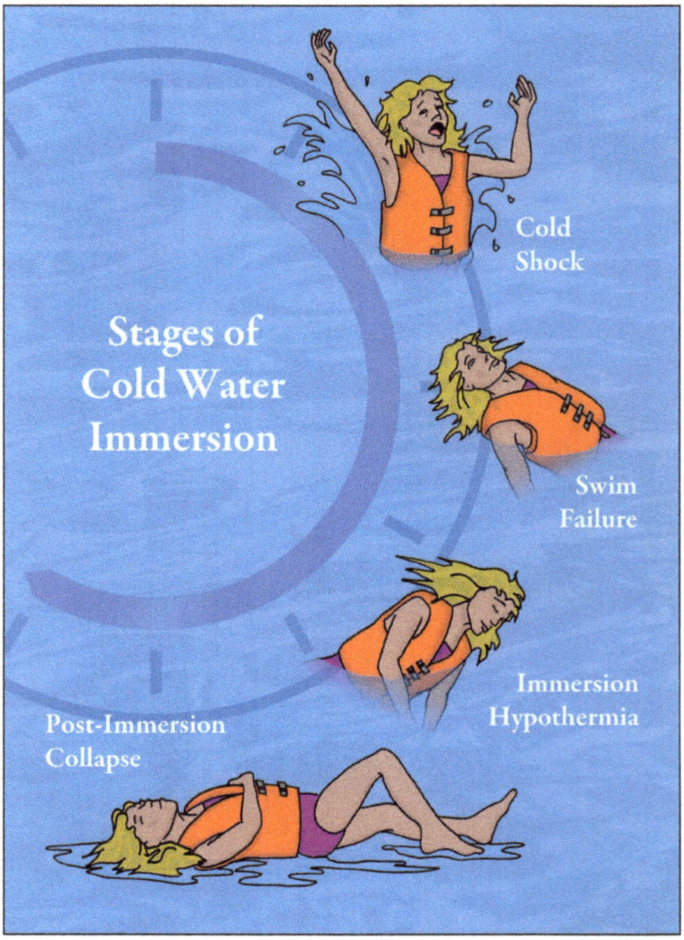

Figure 2.52 Stages of cold water immersion.

Stage 2—Swim failure: Up to 30 minutes after immersion, the muscles in the arms and legs start to lose dexterity and strength, making it difficult to swim or pull oneself out of the water. Death occurs by drowning.

Stage 3—Immersion hypothermia: After 30 minutes of submersion, the body is robbed of body heat and the victim becomes hypothermic because the body is losing heat faster than it can produce it. Severe hypothermia leads to unconsciousness and death, with or without drowning.

Stage 4—Postimmersion collapse: After a person is pulled from cold water, he or she is still in danger due to a change in blood pressure and heart rhythm. Heart complications result when cold blood is released from the extremities into the core of the body.

New York has become the first state to require life jackets to be worn by everyone in small boats for the coldest half of the year. More boating accidents happen in the summer months, yet the death rate increases drastically in colder weather, from 8% nationally to 25% in November for the year 2008. A person falling into cold water may experience shock as well

Table 2.4 Survival Times for Immersion in Cold Water

Water Temperature in Degrees Fahrenheit	Exhaustion/Unconsciousness	Survival Time
32.5	Under 15 minutes	15–45 minutes
32.5–40	15–30 minutes	30–90 minutes
40–50	30–60 minutes	1–3 hours
50–60	1–2 hours	1–6 hours
60–70	2–7 hours	2–40 hours
70–80	2–12 hours	3 hours to indefinitely

Source: ODNR Watercraft Safe Boating Course, Ohio Department of Natural Resources, Division of Watercraft, Columbus, Ohio.

as a cold water gasping reflex, causing the swimmer to suddenly inhale water. Immersion in water that is colder than 40°F can lead to hypothermia and unconsciousness in roughly 15 minutes. Colder weather is also responsible for fewer boaters on the water, which may have been able to render assistance to immersed boaters.

As of November 1, 2009, all boaters in a vessel less than 21 feet in length must wear a U.S. Coast Guard–approved life jacket while on New York's coastal waters, lakes, rivers, and other waterways. They must also be worn by anyone being towed, such as a water skier or tuber, and by all riders of a personal watercraft. The rule will remain in effect until May 1 of each year.[27] Table 2.4 shows the survival time for a victim suddenly immersed in cold water.

Alcohol

Alcohol intensifies the effects of wind, heat, boat motion, and fatigue, which adversely affects balance, judgment, and reaction time. These stressors weaken the body, making the chance of an accident much greater. Sitting in the sun increases your body heat, and this in turn causes sweating. As a person rides in a boat, his or her body constantly adjusts to the position of the boat. This constant adjustment increases body heat and fatigue. Sweating and alcohol consumption cause severe dehydration. Dehydration causes fatigue, irritability, headaches, and sleepiness. All these factors increase the risk of an accident. Research has proven that one-third of the amount of alcohol it takes to make a person legally intoxicated on land can make a boater equally impaired on the water. Alcohol use impairs judgment and slows reaction time. Most people can become impaired with only one drink. It makes it difficult for the operator to pay attention and perform simple tasks, such as keeping track of other vessels operating in the immediate area. In emergency situations, this can be critical if the operator is forced to make an immediate decision. For these reasons, alcohol consumption while boating significantly increases the likelihood of accidents. Table 2.5 shows areas of impairment due to varying blood alcohol concentration (BAC) while boating.

Alcohol use also contributes to one-third of all fatal boating accidents nationwide. The statistics for alcohol-related boating fatalities are believed to be lower than the actual amount for several reasons. Offenders are reluctant to report alcohol use in fear of retribution. Reporting may also be delayed for up to 12 hours to allow the offender to sober up before reporting the accident. A delay in the recovery of the decedent also allows the

Table 2.5 Areas of Impairment

Blood Alcohol Concentration (BAC)	Type of Impairment
0.01–0.02	Divided attention, reaction time, and visual function
0.03–0.04	Eye movement control, steadiness, and emergency response
0.05–0.08	Information processing and judgment
Over 0.08	Concentrated attention and speed control
0.09 and higher	Total impairment of motor skills

Source: ODNR, Division of Watercraft, Safe Boating Course, Ohio Department of Natural Resources, Division of Watercraft, Columbus, Ohio.

effects of decomposition to render the interpretation of the blood alcohol concentration and degree of impairment at the time of the accident invalid. The following accidents are representative of typical alcohol-related boating accidents:

- Two vessels were traveling toward each other on a narrow waterway and met at a blind curve. One operator attempted to cut the corner, placing him on the wrong side of the channel and in the path of the oncoming vessel, causing a collision. Both occupants of the second vessel were killed on impact. The first vessel operator's blood alcohol level was 0.05%.
- A victim fell overboard attempting to do a headstand on the bow of a vessel while it was under way. The victim was the original operator of the vessel and had been relieved of command due to his intoxication. The others on board attempted to stop the victim from falling overboard, but failed. The victim fell off the bow and was run over by the boat and struck by the propeller. His blood alcohol level was 0.12%. The victim was not wearing a life jacket and may have survived his injuries if he had been wearing one.

- Several vessels were tied together in a raft-up. The victim was stepping from the swim platform of one vessel to the swim platform of the other when he lost his balance and fell into the water. He was intoxicated, was not wearing a life jacket, and drowned. His blood alcohol level was 0.20%.
- Two motorboat operators were racing each other. The operator of the first vessel was slightly ahead and pulled in front of the second vessel, causing a collision. The impact killed the operator of the first vessel. His blood alcohol level was 0.05%, and the operator of the second vessel had a blood alcohol level of 0.09%.
- June 10, 2006, two passengers in a 24-foot cabin cruiser lost their lives when the boat collided with a concrete bridge abutment in the dark. The vessel then veered toward shore and ran aground. Blunt force trauma from the collision with the bridge abutment was responsible for the death of one passenger, while the other was thrown overboard and drowned. Alcohol was a major factor in this accident. One body was still on board when the vessel was discovered the next morning on shore. The body of the victim that was thrown overboard was recovered four days later. The boat operator was not seriously injured and left the scene of the accident without reporting it.[28]

Drug Use, to Include Illegal/Illicit Drugs and Prescription Drugs for Sedation, Anxiety, Sleep, Pain, etc.

Drug use may also play a role in a boating fatality. Similar to alcohol, the effect of a given drug level on behavior and motor skills in one person may be different in another. According to the Ohio Revised Code Statute 1547.11, in regard to illegal drug use, an operator can be charged with operating under the influence of a controlled substance if the following restrictions of nanograms per milliliter of the person's whole blood are found:

- At least 500 nanograms of amphetamine
- At least 150 nanograms of cocaine
- At least 50 nanograms of cocaine metabolite
- At least 50 nanograms of heroin
- At least 10 nanograms of heroin metabolite
- At least 10 nanograms of LSD
- At least 2 nanograms of marijuana

Many times, it cannot be determined whether or not drugs affected the operator's abilities, since only the inactive breakdown products may be detectable, and therefore the level of impairment cannot be assessed. This sometimes makes the evaluation of drug-related accidents difficult to determine.

Causes of Injury to PWC Operators

Injuries sustained while operating a personal watercraft are complicated because the operator is in an exposed position, sitting on the craft rather than confined in the vessel. Most of these accidents are attributed to operator inexperience and the fact that a PWC operator has no control over the vessel when the throttle is not activated. The natural reaction for an operator about to strike another vessel is to release the throttle. The majority of PWC accidents involve two vessels striking each other, and studies show that in the majority of these accidents, the operators know each other and are riding together. PWC accidents involve two distinct types of activity. This includes following each other, often at too close of a proximity to one another, and operators making radical movements, such as donuts, playing chicken, or most often attempting to spray each other. Consider these accidents:

- The operator of a PWC was attempting to spray his mother, who was sitting on the beach, but he lost control of the vessel and struck her instead. The blunt force impact broke all her ribs on one side of her body and caused severe internal injuries, which led to her death.
- A first-time PWC operator was approaching the shore and was unable to maneuver since she had let go of the throttle and lost her steering capability. She grounded the vessel and was thrown into the water. The fall rendered her unconscious but her life jacket kept her afloat.
- An 18-year-old woman lost her life when the motorboat in which she was a passenger turned into the path of a 10-foot personal watercraft, causing a collision. The operator of the PWC was unable to take evasive action and struck the motorboat amidships on the port side. The point of impact was the seating location of the victim. The operators of the PWC and motorboat were not injured.

Most fatal boating accidents could have been prevented. Even accidents related to the environment could have been prevented if the operator recognized the warning signs, had not made poor decisions, or had proper boating knowledge and skills. Many accidents involving equipment failure could also have been prevented if proper maintenance had taken place. Thus, in virtually every boating accident, operator error is the ultimate reason for the accident.

Vessel Examination

The investigator must take the time to do a thorough examination of the vessels involved in a fatal boating accident. The omission of any one piece of evidence could be a crucial error in determining the cause of the accident, position of operators or passengers, and wound patterns.

The first observation should be to determine any evidence of contact. This contact may have been from vessel to vessel or from vessel to victim. Evidence of contact would utilize the theory of transfer, which states that any time objects come in contact with one another, material from one object will be found adhering to the other object. For example, if a red boat and blue boat collide, the red boat will have blue paint transfer marks and the blue boat will have red paint transfer marks. Paint transfer is a reliable indicator of point of contact. Some examples of material transfer may include:

- Human tissue
- Blood
- Hair
- Paint
- Skin

Next, the investigator should document damage patterns. Damage will help to determine the direction of travel of the vessels involved, approximate speed, and proximity to other vessels or persons in the water. Damage patterns, coupled with material transfer and body injuries, will assist the investigator in determining who was operating the vessel as well as the location and position of passengers. Some examples of damage patterns may include:

- Ripping, gouging, and tearing of metal or fiberglass
- Propeller damage
- Imprints or marks made by housings and rub rails
- Needle slap viewed under ultraviolet light; the soft metal backing of the speedometer will be damaged by the speedometer needle slapping the metal upon impact. This is a reliable indicator of speed at impact

After these observations, the investigator should check the vessel for proper operation as well as any malfunctioning controls that may have contributed to the accident. Before any controls are altered, photographs should be taken to document the condition and position found. Observe the steering mechanism of the vessel. Document in notes and photograph the steering wheel or rudder position, out drive and trim position, and trim tabs. Document the position first and then check these for proper function.

Photographs and documentation of the gear shift should also be done. Document the position of the throttle. Many vessels have two throttles side by side that operate dual engines. On occasion, the accidental force from the side may cause the throttles to obscure the paths of each other. This may cause the operator to inadvertently throttle up both engines when the intention is to only throttle one engine. This can become a major factor in the cause of an accident because many of these dual-engine vessels are steered by altering the power in the engines rather than using the steering mechanism.

It is best to document all these observations with both notes and photographs. Photographs prevent any chance of error or debate as to how the evidence was found. Photographs to be taken should include:

- Position of controls, switches, and key safety devices.
- A view from the helm (side), which may indicate a possible obstructed view of the operator.
- Any mechanical failures or defects.
- Interior contact points where blood, hair, tissue, clothing marks, or deposits are found.
- Damage to the windshield.
- Photograph injury patterns on the victims. Injury patterns and interior contact points will assist in determining where the occupant was at the time of impact and who was driving, and are important for accident reconstruction.

For body photographs, take a photo of the gross (overall) condition of the body, any external injuries, and injury patterns. The investigator should also try to photograph any sunken objects from the surface, if water clarity and depth permit the taking of such a photograph. In cases of deeper water or poor water clarity, evidence can be marked utilizing floats and photographing the floats on the surface. Then notes can explain what the floats represent. This allows the investigator to document the location of specific items for accident reconstruction as well as court presentation. An aerial view of the crash site may also prove helpful in documenting nearby land, navigation aids, and other objects that may be relative to the area. Although current aerial photographs are best, some agencies do not have access to aircraft to take these photos. Some alternatives may be the assistance of neighboring agencies, such as the local sheriff's office or the highway patrol. Aerial photos are also available on the Internet from websites such as www.googleearth.com, although these are only updated in two- to three-month increments.

Another important factor to consider in a boating fatality is carbon monoxide poisoning. Carbon monoxide is an invisible, odorless, tasteless gas that is produced when a carbon-based fuel burns. It can make one sick in seconds, and in high concentrations, it can kill a person in just a few breaths. Check vessel ports to make sure they are clear and free of obstructions that may hinder venting of fumes. Sources of carbon monoxide on a boat may include gasoline engines, heaters, stoves, and generators. Early symptoms of carbon monoxide poisoning include eye irritation, dizziness, nausea, headache, and weakness. Interviews with fellow boaters may determine that the decedent was complaining of these symptoms.

Common Causes of Carbon Monoxide Poisoning While Boating

1. **Swimming under swim deck.** Many vessels have an attached swim platform along the stern of the vessel, near the engine exhaust. The platform concentrates the fumes put off from the gasoline engine and prevents them from being blown free

of the vessel. Swimmers who swim underneath these platforms can breathe high concentrations of carbon monoxide fumes, which can be fatal.

2. **Blocked exhaust outlets.** Care must be taken to ensure that exhaust outlets are free from obstructions that can block them, causing carbon monoxide fumes to accumulate in the cabin or cockpit area.
3. **Another vessel alongside.** Other vessels in the immediate vicinity can produce fumes that can accumulate in the cabin of a vessel. Vessels with running engines should maintain a minimum distance of 20 feet to prevent this from occurring.
4. **Teak surfing.** Swimmers must avoid holding on to a swim platform while a vessel is under way. Vessels that are dragging a swimmer in this fashion, or water skiers less than 20 feet from a vessel, can expose users to carbon monoxide poisoning. If swimmers are utilizing a swim platform, all gasoline engines must be off.
5. **Slow speeds.** Vessels operating at a slow speed or idling for long periods of time can cause carbon monoxide fumes to enter the cabin areas of the vessel.

Mammalian Dive Reflex/Cold Water Near Drowning

On June 10, 1986, Michelle Funk, a 2 ½-year-old, was submerged in an icy creek near Salt Lake City for 66 minutes. When rescuers finally pulled her from the water, her body was cold and blue and she had no pulse and was not breathing. Rescuers began CPR and continued it during her life flight to the hospital. Her body was gradually warmed with warm air and fluids. When she arrived at the hospital, her body temperature was 66°F. Factors that encouraged doctors to continue life-saving efforts was her lack of any physical injuries, coupled with the fact that oxygen levels and other gases within her blood were good, considering the circumstances. Two months after the accident, she was talking and had normal motor skills except for a slight tremor in her hands, which gradually disappeared (see Appendix F).

Many would ask, "How was this possible?" that a child could go without oxygen to the brain for an extended period of time and have a full recovery without any brain damage? The answer is Mammalian Dive Reflex, also known as the diving response. This phenomenon is found in aquatic mammals such as dolphins, muskrats, seals, and otters. It is triggered by chilling and wetting the nostrils while breath holding.

Mammalian Dive Reflex is a set of physiological responses to immersion that overrides the basic response to stimulus found in all air-breathing vertebrates. Cold water slows the heartbeat, stops breathing, and redistributes blood flow to organs that need blood and oxygen (heart, lungs, brain). The cold temperature reduces the brain's need for oxygen and allows survival longer without air. This optimizes respiration by distributing oxygen reserves to the heart and brain, enabling submersion for long periods of time. To increase the chances of reviving the victim, quick and continued resuscitation efforts are required, even starting CPR while still in the water. Rescue efforts must include aggressive CPR, water removal from the lungs, and slow rewarming of the body (rewarming too quickly can cause shock and heart issues). Once at the hospital, heated humidified oxygen is administered to rewarm the lungs and heart. This will cause the blood to circulate more normal, causing the body to generate its own heat. This rewarming process will take one to three hours.

Resuscitation efforts should last long enough to rewarm the body to normal temperature. If there is still no response, rescue efforts cease.

Factors affecting survival:

- Length of submersion
- Water temperature
- Victim age
- How quick and effective rescue efforts are done

Cleaner water is optimal. Muddy water has poorer results as water impurities are introduced into their system. Younger aged victims mean better survival rate as they are more capable of surviving low oxygen periods and their bodies cool quicker. The colder the water, the better chance of survival. Victims don't do well in water warmer than 70°F. Recovery of victims from water colder than 70°F within an hour, the survival potential is good assuming they don't have life-threatening injuries.

It is maintained by the neural processing via the carotid chemoreceptors.

The most obvious effects are on the cardiovascular system, which displays peripheral vasoconstriction, slowed heart rate, redistributed blood to vital organs, release of red blood cells stored in the spleen and in humans, heart rhythm irregularities.

Environmental Considerations

Water is one of our most powerful natural resources. Even water with a minimal current has an incredible and relentless power to cause damage to virtually everything it comes in contact with. Add a submerged or floating body to the equation and the result can be catastrophic. Moving water pushes against objects continuously, causing endless amounts of damage that have the potential of being interpreted erroneously. It is important for the investigator to be familiar with the varying types of environmental conditions that may cause postmortem injuries to submerged bodies. This will allow a more accurate on-scene assessment of the recovery location, which could possibly help explain injuries to the decedent's body.

Low-Head Dams Commonly referred to as "the drowning machine," a low-head dam to the untrained eye can appear quite harmless, especially when viewed from a boat upstream, but the hidden dangers of the hydraulic can hold persons in the boil of the dam for extended periods of time, and rescuers may fall victim to the powerful hydraulic pull as well.

CASE STUDY

September 1975 in Binghamton, New York, three firefighters drowned during an unsuccessful rescue attempt, and three others narrowly escaped the dangerous hydraulic of a low-head dam.

Low-head dams are not really dams at all. They are usually no more than 10 feet in height and allow water to flow over them rather than holding water back. They were originally built to provide water for grain mills and early hydraulic generators, and to control lake levels. The flow of water over the top creates a hydraulic pull upstream, which can hold bodies and even quite large objects like boats and whole trees against the uniform surface of the dam. The water flowing over the dam creates a void called a trough that must

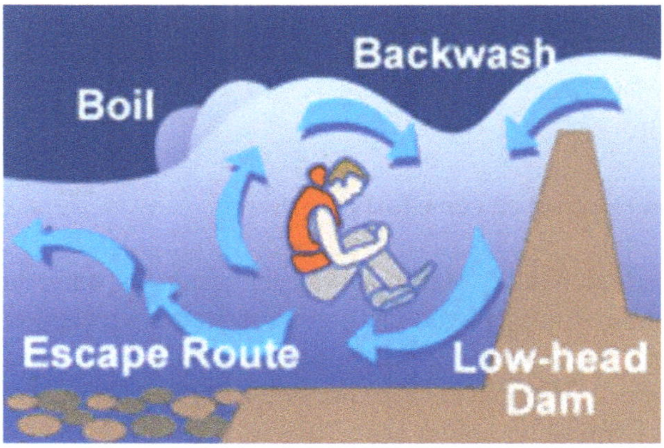

Figure 2.53 Low-head dam diagram showing dangerous hydraulic that traps victims against the foot of the dam.

be filled. Water downstream from the dam is pulled upstream to fill the void. If viewed from the side, a person can see that the water downstream from the dam is actually moving upstream, trapping any object in the boil. This boil recirculates the water at the base of the dam in a circular motion (Figure 2.53), which constantly churns objects over and over. This recirculating current traps bodies and debris against the face of the dam, pushes them underwater, and then upon surfacing, draws them back toward the dam. Air bubbles mixing in the water drastically decrease its buoyancy, making swimming impossible and staying afloat extremely difficult, even with a life jacket on. The sides of the dam are usually blocked by sheer concrete walls and debris preventing any chance for escape. Exposed rebar, concrete, and rock can cause massive lacerations and abrasive wounds to the surface of the skin.

Strainers A strainer is something on the surface of the water that allows water to pass through it but not solid objects, like boats and people. Strainers are likely to consist of fallen trees, old fencing, guardrails, or other debris hung up along a river. The force of the current holds objects against the strainer or may even force objects under water. Strainers will hinder postmortem wandering of a body and have been known to trap bodies and hold them stationary for weeks (Figures 2.54 and 2.55).

CASE STUDY

A woman lost her life when the 12-foot kayak she was paddling with her husband capsized. The couple had attempted the rain-swollen creek, which was about 1 foot above normal, 62°F (17°C), and muddy. Both paddlers were experienced boaters and good swimmers. Both were wearing life jackets and had taken a safe boating course. After launching, they floated ¼ mile downstream when they went sideways in a riffle above a large sycamore tree that had fallen across the creek channel. They capsized and floated into the tree feet first. The husband managed to grab hold and pull himself up. The victim disappeared under the log strainer and did not resurface. After several attempts to find his wife, the survivor forded across the stream, ran to a roadway, and called for help. Rescue personnel recovered his wife's body approximately six hours later. The coroner ruled her death an accidental drowning.[29]

Figure 2.54 Natural strainer in moving water.

Figure 2.55 Man-made strainer in moving water.

Natural Hydraulics

Much the same principle as a low-head dam, a natural hydraulic is comprised of a large submerged boulder in a swift current. Water flowing over the boulder on the surface creates a recirculating current as the water plunges behind it and then flows back upstream. This water is extremely aerated and will appear white and foamy from the constant churning of the water. This hydraulic may trap objects for extended periods of time.

Boulders and Debris Submerged boulders and debris can be struck by a floating body, causing lacerations, abrasions, and even broken bones. Undercut rocks, which have an underside void, can hold bodies that have been forced under water by strong currents for extended periods of time, sometimes weeks. (Figure 2.56).

Bridge Abutments Bridge abutments are often the site of collected debris that may accumulate and form strainers. During flood conditions, larger debris such as whole trees may hang up and form a dam that holds back large quantities of water and other debris, including bodies. Abandoned structures near rivers, such as old bridges and mills, are seldom destroyed. Concrete structures may crumble and wash away, leaving exposed rebar and reinforcements. These submerged obstacles may be difficult to detect from the surface, yet submerged bodies may hang up on them or become impaled. These dams may limit or hinder postmortem wandering and hold bodies until another flood situation arises to build up enough force to break the dam free. Postmortem injuries may include lacerations, punctures, or evidence of impalement (Figure 2.57).

Floodwaters Following storms and heavy rain, rivers often reach the flood stage, which causes a normally flowing river to peak above its banks. As the river level rises, the water picks up debris from the riverbanks. The water occupies floodplains and flows through trees, brush, and fences, creating a strainer-like hazard. Floodwaters create faster-flowing currents, which may cause bodies to strike objects at an incredible force, causing multiple postmortem injuries, including broken bones. If a river seems to have more floating debris than usual, this is an indication the river level is rising.

Figure 2.56 Photo of undercut rock.

Figure 2.57 Bridge abutment where bodies can get trapped in debris.

Ice There is a potential for ice to abrade and fracture skeletal remains and bones as well as crushing or tearing flesh. Bones may be frozen and compressed within the ice, ground between blocks of ice and debris, or simply crushed between ice floes as they break up and pound together during warm spells or spring thaw.

Vegetation Vegetation such as various aquatic plants like seaweed may impede the downstream progression of a body or its parts. This delay may contribute to the disarticulation of the body, causing portions of the remains to drop off at varying rates and locations. The head and hands are most likely to disarticulate from the body early during decomposition, with the cranium losing the mandible and hyoid bone in the process. Body parts resting at the bottom of a deep channel and covered with adipocere will disarticulate and abrade at different rates than a body sweeping downstream or drying in the sun on land.

Vertical Drops and Waterfalls Most people are surprised to learn just how calm the area below a waterfall can be. Contrary to the strong currents observed on the surface, the deep pools below offer a calm and still area where debris and bodies may collect. As with bodies located within a current, the body will remain stationary until refloat begins. In areas near-vertical drops in a river or waterfalls, large boulders and undercut rocks are usually plentiful, where bodies can be trapped. While entrapped in the strong current, it is not uncommon for the water to remove clothing from the body. If the body has plunged over a vertical drop or waterfall, massive internal injuries may be present, such as skull fractures, multiple broken bones, and ruptured internal organs. Because the water on the surface is white and foamy from extreme aeration, locating the body may be severely hampered (Figure 2.58).

Current and Wave Action As refloat begins, the body begins to gain buoyancy due to gas buildup within the body cavities, organs, and soft tissues, and travels along the bottom of the waterway. This travel will be greatly accelerated if a current or wave action is present. In most cases, postmortem injuries will only be superficial scrapes and scratches, referred to

Figure 2.58 Vertical drops may cause postmortem wounding and even broken bones.

as travel abrasions. If the current is fast moving, there may be broken bones from the body striking solid, immovable objects such as rocks, bridge pilings, or other debris.

High and Low Tide Tide can have an adverse effect on witness accounts as it pertains to the last seen point of the victim. Interviews of any potential witnesses should take place during the same time of day that the incident occurred. This will allow the witness a direct correlation as to the distance from shore the victim was last seen. Tidal information can be found at www.freetidetables.com. This site offers searches by state, region, and tide station, as well as maps and satellite imaging. If a drowning occurred during high tide, it may be possible to locate the body during low tide without the need for divers.

Chemicals and Pathogens Contaminants or water pollutants come in three basic forms. They are biological, chemical, and nuclear. Each one of these has the potential to seriously injure or kill a person. Since this topic is quite extensive, only a general overview will be provided to stress the importance of exercising caution in each of these environments.

Natural bodies of water that appear perfectly clean may contain millions of life-threatening biological contaminants referred to as pathogens. For instance, a very dangerous bacterium known as *Vibrio cholerae* is prominent in the lakes of Colorado, which leads to severe diarrhea, causing the victim to lose 10–15 liters of fluid per day. Death occurs in up to 60% of untreated cases. One of the most common ways for these harmful bacteria to be introduced into our waterways is through the dumping of raw sewage. The bacterium contained in this sewage is called *Escherichia coli*, which is found in human feces.

Certain chemicals, such as acids, may cause severe and immediate injury to the body, while others may have no external effect but can cause internal injury, paralysis, or death. Many flammable liquids are considered carcinogens (cancer-causing agents). Other chemicals, such as formaldehyde in high concentrations (50–100 ppm), can cause inflammation of the lungs and death. Most people are familiar with the rotten-egg smell of sulfur-containing gases, but what they don't know is that it is extremely toxic. Hydrogen sulfide is an asphyxiant that paralyzes the nerves in the brain that control the sense of smell, and with continued high-level exposure, one becomes unable to detect this gas by smell.

Toxic chemicals and pathogens may complicate the drowning process as well as pose a threat to any rescue personnel involved. During Hurricane Katrina, waterborne bacteria were circulating in the floodwaters, causing five deaths from diseased water. The deaths were caused by *Vibrio vulnificus*, bacteria common in warm Gulf water, which is usually spread by eating contaminated food, but can penetrate open wounds as well. Rescue personnel need to be aware of these hazards and exercise extreme caution by wearing appropriate protective gear.[30]

Most sources of nuclear pollutants are in the form of radiation, which enters the water through accidents at nuclear power plants and accidental or intentional dumping of nuclear waste.

For assistance in dealing with these polluted environments, the investigator can contact CHEMTREC, which stands for Chemical Transportation Emergency Center, located in Washington, D.C. CHEMTREC operates 24/7 and can be reached at 1-800-262-8200 or www.chemtrec.com.[23]

Electrical Hazards Electrical hazards in and around swimming areas, such as pools, hot tubs, and spas, can lead to multiple deaths or injuries. This occurs when one person becomes incapacitated by an electrical current in the water, and others jump into the water to save them, unaware of the hidden dangers, which results in multiple electrocutions. Hazards may exist with faulty underwater lighting, aging electrical wiring, the use of sump pumps, power washers and vacuums that are not grounded, electrical appliances such as televisions and radios, and extension cords falling into the water. All these hazards present an even greater risk if they are not protected with a ground fault circuit interrupter (GFCI), which is the best safety device to prevent electrocution (Figure 2.59). If a GFCI outlet is not installed, check the circuit box. Newer homes have a special GFCI circuit switch located inside the circuit box that responds in the same manner as the GFCI outlet. Both of these devices cut off the electrical current upon a circuit overload or short (Figure 2.60). Older facilities may be the greatest risk since they have underwater lighting fixtures that have degraded over time and have gone uninspected for years, as well as being installed before the existence of GFCI outlets.

Figure 2.59 Ground fault circuit interrupter (GFCI) outlet.

Figure 2.60 GFCI circuit switch in the breaker panel.

CASE STUDY

In May 2002, a 14-year-old girl from Arlington, Texas, was electrocuted as a result of wiring problems in an apartment swimming pool's underwater lights which caused the water to become charged with electricity. A 16-year-old boy was seriously shocked when he jumped into the pool to try to save her. Another teenager used a fiberglass shepherd's hook (a nonconductive material) to pull them both from the water.[31]

Other potential risks are overhead power lines, junction boxes, swimming during a thunderstorm, and outdoor receptacles. If electrocution is suspected, the investigator can conduct a test on the scene by doing the following:

- Plug a nightlight into the outlet and turn it on.
- Press the TEST button on the GFCI outlet. Did the light go out? If not, the GFCI outlet is faulty.
- Press the RESET button. Did the light come back on? If not, the GFCI outlet is faulty.

Wear rubber-soled shoes while conducting this test, especially if outdoors or standing on wet ground.

For assistance or information about electrical safety in and around pools, hot tubs, or spas, or to report a product-related injury, contact the U.S. Consumer Product Safety Commission (CPSC) at 1-800-638-2772 or www.cpsc.gov.

Pool Drains An issue gaining more attention regarding public swimming pools is the dangers of defective swimming pool drains. Since 1980, dozens of children between the ages of two and fourteen have been seriously injured or died due to body part entrapment involving the drains of swimming pools, wading pools, or spas. Under normal operation, pipes leading from pool drains to pumps carry water from the pool, creating suction. If the drain becomes blocked, the pressure increases as the pump draws water from around the obstruction. This increased suction can entrap parts of a person's body, including hair, clothing, and jewelry, causing the person to be held underwater until the suction is relieved by turning off the pump. In deep water, this entrapment can lead to drowning since the victim cannot free him- or herself from the powerful suction. In shallower water, such as a wading pool, if the drain is obstructed by having a child sit on it, the suction can cause disembowelment.

CASE STUDY

In Minnesota, a six-year-old girl suffered a terrible injury when she sat on a pool drain, causing an intense suction that ruptured her rectum and sucked out most of her intestines. She was at a golf club with her family, using the wading pool. When she got out of the wading pool, she walked several feet then collapsed. Because external injuries were not apparent, it was first believed that she was suffering from a heat stroke. It was not until later that it was discovered that the suction created a 2-inch tear in her rectum, through which a large portion of her intestines was sucked into the drain. A search of the pool drain revealed her intestines. Surgeons were amazed that the girl survived the ordeal, yet she would be required to be fed intravenously and wear a colostomy bag for the rest of her life. A search of the pool area revealed a missing pool drain cover. The girl died the following year.

A bill was introduced into legislation in 2007 that requires all pool drains to have a sensor installed that would release suction in the event the drain becomes blocked.[25] Approved drain covers have features such as scalloped edges that decrease suction, or smooth edges that allow hair to be pulled out easily. The federal regulation reads as follows:

a) Consumer Product Safety Rule—The requirements described in subsection (b) shall be treated as a consumer product safety rule issued by the Consumer Product Safety Commission under the Consumer Product Safety Act (15 U.S.C. 2051 et seq.).
b) Drain Cover Standard—Effective one year after the date of enactment of this title, each swimming pool or spa drain cover manufactured, distributed, or entered

> into commerce in the United States shall conform to the entrapment protection standards of the ASME/ANSI A112.19.8 performance standard, or any successor standard regulating such swimming pool or drain cover.

In short, all public pools and spas were required to comply by December 19, 2008, by installing drain covers that have an antientrapment system such as the Safety Vacuum Release System (SVRS). Pools must install the device, which is automatically activated when a blockage is detected.[32,33]

The VGB Act is named after Virginia Graeme Baker, granddaughter of former secretary of state James A. Baker III. In 2002, Virginia Baker, at the age of seven, died in a spa after the powerful suction of a drain entrapped her underwater. The Bakers joined Safe Kids USA in a three-year campaign for this legislation.

References

1. Hendrick, W., and Zafares, A. 1998. *Homicide by drowning manual.* Hurley, NY: Lifeguard Systems.
2. Geberth, V. 1996. *Practical homicide investigation: Tactics, procedures and forensic techniques.* 3rd ed. Boca Raton, FL: CRC Press.
3. Erskine, K. 2003. *Devil's triangle: A guide to drownproofing divers.* West Conshohocken, PA: Infinity Publishing.
4. *Forbes* Magazine, April 7, 2014, Kashnir Hill.
5. NAPSG Foundation, 5335 Wisconsin Ave., suite 440, Washington, DC, 20015.
6. Drone, D. J. December 10, 2018.
7. The Austin Chronicle, November 23, 2018.
8. Anthropological Research Facility at the University of Tennessee, Knoxville, Galloway et al., 1989.
9. AeroWorks Academy, Professional UAS Training, Somers, Wisconsin, USA, Adam Andrews. S.W.A.R.M. Network.
10. Deep Trekker, Inc., 830 Trillium Dr., Kitchener, Ontario, Canada N2R1K4.
11. Beaver County Times. "Police Lose Sight of Body in Ohio River, Drone Shows Distinctive Features of Remains" article, November 2017.
12. http://www.dispatch.com/.../sonar.ART_ART_07-05-07_B1_3577443.html (accessed October 19, 2009).
13. http://gralston1.home.mindspring.com/lakecumberland.html (accessed October 19, 2009).
14. http://www.startribune.com/local/35830499.html?elr...DW3ckUiD3aPc (accessed May 16, 2009).
15. Haglund, W. 1997. *Forensic taphonomy.* Boca Raton, FL: CRC Press.
16. Teather, R. 1994. *Encyclopedia of underwater investigations.* Flagstaff, AZ: Best Publishing.
17. http://crime.about.com/od/murder/a/susan_smith_3.htm. (accessed January 25, 2010).
18. Donohue, W. A. 1993. Michigan State Police, operation star: Submerged transportation accident research. *Searchlines* 10(1), January/February.
19. http://archpedi.highwire.org/cgi/content/summary/135/11/998 (accessed April 4, 2009).
20. Divers Alert Network. 1999. *DAN report on decompression illness and diving fatalities.* Durham, NC.
21. TRI Laboratory Director Edward Golla, PhD, CIH, TRI Air Testing, Inc.
22. Erskine, K. 2008. *Thrill and danger.* Baltimore, MD: Publish America.
23. Euclid, Ohio Police Department, September 2006.
24. http://www.azcentral.com/news/articles/2009/04/13/20090413ToddlerDrowns13-ON.html (accessed April 3, 2009).
25. http://www.menunderwater/uwgames.com (accessed April 3, 2009).

26. Sauvageau, A., and Racette, S. 2006. Aqua-eroticum: An unusual autoerotic fatality in a lake involving a home-made diving apparatus. *J Forensic Sci* 51(1): 137–39.
27. National Boating Fatalities Report. May 2003. Ottawa, ON, Canada: Lifesaving Society.
28. http://www.lifesaving.ca/content/english/pdf/2003-NatlBoatingRepFinal.pdf (accessed May 10, 2009).
29. Ray, S. 1997. *Swift water rescue*. Asheville, NC: CFS Press.
30. http://www.cdc.gov/ncbddd/hurricanes/environmental.htm (accessed May 19, 2009).
31. Barsky, S. 1993. *Diving in high risk environments*. Fort Collins, CO: Dive Rescue Intl.
32. http://www.cpsc.gov/cpscpub/prerel/prhtml03/03125.html (accessed May 19, 2009).
33. U.S. Government, Code of Federal Regulations, 16 CFR 1207.

On-Scene Body Assessment

3

KEVIN L. ERSKINE AND
ERICA J. ARMSTRONG

Introduction

The determination of the cause and manner of death in a water-related death presents many challenges, and surmounting those challenges requires collaboration between on-scene investigators and the pathologist. To aid the pathologist in this determination, all investigative information must be diligently documented. Due to the lack of specialized training for responding officers and investigators, much valuable information is not observed or recorded, which may lead all those involved in the investigation to an erroneous conclusion. Upon location or recovery of a body near or within a watery environment, and after medical and first responders have attempted resuscitation or determined that vital signs are absent, an on-scene assessment is mandatory. Protective examination gloves should be worn during the examination of the body, and care should be taken not to extensively disturb articles of clothing or other on-body artifacts and debris. This assessment must be done promptly and thoroughly since after-death changes of the body will progressively continue, potentially altering the interpretation of findings.

The most efficient procedure to document the findings of an on-scene body assessment is to use a standard body recovery checklist (Appendix C). This allows the investigator to record observations made during the assessment and accurately document injuries by using the appropriate supplement form. Each supplement provides a diagram of a specific body part to allow the investigator to draw injuries in the location in which they are found on the decedent. The investigator can then make notations beside the drawing to document specifics about that injury. For instance, if a laceration is observed on the forehead of the decedent, the investigator would use the "head and neck supplement" to draw the injury in its location. Notes would then be included to describe the appearance of the injury, such as "a laceration on the left side of the forehead with jagged edging; blood is absent and bruising surrounds the wound." The inclusion of precise measurements and enumeration of injuries is best left to the pathologist who will perform these as part of a complete autopsy. Approximation and general description with mention of any limitations to the examination are acceptable to include. This will minimize conflicts in interpretation, which may be created by discrepancies in measurements and enumerations and may become points of contention during trial preparation or court proceedings.

Postmortem Wandering

Prior to the assessment of a recovered body, it must first be located. The position of a body within a vast and deep waterway is dependent on not only topography but also a number of other factors. In freshwater, once the body has landed on the bottom, it will not move, even in a current, until refloat begins. With the passage of time and during the early stages of refloat, the body will travel along the bottom until it gains enough buoyancy to rise completely to the surface. This is due in large part to the gases formed within the body as a result of bacterial action within the body and will cause the body to resurface. The factors affecting refloat are:

- **Last meal:** Meals high in carbohydrates and carbonated beverages produce gases very quickly.
- **Temperature:** Bacterial action is increased in warmer temperatures, which will cause refloat sooner than in cooler water.
- **Water depth:** Greater depths affect both water temperature and compression of body tissue. In depths of 200 feet or greater, bodies may not refloat at all.
- **Body mass:** Bodies containing a higher quantity of body fat will refloat more quickly than leaner ones under similar conditions. This is due to greater buoyancy of body fat and the insulation effect of body fat, which contributes to more rapid putrefaction.
- **Health:** An individual with a bacterial infection, sepsis, or high fever prior to death will tend to decompose at a faster rate.

One might ask if it is possible to have a body that stays on the surface without sinking. In this instance, the body may stay at the surface if killed in another location, allowed to decompose (thus contributing to a faster refloat), and then dumped into a waterway. Air trapped within the lungs of an individual killed prior to submersion may also contribute to floating. A body within the saltwater will float at various depths, including near or on the surface, dependent upon the salinity of the water. Finally, clothing that allows the trapping of enough air will allow the body to float, and this scenario is particularly common in clothed infants.

General Body Assessment

After first noting and documenting the position of the body (i.e., supine, prone, fetal, on one side or the other, or even entrapped within a vessel or vehicle compartment), an on-scene body assessment is done by beginning at the head and checking all around the head, face, neck, behind the ears, and back of the head. Inspection of as much body surface area as possible should be done, from head to toe, right and left sides, and the back of the body, with the assistance of another to help roll the body for visualization of the back. Visualization of various body crevices can also be done, such as by lifting the arms to inspect the armpits, extension and turning of the neck, and parting of the legs to inspect the groin and genitalia. Clothing, debris, and the condition of the body may preclude complete visualization of all of the body surfaces, however. Determination and documentation of the body, hair, and any clothing or personal effects as wet, moist, dry, or soiled should also be done during the initial assessment. If the body is located within a vessel or vehicle, it may be transported in its entirety to the office of the coroner/medical examiner (C/ME); thus, on-scene body assessment may be further limited. The forensic scientist and pathologist will examine the entire body, including crevices and orifices before and during the autopsy, including after all clothing and debris have been removed. Additionally, if the body is received inside of a vehicle or vessel, it will be examined first as it is situated, prior to removal. When the assessment is done systematically, the investigator stands a much greater chance of conducting a thorough search. If done haphazardly, an important finding may be missed.

Diatoms are microscopic algae with a silica outer shell. They are found in soil, air, and natural and man-made bodies of water, and a given geographical location can give rise to its own signature mix of species. The identification of diatoms in human tissues has been used as supportive or definitive evidence of drowning and in pinpointing the geographical location in which the drowning event took place. When a body is recovered, it is recommended that the recovery divers obtain a water sample from the immediate area of recovery. This will aid the lab in establishing a diatom signature for the body of water, which can then be compared to diatoms extracted from the tissues and body fluids. Diatom testing is not widely available and is not routinely performed (or not performed at all) at C/ME offices, and samples may have to be sent to specialized reference laboratories for analysis utilizing the expertise of the forensic geologist.

CASE STUDY

In May 1996, the body of a woman was found in the Hudson River in Ulster County, New York. The autopsy findings revealed evidence of strangulation and drowning. A witness came forward with information stating he believed the drowning occurred in her bathtub. Police obtained water samples from the Hudson River and the decedent's bathtub and submitted them to the lab for diatom analysis. The diatoms found in the bathtub water did not match the diatoms found in the decedent. Diatoms found in the river did match those of the victim. When this information was presented to the "eyewitness," he recanted his original story and investigators were able to confirm her drowning occurred in the river and her live-in companion played a role in her death. Diatoms from the decedent and articles belonging to the accused and in the Hudson River led to a conviction of the suspect.

Ocular Changes

During interviewing and interrogation training, it has been said that a suspect will not look his or her interviewer in the eye because it is believed that "the eyes are the window to the soul" and they will reveal when someone is lying. The same holds true for a water-related death. Much information can be obtained by just looking into the eyes of the victim. Ocular changes are easy to identify and may immediately indicate foul play to the on-scene investigator.

To conduct an on-scene observation of each eye, the investigator must place an index finger on the upper eyelid and the thumb below the eye on the lower eyelid and spread the eye open, revealing the eyeball along with the **sclera** (plural form is *sclerae*), which is the white portion of the eye. The **conjunctiva** (plural form is *conjunctivae*) of each eye must also be inspected. This is the pink, glistening portion lining the inner upper and lower eyelids and the lower portion of the eyeballs. This lining can be examined by gently pulling forward and turning the upper and lower eyelids partially inside out. On decomposing bodies, the skin may be quite fragile and easily removed, even with gentle manipulation, and if this occurs, it should be documented and communicated to the C/ME death investigator or pathologist. Check both the sclerae and conjunctivae for **petechiae**. Petechiae (singular form is *petechia*) are hemorrhages that appear as multiple small, round, red or red-brown spots (Figure 3.1). They may be present elsewhere, such as the outer eyelids, forehead, cheeks, inner lips, neck, and other body regions. If the body was recovered in a sandy area and sand or other debris is present about the face and body crevices, it may be necessary to first flush the eyes with clean water, and if this is done, it must be recorded and directly communicated to the C/ME's death investigator or pathologist (Figure 3.2). This is required because small grains of sand or dirt in the eye may appear as petechiae, which may lead the investigator to an erroneous conclusion. Also take note of the position of the body when recovered, since an individual in a prone or partially prone position (with face down and slightly on one side) for an extended period of time may present with congestion of the sclera and conjunctivae accompanied by petechiae as a result of prolonged positioning. Petechiae (also referred to as petechial hemorrhages) are usually caused by increased pressure within the venous system, particularly the veins within the head and neck, from the larger jugular veins to the tiny veins and capillaries that drain the conjunctivae, and are prominent in certain types of asphyxial deaths.[1] This increased pressure can occur as a result of an outside compressive force placed on the face, neck, chest, or abdomen, causing obstruction of blood flow back to the heart, with engorgement of the veins above the level of the applied pressure, such as in homicidal ligature strangulation. The veins become engorged to the point of bursting, resulting in the spots you may observe. Pressure applied to the neck, specifically, may result in compression of not only the jugular veins but also the carotid arteries if enough force is applied. Compression of the carotid arteries restricts blood flow from the heart to the head and brain, which can cause fainting or death, but alone is not the direct cause of the petechiae.

Petechiae may be seen in other types of natural and non-natural deaths, including deaths from acute heart failure, seizures, bleeding disorders, bacterial infection, traumatic/mechanical asphyxia, suffocation, and carotid sleeper holds accompanied by struggle.

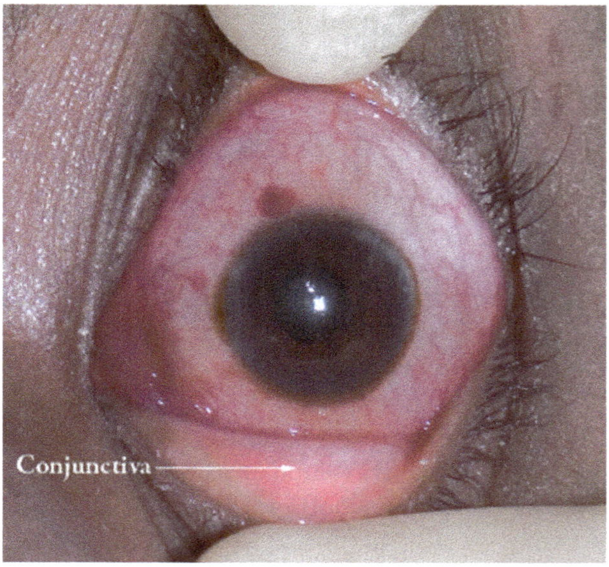

Figure 3.1 Petechiae with congestion of sclera.

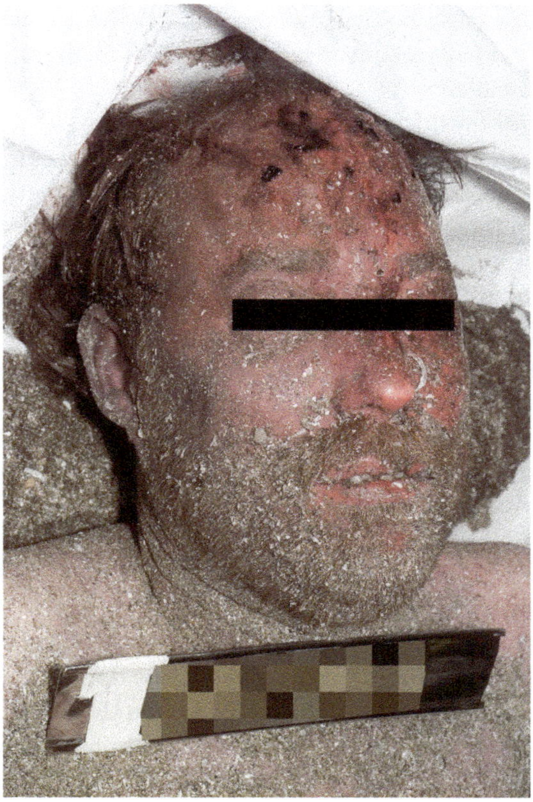

Figure 3.2 Adherent sand and other aquatic debris of face.

Petechial hemorrhages may also be noted in individuals after a violent episode of coughing. Deaths involving sudden cardiac or cardiorespiratory arrest in general, which may have a wide variety of natural and non-natural causes, may be accompanied by petechiae.

Petechial hemorrhages are seen in the majority of homicidal ligature strangulation and manual strangulation deaths and occasionally suicidal hangings, particularly in individuals who were partially suspended. The intermittent and variable compressive forces applied during homicidal ligature strangulation allow enough blood flow into the head via the carotid arteries but preclude adequate drainage of blood from the veins of the head, including those that drain the sclerae and conjunctivae, leading to engorgement and rupture of the veins with the formation of petechiae. Petechial hemorrhages are seen less frequently in suicidal hangings as the weight of the head against the ligature causes complete compression of the carotid arteries and jugular veins simultaneously. Thus, there is not enough increase in pressure to cause vessel engorgement, rupture, and petechiae.

Aggressive cardiopulmonary resuscitation (CPR) may also give rise to petechiae, including resuscitation of a drowning victim. This emphasizes the importance of inquiring and documenting whether or not CPR was performed upon rescue.

In light of all the potential causes, the discovery of petechiae during an on-scene body assessment may be a red flag indicator of foul play, which in turn may change the emphasis and direction of the investigation. It should be emphasized that the presence of petechiae is not *specific* for foul play, as there may be other causes. Furthermore, the absence of petechiae does not rule out foul play. To the careful observer, petechiae will be readily detectable on a fresh body. However, in an individual who has been dead for a prolonged period with evidence of advanced decomposition, detection of the same may be more difficult or not possible.

Next, the investigator must look for ***tache noire,*** which is an after-death (postmortem) artifact of drying of the sclera left exposed by partially opened eyes in a deceased individual. It is a French phrase translated as "black spot." Again, the investigator will spread open the eye with thumb and index finger and observe the sclera, cornea, and iris. The **cornea** is the transparent convex refractile structure that overlies the colored portion of the eye called the **iris,** which surrounds an opening to the eye called the **pupil.** Tache noire will appear as a horizontal red, brown, or black band across the sclera but will not be visible over the cornea/iris region (Figure 3.3). It begins to appear just after death as a band of red discoloration becoming darker (brown) and more fully developed by approximately two hours, with greater darkening (brown-black) beyond this time. If the eyes are wide open, the drying and discoloration will involve more of the scleral surface area. It should not be misinterpreted as an injury to the eye. Since it has permanency, once it is established, submersion in water will not cause it to disappear. In circumstances where bodies are found floating face down and unobstructed, tache noire should not be present. If there are obstructions such as logs and other moving or fixed large debris present at the recovery site or somewhere along the area traveled by the body, there may be explanations for the presence of the tache noire (i.e., a body with eyes partially opened that became entangled in a face-up unsubmerged position with exposure to air). On the contrary, if the body is found floating face down in the water and tache noire is present without evidence of obstruction or entanglement, this may be a red flag indicator of foul play since at some point after death, perhaps in another location/crime scene altogether, the eyeballs were exposed to air prior to being submerged.

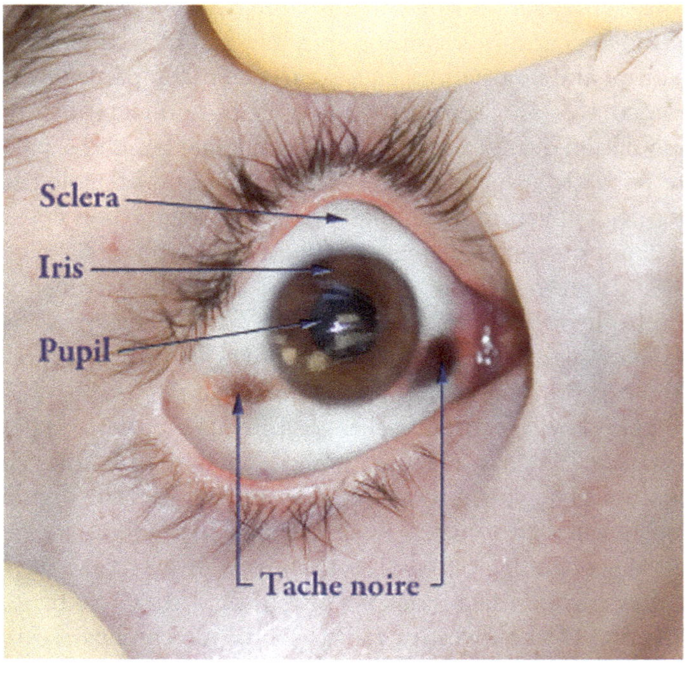

Figure 3.3 Tache noire.

CASE STUDY

The body of a 22-year-old female was recovered face down in a river. An on-scene body assessment revealed tache noire in both eyes. She was reported missing two days before by her mother. She had gone out that night to the local bar and never returned home. Many described her as an attractive girl who was very outdoorsy. She liked to take walks along the scenic river in which she was found. There had been some recent rainfall, which caused the river to rise, creating some rushing water. The temperature had been unseasonably warm all week. Bar patrons saw the local sex offender approach her in the bar, only to be turned away by her. Some bar patrons thought they saw him follow her out of the bar, but he maintains he is innocent after a lengthy interrogation. A river walk was conducted by the investigator, which revealed a large strainer along the route. There were many large tree branches caught up against some rocks in the river, which kept the branches pinned there even in the strong current. The investigation finally revealed that she had taken a walk along the river after leaving the bar and slipped into the rushing river, causing her to drown. Her body had been caught in the strainer, which held her against the rocks for two days, causing her eyes to be exposed to air. The incident was ruled an accident by the investigating agency.

Another ocular change is called **corneal opacity.** This change is not specifically related to or caused by exposure to air but is enhanced or accelerated by such exposure. On an individual who has died with the eyes open, a thin, whitish film will form over the surface of the cornea within minutes of death, and within two to three hours of death, corneal opacity will develop, giving the cornea a frosted glass appearance (Figure 3.4). If the individual dies with the eyes closed, the appearance of the corneal film will be delayed by several hours, and the appearance of the corneal opacity may be delayed over 24 hours.

Foam Column/Foam Cone

Another observation that will be more obvious to the investigator is the appearance of a white or pink foamy substance exuding from the mouth or nose, known as the **foam column** or **foam cone.** The foam is a mixture of water, air surfactant, blood proteins, and blood formed within the lungs, which may have a consistency of meringue. Even if not immediately apparent, it may become more noticeable upon moving the victim during recovery. This foam may be observed for some time after the body has been removed from the water. The presence of foam is not 100% specific for drowning and may be seen in other deaths, such as drug and prescription medication overdoses. An image of the foam cone appears in Figure 1.7.

Rigor Mortis (Rigidity)

Rigor mortis is caused by the irreversible locking together of the contractile proteins of the skeletal muscle cells as the biochemical energy needed for muscle contraction is depleted

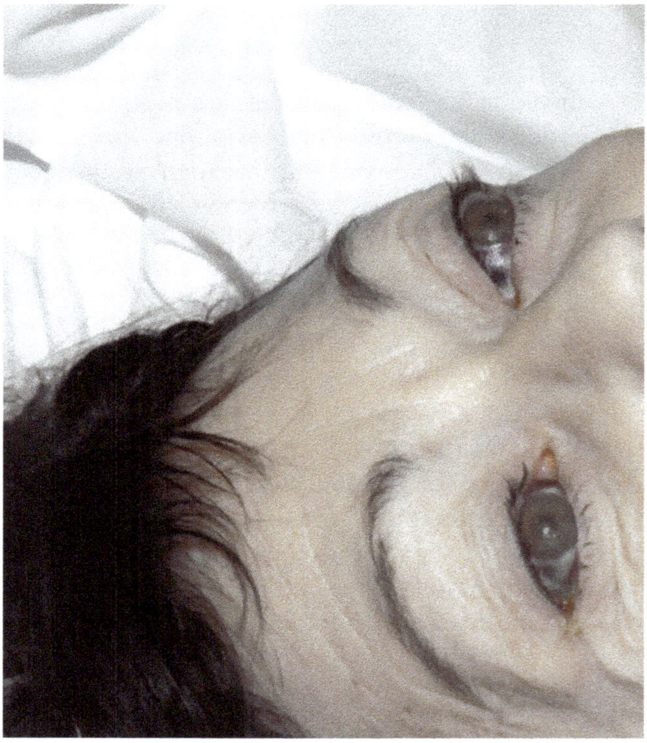

Figure 3.4 Corneal opacity.

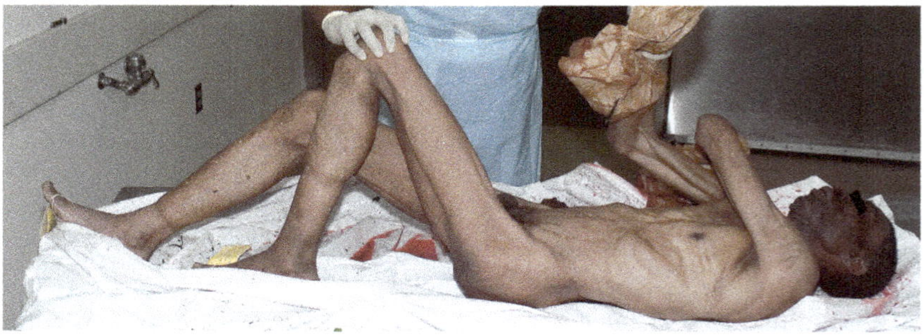

Figure 3.5 Rigor mortis of arms and legs.

upon death. This depletion causes the muscles of the limbs, jaw, and other regions to become "frozen" in the position the body was in at the time of death (Figure 3.5). After an initial brief flaccid period in which the limbs and jaw are easily and passively movable, rigor mortis will be noticeable as stiffening of the limbs and joints. In a temperate environment and in an individual of normal body habitus, it is noticeable within 30 minutes to 2 hours and becomes fully established by 6–12 hours. In an environment in which the entire body is exposed to a relatively constant and even temperature, it involves all of the skeletal muscles at the same time and at the same rate, but becomes more readily evident in the smaller muscles first (i.e., the muscles of the jaw) due to the lesser volume of tissue, followed by the larger muscles. It becomes less readily evident in the same order by 24–36 hours due to the disassociation of the contractile proteins with the onset of decomposition. By the time the rigor in the larger muscles (such as those of the thigh) is fully established, it may become less evident in the smaller muscles, which may seem flaccid, because the rigor is already starting to leave the body. Rigor mortis also occurs in the involuntary muscles, including the muscles of the hair follicles (**gooseflesh** or **cutis anserina**) and the seminal vesicles of the male reproductive system, causing the expulsion of semen, which may be visible as a whitish fluid on the thighs or as staining on adjacent clothing or undergarments. The pronounced patency of the anus resulting from loss of rigor of the anal sphincter muscles may be overinterpreted as anal penetration in relation to a sexual assault.

This finding must not automatically be considered a red flag indicator of foul play and must be interpreted within the context of the information garnered from the scene investigation and autopsy. Once rigor has passed, muscles lose their stiffness, which will not reform. This is sometimes referred to as **secondary flaccidity**. Frozen bodies in which the muscle tissues are also rendered stiff may be misinterpreted as having rigor mortis. Extreme heat may cause coagulation of the muscle protein with stiffening of the limbs, mimicking rigor mortis, such as in the case of an individual dying in a house fire in which the contact with heat and flames causes the limbs to retract into a boxer's stance or **pugilistic** position.

Several factors may hasten the onset of rigor, and these include:

- Excessive environmental heat
- Hyperthermia
- Disease or infection
- Violent struggling prior to death
- Seizures
- Poisoning

Factors known to slow the onset of rigor include cold environmental temperature and low muscle mass (elderly, infants/young children, and the debilitated).

Although not conclusive, the determination of the degree of rigor can aid in the approximation of the time of death. For example, if an investigator determines that the small muscles are flaccid (and thus the joints more easily movable) and larger muscles are in full rigor, this will indicate that the body has already fully established rigor and it is starting to leave the body. Remember, the rigor is more readily evident in the smaller muscles first, then the larger ones. Therefore, in this example, it can be opined that the individual has been dead for approximately 12–14 hours.

Rigor may also indicate body positioning at the time of death: a body in full rigor found supine on the ground with the limbs positioned as if the body had been sitting in a chair needs explanation as to how the body came to rest on the ground and the ruling out of foul play.

To record the degree of rigor, the investigator must physically manipulate the limbs around their corresponding joints to which the muscles are attached. If the muscles are in any degree of rigor, the extent to which the joints can be flexed, extended, or rotated will be limited. All joints should be *gently* manipulated to check for the degree of rigor. If forceful flexion and extension of the joints are applied, fully established rigor may be "broken," and upon manipulation by the next assessor (i.e., by the pathologist during the autopsy), the lessened or lack of appreciable rigor will result in misclassification as to the degree of the rigor. Rigor that has only partially developed may reform to an extent after manipulation has broken it. If the rigor is inadvertently broken, it should be noted in the investigator's report and verbally communicated to the C/ME or representative.

The small joints with their attached musculature are contained within or attached to the following anatomic structures, which can be assessed for degree of rigor:

- Jaw
- Hands/wrist/fingers
- Feet/ankles/toes
- Elbows
- Shoulders

The larger joints with their attached musculature are contained within or attached to the following anatomic structures, which can also be assessed for degree of rigor:

- Hips/thighs
- Knees
- Neck
- Arms at the shoulders

The degree of rigor for each region can be rated on a scale of 1–10, with 1 designating the rigor as absent, 5 as moderate, and 10 as fully established, and is based on the subjective observation of one observer's opinion and allows comparison between various muscle groups. The degree of rigor can be further or alternatively qualified using the following descriptors:

- Not detectable (absent)
- Not yet fully established (partial)
- In the process of leaving the body (passing)
- Fully established (full, complete)

In partial rigor, in which the rigor is not fully established, the body will likely be warm to the touch, and this should be noted. In the instance where rigor is leaving the body, the body will likely not be warm to the touch (unless in a very warm environment), and there may be other early signs of decomposition; these changes should also be noted. Additionally, with a body that has no detectable rigor and is warm (with blanchable lividity—to be discussed in the next section), the individual is likely to be very recently deceased, whereas one without detectable rigor that is cool to the touch (unless in a very cool environment) has been dead much longer and may have the additional signs of decomposition. The latter instance assumes temperate conditions and the absence of breezes or cooled air currents. The description of additional changes alongside a particular rating aids in the best estimation of the interval of time after death and the time of death itself when considered within the context of all investigative information. Changes in the body related to decomposition will be discussed subsequently.

Cadaveric spasm, also referred to as **instantaneous rigor** or **death grip**, simulates the stiffening of rigor mortis but does not develop gradually. Rather, it is instant upon death, capturing the last activity of the individual just before death. It is more commonly observed as tight gripping and flexion of the fingers in deaths preceded by vigorous struggle, intense fear, or intense excitement, and may be seen in cases of drowning in which aquatic vegetation or other debris is found gripped within the hands, indicating that the person was alive during the submersion event. It can involve any muscle group of the body, however. Such tight gripping cannot be simulated after death, such as by placing a gun in the hand of a "suicide" victim (staged homicide).

Livor Mortis (Lividity)

Lividity or livor mortis is caused by the gravitational pooling of the blood under the skin when the blood circulation has greatly slowed (heart failure) or ceased (death). It usually appears as a red, blue, or purple discoloration of the dependent regions of the body and can indicate the position of the body prior to and after death. In addition to noting the location of the lividity, it is important to specifically note the color of the lividity. In deaths due to carbon monoxide, cyanide, or fluoroacetate poisoning and hypothermia, the lividity may appear bright pink or cherry red. The lividity in refrigerated or cold bodies may have a similar appearance. The lividity in deaths resulting from hydrogen sulfide, sodium chlorate, or inorganic nitrite poisoning may appear brown. There will be blanching (focal absence of the lividity created by compression of the skin) where the body contacts a surface or object, and any texture or pattern of a surface or object will be transferred to the skin's surface as an impression (Figure 3.6A and B). Lividity may be misinterpreted as bruising and may even mask true bruising. It may be inapparent in dark-skinned individuals upon external

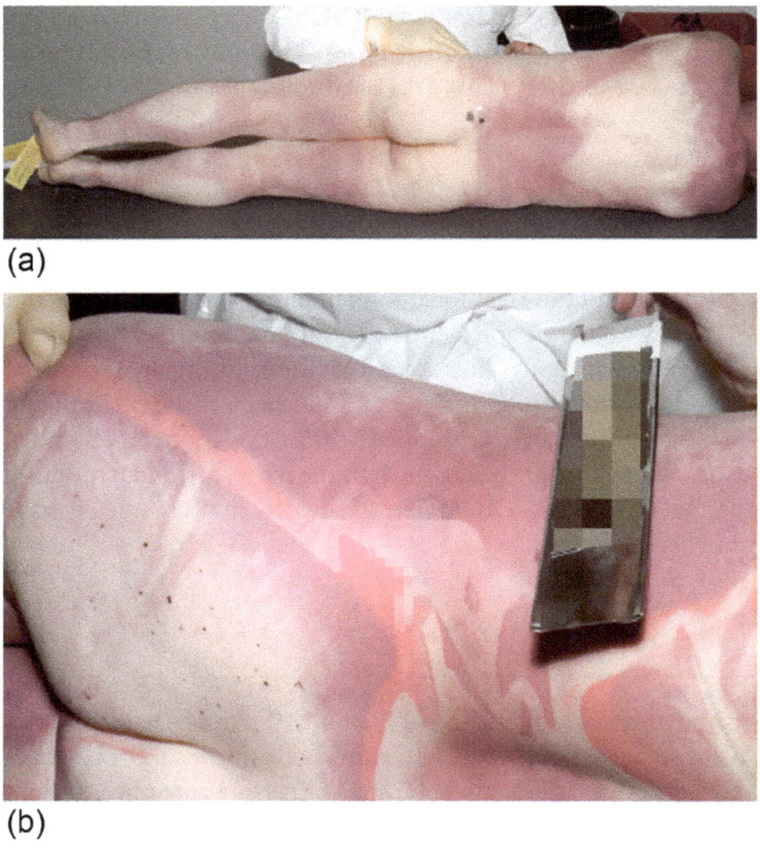

Figure 3.6 Lividity (A) and a patterned lividity from contact with a bed sheet (B).

examination but will be apparent to the pathologist upon inspection of the internal organs and undersurface of the scalp as these structures can exhibit the same kind of dependent pooling of blood. Lividity may be absent in drowning due to the water pressure exerted on the body, or if present, it may be difficult to interpret because of its blotchy, uneven distribution. Lividity may be very light or not visible in individuals who have lost a large amount of blood due to injury or who are anemic.

Lividity usually develops within 30 minutes to 2–4 hours after death and is well developed by 8–12 hours. Lividity is blanchable upon compression of the skin within this 12-hour period, but becomes fixed (nonblanchable) at approximately 12–18 hours. This may assist one in approximating the time since death based on the fixed vs. nonfixed state of the lividity. If lividity has not been fixed and the body is subsequently moved, it will reestablish itself, moving again to the dependent areas of the body. During reestablishment of the lividity, the original locations may have a lighter, blotchy appearance before the blood moves completely to the new position. If the body is found in a position contrary to the location of *fixed* lividity (i.e., found in a prone position with the lividity located on the back of the body), then the body has been moved by something or someone, which may be a red flag indicator or otherwise needs a plausible explanation.

Current lividity is caused by the force of moving water, pushing blood to the extremities located downstream to the rest of the body. Body parts in the upstream position will appear lighter as a result of the blood being pushed out of those regions.

Tardieu spots represent a special kind of advanced lividity, which appear as petechiae or larger patches of hemorrhage *confined to the area of lividity.* These hemorrhages are especially prominent in the arms and legs of individuals suspended by hanging or in deaths due to other causes where the limb or other part of the body may have been hanging over something, such as a bed or chair. Figure 8.11 features an example of Tardieu spots.

Lividity vs. Bruising (Contusion)

Lividity is sometimes misinterpreted as antemortem bruising or contusion. Lividity is generally more widespread and thus less focal than antemortem contusion. To determine the difference, the investigator can apply gentle pressure on an area of lividity with a thumb or finger. This pressure will push the pooled blood out of the area, creating a paler area of blanching. Blood will not vacate this area if it is a bruise (provided the lividity has not yet been fixed) because the blood is trapped within the connective tissues beneath the skin. Bruises usually appear slightly darker than the overlying or surrounding lividity and may be accompanied by swelling. Otherwise, the lividity may completely obscure bruising, especially if it has become fixed.

Algor Mortis

Algor mortis is the postmortem cooling of the body. After death, heat is transferred from the body to a solid surface, fluid, or into the air via the physical processes of conduction, radiation, or convection.[2] Cooling will continue at a certain rate until the body reaches the ambient temperature. As previously mentioned in Chapter 1, the rate of cooling occurs much more rapidly with immersion in cold water. Since the skin is the closest to the air, cooling occurs more rapidly there, and thus the measurement of the *core* temperature gives a better representation of the body's temperature. The core body temperature can be measured by either placing a thermometer through a small incision of the upper right abdominal quadrant into the liver or inserting the thermometer into the rectum (personal protective equipment or gloves must be worn and proper disposal done after measurement). This measurement may be done by the C/ME investigator or pathologist, ideally on the scene, since the measured body temperature would conceivably be closer to the time of death. This may also be done upon arrival of the body at the C/ME office.

Under controlled laboratory conditions of ambient temperature, it has been demonstrated that a body will cool at a certain rate over time: 1.5°F per hour for the first 12 hours after death, then 1°F for the next 12–18 hours. As an adjunct to the known approximate cooling rates, a formula can be applied to help further approximate the **postmortem interval** (PMI) or the amount of time elapsed since death. This is called Moritz's formula: 98.6°F – rectal temperature/1.5 = hours since death).[2] This formula assumes that the body temperature at the time of death is normal (98.6°F), which may or may not be the case and may be unknown. This formula will be further compounded if the body temperature at death is much higher or much lower than normal. Application of formula and knowledge of rates of cooling can only be applied in ideal conditions of a temperate, ambient environment without wind currents or cold water immersion. Additionally, there are many variables that can affect the rate of cooling, such as clothing, body habitus (obese vs. thin), weather, temperature of surface or object in contact with the body, and body temperature at the time of death. Medical conditions, use of illicit drugs or certain medications, head injury, and heat stroke are additional variables.[2] The frequent lack of ideal environmental conditions and the presence of variables make the estimation of time since death using algor mortis tenuous.

Physical Wounding of the Body

There are three terms used to describe the time frames in which a body can be wounded: antemortem (before death), agonal (at the time of death), and postmortem (after death). Knowledge of these terms will assist the investigator in understanding the autopsy report. These time frames, coupled with the location and extent of the wounds on the body, may help reveal the cause of death and may be a red flag indicator of foul play.

Any injury inflicted on the body before death is designated as **antemortem wounding.** Injuries sustained while the heart is still beating, in which there are blood pressure and blood flow to the skin and tissues, appear red to red-brown due to bleeding or hemorrhage arising from the damaged tissue and blood vessels. The pathologist may be able to confirm that the injury is antemortem and determine if an individual survived for a period of time prior to death by examining a biopsy of the injured tissue under the microscope for the presence of hemorrhage, inflammation, and healing. Examples of antemortem wounding are defensive wounds. These are usually blunt force injuries (abrasions, contusions, and lacerations) but may also result from sharp force injury, such as injuries inflicted by a knife. They are found on parts of the body commonly used to ward off an attacker and include the back of the hands and the outer surface of the forearms, or on the legs and feet of a victim attacked while supine on the ground. An individual warding off an attack from a knife may sustain cuts on the palms or webs of the fingers and thumb. In cases of vehicles containing occupants submerged in water, it is common to find antemortem wounding on the victims because of trauma sustained upon impact with the water and with the surfaces and objects within the interior compartment.

Swimmers hit by the propeller of a boat are usually in the water in a vertical or swimming position, attempting to avoid the boat. Antemortem propeller injuries in these individuals will involve the arms, legs, forearms, and hands. They may also be found on the face or side of the head. Propeller injuries appear as multiple, parallel striations or deep cuts. The size of the propeller blades striking the body can be estimated based on the measurements and spacing of the injuries inflicted on the body. Smaller, high-speed propellers leave injuries very close together. Larger crafts with slower engines and larger heavier propellers will leave injuries farther apart and often inches deep. Measurements of propeller injuries will be performed at autopsy and incorporated into the autopsy report. These measurements can be directly communicated with the accident investigator early on to aid him or her in the reconstruction of a watercraft accident or potentially in the identification of a vessel involved in a hit-skip incident.

An individual who still has cardiac activity and thus blood flow to the skin and tissues who receives aggressive CPR may sustain abrasions and contusions of the face, chest, and upper arms during intubation, chest compression, and lifting. Upon autopsy examination, the pathologist may additionally find contusions and other hemorrhages of the tongue, the lining of the oral cavity, throat, and soft tissues of the internal chest plate. Rarely, small tears or areas of bleeding over the surface of the liver may be discovered at autopsy.

One must keep in mind that the injuries sustained prior to death in an individual submerged in water for prolonged periods of time may have minimal to no hemorrhage visible as a result of leaching of the blood out of the wound into the surrounding water. These injuries will appear pale and may be mistaken for postmortem injuries.

Agonal wounding involves injuries sustained at the time of death. In cases of agonal lethal head injuries sustained just prior to submersion, there will be little or no hemorrhage or bleeding due to cardiopulmonary arrest followed by rapid cessation of blood pressure and blood flow to the injured site(s).

Postmortem wounding involves injuries sustained after death, particularly blunt force injury, causing abrasion and laceration of the skin. Since these injuries are sustained after cessation of heart activity, they will lack hemorrhage and have a pale appearance, but it must again be emphasized that antemortem injuries that have been submerged for prolonged periods may have a similar appearance. Additionally, deciphering antemortem vs. postmortem wounding in significantly decomposed bodies may be difficult or impossible. In cases of submerged bodies, they may occur when the body is at the bottom of a lake or other body of water, during the early stages of refloat, or when the body is floating on the surface. While on the bottom, the body may strike submerged objects such as debris, rocks, and trees. During refloat, when the body is lifted off the bottom and postmortem wandering commences, the body may again impact rocks and debris as it travels. By virtue of the downward positioning of the face, arms, and legs, the exposed regions of the body (forehead/eyebrows, nose, elbows, knees, and back of hands and feet) will sustain abrasions, lacerations, and cuts upon impact. The abrasions are also known as **travel abrasions** and can appear as single or multiple linear and parallel injuries (Figure 3.7). Travel abrasions located on the extremities should not be confused with defensive-type injuries, which tend

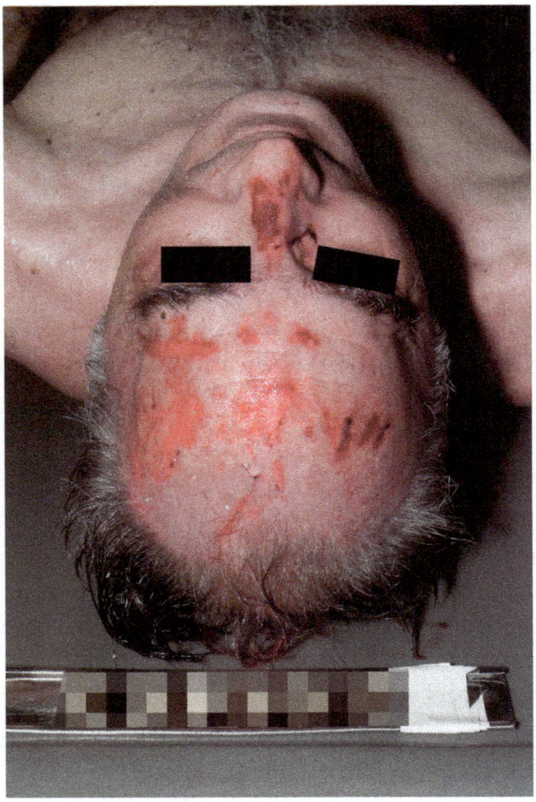

Figure 3.7 Travel abrasions of the face.

to be more randomly distributed. On the surface, the most common cause of postmortem wounding is an impact with a watercraft. In these cases, injuries caused by propeller blades will be located on the shoulders and back as the body is floating in a face-down position with the exposure of these surfaces. Wounds may also be found on the back of the head, neck, and buttocks.

Aggressive CPR on a nearly dead or dead individual may also give rise to postmortem injuries, usually in the form of abrasions, causing injury to the face, mouth, and chest. Finally, handling of the body during recovery and transport may also introduce postmortem injury, usually in the form of abrasion. Postmortem abrasions in particular tend to have a parched yellow-orange appearance, which becomes more pronounced with drying; an example of this is shown in Figure 7.6.

Anthropophagy

Anthropophagy is the feeding on the human body by animal or insect life, whether within or out of the water. Bodies in water with exposure of body parts or body regions and bodies on land are prone to predation by any number of native insects or animals, including insect larvae, ants, roaches, dogs, cats, waterfowl, and rodents. In freshwater, this is most commonly due to feeding by fish, turtles, and crustaceans. In the saltwater environment, it may include larger sea life or microscopic organisms such as sea lice. The injuries produced initially involve accessible areas, including the tips of the fingers, lips, toes, ears, eyelids, and any preexisting open wound, and may become more extensive with continued feeding. The appearance, number, and pattern of these injuries may give the initial impression of foul play. Extensive predation may include dismemberment with scattering or consumption of body parts or skeletonization. Location of scattered body parts will lengthen recovery time and may require other technological and scientific expertise to locate the parts, identify them as human, and determine the completeness of the body or skeleton. The postmortem injuries will appear bloodless; however, the determination of the absence of hemorrhage may be difficult or impossible in cases of advanced decomposition. The location, pattern, and depth of animal- or insect-induced injuries may assist the investigator or animal/insect expert in determining the identification of the animal. An example of this phenomenon appears in Figures 7.6 and 7.7A and B.

Maggots

Maggots are the larval form of flies. Flies lay their eggs in small and sometimes large bulky clusters on accessible unsubmerged areas, crevices, and cavities of the body, preferring moist areas such as the eyes, nostrils, scalp, lips, ear canals, and open wounds. Individually, these are tiny, round to ovoid, tan-white structures that resemble seeds or grains of rice. Egg laying occurs within 1–2 hours of death. The mobile larvae will be noted by approximately 24 hours, depending on the species. If undisturbed on land, within 2–3 weeks, they will pupate, forming a hardened brown outer covering remaining on or around the body or burrowed within the surrounding soil. Maggots will enter anatomic openings, wounds, and body cavities and feed off of the body tissues and organs. Maggots feeding on the skin may leave multiple, small, round (2–4 mm in diameter) holes, leaving a lace-like or web-like pattern on the skin that may be misinterpreted as antemortem blunt, sharp, or other penetrating injury. With time and if left undisturbed, masses of maggots will completely consume the flesh and expose the bones (skeletonization). Their activities constitute a type of anthropophagy (Figure 3.8). Submerged bodies that contain maggots

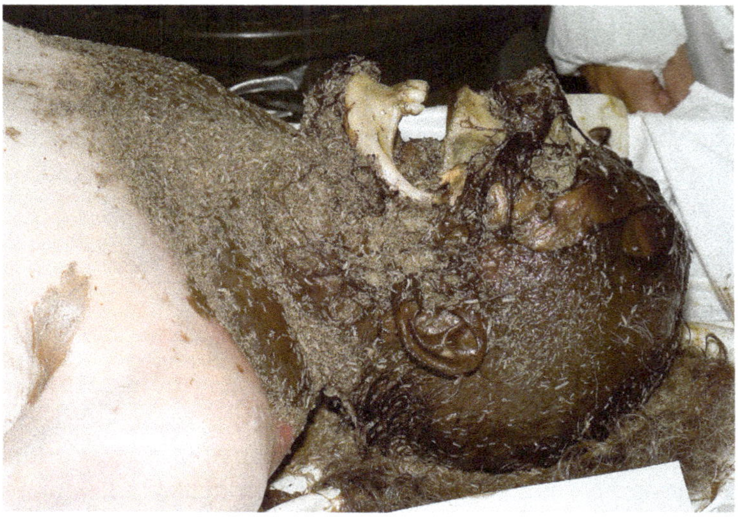

Figure 3.8 Near-complete skeletonization of face by maggot mass.

may be a red flag indicator of foul play, potentially representing a case of an individual killed on land and allowed to remain there for a time, allowing exposure to egg-laying flies, and then subsequently dumped in a body of water. This scenario could also simply represent the exposure of a floating body caused by temporary entanglement in debris. A forensic entomologist who has extensive knowledge of insects can be consulted on how to collect maggots (or any dead flies and pupae) or may be called upon to personally perform the collection. Maggots may also be collected at the time of autopsy and submitted to the forensic entomologist and even the forensic toxicologist for study and testing.

The forensic entomologist can determine the fly species by rearing the live maggots to the adult stage. Knowledge of the normal geographical origin of a particular fly may assist in determining the geographical origin of the body and potentially whether the body has been moved from one location to another or has otherwise traveled a great distance. Determination of the fly species and developmental stage of the maggots can also assist in the estimation of the time elapsed since death or the PMI.

Forensic toxicology involves the detection of drugs, medications, and chemicals in body fluids, tissues, and other sources. Maggots can be processed for testing for various drugs, medications, and chemicals. The detection of substances no longer present in a body with advanced decomposition, lacking obtainable body fluids and tissues, can be invaluable in aiding in the determination of a cause of death or a contributing factor in the death. Human DNA may also be extracted from maggots for the purpose of identification, particularly in an unknown victim or a victim who has been rendered unrecognizable secondary to extensive dismemberment.

Decomposition

Decomposition involves the disintegration of the body's tissues and begins immediately after death. It incorporates the passing of rigor mortis as the contractile proteins of the skeletal muscle disassociate. It involves two general processes: putrefaction and autolysis. **Putrefaction** is the breakdown of the body tissues by bacteria and is what is most notable by sight and smell upon initial assessment of a decomposing body. Gaseous metabolic byproducts, including methane, ammonia, hydrogen sulfide, and mercaptans produced by bacteria, give rise to the disagreeable odor of putrefaction. **Adipocere** is a special type of putrefaction seen most commonly in bodies submerged for extended periods or bodies in damp or warm environments for extended periods. It is produced as a result of the breakdown of the body's fat by a combination of the actions of bacteria and endogenous enzymes producing a chalky, gray-tan-white, rancid-smelling substance in areas under the skin or other internal body regions where fatty tissue resides. Adipocere takes weeks to months to develop. **Autolysis** is the dissolution of the body tissues caused by endogenous enzymes. If the body has been exposed to dry, warm, or hot air for a time, dehydration of the skin and underlying tissues will result in **mummification**, starting with the most exposed body parts, such as the nose, lips, fingers, and toes. Mummification can also involve broad skin regions of the face, torso, arms, and legs. These regions will gradually develop a leathery yellow-orange to dark-brown-black texture and appearance. Examples of mummification and adipocere appear in Figures 9.3 and 9.4.

In a temperate environment, as a body starts to decompose, it will start to change in appearance. In the early stages, between 12 and 24 hours, the skin color will change from a bluish hue to almost green, starting initially on the right lower quadrant of the abdomen and spreading over the entire abdomen. The other regions of the body also become discolored, ranging from green to green-red. If the environment is dry, mummification may become the predominant component of decomposition. Within 24–36 hours the skin may have a generalized dark green, red, or sometimes dark purple appearance, and there may be drying of the nose, lips, fingertips, and toes exposed or not protected by clothing or other covering.

By approximately 36–48 hours, marbling has developed, appearing as a red, green, brown, or black branch-like discoloration along with the distribution of superficial blood vessels as a result of the bacteria-mediated breakdown of red blood cells within the blood vessels. Also, by this time, the face and body begin to swell noticeably, giving rise to a bloated appearance and the appearance of increased weight or obesity. Drainage of bloody fluid from the nose and mouth with pooling under the head or around the face and staining of the underlying surface may be evident. This fluid is referred to as **purge** and is commonly misinterpreted by law enforcement as arising from some type of trauma to the face or head (Figure 3.9). Areas of normally pliable or loose skin, such as the lips, eyelids, and scrotum, become drastically swollen. The eyeballs, lips, abdomen, and scrotum may become greatly distended and protruded secondary to bacteria-mediated gas production. By 72 hours, the entire body is involved and purge is maximally present. The decompositional changes occurring in the region of the neck may accentuate the normal horizontal folds of skin, giving the appearance of ligature marks. This normal anatomic folding of the skin in this region also gives it relative protection from decomposition and will appear lighter in color due to the blanching from contact with the opposing skin folds. The pathologist will examine this region closely for signs of any injury, including injury to the underlying neck structures.

Significant decomposition with bloating and discoloration may make the determination of race, body build, and identification difficult, if not impossible. Examination of the texture of the scalp, armpit (axillary), or pubic hair may be of some help. Examination of the areas of the skin relatively spared from decomposition may also be helpful. If the

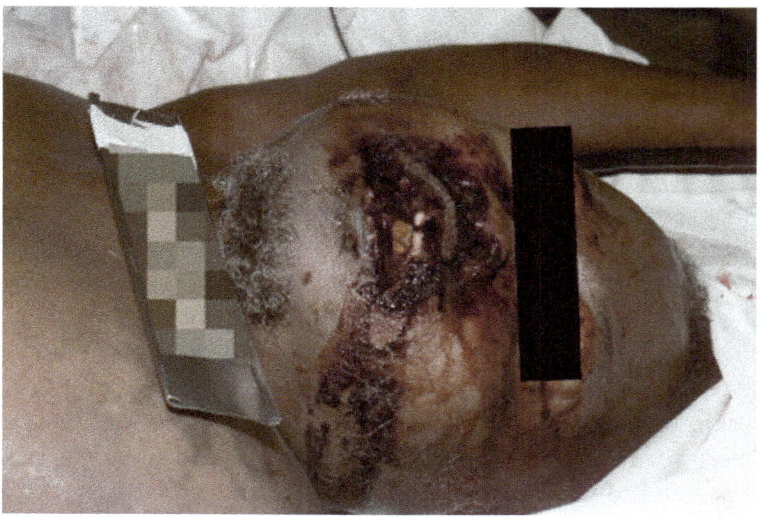

Figure 3.9 Decompositional changes of the face with bloody purge from nose and mouth.

identity of the decedent is uncertain, scientific establishment or confirmation of identity by means of fingerprinting or dental and DNA comparisons may be necessary. A presumptive identification may be made with visual recognition of distinct tattoos, scars, moles, or other personal effects found on or near the body. On bodies with several days of decomposition, any tattoos present become even clearer upon gentle pushing of the overlying loosened outer layer of skin to one side of the tattoo, as the ink of the tattoo will also be embedded within the deeper skin layers (Figure 3.10).

By four to seven days and as early as two to three days, **skin slippage** may be apparent anywhere on the body, including the hands and feet, where the entire skin, along with the fingernails and toenails, loosens, allowing removal of the skin in its entirety, as if removing a glove or sock. In fact, the entire skin of the scalp, along with the hair, will become partially or completely detached, especially upon moving and other manipulation of the body (Figure 3.11A and B). Skin slippage occurs as a result of the putrefactive and autolytic processes causing separation of the outer layer of the skin or epidermis from its underlying attachments. The skin becomes quite fragile and is easily torn upon handling, such as that done with moving and transporting the body. In the case of an unidentified or tentatively identified individual, care must be taken to preserve the skin of the fingers, which may be amenable to fingerprinting. The focal detachment of skin secondary to skin slippage may create blisters that accumulate yellow or red-tinged fluid that may rupture and leak, causing staining of adjacent clothing and surfaces. These areas may later dry and darken and appear as injury, specifically abrasions.

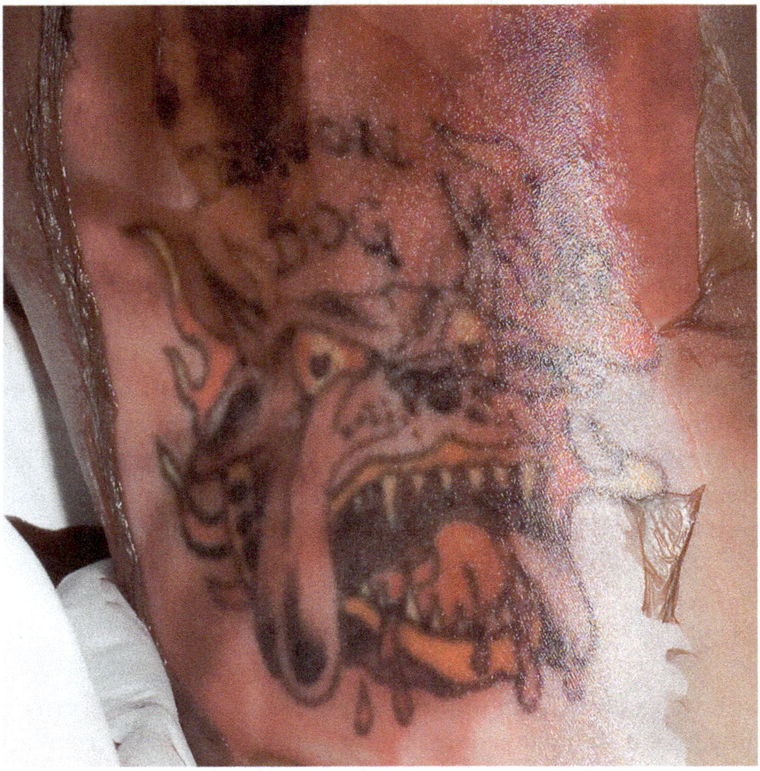

Figure 3.10 Detailed tattoo after removal of loosened skin due to decomposition.

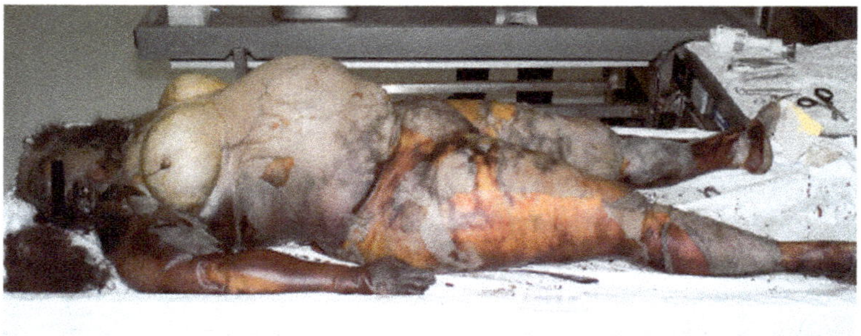

(a)

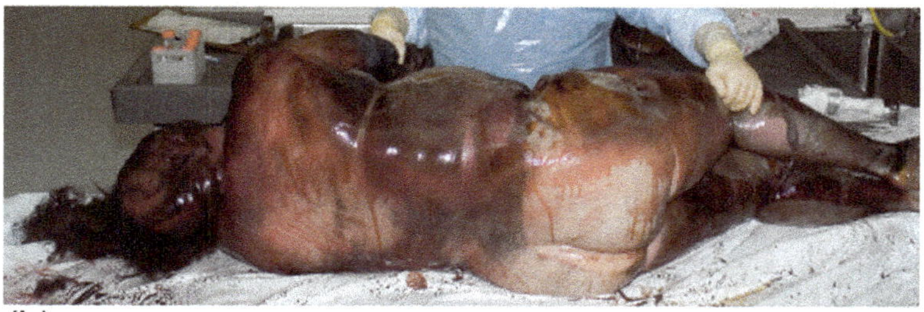

(b)

Figure 3.11 Decomposition of the entire body, including discoloration, skin slippage, bloating, mummification of lower arms, legs, and thighs, and marbling of abdomen and thighs (A) and near-total detachment of scalp with hair (B).

The overall process of decomposition will be hastened by obesity, heavy clothing, warm/hot environmental temperature, or infection. It will be slowed by cooler temperatures, including submersion in cool or cold water. Generally, newborn babies decompose less quickly because they contain a lesser bacterial burden and fewer different types of bacteria than adults. Areas of the body protected by clothing, wrappings, objects, other surfaces, or overhead structures will decompose more slowly or be relatively spared of the changes.

Within weeks to months to years, and with the succession of insects and animal feeding, an exposed body may be reduced to a skeleton. Protected, covered bodies will have varying degrees of decomposition, dependent upon environmental conditions. With extremes of decomposition, including partial and complete skeletonization, openings may develop on the body created by animal or insect feeding. Skin and internal organs progressively soften, detach, and liquefy, so handling of the body or any body sections or body parts must be done with extreme care so that the body remains as intact as possible. Eventually, all of the soft tissue disappears, leaving only skeletal remains (Figure 3.12). The expertise of the forensic anthropologist will be needed and be of great assistance in the inventory of recovered bones, starting at the scene and continuing on to autopsy.

Fingerprinting the Deceased in Water-Related Deaths

One of several ways to identify an unidentified decedent is via fingerprint examination. Sources for fingerprint comparison include antemortem prints from arrest records, military service files, and some governmental files. To aid in a positive identification of the body, it will be necessary to obtain fingerprints. Generally, this is conducted at the

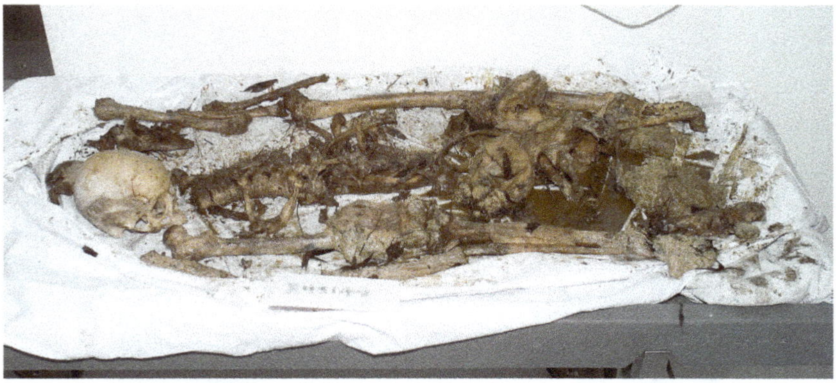

Figure 3.12 Skeletal remains.

C/ME's office by law enforcement after hand examination and autopsy procedures have been completed, especially in violent or suspicious deaths, including water-related deaths, where the hands will likely have been bagged at the scene. This may also be conducted in forensic laboratories whereby the hand, portions of fingers, or the skin of fingers have been submitted separately.

In cases of a prolonged submersion of a body, fingerprinting can prove to be difficult due to postmortem changes of decomposition. **Wauschaut**, commonly referred to as **washerwoman's hands**, is the wrinkling of the skin on the hands and feet caused by prolonged submersion. This phenomenon can be observed on the immersed skin of the living or deceased and is usually visible within several minutes of immersion. With time, changes of postmortem decomposition will ensue, leading to increased fragility and partial or complete detachment of the skin, importantly that of the hands. The wrinkles resulting from immersion or early decomposition can be smoothed by injection of water into the fingertips by using a hypodermic needle, thus revealing again the ridge characteristics. The water is injected just under the first finger crease. A string should then be tied above the injection site to prevent the water from leaking out during the printing process.

In moderate or more advanced decomposition and with the continued development of skin slippage and degloving, the degloved skin can be removed from the decedent's hand like a glove and placed over one's own gloved hand and rolled into the printing ink (Figure 3.13). Since decomposition with or without immersion can produce a moist or wet skin surface, chemical drying may be necessary, such as via the use of ninhydrin spray.[3] If the body is found with skin already gone (degloved) and otherwise absent, the underlying dermis can be fingerprinted and chemical drying of the surface may again be necessary.

In cases where the fingers are dried or mummified, the fingers are cut off using bolt cutters or autopsy cutting instruments. The fingers are then placed in a pan of undiluted Downy fabric softener. Any brand can be used, but Downy works best.[4] After several hours, and upon injection with water or other tissue builders, the skin will be pliable enough to get usable prints. Another option is to use plumber's putty. The putty is rolled into a ball about the size of a golf ball, and the fingerprint paper is placed on the putty. When the finger is pressed against the paper, the putty forms around the finger. This technique allows the fingerprint paper to conform to the finger rather than attempting to make the finger conform to the paper. Prints from dried and hard fingers may also be obtained with the technique that uses black fingerprint powder, which is brushed onto the friction ridges of

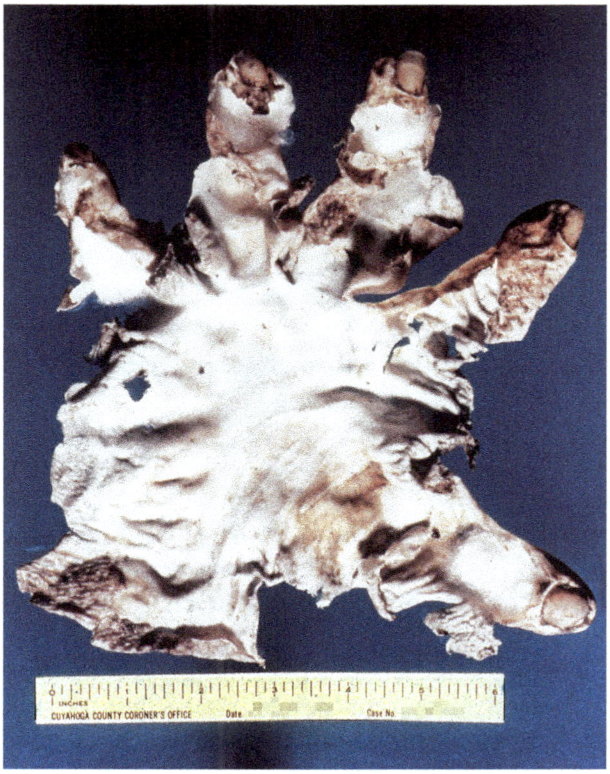

Figure 3.13 Degloved skin removed from the hand.

the print using a standard powder brush. The fingerprints are then obtained by applying Silly Putty® or a similar substance over the fingerprint and lifting. The putty will conform to imperfections in the skin and lift the entire print much more efficiently than expensive tapes. The light color of the putty will contrast nicely with the dark powder, allowing the investigator to photograph the prints.

If the investigator is using a postmortem fingerprinting kit, it will include a fingerprinting spoon. This is simply a curved device that allows the investigator to place a fingerprint card on the inside portion of the spoon. First, the fingers are inked using a standard inked fingerprinting pad, and then the card is placed on the spoon, which is rolled over the fingertips. To make the card easier to work with, it can be cut into two separate strips, one for each hand. Several attempts may be necessary to obtain a usable print. Once a good print is obtained, that portion of the strip can be cut and placed in the corresponding section of the full fingerprint card.

Regardless of the method used to obtain individual fingerprints, prints of the four fingers together on each hand should also be obtained. This allows the print examiner to ensure that each obtained print is placed in the correct corresponding section for each finger on the fingerprint card.

Fingerprinting Decomposed Human Remains

Two methods: Live scan technology and casting mediums

Live Scan

Live scan utilizes a touch screen panel on a scanner that captures friction ridge detail and guides the user through the fingerprinting process. It uses silicone pads to highlight ridge patterns, allowing the system to capture the enhanced prints.

Complications frequently encountered with badly decomposed bodies are the oily skin surface resulting from the decomposition of by-products. This can be resolved by cleaning the area with 70% isopropyl alcohol.

Care must be taken not to apply too much pressure, which can flatten out the friction ridges. Not enough pressure, on the other hand, can result in failure to capture adequate impressions.

Casting Mediums

Some morgues use a casting material called Mikrosil, which is a casting material often used for bite mark impressions as well as other artifact impressions. Mikrosil is formulated to pick up small details while providing high contrast for microscopic comparisons, good releasing ability and a short setting time.

The lack of easily manipulating the hands and fingers due to rigor Mortis is easily overcome by applying Mikrosil to the palmar surfaces. Cleaning the skin with isopropyl alcohol will allow the Mikrosil to adhere to the skin more efficiently by removing the oily by-product of decomposition mentioned earlier.

Removal of the casting material after it has set renders an excellent reproduction of Ridge detail. It shall be noted that this casting is a reverse image instead of the orientation normally produced from an inked print.

This casted impression can then be inked using standard fingerprinting ink and rolled onto a fingerprint card.

After obtaining fingerprints using either of these methods, the results can be entered for a search in the AFIS database. [5]

In the absence of local fingerprinting expertise, in difficult and badly damaged or decomposed bodies, and as a last resort, the hand can be amputated at the wrist, placed in a formalin fixative, and submitted to the Identification Divisions of the FBI for examination and identification—an effort that will be coordinated by the C/ME office.[6]

References

1. Ely, S. F., and Hirsch, C. S. 2000. Asphyxial deaths and petechiae: A review. *J Forensic Sci* 45(6):1274–77.
2. Perper, J. A. 2006. Time of death and changes after death. In *Medicolegal investigation of death—Guidelines for the application of pathology to crime investigation*, ed. W. U. Spitz, 87–128. 4th ed. Springfield, IL: Charles C Thomas Publisher Ltd.
3. Kahana, T., et al. 2001. Fingerprinting the deceased: Traditional and new techniques. *J Forensic Sci* 46(4):908–12.
4. Hallcox, J., and Welch, A. 2006. *Bodies we've buried—Inside the national forensic academy, the world's top CSI training school*. New York: Berkley Book Company Group.
5. Evidence Technology Magazine, volume 3, number 4-July/August 2005, p. 30–33.
6. Spitz, D. J. 2006. Identification of human remains. In *Medicolegal investigation of deaths—Guidelines for the application of pathology to crime investigation*, ed. W. U. Spitz, 184–225. 4th ed. Springfield, IL: Charles C Thomas Publisher Ltd.

Case Investigation
Obtaining Decedent, Witness, Suspect, and First Responder Information

4

KEVIN L. ERSKINE

Parabon Snapshot

Investigation into the cause of death for any unidentified individual cannot begin until the identity of the victim is known. In the past, estimations and a lot of luck were needed to identify skeletal or badly decomposed remains. Yet today, modern technology has made it much simpler. The new technology, called Parabon Snapshot, allows an investigator to obtain a photographic image of the deceased by using a sample of the victim's DNA. DNA carries genetics, which determines a person's physical characteristics, producing a wide variety of physical appearances from one person to the next. Snapshot reads these variances and predicts what a person looked like. This process is simply amazing, and the likeness of the person antemortem (before death) is spot on. Using SNP (Single-Nucleotide Polymorphism) technology, Snapshot generates a composite sketch (the process is called DNA phenotyping). These composites include sex, freckling, skin, hair and eye color, ancestry and face morphology. Composites reportedly have greater than 90% accuracy.

Types of Analysis Provided

In genetic ancestry, both on a global (European) and a subcontinental (Scandinavian) scale, data is compiled in a report, including a predicted composite sketch of the individual along with detailed supporting information that helps build the composite.

Kinship service provides inferences about the familial relationship between two or more DNA samples, out to 6° of relatedness (second cousins once removed).

How It Works

Phenotyping algorithms are used to predict decedents' appearance and ancestry using DNA extracted from bones. Traditional facial reconstruction is done by a forensic artist trained in Snapshot technology. Tissue depth markers are applied to the skull, based on DNA-determined ancestry and estimated body weight, which produces a face shape from cranial morphology. The final composite is created by blending the two predictions (see Figure 4.1).

The process uses bioinformatics pipelines and predictive models developed by Parabon. It reads genetic content from DNA and data sets created that include genotypic (genetic

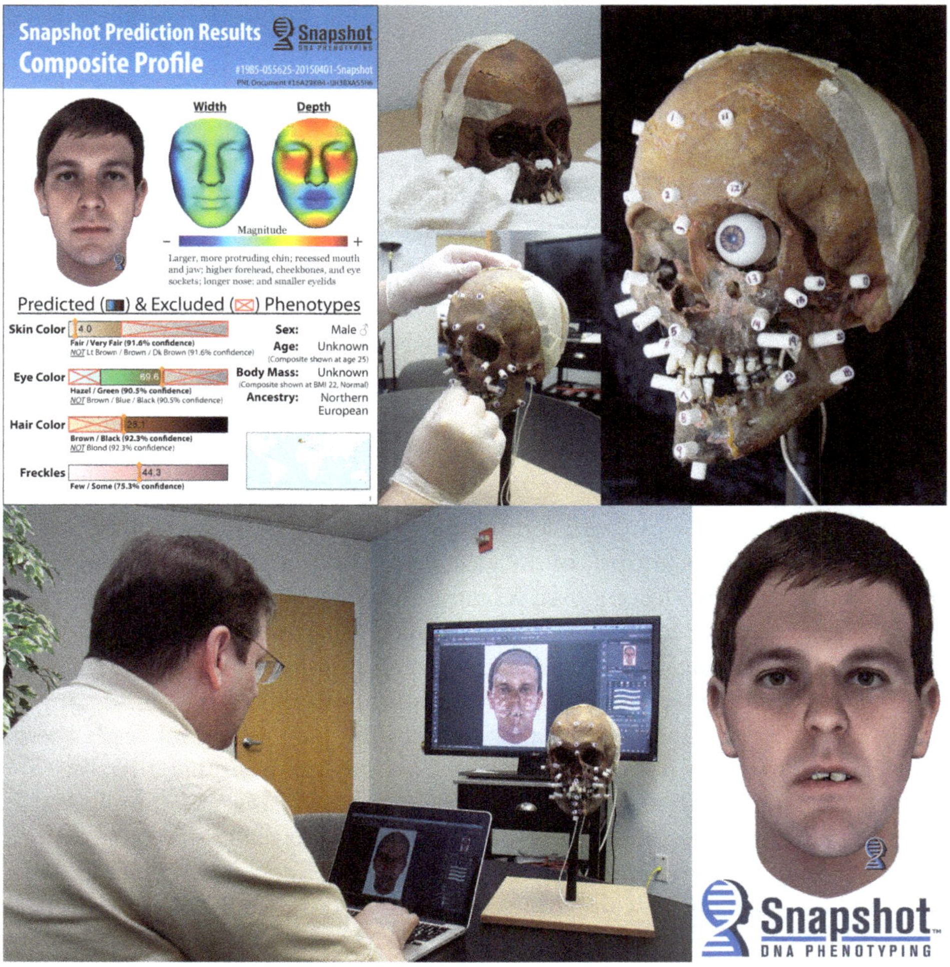

Figure 4.1 Parabon photo of a skull with depth markers.

content) and phenotypic (traits) data for each of thousands of subjects. Through diligent and repeated application of data mining and machine-learning processes, statistical models translate specific genetic bio markers into forensically relevant trait predictions.

STR (Short Tandem Repeats) is only useful for matching a known subject or database. Snapshot technology uses the information about physical appearance encoded in SNP (Single-Nucleotide Polymorphism) to generate new leads about unknown suspects. Snapshot testing is currently only available to law enforcement agencies to aid in solving open cases. No private use or requests are accepted.

The development of Snapshot was funded by the Department of Defense and was tested on thousands of out-of-sample genotypes. It is extremely accurate in re-creating a victim's likeness and is used by hundreds of law enforcement agencies in the United States and worldwide. Generally, the turn-around time is 45 days from the time the lab receives a DNA sample. The amount of DNA sample that is needed is 1 nanogram (ng), or one billionth of a gram, but more improves the likelihood of genotyping success. Samples of less than 1 ng have been used with lower confidence levels.

Sample quantity needs are based on the following factors:

Total available quantity of extracted DNA

- Its quality
- Mixture level
- Date and method of extraction
- Age of the original biological evidence
- Availability of other biological evidence

Genotyping assay calls for double-stranded DNA (dsDNA) either suspended in elution buffer or distilled water or submitted as a lyophilized product. Cases with only partial STR profiles are accepted. Partial profiles usually indicate some form of contamination or sample degradation. In many of these instances, Snapshot protocol is still effective. Mixed DNA samples can be used as long as the unknown contributor is the major contributor.

Genetic Genealogy

DNA phenotyping involves the use of DNA to predict physical appearance and description. It can be used to:

- Generate leads where there are no suspects or database hits
- Narrow down suspect lists and/or eliminate suspects
- Help identify human remains cases
- Determine ancestry
- Infer kinship
- Enhance forensic art
- Reconstruct the face/skull

Stages of Snapshot Reconstruction (See Figure 4.2)

- Composite produced from DNA extracted from bone
- Composite with skull overlay

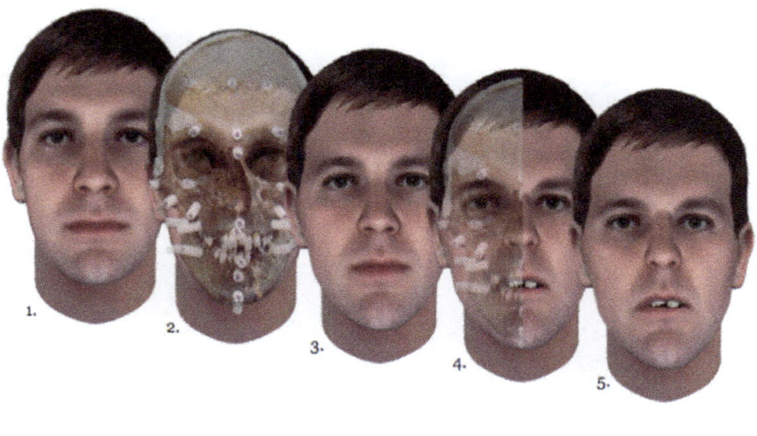

Figure 4.2 Stages of Snapshot Facial Reconstruction. (1) a Snapshot composite produced from DNA extracted from the subject's bone; (2) Snapshot composite with skull overlay; (3) Snapshot composite after re-scaling to conform to skull dimensions; (4) a cutaway image illustrating near final composite; (5) final, blended Snapshot composite.

- Re-scaling of composite to conform to skull dimensions
- Cutaway image showing near final composite
- Final blended composite

Forensic art enhancements can also be added to the composite. These enhancements may include body mass index, facial hair, accessories such as eyeglasses, piercings, tattoos, etc. With the addition of facial hair and some accessories, Parabon can create an age progression composite. For instance, by adding gray hair and reading glasses, the composite can look like a person in their 50s. The forensic artists have training in how aging affects body mass and facial features, which change the overall appearance. By default, Snapshot produces composites at the age of 25 years. Based on the investigating officers' beliefs that a subject is either younger or older, the artists can adjust the composite using standard aging principles. Likewise, if a person's body mass is significantly less or larger than the original composite, the forensic artists can adjust the composite to reflect those features.

Benefits of Snapshot Facial Reconstruction

Traditional reconstruction lacks ancestry and pigmentation, causing them to be depicted in gray scale.

Mandible (jaw bone) may be missing from recovered remains. Phenotyping can provide artist with a solid prediction of jaw shape.

Skull evidence can reveal distinguishing facial features that are difficult to predict (Figure 4.3).

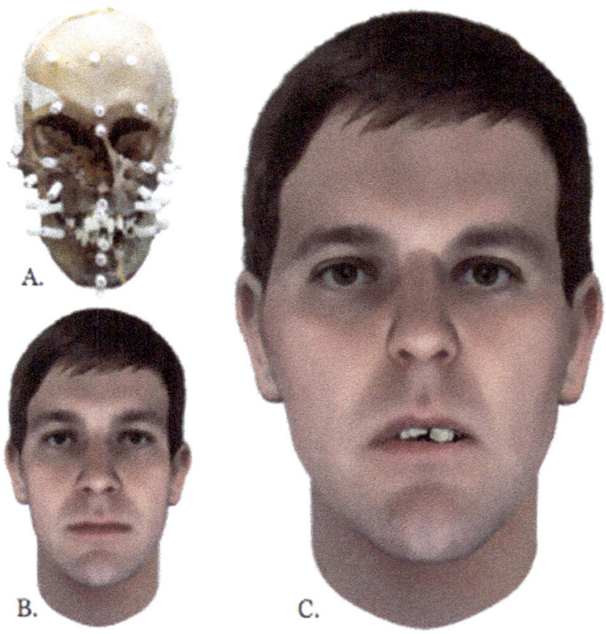

Figure 4.3 When the evidence for a case includes the victim's skull (A), it may be possible to perform forensic facial reconstruction to further enhance the Snapshot prediction (B), resulting in the final blended Snapshot composite (C).

Case Study: Brittani Marcell Assault

September 11, 2008, around noon, Diane Marcell returned home to find her daughter Brittani lying on the floor, covered in blood. An unknown male was standing over her, holding a shovel. The male exited a broken window, leaving behind drops of blood on the glass. For eight years, this attempted murder went unsolved. By mid-2016, the lead detective heard about Parabon Snapshot DNA Phenotyping and decided it might point her in a useful direction. Upon reviewing Snapshot report #APD-NM-08169900, the lead detective, Detective Jodi Gonterman, realized she had only one person on her possible suspect list matching this description (see Figure 4.4). Detective Gonterman was able to arrange for undercover detectives to follow the suspect to obtain an abandoned DNA sample. In time, they were able to observe the suspect drinking from a McDonald's cup and collected it from the trash. DNA was later extracted from the cup and compared to the sample collected from the crime scene. Through traditional STR comparison, the crime lab determined it was a match to the crime scene DNA. A warrant for the suspect, Justin Hansen, was issued, and he was subsequently arrested and charged with this brutal crime. On July 26, 2018, Justin Hansen was sentenced to 18 years in prison for the brutal shovel attack on Brittani Marcell. (This case summary is paraphrased, and it is not intended to diminish the investigative efforts of the detectives involved in this case. I strongly recommend the reader to visit the Parabon Nanolabs website at www.snapshot.parabon-nanolabs.com to read about this amazing case regarding the assault on Brittani Marcell.)

Agencies in need of Parabon Snapshot DNA Analysis Service can go to: www.snapshot.parabon-nanolabs.com. Fill out and send the form. This service is for law enforcement use only. No individuals or personal DNA request are permitted.[1]

Carbon-14 Dating to Determine Age and Year of Death

Carbon-14 or radiocarbon dating is a naturally occurring isotope of the element carbon, continually being formed in the atmosphere. Trace amounts of radioactive carbon are found in the natural environment. It is unstable and minutely radioactive. Carbon-14 dating was first used by archaeologists to estimate the age of certain objects between 500 and 50,000 years old. Radiocarbon content of terrestrial organisms is not the same as those of marine organisms because of the marine reservoir effect. Correction factors of the marine reservoir effect for different oceans in the world are established and recorded in a database. This procedure has recently found its way into technology to identify skeletal remains or other unidentified human remains. Nuclear weapons testing over the past 60 years has stirred up environmental levels of Carbon-14. From 1955 to 1963, levels almost doubled, and since that period of time, the levels have been tapering off to more normal.

When a person was born, or more importantly when their body tissues were formed, it plays a huge role in determining how much radio carbon exists within their body. Researchers from the University of Arizona tested subjects with known dates of birth to determine their date of birth or date of death using precise measurements of Carbon-14 levels in different postmortem tissues. To determine date of birth, tooth enamel was the main focus.

Tooth enamel is formed at specific time frames during childhood. The amount of atmospheric radiocarbon determines the amount found within the tooth enamel. For teeth formed after 1965, radiocarbon testing was accurate in determining the date of birth within 1.5 years. Testing of enamel formed prior to 1965 was less accurate. Researchers

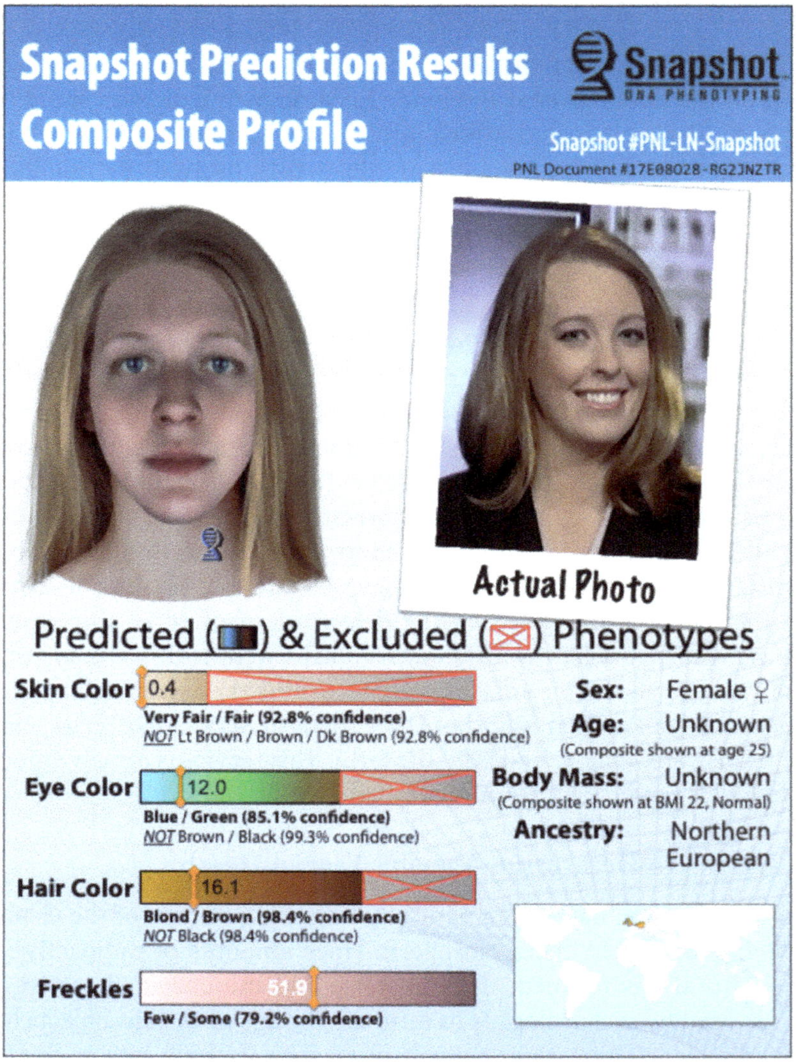

Figure 4.4 Snapshot composite profile and photo.

used radiocarbon levels in the soft tissue to determine the year of death. Different than tooth enamel, soft tissues are always being formed and reformed, which means they are always changing based on changing environmental levels. Blood, fingernails, and hair are the most affective sources which are identical to atmospheric conditions. Thus, the levels in those tissues postmortem would indicate the year of death accurately within three years. In the absence of any future nuclear destinations, this technique will be useful for at least the next 10–20 years. Atmospheric radiocarbon is dispersed uniformly through the entire globe, so this testing should be accurate, regardless of its global location.[2]

Decedent Information

By conducting a victimology, the investigator increases the solvability drastically since most homicidal acts of drowning involve a suspect known to the victim. Drowning is not a crime of opportunity. It would be very difficult for a criminal to plan and execute a drowning of a total stranger. An investigator may not want to accept the fact that a parent or loved one could have possibly drowned a child. But, just as parents beat, stab, strangle, shake, burn, and suffocate their children, they are also capable of drowning them. No matter how badly an investigator may want to write the incident off as an accident, all water-related deaths must be thoroughly investigated.

A victimology consists of all the essential information about the victim. A victimology will require the investigator to conduct a thorough background analysis on the victim to determine every aspect of the victim's life that can be verified, including the victim's identity and age; sex; race; physical description, fitness, and physique; marital status; intelligence and scholastic achievement; lifestyle and sexual orientation; personality style and demeanor; residency (former and present); occupation and financial status; reputation (home and work); medical history (mental and physical); fears; personal habits; alcohol, drug, and social habits; hobbies, clubs, and organization memberships; friends, enemies, and neighbors; recent court actions; teachers, caseworkers, and physicians, including psychiatrists; other siblings; and reports with child services or local police. By learning virtually everything about the victim, an investigator will also learn of any potential suspects.[3]

Relatives, spouses, roommates, neighbors, friends, acquaintances, and physicians may be approached for information, or the information may be gleaned from written and electronic sources.

1. **Identity and age:** These should be obtained and documented using a reputable source, such as a birth certificate and driver's license or any other legal form of picture identification. The decedent's age may assist in answering several questions. First, is the person's age appropriate for where he or she was found? If the age is that of a small child, is it appropriate for that child to be located in the medium in which he or she was found? Could a small child have accessed the waterway easily, or were there barriers that needed to be breached? A small child does not possess the physical strength to climb a fence, open a gate, or ascend multiple stairs. Likewise, an elderly person may not have the stamina or agility to carry out these same tasks.
2. **Sex:** Pay close attention to statements by family members that may indicate the sex of a child was contradictory to their wishes, such as "My husband really wanted a son!" Look for evidence to support these wishes, such as boy toys for a girl or vice versa. Interview the parents separately and inquire about how the other parent interacted with the decedent. In older victims, the sex may have played a role in the competitive sense. A male may have been competing for the affections from a mutual lover, or two males competing for the head of the household. In female victims, look for any signs of jealousy. Is there any indication of an incestuous relationship?
3. **Race:** Are there indications or statements made revealing prejudice or racism? Was a black decedent found in a predominantly white neighborhood or vice versa? Are there reports from school of racial bullying or fights?
4. **Physical description, fitness, and physique:** Does the decedent possess the physical ability to be found in this type of environment? For example, an elderly person in poor physical condition may not be able to access a remote waterway, or a child may not be able to climb a fence or gate to access a public pool. Did a witness have enough time or adequate proximity to give a detailed description about a specific

brand or color of clothing? Does the physical description by witnesses match that of the decedent? If not, there may be multiple victims that haven't been recovered yet. Can a witness on a shoreline accurately give the color of a hat, or wording on a shirt, or even the sexes of the people in a boat a great distance from the shore? Did the lack of abilities, training, and experience to operate equipment and motorized vehicles have any involvement in the death?

5. **Marital status:** Was the decedent married? What was the condition of the marriage? Are there reports of infidelity or a specific lover? What is the marital status of the lover? Were there reports of discovered infidelity?
6. **Intelligence and scholastic achievement:** Did the decedent have a high degree of intelligence? Did the decedent require an extensive amount of tutoring to keep up in school? Did the decedent possess the intelligence to be able to read warning signs posted in the area or assess a dangerous environment? Was a child's scholastic downfall a constant embarrassment to family and peers?
7. **Lifestyle and sexual orientation:** Did the decedent live a high-risk lifestyle, such as frequently visiting bars in a bad neighborhood? Did the decedent fraternize with strangers or people associated with criminal activity? Was the decedent homosexual or questioning his or her sexual orientation? If so, what were the feelings about this of parents, family members, coworkers, and friends? Did the decedent frequent prostitutes?
8. **Personality style and demeanor:** Was the decedent known as a daredevil, risk taker, care-free person, or a jokester? How did peers react to his or her personality traits? Is his or her personality described as abrasive?
9. **Residency (former and present):** Interview former landlords and neighbors to determine living habits and conditions. Did they have many late-night visitors, multiple noise complaints, and questionable characters hanging around? Did they encounter strange noises or odors? Was the decedent reliable, punctual with rent payment, and leave the premises in good condition? Did the decedent miss payments, complain about money problems, or mention adversaries? Was the decedent frequently drunk or high on drugs?
10. **Occupation and financial status:** Was the decedent recently fired from job or collecting unemployment? Was the means of financial support questionable or secretive? Was the decedent believed to be involved in illicit drug sales? Are there bankruptcies or evidence of poor finances, such as late notices, cancellation notices, shut off utilities, repossessions, and foreclosures?
11. **Reputation (home and work):** Was the decedent punctual, trustworthy, frequently absent, or a sick leave abuser? Are there claims or reports of poor bookkeeping, fraud, or embezzlement? Would the decedent have periods of unexplained absences at work? Is he or she known to be honest, friendly, or a recluse? Was there any change in work performance?
12. **Medical history (mental and physical):** Are there multiple unexplained illnesses in the medical history? What is the medical history and list of conditions, including heart disease, stroke, diabetes, seizures, etc.? Was there a recent diagnosis of an illness, terminal or otherwise? Were there multiple trips to the hospital with no known diagnosis? Is there a history of pneumonia or apnea (especially in infant and child deaths), reports of self-inflicted injuries or illnesses, suicide attempts, depression, schizophrenia, or paranoia? Was the decedent a mental or physical burden to the family?

13. **Fears:** Was the decedent afraid of water? A strong fear of water (especially in children) may be an indication of water-related torture or punishment. Are there other fears that don't fit the scenario, such as a person afraid of heights who reportedly fell from a cliff, etc.?
14. **Personal habits:** Did the decedent have a daily routine that might lend an opportunity to a would-be attacker, such as a nightly walk in the park or a nightly swim in the backyard pool? Did the decedent have a healthy lifestyle, or was he or she a high risk for diseases, such as heart disease, high blood pressure, or high cholesterol?
15. **Alcohol, drugs, and social habits:** Did the decedent drink excessively, get drunk or high often, which might lower inhibitions or render him or her defenseless in the event of an assault? Any history of prescription medications, whether prescribed to the decedent or someone else? Was the decedent known to use alcohol with medications?
16. **Hobbies, clubs, or organization memberships:** Did the decedent belong to high-risk clubs or participate in dangerous hobbies such as cliff diving, scuba diving, ice or wreck diving, or surfing? Did he or she participate in clubs that frequently swim in the winter months? Did he or she attempt to join a club or fraternity that conducts hazing rituals? Was the decedent part of religious or satanic cults?
17. **Friends, enemies, and neighbors:** Did close friends notice any recent changes in the decedent's mood, or any recent changes in personal habits, social acceptance, or increase in stressors? Are there any recent reports of assaults with the decedent named as the complainant? Were there any recent fights or threats made toward the decedent or any changes in daily routine noted by acquaintances, friends, or neighbors?
18. **Recent or pending court action and arrest history:** Was the decedent involved in a nasty divorce, child custody battle, bankruptcy, or lawsuits? Were the decedent's wages garnished? Were there any active repossessions or foreclosures on the property? Were there any recent arrests with pending court appearances, or warrants?
19. **Teachers, caseworkers, physicians, including psychiatrists:** Was a child decedent showing signs of mental or physical abuse? Were there any patterns of absence or complaints about specific family members? Was the child withdrawn from the class activity? Did the child draw graphic pictures depicting violence or harmful events? Did the child have any injuries with questionable circumstances or inadvertent admissions of wrongdoing? Did the patient claim to be suicidal or make statements about hurting themselves? Was there any history of overdose or deliberate omission of medication, or any history of other siblings with unexplained illnesses or death?
20. **Other siblings:** Do siblings exhibit signs of abuse or neglect? Have siblings moved into the decedent's bedroom shortly after the death? Did siblings hear or see any changes in the decedent's behavior? Was there any sign that the family has put the incident behind them?
21. **Child/adult protective services:** Were any intervention by child services substantiated or unsubstantiated? Check with the local police department, emergency medical services, or fire department regarding repeated response to residence for medical or legal intervention, adult protective service reports, or intervention—substantiated or unsubstantiated.

During the initial response to an incident, pay particular attention to statements made by the complainant or witnesses. Be cognizant of slang, racist, or derogatory terms used to describe the decedent, such as "The dyke finally got what was coming to her." These statements, although not self-incriminating, may jump-start the investigation as to a possible motive of a criminal act.

Witness Interviewing

At the time of an incident, the investigator may not know who is a witness and who, if anyone, is a suspect, so these techniques can be applied to both. Upon initial contact with any witnesses, be sure to obtain proper identification as well as their address and telephone number. It is likely the investigator will need to conduct additional interviews to clarify information obtained during the course of the investigation. Determine where the witness was located at the time of the incident as well as what they were doing. By having them describe what they were doing, you may be able to determine how much detail they were able to observe firsthand, as opposed to obtaining the information by talking to others. For instance, if they tell you they were involved in a baseball game, their attention to surrounding details would most likely be limited. Have them recount the incident from beginning to end, in their own words, being careful not to unnecessarily interrupt them with questions. Interruptions will interfere with their train of thought, causing them to possibly miss important facts. When their verbal statement is completed, take this opportunity to ask questions and clarify any unclear information. Next, have the witness give a written statement, making sure that any important facts are documented in writing. If the witness is unable to give a written statement for any reason, offer to write one for him or her, making sure documentation indicates you did so. It is very important to remember not to abbreviate or paraphrase the witness's statement. Write down his or her exact wording, regardless of whether it makes sense or not. If the witness uses poor grammar or other grammatical errors, don't correct the statement. Write down the exact wording used. This information may prove to validate or contradict information obtained later. For some investigators, it is easier to detect discrepancies in a statement by viewing the written words. For this reason, it is very beneficial to have recorded statements typed out by a stenographer. If the investigator possesses statement analysis training, he or she can review the written statement to look for signs of deception or deliberate attempts to provide false information.

A helpful technique to utilize during the interview process is repetitive questioning. This technique has several advantages. First, repetitive questioning will allow the investigator to clarify any information that may be confusing, unclear, or needs to be elaborated on. Second, the interviewee may have forgotten how he or she answered the question the first time, which is often the case with deceptive persons. Perhaps the most beneficial reason is that an intentionally deceptive person will begin to think the investigator doesn't believe the first story they told, so they will begin to deviate from the original story, possibly changing important facts about their involvement. This is their attempt to make the story more believable. Needless to say, once a person changes his or her story, it is a sign of deception. The investigator must now question why the person is being deceptive. Is it to limit his or her involvement or hide guilt?

Finally, utilize the "show me" technique. This requires interviewees to reenact exactly what they were doing just prior to the incident and act out what they did, where they went, and what they said. Don't let them just stand there and tell you; have them physically show you their actions. The show me technique has several advantages. First, it will allow the witness to relive the incident in his or her own mind, which will stimulate recall. By reliving the incident, the witness will most likely remember or reveal something he or she didn't tell you initially. Second, this technique may assist the dive team in locating the body. Most importantly, this technique will reveal any discrepancies in the witness's story, whether intentional or not.[4]

CASE STUDY

A man reported two boys missing that he had observed in a boat in a nearby pond. Upon his initial interview, he stated he was at the top of a cliff adjacent to the pond birdwatching when he saw two boys in a small rowboat. A short time later, he heard a scream and ran to the edge of the cliff, only to find the rowboat overturned and no sign of the boys. He immediately called for assistance. During his initial interview, he stated the overturned boat was at the base of the cliff. A line of sight was drawn and divers were deployed in this area and, after six hours of searching, did not locate either of the missing boys. A second interview with the birdwatcher was conducted using the show me technique. The interviewer had the birdwatcher reenact exactly what he had done after hearing the scream. The birdwatcher ran near the edge of the cliff, but not right to the end. He stated he was afraid of heights and did not go out to the far reaches of the cliff. A second line of sight was drawn, and divers were deployed in this new location. Within thirty minutes, they located both boys on the bottom of the lake (Figure 4.5).

Figure 4.5 Birdwatcher witnessing overturned boat with missing boys.

If the incident was a child drowning in a bathtub and his mother was giving the bath and says, "I was only gone a few minutes to answer the phone," the show me technique may reveal if she was even able to hear the phone ring at the time of the incident. Were house windows open at the time with loud noises coming from outside? Was the stereo or television on, adding further background noise? Was she able to hear the splash from the kitchen, like her statement reflects? The show me technique will ultimately answer these questions. Could this really have happened the way the witness says it did? Again, once discrepancies are revealed, the investigator will be required to push forward, demanding further explanation.

I recall several drowning incidents I have responded to, to find the only witness to the incident sitting in his or her car away from the search area. All too often, a witness is interviewed and then abandoned to go conduct a search. Care must be taken to maintain constant contact with the witness. Ideally, witnesses can guide searchers to the last seen point by directing them where to go from shore.

In July 2005, we had a swimmer reported missing at Perkins Beach, which is a non-swimming area at Edgewater Park, Ohio. When I arrived at the scene, several other units had arrived ahead of me and were already searching the waters of Lake Erie for the missing swimmer. I asked where the reporting person was located, and I was told the female complainant was sitting in the parking lot by her vehicle. This was a fair distance from the search area. Our lifeguards were in the water doing surface dives in an attempt to locate the missing swimmer. I quickly met the complainant, the swimmer's girlfriend, and led her to the water's edge. I asked her to advise me if the guards were in the right location. She indicated they were not and told me to move them to the left about 30 feet. I directed the guards to move to the location she indicated and a short time later, her boyfriend was found.

Maintaining contact may also reveal an alternative location where the potential victim may be located. A girl reported her little brother missing at our main swimming beach, last seen in the water. The lifeguards cleared the water and obtained volunteers to form a human chain. They began to conduct a search of the 3- to 4-foot waves using the human chain. I kept constant contact with the sister, asking multiple questions, such as "Does he know how to swim? Would he enter the water alone? Does he have a favorite location in the park he likes to visit? Do you have any relatives or friends living in the area?" Suddenly, she spoke up and stated their grandparents lived a couple of blocks from the park. I sent a cruiser to the grandparents' home, and the missing boy was sitting on their couch. This prevented a potential disaster had we decided to deploy divers into the heavy surf. Contact with the complainant will also prevent him or her from locating the missing person somewhere else on his or her own and leaving the location, with searchers frantically looking for a victim who is no longer there.

Suspect Interviewing

The investigator must determine if this incident is an accident, suicide, or homicide. Practically speaking, in most incidents of a water-related death, the outcome of the case will rely heavily upon the evidence collected, the autopsy results of the decedent, and any information the investigator is able to obtain. If there is no trauma to the body, does that mean the manner of death is an accident? Since evidence and autopsy findings cannot determine whether a victim deliberately jumped into the water to commit suicide, fell into the water by accident, or was forced into the water in a homicidal act, any indication of foul play will hinge solely on the statements made by the complainant or witnesses. For this reason, it is imperative the investigator possess the necessary training and experience in nonverbal communication (body language) and statement analysis.

While conducting interviews, it is important to remember one simple fact: the human brain (mind) always wants to tell the truth. This is based on the individual's recall as he or she relives the incident in chronological order, the exact way it happened. When a deceptive person wishes to either withhold information to limit his or her involvement or change facts to conceal his or her guilt, he or she must continuously remember to make a conscious effort to deceive. Once an interviewee becomes more comfortable with the interview, he or she will let his or her guard down and begin to deviate from his or her untruthfulness and begin to unknowingly tell the truth. This will cause hesitations in his or her thought process, which may cause the person to stammer, hesitate, or correct statements previously made, such as in the interview of Scott Peterson.

CASE STUDY

I recall several years ago watching the *Tonight Show* hosted by Jay Leno. He had a pregnant actress named Jennifer Garner as a guest. During the first portion of Mr. Leno's interview, he asked her: "Do you know if you are having a boy or a girl?" Ms. Garner laughed and replied that she did know the sex of her baby but decided this information was something she and her husband wanted to keep a secret. She indicated that their baby's sex was an important secret that she and her husband held dear to their hearts. (It was very apparent to the viewing audience, myself included, that she did not want to reveal the sex of her unborn child.) Later in the interview, when she reached her comfort zone, she referred to the baby as "she." Jay Leno immediately picked up on this and told her she had just revealed she was having a daughter. She appeared noticeably upset for having revealed her best-kept secret.

Attention to minute details such as the one word *she* in this case can make or break not only a witness statement but, quite possibly, a whole case. While this interview was innocent in nature, other nationally publicized cases have had similar indications of deception. When Susan Smith appeared on national television to plead for the safe return of her two sons, allegedly kidnapped by a black male suspect who had carjacked her vehicle, she spoke of her sons in the past tense. She stated, "I **loved** my children; my children **needed** me." She spoke of them in the past tense because in her mind, she knew they were already dead. Other key wording in her statements included the phrase, "I would like to say to **whoever** has my children that **they** please, I mean please bring them home to us where they belong." She used the words *whoever* and *they.* If the last thing you remember is a black male driving away with your children in your car, you would refer to the suspect as *him* or *he,* not *whoever* and *they.* Because she is making up the story, she cannot relate to it. She doesn't see one man driving away with her kids because it never happened.[5]

On January 28, 2003, Diane Sawyer of ABC's *Good Morning America* interviewed Scott Peterson about the disappearance of his pregnant wife, Laci Peterson, and their unborn son, Connor. Ms. Sawyer inquired about the condition of his marriage to his wife Laci by asking, "What kind of marriage was it?" Scott Peterson's reply was: "God, the first word that comes to mind is, you know, glorious. I mean we took care of each other very well. She **was** amazing. She **is** amazing." When asked about his unborn son, due to be born within weeks, he responded, "That **was,** it's so hard." In both responses, he catches himself speaking of both of them in the past tense and corrects himself.[6]

Other clues to be cognizant of are statements made about a specific area the suspect may have traveled to. This will seem to be an out-of-the-way place that will not coincide with the rest of the story. This location will most likely be involved in the incident. In fear that he or she may have been seen there, the suspect will make up some sort of excuse for having been at that location. This was the case, once again, in the disappearance of Laci Peterson and her unborn son. Scott Peterson claimed he went fishing in San Francisco Bay the day his wife disappeared. Investigators believed this was the time and location where he dumped the remains of his wife and their unborn son. Fearing someone might have seen him at that location, he offered the reasoning that he had gone fishing.[7]

Second Interview

If the interviewer detects inconsistencies in an individual's statement about a specific incident, it is highly advisable to conduct a second interview with that person. The interviewer should respond to the individual's residence unannounced. An effective ruse is to claim you misplaced their original written statement and need to acquire another one. Television detective Columbo was famous for this technique. He always appeared to be the most unorganized, absent-minded person in the world. This second interview will serve several purposes. First, it requires deceptive persons to remember the first lie they told you and will often reveal major changes in their version of what happened. Second, it allows the investigator to observe the actions and activities in the home of the deceased. Are there indications the family is planning to move? Have other siblings moved into the bedroom of the decedent? Are the decedent's belongings packed away already or possibly placed out in the garbage? There may be multiple indications of abnormal behavior that could reinforce your initial suspicions of untruthfulness, leading you to believe this incident is more than an unfortunate accident.

After obtaining the second written statement, compare the two and look for indiscrepancies. Again, the witness may sense the first version was hard to believe, so he or she will embellish or change it altogether to make it easier to believe.

Determining Accuracy of Statements Obtained at Scene

An investigator may only get one chance to conduct an interview with anyone involved in an incident. Witnesses may not be available in the future, or they may begin to forget important details about the specific incident when interviewed at a later date. Likewise, any potential suspect may be providing information in which he or she is not aware that it implicates him or her in the incident. As mentioned earlier, high-profile cases were broken wide open by using statement analysis skills. For this reason, it is imperative for the investigator to be able to determine the accuracy of the information that he obtains at the scene. If he is able to determine discrepancies, he can require clarification while on the scene, possibly catching a wrongdoer off guard and causing him or her to offer an inadvertent admission of guilt. When conducting interviews on the scene, ask yourself the following questions:

1. Does the evidence conflict with statements given by the complainant, witness, or possible suspect?
2. Are witness accounts conflicting drastically or are there major holes in the witness's story?
3. Is the complainant or suspect showing signs of deception or untruthfulness?
4. Are there discrepancies in the statements after the incident reenactment is conducted, or inadvertent admissions of guilt?
5. Do witness accounts change drastically during a second interview? Minute details may change or might be added due to recall, but a total change of the story is a red flag indicator of deception.
6. Are subtle hints of deception or untruthfulness apparent in a video, or audiotaped statement, or accidental admissions of guilt?

CASE STUDY

On November 15, 1990, Billy Blankenship, a two-year-old boy, was reported to have fallen down a stairway, causing a massive skull fracture. The incident was reported by his babysitter, Tawny Gunter. During an incident interview, Gunter stated that she was in the kitchen when she heard a thump, thump. She ran to the stairway and found Billy lying at the bottom of the stairs, unconscious. He died from his head injuries. There was no cause for an investigation until eight years later when a three-month-old baby died while in the care of Gunter, and three other children were injured at Gunter's house between 1991 and 1997. The autopsy of the three-year-old could not determine the cause of death. Investigators went to Gunter's house and had her reenact the incident on videotape, and no fault could be determined. A different medical examiner reviewed the skull x-rays of Billy Blankenship and found a skull fracture inconsistent with a fall down the stairs. Investigators returned to Gunter's home to videotape a reenactment of the Blankenship incident. During the reenactment, she stated she was in the kitchen and heard a thump, thump. She stated she ran to the top of the stairs and saw Billy lying on the floor at the bottom. She then walked to the bottom of the stairs and stated, "Billy was whimpering. I thought I had just knocked the air out of him." During a review of the videotape, this inadvertent admission was detected by the investigators, which revealed that she was not only present for the fall but had actually caused it. She later admitted to grabbing Billy in a fit of rage and causing him to fall over the side of a staircase. On November 15, 1999, Gunter pleaded guilty to voluntary manslaughter and received the maximum sentence of 15 years.[8]

Indicators of Deception

It is not the intent here to provide an all-inclusive description of techniques to determine whether or not an individual is lying to you but to offer a brief overview of key indicators that offer a high probability of deception. In order to become an effective interviewer, an individual must seek specialized training, supplemented by reading and personal research and dedication to practice these skills until proficient. An excellent way to practice picking up on key wording is by observing interview-related talk shows on television. Formal and informal interviews can provide a wealth of knowledge about the interviewee if you know what to look for. The following is a list of categories that may alert an interviewer to an evasive or deceptive response and a brief description of each.

1. Unfinished business
2. "I can't"
3. Hypothetically structured phrase
4. Hard question
5. Objection
6. Nonreflective denial of knowledge
7. Maintenance of dignity
8. Interrogatory
9. Projection
10. No proof
11. Accusatory
12. The answer is …
13. Rambling dissertation
14. The answer does not equal the question
15. Denial of presence
16. Speech errors

Unfinished Business

Unfinished business is usually found in statements when an individual has just completed a long description of what has occurred, and he or she ends his or her statement with a phrase such as "That's about it," "That's about all there is," or "I guess that's about all." Such statements should immediately alert the interviewer that there is more to the story than what the person is telling you.

"I Can't"

In this instance, the subject is being completely truthful in stating phrases such as "I can't say," "I can't think of anything," "I can't tell you anything about that," and "I can only tell you this." These statements indicate the subject is verbally prohibiting himself from telling the interviewer any more details about the topic in question.

The Hypothetically Structured Phrase

Use of words such as *could*, *would*, *should*, or *ought* when describing specific facts regarding the incident reveals a hypothetical response. For instance, say an interviewer asks a child molester, "Did you fondle Billy's genitals?" and the subject's response is: "I would say not!" Your first impression is that he is offended by the question, but further examination reveals that the subject really didn't say anything, only that he *would* say something.

Hard Question

Again, the subject is being completely truthful with the interviewer by stating, "That's a hard question." The subject is actually saying he doesn't like the question or that it is simply hard for him to answer, or possibly that he's having difficulty answering the question. If he states, "That's a hard question" and then immediately answers the question with the expected response, it may simply mean that it was hard only because he wanted to answer it accurately, and needed to search his long-term memory to answer it. However, if the subject doesn't answer the question accurately, he is giving an evasive response.

Objection

This response is usually given when the interviewee perceives the question to be that of a sensitive issue. If asked if he stole $5,000 from the bank safe, a suspect isn't going to say yes. So he decides to respond with something like, "I'm not the kind of guy that would do something like that; I have worked here for ten years and I have a good record here and I **could** never do something like that."

Nonreflective Denial of Knowledge

If an interviewee is asked a question in which a pause is normally required to search his long-term memory, but he immediately responds with an "I don't know," "I don't think so," "I guess not," or "I doubt it," with no pause to search his memory, then he is giving an evasive response and probable deception has occurred. For instance, when the interviewer asks a male, "Did you make a comment to Ms. Smith about the size of her breasts?" and his immediate response is, "Not to the best of my knowledge," with no pause to remember, his response is deceptive.

Maintenance of Dignity

This response lets the interviewer know that the question is offensive to the subject. For instance, the question is asked: "Did you fondle Suzie's genitals?" The response is: "I beg your pardon! That is an offensive question!" Or consider this question when asked: "Did you steal any of that sports equipment?" and the response is, "I'm the manager. What kind of question is that to ask of someone in my position?" An honest response would be a simple no.

The Interrogatory Evasive Response

This is when a question is answered with a question. Often, the answer will simply be a repeat of the question, such as "Did you shoot that man?" The response may be: "Did I shoot that man?" You may also get a response such as "How should I know?" "What makes you think I would know?" or "Why are you asking me that?" These are all examples of an evasive response.

Projection

This response allows the subject to admit his own fears but projects fault on someone else. For example, the interviewer asks, "Did you sexually touch your daughter's private parts?" and his response is: "Someone would have to be sick to do that!" In this case, the someone is himself. "Did you break into that store?" "Someone would really have to be stupid to try that. There is so much security and an alarm!"

No Proof

When a question is asked that requires only a yes or no answer, the subject may challenge the interviewer with a "prove it" response. In a burglary, the interviewer asks, "Do you know if the window was broken to gain access to the building?" and the response is: "Is that how they got in? I don't know, I wasn't there, and no one can prove that I was!" Other responses may be: "You'll never prove it," "Show me the proof," "Where's the proof?" or "They'll never prove it!"

Accusatory

When asked a direct question, requiring a yes-or-no answer, the subject may respond with something such as "Are you accusing me of doing that?" His or her claim of an accusation comes from the mind of a guilty person. For instance, when asked, "Did you steal any of the missing money?" the person may respond with answers such as "I don't like being accused of something like that," "I feel like I'm being accused," "Who's accusing me of lying about it?" or "That accusation is false; I have been accused of doing stuff like that before."

The Answer Is …

Again, the interviewer asks a question requiring a simple yes or no answer, yet the subject responds with: "The answer is no." An evasive response such as this allows the subject to respond with a no, without having to lie directly. Literally, he has not said no, he has only said that "the answer is no." Other responses may include "That's a no," "My answer to that is no," "I'll answer that no," or "The answer to that question is no."

Rambling Dissertation

The subject will use any verbal tactic he can to get the interviewer to believe his response to a question is truthful when in fact he is concealing guilt. The subject will provide an overabundance of information than what is necessary to answer the question, literally by rambling.

The Answer Does Not Equal the Question

When asked a direct question about a crime, the subject will respond but not answer the question. For example, if asked, "Did you steal any of the missing money from the safe?" he responds with, "I didn't even know there was any money in the safe; it's not my job to go into the safe." Another example may be: "Did you have a gun on you when you entered the store?" and he responds, "I don't have nutin' to do wit guns!"

Denial of Presence

Even though it is clear that the only two people present for the interview are the subject and the interviewer, the subject will ask if you are asking "him" the question. For instance, when asked "Did you shoot that girl?" he responds with: "Who me? Are you asking me? Is that question for me? Are you talkin' to me?"

Speech Errors

During witnesses' accounts of an incident, they may make an honest mistake in their speech, meaning they tell exactly what they were thinking. For instance, when a female was asked, "What else can you tell me about this incident?" she responded with, "Just that I am doing everything I can to prove that I am guilty." When a suspect was asked, "How do you think this polygraph will come out?" he responded with, "My answers will tree the buth" (instead of "be the truth"). [9]

Again, this information is only a general overview. To fully understand these key phrases and become proficient in their use, formal training is highly recommended, coupled with supplemental reading. I have read many books on the topic of interview and interrogation, and *Identifying Lies in Disguise* by Wendell Rudacille is by far the best book I have found to date.

A fellow officer once told me that body language and statement analysis training is one of the greatest tools law enforcement officers can develop. But, once proficient in its use, "You will be a very unhappy man." I asked him what he meant by that statement, and he said, "You will always know when you are being lied to—by your wife, your kids, and your friends." He was right!

Nonverbal Communication

During the interview process, it will be necessary for the investigator to be cognizant of body language and how it pertains to a deceptive person. Body language, coupled with good statement analysis skills, can reveal much about the validity of any statement obtained. Like statement analysis, body language, or nonverbal communication, requires formal training and adequate practice in observing and recognizing deception.

It is very advantageous to videotape any statements made during the course of the investigation. Although it is not always practical, not only can a videotape reveal spontaneous utterances of deception or guilt, but it also allows others who have the expertise to observe the interview and possibly observe deception, such as the Billy Blankenship case previously mentioned.

Telling lies causes anxiety in most people, which elevates their stress level. This stress causes their body to react by making movements such as changing body positioning by shifting in their seat, touching their face with their hands, shifting their eyes, or even pointless gestures such as picking lint off their clothing or smoothing nonexistent wrinkles in clothing.

It is believed that the eyes are "the window to the soul." For this reason, generally speaking, a deceptive person will not look his or her interviewer in the eye while telling a lie, in fear the interviewer will be able to "see what they are thinking." They will maintain eye contact throughout their statement, but at the point of deception their eyes will involuntarily shift, often from side to side or down, as if in shame.

Physical Gestures

Here are a few physical gestures an investigator may observe during the interview and a brief description of each:

Head position: If tilted to the side, the person is being cooperative, interested, and truthful. If his or her chin is resting on his or her chest, this is a sign of probable deception.

Eyes: If he or she breaks eye contact, this indicates probable deception. Looking at the ceiling and blinking indicate ready to confess. Pupils fully dilated indicate probable deception. Closed eyes mean the person is mentally trying to escape the situation (deception), and rapid blinking means high stress and probably lying.

Mouth: Frequent fake smiles mean deception. Dry mouth or a hoarse voice means high stress and probable deception. Biting of the lower lip means the person is physically preventing himself or herself from giving incriminating information or is possibly ready to confess.

Arms: Crossed and tight to body indicates deception. Away from body indicates relaxed, truthful.

Hands: Covering both eyes means attempting to mentally escape, probable deception. Hands over mouth means the person doesn't want to talk or is lying. Hands on chin indicate truthfulness.

Legs: Open with hands folded in lap indicates truthful. Crossed (especially with men) means deceptive.

Again, formal extensive training is required to fully understand the use of body language during an interview, and the more an interviewer practices these techniques, the more proficient he or she will become in their use.

Why People Lie and How They Attempt to Conceal It

Children learn from a very early age to lie to avoid pain, both mental and physical. When parents inquire about a specific incident in which the child was involved, they urge the child to tell the truth. When the child is truthful and admits fault, the parent responds with a physical correction, often in the form of a spanking. The next time the child is questioned about an incident, he or she lies to avoid physical correction and confrontation.

People lie for any number of reasons, such as embarrassment, acceptance of fault or blame, and especially acceptance of guilt. For most people, though, lying is very difficult, yet they choose to lie rather than get caught in any wrongdoing. But telling a flat-out lie is extremely difficult for most people, so they choose to use a form of deception called verbal evasion, which to an untrained listener may seem like the truth. In telling direct lies, the person will experience varying degrees of anxiety, remorse, or shame in fear of the consequences to them if the lie is discovered. For police officers, failure to detect deception in the verbal responses of individuals they deal with on a daily basis can result in serious physical injury or death. For this reason, the importance of statement analysis training cannot be overemphasized, and criminals are successfully eluding detection, interrogation, and even arrest.[9]

Child Witnesses

Children make excellent witnesses because they do not exaggerate or embellish their account of what occurred like adults do. Frequently, statements and observations by adults are enhanced or altered based on individual experiences, prejudices, or beliefs from everyday activities and watching television. For instance, an adult may state he or she knew the decedent was drowning because the persons was waving his arms, splashing a lot, and calling for help. This is how a drowning is portrayed on television and is a common misconception for that reason. Even if these actions did not occur, this is their perception of what a drowning person does, and this is what they will tell you occurred, possibly leading to conflicting statements. Yet a child would most likely describe only what they saw. Usually, if adults are present at the scene of an incident, children are overlooked, when in fact the more accurate information may come from the child. A credible witness is one who can understand what is going on around him or her, remember events and relate knowledge of the events intelligently, and appreciate what it means to tell the truth. When interviewing children and taking their statements, the investigator must approach a child in much the same manner as a judge. The investigator must ask him or her if they understand the importance of telling the truth, the consequences of lying to the police, and determine if anyone has told them to lie to the police. Also, the investigator must exercise great care during the interview process to avoid planting ideas or information in their minds. Open-ended questions requiring explanation are better suited for this process.

Interviews of Rescue and Recovery Personnel

Upon arrival at the scene, it must be established if resuscitation attempts were made on the decedent. Attempts to revive a potential drowning victim can cause misleading observations on scene, possibly leading the investigator to erroneous conclusions. The following questions need to be answered by conducting an interview with any potential rescue or recovery personnel, who will include any ambulance attendants, firemen, police officers, rescue/recovery divers, and good Samaritans who may have attempted CPR.

1. Was the body moved in any way?
2. Was the scene altered in any way?
3. Was CPR or first aid rendered?
4. During recovery, was the body wounded in any way?
5. Recovery divers: Specifics about the water, such as depth, temperature, visibility, bottom composition, and surface or submerged debris that may have wounded the body?
6. Indoor scenes: Anything they may have touched or moved?
7. Condition and position of the complainant upon their arrival: Overly upset, backward, uncooperative, wearing wet or dry clothing, any noticeable injuries?
8. Anything heard before police arrival, such as admissions of guilt, blame, and the identity of the perpetrator?
9. Any observation out of the ordinary?

During all the interviews conducted in the investigation of a water-related death, the investigator must maintain belief in the possibility that this tragedy was more than just an accident. If at any given moment, information obtained heightens the investigator's suspicion, any and all leads must be thoroughly investigated. To rule out foul play, it must first be seriously considered.

Case Investigation Assistance

CODIS-Combined DNA Index System

- Created and maintained by FBI
- Three levels

- Local DNA where DNA profiles originate
- State DNA which allows labs within states to share information
- National DNA Index System allows states to compare DNA information

The software has different databases, such as missing persons, convicted offenders, and forensic samples collected from crime scenes.

- It does not include any personal identifying information, such as the name of the contributor (for privacy reasons).
- Uploading agencies are notified of any hits to their sample.
- All 50 states, the District of Columbia, federal law enforcement, Army laboratory and Puerto Rico participate in CODIS.
- The missing persons database helps identify missing using known samples of missing persons as well as those of relatives of missing persons.
- As of March 2018, offender database contains more than 13 million profiles, more than 3 million arrestees and 840,000 forensic profiles.
- International police agencies can submit a request to the FBI to search the U.S. database if the request meets inclusionary standards.

VIDOCQ Society

It is a members-only crime-solving club that meets third Thursday of every month in Philadelphia, PA. It is named after Eugene Francois Vidocq, a 19th-century French detective who aided police using psychology of the criminal to solve cold case homicides.

Vidocq was a former criminal himself and used that experience to look at a crime from the psychological perspective.

During Society meetings, members listen to law enforcement officials from around the world who present cold cases for review.

Members are forensic professionals, current and former FBI profilers, homicide investigators, scientists, psychologists, prosecutors, and coroners.

Membership is by invitation only, and participants must commit to attend at least one meeting per year.

Formed in 1990, solved the first case in 1991, clearing an innocent man of involvement in a murder in Little Rock, Arkansas.

Case Considerations:

1. Unsolved deaths for more than 2 years
2. Victims cannot have been involved in criminal activity, such as prostitutes or drug dealers
3. Case must be formally presented to members from appropriate law enforcement officials
4. Services are not charged
5. Society pays for travel expenses of law enforcement officials that come to present their case

For case assistance, contact the Vidocq Society at Vidocq.org to complete and send the request for assistance.

References

1. A&E Real Crime, Tawny Gunter: When Babysitter's Kill, 11/12/2018.
2. National Institute of Justice, Journal no. 269, March 2012.
3. Geberth, V. 1996. *Practical homicide investigation: Tactics, procedures and forensic techniques*. 3rd ed. Boca Raton, FL: Taylor and Francis.
4. Hendrick, W., and Zafares, A. 1998. *Homicide by drowning training manual*. Hurley, NY: Lifeguard Systems.
5. http://www.statementanalysis.com/smith (accessed May 18, 2009).
6. http://www.findlaci2003.us/interview-sawyer.html (accessed May 18, 2009).
7. http://www.findlaci2003.us (accessed May 18, 2009).
8. Kierra Harrison Foundation. 2002. Blankenship, B. January 11.
9. Rudacille, W. 1999. *Identifying lies in disguise*. Dubuque, IA: Kendall Hunt.

Pretrial Preparation for the Field Investigator 5

KEVIN L. ERSKINE

Incident Report

When compiling and writing an incident report, it is important to remain unbiased in the terminology used to describe the incident. Because history dictates our predisposed opinion to believe that all water-related incidents are accidental drowning, it would be easy to make the mistake of titling the incident report as such. It is much more efficient to use terminologies such as *water-related incident*, *death of undetermined origin*, or *death—unknown cause*. If the death is later ruled an accidental drowning, a supplemental form can be added to the report listing the incident as an accidental drowning. Defense attorneys can make a witness appear inadequate and confused on the witness stand by playing on these words. For instance, an attorney might ask of a witness, "Why was the incident investigated at all if the initial report ruled it an accidental drowning?" "Why has my client been charged with a crime if the initial responding officer declared the incident to be an accident?" The use of unbiased terminology in the beginning will eliminate this confusion.

When taking the initial report, a standard information gathering incident form should be utilized for every incident. This form outlines the details needed to conduct the most thorough investigation into the incident as possible. This will allow the gathering of crucial scene evidence as well as obtaining written and verbal statements from any known witnesses. As you walk into the scene of the incident, remain open-minded and don't take anything for granted. Do not make any assumptions, be observant, and document as much as possible by taking extensive notes. What is the body position of the decedent? Is the body wet, damp, or dry? Are there any smells you recognize, such as feces, alcohol, or vomit? Is the complainant wet? Does the evidence make sense? Does the evidence support what the witnesses are saying happened?

The final report should include as many details as possible. It should be written in layperson's terms so that anyone reading it can understand it. Supplemental notes can be used and kept by the investigator but should not be included in the body of the report. The report should only contain facts, which can be substantiated by evidence or witness testimony. Hunches, speculations, and opinions should not be included. Investigative notes in an open case that are made by an investigator are not subject to public record requests as long as they are not included in the body of the report.

Chain of Evidence and Exhibits

As with any evidence in a criminal prosecution, it is imperative that the proper chain of evidence is maintained. Any evidence obtained must have an attached chain of custody tag that documents who recovered it, the date and location recovered, a description of the evidence, and a detailed listing of virtually everyone who has possessed it. One common person overlooked is a recovery diver. The diver surfaces with the item and hands it to a surface support person on a boat or onshore. That person attaches a tag and affixes his or her information to start the chain of custody. Because the diver is wet and often still in the water, his or her name is often omitted from the chain of custody. An efficient way to avoid this mistake is to train surface support personnel to print the diver's name on the evidence tag as soon as it is recovered. This documents who found it so that at a later time, when the diver has exited the water, he or she can sign the tag. It is not uncommon for defense attorneys to be present during recovery efforts to locate evidence; therefore, every effort must be made to ensure proper documentation is completed. If the defense attorney can put any doubt at all into the chain of custody, that piece of evidence will be declared inadmissible.

So, in an instance where a recovered gun, for example, is placed into an evidence room pending ballistic testing, the evidence technician must affix his or her signature to the tag, having received it from the support personnel. When the gun is taken to the lab, the transporting officer must sign the chain of custody as well as every laboratory technician who handles or analyzes the weapon until it is taken back to the evidence room. This procedure assures the court that the evidence presented in court is the same evidence that was recovered from the scene and that the exhibit has not been tampered with illicitly for court proceedings.

Planning the prosecution of a case will require the investigator and the prosecutor to collaborate on what items are to be introduced as evidence and having that evidence properly prepared as an exhibit for the court. Together, you must decide what items you want to use. You must consider what is relevant to the case as well as what is necessary to prove a point being made. The rules of evidence will dictate what items will be admissible by the judge as an exhibit. The investigator must ensure that the proper chain of custody is followed when retrieving any evidence to be used for court purposes. The chain of evidence requires signatures of anyone handling the evidence, from the evidence technician who releases it from the evidence room to the officer bringing it to court and anyone else who takes possession of the item. If any one of these signatures is absent, the item could be found to be tainted and ruled inadmissible.

In preparation of exhibits, it is necessary to produce an exhibit packet that can be distributed to the required parties in court, including a copy for the judge as well as the defense. The packet will include a cover page, which is primarily the exhibit list, followed by each individually labeled exhibit. These exhibits are marked according to a directive provided by the court, usually with color-coded stickers to identify them as exhibits specifically for the prosecution/plaintiff or defense. One copy of the exhibit packet must be provided to the defense by the deadline on the pretrial order. It can be mailed or hand-delivered.

The exhibit packet is not filed with the court until the trial itself. Nothing is presented to the judge until the hearing is in progress, and you have reached the portion of the case when you wish to refer to that specific piece of evidence. The decision as to what items will be admitted as exhibits rests solely with the judge presiding over the case.

The rules of evidence will dictate what evidence will be admitted into court. For instance, a witness can only testify to information he or she knows firsthand. Hearsay (secondhand knowledge) testimony is not allowed. Testimony and exhibits must be relevant to the case.

Items used to present a case are called exhibits. Exhibits may include photographs; records such as police reports, medical records, bills, appraisals, inspections, etc. Basically, any item of evidentiary value that is relevant to the case is considered an exhibit.

During the court proceedings, a prosecutor in a criminal prosecution, or an attorney in a civil matter, has to introduce the exhibit to the court. The witness who will testify to its relevance must have knowledge about the exhibit and be able to explain this relevance to the court. For example, a letter may be introduced that has been written by the defendant. The witness may testify that he or she knows the letter was written by the defendant because he or she has known that person for many years and recognizes the handwriting. However, you could not introduce a photograph of an item the witness has never seen and expect him or her to testify to its relevance.

Pretrial Interviews

A witness for the prosecution should never take the stand to testify without having been subjected to a pretrial interview with the prosecutor. This interview should be conducted in a secluded location, out of sight and sound of the general public. This interview is conducted to review the evidence to be presented and identify any weak areas of the case. It will also prepare the witness and prosecutor for any potential discrepancies that may surface during the witness's testimony. After the interview is completed, the witness will have a full understanding of what is expected of him or her and what questions will be asked. The prosecutor will know what to expect from the witness, so there are no surprises during the testimony. Pretrial interviews are a standard procedure in most jurisdictions and should never be considered optional.

Eyewitness Testimony vs. Circumstantial Evidence

Contrary to popular belief, circumstantial evidence can be more compelling than eyewitness testimony. A DNA match of blood from the victim found on a suspect's clothing, a ballistic match of a bullet removed from a decedent to the gun of a suspect, or credit card records that place a suspect at the scene of a crime are all examples of circumstantial evidence.

In contrast, a psychological study has shown that witnesses are not very good at identifying people they have seen only once, especially for a very short time. The study revealed error rates as high as 50%, which is an alarming rate considering many convictions are made on the testimony of eyewitnesses. The study also showed that witness accuracy is also greatly diminished by stress, and cross-racial identifications are especially unreliable. Study results (based on 179 eyewitness misidentification cases in the first 239 DNA exonerations) showed the following:

1. The number of witnesses misidentifying the same defendant:
   - 62% with one witness
   - 25% with two witnesses
   - 13% with three or more witnesses
2. Eyewitness misidentification as the central cause:
   - 50%—just misidentification
   - 48%—with invalidated or improper forensic science
   - 8%—with false confession or admission
   - 8%—with informant testimony[1]

It is important to remember that while working a case, evidence is much more reliable than witness statements and eyewitness accounts. Witness recollection is too easily swayed by the personal experiences of the witness as well as preexisting prejudices. The following case study is an example of prejudice, as well as tunnel vision by the investigator once accusatory statements are made toward any possible suspect.

CASE STUDY

One night in 1982, three young girls were sleeping alone in a Shreveport, Louisiana, home when a man in cowboy boots came into the house and raped the oldest girl, who was ten years old. When police started to investigate the rape, the three girls all remembered the attack differently. One police report said the ten-year-old victim didn't see her attacker's face. Another report, which wasn't introduced at trial, said she identified Calvin Willis, a black man who lived in the neighborhood. The girl's mother testified at trial that neighbors had mentioned Willis's name when discussing who might have committed the crime. The victim testified that she was shown photos and told to pick the man without a full beard. She testified that she didn't pick anyone. Police said she picked Willis. Willis was convicted by a jury and sentenced to life in prison. In 2003, DNA testing proved Willis's innocence and he was released. He had served nearly 22 years in prison for a crime he didn't commit.[1]

During cross-examination, a defense attorney will make every effort to refute the testimony of an eyewitness by inquiring about the lighting, duration of the encounter, stress experienced by the witness, and any other facts that may undermine the reliability of the witness. In most cases, though, the jury will often believe the testimony of an eyewitness despite a successful cross-examination because they are not aware of the studies that cast doubt on this testimony. Juries will also tend to place more weight on the testimony of a witness that displays more confidence. They tend to view a nervous person as untruthful, yet many practiced liars are confident and cool on the witness stand. Many first-time witnesses are nervous about testifying.

One must also consider cultural differences. Many Americans want a person to "look them in the eye" when telling the truth, yet in many countries, it is more respectful to keep your gaze downward. In short, when the prosecution plans on using the testimony of an eyewitness, every effort should be made by the investigator to qualify the testimony with other articulable facts or evidence.[2]

Child Witnesses

Historically, courts have assumed adult testimony to be more reliable than the testimony of children. Studies have shown this to be distinctly contradictive in that child witnesses tend to be more accurate than adults because they base their memory on actual events. Memories are captured and stored in two different parts of the mind. Children depend more on the part of the mind that relies on what actually happened, while adults depend more on the meaning of what happened. As a result, adults are more susceptible to false or altered memories than children. The ability to extract meaning from an event develops slowly over time. Therefore, children are more likely to give accurate accounts of what occurred because their memory is not based on personal experiences, biased opinions, what the actual event meant to them, or how it affected them personally.

Because witness testimony is often the primary evidence in criminal prosecutions, false memories could be the main reason for the convictions of innocent people. Children do not have the same amount of intellectual experiences as an adult when it comes to deriving meaning from an incident, so meaning-based testimony is less likely to influence the testimony of a child.[3]

Expert Witnesses

The difference between a witness and an expert witness is that expert testimony generally holds more weight than that of any other witness, and an expert is permitted to offer his or her opinion. Expert opinion is always subjected to scrutiny, but in many instances, it has tipped the scales of justice in the direction of an acquittal or conviction.

Once the expert has been sworn in on the witness stand, the prosecutor will ask him or her to give testimony regarding his or her qualifications and experience. This is to establish the witness as an expert and to persuade the court to give more weight to his or her testimony rather than an expert for the defense.

When an expert testifies, he or she should speak clearly and slowly so that he or she can ensure understanding. As with all witnesses, the expert must ensure that he or she understands the questions being asked of him or her. Expert witnesses should keep their reply brief but complete. The expert should refrain from giving expert opinions unless specifically asked.

The defense may cross-examine the expert's qualifications to try to discredit the testimony about to be given, suggesting he or she is not qualified to be regarded by the court as an expert. Whether or not an expert is qualified to give testimony as an expert is for the court to determine. When a court is presented with more than one expert with conflicting opinions, the court must decide on whom to place greater reliance. One of the factors will be a comparison of the training and experience of the experts as well as their general credibility.

During the testimony of the expert, the defense will seek to cut short the expert's testimony or answers to questions. The court should then be asked to allow the expert to finish. When the testimony is complete, the defense will conduct cross-examination in an attempt to weaken, disqualify, or destroy the prosecution's case. A common practice is to get the expert to give an opinion outside of his or her expertise. The defense will attempt to get the expert to contradict his or her testimony.

During reexamination by the prosecution, no new evidence can be presented. This is limited to explaining matters arising out of the cross-examination.

In order for the prosecution to discredit the expert for the defense, the prosecutor must challenge his or her competence by asking questions about training and experience. The prosecution should have prepared questions for cross-examination before trial. While the defense expert is testifying, the expert for the prosecution should sit near the prosecutor to assist with questions. The prosecution may only call for further evidence when the need for it arises *ex improviso:* where no human ingenuity could have foreseen the need for it.[4]

Video and Audio Recordings

Videotaped evidence and video documentation of a crime scene often present a challenge for the prosecuting attorney in the case. Many courts maintain that actual documentation of a crime scene is much too dramatic for the eyes of a jury and may gain a sympathetic vote in favor of the prosecution. Many jurisdictions will only allow black-and-white still photography, especially in cases where extreme trauma is present. The exception to this practice is in cases where the video may offer evidence that will directly refute testimony by the defense. Anytime a video is entered as a court exhibit, be prepared to defend its use because the defense will always object.

When presenting audio recordings of interviews with witnesses and suspects alike, the prosecution will simplify the process if they have taken the time to also include a typed manuscript of the entire audio recording. This allows for clarification of what is said when portions of the audio recording are difficult to understand, either by mumbling of the subject being interviewed or other noises that affect the quality of the recording. Any trained stenographer can produce a typed manuscript from an audio recording. Preparing ahead of time will eliminate any confusion during the court proceedings. As with any evidence, make sure the chain of custody is completed properly and that the video or audio recording has the appropriate documentation declaring who made the recording, the date recorded, and the corresponding case number.

Testifying in Court: Credibility, Appearance, and Demeanor

When you first enter the courtroom, your first impression of the judge, jury, and attorneys will have a direct effect on how you will be treated and how your testimony will be accepted. The investigator's appearance alone may be enough to sway the court's opinion toward acceptance.

As a professional, the investigator must be prepared to testify in court regarding the investigation and corresponding evidence. He or she must present the case in a clear, concise, and confident manner to establish his or her credibility with the jury. The investigator must appear and act professionally, both inside and outside the courtroom. You can never be sure who is sizing you up before you even enter the courtroom to take the stand. When appropriate, the investigator should appear in his or her departmental uniform. If testifying in plain clothes, he or she should wear business attire. Common attire in court for men includes dark-colored or neutral browns and beiges and should include a business-type suit jacket with a tie. The proper dress for women is also business attire of similar color in the form of skirts or pantsuits. Shoes should be worn with appropriate leg coverings (pantyhose or dress socks). Women's shoes should also be close-toed and of reasonable support and height (i.e., no stilettos). Limit the loud ties and excessive jewelry and avoid flashy colors.

When being sworn in, make eye contact with the jurors and clearly state, "I do." Once seated, look directly at the prosecutor during questioning, and then make eye contact with the jurors during your answer. This displays confidence in your testimony as well as reassuring your knowledge in the case. All questions should be answered verbally and avoid nodding. Nodding will prompt the court reporter to question your response and may be viewed as a sign of disrespect for the court. Sit upright with your hands neatly folded in your lap. During questioning, make sure you understand the question before attempting to answer it. If either attorney objects during your answer, immediately stop talking until the judge makes a ruling on the objection, then continue. Once a statement is made, it remains in the minds of jurors, even if stricken from the record.

During cross-examination, stay cool and do not let the defense attorney engage you in an argument. The defense attorney will make every effort to put you on the defense to raise your stress level in hopes that you will make an error in your testimony. Even if an attorney is in your face shouting at you, calmly respond with the appropriate answer. If you make a mistake, admit it and don't try to cover it up. Once the defense catches you in a lie, your testimony is useless. If you are assisting the prosecutor in questions of other witnesses, avoid asking questions you don't already know the answer to. This gives the appearance of a witch-hunt, and the answer may contradict points already established in the case. The most important thing to remember above all is to "tell the truth, the whole truth, and nothing but the truth, so help you God."[5]

Criminal vs. Civil Proceedings

Criminal trials differ from civil trials in several important aspects. In criminal cases, the case is always prosecuted on behalf of the state, not on behalf of a plaintiff, such as a victim or an individual citizen. In civil cases, the remedy sought is usually of monetary concerns or cost of damages, whereas in a criminal prosecution, someone's freedom is at stake, or even his or her life. The biggest difference between the two trials is the burden of proof. In civil cases, the defendant must be found negligent by a *preponderance* of the evidence. This means that the jury must find the plaintiff's evidence more convincing than that offered by the defendant. Even if the evidence is more convincing ever so slightly, the ruling will fall in favor of the plaintiff.

In a criminal case, the prosecution must prove *guilt beyond a reasonable doubt.* This is obviously a much more difficult burden to prove. In order for a jury to find a defendant guilty, they must be convinced by proof of such convincing character that a reasonable person would not hesitate to rely and act upon it in the most important of his or her own affairs. If after hearing all the evidence a jury has any reasonable doubt, the verdict must be not guilty. The prosecution may have a very strong case against the defendant, yet given the strong burden of proof, if there is any cast of doubt, the jury must return a not guilty verdict.

Another difference between criminal and civil cases is the amount of discovery permitted. In civil cases, there is a very broad discovery. In civil cases, both sides are permitted to take a deposition from witnesses in the presence of a court reporter. As a result of this face-to-face meeting, both sides can make a judgment about that particular witness, assessing whether he or she will be a compelling witness or not, and prepare their cross-examination of the witness accordingly.

In a criminal prosecution, many jurisdictions don't even require the prosecution to divulge the names of witnesses to testify, let alone subjecting them to a pretrial deposition by the defense.

In short, in criminal cases, the amount of information provided to the defense will be much less than what is provided in a civil trial.

In either case, the investigator must be prepared to present the most accurate account of the incident as humanly possible. Even in cases where there is no cause for a criminal prosecution, wrongful death suits can be expected a high percentage of the time. Wrongful death cases are filed when a person's death is caused by a wrongful act or negligence on the part of the defendant. Actions may be filed on behalf of the decedent by immediate family members, such as a child of a mother or father, or a spouse of the decedent.

CASE STUDY

This California wrongful death case involves four-year-old Yoni Gottesman. According to news reports, the boy was swimming at the Cathedral Oaks Athletic Club in Santa Barbara, California, in 2005. Staff at the club did not watch Yoni while he was in the pool with many other children and he drowned. His parents filed a wrongful death lawsuit against the club and were awarded a record $13.8 million in compensatory damages for the loss of the love and companionship of their son, as well as funeral and burial costs. It is thought to be the largest verdict in a drowning case in California's history.[6]

A wrongful death case will claim that the death could have easily been avoided if not for the negligence exhibited by the defendant. Damages are assessed in a number of ways for wrongful death cases. The claims usually rest on the financial loss of the plaintiff as a result of the death. Even if the decedent was not currently making money at the time of his or her death, the damages offered are based upon the earning potential of that individual.

In cases of boating fatalities, there are many types of negligence that may lead to serious injury or death. Sometimes operators are inattentive, operating at excessive speed, or in a careless or reckless manner. With jet skis or personal watercraft accidents, inexperienced operators are often the cause of accidents. While the use of these watercrafts can be extremely fun, they can also be hazardous if proper caution is not exercised. Personal watercrafts are operated differently than your average boat, so they require special skills and attentiveness to handle them properly. In many cases, these accidents are caused by an intoxicated driver. Some examples of wrongful death cases filed in the United States involving drowning accidents include:

- Beaches, pools, and other bodies of water that were improperly supervised
- Lifeguard negligence or incompetence
- Fall accidents from piers or docks
- Personal injuries and deaths involving defective boats and other water products

CASE STUDIES

ANDREA YATES (WITNESS CREDIBILITY)

On June 20, 2001, after her husband left for work, Andrea Yates filled the family bathtub with water and drowned her five children, starting with her three youngest: Luke, Paul, and John. She placed their bodies next to each other on her bed, placing an arm of each boy over another. The infant, Mary, had been in the bathroom in her bassinet crying. She became the fourth victim. When her eldest, Noah, entered the room, Mary's body was still in the bathtub. After asking his mother what was wrong with Mary, he fled. Yates caught him and dragged him back to the bathroom, where she drowned him in the tub next to Mary. She took Mary into the bedroom and placed her on the bed and covered the four children with a sheet, leaving Noah in the tub. Yates then called 911 and reported that she had just killed her children.

During her trial, the jury rejected her insanity defense and found her guilty of five counts of murder. The prosecution had sought the death penalty, but the jury refused that option. The judge sentenced Yates to life imprisonment with eligibility for parole in 40 years. On January 6, 2005, the Texas Court of Appeals reversed her conviction based on false testimony by a prosecution witness. California psychiatrist Dr. Park Dietz stated that shortly before the killings, an episode of *Law and Order* had aired featuring a woman who had drowned her children and was acquitted of murder by reason of insanity. A former writer for *Law and Order* reported that no such episode existed. The appellate court held that the jury may have been swayed by the false testimony, and thus a new trial would be necessary.

On July 26, 2006, after three days of deliberations, Yates was found not guilty by reason of insanity and was committed to a state mental hospital. In 2007, Yates was moved to a minimum security mental facility.[7]

SUSAN SMITH (VIDEO ADMISSIBILITY)

On October 25, 1994, in Union, South Carolina, Susan Smith claimed a black male had carjacked her vehicle at gunpoint and drove off with her two sons in the back seat. A nine-day search ensued to find the missing boys and her car. She appeared on national TV and made a tearful plea for the safe return of her sons.

On December 12, 1994, Susan Smith was charged with two counts of first-degree murder in connection with the drowning deaths of her sons. During her trial, she claimed she was suicidal and had driven her car to John D. Long Lake to commit suicide. She claimed she didn't want her children to live without a mother, and she was planning to kill herself and take her sons with her. She pulled her car onto the boat ramp at the lake, got out, and the car rolled into the water with Michael and Alex still inside. She was found guilty of two counts of murder.

During the penalty phase of her trial, the prosecution was seeking the death penalty. Smith claimed that although she had contemplated suicide, she changed her mind and got out of the car. The car rolled into the lake, and she did not have time to rescue her sons before the car sank.

The prosecution made a video reenacting her vehicle rolling down the boat ramp and sinking in John D. Long Lake. The reenactment was videotaped from the shore while another camera was mounted inside the car where Michael and Alex were sitting. The car floated for nearly six minutes and showed a view of what the boys went through as the water level rose inside the car. The defense objected to the video, claiming the daylight and divers floating in the water depicted a false sense of rescue that Smith, alone in the dark, would not have had. The judge allowed the video based on relevance. In the judge's opinion, the video proved that there was ample time for Smith to effect a rescue of the boys before the car sank.

The jury sat and watched as the car floated for 5 minutes and 52 seconds. There was not a dry eye in the courtroom as everyone watched the car bobbing in the water, realizing the terror the boys had gone through, strapped in their car seats, and watching the water rise. There was nothing they could do.

After only 2½ hours of deliberation, the jury handed down the verdict of life in prison based on other facts in the case.[8]

SCOTT PETERSON'S INTERVIEW WITH DIANE SAWYER—ABC'S *GOOD MORNING AMERICA*, JANUARY 28, 2003 (VIDEO ADMISSIBILITY)

On September 22, 2004, prosecutors presented a taped interview of murder suspect Scott Peterson with Diane Sawyer from ABC's *Good Morning America.* Scott Peterson had maintained his innocence throughout his trial, and the interview would prove his statements of cooperating with the investigation of the disappearance of his wife, Laci, and unborn son to be contradictory. A portion of the transcript is as follows:

Peterson: I told the police immediately [*referring to his affair with his mistress, Amber Frey*].

When Sawyer pressed him for a more specific time frame, he said he told them on Christmas Eve, the night he reported his 27-year-old wife missing.

Peterson: Yeah, December 24 on.

Peterson told Sawyer that his wife was aware of the affair.

Peterson: It was not positive obviously, you know, it was inappropriate. But it was not something we weren't dealing with.

Peterson claimed he and his wife never even had a fight over his extramarital affair, adding that he never laid a hand on her and hoped she would be found alive.

Peterson: You know, I can't say that even, you know, she was okay with the idea, but it wasn't—it wasn't anything that would break us apart.

Sawyer: Do you really expect people to believe that an 8½-month pregnant woman learns her husband has had an affair and is saintly and casual about it, accommodating, makes peace with it?

Peterson: No one knows our relationship but us.

Sawyer: What kind of marriage was it?

Peterson: God, the first word that comes to mind is, you know, glorious. I mean we took care of each other very well. She *was* amazing. She *is* amazing. *Asked about his son that was due within weeks, he responded:*

Peterson: That was, it's so hard.

Sawyer: You haven't mentioned your son.

Peterson: Hmm [*Long pause*]. That was, it's so hard. I can't go in there [*referring to the baby's room*]. That door is closed until there is someone to put in there.

Sawyer: I think everybody at home wants the answer to the same question. Did you kill your wife?

Peterson: No. No. I did not. And I had nothing to do with her disappearance.

Peterson: Violence towards women is unapproachable. It is the most disgusting act to me. [Refer to Chapter 4 under "Indicators of Deception" regarding this statement.]

Scott Peterson lied in his interview. He never told the police about his affair with Amber Frey and denied the relationship when asked about it on December 30, 2002. He stated he never tried to conceal the affair from the police. The police learned of the affair from Amber Frey, who began to secretly cooperate with the police on December 30. Peterson did not admit the affair until January 24, 2003, when Frey held a press conference at the police station.

When asked about his relationship with his missing wife, he speaks of her in the past tense: "She *was* amazing." He then corrects himself: "She *is* amazing." When asked about his unborn son, he again speaks in the past tense: "That was, it's so hard." He spoke of how difficult it is to go into the baby's room. "That door is closed until there is someone to put in there." Police learned he had converted the baby's room into a storage room when they served a search warrant on his home on February 18, 2003. (This activity is discussed in Chapter 4 in the "Second Interview" section.)

This interview helped convince many people that their suspicions regarding Peterson's guilt were relevant, and critics believed it to be a breakthrough for the prosecution in the case.[9]

Wrongful Death Lawsuit Filed against Rafting Company

According to the suit that was filed by the family of a 52-year-old woman decedent, the woman was kayaking with a large guided party on June 27, 2008, when the inflatable raft she and another woman were in capsized as they tried to get by a series of rocks. The suit contends that they became entrapped in an unusually high flow of water. The decedent was able to push the other woman out of the area but remained trapped herself. The decedent drowned, and her body couldn't be recovered until it finally washed free, several days after her death.

The plaintiffs sought $4 million for her wrongful death; $1.5 million for lost wages, savings, and services; $2 million for loss of companionship; and $500,000 for the decedent's anguish for the drowning and burial costs.

The suit contends that the rafting company should have provided the decedent with sufficient instruction and neglected to have properly trained guides, assuring her safety. The suit also contends that the rafting company should have realized that the decedent and her female companion lacked experience and were depending on the guides to help them navigate safely through the dangerous rapids.[10]

In civil cases of wrongful deaths, many different aspects of the case may become scrutinized, and it is important for the investigator to be aware of this. Unlike criminal proceedings, which usually attempt to determine "Who is to blame for the death?" a civil proceeding may examine other aspects of the case, based on legal issues as well as limitations placed on coverage of an insured client. As evident in the following case study, liability was not the issue. The time of death became a factor when two boys were found trapped in the soft mud at the edge of a pond. The Illinois Supreme Court was asked to determine whether the incidents regarding the deaths of both boys constituted a single or multiple occurrences. The property owner's insurer agreed to settle the claims for an amount equal to the policy's limits. However, the parties disputed which policy limit applied. The insurer's policy provided for a general aggregate limit of $2 million. The policy also contained a $1 million limit for each occurrence. The court needed to decide if the incident was one or two occurrences, and therefore whether there was an obligation to pay $1 million or $2 million.

CASE STUDY

At about 5 p.m. on April 30, 1997, Laura Shackelford watched her 14-year-old son Everett Hodgins leave her home. Hodgins left with his 15-year-old friend, Justice Carr. Shackelford believed the two boys were planning to go fishing in a nearby cooling lake. The two boys did not return that night. Around 10:30 p.m., Donna Fay, Justice Carr's mother, reported her son missing. The police responded that night and conducted a search, but they were not able to locate either boy at that time.

On May 3, 1997, the boys' bodies were found in an excavation pit on land near Justice Carr's home. The land belonged to Donald Parrish. At the time, Parrish conducted a business on the property. Parrish was insured by Addison Insurance Company. The pit in which the boys were found was partially filled with water. The sand and clay around the pit were saturated, creating what an engineer testified to be a "quick" condition. A quick condition is one in which a cushion of water prevents the soil from supporting a load of weight and can result in that load sinking and becoming trapped.

Carr and Hodgins fell prey to this condition. The boys were found at the edge of the pool of water, trapped in the wet clay and sand. Justice Carr was found facing the north bank of the pit. The lower half of his body was partially submerged in the water, and both of his legs were trapped in the sand and clay. Everett Hodgins was found facing south, toward Carr and the water. Hodgins had one leg trapped in the sand, and his other leg was free. Although the two boys were facing different directions, both bodies were in close proximity and physically touching. Both boys had been exposed to the cold water and weather during the time they had been missing. The doctor who performed the autopsies concluded that the immediate cause of Hodgins' death was hypothermia. He determined that the immediate cause of Carr's death was drowning secondary to hypothermia. Addison's forensic expert concurred in his findings. Neither doctor could conclude with any certainty the time of death of either boy, nor how closely in time the boys had perished.

Investigators at the scene concluded that the boys had been trapped while returning home to get out of a storm that swept in during the evening of April 30. The boys used this property as a shortcut to Carr's house, which was very close to the pit. The investigators concluded that when the boys reached the pit, Carr attempted to jump across the water and, in doing so, became trapped. The investigators also concluded that Hodgins then attempted to help his friend out of the sand and clay but became trapped himself. However, the investigators could not conclude how much time had elapsed between Carr's and Hodgins' entrapments, or whether the two boys were even together when Carr was trapped.

The trial court found that the deaths of Carr and Hodgins were the result of two occurrences. The court acknowledged that the evidence could be viewed in ways that tend to support both sides. However, the court found the evidence sufficient to show that the causes of death were different and that the circumstances immediately prior to the deaths were different.

The appellate court reversed and concluded that the deaths of Carr and Hodgins were so closely linked in time and space as to be considered by a reasonable person as one occurrence.[11]

References

1. http://www.innocenceproject.org/understand/Eyewitness-Misidentification.php (accessed December 6, 2009).
2. Dorf, M. 2001. *Find law legal commentary.* New York: Columbia University.
3. Kask, K. *How to improve child and adult witnesses.* http://www.sciencedaily.com/releases/2008/09/080916143854.htm (accessed December 10, 2009).
4. Daley, T. 1996. Pretrial preparations can improve a physician's value as an expert witness. *Can Med Assoc J* 154(4):573–5.
5. Murray, J. 2008. *Expert's guide to successful legal testimony.* Austin, TX: Thomas Investigative Publications.
6. http://accident-law.freeadvice.com/wrongful_death/califronia-wrongful-death-drowning.htm (accessed December 15, 2009).
7. http://www.cbsnews.com/stories/2006/07/26/national/main1837248.shtml (accessed December 15, 2009).
8. http://en.wikipedia.org/wiki/Susan_Smith (accessed October 29, 2009).
9. Clark, C., and Silverman, S. Peterson trial: Jurors hear Scott's voice. http://www.people.com/people/article/0,,697862,00.html (accessed December 15, 2009).
10. http://www.mountainbuzz.com/forums/f11/body-in-blossom-bar-20283.html (accessed October 29, 2009).
11. http://www.state.il.us/court/opinions/SupremeCourt/2009/January/105752.pdfClick here to enter text. (accessed January 20, 2010).

Medicolegal Investigation of Deaths

Initial Processing

6

ERICA J. ARMSTRONG

As previously stated, the coroner/medical examiner (C/ME) is charged with investigating sudden, unexplained, and suspicious deaths with the help of trained staff who are involved to some degree at every level, from the scene to the autopsy and beyond. This charge encompasses medicolegal death investigation. An important goal of medicolegal death investigation is the determination of the cause and manner of death. The utilization and application of standard operating procedures, protocols, and scientific analyses not only facilitates this goal but also aids outside investigators such as law enforcement in the reconstruction of the death circumstances.

After a death is reported to the C/ME, and that death has been determined to meet the criteria for a C/ME case, the death investigation begins or, more precisely, continues, sometimes with a visit to the death scene by medicolegal death investigator and/or pathologist, especially in water-related deaths. This may include securing and preserving evidence, including the body itself, at the scene, which involves the initiation of the chain of custody process. A tag labeled with decedent identifying information is attached to the body such as the wrist, ankle, or toes. The body is placed in a clean body bag which is closed by a zipper and secured ideally with a tamper-evident seal. Alternatively, the tagged body may be covered with a clean white sheet. Bodies discovered in cars (passenger compartment or trunk) may arrive as found, covered with a clean white sheet, via towing on a flatbed truck. Bodies found buried in or lying on soil may arrive along with the soil, which can be examined, x-rayed, and sampled for additional evidence.

Each department within the C/ME office becomes involved at some level with the death investigation. While variations among C/ME offices exist, a typical C/ME office may contain the following departments, dependent upon many factors, including the physical capacity of the building, number and expertise of the staff, whether or not outside laboratories are utilized, and budgetary constraints:

- Death investigative unit
- Decedent intake/receiving/release department
- Decedent property department
- Photography/digital imaging department
- Trace evidence/DNA departments
- Pathology/biology/histology departments
- Toxicology and drug chemistry departments
- Administration, secretarial, information technology, statistics, and building maintenance departments

The identification of the decedent may have been initially confirmed at the previous place of confinement (hospital, nursing, or hospice facility) as indicated on the identification bracelet placed by that facility around one of the wrists or ankles or on the toe tag. If the identification has been established at the scene, it is conveyed to the medicolegal death investigator and appropriate tagging is applied to the body. Upon receipt into the receiving department and following the breaking of the tamper-evident seal, the identification is rechecked and a uniquely identifying case number is assigned, if not already done at the time of assumption of jurisdiction. If the decedent is received as "unidentified," prompt action will be taken to establish identity by one or more of a number of different methods: visual recognition (face, unique body markings, identification cards, clothing, personal effects), fingerprint comparison, dental x-ray comparison, body x-ray comparison, DNA comparison, and anthropological examination of skeletal remains (Figure 6.1). Dentures worn by a decedent may have the name inscribed on one of the inner surfaces, which serves as preliminary identification (Figure 6.2).

When traditional scientific modes of identification cannot be applied or fail due to extreme decomposition with skeletonization of the head or severe facial injury, forensic facial reconstruction may become necessary. Available techniques are generally divided into two-dimensional (2D) or three-dimensional (3D). 2D techniques combine anthropological and artistry expertise along with computer software technology to render a profile from photographic or radiographic images. Advances in computerization and software technology have also rapidly improved outcomes of 3D facial reconstruction, which also combines anthropological and artistry expertise by using manual reconstruction to apply clay or plastic to a skull or skull replica.

Basic identifying attributes such as age, race, sex, hair color, eye color, condition of teeth, height, and weight are assessed and recorded. Photographic documentation preferably using digital imaging technology of the decedent is performed. Decedents are placed in temporary, secured storage at refrigeration or freezing temperatures between scientific procedures or until claimed and removed by funeral home personnel in order to preserve the body as much as possible.

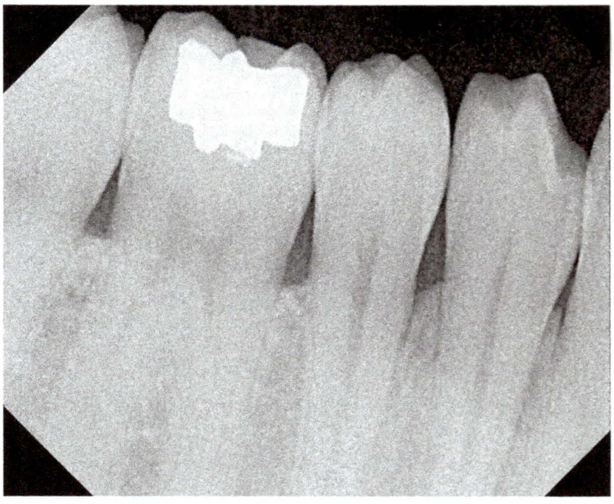

Figure 6.1 Dental x-ray featuring dental filling in one tooth.

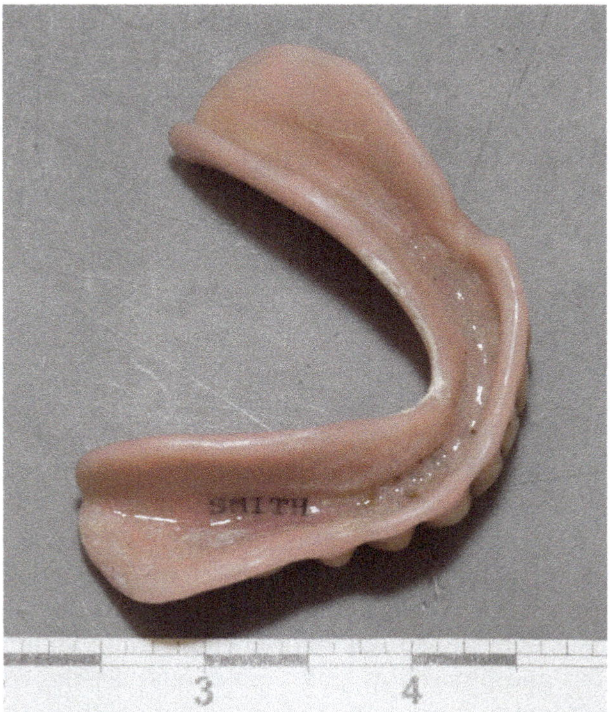

Figure 6.2 Dentures with an inscription of the last name.

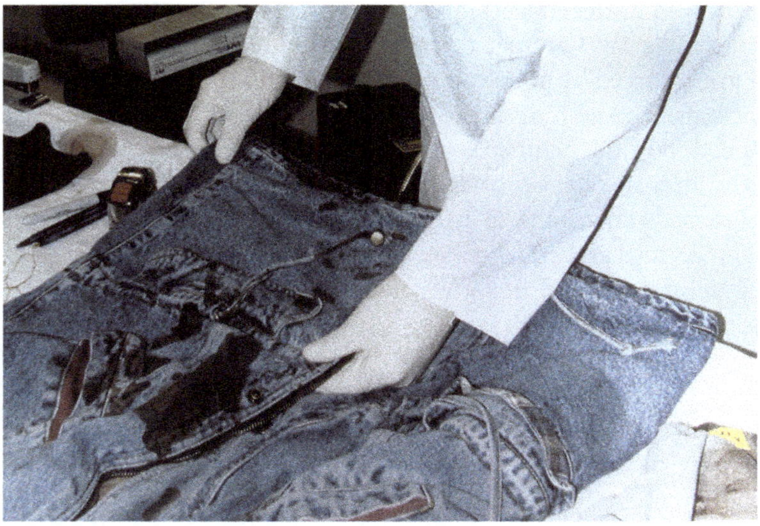

Figure 6.3 Clothing examination.

Clothing or personal effects that may accompany the body are documented and secured within the department in charge of personal property and are released to the funeral home. Clothing and personal effects will be retained, photographed, and further examined and analyzed in all homicidal deaths, certain other types of violent deaths, and deaths occurring under suspicious circumstances (Figure 6.3). Medications obtained from the death scene are inventoried and retained in secured locations such as the toxicology laboratory. Illicit drugs and drug paraphernalia may be similarly obtained and inventoried, but this task may also be handled by the law enforcement agency dedicated to the investigation of drug-related deaths. The forensic pathologist may need to access the drug or medication inventory record to aid in decision-making relative to postmortem toxicological testing. If paper bags have been placed over the hands of the decedent in efforts to preserve evidence, care is taken not to disturb the bags, pending examination by a forensic scientist. Bagging of hands with plastic bags is never acceptable, as condensation formed on a cooling body may collect and promote the growth of bacteria and mold, which may further compromise the integrity of evidence present on the hands (Figure 6.4).

If consent for harvesting of the eyes, bones, connective tissues, skin, or organs has been given by the legal next-of-kin, or in accordance with pre-death donor registry information, harvesting will take place after initial forensic examinations are done and prior to autopsy if one is warranted. Harvesting of eyes, skin, connective tissue, and bone can take place within the C/ME office if it is set up to accommodate those procedures. Harvesting of solid organs usually takes place within the hospital, and in the case of homicides or suspicious deaths, hands will be bagged and confiscation of clothing will be or should have been done at the hospital by the police or C/ME death investigators. Organs with visible signs of injury or disease are generally not harvested, and consultation with the C/ME or designated pathologist can be provided if unusual or uncertain findings are encountered. After all examinations and procedures have been completed, the decedent, along with personal effects, is released to the care of the funeral home that the family has chosen in the interim time period.

Early on in medicolegal death investigation, including at the scene, the forensic scientist may become involved in the collection and scientific analysis of trace evidence, including DNA-containing material. **Forensic science** is the application of science to criminal and civil laws that are enforced by police agencies working in the criminal justice system.[1] The **forensic scientist** is the key individual trained and skilled in utilizing technologies that allow the application of the principles of the physical and natural sciences to the analysis of evidence.[2] The forensic scientist understands the validity and limitations of technologies based on experience and results of peer-reviewed studies and can communicate those during pretrial meetings and court testimony. The forensic scientist handles and analyzes many types of substances and materials, including hair, fibers, glass, paint chips, soil,

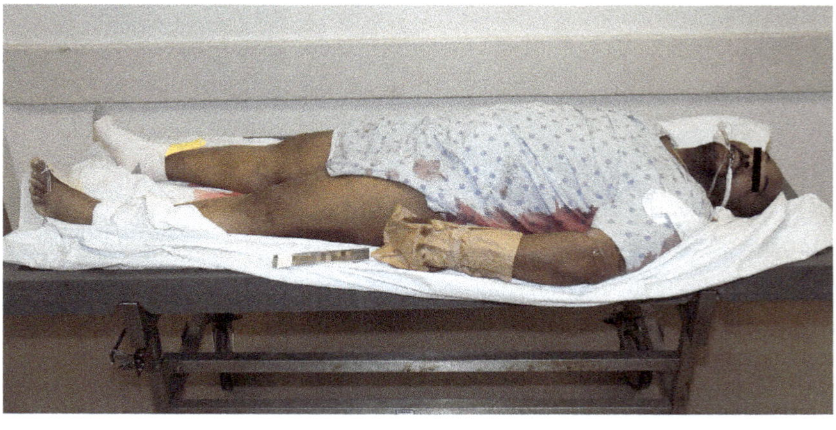

Figure 6.4 Properly bagged hand utilizing paper bag.

gunshot residue, and unknown materials that constitute **trace evidence**. These substances and materials may possess properties allowing transfer from object to object, person to person, or object to person, and vice versa. This concept is known as **Locard's exchange principle.**[2] These properties may also allow for class or individual characterization and can assist in the identification and determination of the origin of a substance or material. Trace evidence may be collected from the clothing or the body or submitted separately by police investigators with the assistance of their own scientific investigators. Evidence submitted separately by police investigators is required to be submitted to the trace evidence laboratory with the proper **chain of custody**. Items must be placed in proper containers, be sealed, be dated, be signed, have the location/origin clearly stated, and have the type of testing requested clearly stated *prior* to submission to the laboratory (Figure 6.5A and B). Upon submission to the laboratory, the laboratory's submission form must be completed. Within the laboratory and between laboratories at the C/ME office, a similar chain of

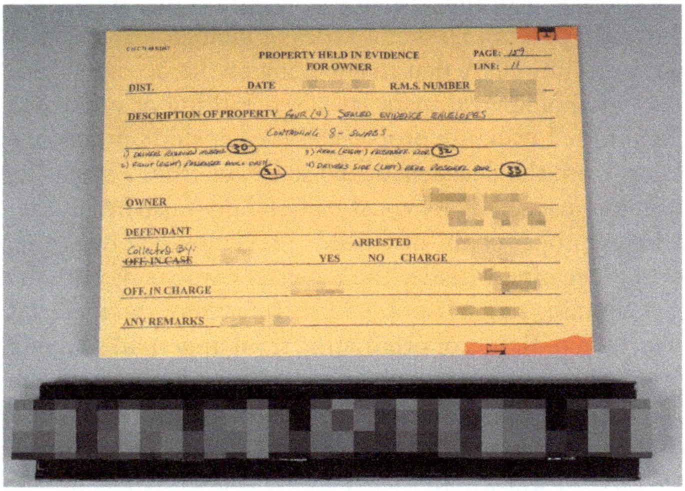

(a)

(b)

Figure 6.5 (A and B) Properly packaged, sealed, and signed evidence envelope.

custody format is maintained and tracked with each opening and testing event. This may be done electronically using specialized proprietary computer programs that allow tracking of each item submitted to, tested in, and released from a forensic laboratory via barcoded identifiers. Tracking information can be produced should an inquiry regarding the handling and testing of evidence arise.[1] The chain of custody protocol is one of many laboratory standards that forensic laboratories must adhere to in order to maintain a current accreditation status provided by the American Society of Crime Lab Directors (ASCLD), following periodic inspection and evaluation. The proper handling and submission of evidence along with documentation and guarding the integrity of the chain of custody are essential in order to be able to withstand any future court proceedings.

Human **deoxyribonucleic acid** (DNA) is a complex of molecules that can be of extreme importance in death investigation and resolution of criminal cases during court proceedings. It is contained within the nucleus of cells which make up the tissues and organs of our body and contains the genetic instructions for our development and the many bodily functions. DNA is contained in the 23 pairs of chromosomes (one chromosome of each pair inherited from each parent). Different types of biological material may contain cells and any cells would contain DNA that may belong to the deceased individual or is of a foreign origin. Suspected biological material from clothing or other items/evidence may be collected and submitted utilizing proper chain-of-custody procedure by law enforcement from the scene, from the decedent at the scene, or from a suspect(s). Once received at the C/ME's office, the suspected biological material may also be collected and submitted from the body utilizing proper chain-of-custody procedure before and during an autopsy. Preliminary tests to determine whether the material consists of human tissue or human blood or whether it contains semen can be done. This biological material, whether blood, semen, urine, saliva, hair, or tissue, or originating from fingernail scrapings, swabbed body surfaces and cavities, clothing, or other objects, can be analyzed for the presence of DNA.

Human DNA has numerous, short nonfunctional repetitive locations or **loci**. The short repetitive loci are known as **short tandem repeats (STRs)** and form patterns that are unique to each individual. They are known for their stability and withstand harsher environmental conditions. Following laboratory techniques that extract, copy, and separate the DNA from the biological sample, the **STR DNA typing** technique is applied in order to obtain a profile based on the identification of a number of unique regions called **loci** (Figure 6.6). [3,4] Once obtained, this unique profile can be subsequently compared to the victim's DNA for the purpose of inclusion or exclusion of the victim, as the individual that was in contact with an object such as a weapon or was wearing or in contact with an item of clothing.[3,4] Similarly, the DNA profile extracted from a biological sample submitted from a crime scene can be compared to the suspect to include or exclude that individual's involvement in a crime or presence at a scene. Biological material, including blood, may also be submitted from the victim at the time of autopsy, serving as a DNA standard or reference sample to which other DNA-containing biological samples obtained elsewhere can be compared.

DNA profiles can be entered into the Combined DNA Index System (CODIS), a national database of DNA profiles from convicted offenders, missing persons, and material recovered from crime scenes, to assist in the identification of suspects or victims or in the linkage of crimes based on the finding of identical profiles at multiple scenes.[5] DNA profiles can also be entered into local database systems as well. DNA comparison is also used to establish or confirm paternity, maternity, or other genetic relationship, such as between siblings.

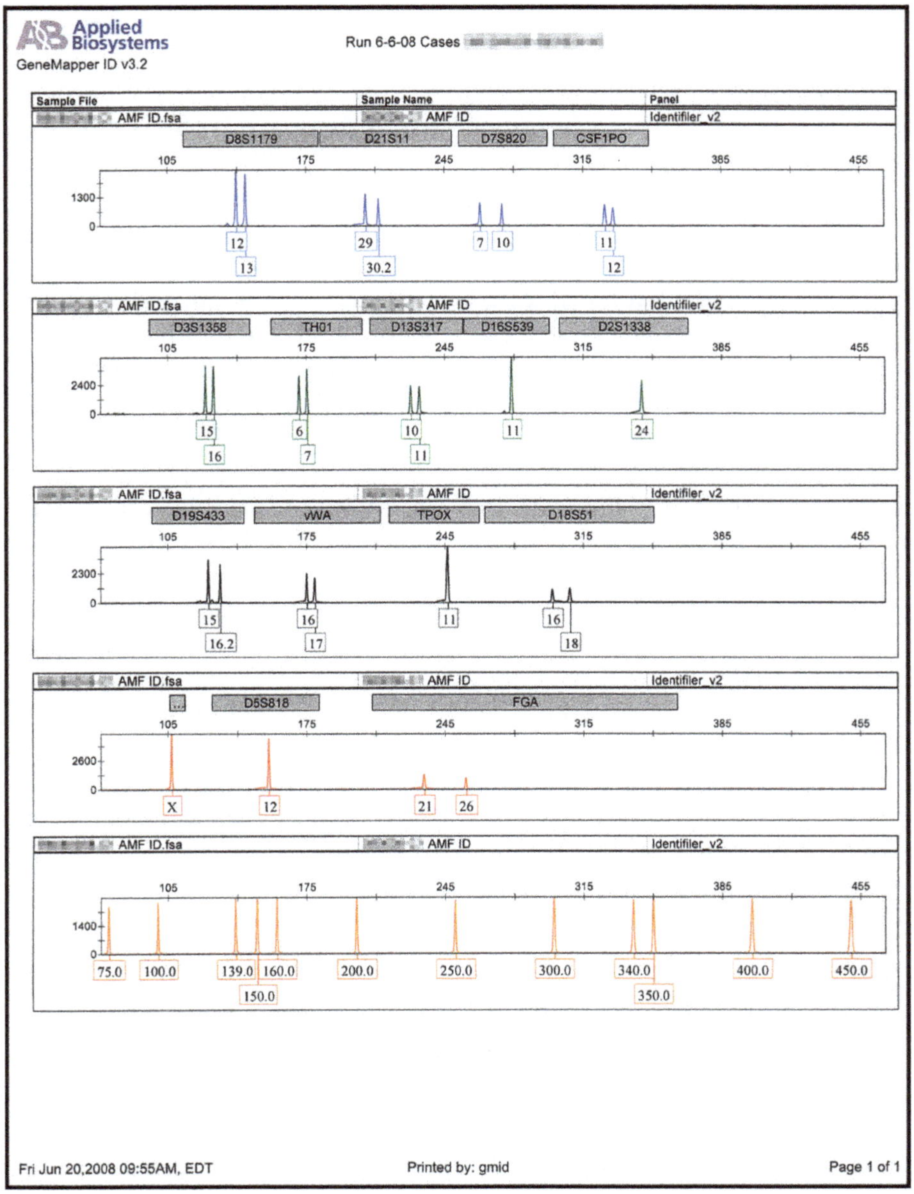

Figure 6.6 DNA profile resulting from the amplification of several genetic loci of one individual.

DNA technology has utility in many deaths, including certain water-related deaths, in regard to the establishment and confirmation of identity. Fresh human tissue recovered after a shark attack in which there had been significant dismemberment of the body was shown to be suitable for DNA extraction, as shown in one case report.[6] Positive identification can be obtained via comparison of a DNA profile extracted from the biological material of a known individual (i.e., recovered from a toothbrush or from tissues retained in hospital pathology departments recovered during a previous surgical procedure) with that of an unknown victim, with subsequent matching and identification. However, decomposed, submerged remains in which DNA may be significantly degraded may necessitate analysis of maternally inherited mitochondrial DNA or may otherwise be unsuitable for any type of DNA analysis.

After initial processing, a decision must be made as to whether the history and the circumstances warrant further investigation with an autopsy. It is often presumed that all deaths that have come under the jurisdiction of the C/ME will further require an autopsy prior to the determination of the cause and manner of death. This is true for every case, however. A daily review process of the death circumstances, including a review of the medical history and any available medical records and other reports, is done, and an autopsy will be performed in some but not all cases. Decedents who will not have an autopsy performed will receive a thorough external examination of the body, with a notation of scars, other unique marks, injury, and evidence of therapeutic intervention. Bodily fluids such as blood, urine, and eye fluid (vitreous humor) will be collected for possible chemistry and toxicological analysis. A DNA reference sample may also be collected, and the decedent may be fingerprinted, especially in instances in which the identification is tentative or the decedent is unidentified. If not already received, additional medical records, emergency medical response run reports, police reports, and any other relevant investigative reports will be requested and reviewed. Although medical records are considered protected health information under the Health Insurance Portability and Accountability Act (HIPAA) of 1996, they can be disclosed to law enforcement and C/MEs in order for them to carry out their authorized duties.[7]

After a review of the circumstances, records, reports, and test results, the determination as to the cause and manner of death will be made and entered onto the death certificate. If an autopsy was performed, the findings of the autopsy in addition to the review of all of the above will be considered altogether, with subsequent determination of cause and manner of death and completion of the death certificate.

Usually before or during the time the decedent has been conveyed to the office of the C/ME notification to the legal next-of-kin has been made, or attempts are being made to notify the family so that they can commence plans for final disposition. After examinations, procedures, and any needed establishment or confirmation of identification have taken place, the decedent can be released to the funeral home. If diligent attempts to locate legal next of kin have been made without success or with family members or acquaintances unwilling or financially unable to claim the decedent, arrangements will be made for city or county burial or cremation.

An individual may remain unidentified after all attempts have been made to establish identity. Specific information, such as original photographs, facial reconstruction images, circumstantial details, demographic information, physical characteristics, dental information, C/ME case numbers, and other information, can be entered into the National Missing and Unidentified Persons System (NamUS) database, which performs a search for matching information pertaining to missing individuals contained within the database.[8]

References

1. Gupta, S., Gupta, V., Vij, H., et al. 2015. Forensic facial reconstruction: The final frontier. *J Clin Diagn Res* 9(9):ZE26–28.
2. Saferstein, R. 2018. Introduction and the crime scene. In Richard Saferstein (Ed.), *Criminalistics: An Introduction to Forensic Science*, pp. 1–29 and pp. 42–48. 12th ed. Boston, MA: Pearson Education.

3. Pinckard, J. K. 2008. Memorial Eckert Paper for 2007—Forensic DNA analysis for the medical examiner. *Am J Forensic Med Pathol* 29(4):375–81.
4. Saferstein, R. 2018. DNA: The indispensable forensic science tool. In *Criminalistics: An Introduction to Forensic Science*, pp. 397–425. 12th ed. Boston, MA: Pearson Education.
5. CODIS and NDIS fact sheet. https://www.fbi.gov/services/laboratory/biometric-analysis/codis/codis-and-ndis-fact-sheet (accessed April 5, 2020).
6. Byard, R. W., James, R. A., and Heath, K. J. 2000. Recovery of human remains after shark attack (case report). *Am J Forensic Med Pathol* 27(3):256–59.
7. U.S. Department of Health and Human Services. Health information privacy-When does the privacy rule allow covered entities to disclose protected health information to law enforcement officials? https://www.hhs.gov/hipaa/for-professionals/faq/505/what-does-the-privacy-rule-allow-covered-entities-to-disclose-to-law-enforcement-officials/index.html (accessed October 20, 2019).
8. National Missing and Unidentified Persons System (NamUS). http://www.namus.gov (accessed October 20, 2019).

The Medicolegal Autopsy

7

ERICA J. ARMSTRONG

Introduction

Under certain circumstances, a coroner/medical examiner (C/ME) must further investigate a death by way of the autopsy. This is especially true for water-related deaths. Of all the deaths that come under the C/ME's jurisdiction, 40–50% of those deaths will be autopsied.[1] An autopsy is performed to establish the cause and manner of death as defined in Chapter 1, and to be defined further in this chapter. It is a systematic, scientific, examination that usually takes one to two hours to complete. Complex autopsies may take several hours to complete and may include next-day examination or require several days of examination. This chapter provides a general overview of autopsies performed in the medicolegal or forensic setting.

Autopsies that are performed in hospitals require the consent of the legal next of kin, who may allow the performance of a complete autopsy or examination of only limited regions and organs (i.e., brain-only autopsy). In hospital autopsies, photographic documentation of the body, examination of the internal neck structures, examination of the back of the body, and toxicological testing may not be done. Hospital autopsies do provide correlation between diagnoses and clinical signs and symptoms and can help characterize the extent of disease and the effectiveness of therapy, as well as determine the cause of death. Pathologists based in hospitals perform these autopsies and have direct access to the decedent's medical records and their treating physicians.

By contrast, consent from the legal next-of-kin to perform an autopsy is not required for deaths that have come under the C/ME's jurisdiction. The C/ME autopsy is also not limited to a body site or region, and the forensic pathologist will perform a complete autopsy, sampling only the tissues and body fluids necessary to confidently make a determination of cause and manner of death. This is important to note since the forensic pathologist may have little to no available medical history to start with, and the circumstantial information may be limited in amount and scope. Members of the family other than the legal next-of-kin may express wishes for or against the performance of an autopsy. It is important to know who the *legal* next-of kin is since this is the spokesperson for the family who should communicate the collective or majority wishes for or against an autopsy. The legal next-of-kin may request that an autopsy be done when one is not deemed necessary by the C/ME. Thought and care are exercised to try and answer the family's questions, whether or not an autopsy is ultimately performed. A request that an autopsy *not* be performed will be considered on a case-by-case basis. Often, this request is due to religious or personal reasons. Care and consideration for potential compromise of any future inquiries or criminal and civil legal proceedings will be exercised and expressed to the family before the decision to honor the family's wish is made. This is particularly applicable for homicidal deaths, in which the ongoing and anticipated investigative and legal proceedings are best served with the inclusion of a forensic autopsy.

Medicolegal autopsies (synonymous to forensic autopsies) provide benefits in addition to those provided by hospital autopsies, including confirmation or establishment of identification, correlation of injury with the death circumstances, uncovering of previously undiagnosed natural disease, recovering of evidence, and estimation of the time of death. The information and evidence gathered by the forensic pathologist is useful and sometimes vital for law enforcement in the resolution of their cases. A continual open line of communication regarding autopsy and scientific findings and field investigation findings is essential, as the investigation may be ongoing even after the autopsy has been completed, and questions may arise along the way from either party.

The major components of a medicolegal autopsy are the scene investigation (medical facility or elsewhere), autopsy performance, and toxicological testing. Prior to commencing a medicolegal autopsy, the forensic pathologist will have access to death scene information, sometimes police and medical records, and scene photographs, and may have personally attended the scene. Verbal communication with doctors, police investigators, other first responders, and family members may also take place. First responders who have been exposed to biological fluids may formally request that the forensic pathologist facilitate infectious disease testing on the decedent as part of the autopsy. If a scene visitation was not warranted, a narrative of the general information regarding the circumstances surrounding the death, provided verbally to the medicolegal death investigator, will be reviewed.

Before an autopsy can begin, certain important tasks must first be completed. It cannot be overemphasized that checking the identity or starting the identification process is mandatory. Clothing, personal effects, and on-body bindings, wrappings, and ligatures will be removed, retained, and examined, especially in homicidal or suspicious deaths. Clothing that remains on burned victims in which arson is suspected or has not been ruled out, will be collected for testing for accelerants. Clothing with defects caused by bullets or other objects will be retained and later compared to the wounds on the body, if present, and to the objects that may have caused the defects. Hand examination, fingernail scrapings, trace metal detection testing on hands, and sampling for gunshot residue need to be completed in certain cases, prior to the autopsy. Examination using an alternate light source for the detection of biological stains on the body, clothing, and wrappings may also be done and must be done prior to the autopsy. In certain instances, sampling and detection may be hindered or compromised such as in cases involving prolonged submersion or body decomposition.

In certain cases, performance imaging studies is necessary. This commonly involves the performance of an x-ray. Victims who have sustained gunshot wounds, stab wounds, or other penetrating injury will be x-rayed to look for retained projectiles or pieces of a weapon that may have broken off into the body (Figure 7.1). Projectiles and weapon fragments seen on x-ray will be retrieved from the body, as these items constitute evidence and their characteristics may facilitate matching to or associating with their origin. Pedestrian victims sustaining injures known or suspected to be caused by being struck by a motor vehicle will be x-rayed to look for skeletal injury such as bone fractures, especially of the lower extremities. This would be necessary for pedestrians or cyclists found on the side of the road, down a roadside embankment, or in roadside waterways (ditches, streams, rivers, etc.). X-rays will be performed on infants and children to look for recent or old bone fractures, including patterns of fractures suspicious for or consistent with child abuse and neglect. X-rays may be performed to look for fractures of other bones that may have been

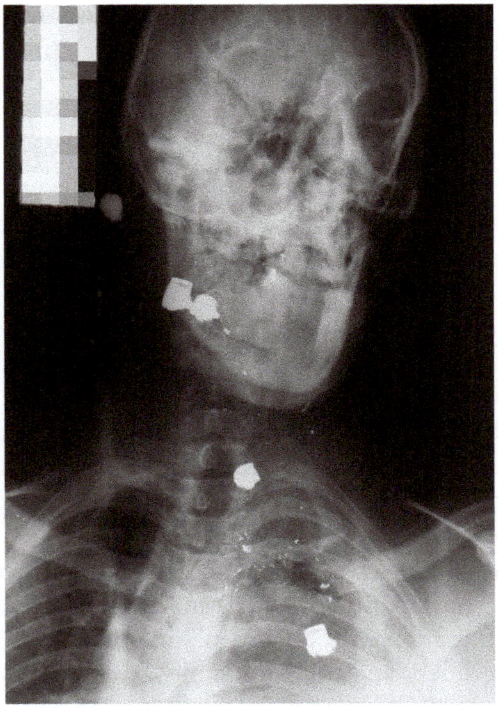

Figure 7.1 X-ray film of head, neck, and upper chest showing retained bullets.

suspected but not documented in the hospital or nursing facility prior to death. X-rays may also be done to look for air within the body cavities in victims sustaining penetrating injury or victims of suspected barotrauma. X-rays will always be taken on victims who are burned beyond recognition to identify any unique skeletal attributes (shape of the sinuses within the head or presence of old rib fractures) and evidence of surgery (prosthetic hip replacement, coronary artery bypass surgery), which may help establish or confirm the decedent's identity via comparison with x-rays retained at a hospital from a previous admission. Moreover, a charred body may not necessarily represent a death due to fire, but a death by other means, including homicidal (i.e., gunshot wound) with subsequent attempts to destroy all evidence with fire. In the case of a charred victim who sustained gunshot wounds, the x-ray may reveal retained projectiles.

The imaging technologies Computed Tomography (CT) and Magnetic Resonance Imaging (MRI) have long since been used on patients in the hospital setting and are being increasingly applied to the postmortem setting. In C/ME offices possessing the budget, infrastructure, and specialized personnel, these technologies have been used as an adjunct in the traditional forensic autopsy in the identification and reconstruction of injuries such as skull fractures, the location of foreign bodies such as knife tip fragments, and diagnosis of decompression sickness in fatal SCUBA diving accidents.[2]

External Examination: General Information

The aim of the medicolegal autopsy is to identify and document injury and disease and to determine if one, the other, or both constitute a cause of death. Photographic documentation is an integral part throughout the autopsy, and the images will be stored, linked by a uniquely identifying case number, indefinitely. As with any procedure involving contact with biological materials, universal precautions, including the wearing of disposable gowns, gloves, and masks, are practiced in the autopsy suite to minimize contracting and transmitting infectious disease.

The autopsy begins with an external examination, with verifying and recording of the identifying characteristics, such as height, weight, hair and eye color, and race. The nutritional state is also assessed (i.e., well nourished, emaciated, or obese). The degree and location of rigor mortis and the location, color, and state (fixed or blanchable) of the livor mortis are recorded. Assessment of the presence or absence of body warmth is made and in some instances, the actual core body temperature may also be taken and recorded. Any changes of decomposition, beginning with loss of rigor mortis, will be noted. Subsequent examination of the head, neck, trunk, extremities, genitalia, body openings, and body crevasses for scars, tattoos, skin changes, deformity, and injuries is done. Typically, external findings will be measured in inches. Evidence of resuscitation, therapeutic intervention, embalming, or organ and tissue harvesting will be noted.

In certain cases in which foul play or homicidal circumstances are suspected or evident, before the external examination by the pathologist is done, and before any washing of the body is done, examination with documentation of any foreign material (i.e., hairs, fibers, vegetation, dirt and debris, glass, paint chips, adherent residue) will be necessary. Collection with proper submission as trace evidence may be done depending on the death circumstances, or alternatively a forensic scientist may be called into the autopsy suite to perform such collections prior to the autopsy. In cases of obvious or suspected sexual assault, oral, vaginal, and rectal swabs in females, and oral and rectal swabs in males will be taken for subsequent examination for the presence of sperm, sperm DNA, or other foreign DNA.

Bite marks represent a potential source of foreign DNA and must be photographically documented and swabbed using sterile technique for possible scientific analysis, prior to any washing (Figure 7.2). A forensic dentist or odontologist may also be called in to examine a bite mark for any identifying or distinguishing characteristics.

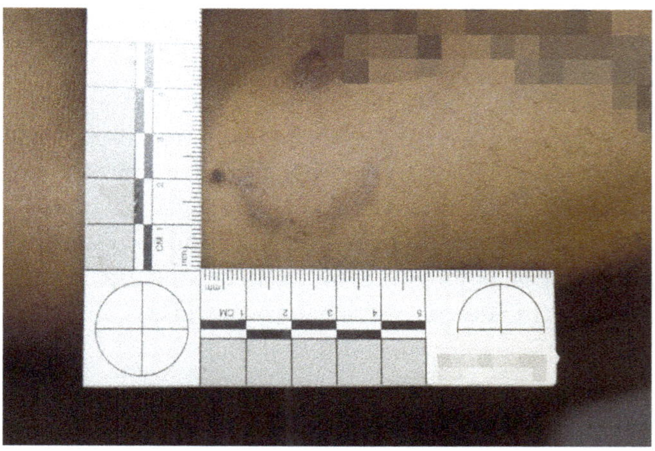

Figure 7.2 Semicircular bite mark scar taken with a two-dimensional ruler.

In all cases and where possible, collection of a clear and slightly viscous fluid from the eyes **(vitreous humor)** will be done, and the fluid will be sent to the postmortem forensic toxicology and chemistry labs to test for certain drugs, alcohols, poisons, medications, and electrolytes.

In certain cases (i.e., death from obvious or suspected homicidal violence or motor vehicle accidents), the body will be photographed head to toe, front to back, and/or by region, as is, prior to washing and removal of any therapeutic devices, if present. Following removal of these items, the body will subsequently receive the same series of photographs. The number of photographs taken is dictated by the number, location, and unique characteristics of external changes, including injuries, at the discretion of the forensic pathologist performing the autopsy.

Individuals with significant changes of decomposition are carefully examined for signs of injury or disease. Extreme changes of decomposition may obscure these signs, however. An extremely decomposed body may have little left in the way of recognizable internal organs, that may have been consumed by the bacteria, larvae, insects, and molds (Figure 7.3). If there are fly larvae present, they will be observed entering and feeding on the most accessible, moist, and *unsubmerged* areas, including eyes, nostrils, ear openings, groin, anus, dehisced surgical incisions, and *inflicted wounds* (Figure 7.4). Concentration of fly larvae on areas of the body other than anatomic openings is important to note because these areas may represent wounds such as stab wounds, gunshot wounds, or other penetrating injury. X-ray of the body in the region of the defects in addition to a search for internal injury connected with these defects along with any retained foreign material would then be necessary. Large concentrations of maggots upon and within the body can generate heat, thereby slowing the rate of body cooling and further contributing to heat-accelerated decompositional changes. Fly larvae undergo multiple stages of development prior to pupation, and the largest among them may represent the oldest, and thus the ones that have been feeding the longest. Representative larvae, especially the largest ones, can

Figure 7.3 Body in advanced stage of decomposition with skeletonization, without recognizable internal organs of the chest and abdominal cavities.

Figure 7.4 Masses of maggots concentrated around eyes and the mouth and on the neck.

be collected for or by the forensic entomologist and preserved for subsequent examination and approximation of the postmortem interval. With proper handling, live larvae can be reared into flies and the determination of the species of flies, which may exist only in certain habitats or at certain times of the year, may help determine not only the time of death but also the location of death.[3] Larvae can be analyzed in the toxicology lab for the presence of drugs and poisons ingested while feeding on the body of the decedent who had initially consumed a drug or poison. The presence of a drug or poison may provide a clue as to the cause of death or contributing factors such as illicit drug use. They can also be analyzed for human DNA, which may assist in the establishment or confirmation of identification.[4] With continued decomposition over an extended period of time and under the right environmental conditions, a succession of insects may continue to colonize and feed off the body or off the insects that are feeding on the body. These include beetles, centipedes, millipedes, and spiders. Their presence may have utility, albeit limited, in postmortem interval approximation. Dried, mummified remains recovered after months or years from within a closed and protected structure may be colonized only by beetles that feed upon the body leaving masses of brown, stringy, segmented, soft material known as **peritrophic membranes**. The membranes consist of the intestinal lining of the beetle extruded along with the fecal material upon defecation (Figure 7.5).[3] Remains submerged for prolonged periods in aquatic habitats may become colonized by various aquatic larvae and insects, which have been used to estimate the minimum **postmortem submersion interval** (PMSI).[5]

External changes related to **postmortem predation** or **anthropophagy** by common insect larvae, roaches, ants, beetles, rodents, domestic and wild canines, and domestic

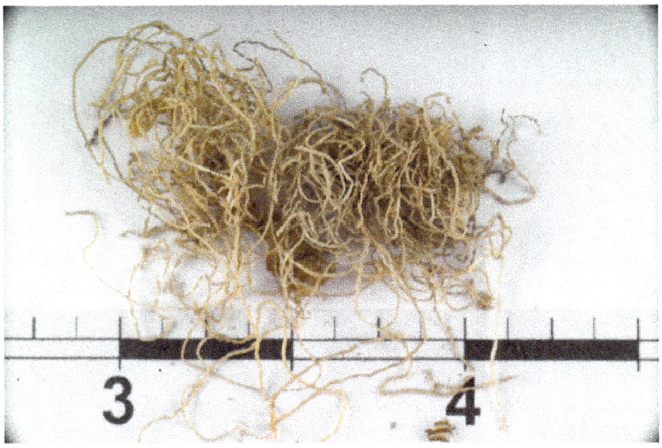

Figure 7.5 Peritrophic membranes from beetles.

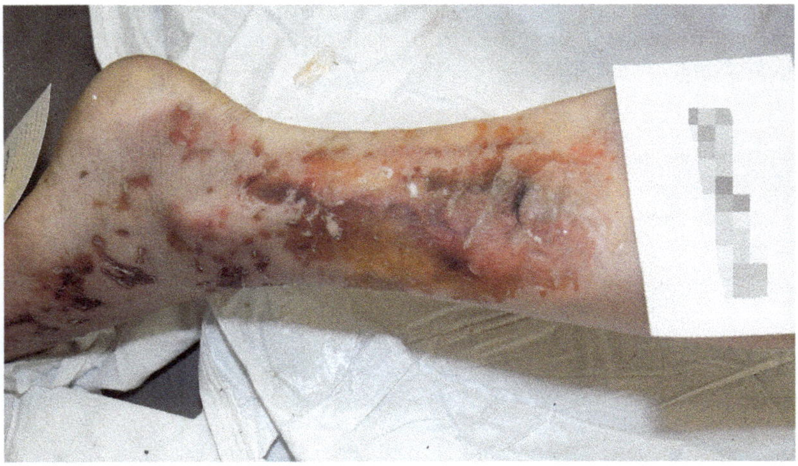

Figure 7.6 Postmortem abrasions of distal lower extremity due to anthropophagy by insects.

and wild felines will be noted. In general, the accessible parts of the body are favored by these creatures, especially the face, and the defects will generally be bloodless and without hemorrhage. With larger animals, scavenging may continue to the point of dismemberment, with scattering of the remains for some distance. The mouthparts from insects tend to leave superficial, yellow, irregular, and linear abrasions with rounded edges on the skin (Figure 7.6). Over time, these abrasions may appear redder or darker and may ooze bloody fluid, thus taking on an antemortem appearance, in areas of lividity. Upon exposure and over time, these abrasions will dry and appear parched and yellow. Rodents and larger predators (land or aquatic) may leave larger defects or defects with patterns of injuries around the edges and on the bones caused by gnawing of the teeth (Figure 7.7A and B). The dimensions and spacing of the injuries may exhibit a pattern which may help identify the animal that caused it.

The examination of skeletonized remains is aided by the expertise of the forensic anthropologist and the forensic dentist, who will work alongside the forensic pathologist whether on scene or in the autopsy suite. An inventory of all recovered bones (and teeth) must be initially done and an effort to locate the hyoid bone made (Figure 7.8 A). The **hyoid**

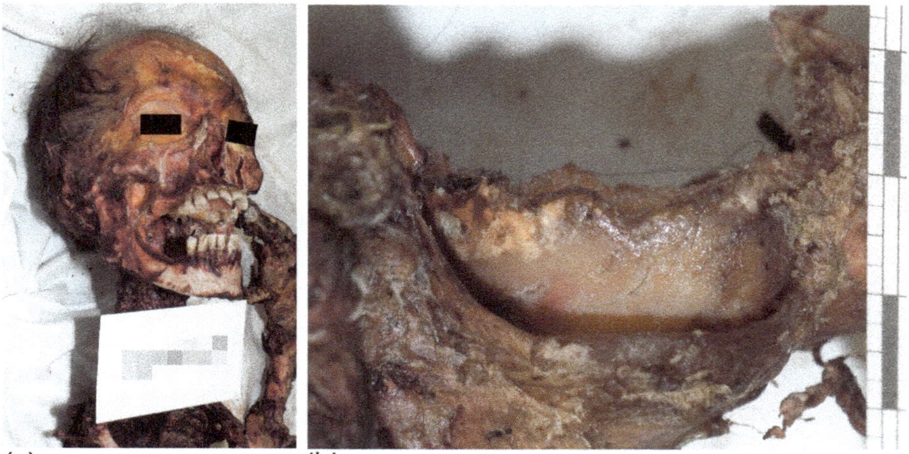

(a) (b)

Figure 7.7 (A) Anthropophagy by pet dog with near total absence of facial skin and nose. (B) Anthropophagy by pet dog showing curvilinear oblique teeth marks and gnawed, jagged edges on piece of bone.

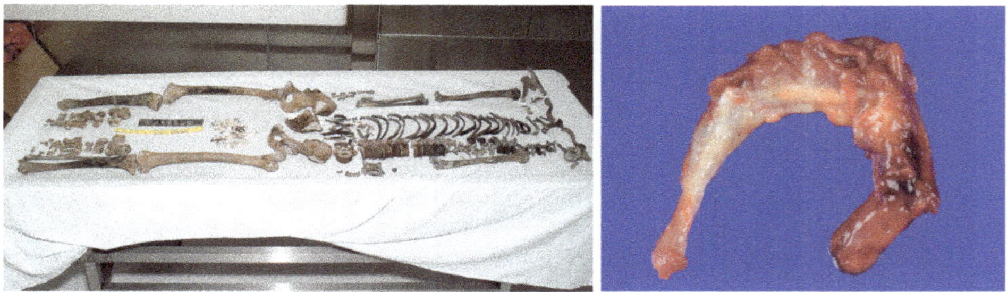

(a) (b)

Figure 7.8 (A) Skeletonized human remains arranged anatomically, including ribs and upper extremity bones (right half of photograph) and pelvis and lower extremity bones (left half of photograph). (B) Hyoid bone with fracture and dark red area of hemorrhage.

bone is a c-shaped bone that sits above the thyroid cartilage (colloquially known as the Adam's apple) and may be fractured in cases of homicidal strangulation and suicidal hanging (Figure 7.8B). Any attached skin and soft tissue will be removed so that all surfaces of the bones can be seen in order to aid in the determination of age, sex, race, evidence of injury, and identification. This is done by boiling the bones in soapy water, which allows for easy manual removal of the attached tissue without having to use blunt or sharp instruments, which may leave unwanted tool markings on the bones. X-ray of the bones with any attached soft tissue will be done before and after any manipulation so as not to miss any attached or embedded objects with potential evidentiary value. Examination with inventory of the teeth with x-ray will be done by the forensic dentist, and this may aid in identification of the decedent by dental x-ray film comparison. After inventory and examination of the bones, a segment of bone such as the femur can be excised and submitted for possible DNA extraction, which could aid in the establishment or confirmation of identification of the decedent.

Description of External Findings

External findings are described as if the body is in **anatomic position,** in which the body is standing straight with legs spread slightly apart and hands down at the sides with palms facing up (Figure 7.9). During the autopsy, the body is lying supine on the autopsy table and examined as if in anatomic position. The external findings are generally described and sequentially enumerated from the top to the bottom of the body, and from front to back. For injuries, the order of their description is as they are seen and is not indicative of the order in which they were sustained. The findings may additionally be described by body regions: head, neck, trunk/torso, upper extremities, and lower extremities. Injuries may be prioritized and described based on severity. Injuries of similar type may be grouped and enumerated, with reference to the body region(s) affected.

A variety of anatomic terms can be used to describe the exact location of injuries and pathological changes. This allows the reader to conceptualize the location of injuries and pathological findings on or in the body, especially if not all of the findings are documented by photographs. The description may be accompanied by a body diagram with markings designating the location of the findings.

Anatomic terms that describe the location of certain findings refer to both external and internal structures. Many of these terms have opposites or counterparts. Certain terms have reference to planes or the *midline of the body,* an imaginary line down the front

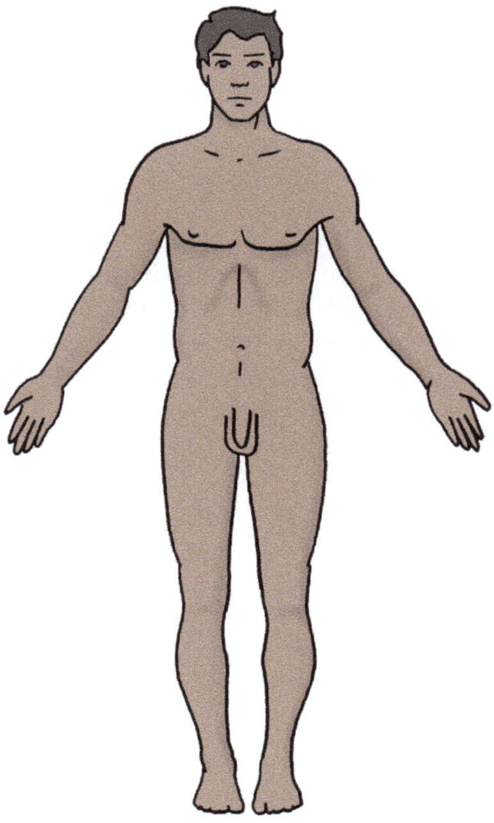

Figure 7.9 Anatomic position of the body.

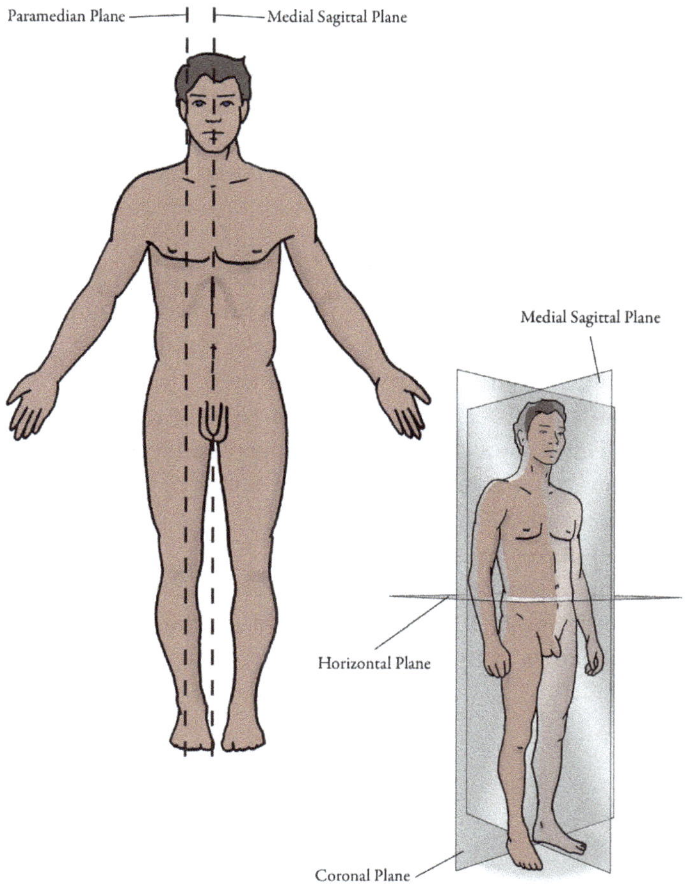

Figure 7.10 Anatomic planes.

or back of the body that divides the body into equal halves: **medial sagittal plane** (on the midline), **paramedian plane** (to one side of the midline), and **coronal plane** (divides body into front and back or anterior and posterior along a longitudinal line extending top to bottom) (Figure 7.10). Other terms have reference to specific directional regions or faces of the body or body part or are root words that can be combined with an anatomic structure (i.e., supraclavicular—above the collar bone) (Figure 7.11):

- Anterior (front) — Posterior (back)
- Superior (top) — Inferior (bottom)
- Supra- (above) — Infra- (below)
- Proximal (nearest to origin) — Distal (farthest from origin)
- Medial (inner) — Lateral (outer)
- Dorsal (posterior, upper surface) — Ventral (anterior, under surface)
- Flexor/volar/palmar (inner surface) — Extensor (outer surface)
- Median (middle) — Paramedian (next to the middle)

Some terms are used to describe discrete injuries or pathological changes located on the same side **(ipsilateral)** or the opposite side **(contralateral)** of another injury,

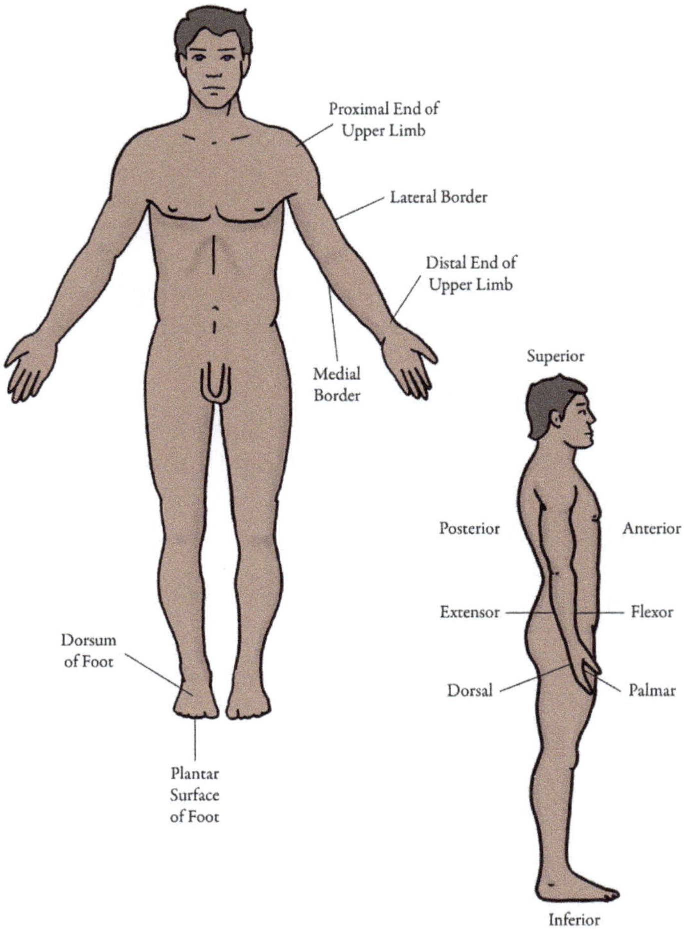

Figure 7.11 Anatomic body designations.

pathological change, or fixed anatomic structure. For example: "The entrance gunshot wound is located on the right abdomen contralateral to the previously described contusion." Clusters of injuries may be described as being located on one side of the body **(unilateral)** or both sides **(bilateral),** and may be sequestered in one area **(focal)** or spread all over **(diffuse).**

Common body regions or structures of the trunk and extremities are used as reference points when describing injuries or other changes. Reference points of the face include:

- Forehead
- Eyebrows
- Nose (bridge, nostrils)
- Lips (upper and lower)
- Chin
- Cheeks
- Jaw/mandible
- Ear/pinna

Regions of the head include:

- Frontal (front)
- Parietal (side)
- Occipital (back)
- Temporal (side, temple)
- Vertex (top)

Pathological changes and injuries will be described according to certain landmarks and regions of the trunk and extremities. Some examples are (Figure 7.12):

- Collar bone (clavicle), right and left
- Costal margin (lower border of the ribs), right and left
- Quadrants of the abdomen, upper and lower, right and left
- Patella (knee cap)
- Lumbrosacral (lower back)
- Gluteal, gluteal fold (buttocks)
- Antecubital fossa (recess opposite each elbow)

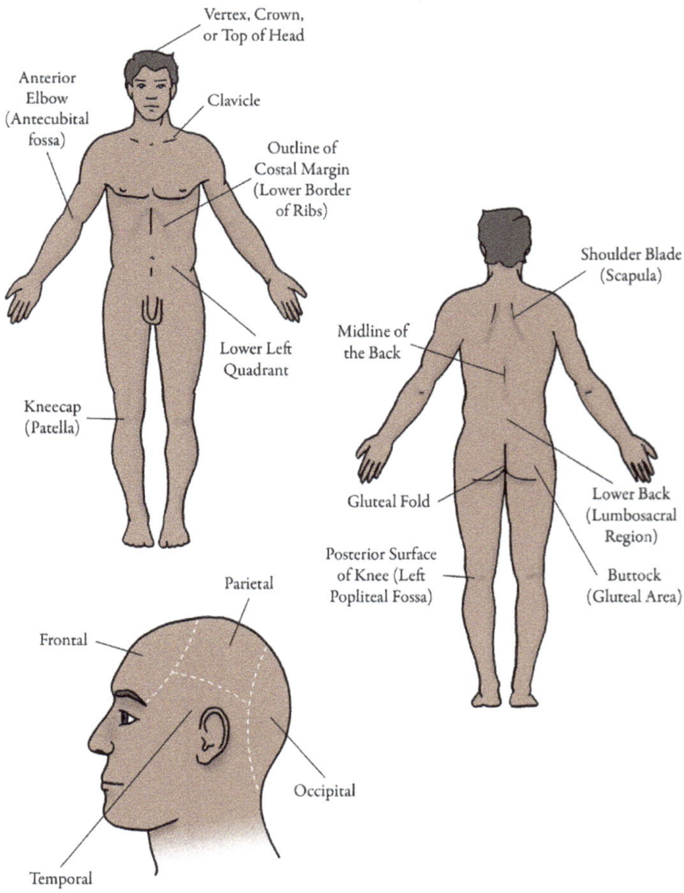

Figure 7.12 Selected body landmarks.

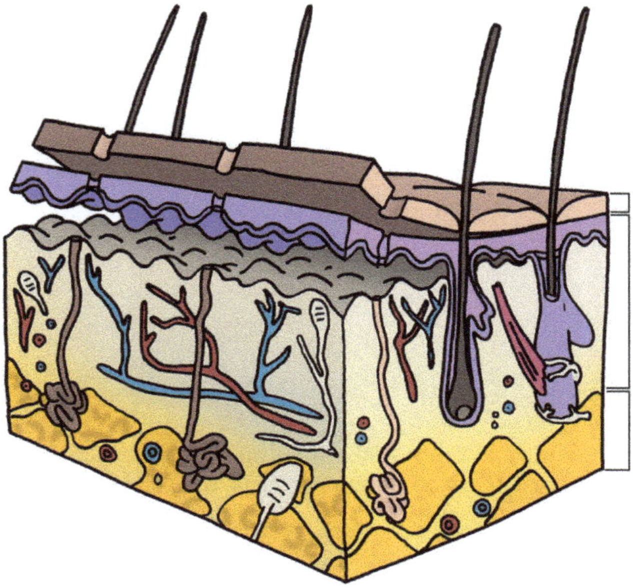

Figure 7.13 Layers of the skin.

- Popliteal fossa (recess back of each knee)
- Posterior midline (midline of back)
- Shoulder blades

Changes on the skin may be described in reference to the layers of the skin involved. The skin is divided into the outer layer (epidermis), middle layer (dermis), and the inner layer (subcutaneous layer or subcutis), and injuries and other changes may involve one or more of these layers (Figure 7.13).

Injuries

External injuries can be classified and described as blunt, sharp, or penetrating. Other specialized types are thermal, electrothermal, and chemical. Injuries sustained in life (i.e., with the presence of a pulse, blood pressure, and blood flow to the injured areas) will have evidence of bleeding or hemorrhage, which may not be visible externally and may involve underlying tissue and organs. Injuries sustained prior to death, followed by prolonged submersion of the body, may appear bloodless and thus postmortem. It must be specifically emphasized that the absence of visible external injury does not rule out injury, especially blunt force injury, since it may not be apparent until inspection of the layers under the skin and the internal tissues and organs is done. Notation of any *patterned injury*, which may represent complete or partial profiles or outlines of an object, is extremely important. A patterned injury is photographically documented with the inclusion of a special right-angled two-dimensional ruler next to the injury (Figure 7.14). The resultant photograph can be physically or digitally superimposed upon the object or photograph of the object (taken in a similar fashion) for comparison or matching. *Patterns of injury* appear as multiple injuries clustered on certain parts or regions of the body: scrapes, bruises, or cuts of the dorsal/palmar hands, finger webs, or extensor forearm (defensive injuries); needle

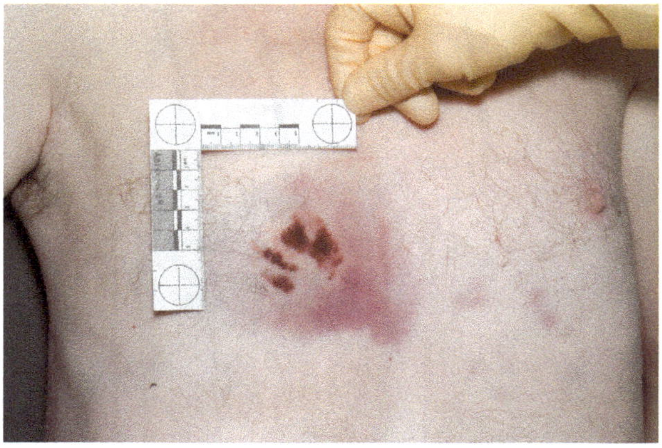

Figure 7.14 Patterned injury from impact of the chest with a small camera, causing contusion with eccentrically located brown abrasion, taken with a two-dimensional ruler.

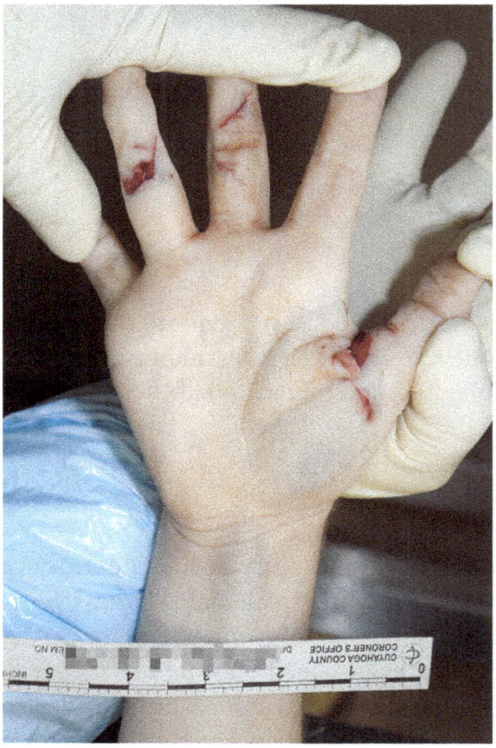

Figure 7.15 Defensive injuries: Incised wounds of the thumb and the third and fourth fingers due to victim grabbing a knife.

punctures of the antecubital fossa (intravenous drug abuse or therapeutic access of veins); horizontal cuts on the volar wrist (suicidal cuts); or evenly spaced linear chop wounds (boat propeller injuries) (Figure 7.15). Injuries caused by therapeutic intervention (also known as artifacts), including cardiopulmonary resuscitation and surgery, may leave a variety of blunt, sharp, and penetrating injuries that must be distinguished from injury sustained or inflicted prior to medical treatment.

Blunt Force Injury

Blunt force injury is the most common type of injury, whether it results in death or not. It is the result of body or body part impacting a blunt surface or conversely as a result of a region of the body being *impacted by* some type of blunt object or surface. Upon impact caused by an object striking a body region, a transfer of energy occurs which is dependent on the mass of the object and the velocity at which the object strikes the body ($E = MV^2$).[6] An increment in the velocity of impact will result in transfer of greater energy than the same increment in the mass of the object. With sufficient object mass or velocity of application of the impact, tissue disruption with injury and disturbance of structure and function of the impacted region can result. The characteristics of the object, along with the amount of surface area on the body affected and the characteristics of the area of the body impacted, in part determine the extent of injury. In general, the shorter the time of infliction, the smaller the surface area impacted; the greater the mass of the object, and the faster the impact is applied, the greater the damage to the body.[6] For example, an impact to the upper posterior trunk or torso (the upper back) with a wooden paddle would cause less injury than an impact with the heel of a stiletto shoe applied with the same force since the energy from the paddle would be dispersed over a broader surface area. Thin skin, aged skin, and skin overlying bony surfaces (i.e., head and elbow regions) are particularly susceptible to injury. Internally, bone and cartilage will be more resistant to internally transmitted forces than liver or spleen by virtue of the inherent structural characteristics of these tissues whereby bone and cartilage would be more resistant to forceful impact than liver or spleen.

The resulting injury caused by blunt impacts or forces can manifest as an abrasion, contusion, or laceration of the skin, or fracture of the bone. The injury may be of a single type or combination of more than one type. Damage to the underlying soft tissues and internal organs may be included and may take the form of hemorrhage, contusion, or laceration, and may not be visible externally. The effects of injury can be local and confined to one area or more extensive and widespread and associated with complications such as shock from blood loss, organ and tissue death from loss of blood flow, formation of blood clots that may travel to the heart and lung, infection, and multiple organ failure. Depending on the extent of injury death may occur quickly or be delayed with the development of pre-death complications.

Abrasions (commonly known as scrapes) arise from impact, causing tangential or compressive force with friction and removal of the epidermis or epidermis with dermis. An abrasion may be linear (scratch), broad (road rash, brush burn), elongate/oblong (graze), impact (imprint of object), stretch, or postmortem (Figure 7.16). It may take on the shape of the object that produced it (patterned injury). Recent abrasions appear red, red-brown, or tan, with or without bleeding or oozing of a reddish sticky serum. With healing, a brown scab **(eschar)** will form and eventually fall off, leaving no trace of injury, a light (hypopigmented) scar, or a dark (hyperpigmented) scar. **Graze abrasions** deserve special mention since they may represent impact from a bullet skimming across the surface of the skin, creating a superficial elongated oblong injury (Figure 7.17A). A special type of graze abrasion is the **tangential abrasion,** which is a slightly deeper form of a graze abrasion with the addition of angled tags of skin that point in the direction from which the bullet came (Figure 7.17B). Sometimes abrasions will have heaped-up skin at one edge, which may give clues as to the direction from which the impact originated. Postmortem abrasions are

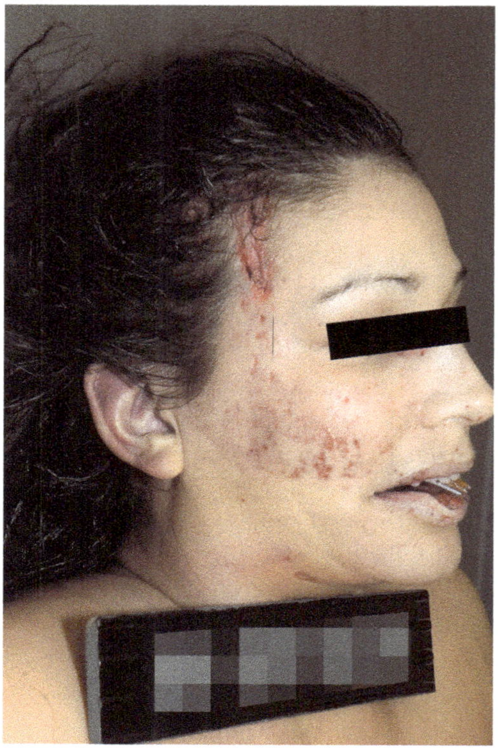

Figure 7.16 Abrasions of the cheek of passenger from impact by shattered tempered glass.

typically yellow to yellow-orange with a parched appearance. Abrasions, initially faint or invisible, may become even more apparent after the skin has been allowed to dry further. Abrasions often harden and appear darker after a period time of being exposed to air.

Contusions arise from crushing, squeezing, or compressive forces that cause tearing and rupturing of the subcutaneous blood vessels with resultant hemorrhage. The overlying skin usually remains intact, however, and the contusions may be accompanied by other blunt force injuries, such as abrasion or laceration (i.e., abraded contusion or lacerated contusion). The bleeding that results from contusion may accumulate within pockets of subcutaneous tissue or within damaged organs and is referred to as a **hematoma. Bruise, ecchymosis,** or **purpura** are other similar terms that may be used. Ecchymosis and purpura involve leakage of blood from a blood vessel under the skin, usually spontaneously or with very little force of impact. Ecchymosis may also develop in an area that overlies a bone fracture, as a result of leakage and migration of blood from the fracture site. Ecchymosis is particularly prone to develop during and after access of the superficial veins of the skin by syringes or placement of catheters. Contusions may take a short time to appear after impact, but usually and initially appear blue, purple, or red, or a combination of those colors (Figure 7.18). They can have rounded or irregular borders that may merge into adjacent contusions or other injuries. They may be initially faint or invisible, becoming more distinct after the performance of the autopsy, and even the following day. Like abrasions, they may also be patterned. They may be masked by livor mortis, but can usually be distinguished by the forensic pathologist by incising into the skin of the discolored area: contusions will have red hemorrhage that has infiltrated into the subcutaneous tissues, remaining fixed without leakage, as would occur with incision into an area of livor. Blood

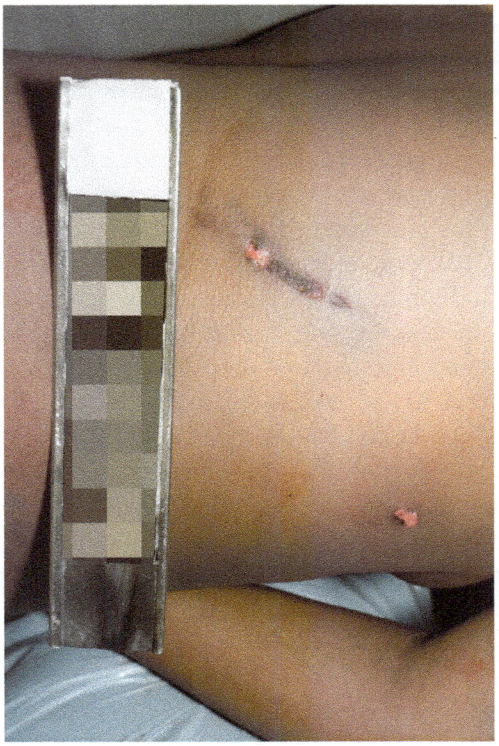

Figure 7.17 (A) Graze abrasion of posterolateral lower right trunk. (B) Tangential abrasion of posterior neck with a single skin tag pointing leftward, indicating a left-to-right direction of travel of the projectile.

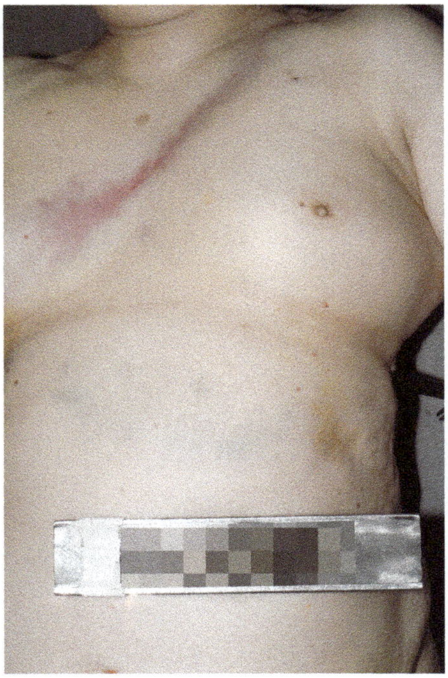

Figure 7.18 Oblique contusion from left shoulder across the chest of the driver of an automobile.

may also migrate into the soft tissues, especially fatty tissues, upon pressure or impact occurring after death such as during attempts to lift and remove a dead body. Contusions on the lateral and more commonly the medial surfaces of the upper arms of deceased individuals who have been carried by the arms are examples of *postmortem contusions* by virtue of their location and correlation with the terminal historical circumstances (Figure 7.19). A blunt impact that would ordinarily cause a contusion may give rise to very little or no hemorrhage if sustained contemporaneously with injury to the brainstem, with the ensuing rapid death.[6] Chronic liver disease, bleeding disorders, and blood-thinning medications predispose individuals to easy bruising. Elderly individuals with paper-thin skin and fragile blood vessels are prone to skin tears and bruising, sometimes with the slightest impact. The number and distribution of these injuries on a deceased individual may sometimes arouse suspicion of trauma due to foul play (Figure 7.20). The recognition of contusions in darker-skinned individuals may be challenging and not appreciated until inspection of the tissues immediately under the skin is done at the time of autopsy.

Over time, a contusion on a living person will heal and change color, usually changing to green, yellow, and brown, representing the breakdown of the red blood cell protein hemoglobin. The sequence and succession of the changes of color of a contusion are not uniform and do not occur at any predictable rate. The aging of bruises by the forensic pathologist by microscopic examination of a small biopsy of skin is tenuous at best.

The appearance under the microscope of cellular swelling and death, inflammatory cells, and the breakdown product of red blood cells, called **hemosiderin,** may provide a clue that the individual sustained the contusion and then lived for some time afterward known as the **survival interval.** The microscopic appearance of these changes beginning with the appearance of fresh bleeding or hemorrhage is called **vital reaction** and can be seen in conjunction with abrasions and lacerations as well. Designation of contusions as recent may be inexact, since overlap in the appearance and color of recently inflicted contusions vs. older ones has been shown. The forensic pathologist is left with describing the contusion based on the subjective appearance, knowing that only yellow or partly yellow contusions give some information as to the age (resolving and at least 18 hours of age).[7]

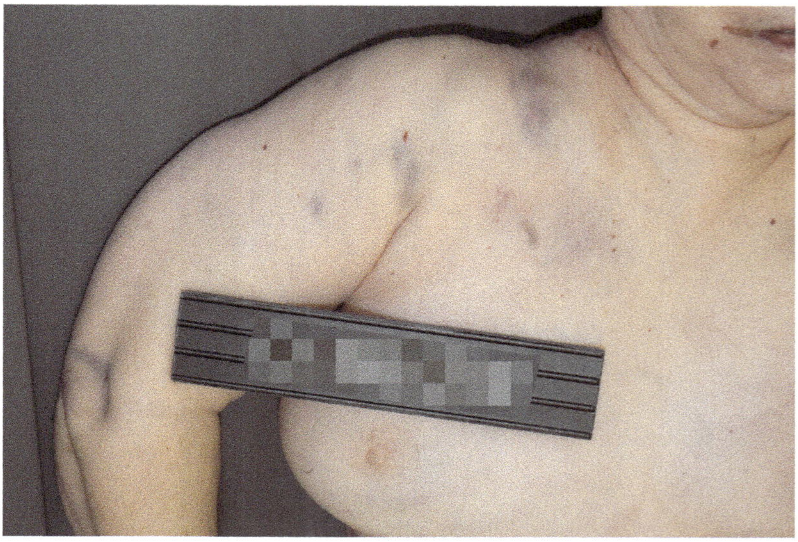

Figure 7.19 Postmortem contusions of proximal arm from lifting of body.

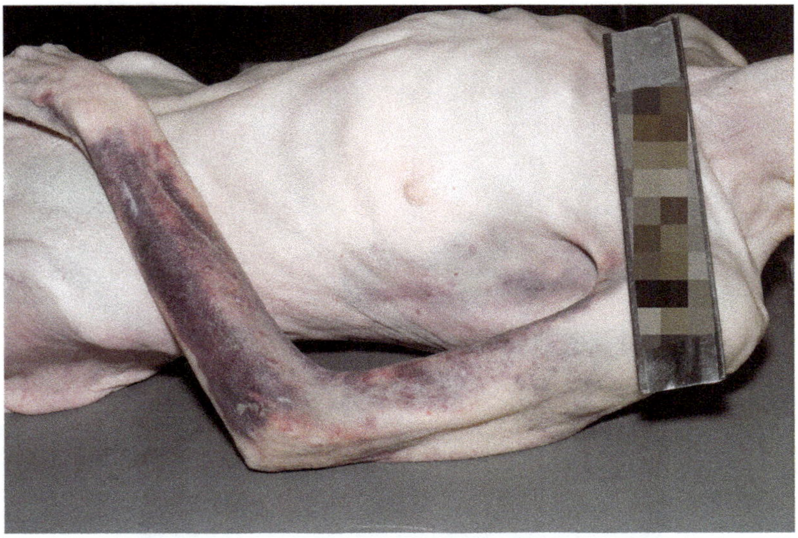

Figure 7.20 Senile purpura/ecchymosis on forearm of an extremely thin 78-year-old female.

Lacerations, or tears, are caused by stretching, shearing, and crushing forces. On the skin, they appear as tears, with or without abrasion of the edges or contusion of the depths. Lacerations are sometimes misidentified as incised or stab wounds, which are sharp force injuries. Sharp force injuries have clean, sharp edges. By contrast, the edges of lacerations are usually (but not always) irregular, and upon close inspection, one may observe the bridging of connective tissue, nerves, and blood vessels across the wound (Figure 7.21). Lacerations can occur anywhere on the body but are particularly prone to appear upon impact in areas of the body where skin overlies bone, such as the head, eyebrows, and knees. Lacerations to the head can bleed profusely, a particularly dangerous situation in an intoxicated, stuporous individual who is unaware and/or unable to stop the bleeding with risk of death from extensive blood loss **(exsanguination)** even from a single, seemingly small and inconsequential injury. Blunt force impacts causing laceration may also create a pocket of skin that has become detached from its underpinnings. The orientation of the pocket of the tissue can give clues to the directionality of the blow or impact. The orientation and size of an adjacent abrasion can also give clues to directionality. Blunt forces caused by penetrating projectiles such as bullets or forces that cause bone fracture with fragmentation and displacement, rapid deceleration of the body such as in motor vehicle accidents, or compression of large regions of the body, may give rise to lacerations of the internal anatomy, such as the blood vessels, heart, lungs, liver, and intestines.

The forces necessary to cause **skeletal fracture** is usually significantly greater but may be dependent on the condition of the bones at the time of impact. Under normal circumstances, significant force is needed to cause fracture to bones such as the long bones of the arms and legs, pelvis, and skull. However, individuals who are malnourished, who are infants or children with genetic bone diseases, or who are elderly, may have weaker bones that are more prone to fracturing with less force or impact. Elderly individuals with advanced osteoporosis may sustain a hip fracture by just simply taking a step while walking upright. Individuals with metastatic cancer may also have weakened bones due to infiltration by the cancer, and sustain a **pathological fracture** with little or no force or impact. Fractures may be visible externally as obvious deformity, sometimes with

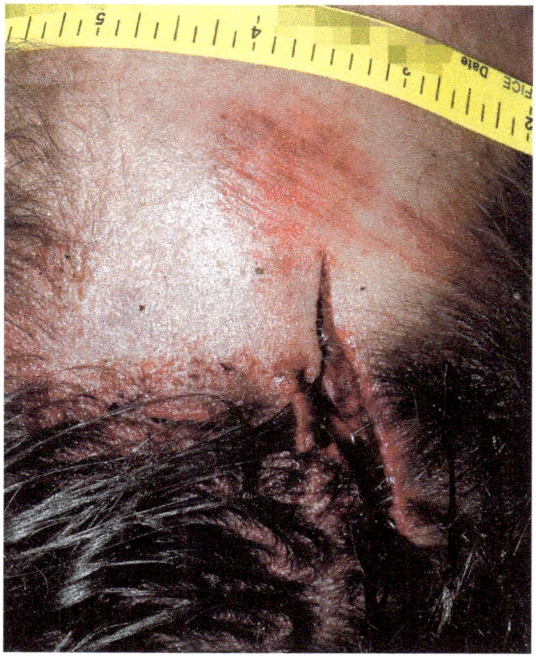

Figure 7.21 Laceration of the right frontal scalp-forehead region with bridging of connective tissues across wound.

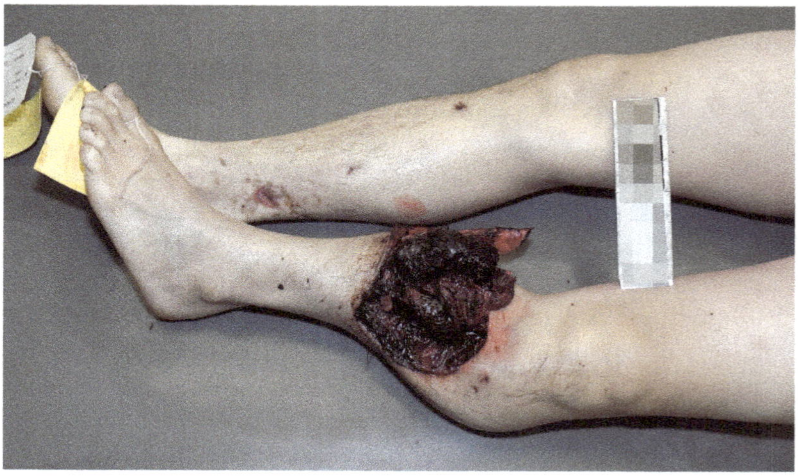

Figure 7.22 Compound fracture of the left tibia and fibula.

protrusion through the skin **(compound/open fracture),** and otherwise illuminated by an x-ray (Figure 7.22). Consultation with the forensic radiologist in the detection of or confirmation of suspected fractures seen initially by the forensic pathologist is vital. Bone is a special type of connective tissue that is mineralized, possessing the capacity, although limited, to bend or deform. Compressive, tensile (pulling), or shearing (angled) forces that breach that capacity will cause fracture of the bone. Particular types of fractures may give clues as to their origin. Symmetrical fracture of the thigh bone (femur) and lower leg bones (tibia and fibula) may represent **bumper fractures,** which can result when a pedestrian is struck by a car, sports utility vehicle, or small truck. Fractures of the pelvis represent severe lateral, anterior-posterior, or shear forces, such as those produced in motor vehicle accidents and falls from heights. Fractures of the lateral aspects of the ribs, especially with underlying injury to the heart and lungs, represent compressive forces to the chest. Focal depressed fractures of the skull may represent impact with a narrow blunt object (i.e., a hammer, corner of a brick, or corner of a table). Fractures resulting in multiple fragments of bone **(comminuted)** represent high-energy impact, crushing injury such as by heavy industrial machinery, or rollover injury caused by a vehicle. Fractures of the spinal column or vertebral bodies may result from direct impact due to falls and motor vehicle accidents or from severe flexion or extension of the neck and torso, with or without injury to the underlying spinal cord. Child abuse may manifest with a constellation of recent, healing, or healed injuries and include rib fractures adjacent to the spine, skull fracture, and fracture of the ends of the long bones of the upper and lower extremities. The cause of death in child-abuse-related cases involving blunt force injury is often due to a combination of skull and brain injury **(craniocerebral),** including skull fractures, hemorrhages of the backs of the eyeballs **(retinal hemorrhages),** bleeding over the surface of the brain **(subdural and subarachnoid hemorrhage),** tears and bleeding within the brain tissue, or injury to the upper/cervical spinal cord (Figure 7.23).

Blunt force injury to the head may have a number of external clues that internal brain injury of varying extent is also present. Purple-red ecchymosis (raccoon eyes, **periorbital ecchymosis)** of the eyelids without involvement of the eyebrows or other protruding structures of the face, is a sign of fracture with hemorrhage of the anterior region of the base of the inside of the skull **(orbital roof fracture),** often with injury to the brain, and is seen in falls with impact to the back of the head and gunshot wounds to the head (Figures 7.24 and 7.25). Bruising of the eyelids *accompanied by* bruising, abrasion, or laceration to the nearby protruding structures of the face (eyebrows, nose, and cheeks) most likely represents direct blunt impact to the upper face region. It conceivably could also represent a direct blow to the face, causing the victim to fall and impact the back of his or her head, with subsequent development of periorbital ecchymosis. Purple-red ecchymosis behind the ears **(Battle's sign)** represents fracture with hemorrhage of the middle region of the base of the inside of the skull or middle cranial fossae **(hinge fracture),** often with brain injury, seen in motor

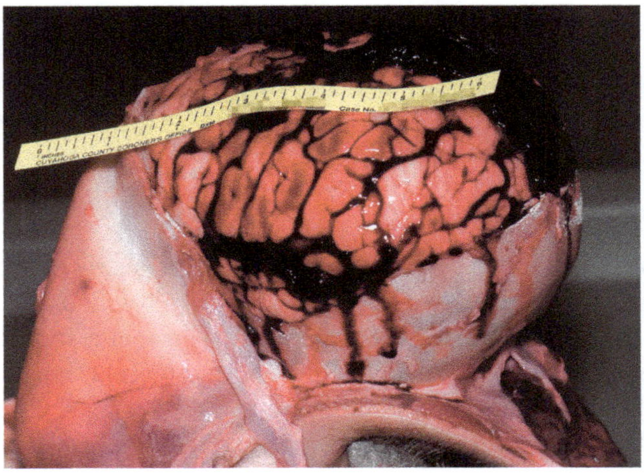

Figure 7.23 Subdural and subarachnoid hemorrhage of the brain in a fatally abused child.

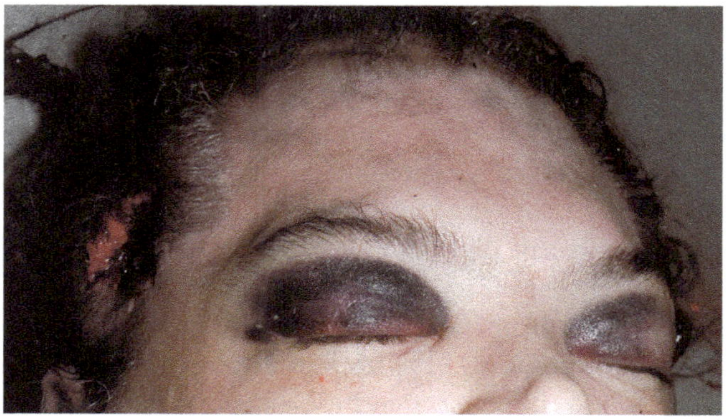

Figure 7.24 Periorbital ecchymosis due to self-inflicted gunshot wound of the head.

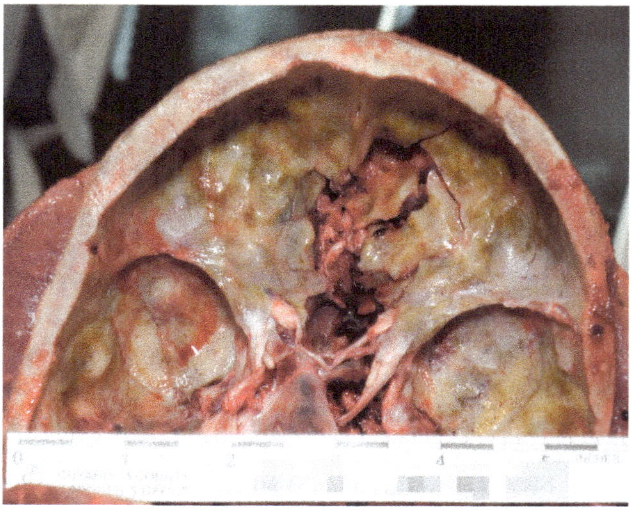

Figure 7.25 Fractures of the anterior right base of the skull above the eyes (orbital roof) due to self-inflicted gunshot wound of the head.

vehicle accidents (Figure 7.26A and B). Visible deformity of the face with movement of the fractured bone on palpation (fractures of the bones around the eyes, cheek bone, and jaw bones) represents blunt force injury to the face, such as those sustained in assaults, motor vehicle accidents, falls, and gunshot or shotgun wounds to the head (Figure 7.27).

Sharp Force Injury

Sharp force injuries are caused by objects with sharp or nearly sharp edges or points, including knives, screwdrivers, scissors, ice picks, broken glass, and axes. The wounds they produce typically have smooth distinct edges and vary in shape, including round, linear, curvilinear, gaping, or slit-like. They can be divided into incised wounds (cuts or slashes), stab wounds, or chop wounds. Chop wounds are a special category of sharp force injury caused by heavy objects with relatively sharp edges, such as axes and boat propeller blades. The wounds produced by these objects may incorporate a combination of sharp and blunt force injury and may have irregular abraded and contused edges.

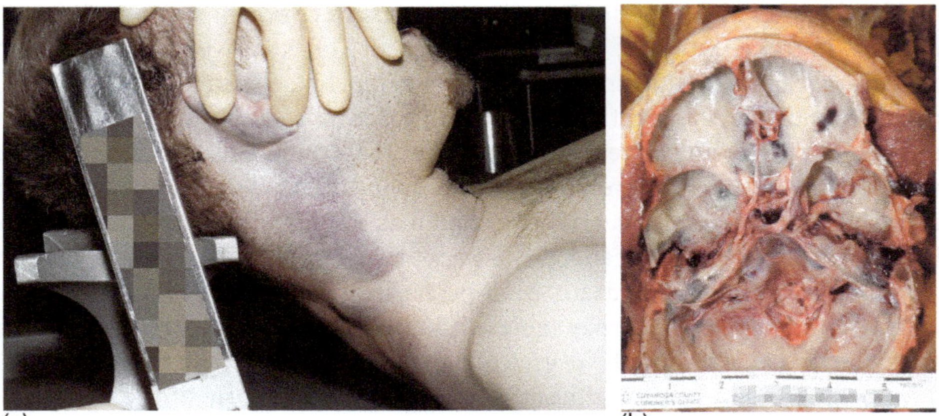

(a) (b)

Figure 7.26 (A) Battle's sign. (B) Linear fracture through right and left middle cranial fossae (hinge fracture).

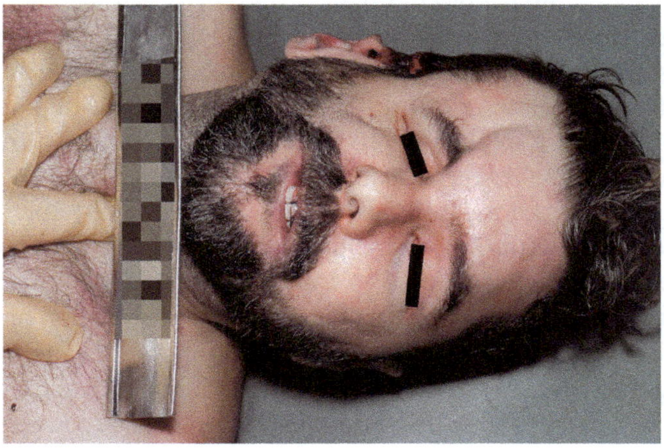

Figure 7.27 Multiple fractures of the facial bones with deformity.

There are basic differences between incised and stab wounds. Typically, incised wounds are superficial, being longer on the skin than they go deep into the skin, and are caused by dragging the perpendicular or nearly perpendicular blade across the skin's surface. Incised wounds that are very superficial do not bleed to a great extent. By contrast, stab wounds extend deeper into the body and thus are greater in depth than the length on the skin surface, and have a greater propensity to involve injury to the internal organs and blood vessels. The skin has some resistance to penetration, but once breached, especially when the instrument has a very sharp edge, it takes very little perpendicular or obliquely applied force to extend the wound into the underlying tissue and organs, unless bone or cartilage is encountered.

The extent of blood loss can vary. Death can result from exsanguination from superficial incised wounds as a result of severing of the arteries and veins just beneath the skin. Incised wounds of the scalp, an area with a great concentration of blood vessels, may bleed profusely, including to the point of death due to exsanguination. Other examples of fatal incised wounds are those of the neck with injury to the underlying carotid and jugular blood vessels and wounds of the inner wrist surface accompanied by injury to the radial artery. In those instances, there may be evidence of extensive bleeding at the death scene with large pools of liquid and/or clotted blood and blood spatter on various surfaces. Deep stab wounds may have little in the way of external bleeding, and thus little blood at the scene, due to closing or reapproximation of the wound edges. Death as a result of stab wounds may be due predominantly to internal bleeding with accumulation of blood within the chest or abdominal cavities or a combination of internal and external bleeding.

The location, configuration, and clustering of sharp force injury can give clues to the circumstances surrounding the death. Multiple horizontal and parallel incised wounds of the wrist(s), forearm(s), or neck may represent **hesitation wounds** of a suicidal nature, in which the individual is testing the degree of pain such injuries would bring (Figure 7.28). Much less common are homicidal hesitation wounds, particularly of the neck, inflicted by an assailant and often preceding one or several long and progressively deeper incised wounds of the same region. V-shaped or L-shaped stab wounds may indicate two or more wounds inflicted in the same area with movement or twisting of the knife or victim (Figure 7.29). Small, paired, round stab wounds may represent injuries produced by a two-pronged fork or similar object. Small, paired, or single rectangular or triangular stab wounds may represent injuries produced by a pair of scissors or similar object (Figure 7.30). A stab wound that is gaping or slit-like is not necessarily indicative of the shape of the knife, but indicative of the arrangement of the elastic fibers located under the skin that support and give elasticity to the skin, called **Langer's lines.**[8] The edges of a gaping stab wound will be reapproximated so an overall measurement can be done and to facilitate identification and measurement of any blunted end(s) and identification any sharp or angled end(s) (Figure 7.31). This may aid in the determination as to whether a single- or double-edged knife was used to inflict the wound. Multiple parallel, spaced, similar-sized incised or chop wounds distributed over a broad region of a body recovered from water may be representative of injuries caused by boat propellers. A serrated knife dragged at an angle across the skin may leave parallel, linear, evenly spaced abrasions that may, depending on the angle the knife was applied to the skin, be consistent with the knife

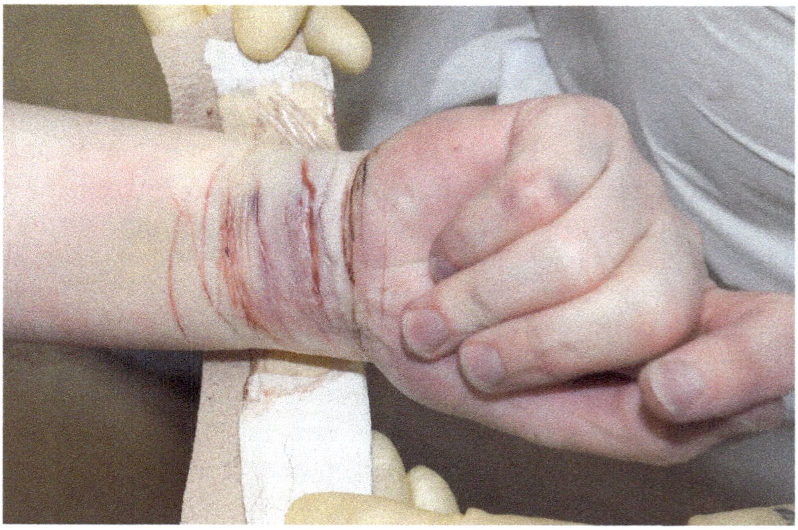

Figure 7.28 Suicidal hesitation incised wounds of the volar wrist.

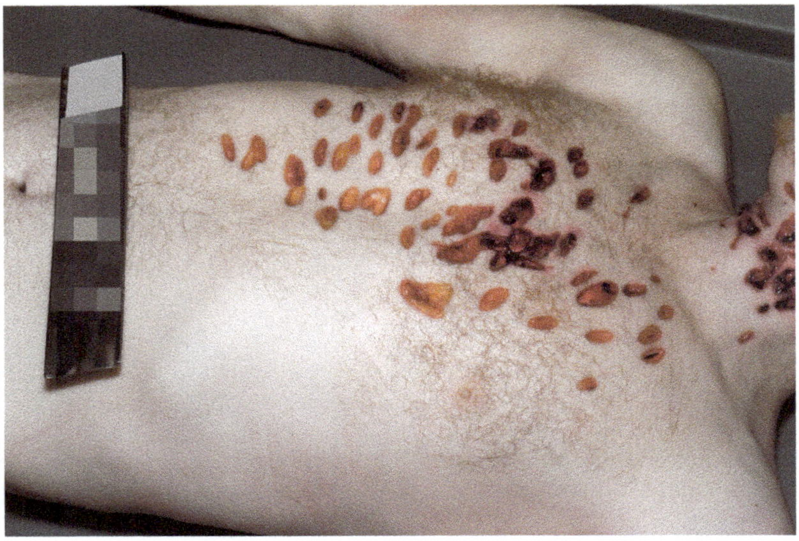

Figure 7.29 L- and V-shaped stab wounds of the chest and abdomen.

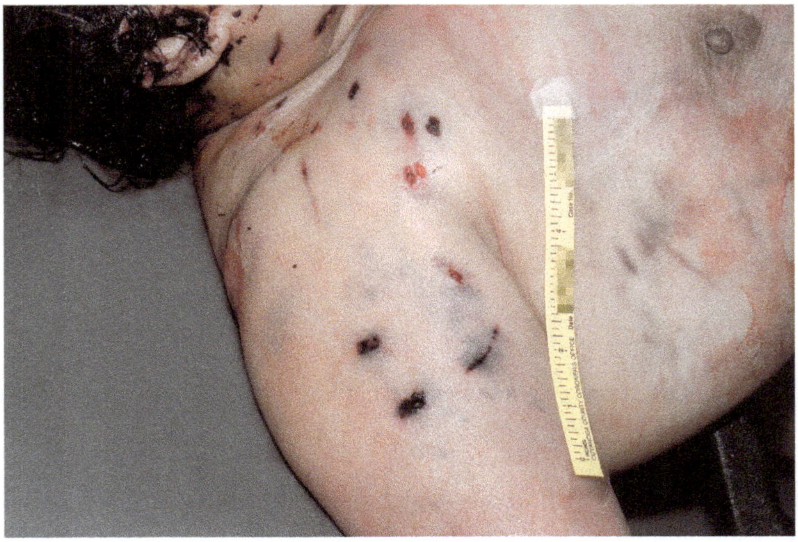

Figure 7.30 Stab wounds of the right shoulder caused by scissors.

that caused the abrasions (Figure 7.32). Contrary to common belief, the handedness of an assailant cannot be determined by the characteristics of incised or stab wounds alone. The forensic pathologist must be presented with the additional investigative information of the relative positions of assailant and the victim at the time the injury was inflicted, before rendering opinions about whether the assailant was right or left handed.

The description of a sharp force injury includes measurement of external dimensions in inches, description of the orientation of the wound (oblique, horizontal, or vertical), description of the path of injury and organs and tissues injured, description of the maximum depth of penetration, and the course and direction (i.e., front to back, right to left, and downward). If a stab wound involves bone or cartilage, description and photographic documentation of any markings left on these structures will be made. The pattern of

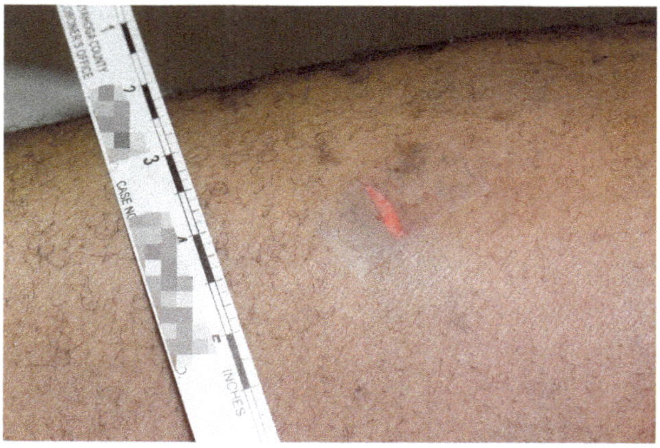

Figure 7.31 Reapproximation of stab wound of anterior left thigh using transparent tape, featuring blunted, squared off end (lower) and V-shaped opposite end (upper).

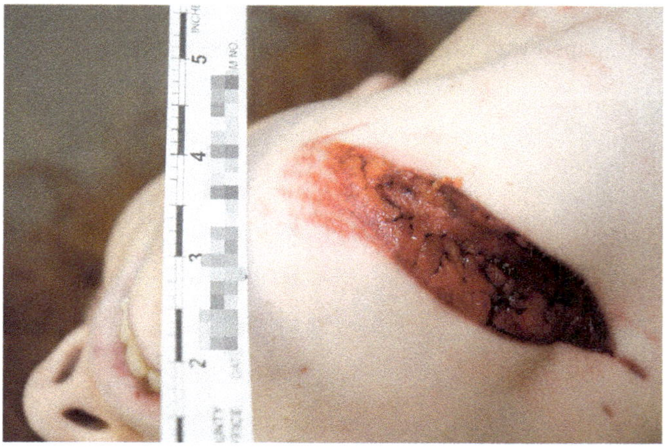

Figure 7.32 Homicidal incised wound of neck from knife with serrated blade, featuring parallel abrasions at one end of wound.

markings or **tool marks** left behind has evidentiary value and could be potentially linked to the instrument that made them (Figure 7.33).

Firearm Injury

A bullet fired from a handgun is a rapidly moving projectile that possesses kinetic energy (a product of projectile mass and velocity) that will be dispersed upon penetration of the skin or other target. It exits the muzzle of the gun spinning along a longitudinal axis, initially in a relatively straight trajectory, and with little deviation from the longitudinal axis **(yaw).**[8]

Upon perforation of the skin, a partial or complete (eccentric or circumferential) rim of abrasion around the margin is created. As it continues into the body, the kinetic energy possessed by the bullet is dispersed in waves into the surrounding soft tissue, organs, and bone, producing a variety of internal injury and hemorrhage close to or a distance away from the path of injury directly created by the bullet. The degree of injury is dependent on certain characteristics of the bullet and gunpowder, and those characteristics that result

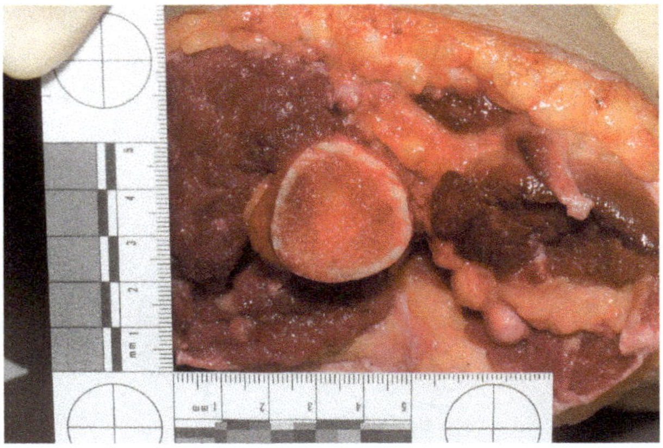

Figure 7.33 Tool marks on cut surface of femur caused by a saw featuring oblique striations across bone, from dismembered victim of multiple gunshot wounds.

in higher velocity or mass will create more tissue damage. As the bullet continues through the body and the various tissues, it will yaw and wobble to a greater extent, and if still possessing sufficient energy, it will exit, generally creating a larger, more irregular wound. Without sufficient energy, it will be retained within the body or just under the skin where it would have exited. The loss of energy is due in part to the types of tissue perforated (i.e., bone) and characteristics built into the bullet or cartridge (i.e., small caliber bullets or hollow point bullets).

The shot or pellets from a shotgun shell fired at close range will all enter the body, creating a large wound of entry around the margin. When fired from an increasing range, the birdshot or buckshot will emerge from the shell with gradual spreading and create scalloping of the wound edges and satellite perforations of increasing spread around the main wound (Figure 7.34). The components of the shotgun shell (cup, wadding, hull, filler material, and shot) rarely exit and may not even enter into the body. The internal injuries caused by shotgun ammunition are extensive at close range, due to the amount of gases released into the tissues and the shredding of tissue produced by the pellets.

Similar to sharp force injury, the description of gunshot or shotgun wounds includes measurement of the external dimensions of the entry and exit wounds, path of injury and organs and tissue injured, and the course and direction of the wound. A description of any bullet(s), bullet fragments, or shot recovered, including the caliber of the bullet (or diameter of a pellet), presence of a jacket, presence of shotgun shell components, degree of bullet deformity, and location in body where recovered, is provided. Occasionally, retained projectiles from remote gunshot or shotgun wounds may be encountered and initially recognized on x-ray. These projectiles (**souvenir** bullets or bird- or buckshots) have a dull, gray, oxidized appearance and are recovered from within dense scar tissue without any evidence of recent hemorrhage. All bullets and buckshot illuminated by x-ray will be recovered and described in conjunction with its respective entrance wound. Rarely, a single entrance wound is associated with the recovery of two projectiles which can happen when two projectiles enter through the same wound. In shotgun wounds involving birdshot, a representative numbers of pellets will be recovered.

Entrance gunshot wounds are typically round to ovoid, with a complete or partial rim of abrasion, whereas exit wounds tend to be more irregular and often larger. Due to the

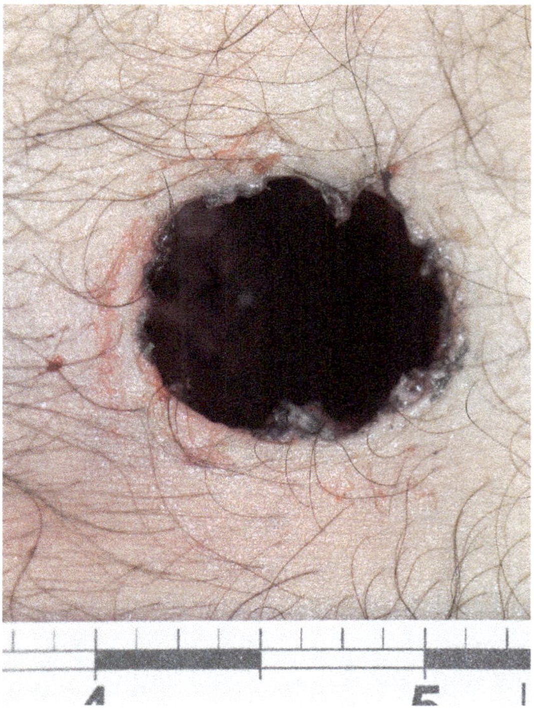

Figure 7.34 Entrance shotgun wound with scalloping of the edges.

presence of underlying bones, the opposite may hold true for contact gunshot wounds of the head, in which the entrance wound is larger and has a cross or star shape, representing skin splitting produced by the expulsion of gas and pressure upon firing the firearm at close range or with direct contact of the muzzle end with the skin. Exit wounds of the head tend to be smaller but still irregular.

Depending on the distance from the end of the muzzle to the body region, the entrance wound may be accompanied by an imprint of the muzzle (contact), fouling by deposition of gunpowder (contact, near contact, or close range), or stippled abrasions **(stippling)** resulting from impacts of burned and unburned gunpowder from an intermediate range (Figure 7.35). The absence of fouling or stippling may represent a distant range or the presence of intervening clothing or objects at the time of discharge of the firearm.[9] Fragmentation of intermediate targets, such as glass, a wooden door, or pavement, may impact the victim, creating larger and more irregular abrasions of varying sizes, called **pseudostippling.**

External and internal injuries produced by shotguns are particularly destructive, and reconstruction of the affected body region to determine the location of the entrance wound and the range of fire may be necessary. Gunshot wounds may also be accompanied by graze or tangential abrasions, and their presence may help determine the direction from which the bullet emerged (and the location of the shooter) or the number of times a firearm was discharged.

Contrary to common belief, the size of the entrance wound cannot be used to determine the caliber of the projectile, as the elasticity of skin, along with the marginal abrasion and effect of gas and heat expelled in close-range discharges, causes an entry wound that may appear smaller than the actual caliber of the projectile.

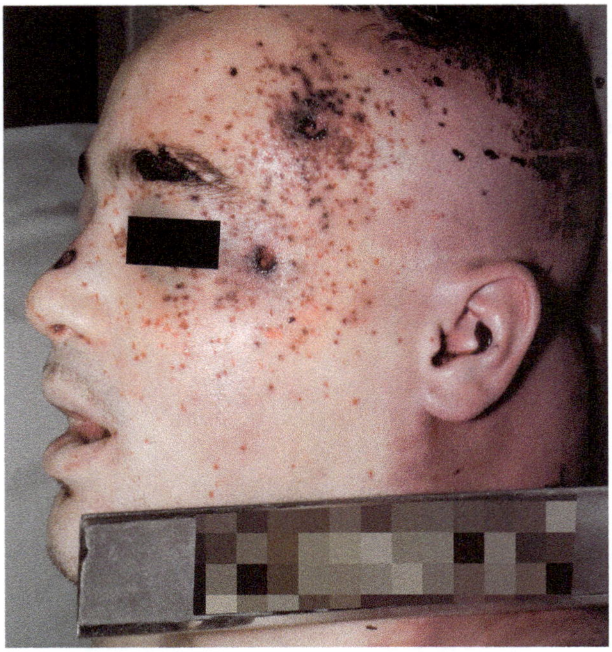

Figure 7.35 Stippling around entrance wounds of the face, intermediate range.

Multiple gunshot wounds will often be enumerated and described separately, and the order of their numbering does not imply the order in which they were sustained. This manner of describing multiple gunshot wounds applies to other enumerated injuries as well. Additionally, numerous gunshot wounds affecting many regions or parts of the body may be grouped and described by body region (i.e., of the head, neck, trunk/torso, and extremities), and a total number of wounds (corresponding to the number of entry wounds with or without an associated exit wound) will be provided. Clusters of entry wounds made by birdshot or buckshot will often have a measurement and description of the maximum horizontal and vertical spread. This may assist police investigators in the determination of the range of fire.

Thermal Injury

Thermal burns of the skin are caused by direct flame, dry/radiant heat, moist/scalding heat, electromagnetic energy or microwaves, or electricity resulting in varying degrees of damage to the layers of skin and underlying tissues. The degree of skin damage is a function of temperature and length of time of contact with heat, whereby high temperatures applied over a short time period will cause significant damage, as would lower temperatures applied over a longer period of time.

The extent of skin injury from thermal burns caused by direct flame or radiant heat is classified into four categories according to the layer(s) affected.[10] **First-degree burns** are superficial with red discoloration; **second-degree burns** involve the epidermis and part of the dermis and appear as blisters; **third-degree burns** involve the entire skin thickness, including blood vessels and nerves, and the skin will have a blanched, leathery appearance and consistency; **fourth-degree burns** are referred to as charring involving not only all layers of the skin but also the underlying fat, muscle, and sometimes bones (Figure 7.36). Fourth-degree burns have a blackened appearance (Figure 7.37). Alternatively, thermal burns may be described based on the depth of involved skin and underlying soft tissues (i.e. partial-thickness versus full-thickness). Even with severe and diffuse fourth-degree injury, the internal organs will often be relatively well-preserved and recognizable (although sometimes hardened by the effects of heat or flame), and blood is often obtainable for carbon monoxide testing.

Each affected region of the body (head, trunk, and each extremity) represents a portion or percentage of the **total body surface area** (TBSA), adding up to 100%. The extent of

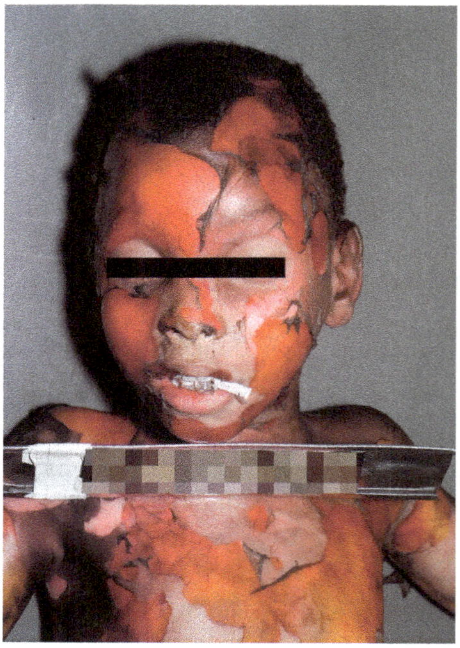

Figure 7.36 Second-degree thermal injury with blisters of face.

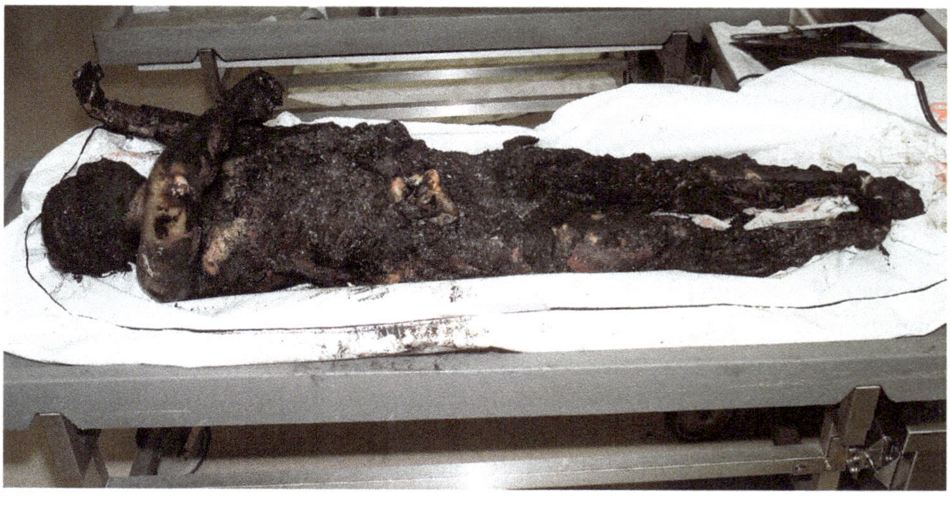

Figure 7.37 Fourth-degree thermal injury (charring).

involvement of the body may be described according to the percent of TBSA involved in addition to the degree of burns. This method of description is used more commonly in hospitals but may be used to describe the injuries at autopsy. Areas spared from thermal injury are important to note and will be correlated with the description of the body position at the scene and the description of any clothing or other objects on or adjacent to the body. These spared areas, especially if on the dependent parts of the body, can also be inspected for the color of the lividity, in which bright pink or cherry-red lividity may indicate carbon monoxide poisoning from the inhalation of smoke by a victim recovered from a structural fire. Scalding injuries from splash or immersion, appearing as reddening with loosening and slippage of the skin, may have a pattern of injury with spared areas of the skin that may provide clues as to how the injury was sustained. A child or infant with scalding burns to the buttocks and lower legs, but sparing gluteal folds and the backs of the knees, may represent abusive injury in which the child or infant was immersed in a hot fluid with defensive flexion at the hips and knees.[10]

Thermal injury may create artifacts that must not be misinterpreted as postmortem changes or inflicted injury. The coagulative or hardening effect of heat or flame that results in third- and fourth-degree injury will cause flexion at the joints of the extremities, with the upper extremities fixed in a position known as **pugilistic attitude** or boxer's stance, and should not be confused with rigor mortis (Figure 7.38).[10] Other artifacts of extreme fire damage include opacification of the corneas, lightening and singeing of the hair, shortening of the extremities due to coagulation of the tissues or consumption by fire, and decrease in the weight of the body. Alteration or destruction of the facial features along with the above artifacts will make visual identification difficult or impossible, necessitating identification by other means. Destruction of the fingers and hands will make fingerprint identification impossible. Other artifacts of extreme heat may mimic sharp or blunt force-inflicted injury, such as splitting of the skin and fracture of the bones (heat fractures). Second- and third-degree injuries appearing with centrally located thermal injury with a red rim at the periphery have been previously designated as antemortem injury (Figure 7.39). This type of injury may also represent postmortem injury in which a heated surface or object was in prolonged contact with the skin after death. Only with the presence of *vital reaction* seen under the microscope can the injury more confidently be designated as antemortem.

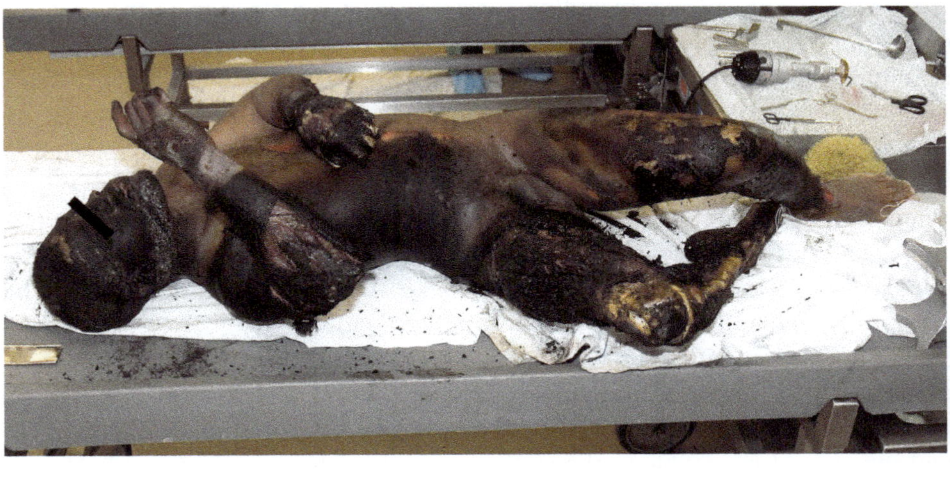

Figure 7.38 Pugilistic attitude of upper extremities.

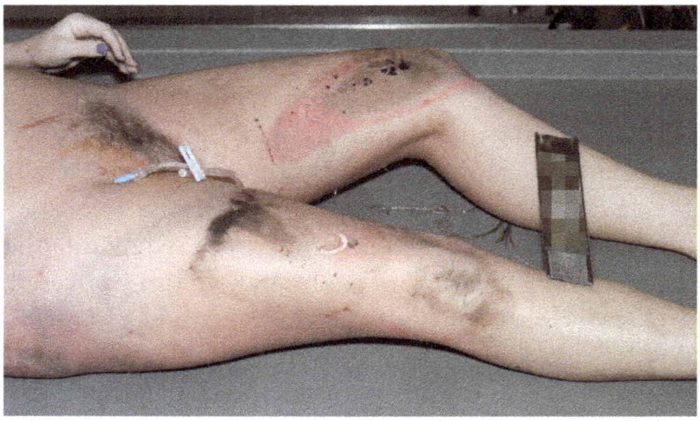

Figure 7.39 Prolonged application of heated object to skin of left lower extremity, featuring rim of red discoloration and centrally located thermal injury.

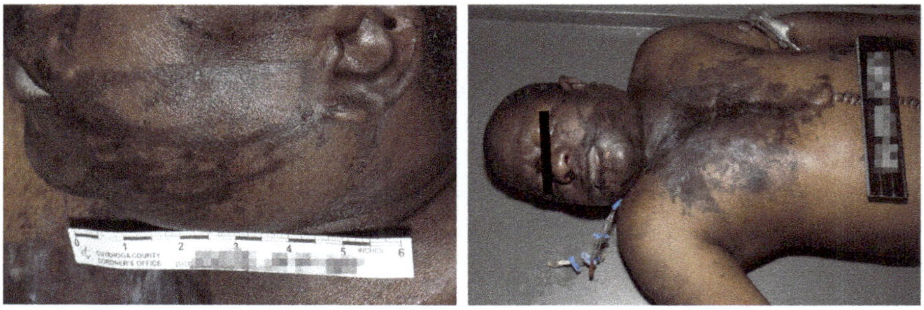

(a) (b)

Figure 7.40 Chemical burns sustained after ingestion and vomiting of sulfuric acid, with drainage pattern of cheek (A) and chest (B).

Chemical burns can mimic thermal injury. Most chemical burns are caused by caustic acidic or basic chemicals. Acidic chemicals produce dry, hardened, darkened, leathery burns as a result of a type of tissue destruction known as coagulative necrosis of the proteins. Basic chemicals, including gasoline, cause liquefaction of the proteins and saponification of the fats with damage that extends deep under the skin, causing more severe injury and swelling. The severity of injury is in part dependent upon the strength and concentration of the chemical and the length of time the chemical was in contact with the skin. Ingestion of acidic and basic chemicals can produce severe internal injury. The act of ingestion and the reflexive vomiting triggered by the chemical may produce patterned injury around the mouth and onto the skin of other body regions (even through clothing) as a result of gravity-assisted dripping and drainage (Figure 7.40A and B). Allergic reactions to antibiotics can result in burn-like reddening and sloughing of the skin but are less commonly seen and mainly involve hospitalized patients.

Smoke inhalation with carbon monoxide and cyanide poisoning are more common causes of death for deceased individuals recovered from a structural fire and may be accompanied by varying degrees of thermal injury. Death due to smoke inhalation without thermal injury is also possible as the victim was not in close proximity to heat or flame. For those that make it to the hospital, death may result from complications of carbon

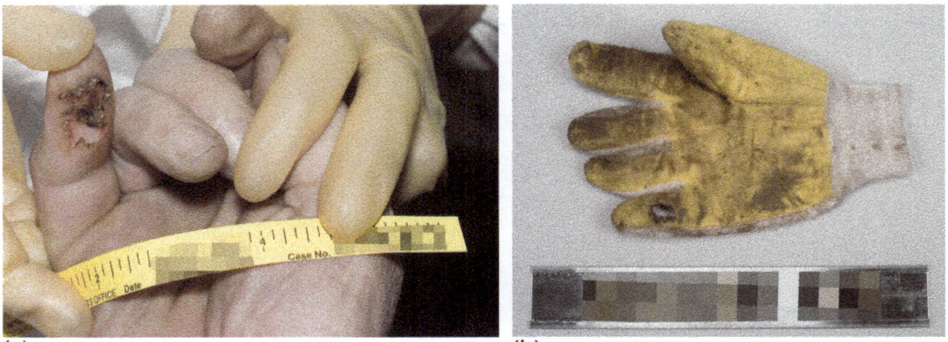

(a) (b)

Figure 7.41 (A) Crater-like electrothermal burn of finger. (B) Corresponding burn of glove.

monoxide and cyanide poisoning or thermal injury to the skin. Complications may also develop secondary to injury to the airway as a result of inhalation of smoke, heated air, or steam.

Deaths due to electrical injury may or may not have outward signs. Low-voltage electrocution, such as that which may be encountered with handling of defective household appliances, will have evidence of skin injury only in approximately one-half of the cases. In these cases, a victim who was near or in contact with an electrical appliance, was heard to shout prior to collapse, and has no electrothermal injuries at the time of autopsy is highly suspicious for death due to low-voltage electrocution. The death of an individual known to be a good swimmer found submerged and unresponsive in a pool equipped with pool lights may be due to electrocution, and there will be no electrothermal injuries. Evaluation of the scene in this instance must include testing of the pool light casing and wiring and questioning of nearby swimmers about any tingling sensations while near any pool lights. High-voltage electrocutions (i.e., direct or indirect contact with power lines or lightning strike) will almost always manifest with thermal injuries, ranging from small crater-like burns to large areas of severe burns, sometimes with amputation of a limb. Crater-like burns with central charring and pale and red peripheral zones of discoloration may be noted on the extremities, such as the palms and soles, representing the entry or exit points of the current (Figure 7.41A). Shoes, gloves, jewelry, and clothing worn by the decedent may be burned, melted, or magnetized (Figure 7.41B).

Internal Examination

With the assistance of a trained pathologist assistant under the direct supervision of the forensic pathologist, the body is opened by means of an incision over the chest and abdomen in the shape of a Y, so that the skin edges can be reflected aside and the rib cage exposed for removal by means of a bone saw (Figure 7.42). This allows inspection of the chest and abdominal organs as they are situated within the chest (thoracic cavity) and abdominal/pelvic cavities. This is also known as an *in situ* examination (Figure 7.43). The forensic pathologist will look for and describe any signs of abnormal anatomy, deformity, infection, injury, or collection of fluids within the cavities and around the organs. Any fluid collections will be measured in milliliters (ml) or cubic centimeters (cc). Notation of any scar tissue (fibrosis and adhesions) or any unusual odor emanating from the body will

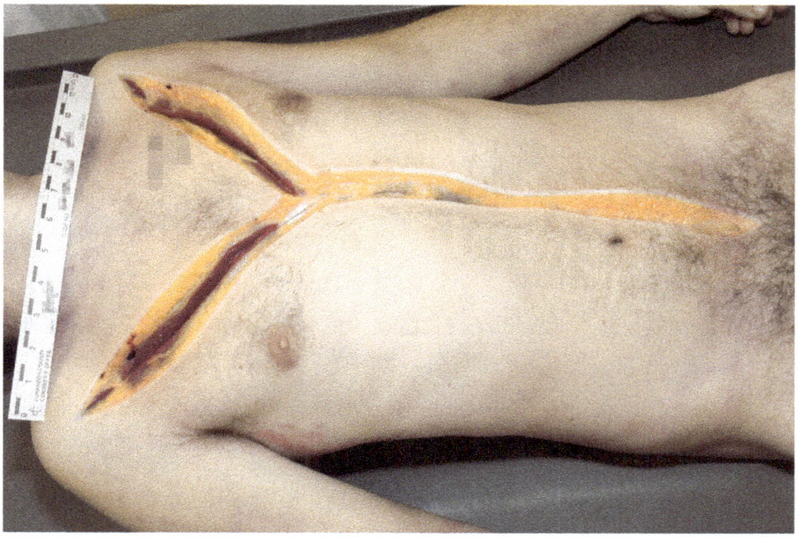

Figure 7.42 Y incision of chest and abdomen.

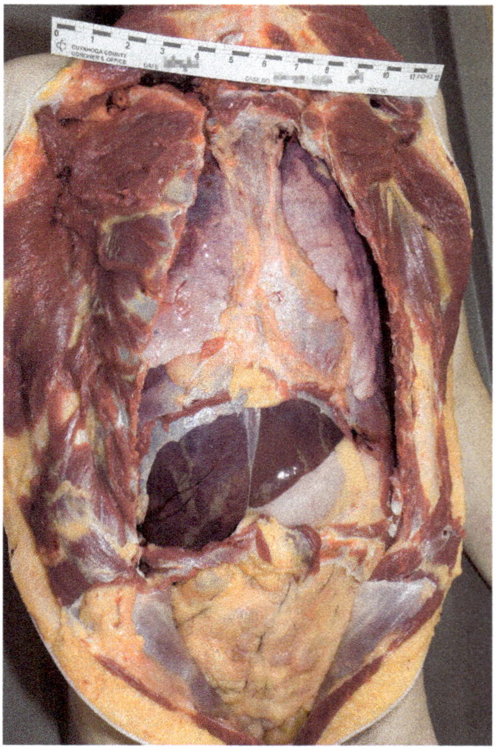

Figure 7.43 Chest and abdominal organs in situ after reflection of skin and removal of chest plate.

be done. The vessels of the lower neck and lower legs in adults, older infants, and children will be tied off during the autopsy and accessed later by the embalmer for the purpose of infusion with embalming fluid in preparation for disposition. The organs and body cavities of smaller infants and fetuses will be later infused with embalming fluid at the funeral home. Furthermore, if the body was received embalmed from the funeral home, description of artifacts of embalming, such as external sutures of the neck (for access to the blood vessels under the collar bones), trocar punctures of the internal organs, the smell of embalming fluid, and the state of fixation of the organs by the embalming fluid, will be described.

Routine sampling of bodily fluids and tissues is an important component of a forensic or medicolegal autopsy. A variety of samples are collected into specimen containers, and properly labeled, packaged, sealed, and submitted to the forensic laboratory in accordance to the proper chain-of-custody protocol. A forensic toxicology laboratory analyzes samples for the presence of drugs of abuse, medications, and poisons. Testing may or may not be ordered by the submitting forensic pathologist and depends on the case circumstances. Certain samples may be submitted to outside or reference laboratories preforming a wider variety of testing or specific testing. Sampling of blood, urine, and vitreous humor can also be done following external-only examination on decedents in which an autopsy was deemed not necessary. Otherwise, this sampling will be done as part of the complete autopsy and further sampling will be done during the internal examination following opening of the body cavities.

If bloodstream infection is suspected and if the postmortem interval has not exceeded 24–36 hours, a sample of blood and sometimes swabs of lung and spleen are taken in a sterile fashion and will be submitted to a lab for testing (microbiological culture) for bacteria or other infectious organisms. This is to be done prior to any other sampling of body fluids. Any accumulation of pus, whether inside the chest or abdominal cavities or over the surface of the brain, will be described and may be sampled and sent for testing for infectious agents. If viral infection is suspected, nasal and throat swabs or small biopsies of tissue may be obtained and sent for viral testing.

Samples of blood are taken directly from the heart and leg vessel with a syringe (Figure 7.44). Blood from the leg vessel may also be taken externally through the skin in the groin region during the external examination. Drops of blood may be placed on a filter paper card serving as a DNA reference sample (Figure 7.45). A sample of urine will be taken directly from the urinary bladder using a syringe, and the entire quantity contained within the urinary bladder will be measured and recorded in milliliters or cubic centimeters. Urine may also be collected from the collection bag that may accompany an individual who has an indwelling bladder catheter since in that case the bladder may contain little or no urine. Bile fluid from the gallbladder will be collected. In some cases

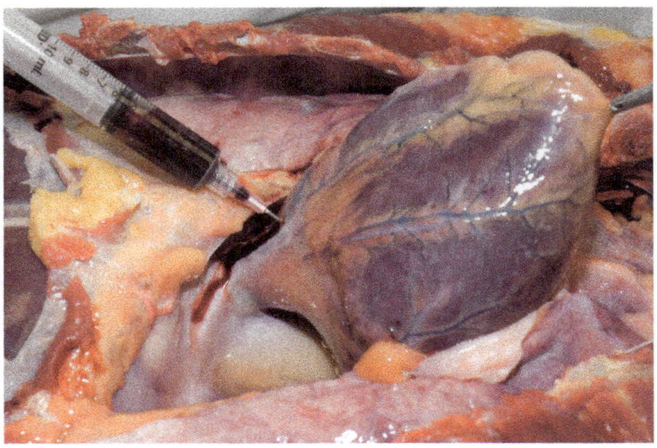

Figure 7.44 Sampling of blood from heart.

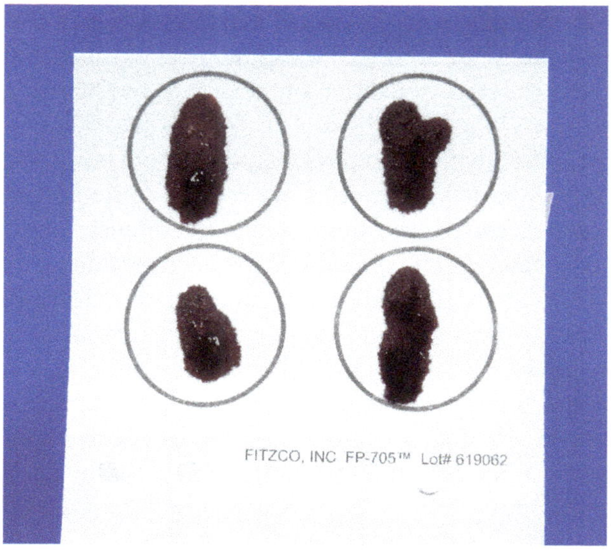

Figure 7.45 Spots of blood on DNA blood spot card.

fluid, from around the spinal cord (cerebral spinal fluid (CSF)) is collected. In cases of suspected meningitis, CSF will also be sent for infectious disease testing. In certain cases, small portions of organs, such as heart muscle, skeletal muscle, liver, or spleen, may be sent for toxicological analysis, especially when there is little fluid blood available for collection. Any contents within the stomach will be examined, measured (milliliters, cubic centimeters, or grams), described, and collected. Additionally, any intact tablets and capsules within the stomach will be recovered, and these will be counted along with notation of any visible identifying marks or inscriptions and may also be photographically documented prior to submission. Packages or small plastic baggies of drugs hastily ingested by an individual **(body stuffer)** to escape detection by police were not meant for long-term transport within the body and are prone to breaking open within the stomach and causing a massive overdose. The packages along with their contents will be collected from the stomach, described, photographically documented, and submitted. The intestines of individuals suspected to have ingested packages of drugs for the purpose of transportation for future sale **(body packers)** will be opened and inspected, and any packages removed, described, photographically documented, and submitted.

All major internal organs are removed in a systematic fashion, weighed in grams, inspected, and dissected into their individual components and basic structures, to look for signs of injury or disease. Organs may be removed in groups (also known as blocks or *en bloc*) or individually. This section will mainly describe removal of organs in blocks. The term for organ removal during autopsy is known as **evisceration.** The organs of fetuses and small infants may be removed all at once, with subsequent dissection into smaller blocks of organs and individual organs. During organ removal, identification of any internal injury in the absence of external injury will be noted. External blunt, sharp, and penetrating injury will be correlated with any internal injury and described. Measurement of discrete findings will be done in millimeters, centimeters, or inches.

The heart with the proximal portion of aorta, lungs with trachea and bronchial tubes, and all attached blood vessels and soft tissue are removed from the thoracic cavity (see Figures 1.1

and 1.2A and B). The upper airway, including the larynx, with or without the attached tongue, may be removed in certain cases. The attached thyroid gland will be included with removal of the upper airway or will be dissected from this region separately, leaving the larynx *in situ*. The liver with diaphragm, spleen, stomach, pancreas, and the proximal part of the small intestine, along with attached blood vessels and soft tissue, is removed from the abdominal cavity (Figure 7.46). The kidneys, adrenal glands, urinary bladder, and reproductive organs are removed from the lower abdominal or pelvic cavity (Figure 7.47). The small and large intestines are removed (Figure 7.48). Finally, after incision of the scalp and removal of the top of the skull with the aid of a bone saw, the brain and its coverings can be inspected for any blood or other fluid accumulation and subsequently removed, and the empty cranial cavity will be inspected for any deformity, pathology, or fracture (Figure 7.49). Depending on the circumstances of the death, the spinal cord, which is connected to the brain and central nervous system, may be removed for examination (Figure 7.50).

All major organs and glands are individually sectioned multiple times using a scalpel to look for structural abnormalities, disease, and injury. A small tissue sample of each major organ is taken and submitted in a fixative solution prior to histological preparation and later examined under the microscope by the forensic pathologist (Figure 7.51). This histological preparation involves standard application of stains called hematoxylin and eosin to each section of tissue in order to bring out the unique characteristics of the tissue and cellular structure (Figure 7.52). The number of samples taken for any given case is dictated by the complexity of the autopsy and the need to adequately characterize the extent of injury or disease. A typical autopsy may include sampling of the heart, lungs, liver, kidneys, and brain, more or less, depending on the case. In certain cases, the pathologist may opt not

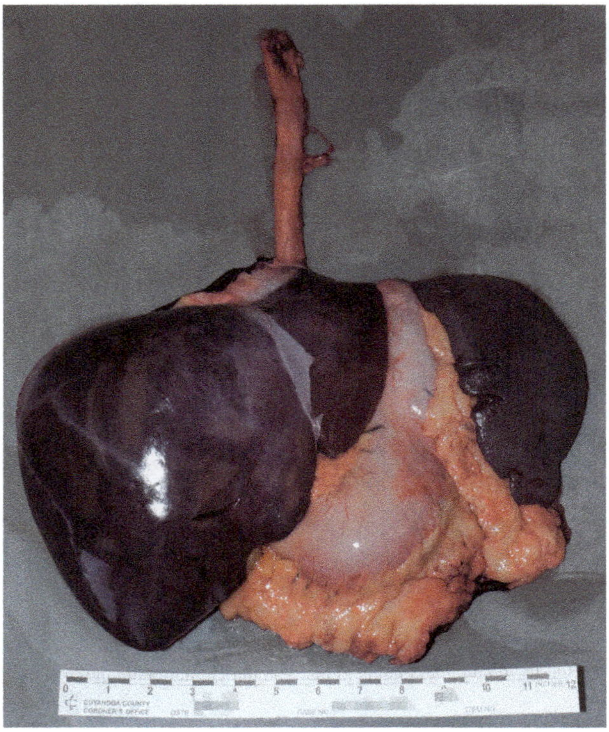

Figure 7.46 Liver block, anterior view, with stomach/esophagus, liver, and spleen.

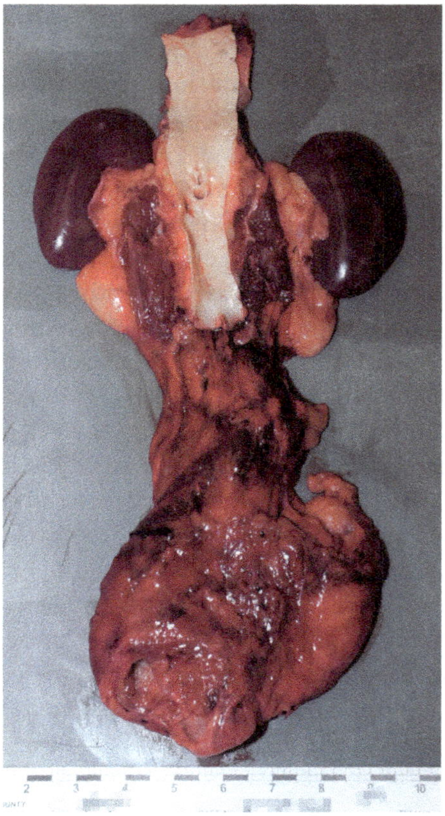

Figure 7.47 Kidney block with kidneys, attached opened aorta, urinary bladder (lower left), and rectum (lower right tubular structure).

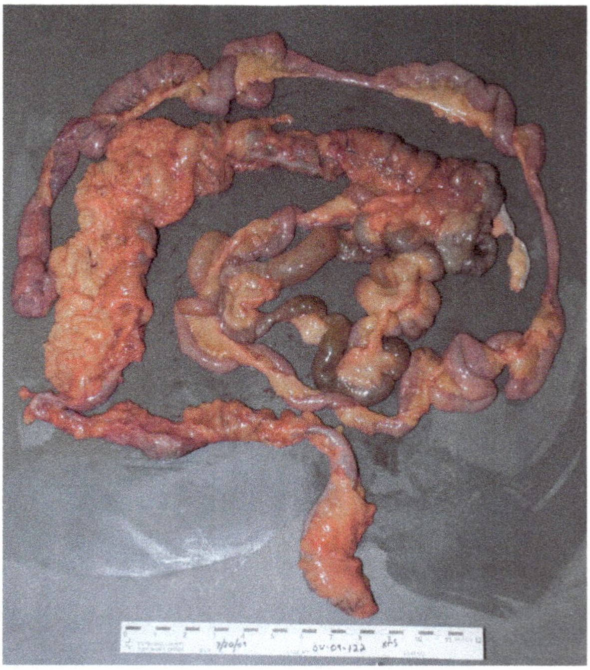

Figure 7.48 Intestines.

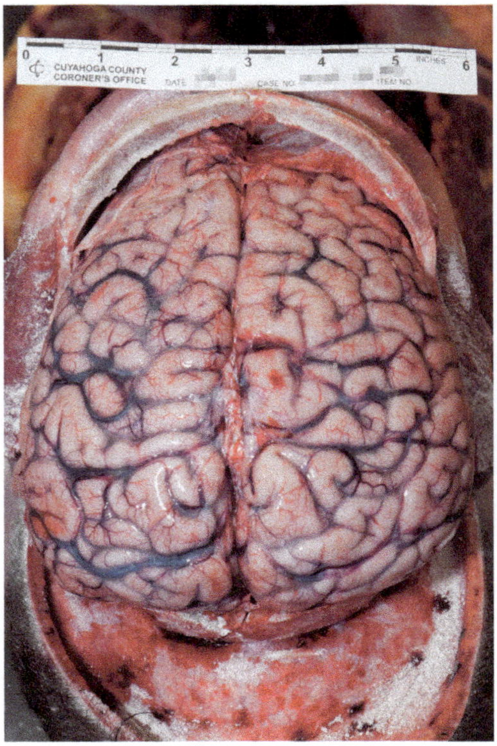

Figure 7.49 Superior surface of brain featuring the two hemispheres.

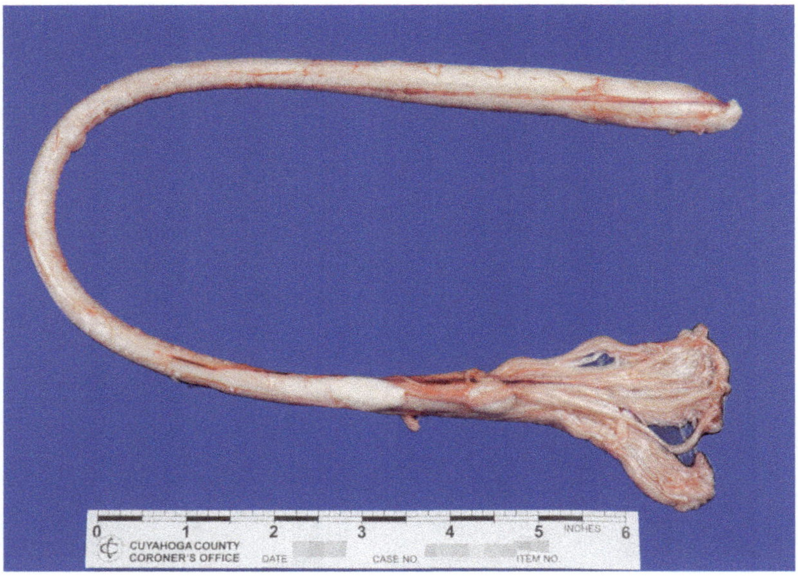

Figure 7.50 Spinal cord.

to submit tissue samples for microscopic examination. Sampling with long-term retention of small portions of tissue in a stock jar containing formalin fixative is routine. These reserved tissues are kept for a pre-defined and often limited time period according to the protocol of the office and is done in the event a future need for a microscopic examination of those tissues arises.

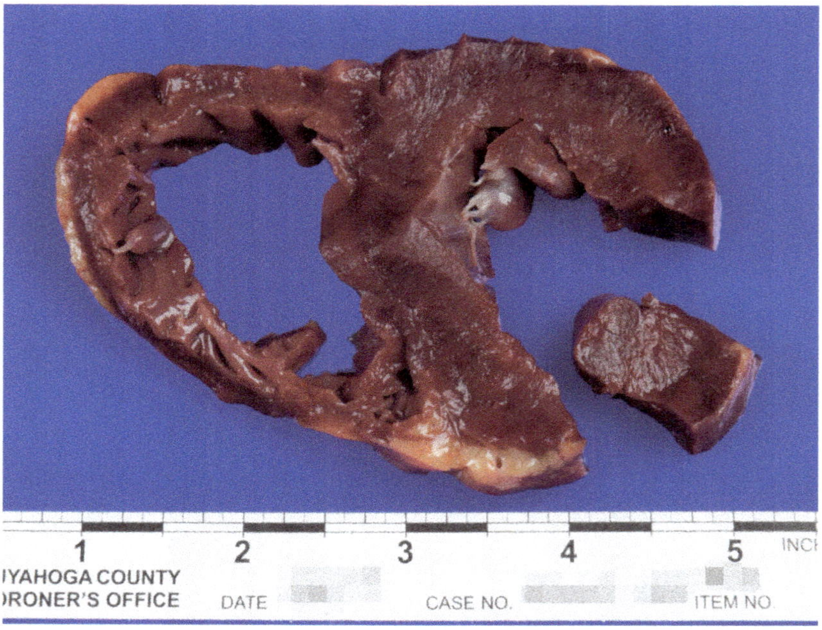

Figure 7.51 Cross section of right and left ventricles with section of the heart muscle to be submitted for histological preparation.

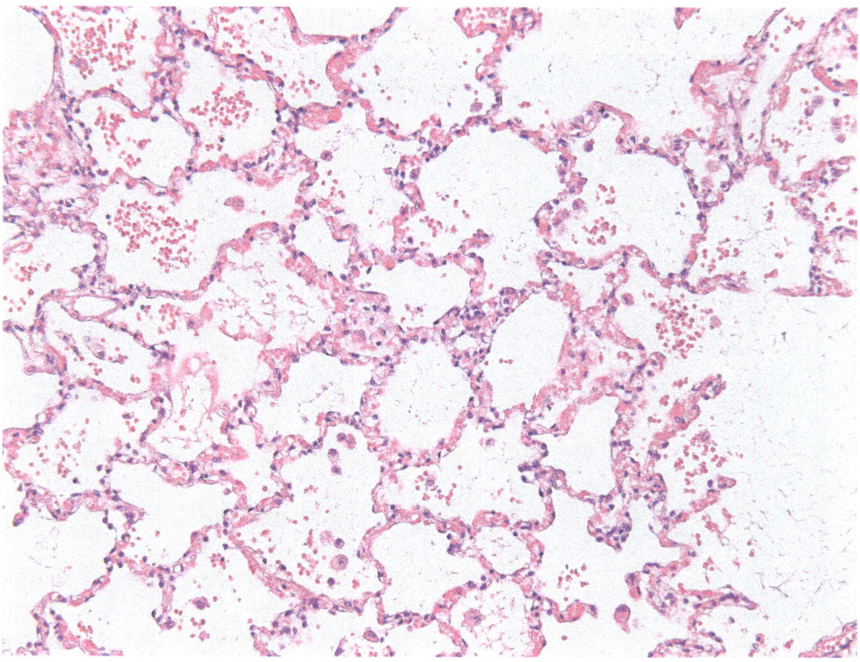

Figure 7.52 Hematoxylin and eosin stain of a section lung tissue featuring alveolar spaces with capillaries containing red blood cells, pneumocytes with blue-purple nuclei lining alveoli, and occasional macrophages with blue-purple nuclei and pink cytoplasm and red blood cells in alveolar spaces (100× magnification).

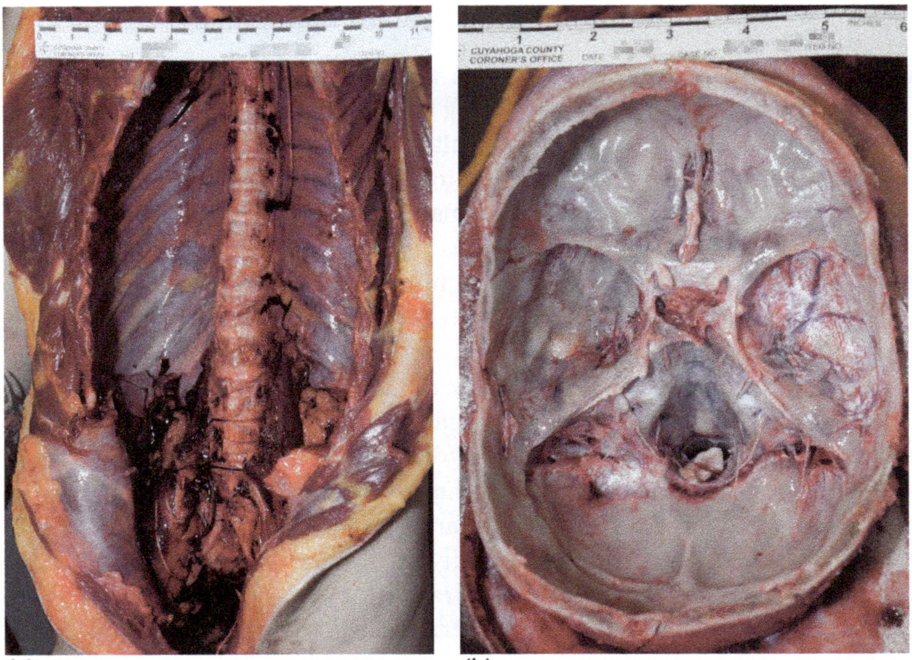

(a) (b)

Figure 7.53 (A) Empty chest and abdominal cavities featuring ribs and spinal column. (B) Empty cranial cavity.

Depending on the circumstances surrounding the death, special autopsy procedures may be performed by the pathologist to look for additional injury or pathology. Individuals with visible or suspected injury to the neck will have inspection with layer-by-layer dissection of the muscles of the neck (cervical strap muscles) and dissection and inspection of the larynx to look for hemorrhage and fracture. Individuals suspected to have injuries of the upper or cervical spine will have dissection of the posterior neck to examine the soft tissues and ligaments for injury and to directly visualize the cervical spinal cord. Infants and children with signs of abusive head injury will have the eyes removed to look for retinal and optic nerve hemorrhage. Dissection of the deep veins within the lower legs will be done to look for any residual blood clot in decedents who have died as a result of blood clots in the lung (pulmonary embolism), as these clots commonly originate from the deep leg veins. Decedents with suspected pressure-related trauma arising from deep diving activity will have inspection of the internal organs, blood vessels, and chest cavity for entrapped air.

Once all the organs have been removed, the empty body cavities, along with the ribs, spine, and pelvis, are examined for disease, deformity, fracture, or other injury (Figure 7.53A and B). Any unsampled organs and tissues are returned back to the body and will be later infused with embalming fluid at the funeral home in preparation for disposition. The skin incisions of the chest, abdomen, and head will be reapposed, and the external body surfaces washed. In most cases, with subsequent preparation and dressing of the decedent at the funeral home, members attending an open-casket viewing will not recognize that an autopsy was performed.

Reporting

The contents of the autopsy or postmortem report may vary by jurisdiction, but most reports will contain the decedent's identifying information, date and time of examination, ancillary toxicological or other testing, consultant reports, description of the external and internal examination of the body, final anatomic diagnoses, and cause and manner of death. Other jurisdictions will include information regarding the reason for examination, a summary of investigative findings, persons in attendance at the autopsy, preliminary diagnoses, microscopic description, and a summary section. In some locales, the autopsy report is a public record. In other locales release of some or all of its contents along with photographs to individuals other than legal next-of-kin, attorneys, or law enforcement may be restricted or prohibited by law. Generally, preliminary, pending, or draft reports are not provided. Release of autopsy photographs may be restricted to legal next-of-kin, law enforcement, and attorneys. A copy of an autopsy report may also be sent to the hospital that was involved in the terminal care of the decedent. Scientific reports such as trace evidence reports are not public records in many locales. Copies of records obtained from medical facilities and other agencies are usually for internal use and are not public records.

Autopsy findings are described in a narrative format known as the **autopsy protocol.** The autopsy protocol contains medical terminology that may be unfamiliar to the lay reader. Upon request, explanation and interpretation of autopsy findings can be provided by the forensic pathologist who performed the autopsy or by the supervising physician C/ME who certified the cause and manner of death.

The autopsy protocol can be generally divided into two sections: the external examination and the internal examination. The *external examination* contains a description of the identifying characteristics, postmortem changes, scars and other marks, evidence of therapy, and evidence of injury. External therapy and injury may also involve internal structures and may be described along with the external changes. The *internal examination* will contain a description of any pathology of the internal organs, often grouped by virtue of how they function (organ system). For example, a description of the digestive system will include information referable to the oral cavity, esophagus, stomach, intestines, appendix, and all related glands. Organs and other anatomic structures that are normal in appearance, size, weight, texture, and consistency will be described as "unremarkable."

The autopsy protocol may also contain a section for description of the microscopic findings of each section of tissue taken. A standard microscopic description from an uncomplicated autopsy may contain a description of sections taken of the heart, lungs, liver, kidneys, and brain. Sections without microscopic abnormality may be described as "nonpathological," "no pathological diagnosis," or "no pathological abnormality."

The autopsy report will include a copy of the toxicology report, which will contain the names and amounts of drugs of abuse, commonly prescribed medications, and poisons that were detected. As part of the chemistry testing, a report of the levels of electrolytes from the analysis of the vitreous fluid sample is also included. Screening tests for general categories of drugs and medications will be reported as "positive" or "negative." Confirmatory testing will have the names and levels of the drugs and medications. Samples may also have been sent to outside reference labs for more esoteric testing, and those results may be reflected within the autopsy report and if significant, the cause of death.

A summary with interpretation of the autopsy and toxicology findings in the context of the historical circumstances and medical history is provided in the autopsy reports at some

C/ME offices. The coroner's verdict also provides a brief narrative summary of the identifying information, brief historical circumstances, records reviewed, medical response and treatment, and the cause and manner of death.

A sample autopsy report appears in Appendix D.

Cause of Death, Manner of Death, and the Death Certificate

Any death that comes under the jurisdiction of the C/ME will have a death certificate completed by a qualified person. While the death certificate is itself a legal document, the statement as to the cause and manner of death is the *opinion* of the certifier based on known information and may be amended at a later time should new information be presented. The completion of the death certificate needs to be done in as timely a manner as possible, as there may be many matters for families, law enforcement, courts, and other entities to settle. The time to completion of the death certificate may be contingent upon receipt of laboratory test results, which may be critical for the determination of the cause of the death. Completion of comprehensive testing can take several weeks to a few months. Deaths with more readily demonstrable or obvious causes are ideally completed in as timely a manner as possible after review of all relevant, accessible information.

The death certificate is a legal document that declares that a person is deceased and serves a multitude of important purposes, including provision of cause and manner of death, provision of a degree of closure for the family, settlement of estates, obtaining of burial permits, making of life insurance claims, determination of the recipient(s) of pension funds, and obtaining of death benefits. Because of the many uses of the death certificate, it is important that the information contained within it is as accurate as possible, and this, in part, is ensured when a high-quality police investigation and medicolegal death investigation have taken place.

The death certificate also has governmental uses. The signatories that comprise the United Nations recognize that the establishment and maintenance of high standards of health within their respective countries have widespread social and economic benefits. The information contained in the death certificate is used by local and national governments for various research and funding programs that target the improvement of health. The World Health Organization (WHO) acts as the agency of the United Nations, with many goals, including the global monitoring of health and death trends. This is done in part by requiring that the signatories compile information about deaths in a standard format so that statistical information can be extracted, analyzed, and compared. Within the United States, the National Center for Health Statistics (NCHS), as part of the Centers for Disease Control and Prevention (CDC), publishes the "U.S. Standard Certificate of Death" as a model for the states' death certificates.[11] It also collects death information from the death certificate prepared by the states and prepares and publishes statistical information that can be used by the WHO for international comparisons. It must first be completed by the certifier (attending physician or physician C/ME), and then registered within the county or state by the funeral director.

The death certificate contains several sections required for completion by the registrar (the funeral director) and the certifier (the physician or C/ME). The first few sections request identifying and demographical information and method and location of disposition, and are completed by the funeral director in conjunction with the family, investigators, and C/ME. The next sections are for completion by the certifier and request information on the date and time of death, the cause and manner of death, other significant or contributing conditions, whether an autopsy was performed, and date, place, and description of any injury.

The **cause of death** is defined as the injury or disease, or a combination of both, that leads to the death of the individual. The injury or disease gives rise to one or more physiological changes or derangements, such as "exsanguination with cardiac arrest," that eventually terminate in death. These derangements, or **mechanisms of death,** are not specific for what caused them, and thus ideally should not appear alone on the death certificate. An example of cause and mechanism of death would be a stab wound of the right thigh with perforation of the femoral artery (cause) with massive hemorrhaging or exsanguination and cardiac arrest (mechanisms) leading to death. The mechanism of death may also be incorporated in the cause of death statement on the death certificate: "Exsanguination with cardiac arrest due to stab wound of right lower extremity with perforation of the femoral artery." The **manner of death** is a designation as to how the death came to be and is classified into one of five categories: natural, accident, homicide, suicide, and undetermined. **Natural** manner of death is defined as death due to disease or the aging process. **Accidental** manner of death is defined as death due to unintentional injury, intoxication, or poisoning. **Homicidal** deaths are deaths due to the direct, *willful* action or inaction of another by way of injury, intoxication, or poisoning. **Suicidal** deaths result from willful self-inflicted injury, intoxication, or poisoning. There are times when the cause of death is known but the manner of death cannot be determined due to insufficient information or uncertainty as to how the death came to be. These deaths are classified as **undetermined.** There are also instances, albeit very few, in which the autopsy and subsequent tests fail to reveal the cause of death. The cause of death in those cases will also be designated as **undetermined.** A significant proportion of all deaths certified by the C/ME in the United States, whether an autopsy was performed or not, are due to natural causes, with deaths due to cardiovascular disease most prevalent.[1]

Application of Medicine and Pathology to Law: The Forensic Pathologist as an Expert Witness

A forensic pathologist possesses specialized knowledge by virtue of education, training, board certifications, experience, professional membership affiliations, scholarly activities, and publication, qualifying him or her as an expert witness as stipulated by the U.S. Federal Rules of Evidence (Article VII, Rules 701–706).[11] Occasionally, the forensic pathologist will be called to provide testimony as an expert witness in criminal or civil proceedings regarding autopsy findings and the cause and manner of death. This may be provided before an actual trial by way of deposition, in which testimony is given under oath in the presence of one or more attorneys and a court recorder. This may otherwise be provided in the usual court setting in the presence of attorneys, the jury, and the judge. Official and legal notification requesting court appearance is provided by the **subpoena.** This court-issued document contains the pathologist's name, the time, date, and location of the court case, the autopsy case number and decedent's name, the defendant's name, and the name of the prosecuting attorney (criminal cases) or other attorneys. Upon receipt, a call should be promptly made to the attorney who caused the issuing of the subpoena to inform him or her that it has been received and determine if a pretrial meeting is in order.

Thorough preparation for testimony, whether for deposition or full trial, is imperative. Review, explanation, and clarification of autopsy findings before providing expert testimony are beneficial for both the pathologist and the attorney, alleviating the possibility for surprise questions asked by the attorney and unexpected answers given by the pathologist. This is ensured by a timely pre-testimony meeting. It is usually the attorney's obligation to call and request a meeting with the pathologist, but unfortunately this is not always done. Depositions also provide attorneys with a kind of preview of the pathologist's court testimony, should it be needed later in trial.

Thorough preparation by the forensic pathologist for court aids in smooth delivery of information at the time of testimony. This in part aids the jury in reaching a verdict. The pathologist will review the entire case, including historical and scene information, medical records, police reports, and other reports. The pathologist should also review his or her curriculum vitae, the number of autopsies performed to date, and the approximate (or actual) number of times he or she has been qualified to testify as an expert witness. It is imperative that the pathologist review any transcripts from prior depositions and trials given for the same case, taking care not to deviate from the content without explanation. Review of trace evidence and DNA findings, or at least review of what items of evidence were examined, refamiliarizes the pathologist with the scope and depth of the case and certain issues and concerns particular to the case. This refamiliarization is greatly enhanced by the pretrial meeting with attorneys, in which the pathologist and forensic scientist(s) should be present. Questions posed to the pathologist in court about details and results of trace evidence and DNA findings are best deflected to the forensic scientist(s) directly involved in examination and testing and who is most qualified to render opinions on the basis of specific training and experience.

With the start of proceedings and after being sworn in, the forensic pathologist must first be qualified as an expert witness and will be asked a series of questions pertaining to his or her education, training, and experience, by the prosecuting or plaintiff's attorney. This will be followed by **direct examination,** whereby a series of questions regarding autopsy and toxicological test findings and the cause and manner of death will be asked. The defense attorney will subsequently conduct the **cross-examination,** with questions limited in scope to the material covered in the direct examination. Sometimes this is followed by redirect and re-cross-examinations usually when some clarification of meaning or concept is sought. In criminal cases, the opinions given by a pathologist or other physician experts during testimony are given within reasonable degree of medical certainty or probability, and speculations, guesses, possibilities, and likelihoods are not allowed. Civil cases are a bit more lenient requiring opinions that are more likely than not or in all probability. Prior to and during testimony, a pathologist may be asked to or may choose to prepare and present body diagrams depicting injuries or provide slide presentations explaining medical and pathological concepts. The pathologist is also often asked to show, explain, and interpret for the jury certain exhibits, including photographs, recovered projectiles, and other objects directly (and sometimes not directly) related to autopsy and toxicological findings.

A professional appearance and calm demeanor along with a clear, audible, and slow rate of speech are requirements for optimal delivery of testimony, relieving the jury from unnecessary distractions. This not only gives the jury time to absorb the answers and explanations, but also allows the court recorder enough time to transcribe them. The pathologist will strive to answer all questions truthfully and completely within his or her area of expertise, pausing after each question is asked to allow for objections from either attorney. If the judge sustains or upholds an objection, then the question must not be answered and the attorney may then rephrase the question. If the judge overrules an objection, then the question must be answered. The pathologist will look at the jury when answering questions and providing explanations, whether asked by the prosecuting or plaintiff's attorney or the defense attorney. If a question is not clear, then the pathologist will politely ask for clarification or repeating of the question. If the pathologist does not know the answer to a question or cannot recall information or events, he or she will answer accordingly without guessing. The pathologist will also abide by any *witness rule* imposed, whereby cases are not discussed until the trial is over, and will not be present in the courtroom during court proceedings prior to giving testimony, unless required. This conduct applies to and should be practiced by *all* expert witnesses. An excellent, concise article by Dr. Charles Wetli, a well-known forensic pathologist, provides the essential information regarding expert witnessing and the pretrial and trial processes for the pathologist or laboratory scientist.[13]

References

1. Hanzlick, R. 2006. Death investigation systems. In *Basic competencies in forensic pathology*, ed. J. A. Prahlow, 15–22. Northfield, IL: College of American Pathologists (CAP).
2. Bollinger, S. A., and Thali, M. J. 2015. Imaging and virtual autopsy: Looking back and forward. *Philos Trans R Soc Lond B* 370:20140253. doi: 10.1098/rstb.20140253 (accessed October 27, 2019).
3. Haskell, N. H. 2006. Forensic entomology. In *Medicolegal investigation of death—Guidelines for the application of pathology to crime investigation*, ed. W. U. Spitz, 149–73. 4th ed. Springfield, IL: Charles C Thomas Publisher Ltd.
4. Campobasso, C. P., Linville, J. G., Wells, J. D., et al. 2005. Forensic genetic analysis of insect gut contents. *Am J Forensic Med Pathol* 26(2):161–65.
5. Wallace, J. R., Merritt, R. W., Kimbirauskas, R., et al. 2008. Caddisflies assist with homicide case: Determining a postmortem submersion interval using aquatic insects. *J Forensic Sci* 53(1):219–21.
6. Henry, T. E. 2003. Blunt force injury. In *Handbook of forensic pathology*, ed. R. C. Froede, 139–46. 2nd ed. Northfield, IL: College of American Pathologists (CAP).
7. Langlois, N. E. I. 2007. The science behind the quest to determine age of bruises—A review of the English language literature. *Forensic Sci Med Pathol* 3:241–51.
8. Prahlow, J. A. 2003. Sharp force injuries. In *Handbook of forensic pathology*, ed. R. C. Froede, 159–73. 2nd ed. Northfield, IL: College of American Pathologists.
9. DiMaio, V. J. M. 1999. *Gunshot wounds—Practical aspects of firearms, ballistics, and forensic techniques*. Boca Raton, FL: CRC Press.
10. Spitz, W. U. 2006. Thermal injuries. In *Medicolegal investigation of death—Guidelines for the application of pathology to crime investigation*, ed. W. U. Spitz, 747–82. 4th ed. Springfield, IL: Charles C Thomas Publisher Ltd.
11. National Center for Health Statistics–National Vital Statistics System. U.S. standard certificate of death. http://www.cdc/gov/nchc/data/dvs/DEATH11-03final-ACC.pdf (accessed October 27, 2019).
12. United States Courts. 2017. Federal rules of evidence. https://www.uscourts.gov/sites/default/files/evidence-rules-procedure-dec2017_0.pdf (accessed October 27, 2019).
13. Wetli, C. V. 1989. On being an expert witness. *Lab Med* 20:545–50.

Asphyxia

8

ERICA J. ARMSTRONG

Water-related deaths may result from bodily injury sustained prior to, upon, or during submersion, whether by blunt force, sharp force, or penetrating injury, or natural disease. Water-related deaths may also be directly due to the effects of inhalation of water or other fluid into the lungs, triggering the drowning process and leading to hypoxia and death due to **asphyxia**. Drowning (discussed in Chapter 1) is a type of asphyxia in which the organs, tissues, and cells are deprived of oxygen via the impairment of O_2 and CO_2 exchange within the pulmonary alveoli. While water-related deaths may have traumatic causes with visible external and internal findings, they may also be due wholly or in part to injury that is not readily apparent or accompanied by very few visible findings. Asphyxia is a unique type of *injury* ranging from little to no internal or external bodily changes to a constellation of supportive findings that help identify the type of asphyxia. Lung congestion and edema are non-specific findings common to many types of asphyxia including drowning, and therefore it is important to be able to recognize other types of asphyxia. The interpretation of autopsy findings (or lack thereof) along with the interpretation of toxicological test results must be done within the context of the historical and scene information before a designation of death due to asphyxia, by whatever means, can be done.

Asphyxia: General Information

Asphyxia is defined as the interference with the uptake or utilization of oxygen with a subsequent reduction in the oxygen level within the blood, cells, tissues, and organs.[1] Loss of consciousness occurs within seconds and may take as long as 13–18 seconds to occur, according to one report of four filmed hangings (two suicides and two autoerotic accidents).[2] Respiratory arrest followed by cardiac arrest ensues after several minutes. In fact, the heart will continue to beat, and there will be a pulse for as long as ten minutes after respiratory arrest.[1] Death due to asphyxia occurs in one of several ways:

- Obstruction of the external airway (nose and mouth)
- Obstruction of the internal airway (oral cavity, larynx, trachea, bronchi, lungs)
- Compression/occlusion of the blood vessels of the neck (carotid arteries, jugular veins)
- Severe flexion of the neck or compression of the chest or abdomen
- Impairment of O_2 utilization by the body's cells
- Displacement of O_2 from the ambient environment

Prolonged interference with O_2 uptake or utilization results in hypoxia or hypoxemia, irreversible cell damage, and eventually cardiopulmonary arrest. The cells within the brain are particularly vulnerable to the prolonged reduction of O_2.

An individual dead as a result of asphyxia may have nothing in the way of external injury. Autopsy findings of lung congestion and swelling (edema) of the brain may be all that is encountered and are nonspecific for asphyxia and may be seen in a number of other deaths, including those due to drug overdoses, cardiovascular disease, and trauma. An infant can be easily overpowered and smothered with little resistance, often resulting in the absence of injuries on the face. A scene consisting of multiple individuals, without visible external injury, found dead within a confined space such as an underground sewer or within a mine suggests an environmental cause due to displacement of ambient oxygen or the presence of carbon monoxide or another gas. These are particularly precarious situations for unsuspecting and experienced rescuers alike.

The historical and scene information gathered by investigators is invaluable in asphyxial deaths. Mothers of infants overwhelmed by parenting and financial obligations or designated caretakers who lack parenting skills or are otherwise without a vested interest in caring for an infant or child not their own, while not proof of foul play, is concerning to investigators evaluating the sudden unexpected death of an infant or child with little or absent visible injury. Utility companies and fire departments can assist in the sampling of the ambient environment to determine the presence of asphyxiants, invaluable information for the investigator and forensic pathologist. In the United States, workplace incidents involving exposure to asphyxiants will be investigated by the Occupational Safety and Health Administration (OSHA) representatives inclusive of an examination of equipment, including personal protective gear, for defects.

Not all asphyxiants can be demonstrated by toxicological analysis of body fluids and tissues, however; thus, without good scene information, the determination of cause and manner of death becomes difficult if not impossible. Overall, most asphyxial deaths are determined to be accidental, but only after completion of a thorough scene investigation and medicolegal autopsy.

Asphyxial deaths can be divided into several categories, essentially based on the compromise of some component of the anatomy or internal impairment of O_2 utilization:

- Suffocation
- Strangulation
- Chemical/gas related
- Atmospheric pressure change
- Other: Natural causes, such as infection and allergic reactions that cause swelling with blockage of the upper airway (tonsillitis, epiglottitis, anaphylaxis), and complication of thermal injury to the upper airway
- Drowning

Suffocation

Asphyxia by suffocation arises when O_2 cannot reach the blood because of a change in the O_2 content of the ambient air, obstruction of the external or internal airways, compression of the trunk/torso, or displacement of O_2 by other gases. These deaths can be accidental, suicidal, or homicidal. Examples include smothering, mechanical asphyxia, and choking. Suicide by placing one's head in a plastic bag after consuming in excess a cocktail of sedative medications is one form of suicidal smothering in which the surrounding O_2 contained within the bag is gradually consumed with continued respiration after the sedative medications have taken effect (Figure 8.1). **Smothering** is a subcategory of suffocation in which there is direct contact with the covering of the external nose and mouth, which,

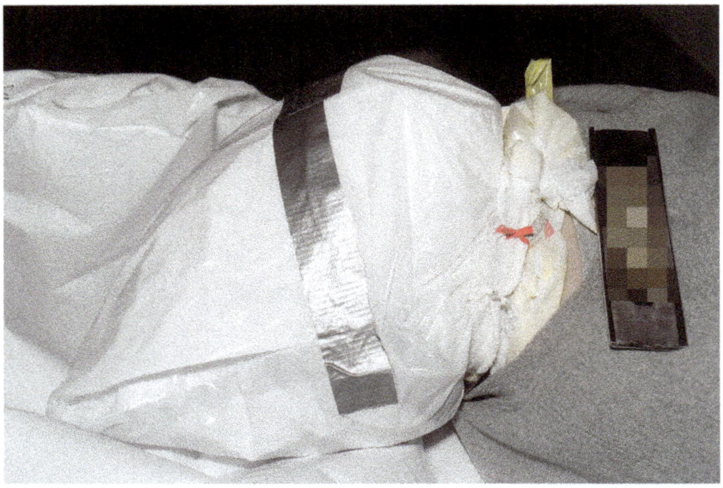

Figure 8.1 Suicidal suffocation by insertion of the head into a plastic bag.

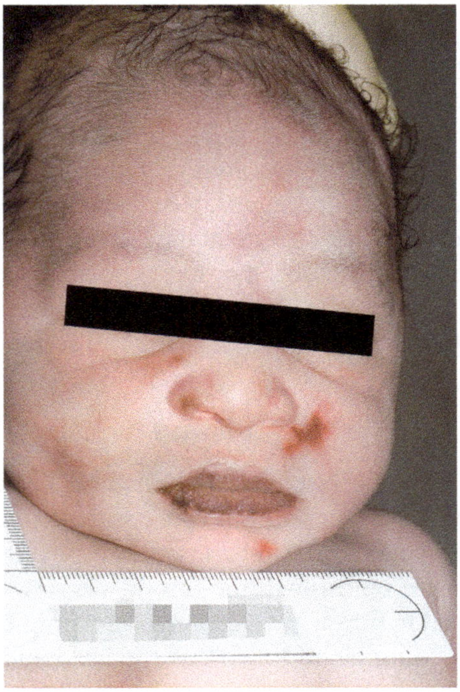

Figure 8.2 Autopsy photograph of smothered infant, featuring abrasions around the nose and mouth and postmortem drying with darkening of lips.

if done with significant force or accompanied by a struggle, may leave abrasions on the face (Figure 8.2). **Mechanical asphyxia** involves compression of the chest or abdomen as a result of the compressive force, whether by a weighty object or a person, preventing the normal expansion and contraction of the chest and abdomen during breathing. Mechanical asphyxia can be subdivided into **positional asphyxia** or **traumatic asphyxia**. A highly intoxicated individual may be unable to extricate himself after getting stuck between the vertical bars of a gate or other similar compromising position, thus succumbing to asphyxia

Figure 8.3 Scene photograph of a highly intoxicated man who collapsed on the stairs upon descent, featuring severe flexion of the neck.

by virtue of position (Figure 8.3). An individual performing underbody car repair can die from traumatic asphyxia after a defective or improperly applied car jack suddenly gives way leading to compression of the chest with fracture of the ribs by the weight of a car. A segment of a bagel with cream cheese retrieved by an emergency medical technician from the airway of an unresponsive woman with advanced multiple sclerosis represents choking in someone unable to chew and swallow normally prepared food and who requires a soft, pureed diet. Information and evidence that a caretaker may have knowingly given improperly prepared food to a compromised individual who subsequently died as a result of choking may have a bearing on the determination of the manner of death (i.e., accident vs. homicide).

Strangulation

Strangulation represents a type of asphyxia in which an object causes compression of the blood vessels of the neck with or without concomitant compression of the larynx or trachea. The major mechanism of death in this type of asphyxia is the impairment of O_2-rich blood flow from the heart up through the carotid arteries within the neck and to the brain, giving rise to cerebral hypoxia. This also involves compression of the jugular veins within the neck, thus impeding blood flow from the head and brain back to the heart. It is the venous compression with intermittent or incomplete compression of the carotid arteries that gives rise to petechial hemorrhages of the face and conjunctivae.[3] These are seen in homicidal ligature and manual strangulation deaths and occasionally in deaths due to suicidal hanging. Additional examples of strangulation are choke/bar arm hold and a carotid sleeper hold. Manual strangulations are always homicidal in manner since one would be unable to maintain compression of his or her own neck vessels after the loss of consciousness since the hand(s) would fall away at that point. Manual strangulations and homicidal ligature strangulations can be accomplished because there is some kind of disparity between the opposing individuals, such as strength or drug or alcohol impairment (i.e., adult vs. infant, male vs. female, or sober adult male vs. highly intoxicated adult male).

The mechanics of hanging differ slightly from that of strangulation. While both require a ligature of some kind to cause neck vessel compression, hanging occurs when gravity along with the weight of the head of a partially or completely suspended body causes the compression, whereas strangulation involves an active force other than gravity transmitted to a ligature or the applied force of part of someone's body. Hangings are more commonly suicidal, followed by accidental. Autoerotic asphyxia by hanging is a type of accidental hanging in which the escape mechanism for relieving the vascular neck compression fails. This ritualistic practice of self-gratification by the euphoric effects of intermittent obstruction of blood flow to the brain is often accompanied by the padding of the ligature for comfort, cross-dressing, binding, or other manipulation of the genitalia, and the display of pornographic materials and evidence of the use of sexual aids.[1] Autoerotic asphyxia by hanging is seen most commonly in men and rarely in women. Another example of accidental hanging is the result of an increasingly popular practice by adolescents who utilize the intermittent compression of the neck vessels by a ligature to achieve a "rush" or "high" and is commonly known as the "choking game." Suicidal strangulations are rare, and one example is the application of a zip tie around one's own neck, in which the tightening of the tie is irreversible, allowing a fixed compressive force on the neck vessels. Accidental strangulations are also rare but have been reported and can occur after clothing becomes caught in a mechanical device or when a child becomes entangled in the cords from draperies or blinds.[4]

The ligature furrow, a linear, often depressed injury of the neck, is a potential finding in strangulation deaths, including hangings. The apposition of the ligature on the neck not only compresses the vessels but can also indent, abrade, or bruise the skin, the extent and depth of which depends upon the characteristics of the ligature, the amount of force (including the force of gravity) or pressure involved, and the length of time the ligature was in contact with the skin. In hangings, narrow ligatures such as ropes and electrical cords tend to leave a more pronounced furrow, while soft and broad ligatures made out of fabric tend to leave a less pronounced furrow or no furrow at all. Any pattern on the surface of the ligature may also be imparted onto the skin (Figure 8.4). Moreover, the injury on the neck may not be depressed to any extent and appear as a superficial linear abrasion or contusion.

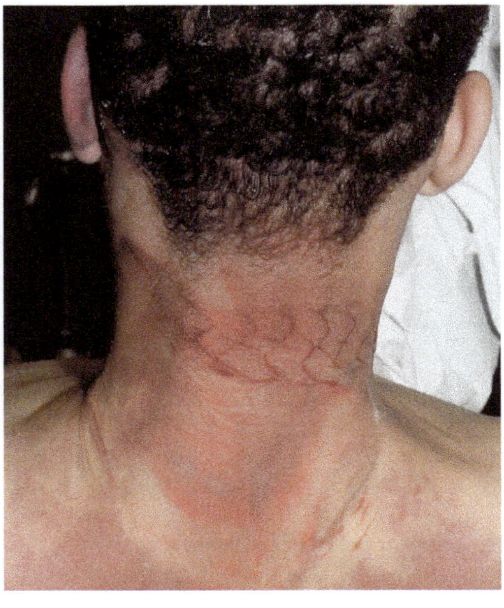

Figure 8.4 Patterned ligature furrow in a suicidal hanging using a woven leather belt.

The location and course of the furrow on the neck can help distinguish or confirm the type of hanging involved and must be correlated with the historical and scene information. In general, the ligature furrow in suicidal and accidental hangings, in which there is some degree of suspension of the body, will extend horizontally around the front of the neck, above the thyroid eminence. This furrow will continue obliquely up both sides of the neck, coming to a point or nearly so, called the **angle of suspension** (Figure 8.5A and B). This endpoint (roughly in the form of an inverted "V") represents the point at which the two ends of the ligature converge, with or without knotting, before being suspended over and affixed to an object such as a rafter or a doorknob (Figure 8.5C). The angle of suspension is usually located on the back or sides of the neck and may be accompanied by additional abrasion of the skin caused by the friction of the knot, if present. In some cases, multiple parallel and intersecting furrows will be visible due to wrapping of the ligature around the neck multiple times or slipping of the ligature from the original position on the neck to another. Additional abrasions associated with the furrow appearing in close proximity on the neck or chin may be present, representing the movement of the ligature during suspension prior to coming to its final resting position. These additional abrasions may also be caused when the decedent is cut down from suspension. It is preferred that the part of the ligature around the neck, including any knot, be left in place by the investigator after the determination of the absence of vital signs has been made by emergency medical personnel. Occasionally upon discovery, the decedent is cut down from the point of suspension or the ligature is removed from around the neck prior to the arrival of investigators. The forward and upward compression of the anterior neck structures by the ligature often causes protrusion with exposure of the tongue, which may dry to a brown-black color, not to be mistaken for trauma (Figure 8.6).

By contrast, the ligature marks or furrows in homicidal strangulation tend to completely encircle the neck with a horizontal course along the anterior surface and coursing over or below the thyroid eminence (Figure 8.7). These marks or furrows may be accompanied by other external blunt or sharp force injuries on the neck, or other parts of the body, such as abrasions, contusions, and incised wounds from the hands, fingertips,

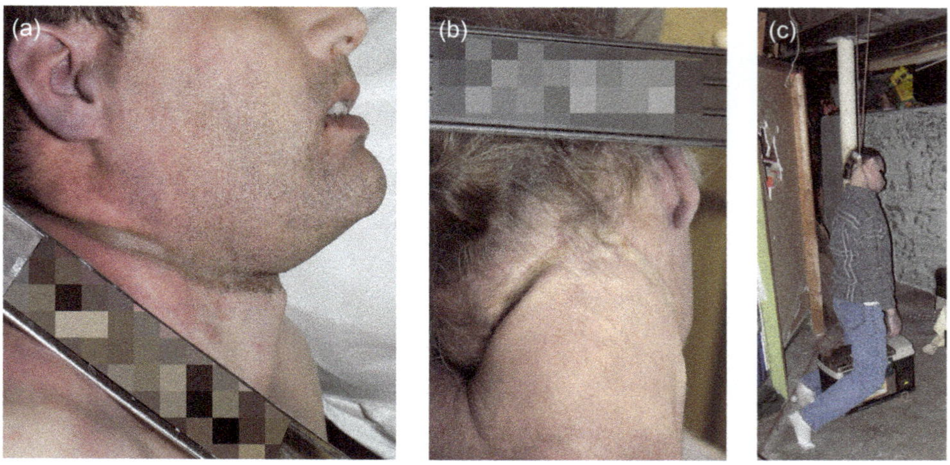

Figure 8.5 Suicidal hangings featuring ligature furrow of the neck above the thyroid eminence and obliquely over the side of the neck (A) and angle of suspension (B). (C) Scene photograph of a suicidal hanging featuring rope ligature suspended over a rafter.

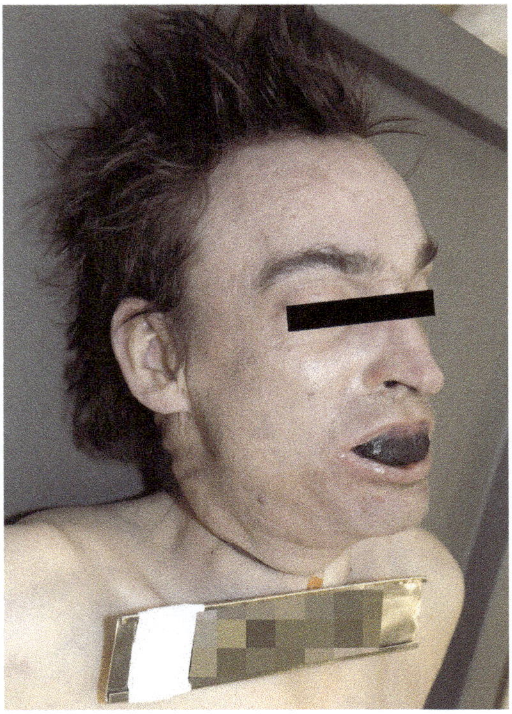

Figure 8.6 Autopsy photograph featuring protrusion with dark discoloration of the tongue due to postmortem drying, in a case of suicidal hanging.

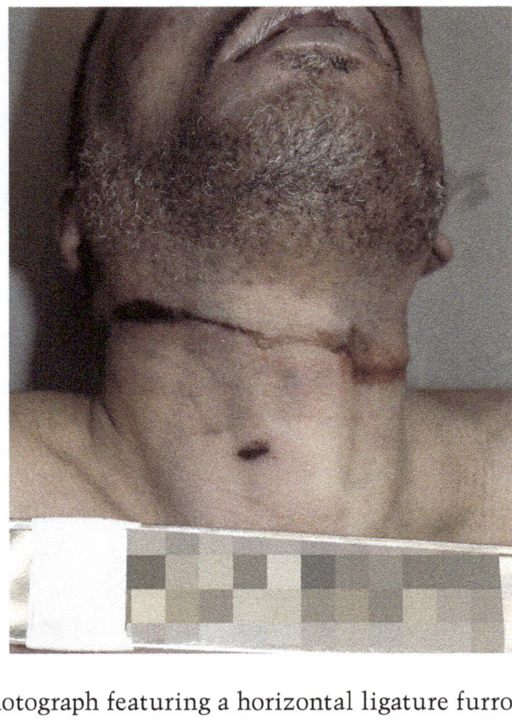

Figure 8.7 Autopsy photograph featuring a horizontal ligature furrow in a case of homicidal ligature strangulation.

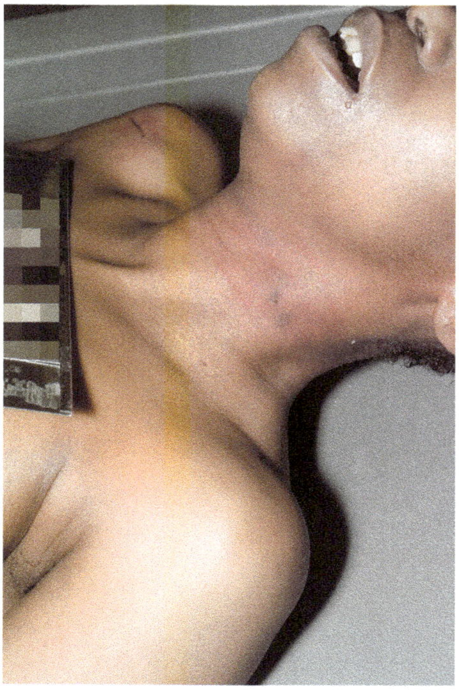

Figure 8.8 Autopsy photograph of a woman who was beaten, stabbed, and strangled, featuring round dark contusions and faint linear horizontal contusions of the neck from the assailant.

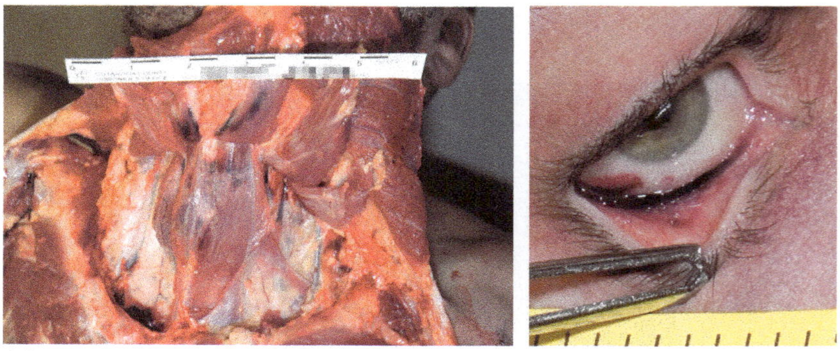

(a) (b)

Figure 8.9 (A) Autopsy photograph of internal neck dissection featuring darker areas of hemorrhage of the cervical strap muscles (reflected superiorly). (B) Autopsy photograph featuring large discrete and confluent conjunctival petechial hemorrhages in a case of homicidal ligature strangulation using a necklace.

fingernails, and any hand/wrist jewelry the assailant or victim may have been wearing at the time of the attack (Figure 8.8). These injuries essentially arise out of the struggle in which the assailant is violently attempting to apply and constrict the ligature, and the victim is desperately attempting to remove it. In the majority of cases, one or more of the internal neck structures (the cervical strap muscles, laryngeal cartilages, and hyoid bone) will show evidence of blunt force injury, and there is frequently petechial hemorrhage of the face, neck, and conjunctivae, above the application point of pressure (Figure 8.9A

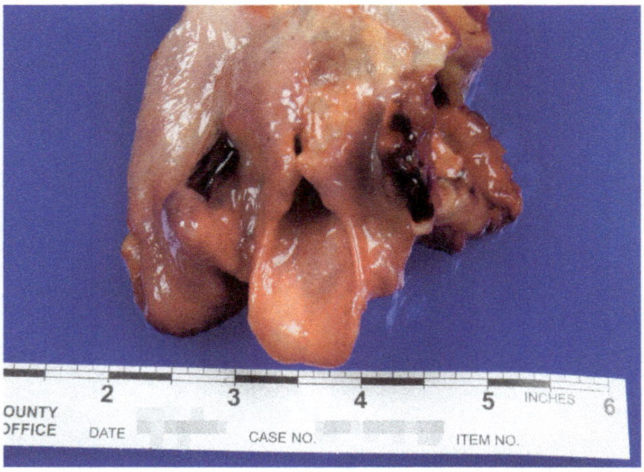

Figure 8.10 Autopsy photograph of larynx featuring fracture with hemorrhage of superior horns of the thyroid cartilage in a motor vehicle accident with overturning, partial ejection, and neck compression.

and B). Fracture of the laryngeal cartilages and hyoid bone, hemorrhage of the cervical strap muscles, and facial and conjunctival petechiae can be seen in suicidal and accidental hangings, with the literature reporting the number of occurrences of one or more of these findings from rare to frequent.[5] The frequency of fractures in suicidal hangings has also been reported to increase with age.[5,6] Fractures of the laryngeal cartilages and hyoid bone can also be seen in other types of accidental blunt force trauma to the neck, such as in motor vehicle accidents with overturning and partial ejection in which part of the vehicle frame comes to rest on the neck (Figure 8.10).

In the rare instance, a hanging may be staged to look like a suicide. The findings of hair entangled within the knot of the ligature with the addition of external blunt force injury in excess of the furrow mark (possibly representing assailant or defensive injuries) and internal injury of the neck structures are suspicious, although not definitive, for homicidal manual or ligature strangulation. Correlation between autopsy findings and scene and historical information (medical and psychiatric) is imperative for the proper determination of the manner of death.

Manual strangulation involves the placement of the assailant's hand, forearm, or flexed upper extremity around or across the neck. Blunt force from compression and squeezing of the assailant's hands will invariably leave injury to the external and internal neck structures and will be accompanied by facial petechiae. Application of the forearm (choke or bar arm hold) or the flexed upper extremity (lateral vascular neck restraint (LVNR) or carotid sleeper hold) will cause compression of the upper airway and the neck vessels, respectively. Airway obstruction due to compression of the larynx and trachea during a choke hold will lead to loss of consciousness. Any resulting fracture of the laryngeal cartilages can lead to a hemorrhage of the surrounding soft tissues and swelling, with subsequent and sometimes delayed airway obstruction, asphyxia, and death. Minimal, focal hemorrhage may be all that is encountered during the inspection of the internal neck structures at autopsy in cases of LVNR.

The autopsy findings in strangulation deaths, including hangings, vary from none to a constellation of findings. Many of the individual findings are less specific for a cause and can be seen in other types of non-asphyxial deaths. A constellation of findings, however,

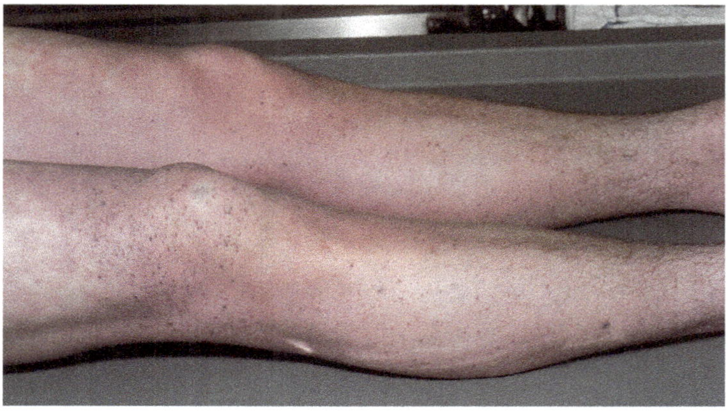

Figure 8.11 Autopsy photograph featuring Tardieu spots of legs in a case of suicidal hanging with prolonged suspension.

is more helpful in identifying an asphyxial cause. Findings include facial and conjunctival petechiae by mechanisms previously discussed. An occasional conjunctival petechial hemorrhage may be produced as a result of cardiopulmonary resuscitation efforts, and care must be taken to not overinterpret their presence in this instance. Facial petechiae are also seen in individuals who have survived an episode of vascular neck compression, including self-inflicted injury, as reported in a case of a man with extensive facial petechiae in an attempt at self-strangulation.[7] Facial congestion, edema or swelling, or bluish discoloration (**cyanosis**) may be present and refer to compression at some point below this region. Tardieu spots, classically appearing only in the regions of lividity, may be seen on the arms and legs of a partially or completely suspended hanging individual (Figure 8.11). Other marks, such as the ligature furrow and other external and internal blunt force injuries to the neck, may be noted. On internal examination, the lungs can appear congested and edematous.

Gas-Related or Chemical Asphyxia

Impairment of O_2 utilization can occur at the cellular level. This occurs because either the cells are unable to use O_2 that has entered the body or ambient O_2 is reduced or not available because it has been displaced or replaced. Classic examples of gases and chemicals causing or contributing to asphyxia include carbon monoxide (CO), methane (CH_4), CO_2, nitrous oxide (N_2O), cyanide (–CN), and hydrogen sulfide (H_2S).

Carbon monoxide is an odorless, colorless, tasteless, and nonirritating gas produced by the incomplete combustion of organic materials, thus emanating from cigarette smoke, cars, boat motors, house fires, charcoal grills, blocked chimneys, defective heating devices, and normally functioning generators operated in confined spaces. Low levels are generated in the body *(in vivo)* as a result of the breakdown of the component of hemoglobin called **heme**, or after exposure to methylene chloride contained in solvents, paint removers, and propellants.[8,9] Rarely, carbon monoxide poisoning may result from contamination of scuba tanks filled by faulty oil-contaminated air compressors. The detrimental effect of CO gas underwater in scuba-related incidents is more severe and increases proportionately as the pressure on the body increases upon continued descent.[10] Most deaths due to carbon monoxide poisoning are accidental, followed by suicidal and, rarely, homicidal. Importantly, individuals complaining of recurrent headaches, dizziness, flu-like symptoms, nausea, and

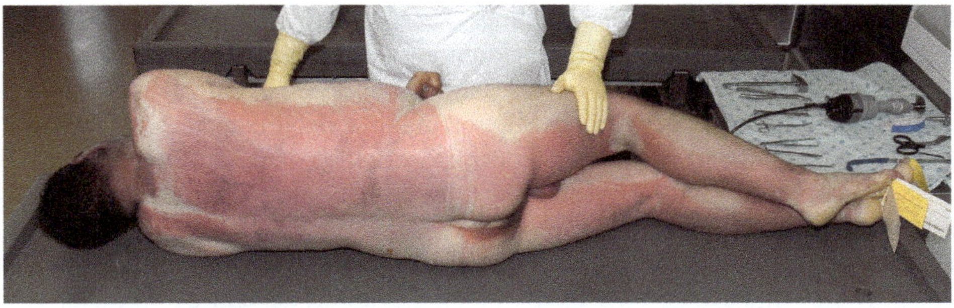

Figure 8.12 Autopsy photograph of cherry-red lividity in a death due to inhalation of charcoal smoke with carbon monoxide poisoning (suicide).

lethargy may be experiencing chronic exposure from some source. There exist occasional news media reports of near deaths due to CO in homes that lacked CO detectors, contained defective furnaces or defective gas stoves, or improperly used indoor generators.

CO binds tightly to the red blood cell protein hemoglobin. Normally, the hemoglobin protein picks up and carries O_2 through the blood circulation and delivers it to the cells that comprise the tissues and organs. It also picks up and carries CO_2, a waste product of a variety of metabolic processes within the body, back to the lungs for exhalation out of the body. CO not only binds tightly to hemoglobin, preventing the binding of O_2, but also displaces the O_2 from the immediate environment and prevents O_2 already bound to hemoglobin from being delivered to the tissues and organs, leading to hypoxia. CO also causes asphyxia by interrupting the production of energy of other cells in the body. In order to reach an elevated blood CO level, there must be active respiration and heart activity (i.e., the individual must be alive). The classic external finding in deaths due to CO is cherry-red or bright-pink lividity, which is a result of the light-sensitive characteristics of the product of CO and hemoglobin, or **carboxyhemoglobin**.[9] This discoloration is also apparent on the nail beds, conjunctivae, and lining of the inner lips and mouth and therefore can be detected even when the skin discoloration is not apparent on darker-skinned individuals. The cherry-red lividity can also be seen in victims of cyanide poisoning, decedents from cold land or aqueous environments, or decedents that have been refrigerated while at the C/ME's office (Figure 8.12). Victims of smoke inhalation from house fires will often have the additional findings of gray-black soot around and within the nostrils and mouth and may have white foam exuding from the nose and mouth. At autopsy, a coating of gray-black soot is usually visible on the lining of the airways, and there will be a bright red discoloration of the organs and skeletal muscle. White or pink foam may also be visible within the airways, which represents the formation and accumulation of edema fluid mixed with air during respiratory efforts prior to death, and is an effect of airway irritation caused by the smoke and direct effects of CO on the heart and circulatory system.[11] The blood also may be notable for the absence of clots that normally form after death, but this change may also be seen in other asphyxial deaths. During the autopsy, a sample of blood is drawn and submitted for testing for the carbon monoxide level, and levels greater than 40–50% are considered lethal. Lower levels of around 20–30% can be lethal in adults with chronic heart and lung disease. Chronic smokers have a constant low level of CO ranging from 8% to 15%, so it is important to know about any history of smoking so that the result of the CO test can be appropriately interpreted within the context of the history, terminal circumstances, and autopsy findings. A negative CO result may indicate death by another means (natural or nonnatural) before the fire, death due to rapid consumption of O_2 from an explosive type of a fire or suffocation due to inhalation of superheated steam with subsequent rapid swelling and obstruction of the upper airway. Lower CO levels may indicate coexistent lethal injury, coexistent intoxication by drugs and medications, death before the fire in a smoker, or impending death due to natural disease occurring slightly before or during the fire. Victims may be resuscitated and rescued from environments with elevated CO, hospitalized, and receive treatment with O_2. Victims treated with O_2 who subsequently die will have low or negative blood CO levels, depending on the duration of O_2 therapy prior to death. Full recovery may ensue, or there may be residual effects from hypoxic damage to the organs, importantly the brain.

Cyanide is an asphyxiant that may be present in many different forms, but most commonly as hydrogen cyanide (HCN) or cyanide salts (potassium cyanide, sodium cyanide, and calcium cyanide). The reaction of the salt with a strong acid produces hydrogen cyanide gas.[8] Sources of cyanide-containing compounds are found in a variety of chemicals, such as insecticides, or are used in the manufacturing of plastics and electroplating and metal polishing; thus, a relatively limited pool of people comprising industrial and laboratory workers have access to or are at risk of exposure.[8,12] Cyanide may also be a by-product of structural fires liberated during the combustion of synthetic materials, and its toxicity is additive to that of CO.[1] Other sources of small amounts of cyanide occur inside the body *(in vivo)* as a result of normal metabolism, metabolism of certain medications, and metabolism of chemicals such as acetonitrile contained in nail polish remover.[8] Ingestion of only small amounts of cyanide by homicidal or suicidal means is the most common route for poisoning, resulting in collapse and death within minutes.[12] The development of symptoms, such as shortness of breath, rapid breathing, change in mental status, metabolic acidosis, and coma may also precede death.[8] In the hospital setting, a high index of suspicion will allow for prompt diagnosis and administration of a cyanide antidote.

At autopsy, cherry-red or bright-pink discoloration of the skin, tissues, and organs may be noted. Additionally, a strong chemical odor similar to bitter almonds may be detected in those who possess the genetic trait to do so. Corrosion of the lining of the mouth, esophagus, and stomach may also be apparent in cases of ingestion of potassium and sodium cyanide.[1] The inhalation of the cyanide gas liberated upon opening the stomach presents a hazard for those in attendance at autopsy, whereby individuals in close proximity may experience an acute episode of shortness of breath and dizziness. This must be immediately recognized so that ventilation and other self-preserving measures can be promptly taken. With a high index of suspicion based on autopsy findings, blood samples will be submitted for specific testing. Interpretation of low levels of cyanide in postmortem blood and urine samples must be done with caution since low levels can be detected in nonsmokers, smokers, and individuals exposed to various chemicals. A specific request for testing for cyanide may be necessary, as this may not be a routine test in some forensic toxicology laboratories.

Cyanide acts as an asphyxiant at the cellular level by blocking the enzyme cytochrome oxidase present in all cells except mature red and white blood cells. This enzyme is partly necessary for cellular respiration and the production of a form of energy called adenosine triphosphate (ATP). The whole process of cellular respiration also requires oxygen, and thus its utilization by the cells is also impaired.

Hydrogen sulfide is a gas originating from the natural environment, organic decomposition, and industry. Specific sources include sewers, septic tanks, the manufacture of petroleum-containing products and paper, natural gas, and volcanoes.[8] It is commonly described as having a rotten egg odor. At higher concentrations in the ambient environment and with prolonged inhalation, its odor becomes undetectable due to paralysis of the olfactory nerves, and respiratory impairment and unconsciousness may ensue.[8] Due to the occupational hazards and past reports of deaths, OSHA regulations restrict the amount of exposure and require training, equipment for detection of the gas, and the use of respiratory protective equipment.[13,14] The action of H_2S is at the cellular level, similar to cyanide. During the scene investigation, blackening of metal objects, including coins, may be noted. At autopsy, a greenish discoloration of the tissues, in addition to the characteristic odor, may be noted. Prompt toxicological testing may reveal elevated sulfate ion or thiosulfate levels.[8]

Asphyxia from the exclusion or displacement of ambient O_2 by other gases has been documented.[1] This includes CO_2, which is encountered in manholes, wells, and silos. The exclusion or displacement of ambient O_2 results in death from suffocation. Entrapment in confined spaces, such as car trunks or refrigerators, in which breathing consumes O_2 while producing CO_2, will lead to asphyxia and death by suffocation. Similarly, the placement of one's head inside of a plastic bag as a suicidal gesture or as an aid to becoming deliberately intoxicated via aerosolized inhalants will lead to the accumulation of CO_2 and asphyxia. The inhalants alone may contain solvents that are directly toxic to the heart, with the potential for causing sudden death. Accidental asphyxia due to the gradual accumulation of CO_2 via rebreathing of exhaled air in a case of autoerotic submersion in a lake (aqua-eroticum) has been reported.[15]

Methane, a component of natural gas and a product of the decay of organic matter, may be encountered in coal mines, marshes, and sewers. With very low ambient O_2 levels caused by displacement by CH_4, consciousness will be lost in seconds and death will rapidly ensue.[1] In cases involving multiple deaths in larger confined spaces, there will often be no specific external or autopsy findings that give any clue as to what may have caused the deaths, and the real danger may still exist, putting unsuspecting rescuers and investigators at risk.

The recreational use of **nitrous oxide** can lead to asphyxia and death.[16] The sources of N_2O, commonly referred to as laughing gas, include anesthetic tanks, whipped cream canisters, and racing fuel tanks. In these cases, supportive autopsy findings may be absent and toxicological testing unrevealing.

Water-Related Deaths due to Atmospheric Pressure Changes

Rapid changes in atmospheric pressure can have direct effects on the lungs, other organs, and blood vessels with potentially fatal consequences, including asphyxia-related complications.[10]

Decreased atmospheric pressure upon rapid ascent during diving using a Self-Contained Underwater Breathing Apparatus (SCUBA), or during other long deep dives while breathing compressed gas mixtures containing nitrogen, causes gas bubbles to rapidly form and accumulate within the tissues and blood vessels faster than it can be exhaled. This leads to the impaired circulation of blood to the joints and brain, giving rise to joint and muscle pain, weakness, and visual impairment. This constellation of symptoms is commonly referred to as decompression sickness, Caisson disease, or "the bends." Death may rarely result due to respiratory failure from the brain or spinal cord damage. Death may also result from **paradoxical embolism** of gas bubbles from the venous to the arterial system and brain through a hole between the upper chambers of the heart, a birth defect known as an atrial septal defect. A similar situation of decreased atmospheric pressure involves a rapid ascent to high elevations in aviators, causing lung and brain swelling within 8–24 hours of the event. In this case, an autopsy may reveal lung evidence of lung damage including congestion, edema in addition to retinal hemorrhage.

The effects of rapid changes in atmospheric pressure may also be encountered by scuba divers in the form of pressure-related trauma (**barotrauma**) to organs susceptible to rupture. This occurs when the internal and external gas pressures are unable to equalize due to rapid ascent *while holding one's breath.* In particular, the alveoli of the lungs will become overexpanded to the point of rupture with the escape of gas into the lining of the lungs (pleura), the pulmonary vessels, the connective tissues surrounding the pulmonary vessels, or distant organs. This can result in gas within the chest cavity (**pneumothorax**), causing lung collapse, gas within the lung tissue (**interstitial emphysema**), gas around the heart (**mediastinal emphysema**), gas under the skin (**subcutaneous emphysema**), and movement or **embolism** of gas bubbles within the blood circulation to distant organs. Gas bubbles within the blood circulation of an organ, much like a blockage by a plaque within a coronary artery, can lead to tissue and cell death (**infarction**) downstream from the blockage, whether in the heart, lungs, brain, or another organ. Lung collapse due to pneumothorax impairs alveolar ventilation and can result in asphyxia with respiratory failure and death if not promptly reversed. Loss of consciousness, chest pain, or stroke-like symptoms are the typical signs and symptoms that can develop after a rapid, uncontrolled ascent. Death due to lung collapse from pneumothorax and severe neurological impairment has occurred as a direct effect of gas embolism. Death may also result from drowning in an incapacitated individual undergoing the effects of barotrauma while submerged. Impairment by drugs and alcohol may also predispose the diver to drowning or barotrauma due to poor decision making and judgment while diving and ascending. Death may also be due to natural causes referable to the cardiovascular or respiratory systems. The accurate determination of the cause and manner of death in these cases necessitates a complete scene investigation with the examination of all diving-related equipment, knowledge of the decedent's medical and psychiatric history, knowledge of the decedent's background and training in scuba diving, and performance of a complete autopsy with toxicological testing.

References

1. Spitz, W. U. 2006. Asphyxia. In *Medicolegal investigation of death—Guidelines for the application of pathology to crime investigation*, ed. W. U. Spitz, 783–845. 4th ed. Springfield, IL: Charles C Thomas Publisher Ltd.
2. Sauvageau, A. 2009. Agonal sequences in four filmed hangings: Analysis of respiratory and movement responses to asphyxia by hanging. *J Forensic Sci* 54(1):192–94.
3. Ely, S. F., and Hirsch, C. S. 2000. Asphyxial deaths and petechiae: A review. *J Forensic Sci* 45(6):1274–77.
4. Russell, D. 1999. Accidental ligature strangulation due to a roller-type massage device. *Am J Forensic Med Pathol* 20(4):354–56.
5. Morild, I. 1996. Fractures of the neck structures in suicidal hanging. *Med Sci Law* 36(1):80–84.

6. Nikolic, S., Micic, J., Atanasijevic, T., et al. 2003. Analysis of neck injuries in hanging. *Am J Forensic Med Pathol* 24(2):179–82.
7. Lambe, A., Puschel, K., and Anders, S. 2009. Extensive petechiae in attempted self-strangulation. *J Forensic Sci* 54(1):212–15.
8. Jentzen, J. M., Mont, E. K., and Revercomb, C. 2003. Volatiles and inhalants (chemical asphyxia). In *Handbook of forensic pathology*, ed. R. C. Froede, 237–41. 2nd ed. Northfield, IL: College of American Pathologists (CAP).
9. Henry, J. B. 1996. *Clinical diagnosis and management by laboratory methods*. 19th ed. Philadelphia, PA: W.B. Saunders Company.
10. Spitz, D. J. 2006. Investigation of bodies in water. In *Medicolegal investigation of death—Guidelines for the application of pathology to crime investigation*, ed. W. U. Spitz, 846–81. 4th ed. Springfield, IL: Charles C Thomas Publisher Ltd.
11. Spitz, W. U. 2006. Thermal injuries. In *Medicolegal investigation of death—Guidelines for the application of pathology to crime investigation*, ed. W. U. Spitz, 747–82. 4th ed. Springfield, IL: Charles C Thomas Publisher Ltd.
12. Musshoff, F., Schmidt, P., Daldrup, T., et al. 2002. Cyanide fatalities: Case studies of four suicides and one homicide. *Am J Forensic Med Pathol* 23(4):315–20.
13. Fuller, D. C., and Suruda, A. J. 2000. Occupationally related hydrogen sulfide deaths in the United States from 1984–1994. *J Occup Environ Med* 42(9):939–42.
14. Hydrogen Sulfide. U.S. Department of Labor–Occupational Health and Safety Administration. https://www.osha.gov/SLTC/hydrogensulfide/hazards.html (accessed March 31, 2020).
15. Sauvageau, A., and Racette, S. 2006. Aqua-eroticum: An unusual autoerotic fatality in a lake involving a home-made diving apparatus. *J Forensic Sci* 51(1):137–39.
16. Wagner, S. A., Clark, M. A., Wesche, D. L., et al. 1992. Asphyxial deaths from the recreational use of nitrous oxide. *J Forensic Sci* 37(4):1008–15.

The Forensic Pathological Aspects of Deaths Due to Drowning and Bodies Recovered from Fluid Environments

9

ERICA J. ARMSTRONG

Introduction

Under controlled circumstances and normal weather conditions, contained bodies of water or other fluids, whether small or vast, pose little threat to those who encounter them. However, the presence of injury, disease, intoxication, human error, dangerous aquatic life, or the malicious intent of another while in or around a liquid medium like water may create an environment that is hostile, placing one at greater risk for death. The medicolegal evaluation of bodies recovered from fluid environments, commonly water, must take into account several possibilities as to how a body became submerged, starting from the point of immersion, and whether or not the immersion/submersion event contributed to or caused the death. These include:

- Natural death preceding or during immersion or submersion
- Homicidal death preceding submersion
- Homicidal death by drowning (forced or precipitated submersion)
- Accidental death by injury or intoxication preceding or during submersion
- Accidental drowning in the context of swim inexperience, nonlethal injury, or non-lethal intoxication/overdose
- Suicidal injury or intoxication preceding or during submersion
- Suicide by drowning, including those assisted by the attachment of weighted object(s) to the body
- Accidental death caused by or precipitated by water temperature extremes (ex. cold water immersion with cold water shock or hypothermia, hot water immersion with hyperthermia)

Below are just a few of the many examples of the types of water-related deaths:

Natural: Sudden blockage of coronary artery with cardiac arrest while wading in a swimming pool.

Accidental: Fracture of the neck with lethal spinal cord injury following a dive from a height into a shallow lake with impact on surface.

Homicidal: Asphyxia by smothering of a small child, subsequently placed in a bathtub filled with water in order to cause wrinkling of the skin, to simulate accidental drowning.

Suicidal: Elderly woman with major depression found in shallow stream with horizontal deep incised wounds of wrists and death due to a combination of exsanguination and drowning.

The determination of death due to drowning, regardless of the manner of drowning, is a diagnosis than can be made only after exclusion of other potential causes, such as those above, and is done in the context of available historical and investigative information. Review of reports that document information including scene attributes, evidence recovery, body recovery efforts, weather and water conditions, indoor scenes, and bystander and medical technician resuscitative efforts, is an essential task of the forensic pathologist as this review provides a contextual foundation upon which the autopsy findings are interpreted. These reports include police reports, technical dive team reports, coast guard reports, and emergency medical services reports as well as the report prepared by the Medicolegal Death Investigator (MDI). Review of any ancillary reports relative to the examination of safety gear, underwater breathing gear, watercraft, or even implanted medical devices such as pacemakers recovered at the time of the autopsy is necessary prior to any final cause and manner of death conclusions. The pathologist will also review medical records that would document the diagnosis and treatment of a drowning victim who may have survived long enough to be hospitalized for a period of time prior to succumbing to complications of drowning. This is vitally important since the supportive findings of drowning may be absent by the time the autopsy is performed. Due to ongoing investigation, many of the above reports and records may not be available in their entirety at the time of autopsy.

The autopsy findings of drowning individually are nonspecific and can be seen in other types of deaths. Each finding itself is considered supportive evidence of drowning. When more than one supportive finding can be identified, the case for drowning is strengthened, especially when they are collectively interpreted within the context of the historical and terminal circumstances. The lack of supportive findings or the presence of weak or insufficient findings, however, will prompt consideration that the death may have resulted from some other cause.

With exclusion of other causes of death, the designation of death due to drowning can be more confidently made. This, however, is only half of what is necessary for death certification, as the death needs to be properly classified as to the manner in which it came to be. Once the death is designated as that due to drowning, the death is automatically no longer considered natural in manner, and therefore must be categorized into one of the remaining four categories discussed in Chapter 1. In near-drowning deaths where the immediate cause of death may be due to seemingly natural conditions such as pneumonia or organ failure, the manner of death is also no longer considered natural since it was precipitated by the unnatural process of drowning. While the autopsy may provide clues allowing for the assignment of manner of death (i.e., the additional finding of suicidal incised wounds of the wrists), the investigative information provided by the C/ME's medicolegal death investigators and police investigators together can add the balance of what is needed for the most accurate determination of the manner of death.

Water-Related Deaths: Initial Processing

The investigation of water-related deaths involves three key components: death scene and circumstance review, autopsy performance, and toxicological testing. Interpretation of all information gleaned from these components must be done in the context of all available historical information in order to facilitate the determination of death due to drowning versus death by another cause. Moreover, interpretation of autopsy findings and any results of laboratory testing are also done within the context of all known information, rather than in isolation of it, as this can also aid in answering additional questions of investigative importance such as:

- Was the victim alive or dead before entering the water?
- Did the victim drown?
- Did injury, natural disease, or physical disability prevent the victim from exiting the water and did they cause or contribute to the death?
- Is the body found seaside indicative of a drowned body washed ashore or a dumped victim of homicidal violence?
- Were the injuries observed on the body at the time of recovery sustained before death or as a result of the water conditions or recovery efforts?
- Is the body temperature measured or estimated on scene consistent with the cold water conditions from which it was recovered and were there also signs of hypothermia?
- What is the approximate time of death or length of time the body was submerged?

After documentation of the death scene, initial processing of the body will occur prior to autopsy. If not already established, the most important task is to identify the decedent, which may include presumptive identification based on recognition of personal effects, such as clothing, jewelry, or tattoos. Locating photo ID-type documents such as a driver's license followed by side-by-side comparison to the decedent can be done. In decedents with intact and preserved facial features, viewing of the body by a relative can add another layer of confirmatory identification. Alongside positive visual identification, the C/ME may additionally utilize more scientific methods to confirm identification such as fingerprint comparison, dental comparison, DNA comparison, or x-ray comparison of unique skeletal anatomy.

Following or during efforts to establish the identity, a review of all available information about the scene, resuscitative attempts, and the decedent's personal history (medical, psychiatric, and social) obtained by the C/ME medicolegal death investigator, police investigators, and medical personnel is done. Some, but usually not all, of the information will be available prior to the autopsy and the greater the amount of pre-autopsy information made available to the pathologist, the better. Additional information is often relayed to the C/ME or forensic pathologist during or after the autopsy. The forensic pathologist may also request any additional follow-up investigative information both verbal and written.

Decomposed or badly injured bodies or bodies with penetrating injuries arriving wearing clothing should be first photographed and then x-rayed to look for loose projectiles or other on-body foreign material and personal effects that may be of evidentiary value and therefore warrant retrieval and submission according to the chain-of-custody protocol.

In suspicious or uncertain death circumstances, the forensic scientist may become involved early on with the documentation (including photographic), collection, examination, and retention of certain items of potential evidentiary value including on-body clothing, personal effects, and foreign material. Unique or unusual findings are then communicated or shown to the forensic pathologist as such findings can provide important interpretive context. For example, the location and the precise way in which binding materials or items used as weights are affixed to the body are vitally important for manner of death determination, especially suicide versus homicide.[1, 2]

The condition of any on-body clothing will be noted as this could be relevant to the victim's appearance when last seen or the characteristics of the environment from which the body was recovered. Wet or stained clothing will be removed and hung in a secured location to allow drying, and otherwise handled with care so as to not disturb any adherent material of potential evidentiary value. Clothing suspected to have been immersed in accelerants will be retained in sealed metal containers, or as otherwise directed, until further testing. Bagged hands will be examined and potentially include scrapings from fingernails depending on the death circumstances. Hands may be examined for trace metal or sampled for gunshot residue in relevant cases, although the yield may be severely limited in the case of a submerged body. Any water or other fluid samples collected and submitted from the scene are retained for possible microscopic or toxicological examinations. Diving equipment, personal watercraft, personal flotation devices, and other safety-related equipment should be retained by the C/ME or other secured location for possible later examination by appropriate experts for defects, evidence of tampering, evidence of alteration, or evidence of improper use. Any findings may be pertinent to cause of death determination made by the forensic pathologist.

Analysis of DNA samples taken from the body or other item for the ultimate purpose of identifying the source (victim versus other) may be of vital importance in establishing or confirming not only the victim's identity, but also in the reconstruction of the death circumstances by police investigators. Sampling for potentionally DNA-containing, foreign biological material such as saliva, blood, and semen may be attempted although the successful recovery of DNA may be limited or precluded in cases of prolonged submersion or decomposition as the sample may become too degraded to be tested.[3,4,5] Successful identification using DNA obtained from dismembered and disarticulated remains submerged for extended time periods has been reported, however.[6,7]

As part of the pre-autopsy initial processing, in cases of tentatively identified or unidentified bodies, fingerprinting may be done which can provide a rapid means of identification. Obtaining fingerprints suitable for comparison can be challenging in cases of prolonged submersion with decomposition, however. When positive identification using more conventional methods of fingerprinting (discussed in Chapter 3) have been unsuccessful, application of special fingerprint enhancement techniques may be necessary with success reported in the literature.[8]

In cases involving submerged vehicles that contain a body or bodies, optimally and if feasible, the entire vehicle should be extricated and transported to the forensic laboratory (which may also be the C/ME's office) for processing. Characteristics, operability, status of operation upon entry into water, and extent of damage as determined by an investigator with the appropriate expertise, as well as the location of recovery of the submerged vehicle may provide potential clues that can assist in the reconstruction of events that led to or caused the submersion which in turn may ultimately have bearing on the manner of death determination.

The Autopsy and the Diagnosis of Drowning and Other Water-Related Injury

It is imperative that all bodies freshly retrieved from an aqueous or other fluid environment receive an autopsy regardless of whether or not the scene findings are strongly in favor of drowning, accidental or otherwise. The omission of an autopsy is tantamount to malpractice on the part of the physician C/ME (the forensic pathologist) and neglect of one's duties as an elected official on the part of the coroner. This applies specifically to cases in which the individual is pronounced deceased on scene, on arrival to the hospital, or shortly thereafter. At times, when the death circumstances are clearly accidental or suicidal, and the individual has had a period of survival in a medical facility prior to death, an autopsy may not be performed. In those instances, review of the first responder reports, medical records and any other relevant documents followed by an external examination of the body will be done prior to the determination of the cause and manner of death and completion of the death certificate. For homicidal drownings with or without an interval survival, best practices warrant autopsy performance.

Once the body is received at the C/ME's office, performance of an autopsy, along with collection of specimens for toxicological analysis, is best commenced quickly, as the changes of decomposition will proceed more quickly in a body recovered from an aqueous environment than in one recovered from dry land, even with prompt refrigeration. Decomposition that has taken place during submersion may alter the body to such an extent as to make identifying the individual and interpretation of injuries difficult or impossible. Significantly decomposed or badly damaged bodies will require imaging studies such as an x-ray to allow assessment for internal injuries or retained foreign materials. Aside from helping to locate retained foreign materials, postmortem imaging studies can be beneficial in other ways. Imaging studies can identify unique anatomic attributes or evidence of prior surgical intervention that can assist in identification of an individual by comparison to medical records. In scuba- or deep diving–related deaths, imaging studies such as x-ray and computed tomography (CT) scanning performed prior to autopsy will facilitate assessment for evidence of air within the body cavities such as air within the chest cavity also known as **pneumothorax** or air within the soft tissues, a sign of subcutaneous emphysema. While the traditional autopsy procedure affords external and internal access to much of the anatomy to allow assessment for findings of drowning, a specialized type of imaging known as postmortem whole body computed tomography (WBCT) has been shown to be increasingly useful as a way to document relevant findings without the invasiveness of a traditional autopsy and can be used in instances of religious or other objections to an autopsy.[9] As an example, excessive fluid and sedimentary material in the sinuses and cavities of the head and chest, mouth, throat, lungs, stomach, and small intestine have been identified in drownings using WBCT technology. Additionally, identification of differences in body fluid and tissue density, as a result of dilution of the blood or sequestering of blood within the organs, has been used in the differentiation of fresh versus saltwater drownings using the same technology.

External Examination

Like in any other autopsy, in water-related deaths an external examination will be performed to record identifying characteristics, degree of rigor mortis, position and color of the lividity, and any decompositional changes. Rigor and livor mortis (lividity) and decomposition were defined and discussed in previous chapters. Rigor mortis will be evident in the earlier postmortem period prior to decomposition, the degree of which will be dependent upon the postmortem interval and water conditions such as water temperature. The time to onset and the degree of the rigor mortis will depend on the degree of muscular activity during the drowning process with greater muscular activity giving rise to quicker onset of rigor mortis. Rigor mortis affects all muscles including the tiny muscles attached to the body hairs known as the **arector pili** muscles. Rigor mortis of these muscles causes the skin change known as **gooseflesh** or **cutis anserina** and has no relation to cold water immersion and is seen in submerged and non-submerged bodies alike (**Figure 9.1**). Lividity may appear anywhere and in any pattern on the body or may not be apparent at all, an effect of the variability of effects of water pressure from flowing water or strong currents. In the absence of those effects, and involving submerged bodies at depth, typically the lividity will be most apparent on the anterior torso and in the face, neck, chest, hands, lower extremities, and feet as a result of prone body positioning, also known as the **drowner's pose**. This pattern of lividity, however, is not a diagnosis of drowning. The color of the lividity may provide additional clues to the death circumstances and direct further testing such as in the case of cherry-red or bright-pink lividity which may indicate carbon monoxide poisoning and require submission of blood to the lab for appropriate testing. The external examination depends significantly on the sense of sight to detect signs of injury and disease. Use of the sense of smell may be important in detecting any chemical odors that may also direct specific testing. Palpation for bony deformity can identify or confirm fracture of a limb seen on pre-autopsy imaging. Palpation can also be utilized to detect entrapped air under the skin also known as **subcutaneous emphysema** which may be a sign of barotrauma in SCUBA-related drowning deaths or a result of blunt force injury causing rib fracture with displacement and puncture of the adjacent lung. The entrapped

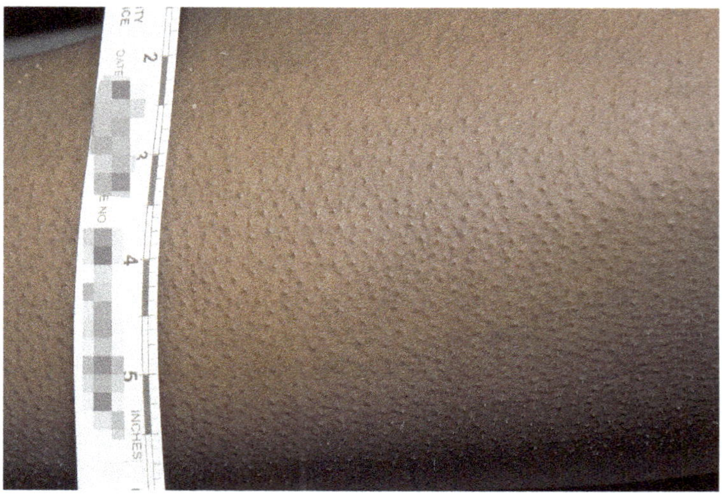

Figure 9.1 Cutis anserina.

air produces a crackling sensation known as crepitance and may be widespread involving contiguous soft tissues and body regions.

External findings in drowning deaths vary. Each finding alone is neither specific nor diagnostic of drowning. Some findings merely indicate that the body or body part has been submerged long enough for changes to be visible. The presence or absence of external findings are dependent on many factors such as the postmortem submersion interval (PMSI), characteristics of the water including but not limited to temperature and current, the time elapsed between recovery and autopsy, resuscitation efforts, and any in-hospital survival time. It is important to note that there may be little to no findings. In other instances in which factors have been at play for prolonged periods, any findings may have been altered or have deteriorated to the point that they cannot be interpreted.

Depending on the manner of entry into the water, topography of nearby shore and underwater environments, water movements, the presence of aquatic organisms, or the presence of watercraft, the body may sustain one or more injuries, sometimes with a pattern or distribution that is indicative of the object or organism that produced them. Swimming pools and other smaller bodies of water may contain additional hazards with the potential of causing injury of various types. Injuries may be blunt, sharp, penetrating, or any combination of these. Injuries must be correctly identified and interpreted as misidentification or misinterpretation can lead to erroneous conclusions which in turn can have legal ramifications. Of the different types of injury, blunt force injury types (abrasions, contusions, and lacerations) are most common. These may have been sustained prior to submersion, on impact with water or objects in or near water, or while submerged, or may have nothing to do with the submersion event. In larger bodies of water, both natural and manmade, the manner of entry, the presence of moving or fixed natural or manmade objects, water current and wave action, underwater topography, and predation by marine or terrestrial animals may individually or collectively play a role. Recovery efforts may cause injury, typically blunt force type injury of the chest, face, neck, or the inner and proximal aspects of the upper extremities. Resuscitative efforts such as moving and positioning of the body for transport or placement of an oral endotracheal tube and chest compressions may cause similar types of injury in the same locations and the presence of petechiae of the sclerae and conjunctivae may be noted. Resuscitative efforts often include the placement of intravascular catheters. When these are removed prior to the autopsy, they can have the same appearance as the puncture marks associated with intravenous drug use. In the hospital, tubes may be placed in the chest and there may be surgical interventions that include skin incisions and this will ordinarily be noted in the medical records. Ordinarily, therapy-associated devices that have been placed on the body are left in place which is most helpful to the forensic pathologist who must interpret the significance of all bodily findings. Without knowledge of the types and extent of recovery or resuscitative efforts or in-hospital therapeutic interventions, these findings may be incorrectly interpreted as some other type of injury such as inflicted injury. For example, surgical incisions made for the placement of chest tubes can look like a stab wounds and can render interpretation difficult when these tubes have been removed by hospital personnel prior to the autopsy.

The presence or absence of injury may also depend on factors that impede or protect the body from being impacted. One example is body buoyancy. Factors that affect body buoyancy include the amount of body fat, the presence of on-body buoyant clothing or flotation devices such as life vests, and the amount of air contained in lungs and intestines and will determine the depth to which the body will sink and affect its potential to come in contact with any underwater objects. Clothing and wet suits may protect the skin from injury. In deeper waters, the body often assumes a classic drowner's pose with the head down and the extremities dangling as it sinks to the bottom. As a result of the body being propelled by wave and current action with dragging against the bottom surface, **travel abrasions and lacerations** may appear on exposed body surfaces, particularly the forehead, backs of the hands, knees, and tops of the feet (**Figure 9.2**). By virtue of their clustering and location on various regions of the body, these postmortem injuries represent a type of patterned injury, and knowledge of the characteristics inherent in the location of recovery is another example of the importance of how knowing about the death scene attributes and circumstances leads to proper interpretation of injury.

Injuries may have a nonspecific pattern and distribution, making it difficult to determine what exactly caused them and how they were caused. By contrast, the location and clustering pattern of injuries can be informative, such as fresh or healed incised wounds clustered on the extremities or inner wrist surfaces, indicative of suicide. Severe injuries of the skin, fractures of the bone, and lacerations with hemorrhage of the internal organs in an individual found submerged in water located at the bottom of a precipice would be highly concerning for a suicidal jump or possibly an accidental fall from a great height. The presence of petechial hemorrhages clustered on the face or conjunctival lining of the eyes accompanied by facial swelling, would be worrisome for either an asphyxial death caused by vascular neck compression or, in the case of scuba-related deaths, **mask squeeze**

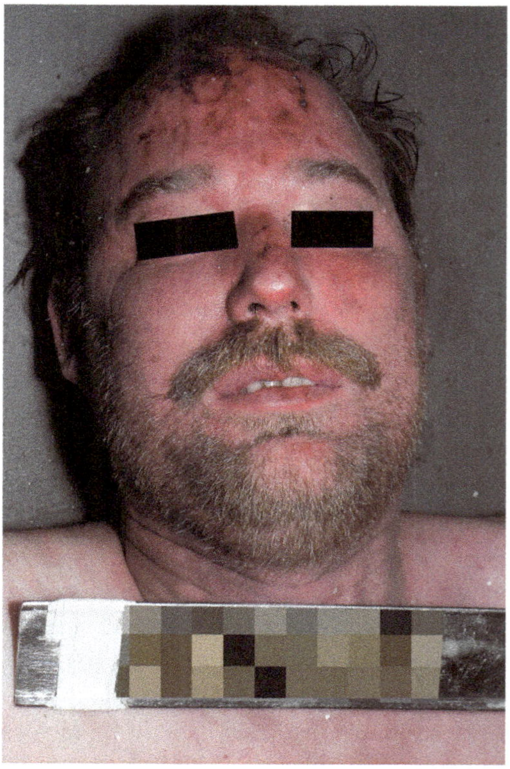

Figure 9.2 (A) Travel abrasions of forehead and nose in drowned individual floating face down and (B) Emphysema aquosum of the lung with voluminous appearance, foamy fluid exuding from bronchus and blotchy dark subpleural hemorrhages.

related to rapid descent without equalization of mask pressure. Moreover, abrasions and contusions may be barely visible initially, especially on wet or moist skin, and the extent of these injuries may not be appreciated until drying of the skin has taken place. In cases of equivocal or suspicious circumstance, next-day examination with redocumentation of all injuries may be additionally revealing or otherwise confirm the initial interpretation. The location, distribution, and characteristics of any blunt force injury, sharp force injury, and gunshot wounds require careful documentation as it may be of investigative importance aiding in the reconstruction of the death circumstances.

Injuries may have been sustained before death (antemortem), after death (postmortem), or both. These include blunt force, sharp force, and penetrating injuries and those caused by encounters with aquatic fauna. Distinguishing antemortem from postmortem injuries can be important not only to help determine the timing of the injury which may be important information to law enforcement investigators, but also when trying to determine whether any injuries were sufficient to be the outright cause of death or otherwise incapacitating enough to precipitate the process of drowning. Antemortem injuries typically have evidence of **vital reaction**, which in the early or acute stage is visually recognized as reddening and possible swelling which are representative of bleeding (hemorrhage) and the onset of inflammation (Figure 9.3 A, B). Similar to blunt, sharp, and penetrating injury, vital reaction from animal bites or stings from jelly fish may be demonstrable. Moreover, the stinging cells or nematocysts of jellyfish can be seen in the epidermal layer of the skin when examined under the microscope and may provide clues to the death circumstances. If there was a survival interval of at least one to two hours such as in a near-drowning event with rescue and hospitalization, the injured tissues will show infiltration of red blood cells (hemorrhage), acute inflammatory cells (neutrophils), and signs of cell death. With prolonged survival of days to week's duration, removal of cellular debris and red blood cells by scavenger cells (macrophages), ingrowth of thin delicate blood vessels (granulation tissue), and the formation of scar tissue will be evident. These are all signs of healing and part of the vital reaction continuum, the extent and characteristics of which are determined in part by the severity of the injury and the length of the time between the injury and

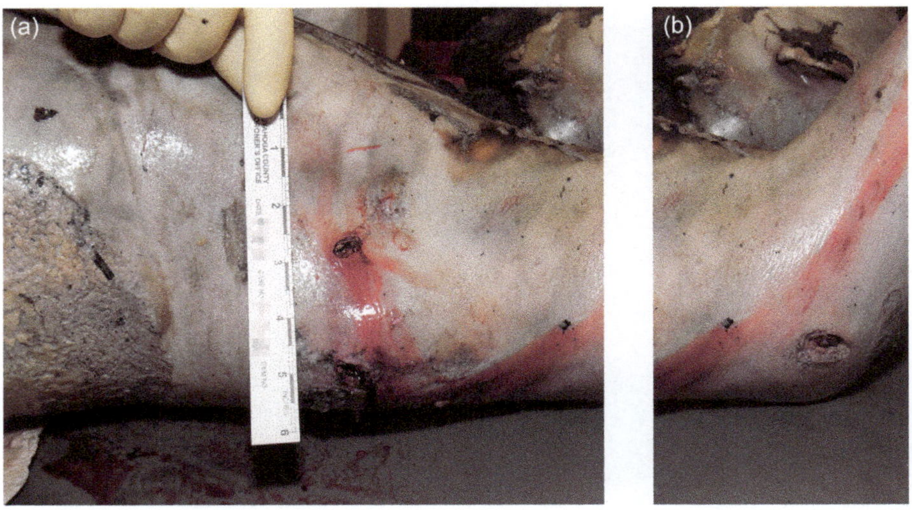

Figure 9.3 (A) Blood stab wounds of left chest on body recovered after prolonged submersion in pond and (B) Bloodless stab wound of left shoulder in the same victim.

death, known as the **survival interval**. The longer the survival interval after the injury was sustained, the longer the time for the changes associated with vital reaction to develop and progress. The degree of the vital reaction as described by the pathologist can be helpful in assisting police investigators in the reconstruction of the timeline of events as they relate to the approximate time that the injury was sustained and events that may have preceded and followed the injury. Postmortem injuries typically lack vital reaction changes. At times, deciphering the difference based on the appearance can be challenging. In those instances, the questionable injuries can be sampled and examined under the microscope (**Figure 9.4**).

Other causes of injury are those that result from animal predation and those that are caused by the time-dependent effects of the immediate environment on the body, known as **taphonomy**. Animal predation-type injury, whether caused by land or aquatic animals, large and small, and whether sustained in the antermortem or postmortem period, includes superficial skin injury, removal of large sections of soft tissue, amputation, dismemberment, evisceration, and fracture and crushing of bones. Patterns of injury characteristic of the type of animal may be evident.

Shark bite wounds are a prototypical patterned animal injury that has the propensity to be not only incapacitating, heightening the risk of drowning, but also rapidly fatal.[10] Attacks on humans by large predatory sharks, such as the great white shark (*Carcharodon carcharias*) in particular, are not necessarily representative of feeding behavior but are believed to be more likely due to either anomalous behavior or defense of territory.[10] As a consequence of prolonged submersion with leaching of blood from wounds, deciphering the difference between antemortem and postmortem injuries in cases of shark and other large animal predation may not be possible, which in turn could make determination of the cause of death impossible as well (i.e., cause of death due to the attack vs. due to something else—like drowning—with subsequent feeding by a large aquatic animal). While the large, deep crescent-shaped injury with jagged edges is one pattern of injury that may be seen, injuries left by shark attacks can range from skin lacerations, abrasions, and incised wounds to loss of limbs and deep viscera. Laceration of major blood vessels, muscle, and soft tissue

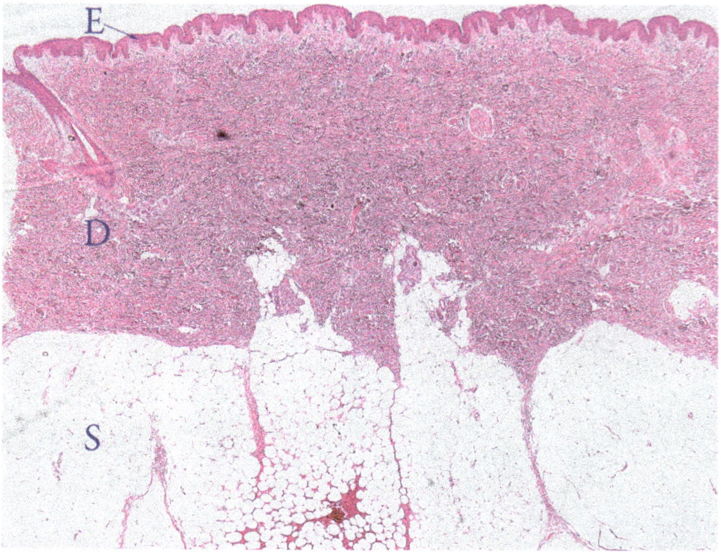

Figure 9.4 Section of scalp skin with contusion featuring epidermis (E), dermis (D), and subcutis (S) (H and E, 40× magnification).

can lead to rapid blood loss. Large lacerations in which there is little or no loss of tissue, may be amenable to reconstruction and potentially reveal a general pattern of the shark bite(s).[10] Similar reconstruction can be done on any recovered clothing as well. Portions of the shark's teeth may be found, grossly or by x-ray, embedded within soft tissue and bone, and the recovery of the teeth could aid in the identification of the species involved. Sharks' teeth have serrated edges, which can leave patterned marks on hard surfaces, such as bone and diving equipment.

Any postmortem injury to the body, whether caused by animal predation or by environmental taphonomic changes can also alter, confound, or obscure true antemortem injury. Interpretation of cadaveric trauma caused by animal activity can be especially problematic.[11] Postmortem injuries may be present secondary to predation or anthropophagy by small aquatic organisms or other organisms, such as fish, crabs, crayfish, and river rats. These injuries are typically located on the accessible regions of the body, especially the face, with partial or complete removal of the eyelids, lips, ears, and nose. Extensive injuries secondary to predation may make visual identification difficult or impossible **(Figure 9.5)**. Bodies found floating in oceanic environments may become colonized by sea lice, microscopic organisms that can consume skin and underlying soft tissue alike, creating artifacts that may mimic inflicted wounds or significantly alter or obscure bona fide ones. Injuries caused by stinging organisms such as jellyfish sustained while in water produce red, linear, rash-like discolorations, similar to ant or roach bites.

Postmortem taphanomic injuries can also be extensive and include dismemberment, disarticulation, tissue loss, bone fracture and skeletonization.[12,13,14] The expertise of the forensic anthropologist will be needed in cases of extreme taphonomic changes, especially skeletonization. Determining whether or not open wounds are antemortem versus postmortem can prove challenging for the forensic pathologist due to a variety factors and circumstances that may be at play. The leaching out of blood through open wounds and decompositional changes can make differentiation between antemortem versus postmortem injury difficult or impossible.

As previously stated, pattern recognition has relevance to both the death investigation and the cause-of-death determination made by the forensic pathologist. Certain types

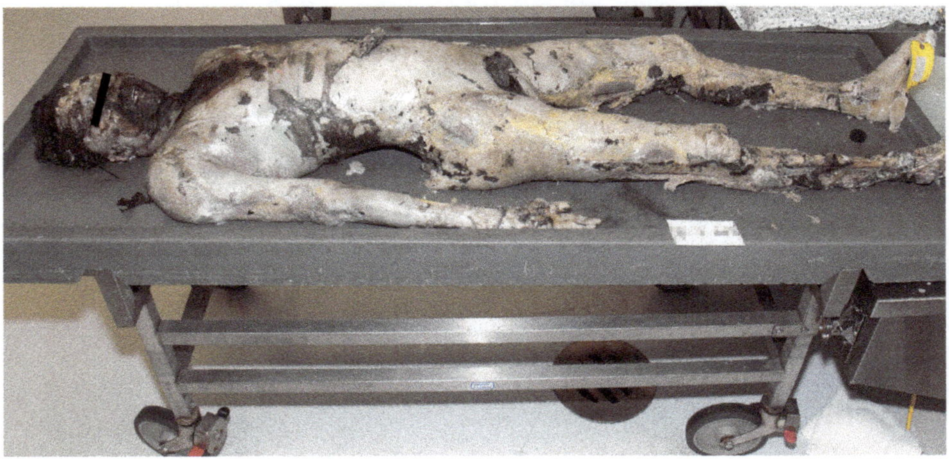

Figure 9.5 Unidentifiable decomposed body of a man removed from a pond with extensive tissue loss due to predation by aquatic fauna.

of injury individually or in aggregate can represent patterned injury resulting in certain circumstances. The increased use of personal watercraft has resulted in an increase in a variety of injuries related to impacts from other watercraft or direct bodily impact. As documented in one study, incapacitating or fatal injuries included aortic injury, brain injury, skeletal and skull fractures, spinal injuries, and injury to the internal abdominal organs.[15] Propeller wounds (**Figure 9.6**) represent an example of patterned injury resulting from contact with watercraft. While the typical scenario involves injuries caused by the propellers of boats and other personal watercraft, other less typical circumstances should be considered such as propeller injuries caused by underwater industrial pumps.[16] Characteristic propeller injuries are chop-like wounds that can have features of both blunt and sharp force type injuries, specifically cuts or incised wounds with abraded edges. Other characterizing features are open wounds, parallel in orientation, with characteristic spacing and multiplicity, particularly when distributed over broad body surfaces such as the torso. Abrasions, contusions, and deep lacerations of the skin and underlying soft tissues and organs may also accompany theses injuries. Impacts with rotating propellers of varying mass, dimension, and velocity can also cause devastating head injury with skull fracture and laceration to the brain as well as fracture and partial or complete amputation of the limbs. The characteristic features of propeller injuries can be compared to the physical features, revolutions, and speed of the propeller of the suspected watercraft and therefore can be helpful in the reconstruction of the death circumstances and the identification of the watercraft, particularly if the incident was a hit-skip or the specific type of watercraft is in question.[17] Propeller injuries can be devastating, rapidly incapacitating, and lethal in and of themselves or otherwise precipitate the drowning process.[18] The determination as to whether these injuries were sustained as a result of impact with the propellers while alive versus impact with a drowned body (i.e. the presence or absence of vital reaction) could have relevance in regard to culpability or negligence on the part of the watercraft operator.

Other unique injury patterns or even the absence of injury may accompany specific death circumstances emphasizing the importance of recognition during the external examination. Individuals who come in contact with caustic or corrosive chemicals while submerged may sustain chemical burn injury. Thermal and chemical, external and

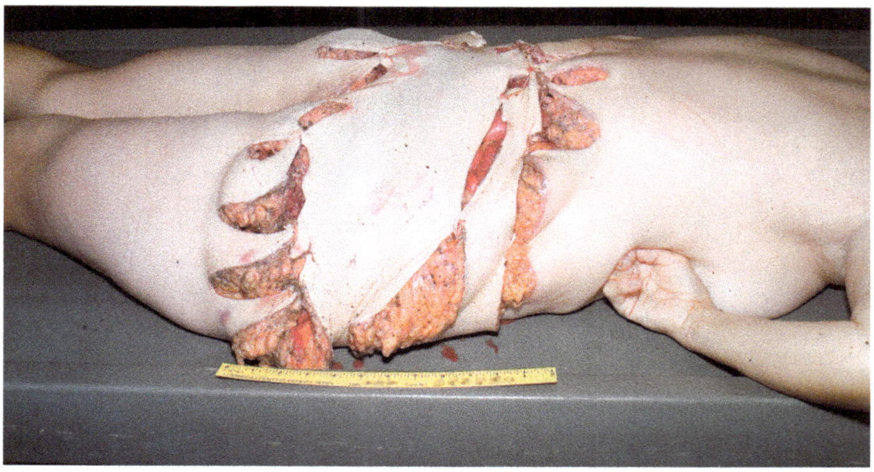

Figure 9.6 Bloodless boat propeller chop wounds of trunk and lower extremity after wound reconstruction.

internal injuries arising from immersion/submersion with drowning in liquid mediums such as gasolines, hot oils, and waxes have been reported.[19, 20] Other injuries may provide clues to the circumstances that may have precipitated a drowning such as the presence of track marks indicating intravenous injection of drugs and the possibility of an overdose or surgical scars indicative of disability. Loss of hair, clothing, jewelry, or patterned contusions or abrasions may be seen in individuals entrapped by pool drains with defective covers. Sitting upon pool drains lacking proper covers or otherwise unsecured covers can result in serious and potentially fatal evisceration/disembowelment injuries produced by the strong suction forces which will be obvious during the external examination of the body.

Physical wounding may be lacking altogether with the presence of petechial hemorrhage as the only sign of vital reactions in certain cases of drowning such as those precipitated by electrocution.[21] Individuals submerged in water while sustaining electrical shock arising from devices and fixtures that carry low-voltage current (i.e., electrified cords, cables, appliances, and defective pool lights) will have no external signs of electrothermal injury due to the lowered skin resistance and heat-protective effect of water. One may find electrothermal injury on the skin of an individual who has come in contact with an electrical current *prior* to submersion, however. In that instance, death may result either from the direct effects of electrocution or otherwise from drowning precipitated by temporary paralysis of the respiratory muscles caused by the electrical current.

The changes conferred by the processes of autolysis and putrefaction, known as decomposition, can add yet another layer of difficulty regarding injury recognition, time of death determination, the location of the death, and the PMSI. While there are some similarities in the appearance of the body seen on external examination, the rate of progression of the changes of decomposition in a submerged body, typically in water, will differ and depend on not only body factors, but also factors inherent in the fluid medium, such as salinity, temperature (especially cooler temperatures), animal predation, colonization by bacteria and plants, wave and current action, and the effects of moving and fixed underwater objects. The general rule is that decomposition of duration of one week in the air equals two weeks in water, which equals eight weeks in the ground.[22] Saltwater portends a slower rate of decomposition than fresh water due to the retardation of bacterial proliferation as a result of the higher salinity. Bodies entrapped in deeper, cooler waters or are otherwise protected from marine predation, may have little in the way of decomposition.[23] In contrast, the body may be nearly or completely defleshed to the point of skeletonization aided by warm temperatures and/or aquatic organisms large and small which may require the expertise of the forensic anthropologist to assist with identification and assessment of taphonomic changes.[23,24] Occasionally, the floating decomposed body may present with the anterior side up allowing the face, chest, and abdomen to be exposed to the air and sun resulting in a dry, darkened, leathery, and sunburnt appearance. The exposed skin of bodies unprotected from strong sun exposure or are otherwise indoors will, in the earlier postmorterm period, have a yellow parched appearance that will gradually shrink, darken, and harden exhibiting a mummified appearance (**Figure 9.7**) Exposed body regions may also be colonized by mold. Exposed areas are also prone to animal predation and colonization by insect larvae causing postmortem injury. Other, more typical external signs of decomposition that may be evident include skin discoloration, sloughing, marbling, and bloating. These findings can mimic bruising, burn injury, and swelling, or otherwise obscure identifying characteristics and true injury. Drainage of reddish fluid from the nose and mouth, known as **purge** may also be found. Purge

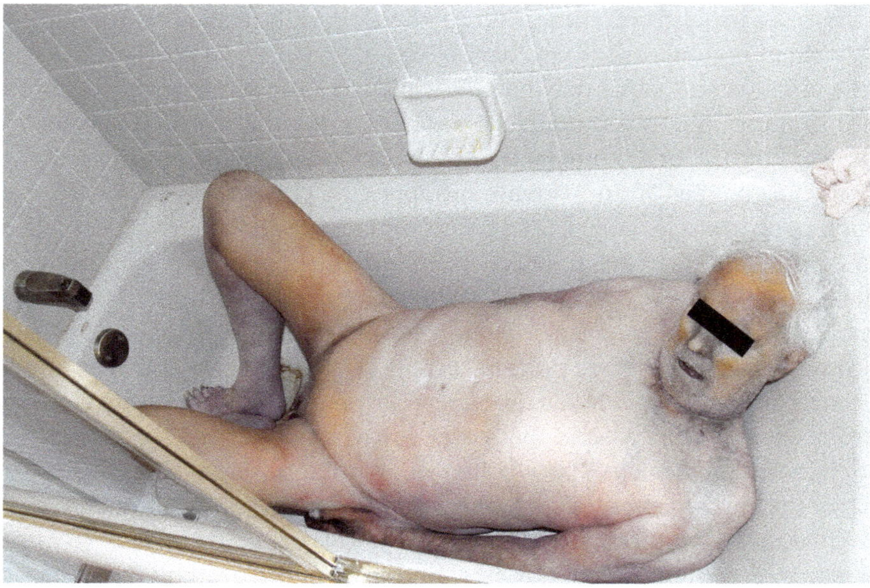

Figure 9.7 Dark-yellow and brown discoloration due to mummification of exposed skin regions in man dead of natural causes while bathing.

fluids originate from the lungs and oral and nasal passages as a result of leakage from decomposing tissue and their blood vessels, propelled out of the oral and nasal openings by the pressurized decompositional gases. A recent illustrative publication by Caruso highlights the key findings and environmental considerations important for interpretive context when examining decomposed, submerged remains.[25]

In bodies that have remained in damp, swampy environments or submerged for a prolonged period of weeks to months or longer, a special kind of decomposition can occur in which the body fats are degraded by a process known as hydrolyis to form a thick, chalky, gray-white substance known as grave wax or **adipocere (Figure 9.8).** The preservative qualities of this substance are well-recognized including preservation of anatomy and skeletal injury as well as toxicological evidence.[26] The timeframe for the development of adipocere is variable depending on factors inherent in different watery environments.

In addition to the classical changes of decomposition, other bodily findings may aid in the determination or confirmation of the PMSI, time of death, and the location of death and will require additional expertise in entomology and botany.[27, 28, 29, 30] These include colonization by land and aquatic insects and their larva, algae, and molds (**Figure 9.9**). Through their knowledge of the appearances, life cycles, and habitat of insect and plant life, forensic entomologists and botanists can be of great investigative value and aid in the reconstruction of the circumstances leading to the death, events following the death with submersion, and in decedent identification.

In bodies with little to no decomposition, or in the case in which there was no resuscitation, the more typical findings associated with either a submersion and/or drowning may be evident. Depending on the interval of time between recovery and the start of the autopsy, the hair and skin may be wet, damp, or dry. The degree of moisture or dryness should be correlated to that of any on-body clothing noted at the time of recovery and emphasizes the importance of communication with law enforcement and other

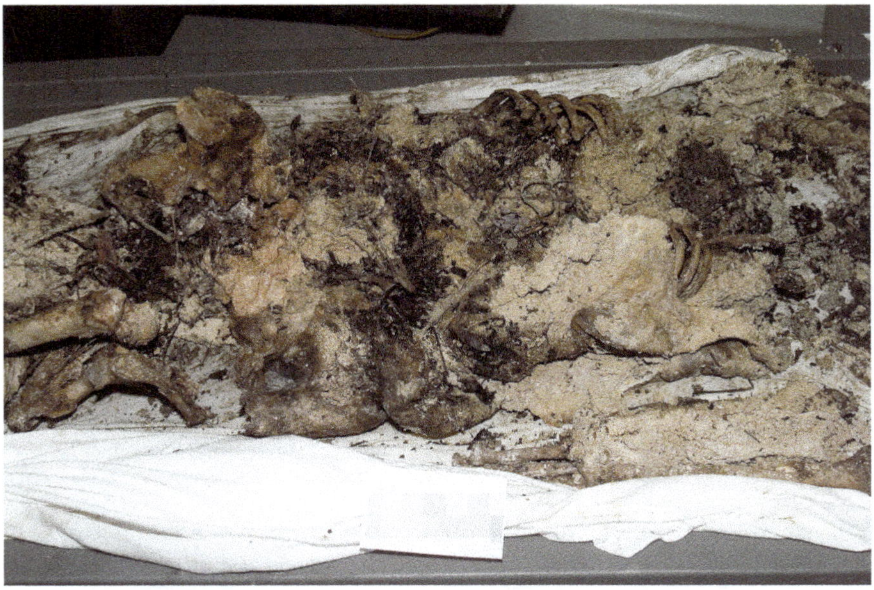

Figure 9.8 Adipocere formation within body cavities after prolonged contact with swampy woodland environment.

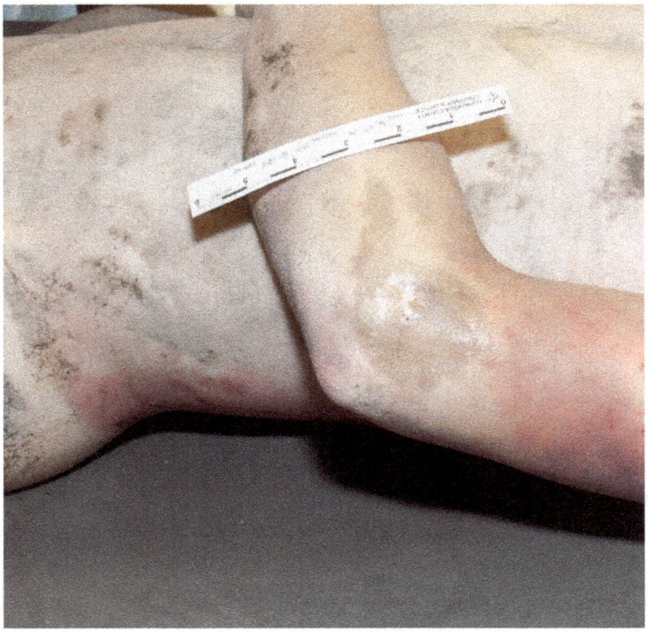

Figure 9.9 Mold growth on exposed skin of submerged drowning victim.

first responders regarding the initial condition of the body. The vital role of the C/ME medicolegal death investigator as the initial point of contact and liaison between all first responders and the forensic pathologist cannot be understated. Pink, white, or red frothy fluid, known as the **foam cone** or **froth cone** (discussed previously in Chapter 1 and shown in Figure 1.7) may be seen in the nostrils or between the lips and made more prominent by pressing on the chest. This fluid is a mixture of residual air and lung fluid, both inhaled

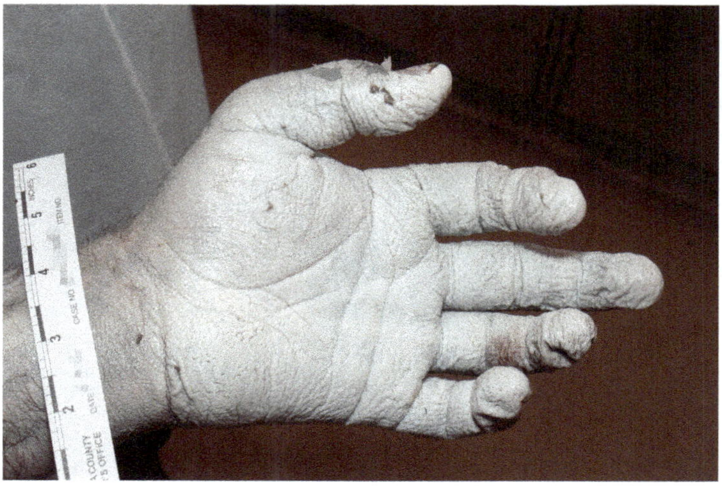

Figure 9.10 Wrinkling and pallor of palm following submersion in bathtub.

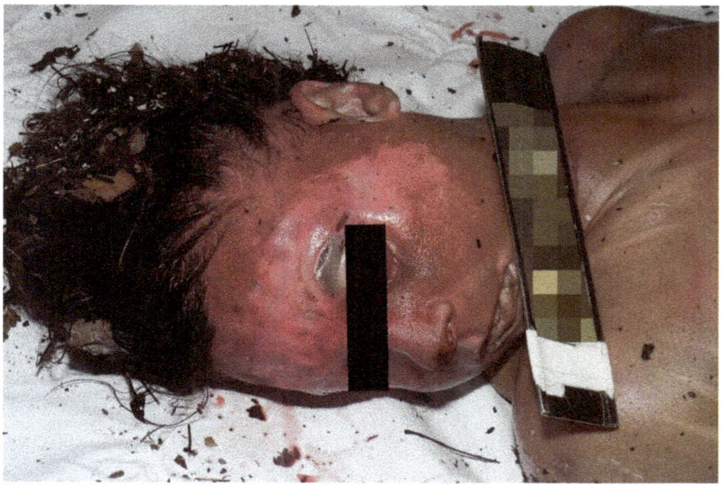

Figure 9.11 Patchy pigmentation and loss of pigmentation of skin following prolonged submersion in cold water.

and produced during the drowning process. The froth or foam cone is not specific for drowning deaths and is seen in other types of deaths such as deaths due to drug overdose, congestive heart failure, asthma, smoke inhalation, and seizures The outdated terminology "washerwoman's hands" has been used to refer to the pale, waterlogged, pruney appearance of skin of the palms and soles as a result of prolonged submersion and is sometimes seen **(Figure 9.10)**. However, with a sufficient interval of time between recovery and autopsy, this finding may not be apparent and can disappear in as little as 20–30 minutes upon exposure to open air, again emphasizing the importance of knowing the appearance and condition of the body upon recovery.[31] In contrast to pallor and wrinkling, regions of the body where skin contacts skin such as the groin, gluteal folds, and armpit regions may appear darkened and is an artifact of the effects of moisture on the skin (**Figure 9.11**)

For bodies recovered from natural water environments, aquatic debris, flora and fauna may be found on the body surfaces or within body crevices. This includes sand, silt, shell fragments, mud, insect larvae, various small aquatic animals, vegetation, mold, and algae. These may be unique to a particular aquatic environment thus after documentation, collection, and preservation of representative material for later comparison may be beneficial or otherwise consultation with the relevant expertise may be in order. These experts can also provide instruction on proper collection and preservation.

In cases suspicious of foul play, consideration that there may have been transfer of biological evidence is necessary and therefore performance of additional sampling during the external exam is in order. This will include sampling of scalp and pubic hair as well as sampling from the body orifices. As for spermatozoa contained in seminal fluid, published literature on the persistence of spermatozoa from *unsubmerged* living and deceased individuals for various lengths of time exists.[32] While the recovery of DNA from submerged biological fluids such as saliva, blood, and semen has be demonstrated, successful recovery is rapidly reduced in the setting of prolonged submersion and decomposition.[3,4,5] As a matter of routine in the thorough workup of a submerged body, particularly in the setting of unknown circumstances, sampling from the oral, vaginal, and rectal cavities can still be performed.

Internal Examination

The internal examination of the body involves systematic inspection of the organs and other anatomic structures within the head, neck, and trunk in search of supportive findings of drowning, injury, and disease processes, just as is done during the external examination. Importantly, the entire neck block should be removed to look for structural injury as well as pathology and to allow visualization of the cervical spine. Any findings may provide clues regarding the terminal events or help direct specific postmortem testing. For example, contusion or laceration of the tongue is a potential indicator of terminal seizure activity that resulted in biting of the tongue which would be relevant in someone known to have a history of seizures, a known risk factor for drowning, and would direct postmortem testing to assess for anti-seizure medication levels. Special procedures and sampling may also be warranted in the work-up of bodies recovered from watery environments. Any findings of natural disease with obvious lethality sufficient enough to preclude the drowning process versus that which could precipitate the drowning process must also be evaluated alongside any found injury.

While there is no one internal finding that is specific for drowning, an aggregate of supportive findings, interpreted within the context of any external findings and the death circumstances, helps to fortify the final determination of drowning as a cause of death. As with any findings, written and photographic documentation is necessary. Certain findings are more readily apparent in more recent or "fresh" drownings. Otherwise, the typical findings become less apparent or absent in the setting of prolonged resuscitative efforts, a lengthy hospital stay, or decomposition. In absence of these factors, lack of or very few supportive findings require consideration that there may have been a disease or injury condition at play that mitigated the drowning process and the associated outward signs or were of sufficient lethal potential to preclude the drowning process altogether. Signs of disease (or pathology) sufficient to explain death may be readily apparent during the inspection and dissection of the organs or upon examination of tissue sections under the microscope. The absence of definitive gross pathology of lethal potential may warrant submission with later microscopic examination of tissue samples and certainly will require toxicological and chemistry testing of bodily fluids collected during this phase of the autopsy.

Classically in drownings, upon removal of the chest plate, the lungs appear voluminous and boggy with touching or overlapping of the medial edges (**Figure 9.12A**). This voluminous appearance is also known as **emphysema aquosum** due to an appearance similar to the type of emphysema commonly caused by chronic tobacco smoking. On palpation, a popping sensation (known as crepitance) may be appreciated and represents residual air within some of the alveoli. Fluid accumulation in the chest cavities known as **pleural effusion** may be present and originates from the lungs. In near-drownings, in which individuals have been placed on life support, multiple organ failure and sometimes **sepsis** (clinical effects of bloodstream infection) develop, resulting in soft and discolored organs and a dusky, friable brain. In near-drowning cases with a period of hospitalization, the lungs may also appear consolidated, dark red, and rubbery, secondary to pneumonia or complications of respiratory failure with prolonged mechanical ventilation. In this context the effusion fluid within the thoracic/pleural and abdominal cavities may be encountered and indicate multiple organ failure. The lungs of drowning victims are typically heavier than normal with combined weights in excess of 1 kg reported in the literature in cases of both saltwater and freshwater drownings and without significant differences observed

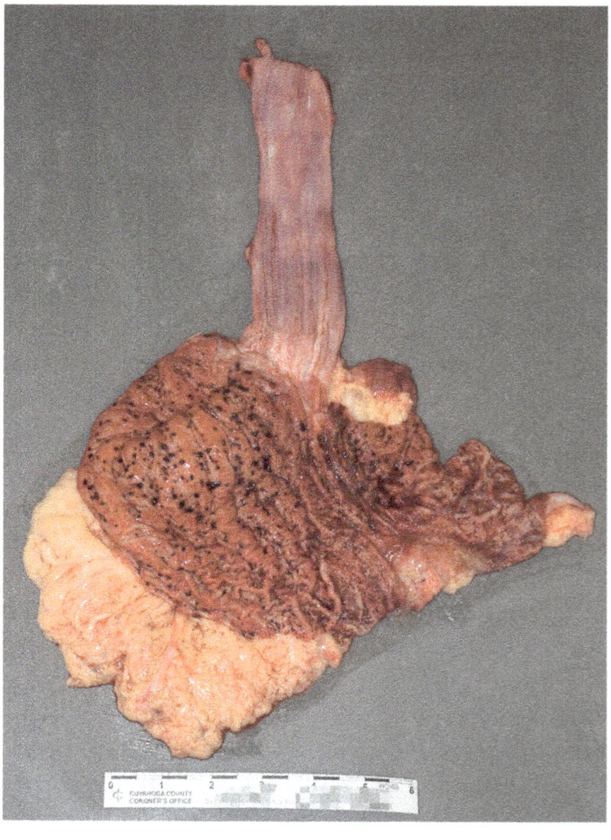

Figure 9.12 (A) Voluminous lungs with filling of the chest cavity and touching of the medial edges, (B) Emphysema aquosum of the lung with voluminous appearance, foamy fluid exuding from bronchus and blotchy dark subpleural hemorrhages, (C) foamy fluid within trachea and bronchial tubes, and (D) Frothy fluid expressed from cut surface of lung in drowning victim.

between fresh water and saltwater cases.[33, 34] Fluid in the lungs in bodies recovered from a watery environment does not necessarily rule out death by other means, whether by natural causes or injury, in which there is contemporaneous submersion and terminal aspiration/inhalation of water. With increased postmortem submersion interval and the onset of decompositional changes, decreased lung weights along with increased amounts of pleural fluid have been reported.[34] As a result of overexpansion with rupture of alveolar capillaries, blotchy, hemorrhagic areas (also referred to a **Paltauf's spots**) may be visible on the pleural surface and deeper within the tissue on further sectioning (**Figure 9.12 B.**). Red-tinged, pink, or white foamy/frothy fluid seen both in the nose and mouth and upon sectioning of the lung tissue originates from the ruptured alveolar capillaries and as a result of being churned up with any inhaled fluid, edema fluid, and residual air during the drowning process. This fluid, often copious in amount, will exude from the lumen of the sectioned larynx, trachea, and bronchial tubes as well as the cut surfaces of the lung parenchyma (**Figure 9.12 C and D**). Compression of the lung tissue often results in even more frothy fluid to flow from the cut surfaces. Contrastingly, the lung weights may not be significant and the amount of frothy fluid found in the lungs and attached airways may be underwhelming and suggestive of a so-called and speculative "dry drowning" (previously discussed in Chapter 1). There may be factors that explain the lack of excess fluid such as in the case of early recovery of the submerged drowning victim followed quickly by death, prolonged cardiorespiratory resuscitation, the effects of cold water immersion, or death from some other cause altogether. Fluid found within the larger airways may have visible silt, mud, shell fragments, and other aquatic debris inhaled during the drowning process. Representative samples of this material can be obtained, preserved, and retained for possible future in comparison to samples collected from the drowning medium to assist in confirming or refuting the drowning location.

On microscopic examination of lung sections, pink edema fluid sometimes mixed with blood (hemorrhagic edema) in a patchy distribution, alongside abnormally expanded alveolar airspaces (emphysema aquosum) can be seen and congestion/engorgement of the blood vessels is common (**Figure 9.13A**). As part of the drowning process or as a result of autolytic changes, the epithelial cells lining the more proximal airways, including the bronchial tubes, slough off into the lumen. Inhaled polymorphous aquatic debris such as sand, silt, shell fragments, diatoms, and fragments of aquatic vegetation may also be found (**Figure 9.13 B, C, and D**). Characteristic features of these debris can be further delineated by utilizing the polarization feature of an equipped microscope or by use of Nomarski interference contrast microscopy. Utilization of such techniques can further facilitate comparison of the lung fluid to the fluid within which the body was submerged. Drowning fluid extracted from lung tissue has been analyzed for the presence of diatoms to assist in the diagnosis of drowning or identification of drowning location. There is some limitation to the interpretation of the presence of diatoms as a marker for drowning due to the widespread domestic, industrial, and environmental distribution and their presence in tissues and organs in persons who have not drowned.[35,36] Conversely, the absence of diatoms does not rule out drowning. In near-drownings in which there is an in-hospital survival interval allowing for the development of complications, the presence of pink (hyaline) membranes lining the alveolar sacs representative of Acute Respiratory Distress Syndrome (ARDS) may be noted. Additionally, bronchopneumonia or the presence of inflammatory cells within the alveolar sacs may be evident (**Figure 9.14**). In air embolism cases, hemorrhage, collapse, and rupture of the alveoli may be detected both grossly and microscopically.

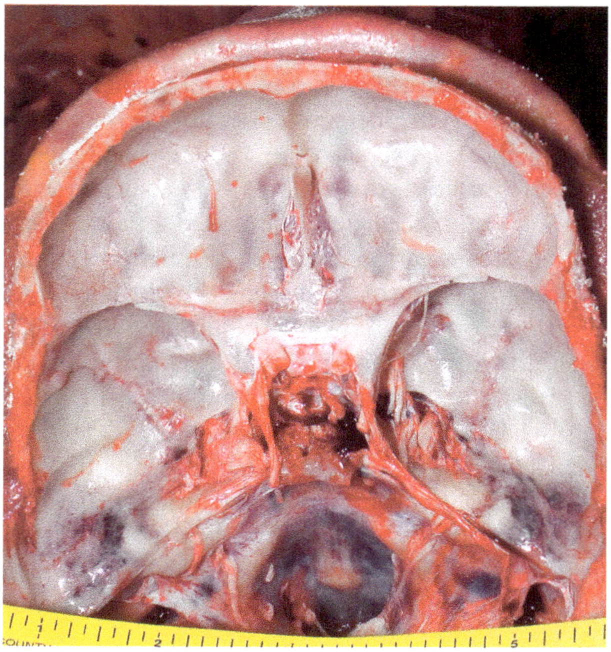

Figure 9.13 (A) Microscopic changes in emphysema aquosum with rupture and expansion of alveolar spaces (left) and pink intra-alveolar edema fluid (right) (H & E, 100× magnification), (B) particulate aquatic debris admixed with cells within airway before (A) and after (B) polarization (H and E, 400× magnification, (C) particulate aquatic debris admixed with cells within airway before (A) and after (B) polarization (H and E, 400× magnification), and (D) diatoms of multiple forms (Nomarski microscopy 40× magnification).

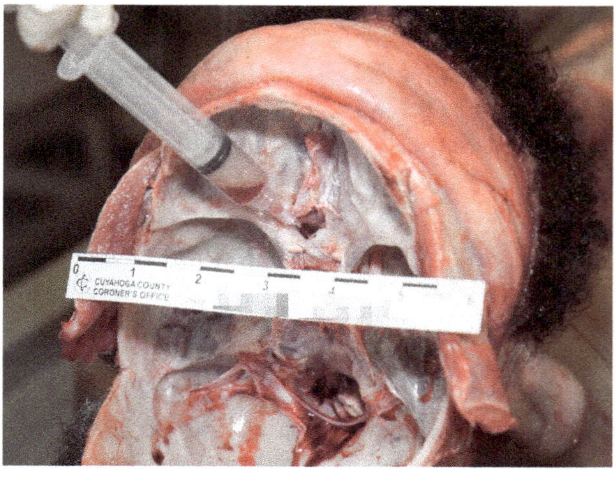

Figure 9.14 A and B Acute bronchopneumonia featuring inflammatory cells within alveoli and pink (hyaline) membranes lining alveoli (H&E 100× magnification).

As a sign of strain on the heart associated with the pathological changes of the lungs, extreme widening or dilatation of the right ventricle, which may also be filled with blood, may be observed (**Figure 9.15**). Sampling with submission of representative sections from the heart followed by microscopic examination is warranted in search for signs of inflammation that could indicate infection or an evolving myocardial infarction as well as

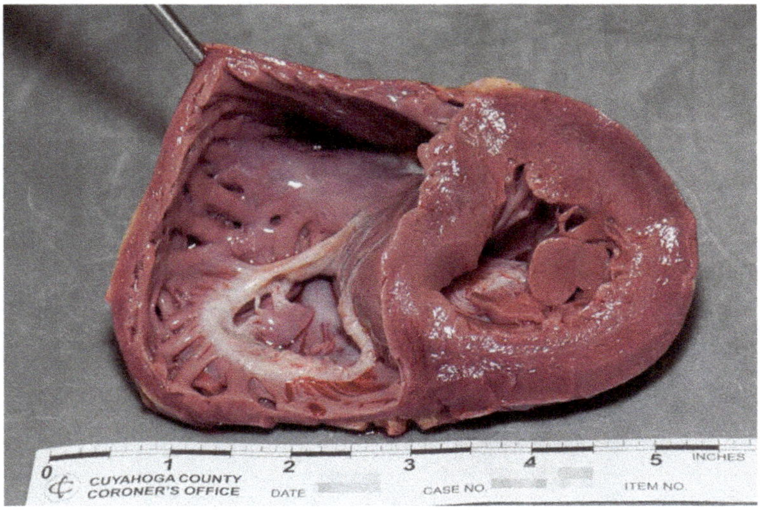

Figure 9.15 Extreme widening (dilatation) of right ventricle of heart.

scar tissue which can be a nidus for conduction system disturbance leading to arrhythmia and sudden cardiac death. Stress-related changes or changes associated with lowered oxygen levels in the heart may be found, including necrosis of the contractile apparatus and enhanced staining characteristics (hypereosinophilia). Gross and microscopic findings in the heart overlap those seen in other types of deaths, stressing the importance of the need for an aggregation of supportive findings and interpreted within the proper context of the death circumstances. Sampling of diseased coronary arteries including those with severe narrowing (stenosis) or blockage by atherosclerotic plaque is warranted and can provide further supportive evidence for progressive and evolving cardiovascular disease sufficient to be an outright cause of death or a precipitating factor in a drowning death.

Varying quantities of watery fluid admixed with aquatic debris may be found in the stomach as a result of active ingestion during the drowning process, terminal agonal swallowing, or passive flow of water into the stomach. The stomach may be full, partly full, or empty. In cases in which a cause of death other than drowning can be demonstrated, such fluid can be considered to be the result of passive entry into the stomach. Antemortem ingestion of water is another consideration. Any odors emanating from the gastric contents will be noted. For example, drinking-alcohol often has a recognizable odor, an effect of the additives and chemicals in alcoholic beverages known as **congeners**. The gastric contents will be collected and measured (typically in milliliters) and a portion or the entire contents will be submitted preferably to the toxicology lab. In cold water drownings, the presence of punctate green-black gastric erosions, also known as **Wischnewski spots or erosions (Figure 9.16)** are representative of a stress response induced by the effects of hypothermia. Microscopically, the necrosis (cell death) with reactive inflammation will be evident and are a sign of vital reaction.

As for the brain, the cerebral cortex may appear swollen due to edema as a result of the pathophysiological complications stemming from a lack of oxygen (hypoxia or anoxia) as a result of the drowning process. This is especially true in children. This appearance has been noted in freshwater drownings, but can be seen in other types of deaths, and is therefore not specific for drowning. A red-gray congested or sometimes dusky appearance

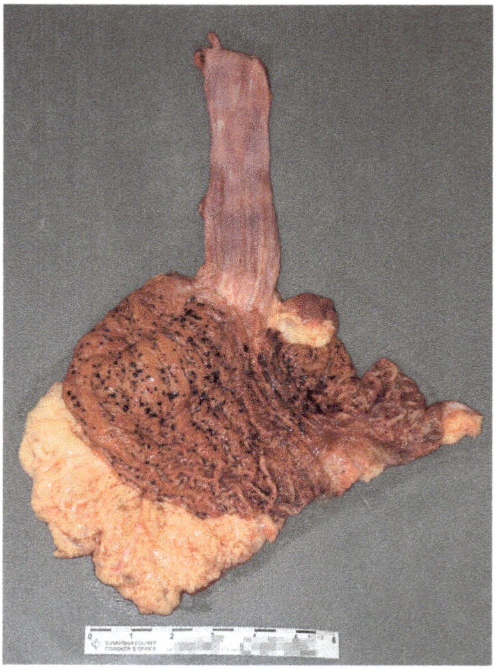

Figure 9.16 Wischbewski's spots (erosions) on lining of stomach.

has been noted in the brains of victims of saltwater drowning, but this appearance is also nonspecific, may not be seen at all, and can be seen in the brains of individuals dead as a result of drug overdose and other types of deaths. As a result of prolonged cardiopulmonary arrest with decreased or lack of blood flow to the brain, followed by resuscitation with an interval of hospital survival, intense histological staining of the neurons known as **neuronal eosinophilia** may be evident on microscopic examination and is a manifestation of anoxic-ischemic encephalopathy, a condition diagnosed clinically **(Figure 9.17)**. The prolonged lack of oxygen may lead to neuronal cell death and dropout with replacement by specialized cells called astrocytes that can be seen in individuals that have been resuscitated from a near-drowning event. The appearance of these cells alongside neuronal cell dropout in tissue sections taken from certain regions of the brain (cerebral cortex, hippocampus, and cerebellum) serve as evidence of a prior prolonged cardiorespiratory arrest, changes seen not only in near-drownings but also from other causes such as cardiovascular disease, drug overdoses, and epileptic seizures. Petechial hemorrhage of the gray and white matter substance of the brain may be the only finding in the brain in deaths due to air embolism and necrosis, or cell death may additionally affect the spinal cord especially in fatal cases with an intervening interval of survival. Upon removal of the brain, the petrous ridges may appear dark purple-red, referred to as **petrous ridge hemorrhage**, which occurs as a result of subcortical congestion with hemorrhage, purportedly as a result of pressure changes in middle ear pressure incurred by a sinking body[37] (**Figure 9.18**). Five to ten milliliters of red-tinged watery fluid sometimes admixed with aquatic debris can at times be aspirated from the **sphenoid sinus** and has been used in quantitative analysis of diatoms to support the diagnosis of drowning[38] (**Figure 9.19**). It should be noted that sphenoid sinus fluid may also be present in non-drowning cases in volumes that overlap with drowning cases. One study comparing drowning and non-drowning cases showed that the average volume

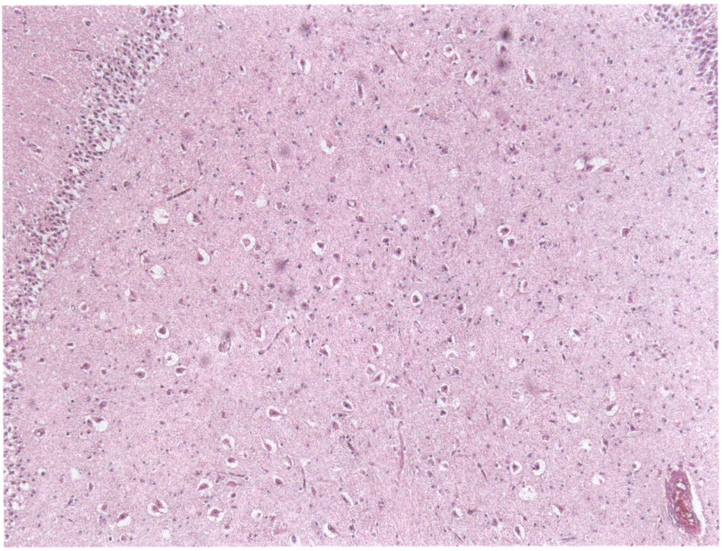

Figure 9.17 Neuronal eosinophilia with intensely pink and shrunken neurons of cerebral cortex (H and E, 100× magnification).

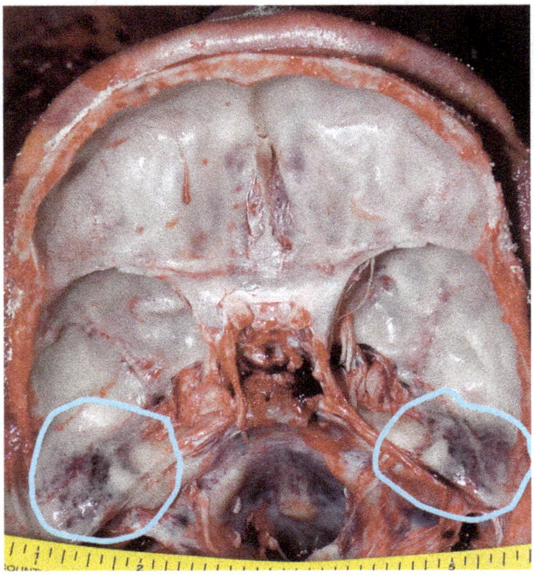

Figure 9.18 Petrous ridge hemorrhage.

of aspirate from non-drowning cases (control group) was smaller.[39] Infants and children have an underdeveloped sphenoid sinus until approximately the age of six or seven; thus, aspiration of fluid with be limited or precluded in those individuals.[40] Inspection of the bilateral middle ear cavities after removal of the temporal bone region of the middle cranial fossa may reveal hemorrhage within the middle ear canal, including rupture of the tympanic membrane, a potential finding in scuba-related deaths.

The finding of hemolytic intimal staining of the aorta in freshwater drownings, purportedly the result of the rupturing of red blood cells with release of the heme pigment,

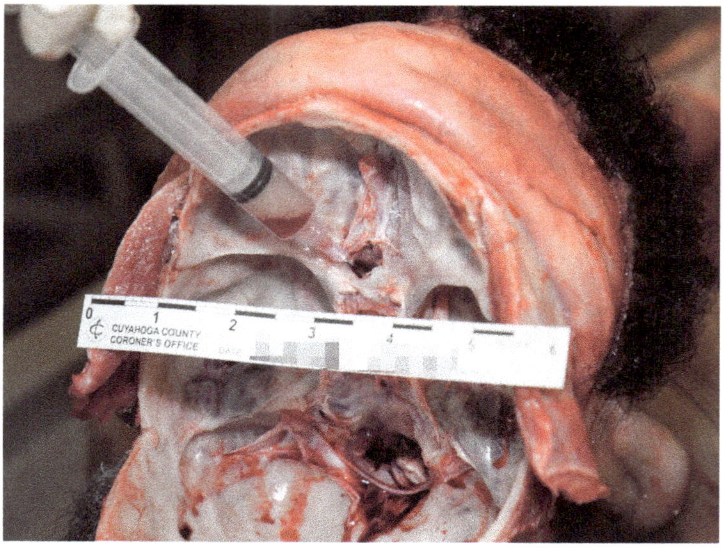

Figure 9.19 Blood-tinged fluid aspirated from sphenoid sinus.

is described, and an added supportive finding with the knowledge that this finding is also seen in other types of deaths and is a common finding in decomposed bodies[41]. Multifocal hemorrhage may be seen in the skeletal muscles of the head, neck, torso, in addition to the sclerae which, in the absence of other evidence of impact or strangulation injury, has been attributed to hypercontraction during struggling in the initial stages of drowning and elevated venous pressure[42,43].

In acute drowning deaths, the remainder of the viscera and soft tissues will exhibit varying degrees of congestion with corresponding changes seen on microscopic examination. In near-drownings with prolonged cardiorespiratory arrest, that include interval hospitalization prior to death, with the onset of complications leading to multiple organ failure, tissue sections from various organs, more commonly the liver and kidneys, may also exhibit signs of cell death and dysfunction.

On internal examination of decomposed remains, the organs and tissues will have a soft consistency, be discolored, and malodorous. The odor of decomposed remains recovered from natural water environments are particularly pungent and take on the odor of the liquid medium (ex. lake water or seawater) which permeates the tissues and fluids. Glandular tissues, the spleen and the brain may be quite soft or liquefied due to the process of autolysis and putrefaction.

As a result of impact with the water surface, bottom surface, fixed or moving above and underwater objects, predation, or collision with watercraft, blunt force or penetrating trauma of various types and patterns of distribution may be found and may or may not correspond to trauma seen on the skin surface. All injuries must be assessed and a determination made as to whether or not the injury or a combination of injuries have enough lethal potential or are otherwise contributory to the death as a result of their incapacitating effects thereby precipitating the drowning process. As a result of therapeutic intervention, a number changes that can technically be classified as injury may also be found and care must be exercised in order to not misinterpret these findings as injuries associated with or acquired during submersion or drowning. Resuscitative or therapy-associated injuries are recognized as such based on the pattern and location and correlation to associated procedures documented in the medical records. Inadvertent misplacement of intravascular catheters such as central line catheters and inguinal catheters can lead to internal bleeding with the accumulation of blood within the chest and abdominal cavities. Intubation with placement of an oral endotracheal tube can result in injury (contusion and laceration) to the lips, mouth, and the mucous membranes that line the back of the throat and upper airway. Placement of chest tube can result in lung punctures and internal bleeding within the chest cavity. Resuscitative chest compressions (manual or mechanical) can result in sternal fracture and anterior rib fractures with or without lung contusion or laceration. Resuscitative compressions can also result in contusion and laceration of the lungs and liver. Resuscitation-associated injury of the internal organs can also result in blood accumulation in the body cavities (hemothorax and hemoperitoneum).

Certain death circumstances and findings on initial evaluation at autopsy such as x-ray and other imaging studies may warrant the performance of special procedures and sampling. Cases in which barotrauma associated with SCUBA and deep-diving are suspected, such as when the skin is crepitant to palpation and the body appears bloated or swollen but without visible signs of decomposition, or when subcutaneous emphysema or thoracic cavity hypodensities are seen on pre-autopsy imaging, examination for entrapped air within blood vessels or body cavities is warranted. This includes subcutaneous dissection of the outer chest wall for the identification of pneumothorax (**Figure 9.20**), examination of the outer surface of the heart and surface of the brain for air bubbles entrapped within blood vessels, or an in situ puncture through the right ventricle in the evaluation for intraventricular air.[44] Assessment and interpretation of bubbles within blood vessels is sometimes difficult since they can be introduced during the initial stages of the autopsy and organ removal **(Figure 9.21).** In deaths following diving into shallow water in which impact of the head onto fixed underwater structures is suspected, inspection of the head to look for scalp contusion, skull fracture, and hemorrhage of the brain coverings (dural and arachnoid) is of particular importance and is part of the routine autopsy. In addition, dissection of the anterior and posterior neck including in situ examination and removal of

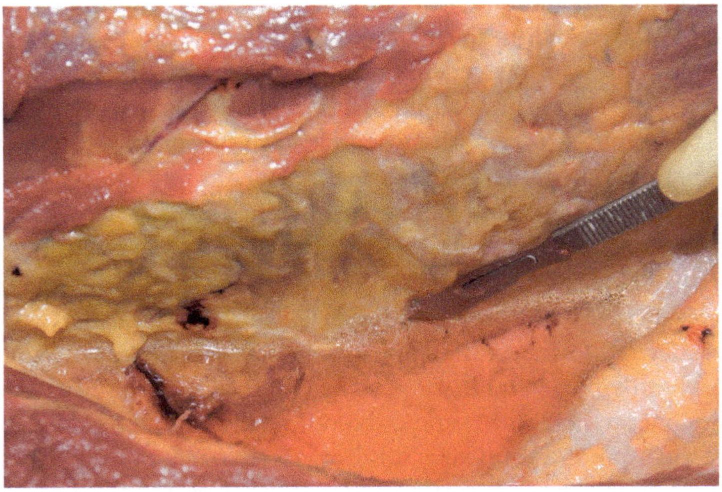

Figure 9.20 Release of air bubbles from inside chest cavity into skin flap after incision of chest wall.

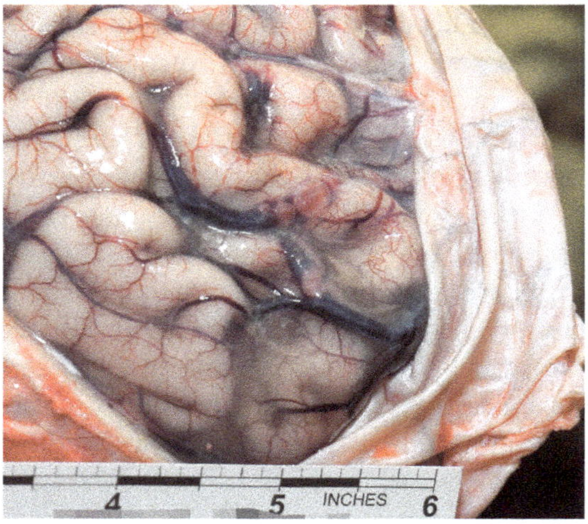

Figure 9.21 Air bubbles within blood vessels overlying brain after removal of chest and abdominal organs.

the spinal cord, is in order to look for cervical spine injury including vertebral fracture(s) and ligament tears, is necessary.[45] Whenever facial petechial hemorrhage or bruising on the outer neck surface is seen, a layer-by-layer dissection with inspection of the anterior neck structures should be done to look for and document any hemorrhages of the cervical strap muscles and associated soft tissues or hemorrhagic fracture of the laryngotracheal skeleton and hyoid bone that could indicate anterior or lateral neck compression caused by asphyxial ligature of manual strangulation or some other type of blunt or compressive force. An autopsy in a water-related death or otherwise unexplained drowning, particularly in the absence of obvious injury or natural disease, should include the dissection with removal and retention of the sinoatrial and atrioventricular nodal tissues, the source of the heart's electrical conduction system. Microscopic examination of these tissues may be warranted in order to look for pathological changes, such as inflammation and scar tissue or narrowing of feeder blood vessels, known to cause or be associated with arrhythmia and sudden cardiac death.[46] In addition, sampling with retention and storage of heart muscle and whole blood is warranted in unexplained water-related deaths inclusive of drowning deaths especially if there was a decedent or family history of fainting spells, arrhythmia, sudden cardiac arrest, seizure-like symptoms, or a family history of sudden unexplained death. Should it become necessary, these samples can be submitted to a laboratory that specializes in genetic testing for cardiac channelopathies as mutations have been identified including those associated with unexplained drowning deaths,[47]

An autopsy in a water-related death would not be complete without sampling and submission for toxicological and chemistry testing. Any results (even negative results) can be very relevant to or otherwise explain the death circumstances as it relates to impairment, incapacitation, medication non-compliance, and disease complication. Often, a great variety of bodily fluids and tissues can be obtained during the autopsy and include heart blood, peripheral (femoral) venous blood, gastric contents, bile, urine, vitreous humor fluid, cerebrospinal fluid (CSF), solid organ tissue, and skeletal muscle. In cases in which exposure to exhaust fumes from boats or other personal watercraft is suspected and especially with the appearance of cherry-red or bright-pink livor mortis and similar discoloration of the internal organs and tissues, blood or extractions from vascular organs such as spleen and lung can be tested for the presence of carbon monoxide. Alcohol testing should be requested on blood and vitreous humor fluid in cases of suspected impairment or in cases in which the odor of drinking alcohol (ethanol) is detected during the internal examination. Otherwise, comprehensive toxicological testing for not only ethanol but also illicit drugs of abuse and medications is essential in order to look for the presence of (qualitative) and level of (quantitative) one or more substances. This testing is typically performed on blood, ideally blood sampled from a peripheral site such as the femoral vein. Testing on portions of solid organs may be necessary in cases of decomposition or massive blood loss due to severe injury, in which very little or no blood or otherwise unsuitable blood is available. In cases of trauma, bloody fluid collections such as subdural hematoma, or soft tissue and intramuscular hematomas can be collected and submitted for testing. Blood collections of this sort can be particularly valuable as they are a kind of time capsule, potentially representing a drug or medication level at the time of the injury that lead to the blood collection. As an anatomically protected type of fluid, relatively resistant to changes induced in the postmortem setting as compared to blood, vitreous humor fluid (or simply vitreous fluid) is the postmortem sample of choice for evaluation of the electrolyte levels, hydration status, kidney function, and blood sugar (glucose) level and is amenable to testing for ethanol, some medications, and certain drugs of abuse. Vitreous fluid along with CSF obtained from the spinal canal have been shown in cases of saltwater drownings to have elevated sodium levels and thus may be a potentially useful adjunct in the confirmation of saltwater drownings.[48,49] Further discussion on postmortem toxicological testing appears in Chapter 10.

Infant/Fetal Toilet Deaths

In cases of fetuses or newborn infants found in toilets or other similar small bodies of water, forensic pathologists are tasked with establishing identity and maternal relationship, determination of the cause of death (drowning vs. other), and the documentation any signs of vitality. This is facilitated by meticulous scene investigation by medicolegal death investigators and law enforcement. Good death scene information provides the necessary context for the interpretation of autopsy findings and further assists in the determination of the manner of death (natural vs. accident vs. homicide vs. undetermined). Depending on the jurisdiction, there may be legal ramifications when the classification of an infant's death is homicide, which represents neonaticide, defined as the deliberated killing of a newborn infant in the first 24 hours of life.[50]

Newborn infants or fetuses recovered from toilets or other fluid-filled confined spaces such as bathtubs, basins, and buckets, may represent death resulting from natural causes including prematurity or various other maternal-fetal pathologies, obstetrical complications with unattended home delivery of an otherwise healthy viable infant, precipitous delivery with accidental drowning, or concealed delivery with accidental drowning or outright homicidal drowning. Because of the inherent physical disparity between a caretaker and an infant or even a small child, child abuse by homicidal drowning, or in conjunction with blunt force trauma and asphyxia such as suffocation, is an additional important consideration.[51] Infant mortality arising from the complications stemming from water birth, a method of easing the birthing process, has also been reported. The autopsy workup in water birth deaths in particular necessitates the identification of not only evidence of breathing but also complications associated with drowning, near-drowning, and infection. [52, 53]

In cases of home birth followed by death, corroboration of the autopsy findings with any statements given by the mother or other witnesses is important.[52] The developmental stage of an older infant or toddler in regard to mobility and access to bodies of water, whether in the bathtub, pool, pond, or other environment, may become particularly relevant in the corroboration or refuting of statements. When involving the death of the fetus or neonate in connection with a birth in the home or other out-of-hospital location, scene indicators of a recent delivery such as blood in the toilet or bathtub, bloody bedding, towels or garments, or the discovery of the placenta are important to seek out and document. In the case of an abandoned infant, DNA comparison of blood from the infant to blood of the suspected mother and to biological material recovered from the scene (bloodied clothing, towel, etc.) can help establish not only biological relationship but also help to confirm maternal physical presence at the scene. It is also very important to locate, retrieve, and submit the placenta and any blood clot, preferably in an appropriate container for biohazardous materials, along with the infant's body. The placenta may not be located because it was disposed of or discovered at a later time in which case a separate submission as a specimen would be required. Local hospitals should be contacted in an effort to confirm or rule out a recent maternal hospital admission for postpartum complications such as retained placenta tissue, excessive bleeding, or infection, and any relevant medical records including the pathology report of the placenta findings must be obtained.

The autopsy in an infant or fetal water-related death, like in other fetal and infant deaths, is preceded by a complete skeletal survey by way of x-ray or computed tomography (CT). Pre-autopsy imaging can aid not only in documenting fractures but also in documenting the presence of air in the lungs or gastrointestinal tract, a potential indicator that the infant was born alive. As an indicator of recent birth, the presence of head molding and the natural skin protectant vernix caseosa deposited on the skin surface should be noted or re-confirmed if noted initially by investigators at the death scene. The autopsy will proceed with the external and internal examination including anthropometric measurements and weighing and dissection of organs. This will aid in the determination of the developmental stage and the degree of maturation. Early on during the internal examination following in situ examination of the organs, and when quantities are available and/or sufficient, sampling and submission of blood for toxicological analysis to look for drugs and medications and for microbial culturing to look for infection is necessary. Results of these analyses may help discern maternal intoxication, maternal infection, or infant/fetal infection. Additional small samples of tissue or blood may be retained for other testing such as possible genetic testing. Documentation of supportive signs of active drowning would be especially important in cases of submersion including notation of any foamy fluid within the nostrils, mouth, lungs, and airways. As far as injury documentation, any patterned or clustered injuries, especially blunt force types and on the face and neck, are worrisome for inflicted injury inclusive of suffocation and strangulation. However, it must be discerned as to whether these injuries may represent resuscitative attempts by caretakers which ideally has been documented (including by way of recorded re-enactment) as part of the investigation of the death circumstances. Documentation of any external or internal signs of infection, natural disease, and birth defects is routine. The finding of natural disease conditions that are inherently lethal, or findings of prematurity and pre-viability in which the fetus is too immature to survive for long or at all outside the uterus, can be helpful in ruling out death by drowning. Signs of maceration signaling intrauterine fetal demise leading to stillbirth would support a historical account of the mother noting no fetal movement prior to giving birth to a stillborn infant or the absence of crying, breathing or other movement upon delivery. Microscopic confirmation of intrauterine fetal demise can be done as certain changes of the tissues and organs will be evident. Gross and microscopic examination of the placenta and any attached umbilical cord, if available, may reveal pathologies associated with premature delivery such as placental abruption, umbilical cord abnormalities, and chorioamnionitis that may be sufficient in degree and severity to explain death by natural means. Gross and microscopic examination of the *infant's* umbilical stump for signs of vital reaction and infection is also important. Evidence of a torn versus cut umbilical cord may be relevant to the described birth events including reference to any implement used to separate the umbilical cord. Microscopic examination of cutaneous, visceral, or skeletal injuries for signs of inflammation and healing stage may be useful in confirming or refuting statements regarding the timing of injury, documenting repeated physical abuse, or clarifying the time line of events leading to death. As part of a routine pediatric autopsy, adequate tissue sampling of all major organs to help identify or rule out disease processes and signs of infection as well as signs of vitality are important. This includes sampling from all lobes of the lung to assess for water inhalation (i.e. emphysema aquosum, lysis of red blood cells, and inhaled debris from water medium) as a marker for drowning and aspiration of amniotic fluid or meconium as markers for distress during birth. Lung inflammation, including pneumonia, may have arisen as a result of maternal infection of the uterus. Gross anatomic and microscopic evidence of heavy lungs with or without foamy exudation, pulmonary congestion, pulmonary edema, aspiration of gastric contents, and pneumonia, may represent complications of near-drowning event and thereby defining an interval of survival.

Retention of additional small portions of organs and bone is routine. This is done should there later arise a need to submit additional sections for microscopic examination to further clarify or characterize a pathological process seen in the original tissue sections. A pediatric pathologist should be consulted in cases with external findings of dysmorphic features and abnormal organ and placenta findings, in order to help discern or characterize any congenital abnormalities or genetic syndromes and determine if any diagnosed condition could be a cause or contributing death factor.

Like in any death of a fetus or infant that has not occurred in the presence of or with the assistance of medical personnel, especially one that is found submerged in confined, water-filled locations such as the toilet or bathtub, efforts to first determine live birth versus stillbirth along with corroboration of maternal and other witness statements are needed. Importantly, this begins even before the autopsy with eliciting statements describing the birth event and any observations of signs of life such as body movements, respiratory efforts and pulsation of the umbilical cord. The finding of signs of lung aeration, air in the gastrointestinal tract and middle ears, food in the stomach, and histological evidence of vital reaction in the umbilical cord stump are helpful criteria in supporting life for a time after birth.[54] With infant drowning, whether as a result of an intentional act by being held under water or as a result unattended or *unintended* water birth, determination of life after birth may be hampered by the pathophysiology of the drowning process. Intervening resuscitative efforts by a parent, bystander, or medical first responder may also hamper this determination during the autopsy. Like with the diagnosis of drowning itself, there is no single test that can reliably determine whether an infant or fetus was born alive, but instead the identification of an aggregate of supportive findings is necessary for this determination. Importantly, microscopic examination may reveal additional clues of aspiration inclusive of fluid and any particulate matter (originating from the drowning medium, amniotic fluid or stomach), over/under expansion of alveoli, pulmonary edema, diffuse alveolar damage, and pneumonia as these can be helpful in the determination of the events that transpired near the time of death or during the interval time of survival prior to death. Comparative microscopic examination of a sample of drowning medium, lung tissue, and gastric material may provide supportive or exclusionary information in regard to location of drowning or evidence of signs of life. Even chemical analysis of the drowning media for comparison with bodily fluids can be done.[51]

Beginning with the in situ examination of the lungs, findings of salmon-colored, puffy, overlapping lungs with blunted edges indicate that respiration has taken place with filling of the lungs with oxygen-containing air. Incompletely aerated lungs, in which the infant did not take complete breaths, may have a mosaic appearance with patches of pink puffy areas alternating with darker sunken areas which represent areas of atelectasis. By contrast, lungs that appear collapsed into the chest cavity, are darker red, have a slightly rubbery consistency much like the liver tissue, have sharp edges, and that lack crepitance on palpation, represent absence of respiration. It is important to keep in mind that the lungs of liveborn infants may be devoid of air and those of stillborn infants may have the appearance of aeration.[54] Furthermore, incompletely developed lungs, such as in the case of prematurity, may not be able to support complete aeration. The so-called **hydrostatic or float test** is a technique applied to the lungs, viscera, and intestines gastrointestinal tract to aid in the determination of life after birth, namely via detection of air contained in these tissues as a result of breathing and swallowing, after birth. For evaluation of aeration of the lungs, preferably the entire heart-lung block rather one lung is resected and placed into a container of water and observed for floating. If the lungs float (i.e., positive float test), this indicates that the infant inspired air into the lungs, and thus was alive for some period of time. If the lung tissue sinks, this indicates that the infant did not take a breath (**Figure 9.22A and B**). A portion of the infant's liver should also be dropped into a small container of tap water to assess for flotation. This serves as an internal control since fresh

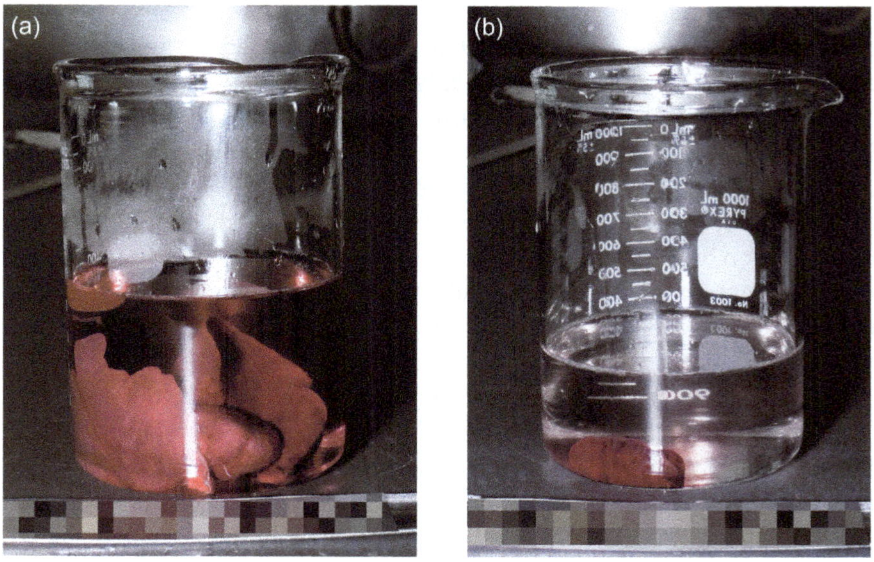

Figure 9.22 (A) Negative float test of lungs with attached heart and (B) portion of lung tissue.

(nondecomposed) liver will sink. If the portion of liver floats, some degree of decomposition with gas production has taken place and would invalidate any positive result seen in the lung test, as the formation of decompositional gases would explain the flotation of the lung tissue. Moreover, a history of airway resuscitation and/or mechanical ventilation, especially when prolonged, would make a positive float test uninterpretable. A negative lung float test also does not rule out the possibility of a liveborn infant in the case of a water birth in which water is inhaled instead of air. Postmortem Computed Tomography (PMCT) has been shown to be a helpful adjunct to the lung float test and possible differentiation between artificially and naturally aerated lungs. [55] Microscopic examination of the lung tissue may be notable for expansion of the alveoli as an indication of inhalation of air. Overexpansion of the alveoli can cause their rupture and may be especially prominent in cases where mouth-to-mouth resuscitation or intubation with mechanical ventilation has been performed. This overexpansion translates to an emphysema-like appearance, similar to that which is seen in drowning. Otherwise, unexpanded lungs will have a collapsed (atelectatic) appearance on both gross and microscopic examinations. The stomach and/or intestines can be submerged in a similar fashion and if air-filled will float resulting in a positive test and would not be interpretable in the setting of decomposition with the production of associated gases. Any food found such as milk within the stomach will provide additional evidence of life after delivery, and the combination of a positive float test with food in the stomach in an infant found in the toilet indicates foul play.

References

1. D'Ovidio C, Rosato E, Carnevale A. An unusual case of murder-suicide: The importance of studying knots. *J Forensic Leg Med* 2017;45:17–20.
2. Todt M, Ast F, Wolff-Maras R, et al. Suicide by drowning: A forensic challenge. *Forensic Sci Int* 2014;240: e22–24.
3. Sweet J, Shutler GG. Analysis of salivary DNA evidence from a bite mark on a body submerged in water. *J Forensic Sci* 1999;44(5):1069–72.
4. Borde YM, Tonnany MB, Champod C. Study on the effects of immersion in river water and seawater on blood, saliva, and sperm placed on objects mimicking crime scene exhibits. *Can Soc Forensic Sci J* 2008;41(3):149–63.
5. Frippiat C, Gastaldi A, Van Grunderbeeck S. Persistence of immersed blood and hair DNA: A preliminary study based on casework. *J Forensic Leg Med* 2017;51:1–8.
6. Crainic K, Paraire F, Leterreux M, et al. Skeletal remains presumed submerged in water for three years identified using PCR-STR analysis. *J Forensic Sci* 2002;47(5):1025–27.
7. Byard RW, James RA, Heath KJ. Recovery of human remains after shark attack (case report). *Am J Forensic Med Pathol* 2000;27(3):256–59.
8. Khoo LS, Hasmi AH, Mahmood MS, Vanezis P. Underwater DVI: Simple fingerprint technique for positive identification. *Forensic Sci Int* 2016;266:e4–e9.
9. Plaetsen SV, De Letter E, Piette M, Van Parys G, Casselman JW, Verstraete K. Postmortem evaluation of drowning with whole body CT. *Forensic Sci Int* 2015;249:35–41.
10. Byard RW, Ross A, Gilbert JD. Pathologic features of fatal shark attacks. *Am J Forensic Med Pathol* 2000;21(3):225–29.
11. Byard RW, Ross A, Gilbert JD. Diagnostic problems associated with cadaveric trauma from animal activity. *Am J Forensic Med Pathol* 2002;23(3):238–44.
12. Vanin S, Zancaner S. Post-mortal lesions in freshwater environment. *Forensic Sci Int* 2011;212(1–3):e18–20.
13. Haglund WD. The disappearance of soft tissue and the disarticulation of human remains from aqueous environments. *J Forensic Sci* 1993;38(4):806–15.

14. Sinton TJ, Byard RW. Pathological features of fatal crocodile attacks in Northern Australia. *J Forensic Sci* 2016;61(6):1553–55.
15. Shatz DV, Kirton OC, McKenney MG, et al. Personal watercraft crash injuries: An emerging problem. *J Trauma* 1998;44(1):198–201.
16. Perilli G, DiBattista B, Montana A, et al. A rare case of a scuba diver's death due to propeller injuries of a desalination pump. *J Forensic Leg Med* 2015;32:21–24.
17. Ihama Y, Ninomiya K, Noguchi M, et al. Fatal propeller injuries: Three autopsy case reports. *J Forensic Leg Med* 2009;16(7):420–23.
18. Xhemali B, Vyshka G, Sinamati A, Shaqiri E. Pattern of lethal trauma among swimmers colliding with a personal watercraft. *Int Marit Health* 2017;68(4):187–89.
19. Capovilla M, Durigon M, de la Grandmaison GL. An original cause of drowning in an industrial environment. *Am J Forensic Med Pathol* 2007;28(1):91–3.
20. Mugdlimath AB, Sane MR, Zine KU, Hiremath RM. Quenching tank: Accidental drowning in hot quenching oil. *Med Leg J* 2017;85(2):108–110.
21. Karger B, Suggeler S, Brinkman B. Electrocution-autopsy study with emphasis on "electrical petechiae". *Forensic Sci Int* 2002;126:210–13.
22. Spitz DJ. Investigation of bodies in water. In *Medicolegal investigation of death—Guidelines for the application of pathology to crime investigation*, ed. W. U. Spitz, 846–81. 4th ed. Springfield, IL: Charles C Thomas Publisher Ltd., 2006.
23. Ellingham STD, Perich P, Tidball-Binz M. The fate of human remains in maritime context and feasibility for forensic humanitarian action to assist in their recovery and identification. *Forensic Sci Int* 2017;279:229–34.
24. Haglund WD, Sorg MH. Human remains in water environments. In *Advances in forensic taphonomy: Method, theory, and archeological perspectives*, eds. WD Haglund and MH Sorg, 201–18. 1st ed. Boca Raton, FL: CRC Press, 2001.
25. Caruso JL. Decomposition changes in bodies recovered from water. *Acad Forensic Pathol* 2016;6(1):19–27.
26. Ubelaker DH, Zarenko KM. Adipocere: What is known after over two centuries of research *Forensic Sci Int* 2011;208:167–72.
27. Heaton V, Lagden A, Moffaat C, Simmons T. Predicting the postmortem submersion interval for human remains recovered from the U.K. waterways. *J Forensic Sci* 2010;55:302–7.
28. Doberentz E, Madea B. Estimating the time of immersion of bodies found in water-an evaluation of a common method to estimate the minimum time interval of immersion. *Revista Espanola de Medicine Legal* 2010;36(2):51–61.
29. Wallace JR, Merritt RW, Kimbirauskas R, et al. Caddisflies assist with homicide case: Determining a postmortem submersion interval using aquatic insects. *J Forensic Sci* 2008;53(1):219–21.
30. Van Daalen MA, De Kat DS, Oude Grotebevelsborg BFL, et al. An aquatic decomposition scoring method to potentially predict the postmortem submersion interval of bodies recovered from the North Sea. *J Forensic Sci* 2017;62(2):369–73.
31. Reh H. Early postmortem course of washerwoman's skin of the fingers. *Rechtsmed Z* 1984;92(3):183–88.
32. Collins KA, Bennett AT. Persistence of spermatozoa and prostatic acid phosphatase in specimens from deceased individuals during varied postmortem intervals. *Am J Forensic Med Pathol* 2001;22(3):228–32.
33. Copeland AR. An assessment of lung weights in drowning cases: The Metro Dade County experience from 1978–1082. *Am J Forensic Med Pathol* 1985;6(4):301–304.
34. Kringsholm B, Filskov A, Kock K. Autopsied cases of drowning in Denmark 1987–1989. *Forensic Sci Int* 1991;52:85–92.
35. Ago K, Hayashi T, Ago M, Ogata M. The number of diatoms recovered from lungs and other organs in drowning deaths in bathwater. *Leg Med* 2011;13:186–90.

36. Kakizaki E, Yukawa N. Simple protocol for extracting diatoms from lung tissues of suspected drowning cases within 3 h: First practical application. *Forensic Sci Int* 2015;251:179–85.
37. Robbins RD, Sekhar HK, Siverls V. Temporal bone histopathologic findings in drowning victims. *Arch Otolaryngol Head Neck Surg* 1988;114(9):1020–23.
38. Lin CY, Yen WC, Hsieh HM, Tsai LC, et al. Diatomological investigation in sphenoid sinus fluid and lung tissue from cases of suspected drowning. *Forensic Sci Int* 2014;244:111–15.
39. Bohnert M, Ropohl D, Pollak S. Forensic medicine significance of the fluid content of the sphenoid sinuses. *Arch Kriminol* 2002;209(5–6):158–64.
40. Spitz WU. Investigation of bodies in water. In *Medicolegal investigation of death-Guidelines for the application of pathology to crime investigation*, ed. W U Spitz, 846–81. 4th ed. Springfield Il: Charles C Thomas Publisher Ltd., 2006.
41. Tsokos MT, Cains G, Byard RW. Hemolytic staining of the intima of the aortic root in freshwater drowning. *Am J Forensic Med Pathol* 2008;29:128–30.
42. Puschel K, Schulz F, Darrmann I, et al. Macromorphology and histology of intramuscular hemorrhage in cases of drowning. *Int J Legal Med* 1999;112(2):101–06.
43. Alexander RT, Jentzen JM. Neck and scleral hemorrhage in drowning. *J Forensic Sci* 2011;56(2):522–25.
44. Spitz WU. Selected procedures at autopsy. In *Medicolegal investigation of death—Guidelines for the application of pathology to crime scene investigation*, ed. W. U. Spitz, 1243–74. 4th ed. Springfield, IL: Charles C Thomas Publisher Ltd., 2006.
45. Voland C, Vilarino R, Grabherr S, et al. Fatal cervical spine injury from diving accident. *Am J Forensic Med Pathol* 2015;36(3):216–18.
46. Gulino SP. Examination of the cardiac conduction system: Forensic application in cases of sudden cardiac death. *Am J Forensic Med Pathol* 2003;24(3):227–38.
47. Tester DJ, Medeiros-Domingo A, Will ML, Ackerman MJ. Unexplained drownings and the cardiac channelopathies: A molecular autopsy series. *Mayo Clin Proc* 2011;86(10):941–47.
48. Garland J, Tse R, Oldmeadow C et al. Elevation of postmortem vitreous humour sodium and chloride levels can be used as a reliable test in cases of suspected saltwater drowning when the immersion time is less than one hour. *Forensic Sci Int* 2016;266:338–342.
49. Garland J, Philcox W, Kilak K, et al. Elevated cerebrospinal fluid sodium and chloride leves in a saltwater drowning death. *Am J Forensic Med Pathol* 2019;40(3):258–61.
50. Phillips B, Ong, BB. Was the infant born alive?: A review of postmortem techniques used to determine live birth in cases of suspected neonaticide. *Acad Forensic Pathol* 2018;8(4):875–93.
51. Griest KJ, Zumwalt RE. Child abuse by drowning. *Pediatrics* 1989;83(1):18–22.
52. Byard RW, Zuccollo JM. Forensic issures in cases of water birth fatalities. *Am J Forensic Med Pathol* 2010;31(3):258–60.
53. Dressler J, Schmidt U, Hanisch U, et al. Neonatal freshwater drowning after birth in the bathroom. *Am J Forensic Med Pathol* 2011;32(2):119–23.
54. Phillips B, Ong BB. “Was the Infant Born Alive?”-A review of postmortem changes used to determine live birth in cases of suspected neonaticide. *Am J Forensic Med Pathol* 2018;8(4):874–93.
55. Mazuchowski EL, Franco DM, Berran PJ, Harcke HT. The virtual hydrostatic test. *Am J Forensic Med Pathol* 2017;38(1):24–28.

The Forensic Toxicological Aspects of Deaths Due to Drowning and Bodies Recovered from Fluid Environments

10

ERICA J. ARMSTRONG

Introduction

A body recovered from within a fluid environment may have an obvious or potentially lethal injury, signs supportive of drowning, a combination of both, or no visible changes. The presence of extensive decomposition or alteration by insects, animals, and aquatic life presents additional challenges for the determination of the identity and cause and manner of death. Historical and scene information can provide vital clues in the reconstruction of terminal events and also play a role in the determination of cause and manner of death. The presence or evidence of use of drugs and prescription medications, whether at the death scene, by history, by review of medical records, or during autopsy, will help to focus postmortem toxicological testing (Figure 10.1). Even in the absence of evidence of drug and medication use, postmortem toxicological testing has relevance and importance. This fact was demonstrated in a retrospective study of a group of deaths in which the initial investigation did not reveal evidence of substance abuse. Subsequent toxicology testing, however, revealed the use of at least one substance that was pertinent to death circumstances in one-third of those cases.[1] The identification of drugs and medications in bodily fluids and tissues can provide clues regarding the medical and psychiatric history and the cause of death. Depending on the specific drug or medication revealed by the testing and with knowledge of its end-organ effects, the level found may be sufficient to preclude the drowning process with few or absent supportive findings of drowning noted at autopsy. In multidrug intoxications, the cumulative or synergistic effects along with any propensity to precipitate drowning must be considered, such as the effect of sedation that causes impairment to a degree that prevents extrication from or leads to collapse with submersion into a watery environment. The knowledge that many medications are used to treat more than one ailment (known as off-label use) is also useful for the forensic pathologist in the construction of the medical and psychiatric history (i.e. some antidepressants are also prescribed for pain, anxiety disorders, and seizure disorders).

Impairment by drugs or alcohol confers increased risk for water-related injury and death, whether due solely to physical injury, drowning, or a combination of both. Medical conditions such as seizure disorder and certain heart ailments, in which medication levels used to treat those conditions are below the therapeutic range, may suddenly decompensate and potentially place an individual at increased risk for drowning or sustaining injury,

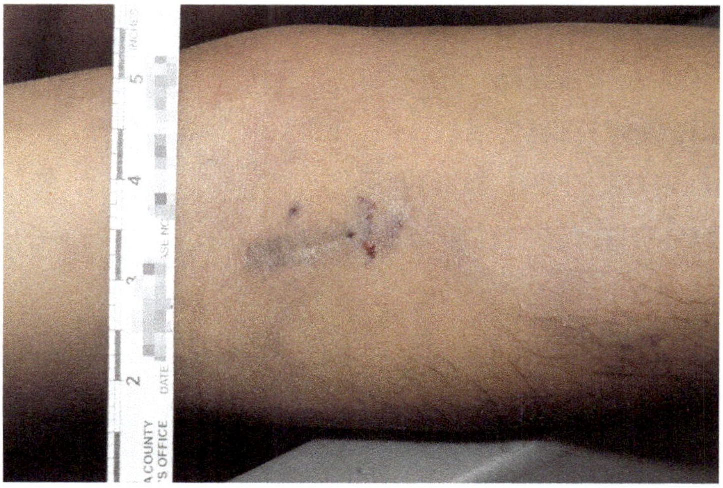

Figure 10.1 Linear track scar with superimposed recent needle punctures on antecubital fossa of a heroin addict.

injury during routine or recreational water-related activities. The effects of exposure to certain chemicals and gases while in or around water are other potential predisposing factors. The results of a comprehensive toxicological analysis can not only reveal the cause of death but also help to provide explanation as to how and why a motor vehicle accident, incapacitating injury, or drowning occurred.

Postmortem forensic toxicology involves the acquisition of body fluids or tissues from the deceased in order to determine the presence (**qualitative analysis**) and amount (**quantitative analysis**) of drugs and medications in order to aid in the determination of whether or not they constitute a direct cause or contributing factor in the death. Any finding must always be interpreted within the context of the information about the circumstances leading to death, death scene information, decedent, history, and autopsy findings. Consultation with a postmortem forensic toxicologist who has extensive knowledge of drugs and medications, their actions within the body, their significance in the postmortem setting, and the technologies used to identify them can be extremely beneficial in the interpretation of test results. When a death is determined to be caused solely by the effects of a drug or medication, the statement on the death certificate may take one of several forms, including "acute intoxication by …" "acute intoxication by the combined effects of …," or "the toxic effect(s) of …" with the inclusion of specific substance(s) identified as the cause of death.

Similar to toxicological testing in a clinical hospital setting, interpretation of results generated from postmortem (forensic) toxicological testing must take into account a number of considerations. Knowledge of the medical and psychiatric history, including diseases that affect the heart, liver, and kidneys and certain mental health disorders, along with medications prescribed to treat those conditions, is necessary. Moreover, a history of substance-use disorder inclusive of the *pattern* of misuse of illicit drugs and medications is important to obtain. Other considerations specific to the postmortem setting are important. Death circumstances, including any recent onset of symptoms relative to a new or pre-existing illness, any interval of in-hospital survival, and the extent of any resuscitative efforts, are necessary to consider. The importance of the autopsy can never be understated as autopsy findings can confirm the history of chronic disease of the organs and chronic drug and medication misuse. Autopsy can also reveal previously unknown but pertinent chronic medical conditions.

Interpretation of results generated from postmortem (forensic) toxicological testing requires a fundamental working knowledge of certain limitations and knowledge of inter-individual and intra-individual differences of how drugs and medications act in the body. Ranges of toxic and lethal levels are reported in the clinical and postmortem toxicology-related literature and reference textbooks and commonly include information regarding the limitations of interpretation of drug and medication levels in the postmortem setting. Drug and medication levels obtained in the clinical setting are not necessarily interchangeable or comparable to those obtained from postmortem testing as the matrix tested may differ in type (i.e. whole blood vs. serum vs. plasma) and the quality of postmortem samples can be a factor (i.e. hemolyzed or decomposed blood). Drug and medication levels generated from postmortem testing are not necessarily reflective of those levels at the time of death, and knowledge of the interval of time following death becomes important as the longer the interval, the more time for a drug or medication to be affected by factors inherent in the blood. Redistribution or continued breakdown of certain drugs and medications can continue in the postmortem period leading to spuriously elevated levels, lower than expected levels, levels that are below the limits of detection, or no drug or medication at all. This postmortem redistribution and breakdown can be exacerbated by conditions seemingly innocuous like body recovery, handling and transport to the C/ME office or in the setting of a prolonged postmortem interval (including postmortem submersion interval) with the onset of decomposition. Concerning the amount of consumption (dose) of a drug or medication, there is variability in what is toxic or lethal and a lethal dose in one individual may not necessarily be lethal for another individual. This highlights the importance of considering whether tolerance to a particular drug or medication based on past use or the *pattern* of use or any period of abstinence are factors. A deceased individual may have a level that is unexpectedly low or at best in the toxic range rather than the expected higher lethal range as a result of lowered or loss of tolerance due to periodic abstinence, such as during incarceration. Genetic factors may also be at play with inter-individual variability in how slow or how rapid a drug or medication is metabolized. Any interval of time before death, in which there would be continued metabolization of a drug or medication, is another important consideration that may also explain lower than expected levels. And finally, due to limitations including those mentioned above, determination of the dose that an individual consumed based on the postmortem test result cannot be reliably done.

Sampling with the submission of bodily fluids and tissues is imperative in all water-related deaths. A variety and abundance of body fluids are available for collection during the autopsy in most cases. Vitreous fluid, blood (central and peripheral), gastric fluid, urine, skeletal muscle, visceral, adipose tissue, sequestered hematomas, and even body hair are all candidates for submission and analysis. The choice of matrices will be limited or suboptimal in cases with prolonged submersion and decomposition, but even with these limitations, qualitative or quantitative results may still be possible.[2] The availability of blood, particularly from the preferred peripheral site, may be limited in cases of extensive injury with massive blood loss or disruption of blood vessels. In decomposed cases in which sufficient quantities of bodily fluids such as blood and urine cannot be obtained, toxicological analysis of adipocere has yielded useful results.[3] In cases in which the urinary bladder is empty, sterile water can be instilled into the bladder and the resulting fluid from the "bladder wash" can be submitted for analysis, which will yield only qualitative information. Qualitative analysis of urine can provide information in regard to either recent and/or historic use of a drug or medication, whereas qualitative and quantitative analysis on blood and vitreous samples can provide evidence of more recent or acute intoxication by a drug or medication.

Sequestered blood clots (also known as hematomas) that form as a result of injury can be a useful testing matrix as they can provide valuable information as to the approximate degree of impairment or compliance with a prescribed medication regimen around the time when the injury was sustained. In essence, these collections represent a kind of time capsule in which the metabolism of certain drugs or medication would be halted as they are no longer being circulated to the liver, the center of metabolism. An example of this type of specimen is the subdural blood clot, which is a collection of blood under the tough membrane that overlies the brain, known as the dura. Subdural blood clots may form in individuals who have sustained blunt force injury to the head. This is a particularly valuable form of the blood sample that can be collected and submitted for analysis of drugs, medications and alcohol, and the resulting levels can reflect the degree of intoxication or impairment just prior to death. Analysis of hematomas resulting from blunt force trauma that have formed elsewhere in the body such as deep within skeletal muscle can reveal similar information.

Other types of tissues can be obtained for testing and may be all that is available in certain cases. In cases of extensive blood loss or decomposition, portions of solid organs, skeletal muscle, bones, and even teeth can be collected and tested. Hair and fingernails may be collected in cases of suspected long-term poisoning by chemicals and heavy metals. Extensively charred bodies often have surprisingly well-preserved internal anatomy including blood vessels containing blood that is readily available for sampling. Testing of teeth and bones in these cases may also be beneficial. Maggots that have fed on the body can be collected and analyzed qualitatively for the presence of drugs and medications.

Acquisition and testing of hospital blood, urine, and other bodily fluid samples taken from patients in the emergency department and early on in the hospitalization are an extremely important part of the medicolegal death investigation of non-natural deaths such as drug overdoses, motor vehicle collision deaths, and water-related deaths. Peripheral blood, typically drawn from the extremities into red-top tubes or into serum separator tubes are the preferred type of blood sample. Bodily fluid samples like blood and urine are kept in the hospital laboratory only for a limited period of time; therefore, time is of the essence in pursuit of these samples. Early-admission hospital samples, especially blood samples, should be obtained as soon as possible in cases of water-related deaths for toxicological analysis. The earliest samples that can be obtained are preferred since they represent the samples taken before significant amounts of medications and intravenous fluids are given, which can have a dilutional effect on drugs and medications of interest and can therefore make an interpretation as to the magnitude of their effects less certain. The passage of time also means that the metabolism of drugs and medications during the period of survival before death continues with further reduction in drug and medication levels. The diagnosis and treatment of patients suspected to have overdosed involve initial screening of the urine for the presence of alcohol, illicit drugs, and certain medications to guide the administration of therapy. Screening provides information on the presence or absence (positive or negative) of a substance in the urine and may or may not be reflective of the presence of those substances in the blood. Blood may be similarly screened with reporting of a positive or negative result only and not an actual numeric value, which represents the drug/medication level or concentration. The reported *blood* level as opposed to any level reported in other matrices such as the urine is an important point of focus as the level in blood can be a good indicator of the acute effects on the organs. Outward signs of acute effects on the brain and central nervous system include impairment of thinking and motor skills. Not all hospital tests for drugs and medications are screening tests. Examples of hospital testing in which levels are reported are serum blood alcohol testing in patients suspected to have acute ethanol intoxication and therapeutic monitoring of certain medications such as those used to treat heart failure and seizures.

Ethanol

Ethanol (aka drinking alcohol, ethyl alcohol, or spirit) is by far the most common substance associated with recreational water-related deaths. Previous studies have shown that drowning was most often the cause of death associated with recreational water activities, with alcohol, with its known physiological and psychological effects, detected in 30–70% of those individuals. [4] A collective analysis of a few past studies has indicated that the risk of death associated with drinking during recreational boating increased approximately ten times with a blood alcohol concentration (BAC) of 0.10 g/100 ml (0.10 g/dl or 0.10 g%), with an increased risk still occurring at lower BACs.[4]

Ethanol is the common ingredient in alcoholic beverages made by the fermentation of sugar (glucose). This substance is also an ingredient in cough medicines, mouthwashes, and other medicinal preparations and is also used as a solvent in industry. It is used therapeutically to treat poisoning by methanol and ethylene glycol (found in some antifreeze fluids). It is also produced in small amounts inside the body (*in vivo*) as a by-product of bacterial metabolism in the intestines.[5] Ethanol is a drug with depressant activity on the central nervous system (CNS) and respiratory system, more apparent with increasing blood levels, and with widespread effects upon emotion, thought processes, and motor skills. Ethanol also has direct toxic effects on the heart, and chronic excessive use can lead to permanent heart disease. The major metabolite of ethanol, **acetaldehyde**, has direct toxic effects on the liver, the gastrointestinal tract, and the pancreas. Chronic excessive alcohol use can cause fatty liver disease, cirrhosis, oral and gastric cancers, and pancreatitis. The CNS and liver effects are increased or potentiated when alcohol is combined with other CNS and respiratory depressants, such as antidepressants, barbiturates, benzodiazepines, opiates, and marijuana.[6] The toxic cardiac effects are also increased when alcohol ingestion is combined with cocaine use. With increasing BAC, subjective or observed changes generally progress from euphoria and relaxation (0.05 g/dl or 0.05%) to impairment of motor, sensory, and cognitive functions (0.18–0.30 g/dl) to coma and death (>0.35 g/dl).[6] These effects cover the seven stages of alcohol intoxication: sobriety, euphoria, excitement, confusion, stupor, coma, and death.[6] These effects are dependent in part upon the frequency and pattern of use, with lessened effects on chronic users for a given BAC.[6] The effects of BAC levels as low as 0.015 g/dl are also detectable in the operation of motorized vehicles, including cars, watercraft, and airplanes.[6] Currently within the United States, an individual with a measured BAC of 0.08 or 0.10 g/dl or greater, operating a noncommercial vehicle, is considered to be operating under the influence.

Upon ingestion and with the passage of time, the distribution of ethanol within the body involves a series of steps: **absorption, distribution, metabolism**, and **excretion**.[7] Upon ingestion, it is *absorbed* by diffusion from the stomach and small intestine into the blood and further distributed via the arterial and venous blood circulation to the body fluids and tissues in proportion to their water content, since ethanol is miscible in water. Ethanol will also diffuse from the pulmonary capillary blood into the alveolar sacs to be exhaled, and this constitutes the basis for breath alcohol testing by breath analyzers. The blood alcohol will gradually rise to a peak concentration after completion of absorption (postabsorptive) before falling owing to metabolism and excretion. A point of *equilibrium* is reached in which maximal diffusion into all of the body compartments (including blood) has taken place, with higher levels or concentrations appearing in compartments or fluids with higher water contents (i.e., blood serum, vitreous fluid, urine, and CSF). Both absorption and elimination of ethanol occur at the point of equilibrium, as these are not abrupt finite phases that happen in succession but rather are taking place simultaneously early on after ingestion. The rise in concentration within the other body fluids will lag that of the blood as absorption and distribution continue. The majority (95%) of ethanol is *metabolized* in the liver initially by **alcohol dehydrogenase** (ADH), in addition to other enzymes. Ethanol is also metabolized to a much smaller extent within the stomach and small intestine by **gastric alcohol dehydrogenase** (GAD). The remainder of ethanol is *excreted* unchanged in the breath, urine, sweat, and feces. With metabolism and excretion, the ethanol levels in all compartments will gradually fall. Ethanol absorption is affected by a number of factors including slowed absorption by the presence of food in the stomach and increased absorption when certain gastric and intestinal inflammatory conditions exist.

Comparison of the ethanol level or concentration measured in the heart or femoral blood samples to that measured in the vitreous fluid, CSF, or urine samples may be useful in determining the phase of the distribution of ethanol. Past experiments under controlled conditions have worked out certain average ratios between blood and vitreous humor, CSF, and urine. For example, in the postpeak or postabsorptive state of diffusion of ethanol, the urine level or concentration averages 1.3 times more than that of blood or a ratio of 1.3:1.[5] A lower ratio would thus be reflective of the absorptive phase in which diffusion of ethanol into the blood predominates early on after ingestion. This would also indicate recent drinking prior to death, with some unabsorbed alcohol still remaining in the stomach, and the BAC would have been higher had the absorption phase continued. Conversely, a ratio greater than 1.3:1 would reflect the elimination phase, in which diffusion into the other compartments, including urine, predominates after the passage of enough time after ingestion. This would indicate less recent drinking. If the result of such comparison is reflective of the postabsorptive state, then the determination of the level, and thus the degree of intoxication at the time of the accident or injury (if known) can be estimated by way of back-calculation using mathematical formulas.[8,9] Calculation of the number of drinks consumed can also be done based preferably on the femoral vein blood alcohol level and after determination that the individual had ceased ethanol ingestion one to two hours prior to the accident, injury, or death and that the individual has surpassed the peak phase of absorption.[8,9] Estimates and calculations may be significantly affected and confounded by an incomplete history and many factors, including those previously mentioned, in addition to increased survival interval, severe internal injury, interindividual variability in the rate of metabolism of ethanol, and administration of medication and intravenous fluids.

The analysis of blood and other body fluids for the presence of ethanol is routinely performed in forensic toxicology laboratories using enzymatic, head space gas chromatographic, and mass spectrophotometric screening and confirmation techniques to achieve identification and quantification. These techniques are performed on a variety of matrices or sample types. Heart blood, femoral blood, vitreous fluid, and urine are the samples most commonly submitted, and the collection of one or more of these samples is contingent upon the availability and the condition of the body. Gastric contents, bile, muscle, liver, brain, CSF, and joint fluid may also be submitted for analysis. The results are generated and included in the toxicology report, along with other results. Ethanol is the most common drug detected in postmortem forensic toxicology, whether alone or in combination with other drugs and medications. Ethanol can be the direct or indirect cause of, or found in, association with accidental, suicidal, homicidal, and natural deaths.

The interpretation of ethanol levels requires awareness of the condition of the body from which the sample was taken (i.e., decomposition, submersion, extensive injury, or disease states) and is enhanced by good scene information and further external and internal examination of the body. The compartment from which the sample was taken (i.e., heart, eyes, or femoral vein) and variables in the methods of sample procurement, handling, and storage prior to analysis (preanalytic variables) must also be considered. Additionally, the effect of environmental conditions on the body, such as temperature and humidity, can affect the resultant ethanol level. The effects of these conditions on the resultant levels can potentially lead to over- or underestimation of the degree of contribution of impairment to the cause of an accident, injury, or drowning event.

In decomposed bodies, the occurrence of postmortem production of ethanol by bacteria, yeast, and molds, which multiply and utilize blood glucose as a nutrient, can occur. Postmortem production of ethanol in blood has been reported to be as high as 0.22 g/dl but is usually not greater than 0.05–0.07 g/dl.[5,10,11] Levels greater than 0.05–0.07 g/dl may represent some component of antemortem ingestion; therefore, a careful review of historical and scene information in the context of autopsy findings is necessary for proper interpretation. Postmortem production of ethanol in putrefied tissues and organs can also occur, usually to a greater extent than in blood, especially in tissues with high glucose or glycogen content, such as the liver. One clue that the presence of ethanol in the tissues is the result of postmortem production by microorganisms is the detection of low-molecular-weight alcohols such as n-propanol, n-butanol, and isobutyric acid.[10,12,13] Moreover, the detection of n-butanol has been shown to be a good indicator of postmortem ethanol production, particularly in bodies that have been submerged for prolonged periods.[13] In severely decomposed bodies, in which blood, urine, and vitreous fluids may be unavailable, skeletal muscle (deep thigh or psoas muscle) has been found to be the best tissue for the analysis of ethanol and the least liable to postmortem production of ethanol.[8] In mild to moderately decomposed bodies, or bodies with severe internal chest and abdominal injury, vitreous fluid is the best sample for measuring ethanol levels, as it is a relatively protected fluid from bacterial contamination and injury, and any resultant level indicates antemortem ingestion. Adequate amounts of quality vitreous fluid become increasingly difficult to obtain with advancing decomposition, however. The level of blood ethanol in a decomposed body in an individual known to have consumed alcohol prior to death will comprise some proportion of antemortem and postmortem ethanol, with a smaller contribution arising from the postmortem production. The extent of the contribution by postmortem production could make the difference in the determination that an individual was impaired during the operation of a motorized vehicle prior to an accident and injury or was not in fact impaired and some other factor, such as mechanical failure, was the cause of the accident and injury. Currently, no proven method can distinguish the *proportion* of antemortem (consumed/ingested) ethanol from postmortem ethanol production in tissues or blood.[10]

It may become necessary to further scientifically differentiate between ethanol blood levels arising from ingestion prior to death and those from postmortem production. One method involves the measurement of urinary metabolites of serotonin, **5-hydroxytryptophol (5-HTOL)** and **5-hydroxyindoleacetic acid (5-HIAA)**, whose production depends in part on one of the enzymes involved in ethanol metabolism. A 5-HTOL/5-HIAA ratio of significantly less than 15 indicates that the ethanol detected is from postmortem production, whereas a ratio of >15 can indicate either antemortem ingestion or postmortem production.[13,14] An additional method for differentiation involves the analysis of urine for **ethyl glucuronide**, which is produced in ethanol metabolism by the liver, but not by the actions of bacteria or yeast. The elimination time of ethyl glucuronide is long; therefore, this analysis is most useful with a shorter postmortem interval, since a longer one increases the risk of postmortem production of ethanol by microorganisms, which, when coupled with the detection of glucuronide, could be misinterpreted as antemortem ingestion.[13] This analysis is also useful in determining recent ethanol ingestion in the poorly controlled or noncompliant diabetic. These individuals normally have increased urinary glucose readily available for fermentation to ethanol (detectable with routine postmortem testing) in the presence of bacteria or yeast.[13]

Interpretation of blood and other body fluid alcohol levels can be particularly problematic in bodies submerged for prolonged periods, which can have lowered ethanol concentrations due to the dilutional effect of water on the body fluids, in individuals known to have consumed ethanol before death.[13] With increased time after death, the onset of decomposition with postmortem production of ethanol in the tissues and body fluids, and diffusion from one body fluid/region to another, also becomes a possibility in conditions of increased water temperature and the presence of severe internal injuries.[13]

Certain disease states, such as diabetes or infection by bacteria or yeast, can give rise to measurable ethanol in the blood, potentially confounding the interpretation of the contribution of ethanol to impairment. Bacterial and yeast infections, particularly of the urinary tract, are a source of microorganisms that migrate and multiply within the bloodstream and tissues, utilizing the glucose there with the production of ethanol as a by-product, within a deceased individual. Deceased, poorly controlled diabetics have an abundant source of blood glucose for use by bacteria, which become much greater in number with the progression of decomposition, with the potential of significant postmortem blood ethanol levels as high as 0.51 g/dl, as reported in one study.[15] The urine in living diabetics with bacterial or yeast infections of the urinary tract may also yield significant levels of ethanol as a result of *in vivo* production.[16] With subsequent death due to complications of diabetes, the vitreous and blood in these same individuals will likely be negative for ethanol, provided they have not consumed alcohol prior to death, the postmortem interval is short, and proper sample handling and storage has been performed. It is important for the forensic pathologist to know if there is a history of diabetes or symptoms of diabetes (excessive thirst, excessive urination, darkening of the skin, and fruity odor of breath) or infection. The death scene may provide clues regarding the medical history of diabetes or infection, such as syringes, insulin bottles, glucose monitors, blood sugar test strips, pill form medications for diabetes (i.e., metformin), and antibiotic medications.

Following death, ethanol present in the stomach or small intestine arising from recent ingestion prior to death will diffuse into nearby structures, such as the chest cavity, pericardial cavity, heart, and lungs, and subsequently into the heart blood, causing falsely elevated levels in the blood sample taken from the heart. This phenomenon is also known as **postmortem redistribution**. This is why a femoral vein blood sample is preferred over a heart blood sample, especially when sampling blood through the skin, such as during an external-only examination of the body. Blind sampling of heart blood with a syringe through the skin of the left side of the chest is also less preferred due to possible aspiration directly from other anatomic sites contaminated with ethanol or through anatomic sites that either contain ethanol or have been contaminated with ethanol. This would include the sampling of fluid effusions within the thoracic cavity, sampling of gastric contents directly from the stomach, sampling of gastric contents aspirated into the lungs during attempted sampling from the nearby heart, or sampling of gastric contents that have entered the thoracic cavity through an injury affecting the stomach and diaphragm. Injury to or rupture of the gastrointestinal tract and urinary bladder is more likely to give rise to contamination as well via diffusion of ethanol. Heart blood is still useful for detecting the presence of ethanol but is usually followed by confirmation and quantitation in the femoral blood sample, if available. Interpretation of ethanol levels from heart blood alone is done with caution.

Preanalytic variables can give rise to spuriously high or low ethanol levels or false negative results, whether samples are taken from live or deceased individuals. These include lack of prompt refrigeration of the body, improper collection and submission, increased time between sampling and analysis, and improper storage conditions. The skin should not be cleaned with any alcohol-containing fluid (i.e. ethanol or isopropanol) prior to percutaneous sampling. Review of medical records regarding the method of skin preparation prior to blood sampling in those receiving therapeutic intervention prior to death may be necessary when ethanol or isopropanol is detected unexpectedly. Review of records from the organ/tissue procurement organization in cases involving postmortem organ/tissue donation may also be necessary with the same unexpected findings. Bodies should be refrigerated promptly after arrival at the C/ME facility. Blood and urine samples should be collected in appropriate tubes containing 1% sodium fluoride powder, which greatly retards the proliferation of microorganisms, including bacteria, and thus either utilization or production of ethanol.[5,13] Diminution or loss of ethanol occurs as a result of volatilization of ethanol or destruction by microorganisms.[5] As previously mentioned, postmortem redistribution may cause spuriously high ethanol levels in heart blood, and therefore, a femoral vein blood sample, if obtainable, should always be submitted at autopsy. This sample can also be obtained through the skin in the groin region in external-only examinations. Blood samples should be promptly conveyed to the toxicology lab and put into refrigeration for temporary storage at 4°C (39°F). Proper handling and storage of blood from infants and children is particularly important, since any true level of ethanol is abnormal and could have serious legal ramifications regarding neglect and abuse if the presence of ethanol is found to be the cause or contributing factor in the death. The determination that a level of ethanol in an infant or child is truly a result of ingestion requires ruling out additional sources, including metabolic diseases, bacterial infections, and formula preparations that may contain substrates for postmortem ethanol production.[13,17]

Psychiatric Medications

Psychiatric medications are prescribed for a variety of psychiatric conditions and include antidepressant, antianxiety, antimanic, antipsychotic, and antiaddiction medications. These medications treat conditions such as depression, anxiety disorder, bipolar disorder, schizophrenia, and drug and alcohol addiction. Because of their actions upon primarily the CNS, these medications have side/adverse effects that may manifest as some degree of motor, cognitive, or sensory impairment. The consumption of these medications in conjunction with certain over-the-counter medications, and/or with alcohol can exaggerate impairment or have serious adverse and potentially lethal consequences due to alteration in their metabolism and blood levels. Medications given for certain other conditions, such as alcoholism (disulfiram) and heroin addiction (methadone), have their own set of side effects and potential for toxicity and death due to elevated blood levels. Short of death due to toxicity, some of these medications have the potential to create varying degrees of impairment and to have direct organ effects, which could place one at risk of water-related injuries or drowning. Their detection in the postmortem setting can provide not only an insight into the person's medical or psychiatric history, but also some explanation as to how and why an injury or drowning was sustained.

The following are but a few examples of adverse effects of some psychiatric medications. The antidepressant paroxetine (Paxil) can produce symptoms of somnolence, agitation, and muscular weakness.[3] This medication is also prescribed for anxiety and obsessive compulsive disorder. One other antidepressant medication, amitriptyline (Elavil, Endep), has been found to impair the skilled performance, such as driving, an effect that is increased with the addition of ethanol.[3] Clinical signs of toxicity and overdosage produced by this medication include seizures, coma, and cardiac arrhythmias.[5] Specifically, cardiac arrhythmias can lead to drops in blood pressure, fainting, and seizure-like activities, potentially life-threatening situations, when combined with water-related activities. Toxicity related to lithium usage, a medication prescribed for bipolar disorder, includes drowsiness, weakness, unsteadiness, and blurred vision. Methadone, which is prescribed for heroin addiction and chronic pain conditions, can give rise to sedation, weakness, and respiratory depression.[5] Overdose and potentially death can occur at therapeutic doses and blood levels, especially in individuals who are naïve to or lack tolerance for this medication.

The detection of medications given for psychiatric conditions can be of great value in determining the cause and manner of death, particularly since it is known that the risk of suicide by a number of means is increased in individuals with certain psychiatric conditions, such as bipolar disorder, depression, and schizophrenia. A recent history of certain precipitating factors, including financial, legal, or relationship difficulties or the death of a loved one, in the context of pertinent toxicological findings in an individual found submerged, is of additional value for determining the accurate cause and manner of death determination. In a study of bodies found in New York City waterways, the cases of suicide (including drownings) had a significant percentage of detection of psychiatric medications, supporting the high incidence of psychiatric illness also documented in that group.[18] In another study of completed suicides (nonoverdose), the proportion of drowning cases was more likely to have antidepressants and benzodiazepines detected than the suicidal deaths by other methods.[19]

Detection of psychiatric medications can also aid in the construction of the medical and psychiatric profile of an unidentified decedent who has no acquaintances or next of kin who can be interviewed. Whether the death is located at the individual's dwelling or common place of habitation, be it the tent out in the woods, a car, or a house, medical papers, prescriptions, pill boxes, and calendars can give the death investigator clues about the medical and psychiatric history. The difficulty arises when a decomposed or nondecomposed unidentified or unidentifiable individual is found away from these dwellings, like in fields, down embankments, or wedged in a break wall at the water's edge. Unique clothing, tattoos and scars, articles of identification, and witness accounts provide death investigators with a good start, if present or available (Figure 10.2). What can propel the case toward a proper determination of cause and manner of death is a sort of toxicological identification through laboratory detection of certain psychiatric medications in body fluids. Even with detection of these substances, determination of the cause and manner of death may still be thwarted if levels are not considered high enough to constitute a cause of death and the autopsy fails to reveal other lethal injury or pathology. On the contrary, the levels may in fact be lethal, but because of insufficient identifying characteristics and other evidence of psychiatric history (including suicidal ideation and prior suicide attempts), the manner of death may be ruled "undetermined," as there may be a lack of certainty as to whether the lethal level resulted from an intentional (suicidal) overdose or an accidental overdose or a homicidal administration. Blood levels may also be found to be within the therapeutic range, thus making the determination of manner of death less certain, especially within the context of negative autopsy findings. One must also keep in mind that a suicidal overdose can involve medications other than those prescribed for psychiatric conditions, so the detection of toxic or lethal levels of traditionally nonpsychiatric medications in an individual with known psychiatric history does not rule out suicide as a manner of death. The detection of psychiatric medications also does not necessarily mean an individual had a mental disorder, as individuals may take medications not prescribed to them for the purpose of self-treatment or experimentation. These are dangerous practices since the individual has not been medically evaluated by a physician, with subsequent proper dosing and counseling on the side effects and potential interferences of normal daily activities, such as work, driving, and recreation. Moreover, and as mentioned previously, a number of psychiatric medications are also prescribed for other chronic medical conditions.

Blood and urine samples obtained at autopsy or during external-only examinations are ideal samples for postmortem testing. Hospital blood and urine samples should also be obtained in pertinent cases. Due to the phenomenon of postmortem redistribution of certain psychiatric medications (i.e., tricyclic antidepressants), the submission of a femoral

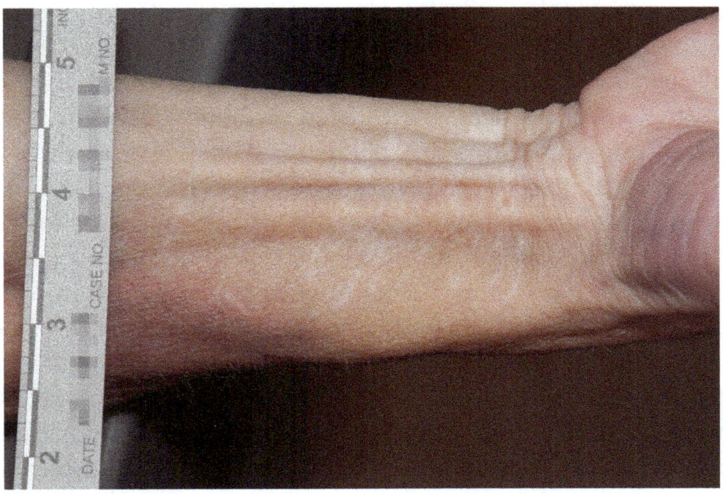

Figure 10.2 Healed incised wound of the wrist.

vein sample is preferred, and the results generated from the analysis of this sample are used for the interpretation of acute toxicity.

The association between the use of psychiatric or psychotrophic medications alone or combined with alcohol and increased risk for accidental drowning has been studied, with results affirming the association and increased risk.[20] Particularly problematic are medications that fall under the benzodiazepine category such as diazepam (Xanax®), which can cause impaired thinking and motor activity. Other medications like citalopram and amitriptyline, which are not known to cause psychomotor impairment, have been associated with arrhythmia, leading to incapacitation while in water and subsequent submersion with drowning and sudden cardiac death during submersion. Like alcohol, these medications have been linked with the prolongation of the QT interval on the electrocardiogram. This abnormality, whether medication-induced or as part of genetic predisposition (i.e. Long-QT Syndrome), is a known potential precursor for arrhythmia and sudden cardiac death. While the association is not the same as causation and further studies are still needed, findings of certain psychiatric medications alone or in combination with alcohol may be useful in the reconstruction of death circumstances, providing some explanation for an accidental drowning in the absence of a more compelling reason.

Illicit Drugs and Medications

Comprehensive toxicological testing will include testing for drugs of abuse and a number of prescription and over-the-counter medications prescribed for many conditions, including seizure disorder, pain, insomnia, fatigue, weight loss, allergies, and hypertension. Testing for many less commonly encountered drugs, medications, and poisons can be performed by outside reference labs. Colorimetric, spectrophotometric, immunological, chromatographic, and mass spectrophotometric methods are commonly used for the detection of substances. Clues suggestive of death due to an accidental overdose, such as fresh or healing needle punctures, skin popping scars, residue in the nostrils or in and around the mouth, excessive numbers of on-body pain medication patches, empty prescription pill bottles, and scattered pills, may be noted during the scene investigation and external examination of the body, though, save for scars and injuries may be inapparent or not present on a submerged body. Upon autopsy, pills in the gastric contents, pulmonary edema, or a full urinary bladder may be noted. Evidence of chronic use of illicit drugs and medications that affect the heart (i.e., dilated cardiomyopathy or hypertensive heart disease) and lungs (i.e., emphysema and pneumonia) may also be detected at autopsy. Moreover, evidence of chronic intravenous drug and medication abuse may be detected upon microscopic examination of tissue from the lungs, liver, and injection sites. Death due to overdose by ingestion, inhalation, or injection is not always readily apparent, however, and there may be no specific anatomic clues prior to toxicological testing. As with other types of medications, the interpretation of levels within blood and other body fluids must take into consideration the condition of the body, sample handling and storage, evidence of disease that can affect metabolism, the potential for postmortem redistribution, and whether the levels represent death by acute intoxication or a recent intoxication followed by slow death. Moreover, genetic variations in the liver metabolism of some medications can result in toxic blood levels at therapeutic doses or affect the metabolism of co-administered medications. A high index of clinical and pathological suspicion in this case may warrant submission of a postmortem blood sample to a reference lab for specific genetic testing.[21,22] Finally, it is important to note physiologic actions and adverse effects of any substance detected and whether they could cause any kind of impairment (alone or in combination), including impairment of motor and sensory abilities and judgment.

Detection of illicit drugs and medications at low or therapeutic levels can be merely incidental, providing evidence of recent use only or, at most, a contributing factor in death, but not necessarily a direct cause of death. Exceptions to this exist, particularly pertaining to medications (including abused medications) that may be lethal even at low and therapeutic ranges, especially in an individual who has not developed tolerance (first-time user) or who has lost tolerance (through temporary cessation of use during incarceration) to the medication. Detection of these substances at toxic or lethal levels may constitute a cause of death when interpreted within the right historical context, and, in the case of autopsy performance, other causes of death have been ruled out. An individual found submerged in a bathtub at a location known to be frequented by intravenous drug abusers, who has only a modest elevation of heroin metabolites in the blood and who at autopsy has a number of fresh and older track marks, would be strongly suspected to have succumbed, at least in part, to a heroin overdose after being placed in the bathtub in attempts to reverse a bad reaction. The contribution of drowning must also be considered in this scenario and may be difficult to discern or prioritize since drowning, and drug overdoses may have similar findings (i.e., the presence of a foam cone and pulmonary edema). By contrast, the detection of a low or subtherapeutic level of an antiseizure medication (or failure to detect any level) in an individual found submerged, with a known history of seizures treated with medication, evokes concern for the contribution of terminal seizures to death. Even with the detection of therapeutic blood levels, consideration for the contribution of seizures to death should still be given, especially if there is a history of a recent change in the type of antiseizure medication, inconsistent use of the medication, or unequivocal witness accounts of seizure activity prior to submersion.

Certain medications and illicit drugs, like opioids and cocaine, have adverse effects that can lead to impairment, affecting various activities, or potentially lethal effects, leading to sudden death at low, moderate, or high blood levels.

Cocaine is a stimulant and acts on the central nervous system by blocking the reuptake of a number of neurotransmitters like dopamine and has direct effects on the heart, blood vessels, and lungs. The effect on the CNS produces intense euphoria and increased alertness, which potentiates addiction, abuse, and death due to overdose. At the death scene, crack pipes, lighters/matches, or kits may be evident. Less commonly, cocaine may be injected intravenously or into skin or muscle, so syringes may be present at the scene. On initial body assessment, perforation of the nasal septum, residue in the nostrils, and burns on the fingers may be the only outward signs of crack/cocaine use. Scars from subcutaneous or intramuscular injection may be seen but not as commonly as with opiate injection. Cocaine overdose or toxicity can lead to uncontrollable hypertension, stroke, heart attacks, seizures, and sudden death. Moreover, death can occur at low, moderate, or high blood levels. Hyperthermia is an additional potential adverse reaction, and evaluation of a scene may reveal attempts to cool or resuscitate an individual, including placement of the individual in a bathtub filled with cold water (immersion or submersion) or shower, so the additional findings of wet hair and clothing and wrinkled skin of the hands and feet would be important to note. Drowning would certainly be considered if one is found submerged in a filled bathtub and should still be considered if the bathtub is empty since the water may have intentionally or passively drained out, especially if the position of the decedent is such that a partially or completely filled bathtub would have allowed coverage of the nose and mouth. Autopsy findings associated with acute or chronic cocaine usage include enlarged heart, myocardial infarct, brain hemorrhage, pulmonary congestion, pulmonary edema, and gray-black discoloration of the lungs (from smoking crack cocaine). Microscopic changes include multiple foci of scar tissue in the heart, acute myocardial infarct, acute hemorrhage of brain tissue, and fluid with the pulmonary alveoli. Additionally, lung sections will reveal increased black pigmentation in the lungs and increased numbers of alveolar macrophages containing black pigment, also known as **crack smoker's lung**.[9]

Opiates and **opioids**, including heroin, morphine, methadone, hydrocodone, oxycodone, and fentanyl, and many others have depressant activity on the central nervous and respiratory systems and have potent analgesic properties. Additional effects include euphoria, pinpoint pupils, sedation, reduced breathing, and respiratory arrest with death, depending on the dose and the individual tolerance to the substance. Inhalation, insufflation, ingestion, and injection are the known routes of use, and with chronic addiction, the route giving the quickest "high" will be preferred (i.e., injection). The stigmata of intravenous heroin injection (needle tracks of arms, hands, feet, neck, legs, and rarely the penile veins) or subcutaneous or intramuscular heroin injection (skin popping) may be noted on the initial scene or at autopsy assessment of the body (Figure 10.3). Prescription pain medications may be crushed and injected or crushed and snorted (insufflation) as well. Drug paraphernalia (needles, spoons, pipes, lighters, residual drug, and empty packages) is more often present in the setting of solitary use, but tends to be absent in the group use situation, having been taken by other users prior to the arrival of law enforcement. As mentioned previously, attempted "resuscitation" by immersion may be done, so the additional findings of wet hair and clothing and wrinkling of the skin of the hands and feet would be pertinent. Victims of an overdose may also be dumped in various places, including natural bodies of water, in such a manner as to give the appearance of a homicide. The manner in which they are dumped (i.e. rolled down an embankment or stuffed in a suitcase) may result in blunt and sharp force injuries, giving the appearance of an assault. At autopsy, there may be pulmonary congestion and edema with heavy lungs,

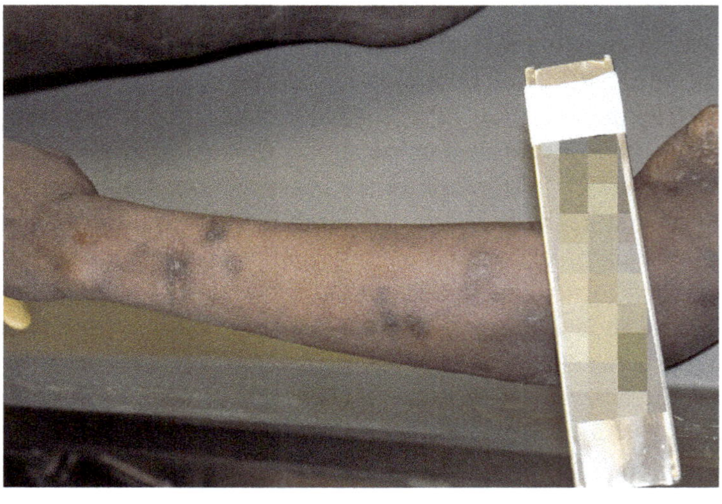

Figure 10.3 Scars on a forearm from skin popping.

foamy fluid within the upper airway, including the mouth, dilated heart chamber(s), and various degrees of congestion of the other organs. Microscopic examination may reveal alveolar edema, pulmonary vascular congestion, polarizable and nonpolarizable insoluble foreign material in the lung tissue and liver, with or without granulomatous inflammatory reaction, and hemorrhage or granulomatous inflammatory reaction in the skin taken from the injection site(s) (Figure 10.4). Clusters of bacteria in sections of the heart/heart valves, lung, liver, brain, and kidney indicate bloodstream infection or sepsis and may be a result of intravenous drug use with contaminated needles or drug and may be accompanied by an inflammatory reaction. Inflammation of the heart and heart valves along with presumed or evidence of bloodstream infection in the form of positive blood cultures can constitute a cause of death (i.e., infective endocarditis with bacteremia and sepsis). Intravenous drug abusers have a high prevalence of viral hepatitis (including hepatitis B and C), and evidence of hepatitis may be seen upon microscopic examination of the liver and proven with viral testing on blood. Kidney disease from chronic heroin abuse is represented microscopically by renal glomerular proteinaceous deposits called amyloid. In cases where death was not immediate, and the individual lingered in a coma for some time before death, pneumonia may be evident. Evidence of recent intravenous injection will be revealed by polarizable insoluble foreign material *within* the blood vessels, especially in lung and liver sections. Evidence of recent insufflation will be manifested by polarizable and nonpolarizable material, without inflammation, within the alveoli. These insoluble materials represent impurities, cutting and bulking agents added to illicit drugs, and filler material from medication pills.

Cannabinoids (marijuana, hashish, and pot) derived from the *Cannabis sativa* plant have CNS effects producing euphoria, drowsiness, and distortion of the sense of time. It is usually smoked in cigarette form but can also be combined with food and eaten. It is also used medically to control nausea and pain.[5] Acute effects include impairment in motor coordination and judgment of time, speed, and distance, factors tied to motor vehicle accidents. In one small study of 11 victims of drowning during whitewater and

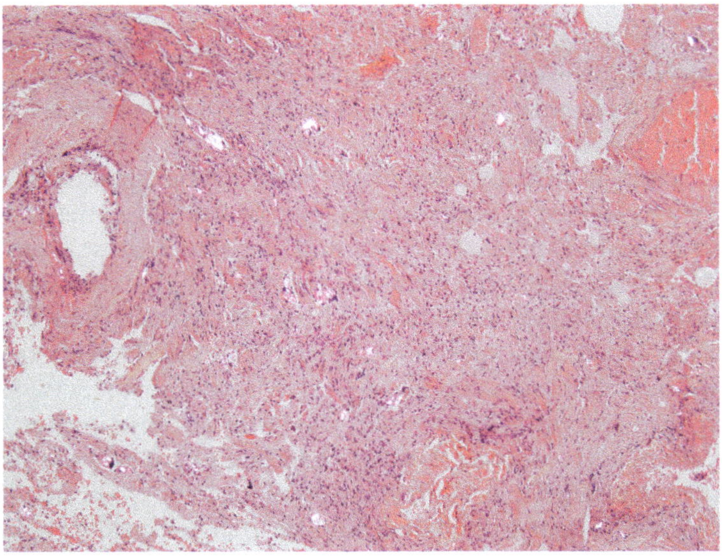

Figure 10.4 Birefringent foreign material in lung tissue of intravenous drug user.

kayaking activities, significant levels of tetrahydrocannabinol (THC), as evidence of acute intoxication, were found in 45% (4) of the victims with the conclusion that the cognitive and delayed response time effects of the substance were factors leading to the drownings.[23] Chronic use can produce hypertension, elevated heart rate, paranoia, and psychosis. Delta 9-tetrahydocannabinol (delta 9-THC) is the most active initial form. 11-Hydroxy-THC (11-OH-THC) and 8-hydroxy-tetrahydrocannabinol (8-OH-THC) are the early active metabolites. Delta-9-THC and 11-OH-THC decline rapidly in the blood approximately three hours after smoking.[5] The carboxylic acid metabolite (11-COOH-THC) is inactive and may remain for days in the blood and weeks in the urine, especially in chronic users. The drug and its metabolites have a propensity to be stored in fatty tissue with continuous metabolism and prolonged presence in the blood and urine. These metabolites are readily measured in blood and urine samples as part of routine comprehensive toxicological analysis. Chronic cannabinoid use causes inflammation of the airways, increased numbers of debris-containing inflammatory cells (macrophages) within the alveoli, asthma-like symptoms, and exacerbation of underlying asthma.

The prevalence (or lack thereof) of illicit drugs and medications varies across all manners of death of water-related causes and is in part dependent on the decedent's medical, psychiatric, and social history. The prevalence of specific illicit drugs may also be related to the geographical location where usage of a particular drug is seen more frequently in one region vs. another. One study regarding drug prevalence in 187 drowning deaths showed that the majority of drowning deaths (across all manners of deaths) were not related to ethanol, illicit drugs, or prescription medications.[24] In the few cases in which substances were detected, not surprisingly, alcohol was more likely associated with accidental drowning. In another study of seventy suicidal drowning deaths, benzodiazepines alone or in combination with other medications for depression, pain, and seizures were detected in 8 out of the 20 cases that were positive for drugs and medications.[25] Cocaine was the only illicit drug detected (three cases).

Carbon Monoxide

The effects of carbon monoxide were explained previously in Chapter 8, including its rare involvement in scuba-related deaths. Moreover, any gas-powered motor, including watercraft, could be a source of this gas.

Boat exhaust arising from house boats and ski boats contains appreciable levels of carbon monoxide (CO) with a real risk of poisoning while on deck or within the cabin or poisoning with subsequent drowning while swimming near the rear exhaust outlet of a running vessel. Ambient CO levels have been measured as high as 27,000 parts per million (ppm) in the stern of boats involved in CO fatalities, whereas the World Health Organization has recommended a cap of personal exposure at 87 ppm.[26] This high level of exposure results in lethal CO blood levels within minutes. Blood CO levels have been reported as high as 59% in victims engaged in swimming by the stern and swim platform, nearest to the exhaust outlet, a significant number of whom died.[26, 27] Exposures have led to toxicity reversed by therapeutic treatment or death due to drowning precipitated by CO poisoning. Low carbon monoxide blood levels give rise to symptoms similar to impairment by drugs and alcohol, motion sickness, and heat stress; thus the danger and need for prompt medical attention may not be immediately recognized. Impairment at low blood levels may also lead to poor judgment and decision making as it pertains to safe vessel operation, leading to increased risk for boating accidents. The circumstances surrounding sudden deaths while boating or drownings associated with recreational (or occupational) boating must be thoroughly investigated, including comprehensive toxicological analysis and specific analysis of the blood for carbon monoxide. Spectrophotometric and chromatographic methods remain the commonly used methods for the detection of carbon monoxide in blood samples.

References

1. Gruszecki, A. C., Booth, J., and Davis, G. G. 2007. The predictive value of history and scene investigation for toxicology results in a medical examiner population. *Am J Forensic Med Pathol* 28(2):103–6.
2. Morini, L., Vignali, C., Tricomi, P., and Groppi, A. 2015. Analytical challenge in postmortem toxicology applied to a human body found into a lake after three years immersion. *J Forensic Sci* 60(5):1383–86.
3. Ubelaker, D. H., and Zarenko, K. M. 2011. Adipocere: What is known after over two centuries of research. *Forensic Sci Int* 208:167–72.
4. Driscoll, T. R., Harrison, J. A., and Steenkamp, M. 2004. Review of the role of alcohol in drowning associated with recreational aquatic activity. *Inj Prev* 10(2):107–13.
5. Baselt, R. C. 2004. *Disposition of toxic drugs and chemicals in man*. 7th ed. Forest City, CA: Biomedical Publications.
6. Garriott, J. C. 1996. Pharmacology and toxicology of ethyl alcohol. In *Medicolegal aspects of alcohol*, ed. J. C. Garriott, 35–63. 3rd ed. Tuscon, AZ: Lawyers and Judges Publishing.
7. Baselt, R. C. 1996. Disposition of alcohol in man. In *Medicolegal aspects of alcohol*, ed. J. C. Garriott, 65–83. 3rd ed. Tuscon, AZ: Lawyers and Judges Publishing.
8. Cooper, W. E., Schwar, T. G., and Smith, L. S. 1979. *Alcohol, drugs, and road traffic*. Capetown: Juta and Company.
9. Stephens, B. G. 2006. Investigation of deaths from drug abuse. In *Medicolegal investigation of death—Guidelines for the application of pathology to crime investigation*, ed. Werner Spitz, 1166–217. 4th ed. Springfield, IL: Charles C Thomas Publisher Ltd.
10. Garriot, J. C. 1996. Analysis for alcohol in postmortem specimens. In *Medicolegal aspects of alchohol*, ed. J. C. Garriott, 151–69. 3rd ed. Tuscon, AZ: Lawyers and Judges Publishing.
11. Zumwalt, R. E., Bost, R. O., and Sunshine, I. 1982. Evaluation of ethanol concentrations in decomposed bodies. *J Forensic Sci* 27:549–54.
12. Moriya, F., and Hashimoto, Y. 2004. Postmortem production of ethanol and n-propanol in the brain of drowned persons. *Am J Forensic Med Pathol* 25(2):131–33.
13. Kugelberg, F. C., and Jones, A. W. 2007. Interpreting results of ethanol analysis in postmortem specimens: A review of the literature. *Forensic Sci Int* 165(1):10–29.
14. Singer, P. P., Graham, R. J., Lewis, R., et al. 2007. Loss of ethanol from vitreous humor in drowning deaths. *J Anal Toxicol* 31(8):522–25.
15. Collison, I. B. 2005. Elevated postmortem ethanol concentrations in an insulin-dependent diabetic. *J Anal Toxicol* 29(7):762–64.
16. Gruszecki, A. C., Robinson, C. A., Kloda, S., et al. 2005. High urine ethanol and negative blood and vitreous ethanol in a diabetic woman: A case report, retrospective case survey, and review of the literature. *Am J Forensic Med Pathol* 26(1):96–98.
17. Bivin, W. S., and Heinen, B. N. 1985. Production of ethanol from infant food formulas by common yeasts. *J Appl Bacteriol* 58:355–57.
18. Lucas, J., Goldfeder, L. B., and Gill, J. R. 2002. Bodies found in the waterways of New York City. *J Forensic Sci* 47(1):137–41.
19. Darke, S., Duflou, J., and Torok, M. 2009. Toxicology and circumstances of completed suicide by means other than overdose. *J Forensic Sci* 54(2):490–94.

20. Pajunen T, Vuori E, Vincenzi F, et al. 2017. Unintentional drowning: role of medicinal drugs and alcohol. *BMC Public Health* 17(1):388. doi: 10.1186/s12889-017-4306-8.
21. Zhou, S. F., Liu, J. P., and Chowbay, B. 2009. Polymorphism of human cytochrome P450 enzymes and its clinical impact. *Drug Metab Rev* 41(2):89–295.
22. Jannetto, P. J., Wong, S. H., Gock, S. B., et al. 2002. Pharmacogenomics as molecular autopsy for postmortem forensic toxicology: Genotyping cytochrome P450 2D6 for oxycodone cases. *J Anal Toxicol* 26(7):438–47.
23. Gorniak, J. M., Jenkins, A. J., Felo, J. A., et al. 2005. Drug prevalence in drowning deaths in Cuyahoga County, Ohio. *Am J Forensic Med Pathol* 26(3):240–43.
24. Copeland, A. R. 1987. Suicide by drowning. *Am J Forensic Med Pathol* 8(1):18–22.
25. Murdock, J., and Kelly, L. 2018. Whitewater rafting and kayaking deaths in Colorado increasing preventative measures by understanding risk factors. *Acad Forensic Pathol* 8(1):44–49.
26. Centers for Disease Control and Prevention–National Institute for Occupational Safety and Health. 2000. House boat-associated carbon monoxide poisonings on Lake Powell—Arizona and Utah. *Morbid Mortal Wkly Rep* 49(49):1105–108.
27. Centers for Disease Control and Prevention–National Institute for Occupational Safety and Health. 2002. Carbon monoxide poisoning resulting from exposure to ski-boat exhaust—Georgia. *Morbid Mortal Wkly Rep* 51(37):829–30.

Water-Related Deaths by Manner

11

ERICA J. ARMSTRONG

The establishment of the cause of water-related deaths is but one task in the certification of death. The assignment of the manner of death is the additional requirement for death certification. Only after a complete analysis of the historical and terminal circumstances, examination of evidence, and interpretation of autopsy and toxicological findings can the most accurate cause and manner of death be applied. Even with such a careful and comprehensive review, incomplete information or uninterpretable findings may warrant the ruling of the cause or manner of death as "undetermined." A homicidal ruling will prompt further legal inquiry and investigation, with the likelihood for future legal and judicial actions utilizing expert testimony regarding evidence and autopsy findings. Immediate family members of a homicide victim may be eligible for state-funded monetary compensation. An accidental ruling involving personal watercraft, safety-related equipment, or pools may evoke questions regarding product defects and the degree of trained supervision, prompting civil litigation. The creation of awareness about certain equipment defects can provide widespread benefit via prompting redesign, with the prevention of future deaths. Even suicidal deaths may prompt questions from families as to whether their loved ones were adequately medicated with the proper psychiatric medication(s). At any point in time, after a water-related death (or any death), after the scene investigation, and after the autopsy, unanticipated questions and concerns may surface. A thorough investigation along with the performance of a complete autopsy, meticulous documentation of all findings, and proper handling of evidence can help answer many important questions, alleviate concerns, and even provide links to new and previously undiscovered information and evidence in unsolved cases.

Homicidal Water-Related Deaths

Homicidal deaths occur as a result of the willful direct or indirect act (by commission or omission) of one or more persons that causes the death of another. In ruling homicides, the coroner/medical examiner (C/ME) is not concerned with whether there was *intent* to kill, which is for the courts to determine. In cases of homicidal water-related deaths, death may have occurred prior to submersion (i.e., strangulation on land with the dumping of the body into a lake) or as a direct result of submersion (i.e., forcibly holding someone's head underwater). An intermediate set of events leading to near death prior to disposing of the victim into a body of water may also have occurred. Rare reports of homicidal deaths due to stabbing and strangulation with subsequent disposal into the bathtub exist. These reports also involved other modalities of incapacitating blunt force and asphyxial injury with disposal of victims, mostly women, usually face down and submerged into filled bathtubs and subsequent drowning.[1] Evidence of intoxication, especially by ethanol, has also been reported in homicides involving bathtubs, but negative toxicological findings still warrant the suspicion for homicidal violence by one or more means.[1] Whatever the scenario, some degree of disparity between assailant and victim is required (i.e., the assailant is stronger, the victim is intoxicated, the victim is a dependent frail elder, the victim is an infant or child, the victim is taken by surprise). The greater the disparity, the less likely one will see defensive-type external injuries, making the circumstances surrounding the death even more mysterious upon initial investigation. It is important to remember that homicidal death does not exclusively involve the direct act of another but additionally includes the *inaction* of an individual responsible for another's care and well-being. Acts of negligence and endangerment that result in death are legally actionable.

CASE STUDY

A ten-month-old previously healthy male infant was found face down in a filled bathtub one late morning. This victim's mother and a close friend shared the apartment where the victim was discovered. The victim's mother, the friend, and two acquaintances had been out all night drinking, and the victim's mother was subsequently dropped off at her boyfriend's house. The friend returned home in the early morning hours. During their nighttime excursion, the victim and the friend's child had been left in the care of a neighbor and babysitter and were returned to their apartment home the following early morning. The still inebriated friend was left in charge of the victim and her five-year-old mentally disabled child. Further police investigation and interviews revealed that the five-year-old was fond of playing with baby dolls in the bathtub and most likely placed the infant victim in the bathtub in an attempt to bathe him and was obviously unaware of the potential consequences. The friend was asleep during that crucial time and only aroused from sleep upon the arrival of the victim's grandparent, who inquired about the whereabouts of his daughter and grandson. It was the friend who made the tragic discovery and the grandfather who began CPR. Emergency medical services were quickly summoned. The infant could not be revived despite approximately 3½ hours of resuscitative efforts by both emergency medical technicians and hospital medical personnel.

A complete autopsy was performed and revealed a healthy infant without significant injury and with evidence of therapeutic intervention. No foam column was seen externally. Internal examination revealed clear fluid within the chest and abdominal cavities due in part to the drowning process and intravenous infusions. The lungs were heavy and severely edematous. Toxicology was significant only for the medicines given in the hospital as part of comfort care measures. After review of the investigative and autopsy information in totality, the cause of death was determined to be drowning and the manner of death was ruled homicide. The mother was charged with child endangerment and entered a plea of guilty and received one-year probation. The friend was charged with reckless homicide and child endangerment and entered a plea of guilty and received sixty days' jail time and two years probation with mandatory Alcoholic Anonymous meetings.

Homicidal drownings are extremely uncommon, whereas other types of homicidal asphyxial deaths (i.e., ligature and manual strangulations) are relatively more common.[2,3] The disguising of a homicidal drowning as an accidental, natural, or suicidal death is an additional important consideration in the investigation of water-related deaths. Moreover, victims may be killed by way of beating, stabbing, or strangulation and disposed of in a body of water in order to ensure that the victim will die, conceal the cause and manner of death, conceal identification, conceal or remove evidence, and ultimately escape legal apprehension. Financial gain may be an additional motive for staging deaths as accidental drownings; thus, the marital, legal, and financial relationships between a victim and the suspect or any persons of interest must be verified and documented as part of the investigation. A death by other means may be presented by the perpetrator to law enforcement and medical personnel with a story of accidental drowning, which, upon further questioning, investigation, and examination of the body, numerous inconsistencies are revealed. Without the presence of injuries, uncovering such inconsistencies becomes much more difficult, especially in infants.

CASE STUDY

An unresponsive six-year-old female child was brought to a hospital emergency department one warm, early summer evening by a frantic caretaker, who reported that the child drowned in the lake. Being unable to swim, the caretaker reportedly summoned a bystander who rescued the child who was "floating" in the lake. This bystander began CPR, which was continued in the caretaker's car on the way to the hospital. Upon arrival, the mysterious bystander reportedly quickly departed. Initial examination in the emergency department revealed an unresponsive child with fixed and dilated pupils and an elevated rectal temperature. Medical personnel became quickly concerned as the child, while dressed in a bathing suit, did not have the appearance of recent submersion, save for the peculiar wrinkling of the skin of the hands only. No sand or aquatic debris was seen in the hair or on the child's body. No foamy fluid was noted upon intubation. Even more alarming were the multitude of contusions, abrasions, a burn, and well-healed scars from head to toe, including a thin ligature-like mark around the neck (Figure 11.1A–C). Police were promptly called and responded to the hospital to view the victim and interview the caretaker. The caretaker was conveyed back to the "scene," and further interviewing revealed an uncooperative individual who was unable to point out the location of where the victim allegedly drowned. Further police investigation did not reveal witnesses to a child in distress, 911 calls, or rescue attempts. Video footage from the hospital did not show the mysterious bystander-rescuer. The caretaker was subsequently arrested, as there were major inconsistencies. A search of the caretaker's home where the victim resided revealed a meticulously clean interior, including the bathroom. Further police investigation also revealed an earlier history of child abuse on the part of the biological mother, who subsequently relinquished her parental rights, giving guardianship to the caretaker. There was further and more recent history that the child had been temporarily placed into foster care due to findings of neglect and abuse while under the care of the caretaker.

A complete autopsy was performed the following day, and the child was in complete rigor with fixed posterior lividity. The autopsy documented all of the recent injuries and scars, including the cluster of discrete and confluent abrasions and

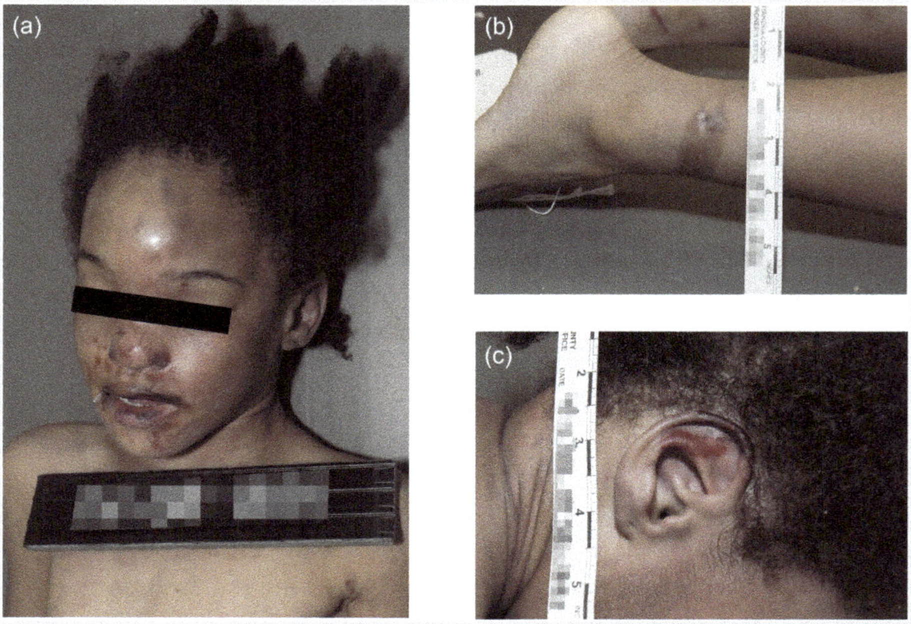

Figure 11.1A–C (A) Abrasions and contusions of the face, (B) scars of the ankles, and (C) thermal injury of the ear.

contusions involving the nose, lips, and chin. The recent injuries were confined to the head and upper and lower extremities. Thermal injury of the right ear was noted. A large contusion with swelling was noted on the forehead. There were a number of acute subgaleal hemorrhages, one of which was associated with a laceration on the back of the head. The linear mark of the neck was a well-healed scar. The wrinkling of the skin of only the hands was noted. No foamy fluid of the airway was noted. There were no internal injuries or other internal supportive findings of drowning. There were no external or internal petechial hemorrhages. X-rays were negative for recent or remote skeletal injury. Subsequent microscopic examination revealed aspiration of gastric contents with acute pneumonia and sickling of the red blood cells without end organ damage. No significant autolysis or putrefaction of the tissues was noted. Hemoglobin electrophoresis revealed a sickle cell trait. Chemistry testing of the vitreous fluid and blood indicated an acidosis. Toxicological analysis was negative. The cause of death was determined to be aspiration with acute pneumonia due to near asphyxia by suffocation (smothering) with the contributory conditions of multiple blunt impacts to the head, trunk, and extremities. The injuries, together with the asphyxial nature of the death (and evidence of a survival component—aspiration, pneumonia, and acidosis), in the context of major historical and investigative inconsistencies, led to the ruling of the manner of death as a homicide. While hypoxia can induce deformation with sickling of the red blood cells, there was no evidence of end organ damage, and thus the finding of sickle cell trait was not considered a contributory condition. Moreover, routine histological preparation of tissue sections can also induce sickling of red blood cells. The elevated temperature was attributed to pneumonia with acidosis, although a body kept in a hot ambient environment, such as a vehicle heated by direct sunlight or the warm outer air, could not be excluded. The wrinkling of the skin of the hands was consistent with the immersion of the hands into a liquid, probably water, to support the story of an alleged drowning.

A multitude of new and old external or internal injuries always concern for chronic child abuse, as represented by the previous case. Deaths associated with child abuse are more often due to blunt force head injury and internal abdominal organ injury and less commonly due to asphyxia. Homicidal drowning can be a form of child abuse, leaving little if any injury and appearing at first glance much like an accidental drowning. This is an uncommon phenomenon, and the usual scenario involves a reportedly unwitnessed event (i.e., the infant was found unresponsive) at home, often in a bathtub, perpetrated on an infant or child between 15 and 30 months of age by the primary caregiver, most commonly the mother, with a delay in seeking medical attention.[4,5] Relatively little force is required to physically submerse and drown an infant, with just enough force needed upon the head or torso to maintain coverage of the nose and mouth. This effort may leave little if any external injury.

Sudden death in an infant with little or no injuries or other anatomic cause of death may have the initial appearance of sudden infant death syndrome (SIDS). SIDS is a diagnosis made by the exclusion of other anatomic, infectious, toxicological, traumatic, and environmental causes of death in an infant age one to twelve months. While studies implicating abnormalities in the neurochemical regulation of cardiorespiratory function coupled with certain environmental risk factors have been published, there remains no definitive structural finding(s) or clinical test for the diagnosis of SIDS.[6] The autopsy findings in SIDS are few and nonspecific, with some similarity to asphyxial deaths (organ congestion and petechial hemorrhage). If a true homicidal drowning presents with incomplete investigative information and little or equivocal supportive findings of submersion and drowning at the scene and at autopsy, the designation of the death as SIDS becomes a possibility. This possibility is increased when the investigation of these deaths lacks detailed documentation of the scene, terminal circumstances, and medical and social history with the completion of a SUIDI-RF form, previously referenced in Chapter 1.

While the autopsy findings supportive of drowning within the context of a body recovered from a watery environment assist in the determination of the cause of death, Copeland recommends extraction of additional information by asking key questions: Who? What? When? Where? Why? How?[2] The victim's identity, information about types of arrests, locations where the victim frequented, and persons with whom he or she interacted can be obtained and used as links to suspects. Confession by the perpetrator as to why (and even how) the incident occurred will obviously be helpful in the investigation, provided that the volunteered information is consistent with the findings produced by a diligent investigation and autopsy. Confession would be particularly crucial in deaths without supportive autopsy findings of drowning or injury, such as a case of electrocution while immersed in the bathtub. Consistent accounts from more than one witness personally unconnected with the homicidal occurrence could be helpful not only in the reporting of what, how, and when the event occurred but also in refuting a perpetrator's inconsistent information. Lastly, a drowning victim found in a location unknown to that person and not normally frequented by him or her, or otherwise not explained by environmental factors such as the effects of water current, should alarm those involved in the death investigation. Historical or autopsy evidence of a medical complication or depression with suicidal attempts or ideation in a drowned individual still makes death due to natural disease, accident, or suicide viable possibilities that need to be ruled out before homicide is applied as the manner of death. Furthermore, these other possibilities may very well form the basis for a defense put forth by the perpetrator.[3]

Suicidal Water-Related Deaths

Suicide involves willful, self-inflicted injury or poisoning. Whether by gunshot, wrist cutting, jumping from a height, intoxication, or drowning, determination of the manner of death requires the collaboration of both the forensic pathologist and law enforcement. Medical and psychiatric history, reports of prior suicide attempts, evidence of recent suicidal ideation including verbalization, and medical records documenting recent psychiatric hospitalizations must be specifically sought during the death investigation. The discovery of suicide notes, whether on paper or in electronic form, is very helpful but only found in a small percentage of cases. Efforts to verify that a handwritten suicide note is consistent with the writing of the decedent should be made. The investigation may also provide other clues that add weight to the designation of death as a suicide, such as recent loss of a job or recent end-of-life preparations (gathering of insurance policies, making of wills, selling or giving away valuables).[7] An imminent arrest, court appearance, or incarceration may trigger the impulsive commission of suicide in an individual who may or may not have a documented clinical history of depression or other psychiatric histories. Findings resulting from toxicological testing can be helpful in the manner of death determination when the initial investigative and autopsy findings suggest otherwise. For example, a death resulting from multiple injuries sustained after a leap from several stories may at first glance appear suicidal until further investigation reveals earlier reports of bizarre behavior, which is confirmed by the finding of phencyclidine (PCP) on toxicological analysis, highlighting the need to reconsider suicide as a manner of death with knowledge of the effects of PCP on behavior and perception. Efforts to rule out accidental or homicidal violence must continue even when initial investigative findings point to suicide. Suicides, in general, may involve multiple modalities (i.e., wrist cutting and gunshot wound of head, multiple stab wounds, and blunt force injury following jump from height) and appear homicidal at first glance. Likewise, suicidal drownings may also involve multiple modalities done by a desperate individual to ensure death when the first method may have been too painful or too slow. These are also known as complex suicides.[8]

CASE STUDY

It was in late winter when a 62-year-old female with a history of bipolar disorder was noted to be missing by her husband after finding a suicide note in the bedroom of their residence. The note expressed feelings of uselessness, remorse, and embarrassment for her past and final suicidal actions. In the note, she also pleaded for her family's forgiveness. Police were summoned by the husband to the residence and directed to a wooded area at the rear of the residence, where it was thought she most likely went. Led by a K-9 with the help of the scent from one of her jackets, she was discovered dressed in a pajama top and bottoms, wearing shoes, face down in a shallow creek. Several pools of blood were noted on rocks and in a patch of snow on the bank approximately 5 feet away. Drops of blood along with a razor blade were also noted nearby on the creek bank, approximately 3 feet away. Footprints were not noted, however. A wound, described by police as a laceration, was noted on the left wrist.

External examination at autopsy revealed a thin, elderly female, compatible with her reported age, with evidence of a unilateral mastectomy with breast reconstruction. Gray-black sediment was noted upon the face and within the nostrils. A foam cone was not seen. Wrinkling of the skin of the hands and forearms was noted. An occasional small recent and resolving contusion was noted on the extremities. On the volar surface of the left wrist was a cluster of multiple, parallel, horizontal, superficial, and deep incised wounds, ranging from 1¼ to 2 inches in length, with transection of the radial artery and vein and acute hemorrhage into the adjacent soft tissues (Figure 11.2A). Hesitation marks consisting of superficial incised wounds were noted at the periphery of the wound cluster. On the volar surface of the right wrist was a superficial incised wound (Figure 11.2B).

Internal examination revealed pale organs. Lungs were remarkable for moderate congestion and edema. The stomach contained approximately a ½ cup of watery gray fluid. Petrous ridge hemorrhage was not appreciated. Aspiration of the sphenoid sinus was not done. The major microscopic findings were pulmonary edema, pulmonary emphysema, breast cancer, and chronic inflammation of the kidneys. Results of toxicological testing were negative. The cause of death was drowning due to incised wounds of the left wrist with exsanguination. The exsanguination was determined to be the dominant component, and thus part of the underlying cause of death that precipitated the very terminal drowning event with a few, although not extensive, supportive findings. The manner of death was ruled a suicide.

The gradual loss of blood leads to loss of blood pressure (shock) with collapse due to loss of physical strength, but with weak vital signs (pulse, respiration, and blood pressure) still obtainable. Collapse within a potentially hostile environment may lead to additional injury, including asphyxia by drowning. After a time of continual blood loss without resuscitation, cardiac arrest with death will follow. The scene investigation was additionally supportive of asphyxia by submersion with covering of the nose and mouth by virtue of her face-down position in the water.

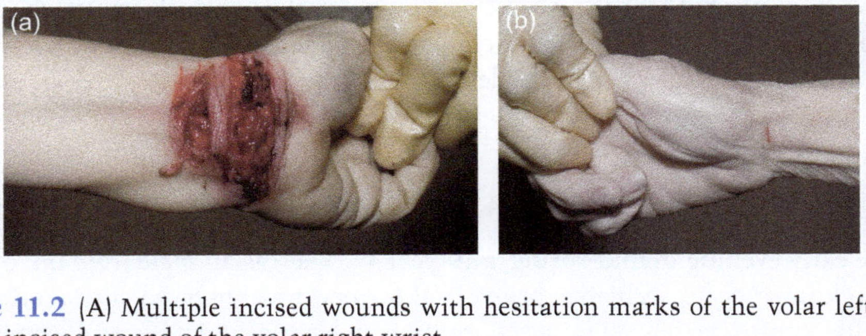

Figure 11.2 (A) Multiple incised wounds with hesitation marks of the volar left wrist and (B) incised wound of the volar right wrist.

Suicidal drownings are uncommon, and the percentages of all suicides vary, depending upon geographic location and access to bodies of water, with rates that vary between 0.85% and 8.9%, as reported in previous studies, with higher rates related to more easy access to large bodies of water, such as lakes, oceans, and rivers.[9–13] A number of studies on suicidal drowning has revealed a particular profile of an individual who has chosen to end his or her life by drowning.[9–13] These individuals tend to be older married or single Caucasian males. A history of depression or other psychiatric illness, such as schizophrenia, has been noted. Certain life stressors, such as declining health, loss of spouse, and financial difficulties, have also been cited. Ethanol is less commonly detected overall, except in the younger individuals less than 40 years of age. Low but sometimes toxic or lethal levels of psychiatric medications have been found. The rate of detection of illicit drugs is low. Suicidal bathtub drownings reportedly have been found to more likely have ethanol and prescription medications detected on toxicological analysis.[9,14] When found, these individuals may be face up or face down in the water.[13,14] As mentioned previously, suicide notes are not commonly found and are noted in a third or less of the cases. Most individuals are clothed, especially those found outdoors. When found unclothed, they either are in the confines of home or have taken off clothing, having placed them, along with other personal effects, nearby, such as in their car or on the shoreline, indicating premeditation and intent. One must also keep in mind that the absence of clothing may be indicative of strong waves, swift currents, and fixed underwater objects that may have stripped the decedent of clothing, including underwear, in cases of drowning in natural bodies of water. Moreover, the force generated by impact with the water secondary to a jump from a great height may also result in the removal of clothing. While men tend to predominate in numbers, suicidal drowning is not an uncommon means of suicide for women who tend to choose less violent means overall. Women who choose drowning as a means to end their life tend to be older; thus, the case of an apparent suicide in a young female, especially 30 years of age or younger, should evoke suspicion for accidental or homicidal violence until proven otherwise.[9] Reports of cases of true suicidal drownings in younger women include a history of severe depression, psychosis, or significant ethanol intoxication.[13]

Unusual and rare circumstances related to suicidal drowning are reported and highlight the degree of desperation that can be at play, in which the individual strives to ensure that death will be certain. One scenario is suicidal drowning subsequent to driving a car into a large body of water, which is rare. Like complex suicides by other means, suicidal drownings involving the attachment of weighty objects and/or tethers and bindings to the body may give the initial appearance of homicidal violence but have been reported.[9,13,14,15,16,17] Of importance in these cases is the documentation of not only the presence of bindings but also the precise way in which the bindings are attached in order to determine whether or not the victim could have affixed the bindings, which will have a direct bearing on the manner of death determination.

CASE STUDY

On one early evening in mid-spring, a 19-year-old Caucasian male from out of state, with no known past psychiatric or medical history, was observed sitting on a local pier. After approximately 30 minutes, multiple independent witnesses observed him tie a rope around his neck prior to securing it to a backpack. Conflicting witness accounts that the male had placed either one or several rocks in the backpack were also given. He was observed by the same witnesses to then jump off the pier into 12 to 15 feet of 56°F (15°C) lake water. Emergency assistance was promptly called. After approximately an 1-hour search, a dive team recovered a lightly but fully dressed unresponsive male with a backpack containing one rock tied with a rope around his neck. Nearly 45 minutes of resuscitative efforts by the medical first responders and hospital emergency room medical personnel were unsuccessful. Pink, frothy fluid was noted in the airway during the resuscitative attempts continued at the hospital.

A complete autopsy revealed a well-developed male without any significant wrinkling of the skin. There was no furrow or other mark on the neck. The only injuries were red abrasions, one of each elbow. Lungs were heavy and voluminous with severe congestion and edema. Watery fluid and a single dime were recovered from the stomach. There were no ulcers or erosions of the lining of the stomach. The heart was enlarged with thickened chambers. There was severe dilatation of the right ventricle. There was a petrous ridge hemorrhage. Aspiration of sphenoid fluid was not done. Microscopic examination was significant for hemorrhagic edema of the lungs and enlarged heart muscle cells. Toxicology was negative. The cause of death was drowning, and the manner of death was suicide.

Accidental Water-Related Deaths

Accidental deaths result from the unintentional and unpredictable direct or contributing effects of injury or poisoning (intoxication). The manner of death may be ruled accidental if the injury or poisoning is listed as the cause of death *or* as a contributing condition on the death certificate. For example, the manner of death in an individual who dies as a result of severe hypertensive heart disease and who also has evidence of *recent* use of cocaine by toxicological testing (considered here as the contributing condition) may be ruled accidental due to the known direct and chronic effects of the cocaine on the heart and vascular system. Similarly, a more acute event, such as a ruptured cerebral artery aneurysm in the setting of *acute* cocaine intoxication, may also be ruled accidental (i.e., cause of death: ruptured cerebral artery aneurysm due to acute cocaine intoxication). In most instances, the nonnatural entity, whether the cause of death or a contributing condition, determines the manner of death. This would also apply to a natural event occurring in a potentially hostile environment such as a body of water. The effects of exertion while swimming in someone with severe coronary artery disease may trigger the development of a myocardial infarct (or exacerbate an already developing one), with subsequent collapse and submersion and drowning. In this example, the cause of death would be drowning *due to* the myocardial infarct. The manner of death in this case is accidental, as it represents a person that was alive with subsequent collapse due to myocardial infarct while in the hostile aqueous environment. By contrast, an individual may have expired just before, during, or very shortly after submersion from a catastrophic natural medical condition; in other words, the person happened to be in or near water at the time of death, which was caused by the natural medical condition. In this case, the manner of death would be natural.

Most direct drownings or injury-associated drownings are accidental and are associated with a number of factors, such as lack of safety education and awareness, impairment, human error, mechanical defect, weather, or an underlying medical condition. Globally, it is the third leading cause of unintentional injury death. In the United States, drowning is the second most common cause of accidental death in infants and children, after motor vehicle accidents.[18] Reports of water-related deaths associated with rare and unusual circumstances have been made. Rare cases of accidental water-related deaths, including drowning, associated with autoeroticism have been reported.[19,20] Electricity-related deaths while immersed in natural bodies of water have also been reported. These reports include electrocution via contact with a submersible water pump while scuba diving and drowning due to electrical shock from contact with dock lights.[21]

Numerous studies of unintentional drownings have uncovered similarities.[22–26] Peak rates of drowning not associated with boating are observed in the very young (less than four years of age) and in adolescents and young adults, with a male gender predominance. Drownings in the very young occur mostly in residential pools and other small bodies of water, while those in adolescents and young adults tend to involve a variety of natural water environments. The prevalence of alcohol, particularly associated with swimming and especially boating activities, has been noted with increasing age, especially between the ages of 24 and 64 years. The presence of illicit drugs has also been reported, but these are not as commonly detected.

Environmental hazards inherent to some natural bodies of water, such as sudden dropoffs and swift currents, have been identified and present a real danger to unsuspecting or inexperienced swimmers of any age. Lack of fencing, fence locks, and adequate supervision are major factors that have been identified in accidental drownings occurring in residential pools, especially involving toddlers and young children, who mostly lack swimming experience and relative strength and coordination, which are impediments to self-extrication. Underlying medical conditions, such as heart disease, seizures, and diabetes, have been identified and implicated as causes or contributing factors in drownings, particularly involving adults. Infants and small children may also suffer from seizures and especially require full-time supervision while in and around bodies of water. Specific hazards for infants and toddlers, such as buckets and bathtubs, have been identified in drownings.[24,27] Particularly, industrial-type buckets partially filled with fluids and other materials to weigh them down present a hazard to toddlers who have high centers of gravity, large heads, and weak neck musculature, allowing for easy head-first submersion with difficulty in self-extrication. In addition to a complete autopsy, examination, and measurement of the bucket with comparison to the infant's and toddler's height measurement should be done. Chemical analysis of retained fluid from the bucket may help to identify contributing factors such as intoxication or chemical injury. Identified risk factors in bathtub drownings in infants and children include inadequate supervision, co-bathing, use of infant bath rings, and a history of seizures.[27] In all infant and children drownings, particularly those involving bathtubs and similar small containers of water or other fluid (bins, sinks, and buckets), it is important to assess whether the infant or child's motor skills are consistent with unassisted access to these locations, if such an account is given to the investigator. Any inconsistency should be further investigated. Finally, the use of residential rainwater collection tanks is increasing in popularity due to the benefits related to water conservation. Child deaths related to the use of these devices have been reported, highlighting the need for continual monitoring of cases of drownings and near drownings alike and for instituting child-proofing measures.[28]

Natural disasters such as hurricanes and floods account for a significant number of episodic accidental deaths. Hurricane Katrina was the deadliest hurricane to strike the United States in over 80 years, with drowning the major cause of death. Deaths due to traumatic injuries and heart conditions were additional significant causes.[29] A study of thirteen flood events in Europe and the United states revealed 247 flood disaster fatalities, with two-thirds of those deaths due to drowning.[30]

A combination of risk factors may also culminate into accidental drowning.

CASE STUDY

On a late spring evening, three men and two teenagers boarded a 40-year-old, recently purchased, 16-foot motorized boat to go fishing in a very large lake. Unbeknownst to the group, a small craft advisory had been issued. Initially, they were not wearing their personal flotation devices. While approximately 1½ miles out from the boating dock, weather conditions began to rapidly deteriorate, with gusty winds at 15 to 20 knots and 4-foot waves. Larger boats had already started heading back to shore. The men quickly put on life jackets and steered the boat back to the shore. The boat was suddenly impacted by a large wave, causing it to break in half, allowing the back half to sink, pitching the men into the water and leaving them to cling to the sinking bow. One of the teenagers broke away and swam to shore to summon help and the Coast Guard was called. The remaining men were recovered from the 49°F (9°C) lake water one to two hours after the accident. All men were conveyed to the local hospital. The two teenagers were treated for hypothermia and released. One man was pronounced dead upon arrival, and the two remaining men could not be resuscitated despite prolonged resuscitative efforts. Further investigation revealed that the personal flotation devices they were wearing were approved for use with waterskiing to help maintain the head of a conscious person afloat, but would not help keep the head of an unconscious person, who had succumbed to waves, strong currents, and cold water, face up.

Autopsy findings were supportive of drowning, including heavy and severely edematous lungs. Petrous ridge hemorrhage was not described. Sphenoid sinus fluid was not aspirated. Two of the men had enlarged hearts, one of which had moderate coronary artery disease. All of the men sustained blunt force injury (abrasions and lacerations). One had a unilateral fracture of the hyoid bone. Two had subgaleal hemorrhage. These injuries were consistent with impacts with the vessel and likely each other. Toxicological analysis of one man's blood sample revealed a femoral BAC of 0.14 g/dl; this was also the same man with coronary artery disease. Marijuana metabolite was found in the urine of another man. For all three men, the cause of death was due to hypothermia and drowning, and the manner of death was ruled accidental.

The investigation concluded that multiple factors contributed to the accident and the fatalities, including the age of the boat, excess load/persons within the boat, lack of boating experience and preparedness, weather conditions, and water temperature. The younger age and absence of chronic disease in the teenagers were probably favorable factors for their survival. The presence of alcohol in one man and marijuana in another were likely additional factors contributing to poor decision making.

As previously stated, intoxication or other impairment does not bode well for survival in the aqueous environment, as demonstrated in the following case. Furthermore, the presence or absence of clothing or the type of clothing may give additional investigative information. For example, the presence of swimwear vs. a heavy coat and jeans, or pajamas vs. work clothes may give temporal clues. The presence of intact jeans with the zipper in the "down" position in an individual later found to have a full urinary bladder and with evidence of acute ethanol intoxication at autopsy is concerning for an accidental fall with submersion after attempting to urinate. These clues can be helpful but are not necessarily absolutes. Furthermore, neatly placed clothing near the point of entry into water is not necessarily 100% specific for suicidal drowning.

CASE STUDY

A 46-year-old male left a popular riverfront restaurant just after midnight. He was in good spirits that evening. He had no known medical or psychiatric history. He suddenly announced to his friends that he intended to swim across the river. He proceeded to remove his outer clothing, leaving on only an undershirt and briefs. He neatly folded these and tucked his socks into his shoes, leaving all items on the dock. He subsequently dove into the river. Friends and witnesses saw the man swim approximately 50 yards upriver before disappearing under water. Police were called and responded, and in turn the Coast Guard and fire rescuers were called. A dive team search could not locate the man. Notification was made to his mother. The search was continued by Coast Guard members using boats and a helicopter. After a three-day search effort, assistance from the local regional emergency response dive team, which had been performing routine drill exercises in the area, was requested. The team located the man at the bottom of the river using sonar technology within the vicinity where he was last seen. Recovery from the 54°F (12°C) water revealed a man wearing undershirt and briefs but with no formal identification. He was conveyed to the coroner's office and officially pronounced dead. Positive identification was made by the mother via visual recognition of the coroner's identification photograph and photographs of his tattoos.

An autopsy revealed a well-developed male compatible with the reported age, viewed initially with clothing on. Sand and silt were present upon the face, trunk, and extremities and within the nostrils (Figure 11.3A and B). Focal skin slippage of the left eyelids and absence of rigor mortis provided evidence of early decomposition consistent with three days of submersion in cool water (Figure 11.3C). The lividity was inapparent. "Washerwoman" changes were described of the hands and feet. An abrasion on the nose was consistent with face-down positioning and contact with the river bottom. Internal examination revealed heavy, edematous lungs, petrous ridge hemorrhage, and reddish fluid in the sphenoid sinus. Two healed rib fractures were noted. The stomach contained 25 ml of tan-gray nondescript fluid, and there were no gastric erosions or ulcers. Microscopic examination revealed hemorrhagic pulmonary edema but no polarizable material. Additional microscopic findings were enlarged heart muscle cells, fatty change of the liver, and mild chronic inflammation of the kidneys. The toxicological analysis was significant for a femoral BAC of 0.17 g/dl, vitreous ethanol concentration of 0.14 g/dl, and urine ethanol

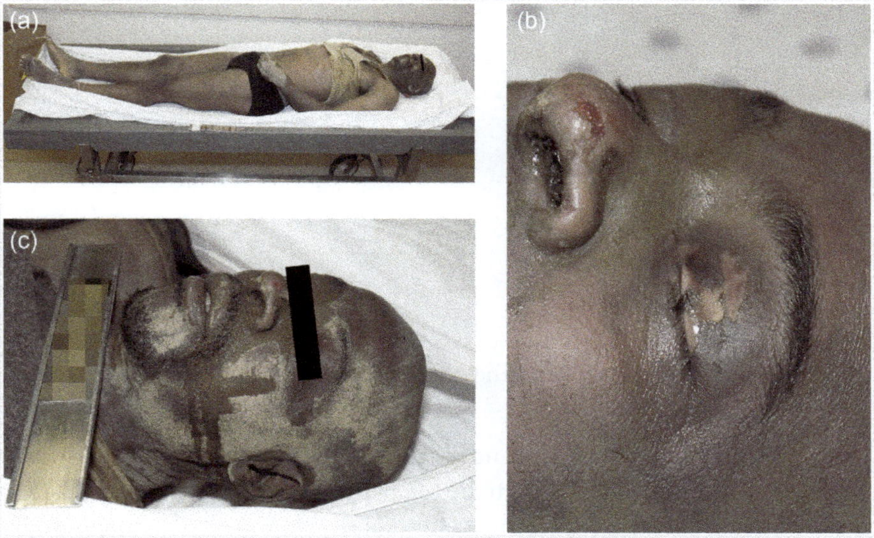

Figure 11.3 Adherent sand and silt on the body (A and B) and skin slippage of left eyelids and abrasion of the nose (C).

concentration of 0.24 g/dl. These findings are consistent with some degree of acute alcohol intoxication, but some degree of dilution secondary to prolonged submersion, in addition to diffusion and postmortem production of ethanol within the body, may also have been present, making the determination of the absorptive status less practical. Further toxicological analysis revealed cocaine, cocaine metabolite, and cocaethylene (product of cocaine and ethanol) in blood and urine samples. The cause of death was drowning, and the manner of death was ruled accidental.

Injuries sustained during a boating accident from impact with another boat or object or contact of parts of the boat with a swimmer can be quickly lethal in and of themselves or cause incapacitation with subsequent submersion and drowning.

CASE STUDY

A 13-year-old child was swimming with a friend in a very large lake while holding on to a log. A swiftly approaching thunderstorm prompted the two to summon a nearby boater for assistance in towing them to the shore. As the boater pulled anchor, the boat began to drift toward the boys, who abandoned the log to swim toward the 23-foot gas-powered vessel. As one boy quickly reached and climbed the swim platform, the boat motor was started but seized shortly thereafter. The second boy had come in contact with the propeller and was pulled underwater. Attempts to free the boy using a rope initially passed under his armpits were done by the boater and passengers, but to no avail. A 911 call was made, and subsequently, the Coast Guard arrived and started CPR on the unresponsive and still partially submerged boy, who was still entangled beneath the stern. The boat, along with the boy and rescuers, was

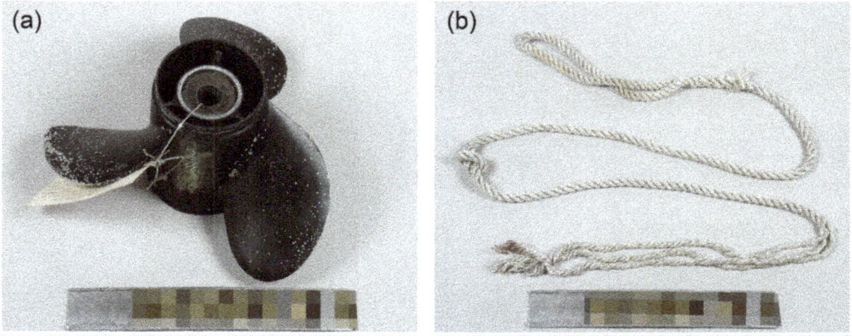

Figure 11.4 Propeller removed from the boat (A) and rope used in attempts to extricate the victim (B).

towed to shore. Additional first responders arrived for assistance. The boy was finally extricated from what was discovered to be the propellers, and severe trauma to his left leg was noted. Approximately 10 minutes of total rescue time had transpired. Shortly thereafter, he was conveyed to the local hospital still in cardiopulmonary arrest and, despite continued resuscitative efforts, was pronounced dead approximately 12 minutes after arrival. Hospital blood tests were significant for hypoxia and acidosis and negative for carbon monoxide and ethanol. Further investigation revealed that the boat was operational and there was no evidence of impairment of the boat operator. A first responder was exposed to the boy's blood and a formal request for infectious disease testing was made. The propeller and rope were conveyed to the coroner's office (Figure 11.4A and B).

The autopsy of the male adolescent revealed multiple, parallel, deep cuts of the lower extremities, with more extensive damage present on the left leg. Additionally, patterned linear abrasions consistent with rope marks were noted, also of the lower extremities. The internal examination was remarkable for hyperinflated, edematous lungs. Petrous ridge hemorrhage was present. The presence or absence of sphenoid sinus fluid was not described. Hemorrhagic edema and emphysema aquosum were described in microscopic sections of lung tissue. Toxicology test results were negative. Testing for infectious disease was negative. The cause of death was due to drowning with a contributing condition of multiple propeller cuts. The manner of death was ruled accidental.

Lack of swimming experience, lack of familiarity with underwater topography, and swimming in locations not designated for recreational swimming confer increased risk for drowning. These factors, combined with swift waters and hidden undercurrents, are a recipe for tragedy.

CASE STUDY

A ten-year-old girl, her two sisters, and a group of friends decided to walk down to a large creek located in a nearby park one mid-spring afternoon. A number of other patrons, later to be witnesses and would-be rescuers, were in the vicinity.

Figure 11.5 (A) Creek with waterfall, (B) Creek with waterfall, and (C) victim rescue.

The scene was that of a large creek, a portion of which coursed under railroad tracks through a man-made concrete tunnel (sluiceway) down to a drop-off of 5 to 7 feet, creating a small waterfall with a resultant hydraulic effect at the bottom before continuing onward down a continual gentle decline (Figure 11.5A). The pool of water at the bottom of the waterfall had a depth of 10 to 12 feet, with vertical recirculation caused by the hydraulic effect, resulting in trapping of objects below the surface (Figure 11.5B).

The incident involved the victim who was unable to swim and one of her sisters, who on a dare decided to slide together over the edge of the tunnel and into the creek. Both girls became submerged, with only one resurfacing. Several bystanders attempted to rescue the girls, with success at the rescue of only one of them. The victim remained submerged. Police were called and responded, along with technical response and dive teams. The dive and technical response teams searched both the calm and more turbulent waters of the creek, respectively. The victim was finally located with the use of a pike pole, approximately 30 feet away from and to one side of the waterfall, and conveyed to dry land (Figure 11.5C). Emergency medical responders determined that there were no vital signs. White foam was visible within the nostrils and mouth.

The autopsy of an otherwise healthy ten-year-old revealed wrinkling of the skin of the hands, blood-tinged foam within the nose and mouth, cutis anserina, and adherent sand and gravel. There were no significant blunt or sharp force injuries. Internal examination revealed severe pulmonary congestion and edema with exudation of foamy fluid from the cut surfaces, petrous ridge hemorrhage, and red-tinged watery fluid within the sphenoid sinus. There were 150 ml of tan and watery fluid within the stomach. The microscopic examination was remarkable for pulmonary congestion and edema and emphysema aquosum. The cause of death was due to asphyxia by drowning, and the manner of death was ruled accidental.

Natural Water-Related Deaths

The classification of a death as natural is done when the death occurs as a result of disease or the aging process. Death due to natural disease can occur relatively predictably, such as that associated with terminal cancer or end-stage liver disease. Natural death can also occur unexpectedly at any time and any place, including near or in an aqueous environment in association with routine or recreational activities. Initial observation of a submersed decedent may lead to the premature conclusion that the death was due to drowning by nonnatural means until further investigated.

Sudden death is generally described as death within 24 hours of the onset of symptoms. For the C/ME, this definition can be expanded to include not only deaths occurring after the onset of symptoms but also instantaneous deaths, deaths occurring before medical diagnosis, and deaths involving individuals found dead outside the confines of a medical facility. The expanded definition encompasses the unexpected nature of some natural deaths. C/MEs are mandated to investigate all sudden and unexpected deaths, the majority of which are found to occur as a result of natural disease, most commonly cardiovascular disease. Water-related deaths may involve catastrophic or insidious natural disease, such as sudden blockage of a coronary artery (thrombosis), cardiac arrhythmia, ruptured cerebral artery aneurysm, massive hemorrhage from a perforated gastric ulcer, massive tumor or infection-related hemorrhage, complications of diabetes, and seizures. The list of potential causes is lengthy. The extent and significance of the natural disease can be such that drowning is precluded because the individual is dead before, during, or very shortly after submersion, with no appreciable effects from airway obstruction, including inhalation of water. Thus, there will be little to no supportive findings consistent with drowning. Care should be exercised, therefore, as to the interpretation of pulmonary edema and petechial hemorrhage of the lungs and other organs, as these may also be present in some natural deaths.

Autopsies involving water-related deaths may reveal an unequivocal anatomic natural cause of death referable to the brain, heart, lungs, gastrointestinal tract, or blood vessels in an individual found in or around an aqueous environment, submerged or not. Correlation with scene findings is always important. Subsequent collapse from the terminal natural condition may end with the person in the water, with or without covering of the nose or mouth by the water. Blunt and sharp force injuries may be sustained as a result of the collapse or with attempts to break one's fall during collapse. It is important to remember that absence of water or other fluid in smaller containers, such as sinks, bins, and bathtubs, where a decedent may be found could mean that water has drained or spilled out and that the person was once partially or completely submerged (findings of a damp body or surroundings may be helpful). Consideration for drowning should be given in this case. An individual found with the head well above the potential waterline, such as in a bathtub (sitting upright), would give weight for a natural cause of death. Likewise, positioning within a bathtub *below* a potential waterline but without evidence that it was recently full (shower running, no waterline, and drain plug in an open position) gives added strength to a subsequent finding of a natural disease at autopsy. In this case, the body and the surroundings may still be wet or damp if the shower was running. The absence of natural disease at autopsy does not rule out a natural cause since sudden death due to natural disease may lack anatomic or microscopic findings, such as those resulting from an abnormal heart rhythm (arrhythmia) or seizures.

CASE STUDY

A 41-year-old Caucasian male had not reported to work one morning and failed to arrive for a medical appointment later in the afternoon. Concerned that his car was

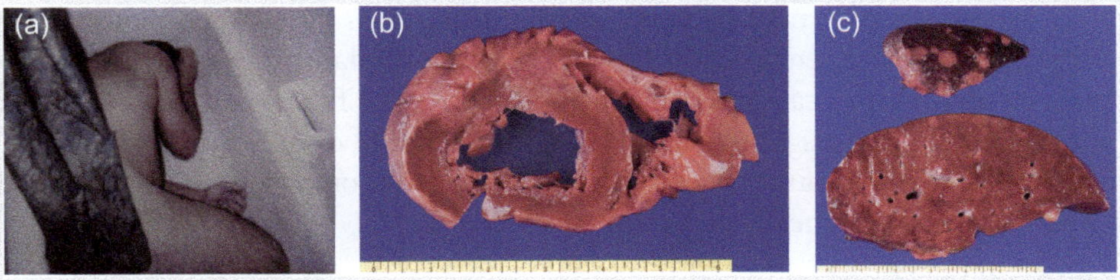

Figure 11.6 (A) Decedent completely within the bathtub. Involvement of the heart (B) and spleen and liver, and (C) by multiple granulomas.

still in the apartment parking lot, the man's sister, who lived in the same apartment building, requested building maintenance and subsequently police to make a welfare check. He was discovered lying nude in a fetal position on his left side in the bathtub (Figure 11.6A). The shower was running (cold), and the drain plug was in the open position, and thus no water had accumulated. Rigor and livor mortis were described by police to be "set in." A search of the apartment revealed medications for a heart condition and the name and office number of a cardiologist treating the man for arrhythmogenic heart disease. A call to the doctor's office revealed that the man had recently called to report that he had received a "shock" from his defibrillator medical device. He was advised to come in for evaluation on the day of his untimely death.

At autopsy, full rigor mortis of the facial muscles and extremities as well as anterior and left lateral fixed livor mortis were noted. An implantable defibrillator was located under the skin of the upper left chest, just beneath a corresponding surgical scar, with wires (leads) extending normally into the right heart chambers. The device was interrogated and deactivated prior to removal by an outside technician. Further internal examination revealed a markedly enlarged heart (720 grams) with severely dilated chambers. Lungs were moderately congested and edematous. The spleen, liver, and lymph nodes adjacent to the lungs (mediastinal and pulmonary hilar) were all enlarged. Multiple tan and rubbery nodules were noted throughout the heart muscle, lung tissue, lymph nodes, spleen, liver, and vertebral bone marrow (Figure 11.6B and C). Microscopic examination revealed a special form of chronic inflammation in the form of multiple noncaseating granulomas. Special histological stains for microorganisms were negative. Toxicological analysis revealed negative results. The results of the defibrillator interrogation were multiple, abnormally fast heartbeats (ventricular tachycardia and ventricular fibrillation) and subsequent multiple shocks from the defibrillator that did not return the heart to a normal rhythm. The cause of death was due to sarcoidosis with the involvement of multiple organs (multivisceral). A review of medical records revealed no previous diagnosis of this condition or cause of the arrhythmia.

Sarcoidosis is a chronic inflammatory disease of uncertain etiology that usually involves the lungs and adjacent lymph nodes. In the United States, it has a greater prevalence among African Americans, particularly women. Involvement of multiple organs occurs in severe cases. Involvement of the heart can cause interference with the heart's normal electrical conductivity, leading to arrhythmias that can result in sudden death despite treatment with medicines, surgery, or defibrillation.

Individuals with physical and mental disabilities are sometimes unable to precisely articulate symptoms they may be experiencing; thus, their caretakers may be unaware of an impending medical emergency. Normal activities of daily living may be continued, whether provided by the caretaker or by the disabled but functional person. Accidents with injury can sometimes result. Physically and mentally disabled individuals can live long lives and develop the same natural diseases, including complications, as those without physical or mental challenges.

CASE STUDY

A 62-year-old woman with a history of mental retardation and deafness had been experiencing flu-like symptoms the preceding several days, according to her elderly mother. One evening, the mother ran a bath for the woman and left her to bathe by herself, as she was able to do so, and this was the normal nightly routine. The mother returned after approximately 25 minutes to find her daughter nude, face down, and submerged in a bathtub full of water. The mother activated her medical alert button to summon emergency assistance. Police and emergency medical services arrived. The woman was removed from the bathtub and placed on the bathroom floor (Figure 11.7A). There were no vital signs. Scene assessment was also made by the death investigator upon subsequent arrival. The woman was conveyed to the coroner's office.

External examination at autopsy was remarkable for severely congested sclerae, conjunctival petechial hemorrhages, damp hair, wrinkled skin of the hands, and a

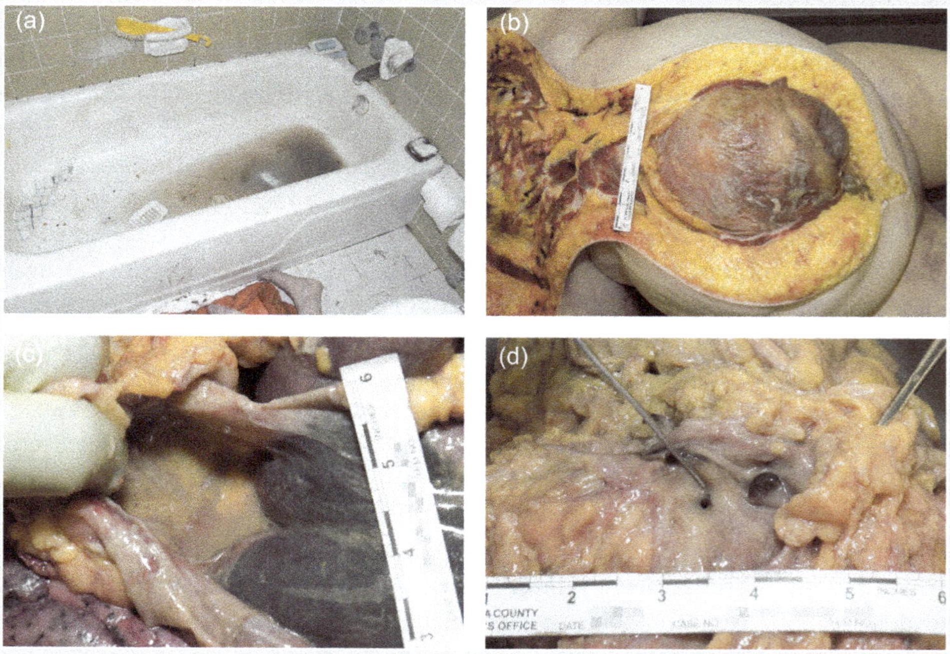

Figure 11.7 (A) Bathtub with water partially drained. (B) Inflamed abdominal cavity (C) containing pus and (D) perforated colonic diverticulum.

markedly distended and firm abdomen. The rigor mortis was complete, and the livor mortis was anterior, posterior, and blanchable. Internal examination was remarkable for a severely inflamed abdominal cavity with the accumulation of pus (Figure 11.7B and C). Further examination revealed a chronic condition of the large intestine called diverticulitis. Specifically, because of this chronic disease, a ¼-inch perforation of the rectosigmoid colon had developed with communication into the abdominal cavity, allowing fecal material and bacteria to stream into the cavity (Figure 11.7D). This was the direct cause of the abdominal infection, and it is likely that the flu-like symptoms were related to sepsis from bloodstream infection by the bacteria. No supportive findings of drowning were present. The cause of death was due to infection within the abdominal cavity as a result of the perforation caused by the diverticulitis. The manner of death was natural, as the historical, scene, and autopsy findings were consistent with collapse and death as a result of overwhelming infection while getting into the filled bathtub.

Seizures can occur spontaneously, without an identifiable cause, or secondary to a number of conditions, including birth-related hypoxia/ischemia, head trauma, stroke, brain tumor, or abnormal brain anatomy. Deaths due to seizures arising spontaneously without an identifiable cause or from natural causes will be ruled as the natural manner of death. Deaths due to seizures resulting from traumatic brain injury will be ruled as accidental, homicidal, or suicidal, depending on the circumstances that precipitated the injury.

Certain types of seizures, arising from abnormal random bursts of neurological impulses, cause uncontrollable motor activity, which can interfere with normal physiology, including breathing, and can also lead to injury and death. Seizures can be controlled by one or more medications, which must be maintained at certain levels in the blood to be effective at suppressing the seizure activity. Patient compliance with the prescribed regimen is a significant factor in the maintenance of therapeutic levels, and thus the suppression of seizure activity, but seizures can still occur, even if the patient is taking the medication(s) as directed. The persistence of uncontrolled seizures will prompt clinical reevaluation with adjustment of doses, changing the type of medication, or adding more medications. Without adequate suppression, the frequency and duration of seizures may lead to complications that then lead to death, including injury and drowning, if seizures are sustained while in or near an aqueous environment.

The increased risk of drowning in someone with a seizure disorder is well known, and recommendations for close supervision during recreational swimming, bathing, or other water-related activity are made continuously, especially for children and infants. The onset of seizures may be unpredictable and go unnoticed prior to a submersion event.

Autopsy findings in individuals who drown during or after a seizure may include those findings supportive of drowning, which in the right historical and scene context, provides the most probable cause of death—drowning due to seizures or drowning with a contributing condition of seizures. In cases in which there are little or no supportive findings of drowning, **sudden unexpected death in epilepsy** (SUDEP) may provide an explanation, especially when an anatomic or toxicological cause of death cannot be found. Particularly in bathtub scenes in which the decedent's head is found well above any potential level of water, SUDEP is a reasonable consideration.

SUDEP involves sudden witnessed or unwitnessed death in an individual with long-standing epilepsy or seizures in which no other anatomic or toxicological explanation for the death is found and after a complete scene investigation.[31,32] This definition excludes seizure-induced drowning deaths. In SUDEP, seizure activity is presumed to precede these deaths. The incidence of this entity is difficult to pinpoint since it has not gained widespread acceptance for use as a cause of death. It is estimated that approximately one in two hundred patients with chronic epilepsy die yearly from SUDEP and 5% to 30% of deaths in patients with epilepsy are due to SUDEP.[29] Risk factors associated with this entity include the history of uncontrollable seizures, the requirement of multiple seizure medications, poor medication compliance, male gender, and sleep. Interestingly, most victims of SUDEP are found in bed or during presumed sleep, and a relevant example could be that of an epileptic who fell asleep upright while taking a warm bath. The mechanism of death in SUDEP is unclear but thought to involve brain-induced cardiac arrhythmia, brain-induced respiratory dysfunction, or both. The neurologic effects of normal sleep have also been postulated as a trigger of seizure activity leading to SUDEP.

Examination of the brains of individuals with a seizure disorder or epilepsy often reveals no structural abnormality. Nevertheless, the autopsy should include careful examination of the brain for scarring of the hippocampal region (including Ammon's horn); abnormal architecture of the gray and white matter, including ectopic gray matter (grossly and microscopically); brain cysts; new and old trauma; and tumors.[31,33] The finding of any of these may provide an explanation as to the origin of the seizures and confirmation of previous clinical neurological diagnosis. A complete autopsy will also naturally include an examination of the heart since structural and microscopic abnormalities of this organ may give rise to seizure-like activity. Documentation of any external injuries along with documentation of contusion of the tongue (from biting during seizure activity) can provide additional supportive evidence of seizure activity. The toxicological analysis may reveal subtherapeutic levels of antiseizure medication(s), but detection of therapeutic levels does not rule out seizures as a cause of death. Histories of a recent change in antiseizure medication, the addition of other antiseizure medications to the regimen, and increased frequency of seizures prior to death are important to note and can add certainty that the cause of death is most likely due to seizures.

Undetermined Water-Related Deaths

There are instances when the investigative and autopsy information are insufficient to allow for the classification of manner of death or to distinguish between two or more possibilities. While the information gleaned from a comprehensive scene investigation and complete autopsy may be sufficient for the determination of a *cause* of death, pinpointing how and why a body became submerged in an aqueous environment may be difficult because the information is lacking or toxicological testing is unrevealing.

Uncommonly, the circumstantial information supports drowning as a cause of death, but the autopsy along with the toxicological testing lack supportive findings of drowning and are unrevealing, respectively. This may arise in the case of a mildly to a moderately decomposed body recovered from a body of water without evidence of injury or with few supportive findings of drowning, and with the detection of ethanol with evidence of endogenous metabolism (and antemortem ingestion). The designation of the cause of death as "probable drowning" or "undetermined" with the manner of death designated as "undetermined" may be applicable here. Rarely, the investigation, autopsy, and toxicological testing fail to reveal both a cause and manner of death or contributing conditions (natural or otherwise), and thus the cause of death will be listed as "undetermined" and the manner of death will also be listed as "undetermined."

CASE STUDY

A 42-year-old man was found with his head, torso, and most of his upper and lower extremities completely submerged in a bathtub filled to the brim with water. The decedent's mother had requested a welfare check on her son after being unable to enter her home where she lived with her son, after being discharged from a short hospital stay. Friends had not heard from or spoken to the man for two days and went to the home in attempts to locate the man. Police were called, arrived, and entered the secured residence to discover the nearly completely submerged and clothed man lying on his right side. His feet and a portion of his upper left arm were not submerged and appeared dried and partially mummified. His feet were resting on the shower curtain and the edge of the bathtub (Figure 11.8). A necklace had become entangled between the lips but was high up enough around the neck so as to not compress the internal neck structures and vessels. The hot water spigot was still running (cold) without overflow of the bathtub due to drainage through the overflow outlet. A folded shirt was noted on the toilet, and a pair of worn socks was in one of the corners of the bathroom. Empty bottles of a sleep aid medication and pain medication were found nearby. No suicide note in any form was found. The rest of the house appeared undisturbed.

This man had a history of heavy alcohol consumption and at times would combine alcohol with his mother's sleep aid medication and his own pain medication,

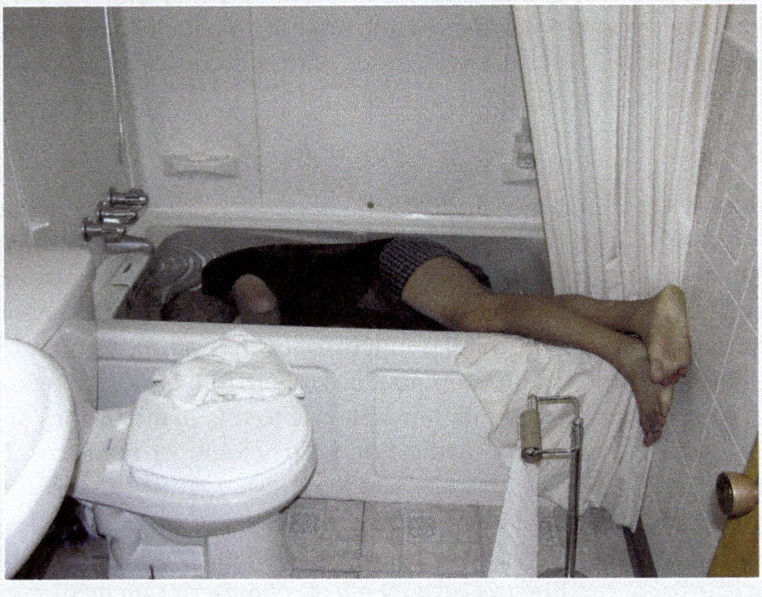

Figure 11.8 Near-complete submersion in a bathtub.

which had been prescribed for an unspecified chronic pain condition. He reportedly had been depressed for an unspecified period of time but had not been clinically diagnosed with a psychiatric condition or on any prescribed psychiatric medication. He suffered the loss of his father and brother within the recent decade. He was the sole caregiver of his mother. A friend reported to the police that during a telephone conversation a few days prior to the man's death, the decedent talked of a recent visit from a female acquaintance with whom he had a "good time." The friend surmised that the man was intoxicated, noting his slurred speech and angry mood while describing the visit. Police investigators were unable to produce verification as to the identity and whereabouts of this female.

Autopsy findings were that of a well-developed, well-nourished male with wrinkling of and pallor of the skin. Rigor was absent, and livor was fixed on the right side of the body. The corneas were cloudy, and there was a focus of skin slippage on the right thigh. There were a number of small abrasions of the face without a discernible pattern or clustering. Two abrasions were of the temple associated with acute subgaleal hemorrhage beneath, indicating blunt impact to this region. A slightly indented, red, and pale patterned mark extended over both lower cheeks corresponding to the necklace. Internal inspection revealed voluminous, congested, and edematous lungs surround by pleural effusion. Foamy fluid was noted within the upper airways. There was a ¼-inch contusion of the tongue. The heart was significantly enlarged with thickened chambers and dilation of the right ventricle. Gross anatomic examination combined with microscopic examination of the heart and kidneys revealed changes consistent with hypertensive cardiovascular disease. The liver was markedly enlarged with severe fatty change and scarring consistent with the history of chronic alcoholism combined with prescription medication abuse. The sphenoid sinus contained 5 ml of blood-red-tinged watery fluid.

The toxicological screening was positive for caffeine, and its presence was otherwise not significant. A subtherapeutic level of zolpidem (Ambien) was found. No ethanol was detected. An electrolyte study of the vitreous fluid was not requested. The cause of death is asphyxia by drowning.

The investigative and autopsy findings in the above case support a cause of death consistent with asphyxia by drowning, but what is the manner of death? A number of significant factors are apparent in this case, making more than one manner of death a possibility. Collapse with drowning from alcoholic seizures due to alcohol withdrawal could constitute an accidental death and is supported by the finding of chronic liver disease, tongue contusion, subgaleal hemorrhage, and lack of ethanol on toxicological analysis. A suicidal death by drowning is not unfathomable due to this man's history of a number of significant life stressors and empty medication bottles found at the scene. However, the overall scene, with the position of his feet and lower legs against the shower curtain and resting on the edge of the bathtub, suggests a sudden collapse, perhaps while getting ready to bathe, which in this man could have been precipitated by a medical- or medication-induced event (cardiac arrhythmia vs. adverse effects of prescription medication, including withdrawal effects) that, combined with drowning, constitutes an accidental death. The prescription medication zolpidem provides sedation and facilitates sleep but has a risk for the development of tolerance and dependence, and its use must be monitored by a physician. Adverse effects with chronic high-dose usage and subsequent withdrawal may cause joint and muscle pain, hallucinations, mood disturbances, agitation, and suicidal ideation, and induce grand mal seizures.[33-36] Homicidal violence must also be ruled out in this case, starting with an additional investigation regarding the existence of a mysterious woman visitor, although it is interesting and provocative that one of the side effects of zolpidem is hallucinations. Cases such as the above require an informed analysis, and the lack or unavailability of information, equivocal results, or uninterpretable findings may require a ruling of the manner of death as undetermined.

References

1. Schmidt, P., and Madea, B. 1995. Homicide in bathtub. *Forensic Sci Int* 72:135–46.
2. Copeland, A. R. 1986. Homicidal drowning. *Forensic Sci Int* 31:247–52.
3. DiMaio, V. J. M. 2000. Homicidal asphyxia. *Am J Forensic Med Pathol* 21(1):1–4.
4. Griest, K. J., and Zumwalt, R. E. 1989. Child abuse by drowning. *Pediatrics* 83(1):41–46.
5. Somers, G. R., Chiasson, D. A., and Smith, C. R. 2006. Pediatric drowning—A 20-year review of autopsied cases. II. Pathologic features. *Am J Forensic Med Pathol* 27(1):20–24.
6. Kinney, H. C., and Thach, B. T. 2009. The sudden infant death syndrome. *N Engl J Med* 361(8):795–805.
7. Lucas, J., Goldfeder, L. B., and Gill, J. R. 2002. Bodies found in waterways of New York City. *J Forensic Sci* 47(1):137–41.
8. Demirci, S., Kamil, H., Zerrin, E., et al. 2009. A series of complex suicide. *Am J Forensic Med Pathol* 30(2):152–54.
9. Byard, R. W., Houldsworth, G., and James, R. A. 2001. Characteristic features of suicidal drowning—A 20-year study. *Am J Forensic Med Pathol* 22(2):134–38.
10. Copeland, A. R. 1987. Suicide by drowning. *Am J Forensic Med Pathol* 8(1):18–22.
11. Avis, S. P. 1993. Suicidal drowning. *J Forensic Sci* 38(6):1422–26.
12. Davis, L. G. 1999. Suicidal drowning in South Florida. *J Forensic Sci* 44(5):902–5.
13. Wirthwein, D. P., Barnard, J. J., and Prahlow, J. A. 2002. Suicide by drowning—A 20-year review. *J Forensic Sci* 47(1):131–36.
14. Racette, S., and Sauvageau, A. 2008. Suicide in the bath using weight and elevation of feet. *Am J Forensic Med Pathol* 29(1):80–82.
15. Stephenson, L., van der Heuvel, C., and Byard, R. 2020. Weighted drownings- an example of augmentation or enhancement of a suicide method. *J Forensic Leg Med* 70:101914. doi: 10.1016/j.jflm.2020.101914.
16. D'Ovidio, C., Rosato, E., and Carnevale, A. 2017. An unusual case of murder-suicide: The importance of studying knots. *J Forensic Leg Med* 45:17–20.
17. Todt, M., Ast, F., Wolff-Maras, R., et al. 2014. Suicide by drowning: A forensic challenge. *Forensic Sci Int* 240:e22–e24.
18. Somers, G. R., Chiasson, D. A., and Smith, C. R. 2005. Pediatric drowning—A 20-year review of autopsied cases. I. Demographic features. *Am J Forensic Med Pathol* 26(4):316–19.
19. Sauvageau, A., and Racette, S. 2006. Aqua-eroticum: An unusual autoerotic fatality in a lake involving a home-made diving apparatus. *J Forensic Sci* 51(1):137–39.
20. Sivaloganathan, S. 1984. Aqua-eroticum—A case of auto-erotic drowning. *Med Sci Law* 24(4):300–2.
21. Jordan, F., Mallonee, S., Reddish-Douglas, M., et. al. Electricity-related deaths on lakes—Oklahoma, 1989–1993. 1996. *Morbid Mort Wkly Rep* 45(21):440–42.
22. World Health Organization. 2009. Violence and injury prevention and disability (VIP), facts about injuries—Drowning. http://www.who.int/violence_injury_prevention/publications/other_injury/en/drowning_factsheet.pdf (accessed May 16, 2020).

23. Browne, M. L., Lewis-Michl, E. L., and Stark A. D. 2003. Unintentional drownings among New York State residents, 1988–1994. *Public Health Rep* 118:448–58.
24. Byard, R. W., and Lipsett, J. 1999. Drowning deaths in toddlers and pre-ambulatory children in South Australia. *Am J Forensic Med Pathol* 20(4):328–32.
25. Lunetta, P., Smith, G. S., Penttila, A., et al. 2004. Unintentional drowning in Finland 1970–2000: A population-based study. *Int J Epidemiol* 33:1053–63.
26. Gorniak, J. M., Jenkins, A. J., Felo, J. A., et al. 2005. Drug prevalence in drowning deaths in Cuyahoga County, Ohio. *Am J Forensic Med Pathol* 26(3):240–43.
27. Somers, G. R., Chiasson, D. A., and Smith, C. R. 2006. Pediatric drowning—A 20-year review of autopsied cases. III. Bathtub drownings. *Am J Forensic Med Pathol* 27(2):113–16.
28. Byard, R. W. 2008. Rainwater tank drowning. *J Forensic Leg Med* 15(8):533–34.
29. Brunkard, J., Namulanda, G., and Ratard, R. 2008. Hurricane Katrina deaths, Louisiana, 2005. *Disaster Med Public Health Prep* 2(4):215–23.
30. Jonkman, S. N., and Kelman, I. 2005. An analysis of the causes and circumstances of flood disaster deaths. *Disasters* 29(1):78–97.
31. Saxena, A., and Ang, L. C. 1993. Epilepsy and bathtub drowning—Important neuropathological observations. *Am J Forensic Med Pathol* 14(2):125–29.
32. Lear-Kaul, K. C., Coughlin, L., and Doberson, M. J. 2005. Sudden unexpected death in epilepsy—A retrospective study. *Am J Forensic Med Pathol* 26(1):11–17.
33. Shields, L. B. E., Hunsaker, D. M., Hunsaker, J. C., 3rd, et al. 2002. Sudden unexpected death in epilepsy—Neuropathologic findings. *Am J Forensic Med Pathol* 23(4):307–17.
34. Sakkas, P., Psarros, C., Masdrakis, V., et al. 1999. Dependence on zolpidem: A case report. *Eur Psychiatry* 14(6):358–59.
35. Boulanger-Rostowsky, L., Fayet, H., Benmoussa, N., et al. 2004. Dependence on zolpidem: A report of two cases. *Encephale* 30(2):153–55.
36. Zolpidem side effects. http://www.drugs.com/sfx/zolpidem-side-effects.html (accessed May 16, 2020).

Personnel Training

12

KEVIN L. ERSKINE

Water-Proofing the Patrol Officer

Introduction

As officers in the public safety field, you are expected to respond to any number of incidents that may include hostile suspects and/or environments. Most agencies provide their officers with ample training for virtually every piece of equipment they carry, such as duty weapon, radio, flashlight, pepper spray, taser, asp, baton, and handcuffs. This equipment is carried on a daily basis to aid the officer with a wide variety of circumstances encountered at any given moment.

One type of call overlooked is the water-related incident. Most often, agencies working directly in or around the water environment, such as marine patrol, possess the necessary training to handle potential threats from the water environment. But agencies that don't have lakes, rivers, and oceans often overlook this potential hazard to their officers.

Officers may be required to respond to a domestic call around a family-built-in pool, or a small fishing pond at the local recreation facility, or an indoor swimming complex. Do these officers have the knowledge, experience, and skill to survive if they are knocked into the water wearing duty boots, ballistic vest, and a heavy duty belt? Can they keep themselves afloat long enough to work their way to safety? Can they subdue the in-water attack of a suspect?

Legal Issue

The potential legal liability of a department is increased if officers are not properly trained. This is based on the standards for failure to properly train personnel as set forth by the *U.S. Supreme Court in City of Canton v Harris*, 489 U.S. 378, 109 S. Ct 1197 (1989). According to this decision, the duties that officers are assigned must be accompanied with adequate training to perform that function. Thus, the design of a water program, including the training component, must specifically address issues most prevalent to that environment and must provide documentation and materials used to defend it. A key question to ask is, "Have I received the necessary training to proficiently handle an encounter in or around water?"

Steps to a Safe Encounter

- Awareness
- Prevention
- Recovery
- Self defense
- Rescue

Awareness

Officers working their specific jurisdictional boundaries should have a good idea about most potential water hazards. But there will always be the unforeseen incidents that will arise, catching the unprepared off guard. These may include incidents near a built-in pool, recreation centers, and ponds or near-private property or boat-docking facilities.

An awareness of these hazards and an organized plan of escape are essential. As a general rule, any area containing water deep enough to knock a person off balance should be considered. This is not limited to water depth over your head. Shallow water can be just as deadly if you are not able to get back on your feet. The bulk and weight of a duty belt may hinder an unassisted recovery. Water deep enough to cover your head can cause drowning.

Prevention

There are certain precautions officers can take before placing themselves in a water-hazard environment that will drastically increase their chances of survival. Donning a PFD (Personal Floatation Device) or lifejacket is a simple way to ensure one's safety. Vest-style jackets are comfortable to wear and allow access to everything on a duty belt. Many marine patrols wear this style on a routine basis. For departments that regularly patrol larger bodies of water such as an ocean, it is highly recommended that the PFD has an E.P.I.R.B. device (Emergency Position-Indicating Radio Beacon) or a strobe light, as well as an audible signal device such as a whistle. These devices will aid in recovery of the officer should other personnel lose sight of them. Agencies should provide these to their officers and have them readily available in the trunk of every cruiser. Agencies may also consider color-coordinated PFDs with identifying features such as sewn-on badge and "POLICE" across the shoulders. This will help the public identify them as well as responding backup. Correctly donning a PFD includes proper size, proper fit, and having all zippers and buckles connected (Figure 12.1).

Placing the suspect between yourself and the hazard is also very beneficial. When approaching the scene, identify the hazard and position yourself so you face the hazard, rather than having your back to it. With your back to the hazard, you have no way of knowing if you are a safe distance away. During your interview stance, you may need to constantly adjust your position to keep the suspect between you and the hazard. By keeping the suspect between you and the water, you are always at an advantage. This also limits escape routes for the suspect.

Nothing is carved in stone, forcing you to stay in an unsafe location. If possible, move the encounter to a safer location. When approaching the scene, identify safe zones where you can move to conduct business. For backyard pools, consider the deck or patio, or even the front yard. Avoid keeping yourself at risk. If possible get out!

Know Your Limitations Officers who can't swim have no business placing themselves in a water environment. If the hazard exists, secure the scene and wait for backup. Nothing would complicate matters worse than responding to a hostile incident and attempting to rescue a fellow officer while also having to subdue a hostile suspect.

Force the subject to come to you. This is the same basic principle as a felony traffic stop. Order the subject out of the hazardous environment. By having the subject come to you, the hazard is immediately eliminated. There will always be situations that won't allow you to apply these precautions, so you must train for worst-case scenarios.

Figure 12.1 PFD shown with an attached strobe light and whistle.

Recovery (Self-Rescue)

These self-rescue techniques should be practiced in a safe controlled water environment such as a pool. To accurately simulate everyday situations, weigh your duty belt and then, for the in-water skills, place diving weights on a belt to represent your duty belt. This prevents any water damage to your actual duty rig.

Upon unexpectedly entering deep waters, it is imperative that you immediately drop your duty belt. The excess weight and bulk of a duty belt may be enough to cause many officers to sink beneath the surface. These officers should make dropping the duty belt a first priority. Many duty belts weigh in excess of 10–15 pounds. Although you may be removing any available defense weapons, your first priority is drowning prevention. Practice removing belt keepers without looking both in and out of the water. Practice calling for backup before ditching your radio. To drop the duty belt, first release the back belt keepers, then the front. If the front keepers are released first, the belt can sag and hinder movement of the legs to keep your head above water. Practicing this technique will help prevent a panic situation which can lead to tunnel vision and complications. Using a back float position may also make it easier to release the belt.

Swim to Safety While Wearing a Duty Belt This is only an option for officers capable of swimming while wearing a duty belt. Work your way toward a safe zone, away from hostile persons or environment.

Fending off Rocks and Debris in Moving Water Keep arms and feet in front of you, using your legs and feet to "fend off" rocks. This requires you to use your arms and legs

Figure 12.2 Feet-first position in moving water.

like shock absorbers to prevent your body from being injured (Figures 12.2 and 12.3). Do not attempt to stand until reaching a safe, shallower area. Foot entrapment occurs when a swimmer's foot becomes wedged in a crack or under a rock below the water surface. The force of the current makes escape difficult. In moving water, face downstream and keep your feet near the surface. Fend off rocks with your feet.

Defense against Strainers Strainers are objects in the water that allow water to pass through or over them, but not a person. Strainers may include a log across the waterway, with water rushing over it. Or it may include low hanging branches, touching the water surface, which can force your head below the surface of the water. If you encounter a strainer, swim toward it head first (Figure 12.4) and then hurl yourself up and over it (Figure 12.5). If you do not gain momentum going into a strainer, the force of the water may pull you under the debris. After clearing the strainer, resume the feet forward position.

Ferrying across a Current If you must move yourself from one side of moving water to the other, such as to grab a rescue rope, swim at a 45° angle to the current. This will allow sideways movement in a current without causing excessive fatigue.

Escape from a Fall onto a Pool Cover In the event you should fall onto a pool cover, try to remain calm and crawl out of the cover. Do not attempt to stand or roll out of the cover. This will only entangle you further, making it difficult to keep your head above water. Even attempting to stand in shallow water is extremely difficult. The cover wraps around your body instantly and squeezes tightly, making movement difficult. Immediately work yourself into a sitting position and begin to crawl out by pushing the sides of the cover off

Figure 12.3 Fending off rocks with your legs in moving water.

Figure 12.4 Build momentum by swimming toward the strainer.

Figure 12.5 Hurl yourself over the strainer then resume the feet-first position.

you. Continue to work yourself free. It may be difficult to keep your head above water but do not panic.

In-water Self-Defense

Escape from the grasp of a suspect (as recommended by the U.S. Lifeguard Association).

Front Head Hold Escape Take a quick breath, tuck your chin down, turn your head to either side and raise your shoulders. Once underwater, bring your hands up to the suspect's elbows or to the underside of the suspect's arms just above the elbows. Push hard up and away from you. Keep your chin tucked, your arms fully extended, and your shoulders raised until you are free. Quickly swim out of reach. Most likely, the suspect is grabbing you to keep his own head above water.

Rear Head Hold Escape Take a quick breath, tuck your chin down, turn your head to either side and raise your shoulders. Submerged with the suspect. You may need to perform a feet-first surface dive to do this. Once underwater, bring your hands up to the suspect's elbows or to the underside of the suspect's arms just above the elbows. Be sure to swim clear of the suspect after working free.

Deployment of Intermediate Weapons If immersed in water over your head, you must be able to keep your head above water as a first priority. This may be done by:

- Treading water with duty belt on.
- Dropping your duty belt.
- Holding on to a stationary object such as a pier or ladder.

If dropping your duty belt is the only feasible option, you must first attempt to retrieve an intermediate weapon such as an ASP, baton, pepper spray, taser, or even your handcuffs. Any of these can be retrieved while unsnapping your belt keepers. The weapon of choice is determined by prior practice to find what is easiest and works best for you. Remember, at this point you are not attempting to subdue the attacker, only escape to preserve your own life.

Improvised Weapons Some field officers may not be equipped with a full duty rig. In this case, it may be necessary for the officer to use an improvised weapon such as a pen, flashlight, handcuffs, or keys. These items, when used properly, can provide more than sufficient protection from any attacker.

Pen Grasp the pen with a full fist, allowing the point of the pen to protrude from the pinky side of the fist. Using the point of the pen, swift sweeping movements with the hand can be done to strike the attacker with disabling blows.

Flashlight Grasp the flashlight with a full fist, similar to a club or nightstick and use swift sweeping motions to strike the attacker.

Handcuffs Handcuffs can be used very effectively as a self-defense weapon. Place both cuffs side by side and grasp them with one hand, leaving the hinge or chain side facing outward. The cuffs can then be swung to strike the opponent, similar to using brass knuckles. You can also move the cuffs in a chopping motion, using the teeth to rip the flesh from your attacker's face and hands. By grabbing just one cuff and leaving the second one hanging free, sweep the hands to swing the cuff and strike your opponent. Connecting to the jaw with either of these techniques can cause severe pain and possibly even break the jaw or knock out teeth (Figures 12.6 and 12.7).

Keys Grasp the key ring by a large key or the key ring itself and swing it in the same manner as the handcuffs. An average sized key ring has a significant amount of weight to cause a blunt, forceful blow to the opponent.

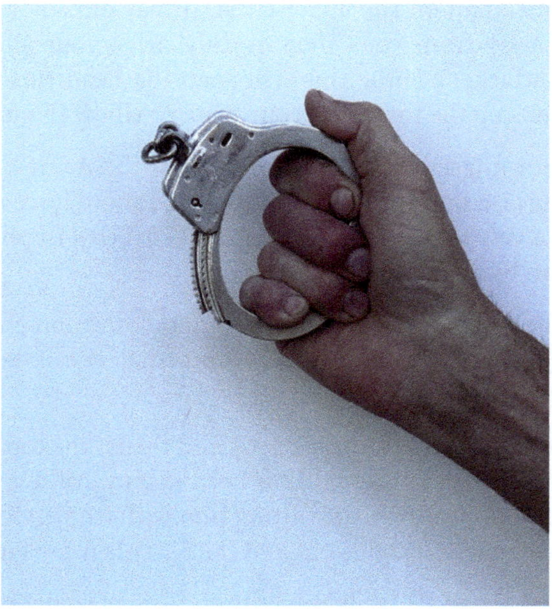

Figure 12.6 Chopping motion to injure your attacker.

Figure 12.7 Swinging the cuffs to strike your attacker.

Deadly Force If your life is in imminent danger, make every attempt to draw your duty weapon or taser from the holster. Under normal circumstances, a taser is not considered deadly force. But, in water over your head (or the head of the attacker), using a taser will totally incapacitate the subject, preventing him from swimming or being able to keep his head above water, which is very likely to cause drowning. Department policies will determine your course of action.

Self-Defense

In most cases, your lower torso will be relatively useless for self-defense. Your legs will primarily be used to keep your head above water. In extreme cases, the legs and feet may be used, but be aware that if the attacker should grab onto your leg or foot, it would be very difficult to keep your head above water. Very little force can be generated by the legs for defense due to water resistance, so the upper torso is primarily used for defense. The suspect's torso will be the only portion exposed as well. Several head and hand techniques are useful and are very effective with just a little practice.

Chin Blast Place your hand on the upper chest. It may already be there in an attempt to push the attacker away from you. Then quickly drive your elbow upward, striking the underside of the attacker's chin. This will snap the head furiously, causing instant disorientation and opens up the throat for your hand or elbow (Figure 12.8).

Throat Jab Force your fingers into the "V" just below the Adam's apple. This will drive even a large person quickly into the fetal position. Add more force and you may damage the wind pipe. This is a very tender area so placement isn't that important, but use enough force to show you mean business (Figure 12.9).

Nose Break Take the palm area of your strong hand and forcefully thrust it upward against the attacker's nose. The subject will be immediately blinded with pain and will cause the eyes to water profusely (Figure 12.10).

Head Butt Grab the back of the suspect's neck and thrust the top of your head upward into the nose of the suspect while you pull his head downward. Even if done wrong, and you drive your head into his face, you are hitting him with tremendous force. In reality, as soon as you deliver this blow, it is lights out and the party is over (Figure 12.11).

Ear Slap This is like taking a sledge hammer to the side of someone's head. Don't punch as you will hurt your hand. Just cup your hand and slap hard, creating a disorienting and disabling vacuum blow (Figure 12.12).

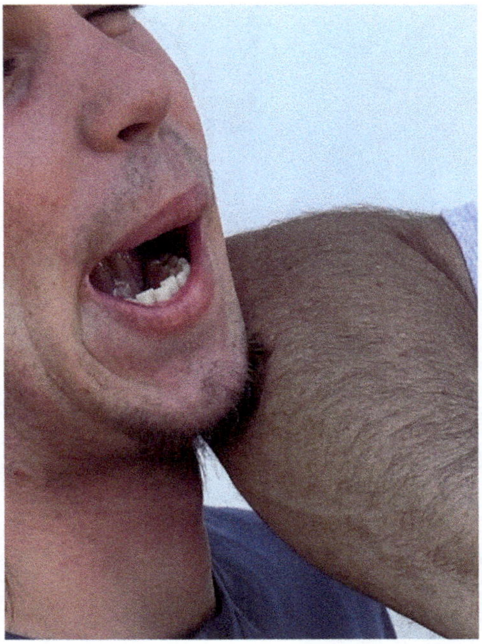

Figure 12.8 Chin blast.

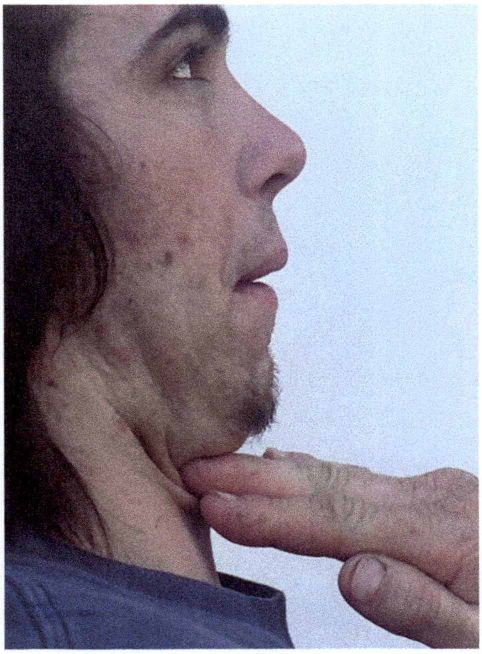

Figure 12.9 Throat jab.

Eye Jab Extend the fingers of one hand and drive them into the attacker's eye. This is a great technique to buy time and merely grazing one eyeball will make both eyes water profusely. If you miss his eye, he will still blink. It's an automatic response. Just touching his eyes will immediately blur his vision severely. If you hit with a full strike, you win the fight (Figure 12.13).

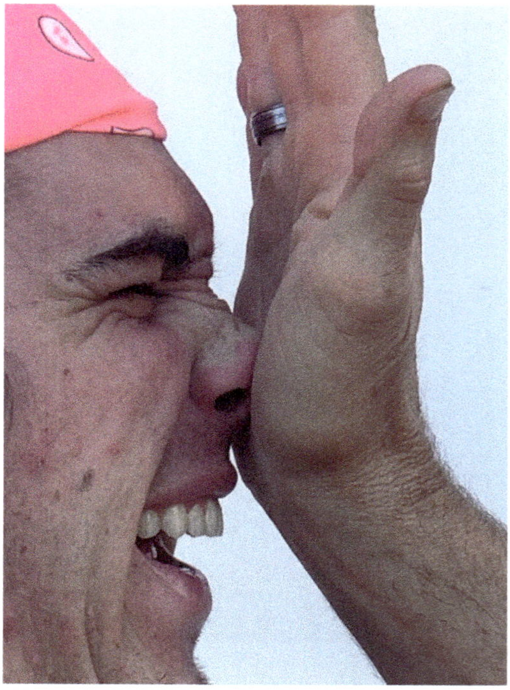

Figure 12.10 Nose break.

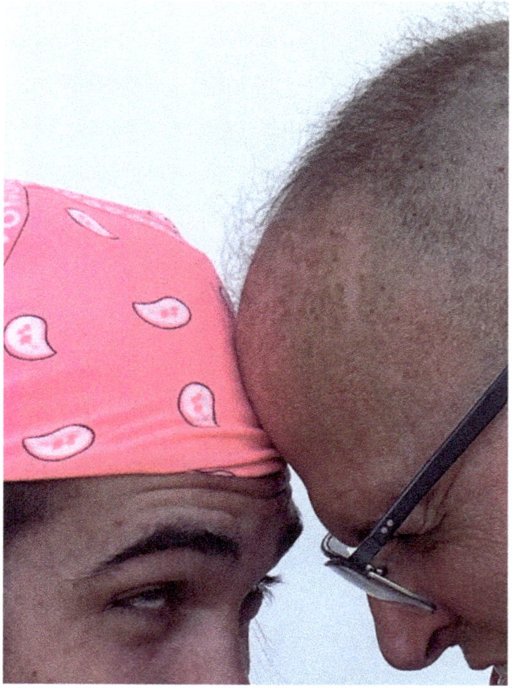

Figure 12.11 Head butt.

Figure 12.12 Ear slap.

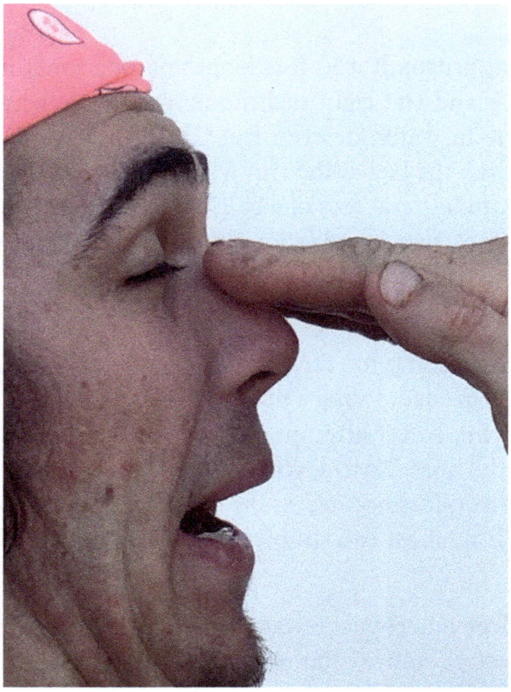

Figure 12.13 Eye jab.

These are just a few ideas to get you thinking about defensive options. If you have other techniques that work well, use them.

Rescue of Others

This rescue sequence starts with the technique safest for the rescuer. As you progress through the sequence, rescuer risk increases.

- Reach
- Throw
- Row (watercraft assisted)
- Go (water entry)

Reach If you have determined that another officer is in immediate need of assistance in the water, and there is a suitable object long enough to reach him, then use it. Proper technique is imperative. If done improperly, you may be pulled into the water as well, complicating the situation drastically. A suitable item might be a branch, canoe paddle, rowing oar, or a similar item. Grasp the item securely with both hands and lay out prone on the ground. Spread your legs to give your torso balance and then move yourself toward the edge of the water. Reach out and tell the person to grab the object and pull them to safety. If you do not possess enough strength to pull them to safety, just tell the person to hold onto the object and pull themselves to safety. Never attempt to reach with an item while standing up. The force of the victim grabbing the reach object will cause you to lose balance and pull you in the water as well. Laying on the ground lowers your center point of gravity and increases your body friction on the ground, making it more difficult to pull you in.

Throw Bag A throw bag is usually a 50-foot length of rope contained in a nylon throwable bag. With some practice and the right technique, the entire length of this rope can be deployed to aid someone in water, or even ice. Grasp the end of the rope in your weak (non-throwing) hand. Grab the bag at the rim with your throwing hand, palm up. Using a movement similar to an underhand toss of a ball, throw the bag over the head of the victim in the water. This will allow the rope to fall within easy grasp of the victim to be pulled to safety. NEVER throw the bag directly to the person as this could strike them in the face and cause injury.

Row In the event that a person is too far from shore to affect a reach or throw rescue, then a go-rescue (boat) may be needed. Using a boat or canoe, don a PFD and enter the boat and row or paddle to the victim. Never attempt a boat rescue without the safety precaution of wearing a PFD. Should the boat capsize, you now become a second victim and complicate the rescue of the first officer. It is not necessary to pull the victim officer into the boat, but do so if possible. The victim officer can simply hold onto the side of the boat and be dragged to safety.

Go (Water Entry) Before entering the water, the rescuer must first don a PFD to assure his own safety. This rescue requires the rescuer to physically grab the victim and drag (or tow) to safety. Quickly surface swim toward the victim and make contact. Grab the victim's shoulders. Turn the victim around, facing downstream and away from the rescuer. Grasp the back of the collar and tow them to shore. A rescue board or other flotation device can aid in offering the victim extra flotation.

Rescue from Others

In the event that you are the officer being rescued using a throw bag, after grabbing the throw rope, simply roll over on your back and hold the rope against your chest. This will allow you to keep your face above water while your back skims the surface of the water. Under no circumstances should you tie the rope to yourself. The tension on the line can cause your body to submerge and the water pressure will prevent you from untying yourself from the line.

Train for worst-case scenario. Just because someone is responding to help doesn't mean they are going to know what to do for you (1).

Diver Training

Introduction

Way too often, public safety agencies form dive teams based solely on its members having been certified by any number of recreational dive organizations. While this practice is a good starting point for divers to learn the basics, such as equalizing and proper weighting and buoyancy control, the more specific skills must be learned from a public safety–specific dive training agency. Lifeguard Systems, Inc. out of Shokan, New York, is one of the best. In this chapter, I will cover the basics, but this is just an overview of training topics needed. This information is not intended to replace seeking expert training but to educate dive teams in considering the vast array of training needs.

During recreational diving certification, agencies promise to certify a person in diving in as little as a weekend of classroom time and some pool exercises. Upon completion of these training requirements, the students are then taken to an open water environment, usually a nearby lake or quarry where they repeat the skills they learned in the pool sessions. While these skills are normally all that is needed for most recreational diving excursions, the public safety diving environment is nothing like the gin-clear water of most vacation diving destinations.

Public safety divers are usually called upon to locate lost persons or evidence in a less than perfect environment. The water is usually as dark and silty as chocolate syrup, making any navigation by sight impossible; it is often cold at depth and contains many unforeseen obstacles that quickly can cause entanglement. Water depth and darkness can induce panic very quickly for someone not properly trained for this harsh diving environment. Specific emergency procedures must be learned and practiced over and over, so any diver finding himself in trouble, has the presence of mind and ability to free himself and affectively surface safely.

Preparing for a Dive Deployment

Anytime a public safety diver is placed in the water, that diver is putting his/her life at risk for the specific task undertaken. So, one must ask themselves if they have acquired all that is necessary to perform this task safely while minimizing any life-threatening obstacles that may come their way. Many skills must be learned and practiced before a diver even attempts to enter the water. One of these skills is proper equipment setup. As stated earlier, Public safety divers are often deployed in less than ideal conditions, so training must also reflect those less-than-ideal conditions. A dive operation may require a diver to respond at night, during harsh weather environments and often times under duress and pressure from loved ones and the media on scene. This pressure can cause even the most seasoned divers to make mistakes during equipment setup.

Dive teams must hold training sessions at different times of the day and the night. A sleepy diver, having responded to the scene from the comfort of his/her bed in the middle of the night, may not be at their best, both mentally and physically. Teams need to practice gear setup both with the aid of a flashlight as well as in total darkness. Blindfolding the divers can simulate darkness as well. It can be very tricky to try setting up the dive and communication gear when one hand is holding a flashlight. Often, a diver will spend more time looking for the flashlight they put down to use both hands for a task, than actually setting up the gear. Training should also be conducted during adverse weather conditions. Pick a heavy rainstorm as a great training opportunity for gear setup, for instance.

In an ideal and perfect world, public safety dive teams would have all the same gear, having been purchased and supplied by the various public safety agencies. Unfortunately this is not always the case. Many newer dive teams start out with each diver using his/her own gear, different in style and operation than the next diver. It is imperative for this reason that teams train to learn the operation and function of all gear used by team members. After all, if a rescue diver is deployed to aid a primary diver in trouble, they must know how to drop the weights, add air to the BC, and so forth. Some BC's have integrated weight systems while others do not. The diver may be wearing hard or soft weights on a weight belt. Underwater in black, cold water and in an entanglement situation is not the time to discover that you are unfamiliar with this diver's gear.

Whether your team is using underwater communication gear or relying on line tug signals, all divers must be fluent on the setup and operation of these systems. Reviewing line tug signals on scene is not the time to learn this task. Likewise, proper set up of communication gear is imperative. Is it a hardwire system or wireless? Are the lines marked in a way to designate the primary diver from backup? Does the comm gear have working batteries and all the necessary hardware required for a safe dive like carabiners, harnesses, etc.? Hand signals must be learned and practiced to accurately direct divers to a last seen point on the surface, before even submerging.

The safest dive operation allows for the diver to be in the water for the shortest amount of time possible to complete the mission. Thus, it is very important that team members are adequately trained on interviewing witnesses on scene to determine an accurate last seen point of the victim. Using the "Show Me" technique, take the witness to water's edge and have them point to the last seen point. Don't rely solely on their description. All too often, people cannot judge distances accurately and are much less accurate describing distances on water. They may say the victim was 20 feet from the shore when in fact the victim was actually 50 feet from the shore.

CASE STUDY

Several years ago, our dive team responded to a call of a missing swimmer. Upon arrival to the scene, another agency with concurrent jurisdiction had already deployed divers in the water to conduct a search. These divers were not able to locate the missing swimmer. I asked where the witnesses were and they told me they were in the parking lot. I ran to the lot and got the girlfriend of the victim, brought her to the water's edge and had her point to where she had last seen her boyfriend. The other agency was not even close to the right area. We placed our divers in the indicated location and within 5 minutes, had the victim located.

There are many types of ropes available on the market that are designed for rescue purposes. These will not be discussed here. Each team must assess their needs and funding and purchase the best ropes possible for the intended use. Kernmantle ropes served our team well. Our hardwire communication gear was also a kernmantle rope. Plastic and other man-made material ropes do not hold knots well and are not recommended for diver use. Use of the proper knots for a specific task is important to know and practice. A rescuer would not want to use a slip knot to tie around a surface rescue victim, for instance, as any tension on the line could suffocate the victim. Practice knot tying in unfavorable conditions. Blindfold the diver and have them tie the knot while wearing dive gloves to start. Then elevate them to the black water environment. Each knot has specific uses and some uses may have more than one appropriate knot. For instance, both the figure 8 follow through and the bowline can be used to tie to a diver's harness but the bowline is much easier to tie blindfolded than the figure 8 follow through. Make sure you are using the right knot for the right task (Figures 12.14 through Figure 12.25).

Here is a list of recommended knots and rescue equipment and the general uses of each.

There are many useful resources that are applicable in learning to tie these knots and determining the specific uses of each. One great online resource is www.animatedknots.com. This site describes each knot use and shows an animated description on how to tie the knots.

In certain instances, it may be necessary for divers to don their dive gear while in the water. This may be because shoreline access is limited by terrain or vegetation or from a small vessel deployment. So teams must train and practice donning gear

Figure 12.14 Bowline-non-slipping anchor knot.

Figure 12.15 Figure 8 follow through – non-slipping anchor knot.

Figure 12.16 Figure 8 loop (also called figure 8 on a bight) – tensionless anchor point for diver and tender.

while in water. A pool setting is a good start but shouldn't end there. Not many dive operations take place in calm clear 80°F water. Choppy surfaces or potential wavy conditions are more the norm, with cold and zero visibility water, so a diver can't look down to find the dive weight buckle to don the belt, for instance. Practice for worst-case scenarios.

Line tender training is just as important, if not more important, than diver training. First off, if your team is deploying divers without a tender, this is a huge safety risk and should not be done. Even with ideal wireless communication systems, there is no way for a diver to maintain accurate positioning while underwater without a tether line. Many times, I have seen divers being deployed without a tether line, only to either end up swimming in circles or observing two divers swim off in totally different directions. Systematic searches are required to find virtually any submerged object and tether-less operations make it impossible to do so. More

Figure 12.17 Square knot-tying two ropes of same or similar diameter together. This knot can easily be passed through a friction device, if needed.

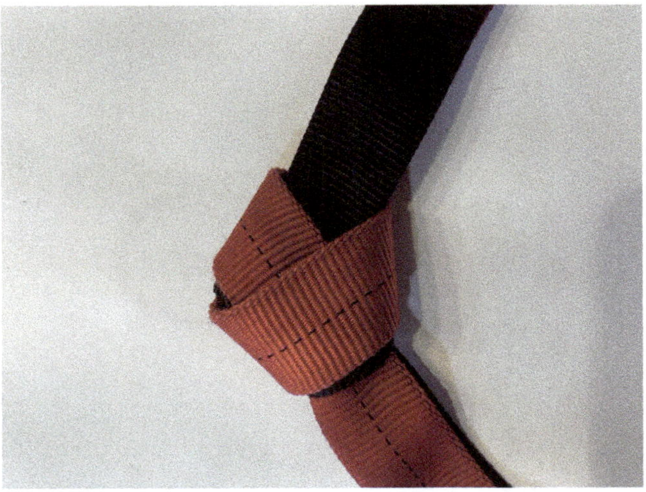

Figure 12.18 Water knot-used to tie harness to diver using tubular webbing, leaders, and runners. This knot can be tightened while being worn by a diver, if needed, without totally untying the knot.

importantly, the dive tender is the life line for the diver. A well-trained tender will know when a diver is not moving, possibly due to an entanglement. Pre-planned and practiced line tug signals will be needed to communicate with a diver that either doesn't have communication gear or has failed communications. A tender will also direct the area and quality of the search pattern. A tether line can also be followed straight to the primary diver should a backup diver need to be deployed for an emergency. By having the backup diver clip a short 3- to 4-foot-long contingency line to the primary diver's tether, it allows him to respond directly to the primary diver. This contingency line allows the backup hands-free response to equalize and do other tasks. Too much time would be wasted searching for a diver in trouble without the use of a tether line.

Figure 12.19 Fisherman's knot-used for tying two ropes together and for tying leaders to use with a Prusik.

Figure 12.20 Prusik knot-mid-line anchor point. This allows the user to anchor equipment such as a rescue pulley to the middle of a rope, without slipping. It is important to note that the wrapping of the prusik knot is done in a way that maximizes the amount of friction applied to the rope it is tied to.

Search Preparation

The target of the search will determine which type of search pattern will be used. For instance, a search for a large object such as a car, with a relatively flat lake bottom, could use the snag search adequately. This type of search would allow the dive team to locate the vehicle in a relatively short time frame because it does not require many switch backs of the diver which requires more time to complete. Likewise, a search for a small item, such as a gun, may require the jack stand search. This type of search is time-consuming and requires much time to set up. Thus, the jack stand would not be used to locate a body, especially, when it is still in rescue mode.

Figure 12.21 8-ring-friction device used for rappelling or controlled deployment of rope, such as ferrying a boat across a river or lowering a rescuer over a cliff.

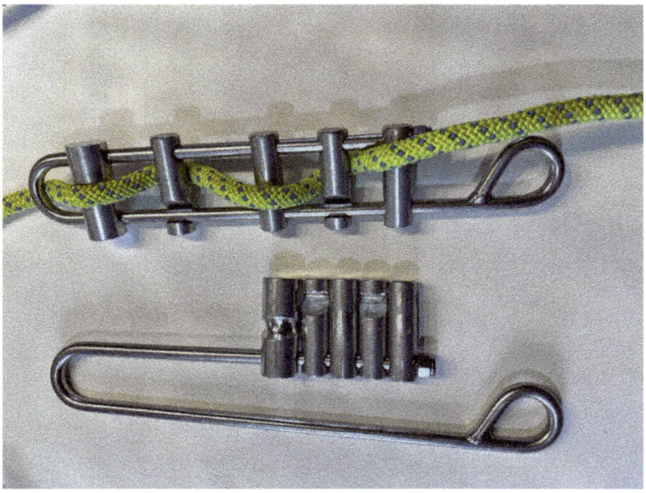

Figure 12.22 Rappel racks-friction device with similar uses as the 8-ring. By adding or removing some of the friction bars, more freedom of movement can be achieved, such as lowering a lighter or much heavier load.

Regardless of the type of search pattern used, all team members need to be familiar with the uses, setup, and emergency procedures of each. During training, have divers simulate different types of emergencies for each type of search. Tenders should be able to determine problems encountered and possess the confidence and expertise in providing emergency protocols to rectify the situation. After the scenario, hold a critique to discuss what was done well and suggestions for improvement. Divers would have great inputs as to how the backup was prepared, including response time.

With any search type, it is ideal to start the searches from the furthest point from the tender and work inward. This procedure is threefold. First, the diver starts the search when he is fresh and energized and closer to the tender when fatigued. Second, it boosts the morale of the diver knowing he is working his way home. Third, and most important,

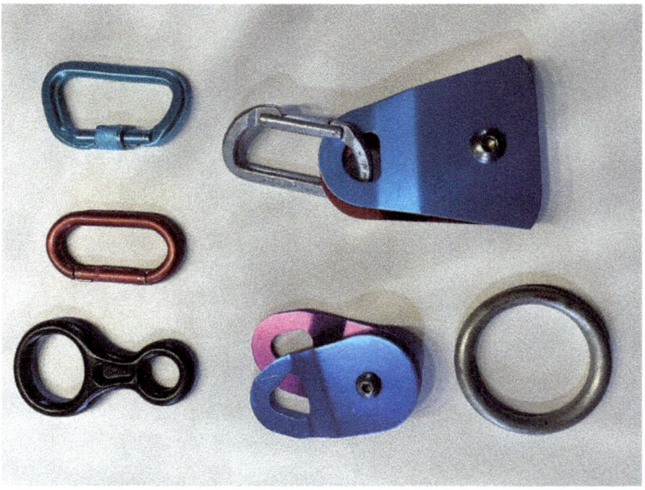

Figure 12.23 Assorted carabiners/rescue pulleys – allowing for attaching equipment and/or rescuers to a rope.

Figure 12.24 Rescue carabiners, larger in size than standard carabiners, allowing a rescuer to quickly make a rope connection such as a "bear hug rescue" in broken ice.

the longer the operation continues, the shorter the response time for the backup diver's deployment.

Many dive team coordinators believe that any training should be in an outdoor environment and not in a pool. With the use of a black-out mask, the black water environment can be simulated while maintaining a safe environment for training. Many entanglement scenarios discussed would be extremely dangerous for training if conducted in an uncontrolled environment. As the team progresses in confidence and ability, more open water training can be conducted.

An added stressor for training is deploying divers without a face mask. This renders the diver sightless, much the same as a black-out mask while also adding the stress of breathing control without a mask. During open water recreational dive training, every

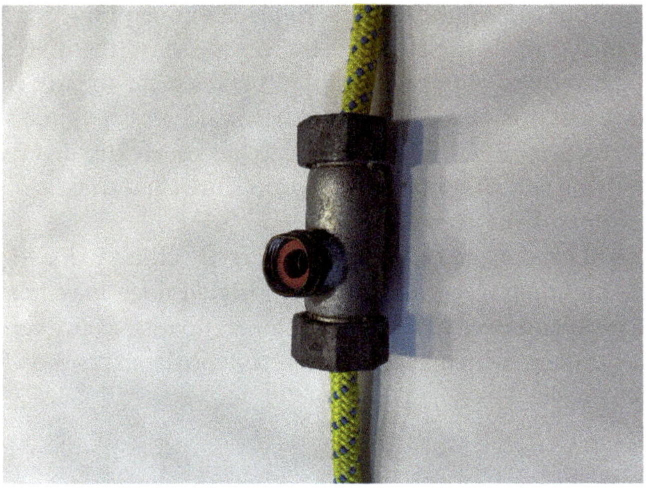

Figure 12.25 Rope washer, a device which is attached to a garden hose, allowing water jets to wash mud and sand from the surface of the rope. Dirt can gradually cause failure of rescue ropes by severing fibers during friction activities, so it is mandatory that rescue ropes be kept clean.

diver is required to remove the mask while under water and then replace or clear the mask. This simple task is done during certification, then for most divers, it is never performed again. Some divers could go for years without the need to recover from an inadvertent mask removal. An accidental mask removal can cause panic for the diver which can lead to life-threatening mistakes.

No dive team would be complete without practicing and becoming proficient in entering and searching submerged vehicles. A great way to start this process is to contact your local impound lot for assistance. Have the lot mark any vehicles that your team can use for training. Our team members donned grungy work clothes, a blacked-out scuba mask, and leather gloves. We strapped an 8″ PVC pipe to the "diver's back." This was to simulate an 80 cubic foot scuba tank. We then practiced entering vehicles in the lot, navigating only by feel. Divers practiced maneuvering between seats, searching the rear floor boards for evidence, and so forth. We also had a baby car seat and baby mannequin strapped in the back seat in which the diver needed to locate the seat and the baby, attempt to release the harness straps, and also learn to cut the harness straps without injuring the baby. Experimentation of different cutting tools for the seat belts revealed surprising results. The seat belt cutting tools (razor blade type) were totally useless. Dive knives were okay but risked injury to the baby, diver, or other occupants. The best tool was the EMT shears that all our divers have attached to their BC to use for entanglement escapes. We had the impound lot flip a couple of the cars in the lot as well to allow divers to navigate inside an overturned vehicle. Next, we practiced using a spring-loaded window punch. By getting low, below the bottom edge of the window glass, divers practiced a window punch out to enter a vehicle with a damaged door. By getting low, the diver prevents any buoyant objects within the car from becoming a missile when the window is punched out. Buoyant objects can strike a diver's face mask with enough force to knock off the mask as well as cause serious injury. After our dry run in the impound lot, it was time to get wet. The same impound company was more than happy to provide an environmentally-safe (all oil and liquids drained from the engine) vehicle to place in one of our marina basins. When the impound company is ready to submerge the vehicle, have the dive team present. This is an excellent opportunity to witness how long it takes a car to sink in a waterway. Our mid-sized sedan took just over three minutes to become completely submerged. Before any diver enters a submerged vehicle, it is imperative to have a backup diver staged at the entry point of the vehicle. This will simplify backup procedures and drastically reduce response time, should the primary diver need assistance.

Dive teams should practice surveying a submerged vehicle prior to removal from the water to determine any damage to the vehicle. This damage may help determine what caused it to enter the water as well as injuries to the occupants. Many vehicles are damaged during the recovery process which can lead to erroneous conclusions if the survey is not done ahead of time.

Rescue Training

A throw bag is a simple tool used by many dive teams for rescue of surface victims. It is usually a nylon bag with 50–75 feet of rope inside. By grasping the end of the rope in the non-dominant hand and the bag in the throwing hand, a rescuer can use an underhand toss (similar to pitching a softball) and deploy the bag to a surface victim. The throw bag is especially effective for a victim who has fallen through ice and is holding onto the ice shelf to stay above water. Use of the bag, while simple in nature, does take some practice to become proficient in its use. Never throw the bag directly at a victim as the bag can strike the victim in the face and knock them unconscious or cause injury. If the victim is holding onto an ice shelf, it could knock them off the ice and possibly cause drowning. The best method is to deploy the bag over the victim's head. This will cause the rope to fall within arm's reach of the victim where they can easily grasp the rope and be pulled to the shore.

For a victim in moving waters, the throw must lead the victim, similar to a passed football. For anyone using the bag, it is important to remember that the rescuer need not be strong enough to pull the victim from the water. They must make sure they can deploy the rope within arm's reach of the victim, and if necessary, the victim can pull himself to safety once the deployed rope is anchored to a stationary object. This is especially effective for a small person or child deploying the bag for an adult rescue.

Dr. Martin Nemiroff was a US Coast Guard Captain who dedicated his life to cold water near-drowning resuscitation. His studies have shown that a victim of cold water near drowning stands a much greater chance of survival if the victim is immediately secured to a backboard. In days of old, rescuers would rush into the water, grab the victim and rush to the shore with the victim's arms and legs flailing about. This action rendered an otherwise savable victim unsavable. Therefore, the dive team must practice securing a victim to a backboard while in the water. Techniques for flipping a face-down victim and C-spine immobilization must be perfected. Having a victim on a backboard sooner also allows for more efficient chest compressions during CPR.

Many dive teams only train for submerged victims and often forget about surface rescue techniques. The probability of a surface victim is overlooked in jurisdictions that do not have a river or moving water environment. But these areas may need to fall back on swift water rescue skills in the event of a flooding situation. During floods, many victims become trapped on rooftops or areas surrounded by fast currents, rendering a walk, wade, or swim to safety very dangerous. Something as simple as swimming a life preserver to a victim in this instance can be difficult if not properly trained. This scenario became a reality on September 14, 2013, in Fort Collins, Colorado, when dive teams were called upon to swim life preservers to victims of a flash flood who were stranded on rooftops. Divers must practice donning a PFD properly and carry a second PFD while surface swimming to a victim. Personnel will quickly realize how difficult and tiresome this task can be while wearing a vest style PFD. If the PFD is of another style, such as the horse collar PFD, this task is virtually impossible. This prior knowledge can be very beneficial when determining a go or no-go response. Swimmers must also practice donning the PFD for the victim. Injuries, panic, or hypothermia may hinder the victim from donning the PFD on their own, so the rescuer may be required to do it for them.

In-water CPR is another skill often overlooked by dive teams. Dr. Martin Nemiroff's research also dictates that immediate CPR and lifesaving efforts drastically increase victim's chances of survival. Therefore, in-water CPR, rescue breathing and oxygen-use skills are also needed. Practice these skills in adverse conditions to prepare for worst-case scenarios. Doing chest compressions and rescue breathing is much more difficult when trying to wade through rough surf as opposed to a padded rug in a heated classroom.

Perhaps, one of the biggest potential concerns for any dive team is the case of an unresponsive diver. Therefore monthly training should always incorporate unresponsive diver scenarios. During training, have the primary diver request assistance in different ways. The diver can call for assistance on the communication gear, use line tug signals, create a free-flow situation by using a pony bottle or by simply not reacting to any communication from surface personnel. All these techniques simulate an actual emergency situation when a backup diver deployment would be needed. This is a great technique to use to evaluate the timely responsiveness of surface support personnel. Tenders must strive to learn the early warning signs such as:

- Fatigued diver
- Increased respirations
- Constant slack in the tether line
- Delayed verbal responses
- Confusion

Upon deployment, the backup diver must secure himself to the primary diver's tether using a contingency line. This is a short length of rope or tubular webbing with carabiners at both ends. By securing one end to himself and the other around the diver's tether line, it allows a hands-free response which allows for other tasks such as equalizing or handling a contingency bottle (backup source of air). Once the backup makes contact with the primary diver and determines unresponsiveness, the backup must act quickly to preserve the life of the primary diver. Dropping his weights should occur automatically with little or no thought. The backup then maintains constant contact with the primary during ascent and immediately notifies topside personnel of an emergency.

Evidence and Body Recovery

Every water-related death starts with the recovery of the body from the water. In some cases, the body may already be out of the water due to bystanders attempting a rescue or possibly by wave action washing it ashore. Although rather unpleasant, recovery of submerged bodies is a very important task that needs to be done properly to prevent valuable evidence from being lost. The only way to be sure this is done is to bag the body where it is found, using a special recovery bag. The bottom of the bag has a high strength mesh that allows water to escape, but retains any forensic evidence. If a dive team attempts to use a regular body bag without the mesh, a disaster would follow. Zipping the bag closed underwater would not allow a large amount of water to escape, which would not only make the bag too heavy to remove from the water, but the added weight and pressure of the water would cause the bag zipper to fail, releasing much of the water and evidence contained in the bag. If all body recoveries took place in 100-foot visibility water, this might be an easy task. But, even in ideal conditions, once a diver contacts the bottom and stirs up silt, visibility is drastically reduced, to zero. Therefore it is required that the dive team practices bagging a body in blacked-out conditions. Attention to detail is needed to make sure the entire body is contained within the bag before attempting to close it. Any current or wave action makes it very difficult to complete this task, especially if the skill is not practiced. When bagging a body, move the bag under the body. Do not move the body to the bag. If bagging the body is not possible for any reason, at a minimum at least bag the hands, head, and feet. These areas are most common locations for evidence retrieval. Upon removing the body from the water, it is critical that an on-scene body assessment is conducted, being careful not to disturb any possible evidence within the bag (See Chapter 3, "On-Scene Body assessment").

In addition to body recoveries, the dive team is often called upon to retrieve evidence from the water. This evidence may be a weapon used in a crime, for example, pieces of a water craft involved in an accident and stolen property. It is important to not only retrieve this evidence properly, so as not to alter its evidentiary value, but to remove it from the water safely, with little or no danger to the recovery diver. Weapons and some smaller types of evidence need to be retrieved using a rigid container such as a PVC cylinder with caps on both ends, or something similar. The container made from a PVC pipe is not only practical to use, as it is very rigid and protects the property inside, but it is easy to use and very inexpensive to make. A section of a PVC pipe about 18 inches long will hold many smaller items, while a longer one of 3–4 feet can be used for rifles. Simply cap one end with a PVC cap glued in place and attach a threaded cap to the other end. This allows the diver to open the cylinder in the water to place the evidence inside before surfacing with the item. These containers will be very buoyant if the cap is kept on, preventing a diver from submerging with it, so the cap may need to be loosened to allow water inside. Once the items are removed from the water, it is important not to open the container to view the evidence. Exposing submerged evidence to air rapidly accelerates the rusting of metal objects such as weapons. Thus, the cylinder should be clearly marked with "CONTAINS WATER" so that lab personnel can take necessary precautions before opening it.

In order to recover heavy objects, such as a safe or boat motor, a diver will be required to use a lift bag. Webbing can be wrapped around the object to form a sling, to which carabiners can be used to attach the sling to the lift bag. A separate air source should be used to inflate the lift bag, not an octopus's or diver's primary air source. Slowly adding air to the bag with short pulses on the inflator will gradually lift the bag. The bag must be filled with just enough air to make the object neutrally buoyant. If too much air is added to the lift bag, the expanding air during ascent may cause the item to surface too rapidly, possibly causing injury or decompression sickness to the diver, or it may cause the item to work free of the sling and plummet back down to the bottom, possibly striking other divers below or damaging the evidence.

For extremely deep recoveries using a lift bag, the stage lifting method should be used. Stage lifting requires the diver to submerge to the item at depth and attach a sling, using tubular webbing. One length of rope, equal to the depth of water, is attached to the sling. There are loops placed every 10 feet along the entire length of the rope. These loops can either be pre-tied in the rope, using a figure 8 loop, or a prusik knot can be attached with a loop. One lift bag is then attached to the loop 10 feet from the surface and inflated. After the lift bag surfaces, a second lift bag is attached to the next loop 10 feet below the surface. This process is repeated, lifting the item 10 feet at a time, until the item is surfaced. This process avoids attaching lift bags at depth and risking a runaway ascent as they rise and the air expands in the bags. It also allows the divers to work at a depth of only 10 feet, after the initial sling attachment, which adds a huge margin of safety. Any practice for divers using lift bags should include blacked-out masks, to prepare them for using this procedure in zero visibility water. Proper use of ropes, slings, and knots should be included. This is a great opportunity for divers to use the learned skill of properly tying knots underwater while blacked out. To calculate the size of the lift bag and the amount of air needed to lift an object, visit www.divestock.se for a lift bag size/volume calculator. You will need to know the object weight, object volume and depth. A Google search of these items can be conducted to determine these calculations.

Drown-Proofing Divers

Open water diver certification is often conducted in water with adequate visibility and subsequent dives as well. Most recreational dives are also conducted in water with good to fair visibility as the dive is often done to view some type of object (such as ship wrecks) or marine life (such as dolphins, manatees, or seals). Unlike recreational diving, public safety diving requires divers to submerge in the worst of conditions, often zero visibility, with potential entanglement hazards which can ultimately become life-threatening. Ideally, divers must not rely on assistance from a backup diver in an entanglement situation, which could ultimately lead to two entangled divers. Therefore, a public-safety diver must be trained to escape these types of hazards, and practice escape techniques often. Here are a few exercises that can be conducted to train divers to escape entanglement situations.

Bed Sheets

Obtain an old full-size bed sheet and cut slits in the sheet about every 3–4 inches, being careful not to cut all the way across the sheet, resulting in cutting pieces off the sheet. When done, you should still have a full sheet, with numerous slits every 3–4 inches. Now, black out the diver's mask (duct tape over the lens works well) and have two separate safety personnel stand in chest-deep water, with the diver between them. These two safety personnel stretch the bed sheet out in front of the blacked-out diver and start to wrap the sheet around the diver, entangling the divers face, body and mask in the sheet. Once the sheet has been completely wrapped around the diver, the diver's mask and regulator are ripped from his mouth and face. Now the blacked-out diver must retrieve the mask and regulator without assistance and free himself from the entanglement unassisted.

Port Hole

This exercise can be conducted using old submerged tires, barrels, or a sheet of plywood with a 2-foot diameter hole cut into it. Whatever is used, the object needs to be situated underwater so that it is suspended at various depths. Again, the diver needs to be blacked out with two safety divers situated on either side of the obstacle. The diver is then led to the obstacle. Once the diver has made contact with the obstacle, he must remove the scuba unit (BC and tank) and feed it through the obstacle, swim through, and then replace the scuba unit on the other side. All this must be done without sight and unassisted. Care must be taken not to lose contact with the scuba unit, which can cause it to separate from the diver and surface. Also the diver would also be negatively buoyant and sink below the obstacle. This scenario requires the diver to maintain control of his equipment under stressful circumstances.

Devil's Triangle

This exercise quickly became the favorite of our dive team as it allows for several variables which really tested the skill of the diver. The obstacle is set up using three 8-foot long 2 × 4 boards. The boards are connected at the ends to form a triangle. We used eye bolts and nuts which allowed us to anchor the triangle at the bottom of a pool using heavy weights on two of the corners. The buoyancy of the boards makes the triangle vertical in the water. It is important to conduct this exercise in a pool setting so that backup (safety divers) can assist the primary diver if a problem occurs. Both safety divers now attach numerous objects to all three sides of the triangle, such as long lengths of wire, rope, and netting. The primary diver is then blacked out and led into the middle of the triangle. Once there, he must wait while the safety divers take several minutes to entangle him. This is done using the wire, rope, and netting, which are wrapped around the diver's body, regulator, tank, hands, and feet. Once completed, the diver is tapped on the head which signals him to begin meticulously (yet calmly) working himself free. It is recommended that all primary divers are regularly equipped with EMT shears in a holster on the BC. Knives are not recommended as they can easily cause an accidental stabbing of a person or gear in an entanglement and they don't cut wire and rope using one hand very easily. The diver uses the EMT shears to cut himself free from the entanglement, totally unassisted. Our team, after much practice, started to get really challenging by tying the diver's arms to the bottom length of the board in the triangle. It is important to remember that diver safety is first priority in any training scenario. If the team is not using underwater communication gear, then a pre-planned panic signal must be established, to allow the primary diver to notify the safety divers that he needs assistance.

Panic and Stress

Virtually every diving fatality has been attributed in some way to diver error. Even in the event of an equipment failure, the failure is caused by poorly maintained equipment, which ultimately is diver error. Many fatalities have been attributed to diver panic. This is because in many cases, a diver is unexpectedly put into a situation in which he has either not been trained for or has not practiced since the certification requirements. For instance, diver certification requires a diver to remove and replace a flooded dive mask without surfacing and unassisted. This is to prepare a diver for an inadvertent removal of the mask. This can be caused for example, by another diver who is descending and accidentally kicks your mask off, or a loose-fitting mask that has not been properly fitted before the dive. This task, as simple as it is, is often never done again after completion of certification requirements.

The *Webster's Dictionary* defines *panic* as "sudden, uncontrollable fear or anxiety, often causing wildly unthinking behavior." Divers who routinely train for the unexpected situation will react to problems underwater with a much calmer, systematic approach to resolve the problem. Therefore, any training that one can do to prepare for these problems will result in a safer, more confident diver. Here are some panic-related training exercises that divers can do to help them remain calm when problems arise.

Equipment Exchange

During the PADI Dive master certification, one of the requirements is to have two divers do an equipment exchange. Although very challenging, it is also very rewarding and serves as a great way to build confidence in an underwater environment. This exercise requires two fully equipped divers in a pool setting. Both divers begin in the shallow end of the pool, holding onto each other's gear with one hand. The divers submerge and begin to buddy breathe off of one regulator. As they buddy breathe, they begin to swim to the deep end of the pool. Once there, they continue to buddy breathe throughout the entire exercise. They start to systematically exchange gear including mask, fins, weight belt, and BC. They continue to buddy breathe and cannot surface. The exercise is complete when both divers are wearing the other diver's gear correctly. This exercise can get complicated if the divers cannot manage their breathing well while buddy breathing. It can also get very difficult when exchanging each other's weight belts as the diver becomes very buoyant after removing their own weight belt. Close contact between the divers is imperative so they can affectively continue to buddy breathe without interruptions. Close attention to the other diver's needs is also required because if one diver keeps the regulator too long for any reason, the other diver can run low on air and begin to panic. Great team work, pre-planning, and equipment familiarization is a must.

Deep Donning of Gear

This exercise is similar to the equipment exchange as it requires all divers involved to don their scuba gear while submerged. The stressor is that there are complete sets of gear submerged in the deep end of a pool, but there is one less set of gear than divers. For instance, if there are four divers, then submerge three sets of gear. Divers must enter the water together and systematically don all gear properly. One diver obviously is left without gear, so it requires all the other divers to work together to make sure the odd man out is supplied with air until the exercise is complete. No one can surface during the exercise, until all gear is worn properly by the divers. This exercise requires great team work, pre-planning, and calmness under stress.

Mask and Regulator Rip Off

If you can make it unscathed through the first two exercises, then this one will be simple. A diver's mask is blacked out, then his regulator and mask are violently ripped off his face. The diver must locate the mask and regulator, don and clear the mask, and then remain submerged. As attempts of this exercise progress, the placement of the ripped off mask can get more and more difficult, placing the mask further from the immediate area of the diver each time. Prior mental planning would dictate that the diver first locate the regulator, then search for and locate the mask, don and clear it. As divers become more proficient with this skill, make it a common practice during any training that it is okay to rip other diver masks off at any given time. Before you know it, divers will become totally comfortable with this task to the point where they hardly even react to the incident. This exercise requires calmness under pressure and self-confidence.

AGA/Full Face Mask Rip Off

Much the same as the mask and regulator rip off, full face mask exercises should be conducted as well. Full face masks, although much more secure to the face do occasionally get dislodged from the face and could get the straps tangled or broken on underwater obstacles. Conduct this exercise the same to build confidence in your divers.

Dropping Weights

It is very beneficial for divers and/or dive teams to read and review diving fatalities. These are published every year by various organizations for public safety divers and DAN (Divers Alert Network) also publishes them every year. While it is not the intent to find blame or fault in other diver deaths, it is a great learning tool to make your divers better. In many diving fatalities, one element stands out more than any other. Diving fatalities almost always include the phrase "the diver's weight belt was still worn." During any certification, agencies stress the importance for divers to drop the weight belt to aid in surfacing in the event of an emergency, yet many fatal incidents indicate this was not done. Many reasons may be offered, such as possibly the diver didn't want to lose the weight belt requiring them to purchase another. Possibly the diver felt they could surface in another manner without dropping the weights. But essentially, in most cases, dropping the weights will make divers buoyant enough to surface in any emergency. So, scenarios must be designed to require divers to drop their weights. This needs to be done frequently so that it is not forgotten during a real-life emergency. Training must also include a safety or backup diver dropping the weights for another diver. This requires all divers to be aware of the various weight systems worn by each and every diver on the team. Imagine a safety diver being deployed to assist the primary diver and upon looking for the weight belt buckle to release it, cannot find it because the diver has an integrated weight system in the BC. This exercise requires team work, equipment familiarization, and repetition.

Underwater Puzzle and Pipe Assembly

Many may recall the movie "Men of Honor" starring Cuba Gooding Jr. who played a Master Navy Diver. Part of the certification depicted in the movie requires the diver to submerge and correctly assemble a valve. This activity is a great beginner's exercise to build confidence and comfort in the underwater environment while concentrating on a specific task. Pool Puzzles for Diabetes was a fundraiser our team participated in every year as part of a fundraising effort. The hosting organization had puzzle pieces cut out of plate steel to form a puzzle measuring approximately 12 feet wide and 6×8 feet high. The event required divers to submerge as a team and put together the puzzle within the allotted time. Teams can also design their own "puzzles" by using threaded pipe sections and elbows to assemble in a pre-designated shape or order. Both of these exercises require the diver to concentrate on a specific task while maintaining correct buoyancy, breathing control and confidence. As divers become more proficient, add some complicating factors to escalate the stress and eventually build more confidence.

These are just a few exercises our team conducted on a regular basis to build confidence in our divers, while lowering stress during an actual entanglement or other problem while on a dive mission. Make sure your team plans for the worst so they can go home at the end of the mission.

Cross-training

There are many benefits to agencies cross-training with each other. This is a great opportunity for agencies that may be responding to an incident together to build a rapport with one another. More importantly, incidents which have multiple agency responses need to be managed by one individual, who is aware of all teams' capabilities and restrictions. More importantly, different agencies may have different types of dive equipment. Some departments still use weight belts and a basic scuba unit, while others may have an AGA or hard helmet type of mask and integrated weights. Imagine a rescue diver from one agency being deployed to assist a diver in trouble from another agency, only to not be able to drop the weight belt because that agency uses integrated weights. The results can be disastrous and deadly. Therefore cross-training which integrates equipment familiarization for all agencies is a must.

Another benefit to cross-training is the ability to build trust among divers. Many dive deployments take place during early morning hours, which may cause a strain on diver availability. Divers from different agencies who know each other personally, and know their capabilities will allow them to work together toward a common goal. This eliminates confusion and competition at the scene and makes better use of available personnel (2).

References

1. Kevin L. Erskine. 2007. *Water-Proofing the Patrol Officer Curriculum*. Richfield, OH: Peace Officer's Training Academy (OPOTA).
2. Kevin L. Erskine. 2003. *Devils Triangle: A Guide to Drown-Proofing Divers*. Conshohacken,PA: Infinity Publishing.

Appendix A

TRI AIR TESTING, INC.
A Texas Research International Company

IS2

INSTRUCTIONS FOR SAMPLING A SCUBA CYLINDER USING A MINI-SAMPLER

Please read the entire set of instructions before sampling

1. The sample will be taken from your SCUBA tank.
2. Attach TRI's double sampling yoke to the cylinder and attach the Mini-Sampler to the other side of the sample yoke.
3. Unscrew the black shipping cap from one of the bottles and screw on the white sampling cap.
4. Record the bottle number on the datasheet.
5. You are ready to take a sample. Open the valve on the air supply. There is no need to adjust the air flow. The Mini-Sampler contains a limiting orifice, which regulates the flow of air.
6. Note that most of the air escapes through the large hole in the fitting while only a small fraction passes through the center needle in the air transfer fitting.
7. Insert the bottle with the white sampling cap onto the needles of the air transfer fitting. (Do not twist the bottle when inserting or removing because it may result in damage to the needles.)
8. Observe the white float inside the bottle; the float will rise with a positive air flow. If this does not occur, cautiously place your finger close to the vent hole, partially restricting the flow. DO NOT COMPLETELY BLOCK THIS HOLE. If the float does not rise, please contact the TRI. To acquire an accurate sample, the bottle must stay in place, with the white float remaining at the top for one minute. **Remove the bottle before the white float is allowed to fall and then shut the tank flow off.**
9. Remove the white sampling cap and replace it with the black shipping cap. **Tighten the black cap securely to prevent loss of the gas sample.** Make sure your air supply valve is shut off and remove the Mini-Sampler from your sample site.
10. Return the bottle and the Mini-Sampler to the foam container and return the package to the TRI (Return shipping label enclosed).

1607 N. Cuernavaca Dr. Ste 500 • Austin, TX 78733-1600 • 1-800-8B0-TEST • FAX (512) 263-7039 alrtesting.com

70-1S-2 Rev 4

TRI Air Testing, Inc.
A Texas Research International Company
1607 N. Cuernavaca Drive, Suite 500
Austin, Texas 78733-1600
(512)263-2101 (800)880-8378 FAX:(512)263-7039
http://www.airtesting.com

For TRI Use Only — Page ______ of ______
TRI Project Number:
TRI Log Number:
Date Logged In: By:

REQUEST FOR LABORATORY ANALYTICAL SERVICES

REPORT RESULTS TO		SEND INVOICE TO	
Name		Purchase Order No.	Client Job No.
Company	Dept.	Name	
Mailing Address		Company	Dept.
City, State, Zip		Mailing Address	
Telephone No.	Telefax No.	City, State, Zip	

Requested Turnaround Time:

Special Instructions: (method, limit of detection required, etc.)

* Explanation of Preservative:

ANALYSIS REQUESTED
(Enter an "X" in the box below to indicate request; Enter a "P" if Preservative added.*)

CLIENT SAMPLE IDENTIFICATION	DATE SAMPLED	MATRIX/ MEDIA	AIR VOLUME (specify units)	Number of Containers												FOR LAB USE ONLY

CHAIN OF CUSTODY			
Relinquished by:	Date/Time	Received by:	Date/Time
Relinquished by:	Date/Time	Received by:	Date/Time
Relinquished by:	Date/Time	Received at Lab by:	Date/Time

Comments:

Sample Condition Upon Receipt:

DISTRIBUTION:
WHITE - TRI Laboratory
YELLOW - TRI Accounting
PINK - Client Copy

D1239

Request for Lab Services, TRI Air Testing, Inc

DSR6

DATA SHEET

All Blanks Must Be Complete
Incomplete Data Will Result in an Invalid Sample
NEED HELP? Call (800) 880-8378; Ask for Compressed Air
After 5PM Central Dial Ext 159

Customer Number ________________
Kit Number ______________________
Order Number ____________________
Report Number ___________________

COMPANY NAME ____________________DATE SAMPLE TAKEN ______________
TYPE OF COMPRESSOR/AIR SOURCE____
SAMPLING FOR____

GAS ONLY ANALYSIS—GAS SAMPLE DATA
TRI'S SAMPLE BOTTLE NO. ________
BOTTLE FLOW TIME ________
MARK THE TYPE OF GAS SAMPLE YOU PUT INTO THE TRI SAMPLE BOTTLE
____ AIR ____ NITROUS OXIDE
____ NITROGEN ____ OTHER GAS
____ OXYGEN
DATE _____ AND TIME _______ GAS SAMPLED

TRI's sample bottle must remain in place for a MINIMUM OF ONE MINUTE WITH THE WHITE FLOAT AWAY FROM THE SAMPLING CAP.
REPLACE BLACK SHIPPING CAP WHEN DONE.

DUPLICATE GAS ONLY ANALYSIS (OTHER THAN AIR)—GAS SAMPLE DATA
TRI'S SAMPLE BOTTLE NO. ________________
BOTTLE FLOW TIME ______________________
MARK THE TYPE OF GAS SAMPLE YOU PUT INTO THE TRI SAMPLE BOTTLE
____ AIR ____ NITROUS OXIDE
____ NITROGEN ____ OTHER GAS
____ OXYGEN
DATE ______ AND TIME ______ GAS SAMPLED

TRI's sample bottle must remain in place for a MINIMUM OF ONE MINUTE WITH THE WHITE FLOAT AWAY FROM THE SAMPLING CAP.
REPLACE BLACK SHIPPING CAP WHEN DONE.

AIR, NITROGEN, OR OXYGEN ONLY APPRECIABLE OR PRONOUNCED ODORI
________ **YES** ________ **NO**

While obtaining the gas sample carefully deflect a portion of the exhaust stream toward the nose and smell. Do not direct the gas stream toward the face.

PRINTED NAME OF PERSON TAKING TEST ___________________________________
PHONE NUMBER ______________ FAX NUMBER _____________ EMAIL _____________
By signing this data sheet, I declare that the sample submitted to TRI was taken according to the instructions provided and was not tampered with to falsify air test results.
Signature of person responsible for air sampling Date
Comments: ____

TRI AIR TESTING, INC. • 1607 N. Cuernavaca Drive, Ste. 500. • Austin, TX 78733-1600 • (800) 880-8378
70-DS-R6 Rev 7

Appendix B: Body Drop Rate Chart

		Current in Knots																			
	10	1	1.5	2	2.5	3	3.5	4	4.5	5	5.5	6	6.5	7	7.5	8	8.5	9	9.5	10
		8	13	17	21	25	29	33	38	42	46	50	54	58	63	67	71	75	79	83
	15	13	19	25	31	38	44	50	56	63	69	75	81	88	94	100	106	113	119	125
	20	17	25	33	42	50	58	67	75	83	92	100	108	117	125	133	142	150	158	167
	25	21	31	42	52	63	73	83	94	104	115	125	135	146	156	167	177	188	198	208
	30	25	38	50	63	75	88	100	113	125	138	150	163	175	188	200	213	225	238	250
Depth in Feet	35	29	44	58	73	88	102	117	131	146	160	175	190	204	219	233	248	263	277	292
	40	33	50	67	83	100	117	133	150	167	183	200	217	233	250	267	283	300	317	333
	45	38	56	75	94	113	131	150	169	188	206	225	244	263	281	300	319	338	356	375
	50	42	63	83	104	125	146	167	188	208	229	250	271	292	313	333	354	375	396	417
	55	46	69	92	115	138	160	183	206	229	252	275	298	321	344	367	390	413	435	458
	60	50	75	100	125	150	175	200	225	250	275	300	325	350	375	400	425	450	475	500
	65	54	81	108	135	163	190	217	244	271	298	325	352	379	406	433	460	488	515	542
	70	58	88	117	146	175	204	233	263	292	321	350	379	408	438	467	496	525	554	583
	75	63	94	125	156	188	219	250	281	313	344	375	406	438	469	500	531	563	594	625

$$\frac{D}{2} \times \frac{C \times 100}{60}$$

D = Depth in feet
C = Current in knots

Appendix C: Checklists and Supplements

Completed by:____
Agency:____
Date/time/location:____________________________________
Case number:____
Coroner/medical examiner notified? yes______ no______
Personnel/dive team members present: ____________________________

Drawing of recovery location? yes______ no ______
Decedent identification: identified? yes______ no______ method of ID______
Tentative ID? yes____ no_____
Recovered in: fresh water _____ salt water _____ domestic water_____
Water type: clean 1 2 3 4 5 6 7 8 9 10 polluted
Water depth (in feet): _____
Water visibility (in feet): _____
Waterway type: still _____ moving _____
Water temperature: _______F _______C
Water sample obtained? yes _____ no _____
Body position: On bottom ________ (check all that apply)
On surface ________
Left side down ______
Right side down _____
Face down ________
Face up ____________
Other ____
Complete or partial submersion (circle one)
If partial, describe which body region(s) submerged: _______________
Clothing/personal effects: present? yes _____ no_____
Description (include whether wet, damp, dry, or soiled): ______________

Body condition/composition (circle or check all that apply):

Wet/damp/dry/soiled (specify region affected):

____

Intact _____
Partial remains _____
Dismemberment _____
Skeletonization: partial ____ complete ____
Anthropophagy: absent ____ present _____
where? _______________

Trauma/wounding (description and location): ____________________________________

____

____

____

(refer to supplements for diagrams)
Ocular changes:
a. Petechiae: right eye _____ left eye _____
b. Tache noire: right eye _____ left eye _____
c. Corneal opacity: right eye _____ left eye _____
CPR performed? yes _____ no _____
Foam column? yes _____ no _____
Rigor mortis: absent 1 2 3 4 5 6 7 8 9 10 fully established (circle one)

Small muscles

Jaw _____
Hands/wrists/fingers _____
Feet/ankles/toes _____
Elbows _____
Shoulders _____

Large muscles

Hips/thighs_____
Knees _____
Neck _____
Arms at shoulders _____
Cadaveric spasm (death grip)? yes _____ no _____

Describe any materials present in grip: _____________

____

Body warm to touch? yes _____ no _____
Core body temperature taken? no _____ yes _____ _____degrees F/C
where taken: _______________
Livor mortis (lividity): present yes _____ no _____
where? _______________ patterned?

Tardieu spots: present _____ absent _____
Current lividity: present yes _____ no _____
where? ______________________
Maggots: present yes _____ no _____
where? ___________________
Sample of maggots obtained? yes _____ no _____
Body decomposition: present yes _____ no _____
(check all that apply):
purge _____
bloating _____
skin discoloration _____
skin slippage/degloving _____
marbling _____
adipocere _____
Wauschaut (dishpan hands or feet): present yes _____ no _____
where? ____
Fingerprinted on scene? yes _____ no _____
Photographs taken? yes ____ no _____ copies to C/ME? (Y/N)
Remarks, including unusual observations: ____
____
____
Investigator's name: _______________________ Agency: _________________
Date/time of report: ____________ Date/time of recovery: ________________
Names of those present during recovery (witnesses and other personnel): _____________
____
____
Occupants and positions found: ____
____
Transmission position: ___________________________
Objects to depress accelerator: _____________________
Radio on/off ________________ Air conditioner or heater on/off _____________
Wipers on/off _________________________
Headlights on/off _____________ Windows up/down _____________________
Doors open/closed _____________ Ignition on/off ________________________
Driver's seat position (measure from front of seat to the accelerator): _________________
Emotional valuables (toys, photos, ornaments, etc.): ___________________________
____
Other valuables or evidence of a crime (camera, business papers, criminal tools, etc.): ____
____
____
Marine growth:____
Exterior damage (use drawing supplement): ___________________________________
____
Are occupant injuries consistent with vehicle damage? __________________________
Drawing supplement attached? yes _____ no _____
Body recovery checklist attached? yes _____ no _____

FULL BODY FRONT VIEW SUPPLEMENT

CASE #____
COMPLETED BY:__________________________________
DATE & TIME:___________________________________

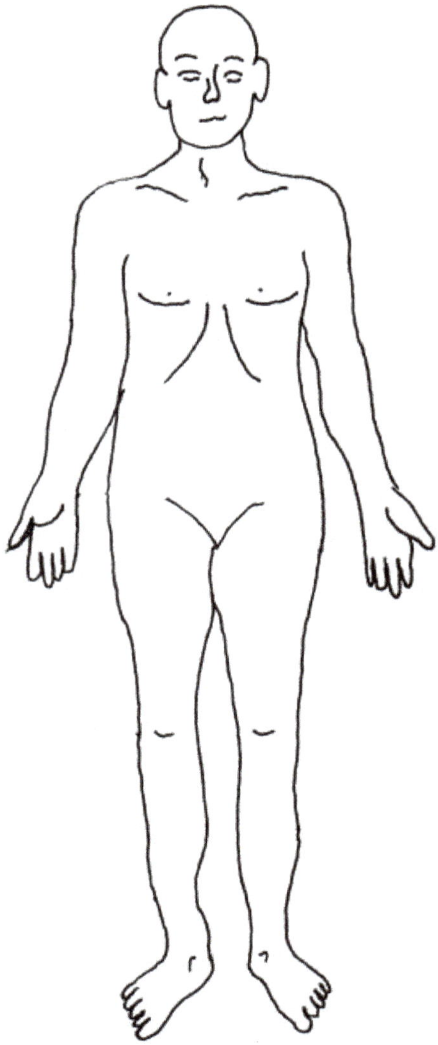

FULL BODY BACK VIEW SUPPLEMENT

CASE #____
COMPLETED BY:________________________________
DATE & TIME:__________________________________

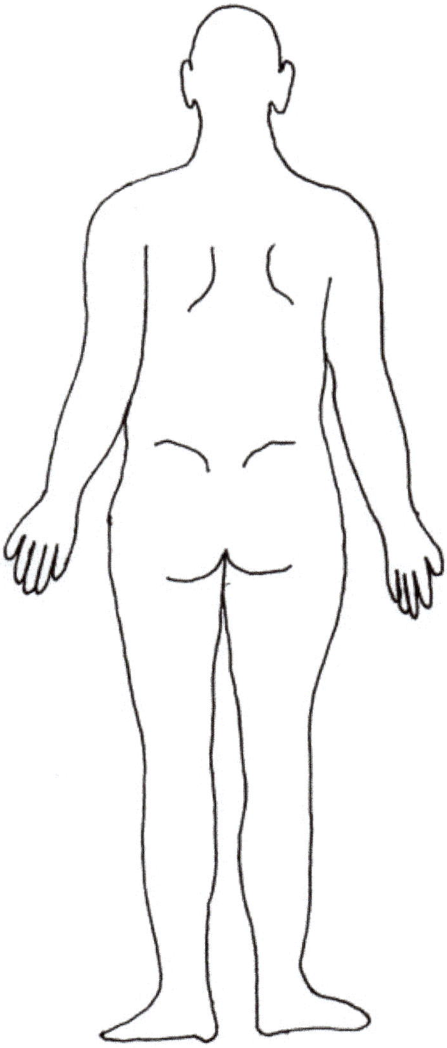

FULL BODY SIDE VIEW SUPPLEMENT

CASE #____
COMPLETED BY:____________________________________
DATE & TIME:______________________________________

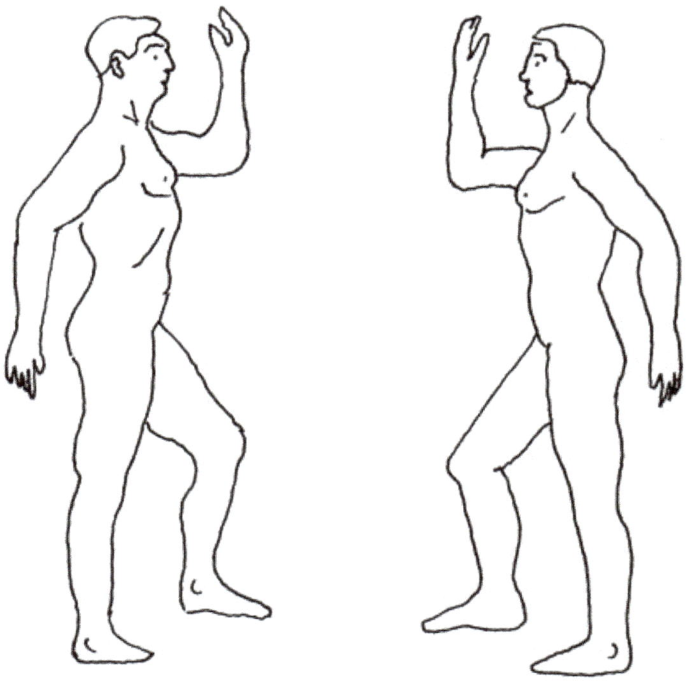

HEAD & NECK SUPPLEMENT

CASE #____
COMPLETED BY:______________________________________
DATE & TIME:_______________________________________

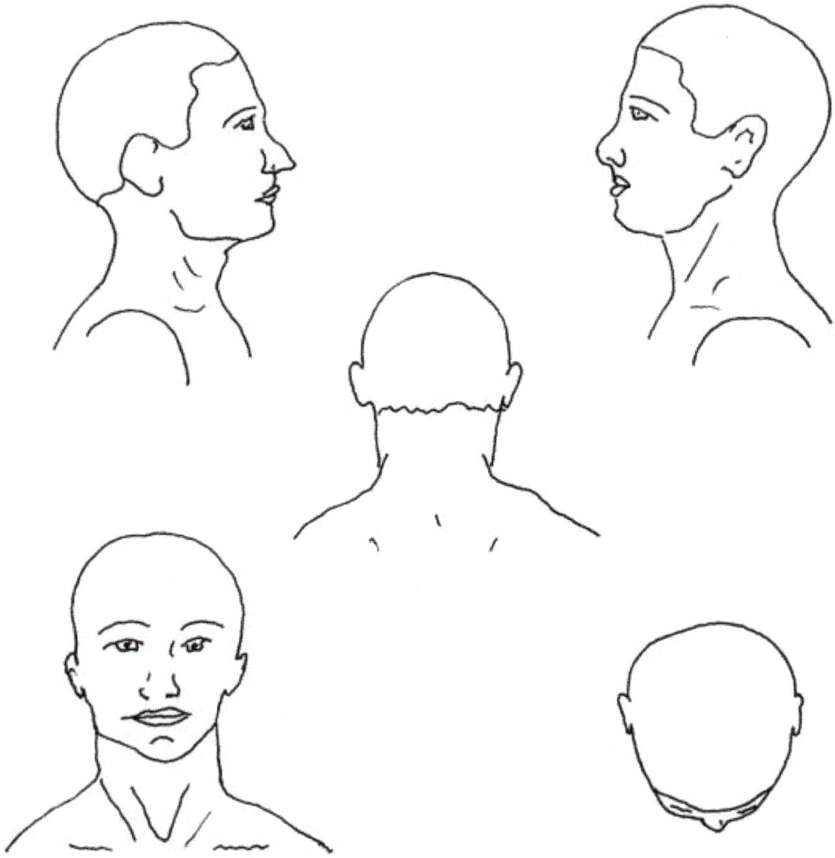

HAND SUPPLEMENT

CASE #____
COMPLETED BY:_____________________________________
DATE & TIME:______________________________________

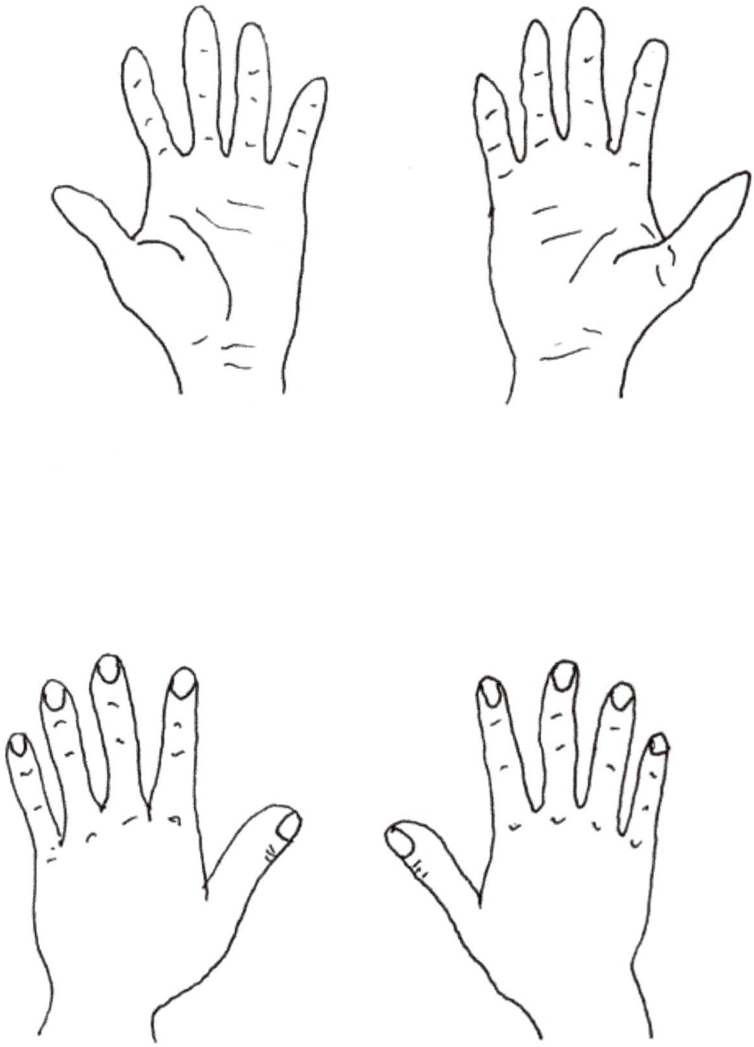

VEHICLE RECOVERY SUPPLEMENT

CASE #____
COMPLETED BY:________________________________
DATE & TIME:_________________________________

Appendix D: Sample Autopsy Report

Scenic County Medical Examiner's Office
678 Market Street, Anytown, Anystate, 65412

Report of Autopsy

Case Number: 00-850

Report of Autopsy of: John Smith
DOB: 1/1/1950

In accordance with Section 123.78 of the Revised Code of Anystate, I, Medical Examiner, certify that an autopsy was performed on the body of John Smith on the 1st day of June 2000 at 9:00 A.M.

The following is the report of autopsy to the best of my knowledge and belief: This person was a male, married, aged 50, of the Caucasian race; had brown eyes, and brown/gray hair, good teeth (dentures), was 70 inches in height, weighing 175 pounds.

Final Anatomic Diagnoses

I. Asphyxia by drowning
  a. Foam column in upper airway
  b. Wrinkling of skin of hands and feet
  c. Aquatic debris (gross and microscopic)
  d. Severe pulmonary congestion and edema
  e. Pleural and epicardial petechial hemorrhages
  f. Emphysema aquosum
  g. Petrous ridge hemorrhage
  h. Fluid in sphenoid sinus (5 ml)
II. Acute ethanol intoxication
III. Hypertensive cardiovascular disease
  a. Cardiomegaly (500 grams)
  b. Left ventricular hypertrophy, moderate
  c. Benign arterio-arteriolar sclerosis of kidneys

VI. Therapeutic intervention:
   a. Oral endotracheal tube placement
   b. Electrocardiogram pad placement
   c. Defibrillation pad placement
   d. Intravenous catheter of left upper extremity
   e. Remote appendectomy

Cause of Death: Asphyxia by drowning

Manner of Death: Accidental

Other Condition(s): Acute ethanol intoxication
Hypertensive cardiovascular disease

Gross Anatomic Description

EXTERNAL EXAMINATION:

The body is that of a well-developed, well-nourished Caucasian male whose appearance is compatible with the reported age of 50. The body is initially viewed fully clothed, wearing a black t-shirt, tan shorts, white underwear, white socks, and gray tennis shoes. A white and yellow metal multilink watch is affixed around the left wrist. A yellow metal band-like ring is on the proximal left fourth finger. These items are removed and placed in secured storage after photographic documentation, prior to autopsy.

The body weighs 175 pounds and is 70 inches in length. The body is cool to the touch. There is full rigor of the facial muscles and extremities. There is red–purple posterior blanching lividity.

The scalp hair is brown with temporal graying, straight, and up to 3½ inches in length. The hair is damp. The irides are brown. The corneas are unremarkable. The conjunctivae are without petechial hemorrhage. The sclerae are unremarkable. The left earlobe is pierced once. The lips are unremarkable. The oral cavity contains upper and lower dentures which are inscribed with the decedent's first and last name. The neck is unremarkable. The chest is symmetrical. The abdomen is flat and unremarkable. The external genitalia, anus, and perineum are unremarkable. The penis is circumcised, and the testicles are descended into the scrotum. The extremities are well developed and symmetrical. There is no palpable crepitus of the skin or accessible bones.

White and slightly blood-tinged foam exudes from the nostrils and mouth. There are pallor and wrinkling of the palms and soles of the hands and feet, respectively. There is cutis anserina of the skin of the forearms. There is adherent brown-black gravel and silt of the body crevices.

IDENTIFYING MARKS AND SCARS:

Trunk:

1. A 2¼-inch, linear, oblique, well-healed surgical scar is on the right lower abdominal quadrant.

EXTERNAL AND INTERNAL EVIDENCE OF RECENT THERAPY:

1. An endotracheal tube is in place within the oral cavity.
2. A total of four electrocardiogram pads are on the body: two on the chest and one on each distal lower extremity.
3. Two defibrillation pads are on the trunk: one on the right chest and one on the posterolateral left chest.
4. An intravenous catheter is inserted into the left antecubital fossa.

EXTERNAL AND INTERNAL EVIDENCE OF RECENT INJURY:

Head:

1. A ¾ × ½ inch red, irregular abrasion is on the tip of the nose.
2. A 1¼ × 1 inch red, irregular abrasion is on the midline of the forehead

Bilateral upper extremities:

1. A ½ × ¼ inch round, red, abraded contusion is on each 2nd, 3rd, and 4th knuckles.

Bilateral lower extremities:

1. A ¾ × ½ inch red, irregular, abrasion is centrally located on each knee.

INTERNAL EXAMINATION:

BODY CAVITIES: The thoracic and abdominal organs are in their normal anatomic positions. The lungs are voluminous with touching of the medial edges. The body cavities contain no adhesions or abnormal collections of fluid. The thickness of the abdominal wall fat is a maximum of 1¼ inches.

ORGAN WEIGHTS:

	(Average weight range)
Heart—500 grams	female/male 250–350/300–350 grams
Right lung—1,100 grams	360–570 grams
Left lung—950 grams	325–480 grams
Spleen—250 grams	100–250 grams
Liver—1,475 grams	1,400–1,600 grams
Right kidney—135 grams	120–150 grams
Left kidney—135 grams	120–150 grams
Brain—1,250 grams	1,200–1,400 grams

NECK: The organs of the neck are removed and examined en bloc. The thyroid gland is resected separately. The soft tissues of the prevertebral fascia of the neck are unremarkable. The hyoid bone and larynx are intact. The tongue is unremarkable externally and upon sectioning.

CARDIOVASCULAR SYSTEM: The aorta and its major branches and the great veins are normally distributed. The intimal surface of the aorta is remarkable for an occasional atheroma. The pericardium is smooth and glistening. The epicardium is remarkable for fine petechial hemorrhages overlying the anterior surface. The coronary arterial system is right dominant. The coronary ostia are patent. There is mild (10% and less) coronary atherosclerosis. There are no thrombi in the atria or ventricles. The foramen ovale is closed. The atrial and ventricular septa are intact. The endocardium is smooth and unremarkable. The cardiac valves are unremarkable. The myocardium is red-brown, of normal consistency, and there are no focal abnormalities. Myocardial wall thicknesses are: left ventricle—1.7 cm, septum—1.7 cm, and right ventricle—0.4 dm. There is moderate concentric left ventricular hypertrophy.

RESPIRATORY SYSTEM: The upper airway is unobstructed; however, it contains white and slightly blood-tinged foam admixed with sand-like debris within the larynx, trachea, and right and left major bronchi. The laryngeal and tracheal mucosa are smooth and unremarkable without petechiae. The pleural surfaces are smooth and shiny, and there is an occasional petechial hemorrhage, bilaterally. The pulmonary arteries contain no emboli. The pulmonary veins are unremarkable. The cut surfaces of the pulmonary parenchyma of all lobes of both lungs are remarkable for copious exudation of blood-tinged foamy fluid. The pulmonary parenchyma is rubbery. There are severe vascular congestion and severe pulmonary edema within all lobes of both lungs.

HEPATOBILLIARY SYSTEM: The liver capsule is smooth and glistening. The parenchyma is dark red-brown, and its consistency is rubbery. There is moderate congestion. The gallbladder contained approximately 15 ml of dark green and slightly viscous fluid. There are no calculi. The extrahepatic biliary ducts are unremarkable, externally and internally.

DIGESTIVE SYSTEM: The esophageal mucosa are gray, wrinkled, and unremarkable. The stomach contains approximately 150 ml of watery, brown fluid, which has an odor consistent with the congeners of ethanol. There are no tablets or capsules. The gastric mucosa has normal rugal folds, and there are no ulcers. The small and large intestines are unremarkable. The appendix is surgically absent. The pancreas is unremarkable, externally and upon sectioning.

RETICULOENDOTHELIAL SYSTEM: The spleen has a smooth and intact capsule. The parenchyma is dark purple and soft. The lymph nodes are unremarkable. The thymus gland is grossly inapparent.

GENITOURINARY SYSTEM: The subcapsular surfaces of the kidneys are slightly granular. The cortices are of normal thickness. The calyces, pelves, and ureters are unremarkable. The urinary bladder contains 50 ml of clear and yellow urine. The mucosa is gray, smooth, and unremarkable. The urinary bladder wall is unremarkable. The testicles, prostate gland, and seminal vesicles are unremarkable, externally and upon sectioning.

ENDOCRINE SYSTEM: The thyroid gland, adrenal glands, and pituitary gland are unremarkable, externally and upon sectioning.

MUSCULOSKELETAL SYSTEM: The clavicles, ribs, sternum, pelvis, and vertebral bodies have no fractures. The diaphragm is intact.

HEAD AND BRAIN: The scalp, subgalea, and skull are unremarkable. The dura and dural sinuses are unremarkable. There are no epidural, subdural, or subarachnoid hemorrhages. The leptomeninges are thin and delicate. The cerebral hemispheres are symmetrical with an unremarkable gyral pattern. There is no evidence of herniation. The intracranial blood vessels have no grossly appreciable atherosclerosis. The cranial nerves are unremarkable. Sections throughout the cerebral hemispheres, brainstem, and cerebellum are unremarkable. There are no hemorrhages in the deep white matter or basal ganglia. The cerebral ventricles contain no blood.

There is subcortical petrous ridge hemorrhage. The sphenoid sinus contains 5 ml of red-tinged watery fluid.

SPINAL CORD: The external and cut surfaces, dura, and meninges are unremarkable. The cut surfaces are unremarkable.

Microscopic Diagnoses

HEART:	Moderate myocyte hypertrophy, section of right and left ventricles
LUNGS:	Acute congestion
	Hemorrhagic edema
	Emphysema aquosum
	Polarizable amorphous debris within bronchi, bronchioles, and alveoli
	LIVER: Acute congestion
KIDNEY:	Mild, benign arterio-arteriolar nephrosclerosis Acute congestion
BRAIN:	No pathological diagnosis, section of cerebellum, hippocampus, and neocortex

Toxicology Results

Drug Screen:	Heart Blood—POSITIVE Ethanol
	Urine—POSITIVE Ethanol
Drug Quantification:	Heart Blood—0.20 g/dl Ethanol
	Femoral Blood—0.18 g/dl Ethanol
	Urine—0.23 g/dl Ethanol
	Vitreous Fluid—0.21 g/dl Ethanol

Appendix E: You Make the Call

The following two incidents are actual cases that involve bodies found in waterways. These cases are presented to allow the reader to review the evidence provided and reach his or her own conclusions as to what actually occurred. An important factor to remember in any investigation is that evidence is always more reliable than testimony or statements made by witnesses or the accused.

Troubled Waters

On May 18, 1998, in Ephrata, Pennsylvania, police rushed to the banks of the Cocalico Creek to find the body of a scantily clad woman. There was no identification on her person, and no one in the area knew who she was. Police interviewed the 19-year-old man who found her. They approached him near the scene, and he appeared nervous and his clothes were wet. While speaking to him, at times he would get down on his hands and knees in a praying-type position. They learned that he lived right across the street with his mother and grandmother. They took him to the police station for an interview.

In the interview, he stated that he was standing by the creek and saw the victim's body floating down the stream. He pulled her out of the creek and began CPR for one minute, and then ran to a nearby house to have someone call 911. Detectives canvassed the neighborhood by the river in an attempt to identify the victim and determine how she died. Detectives assumed this was a drowning since she was found floating face down in the water. The male who found her had a criminal record, which included sexual assault, corrupting a minor, and indecent exposure. After serving nearly a year in prison, he was released just ten weeks prior to this incident.

Police interviewed him all afternoon. First, he told them that he went to the river to go swimming when he found the woman in the water. Later, he stated that he biked to a nearby bridge and witnessed the woman slip into the water and drown. He then stated he saw someone kill her and throw her into the water. He stated that he went home to smoke a cigarette in his bedroom. Detectives asked why he didn't report the attack, and he started to crack. He started crying and said that he was interested in meeting the girl and followed her down to the creek. He ran up behind her and put a cord around her neck. He choked her until she was gasping for air and then threw her into the water. Detectives were puzzled because his statement had changed so much. After conferring with their supervisor, he was arrested for murder, and he quickly retracted his confession and requested an attorney.

Police checked surrounding counties for missing persons, but nothing matched the description of this victim. Twelve hours after her body was found, police asked the media to broadcast her description. A retired trooper recognized her clothing description and reported that his son's girlfriend was wearing those clothes when he saw her that morning. He positively identified the 20-year-old woman as his son's girlfriend by viewing a photograph of her body. The man also stated that his son was missing. He said his son and the girlfriend left the house that morning to take the family dog for a walk. The dog came home wet and alone. The father also stated that his son took a new pair of hip waders with them and gave his girlfriend a pair of running pants to protect her legs from the brush in the area. The pants weren't found on her body, and his son was still missing.

Police spent the night and part of the next day hunting for the son around the river, but no leads were found. A dive team was called to assist. The divers were asked to search the creek and either find the missing son's body or evidence of a crime. The team was advised that the woman's body was found approximately ¼ mile downstream from the bridge where the suspect claimed to have seen her thrown in, but her injuries were not consistent with that story. The woman's injuries were only surface abrasions on her knees.

Divers located a ball against the dam, upstream from the bridge. The current was pulling the ball underwater, and then it would pop back up again. This was repeated over and over. Divers believed that if the missing man's body was anywhere in the river, it was likely trapped in the dam's hydraulic. They had to risk the life of a diver by sending him into this hydraulic, which is like placing a diver in a washing machine. The diver entered the dam by pulling himself along the bottom with one hand while holding his mask on with the other. The missing man's body was not found in the dam area.

The team formed a line across the river, walking shoulder to shoulder, in an effort to search the river bottom. At the feet of one of the searchers, the team located the missing man's body, approximately 4 feet deep, between the dam and the bridge where the suspect claimed to have thrown the female victim into the water. The team meticulously processed the scene and bagged the victim's body before recovery. The man's body had abrasions to the forehead, knuckles, and knees. The team believed the victim's injuries were likely caused by going through the dam's brutal spin cycle. In his pants pocket, they found a dog leash. He was also found to have only socks on his feet, no shoes. The team questioned, "Where were his shoes?" They realized he had been wearing waders but didn't find them on his feet or near his body. The team sent a diver back into the dam to search for the waders.

The suspect started claiming he wrapped a black nylon cord around the female victim's neck and strangled her, but the coroner's findings contradicted this statement by ruling the certified lifeguard's death as a drowning. She also sustained blunt force head trauma. Findings also indicate no evidence of a sexual assault. But, if she wasn't raped, why were her black sweatpants removed and where were they now? Police obtained a search warrant for the suspect's home and found a muddy hammer and a black nylon cord tied to his bed, but no black sweatpants. Police found no evidence to connect the suspect to the deaths. The suspect refused to take a polygraph to corroborate his story. Divers returned to the dam to search for more evidence. They located the waders caught in the rocks at the base of the dam, and a short distance away they also found the female's black sweatpants. The sweatpants were found inside out as if they were removed in a hurry.

Investigators reexamined photographs of the injuries on the female's body and noted abrasions on her knees, possibly indicating she was kneeling on rough concrete. Finally, detectives believed they could fit all the pieces of the puzzle together to determine the outcome of the case and the suspect's role in the deaths.

Tub Drowning in Wolsey

On May 15, 1999, in Wolsey, South Dakota, a 54-year-old wife of a church pastor was found floating face down in the family bathtub. An ambulance was called to the scene, and the medics were met at the door by her husband. They attempted to revive her while her husband stood off to the side crying. She was transported to a hospital, but rescue efforts failed. The sheriff believed the incident to be a tragic accident. As a formality, he asked the reverend to recount what happened that morning.

The reverend stated he got up at seven o'clock in the morning and went to the church. While leaving, his wife was drawing water for her morning bath. He was at the church for 10–15 minutes and then returned home to find his wife face down in the tub, with her head at the faucet end of the tub. The reverend claimed his wife was suicidal, yet no one else, including any family members, could verify that statement.

The autopsy revealed the cause of death to be drowning, but toxicological testing revealed small amounts of oxazepam and lorazepam (both antianxiety medications) in her system. There was also a large amount of temazepam, a sleeping aid. The pathologist believed the amount to be the equivalent of roughly 20 doses. He believed the amount was not enough to kill her but rather caused drowsiness and possibly unconsciousness.

Interviews with other parishioners revealed the reverend was having an affair. Investigators now believed they had a motive for homicide. Investigators returned to the house to collect all the prescription medication they could find, including hers and his. The reverend had two scripts for temazepam. In the reverend's computer, investigators found he had been researching drugs and their effects on people, and temazepam was one of them. This evidence was presented to the grand jury, and the reverend was indicted for murder. He claimed he was innocent.

Investigators interviewed an expert in suicide, and he found no risk factors to be consistent with a suicide. Furthermore, he stated that accidental drowning in a tub occurs when a person is sitting in the tub and falls asleep. His or her body relaxes, and he or she slides down onto his or her back, submerging his or her head. The fact that the victim was found face down in the tub is therefore highly suspicious. Even if she had rolled over, it is not common for people to sit in the tub with their back resting against the faucet.

A computer forensics analyst was consulted to look at the reverend's hard drive on his computer. This analysis revealed extensive research on household accidents, drugs (specifically temazepam), and whether it can be found in tablet or capsule form. All this research was done in the weeks just prior to her death. No capsules or tablets were found in her stomach, which led investigators to believe that someone had fed her the medication without her knowledge by mixing it with something else. The victim's daughter stated her mother loved chocolate milk and bought it by the gallon. Investigators questioned if twenty capsules could be mixed in the chocolate milk without her noticing. Investigators called on a state chemist to conduct a simple yet significant test. He emptied twenty capsules into 300 ml of chocolate milk and mixed it. The entire drug dissolved and could not be seen in the mixture. Next he took a mouthful of the milk and swished it around in his mouth and spit it out. He could not taste the drug, only the chocolate milk. He believed the drug could be consumed by an unsuspecting person. Investigators believed the reverend gave her the chocolate milk mixture, which caused a drug-induced stupor, and dragged her to the bathtub, where he held her head underwater until she drowned.

The defense claimed the victim committed suicide. The reverend admitted to the affair but maintained he did not kill his wife. The defense consulted another suicide expert. He demonstrated a mathematical equation of statistics that refuted the prosecution's prediction that this case was not a suicide. The defense attorney interviewed the victim's younger daughter, who stated her mother was stressed about being overweight and wanted to lose weight before her daughter's wedding. She stated her mother was withdrawn the week before her death. The defense hired a toxicologist, who stated the prosecution had no way of knowing the concentration of the drugs in her stomach. He maintains the belief that the victim took an overdose of sleeping pills.

The defense presented evidence indicating the victim's stomach was pumped at the hospital during efforts to revive her, eliminating the remnants of capsules in her stomach. The defense also presented evidence indicating the reverend wasn't the only person to have access to his computer, and the research on drugs could have been done by the victim. The defense also believed that the victim was washing her hair in the tub when she lost consciousness, accounting for her head toward the faucet end of the tub.

A surprising twist would come at the end of the trial when the defense would present a suicide note, presumably found by the reverend while looking through a reference book he used to prepare sermons. The note was dated May 13, 1999, two days prior to the victim's death. The note had been typed on a computer and was not signed.

The defense had a fingerprint expert examine the note. The reverend's fingerprints were not on the document, nor were his attorney's. The victim had not been fingerprinted after her death, so her fingerprints were'nt available for comparison. The examiner testified that the prints on the note were made by a highly stressed person sweating profusely, like that of a person contemplating suicide.

The prosecution searched the reverend's computer for the suicide note, but it was not there. However, they learned that after they had seized his computer for evidence, he was using another computer. That computer was analyzed by an expert, and the suicide note was found. The date on the suicide note was May 13, 1999, but the file was last modified on August 7, 1999. The defense attorney claimed the note was given to him by the reverend in June.

Appendix F

Victim survival cases after prolonged submersion:

January 19, 2015, St. Charles County, Missouri

Fourteen-year-old John Smith went out onto the ice of Lake Saint Louise with two of his friends. It was a fatal mistake as he fell through the ice and was underwater for a minimum of 15 minutes. Fire Captain Tommy Shine from Wentzville Fire Department arrived on the scene and donned his wet suit. He began using his pike pole to jab at the lake bottom 12 feet down in an attempt to find John. He felt something and pulled it up. It was John's lifeless body. After being rushed to the emergency room, doctors and nurses tried, for 45 minutes, to get a heartbeat before finally allowing his mother to come in and say her final goodbye before they pronounced him dead. As the doctor was walking out of the room, a nurse yelled out, "We have a pulse"! John's heart had suddenly started beating. In the days to follow, John's lungs, full of lake water, started to clear. His brain function slowly started to return to normal. Sixteen days after his lifeless body went into the hospital, John walked out of the hospital. All his body functions returned to normal with no adverse effects from the incident.

(Kay Quinn, 5 On Your Side local information center, St. Louis, Missouri. October 30, 2017)

January 15, 1984, Four-and-a-half-year-old Jimmy Tontlewicz had been submerged for over 20 minutes after falling through the ice of Lake Michigan while sledding with his father. Recovered from the frigid water by Frogman Peter Tomaskiewicz, he was clinically dead. Rescuers and medical teams made a valiant effort to save the boy's life. Eight days after the accident, Jimmy regained consciousness and gradually made a full recovery.

(Eric Levin, *People* magazine, April 2, 1984)

A 14-year-old boy, who jumped into the 6.5-foot depth water in a canal in Milan, Italy, did not come back up. Rescuers formed a human chain and, after 42 minutes of searching, located his body in the 59-degree murky water and brought him to the surface. He had no pulse and was clinically dead. In the hospital, doctors placed him on a life support machine that functioned for his lungs and heart. After a month, he woke up apparently alert and able to talk to his parents and even ask about his favorite soccer team. https://meet.google.com/snc-jmex-wyj

(Alice Park, *Time* Magazine, May 27, 2015)

John Henry-Birtle, a four-year-old boy, stunned doctors after making a full recovery after being submerged for nine minutes at the bottom of a swimming pool. The toddler had fallen into a hotel pool while his family was on vacation in Slough, Berkshire, England, on February 26. When his mother discovered him missing, she jumped into the pool and pulled him out of the water. Hotel staff personnel immediately started CPR and continued until his pulse was restored 40 minutes later. His body was starved of oxygen for 28 minutes and had no pulse for 20 minutes. John-Henry was rushed to the hospital in Oxford, where he spent 13 days on life support. Doctors told his family that he would not have a good quality of life, but he shocked everyone when he walked out of the hospital five weeks later. Two hotel staff members received a Chief Constable Commendation Award for saving the boy's life.

(Liz Dunphy, *Daily Mail*, May 13, 2017)

June 10, 1986, Michelle Funk, a two-and-a-half-year-old girl, 66 minutes submerged in a creek near Salt Lake City. Two months after the accident, she was talking and had normal motor skills except for a slight tremor in her hands.

January 8, 2010, Thomas Hudson, a 6-year-old boy, was trapped under pond ice for 30 minutes in Crookham Common, Berkshire, England. He recovered after undergoing cardiopulmonary bypass surgery.

March 11, 2015, Gardell Martin, 22 months old, had been submerged for 30 minutes in Buffalo Creek, Mifflinburg, PA. He recovered after 1 hour and 41 minutes of CPR.

June 2, 2015, an Italian boy, only known as "Michael", 14 years old, had been submerged in a canal in Milan, Italy, for 42 minutes. He recovered after a full month on life support.

Index

C

D

I

J

K

L

O

P

Q

R

S

T

Y

For Product Safety Concerns and Information please contact our EU
representative GPSR@taylorandfrancis.com
Taylor & Francis Verlag GmbH, Kaufingerstraße 24, 80331 München, Germany

www.ingramcontent.com/pod-product-compliance
Ingram Content Group UK Ltd.
Pitfield, Milton Keynes, MK11 3LW, UK
UKHW052050230926
475702UK00025B/1032

* 9 7 8 0 3 6 7 2 5 1 5 4 3 *